As law schools around the world integrate digital lawyering skills into their core curricula, this book is quickly becoming an indispensable addition to reading lists. From demystifying how technology is impacting legal services and exploring the quintessential skills for successful digital lawyers to an updated chapter on AI that tackles the strengths and shortcomings of Generative AI, this is an ideal, decisive resource for preparing students for the practice of tech-enabled law.

Dr Amanda Turnbull, *Senior Lecturer in Law, University of Waikato, New Zealand, 2025*

The 2nd edition of Technology and Legal Practice: Becoming a Digital Lawyer is being published at a time of intense change in legal practice. There have been many predictions that digital tools will reshape the way in which we engage with law, many of those predictions are still to be borne out. And yet, we do now feel to be on the cusp of a technological shift. Technology and Legal Practice charts many of the areas that may be subject to disruption and provides insights into how law students and legal professionals may harness new technologies rather than being caught unawares by them.

Professor Lisa Webley, *Chair in Legal Education and Research, Birmingham Law School, the University of Birmingham, England, 2026*

As law firms, government agencies, and courts have not only automated document review and assembly, but now turn to the adoption of AI in more aspects of daily practice, every law school should offer a course in Legal Technologies. *Technology and Legal Practice: Becoming a Digital Lawyer* is precisely the text needed for such a course. This second edition presents law students with a collaboration of technologists and legal academics, and is tailored to guide students through the many facets of digital technologies as they mature, exploring the opportunities and challenges this evolution presents to learning and the practice of law. Students and instructors alike will love its up-to-date, authoritative clarity.

David C. Donald, *Emeritus Professor, Faculty of Law, The Chinese University of Hong Kong, 2026*

TECHNOLOGY AND LEGAL PRACTICE

In today's rapidly changing legal landscape, becoming a digital lawyer is vital to success within the legal profession. *Technology and Legal Practice: Becoming a Digital Lawyer* is a toolkit for gaining the key attributes and skills required to utilise technology within legal practice effectively.

Digital technologies have already begun a radical transformation of the legal profession and the justice system. This textbook introduces students to key topics, from the role of blockchain to the use of digital evidence in courtrooms, supported by contemporary case studies and integrated, interactive activities.

The second edition updates reflect the changes that have been brought about by developments in Generative AI since the textbook was first published, along with general updates throughout the book. Using this textbook will allow students to identify, discuss, and reflect on emerging issues and trends within digital lawyering in a critical and informed manner, drawing on both its theoretical basis and accounts of its use in legal practice.

Technology and Legal Practice is ideal for use as a main textbook on modules focused on technology and law, and as a supplementary textbook on modules covering lawyering and legal skills more generally.

Emma Jones is a senior lecturer in law and Director of Sheffield Digital Justice at the University of Sheffield's School of Law. Her research interests focus upon emotions and wellbeing in legal education and the legal profession, and the role of digital technology in legal practice. She leads undergraduate and postgraduate digital lawyering modules and is director of Sheffield Digital Justice, an extra-curricular and multi-disciplinary initiative designed to foster students' critical AI literacy.

Francine Ryan is a senior lecturer in law, Director of the Open Justice Centre at The Open University in the UK, and a qualified solicitor. Her teaching and research interests are clinical legal education with a particular focus on technology and innovation-enhanced learning. She leads a virtual reality courtroom project and a UKRI, Responsible AI funded project: AI Law and Legal Training.

Ann Thanaraj works at the intersection of AI, digital education, and legal practice, and works globally to advance AI-driven, multidisciplinary education. She is creator and founder of "Digital Lawyering" and her research on digital lawyering, cited by the UK House of Lords, shapes policy, legal governance, and curriculum innovation. Having started her career in legal practice before undertaking various leadership roles in higher education, Ann has multiple lenses through which to explore "What Is the Point of Education, Anyway?", a forthcoming literary work that questions multiple facets of education and learning. Ann is Head of Digital and AI Innovations and Chair of AI Operations at Teesside University.

Terry Wong is a technology entrepreneur based in Hong Kong. Born, raised, and educated in the United States, he holds degrees in architecture and management from the Massachusetts Institute of Technology. Terry is the founder and CEO of Cydeas, a global team of system architects, software developers, and user experience designers who invest in, build, and actively manage technology-led businesses, with interests in legal and financial services.

TECHNOLOGY AND LEGAL PRACTICE

Becoming a Digital Lawyer

SECOND EDITION

EMMA JONES,
FRANCINE RYAN,
ANN THANARAJ,
AND TERRY WONG

Routledge
Taylor & Francis Group
LONDON AND NEW YORK

Designed cover image: Shutterstock

Second edition published 2026
by Routledge
4 Park Square, Milton Park, Abingdon, Oxon, OX14 4RN

and by Routledge
605 Third Avenue, New York, NY 10158

Routledge is an imprint of the Taylor & Francis Group, an informa business

First edition published by Routledge 2021

British Library Cataloguing-in-Publication Data
A catalogue record for this book is available from the British Library

Library of Congress Cataloging-in-Publication Data
Names: Jones, Emma (Law teacher) author | Ryan, Francine author | Thanaraj, Ann author | Wong, Terry (Writer of Digital lawyering) author
Title: Technology and legal practice : becoming a digital lawyer / Emma Jones, Francine Ryan, Ann Thanaraj, and Terry Wong.
Description: Second edition. | Abingdon, Oxon [UK] ; New York, NY : Routledge, 2026. | Includes bibliographical references and index. |
Identifiers: LCCN 2025053650 | ISBN 9781032991030 hardback | ISBN 9781032991023 paperback | ISBN 9781003602323 ebook
Subjects: LCSH: Lawyer—Effect of technological innovations on | Practice of law—Automation | Practice of law—Technological innovations | Internet in legal services | Legal services—Automation | Technology and law
Classification: LCC K87 .J66 2026
LC record available at https://lccn.loc.gov/2025053650

ISBN: 978-1-032-99103-0 (hbk)
ISBN: 978-1-032-99102-3 (pbk)
ISBN: 978-1-003-60232-3 (ebk)

DOI: 10.4324/9781003602323

Typeset in ITC Galliard Pro
by Apex CoVantage, LLC

To the educators past, present, and future who inspire learning and innovation.

CONTENTS

ACKNOWLEDGEMENTS

Thank you to Chris Sykes, Lead Designer of BPP Law School, UK, for introducing Emma, Francine, and Ann to Terry.

Thank you to Dr. Graeme Horsman for co-authoring Chapter 8 for its first edition published in 2021. Dr. Horsman is a digital forensics analyst, former EnCase Certified Examiner, Computer Certified Examiner (EnCE), and Certified Computer Examiner (CCE). You can keep up to date on developments in digital forensics and law enforcement as part of your ongoing digital lawyering journey by following Dr. Horsman at @GraemeHorsman on Twitter.

The updated version of Chapter 8 was co-authored with Dr. Rob Ewin. Dr. Ewin is a Detective Inspector currently specialised in digital forensics and the investigation of major and organised crime. His work is grounded in a strong academic foundation, holding a PhD in the relationship between vulnerability and witnesses, and an LLM in Qualifying Law from Liverpool John Moores University. Dr. Ewin's legal scholarship focuses on evidential procedures, particularly the challenges of disclosure and hearsay in criminal proceedings. His LLM, praised for its analytical rigour and clarity, explored the intersection of hearsay evidence and human rights, offering critical insights into procedural fairness, and the treatment of vulnerable witnesses.

1 INTRODUCTION

DEFINING DIGITAL LAWYERING

Emma Jones, Francine Ryan,
Ann Thanaraj, and Terry Wong

WELCOME TO TECHNOLOGY AND LEGAL PRACTICE

BECOMING A DIGITAL LAWYER

This textbook is designed to introduce you to the dynamic, innovative, complex, and fascinating world of digital lawyering—in other words, the use of digital technology within the legal profession. It will give you the opportunity to understand what digital lawyering is, how it has developed, and what role it now plays within legal practice and the delivery of legal services. It will also encourage you to reflect upon your own knowledge and skills and how these can be applied within the digital world. Mind Map 1.1 shows the key topics we will cover, using the title of each chapter.

In exploring digital lawyering, this textbook will take a range of perspectives and approaches, drawing on the viewpoints of its four authors (all of whom wrote this chapter and the conclusion). This includes:

- *A legal perspective*—looking at how laws and regulations have had to, or may have to, adapt to reflect the changes in digital technology and the legal profession.
- *A technical perspective*—looking at the functions and capabilities (sometimes referred to as "affordances") of technology.
- *A sociological perspective*—looking at the impact digital lawyering has upon the profession and wider society.
- *An educational and reflective perspective*—encouraging you to reflect upon your digital and educational experiences and your skills development going forward.

DOI: 10.4324/9781003602323-1

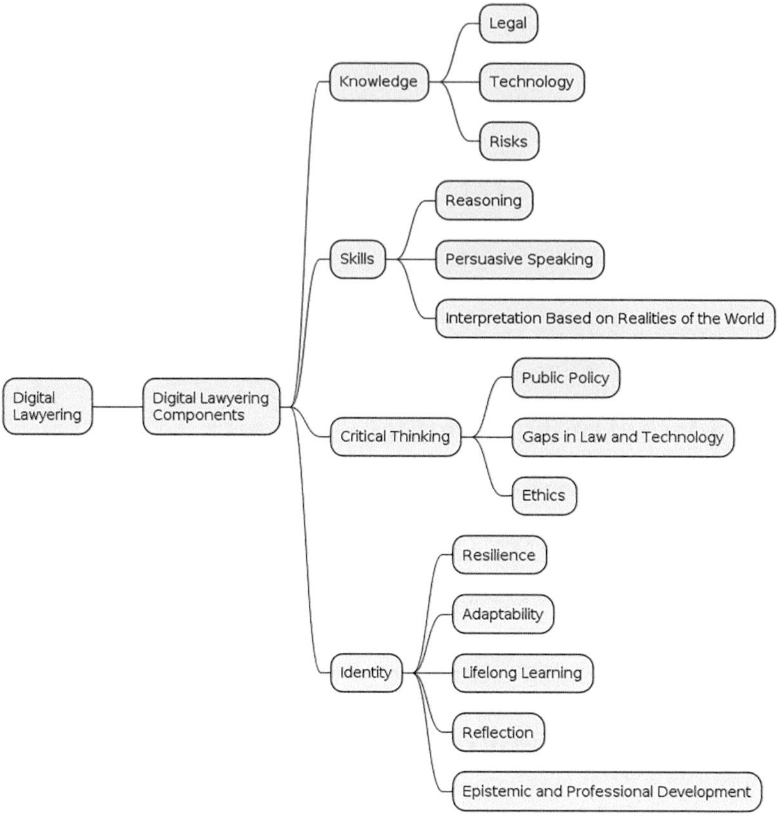

Mind Map 1.1 Topics of chapters

As the four authors, we each have different but equally valuable perspectives, which we will introduce you to later in this chapter. That is the reason that the authors' names are strictly in alphabetical order on the cover!

In this chapter, we will begin by thinking about the role of digital technology within society, definitions of digital technology and digital lawyering, and the relevance of ethics and legal education. We will then explain the way the rest of this book will work. The chapter will finish by explaining the authors' journeys into and within digital lawyering. This will help put each of the chapters we have written in context as you work through the rest of the textbook. Let us begin by considering the role of digital technology within society.

Digital Technology and Society

Digtal technology plays a critical role in shaping our society. It impacts on the way individuals communicate, interact, and think. The advancement of technology has had both positive and negative effects on our lives. It is hard to imagine our existence without access to the internet and smartphones, but we need to be aware of the pervasive effect of technology on our lives too. Technology brings opportunities for innovation and change, but it also brings risk, distrust, and concern. Throughout this textbook, it is important to consider to what extent technological development is a good thing for our society and for our legal system. This may be a good opportunity for you to reflect on your own experiences of technology to help you understand in greater depth the issues raised in this textbook.

Technology is now commonplace in our lives. In July 2025, globally there were 5.76 billion unique mobile phone subscriptions and 5.65 billion people (68.7% of the population) using the internet.[1] Social media reach and adoption is growing in popularity too, with 5.41 billion social media identities in existence.[2] More people than ever are accessing the internet via smartphones and using tablets for activities such as online shopping, watching TV and films, and communicating via social media. Social media, email, and apps are used by governments to engage with their citizens. We now have online services for many aspects of our lives. If you want to apply for a driving licence, file your taxes or start divorce proceedings, all of this can be done online. The United Nations notes that "public services are also becoming more accessible and accountable through blockchain-powered systems, and less bureaucratically burdensome as a result of AI assistance. Big data can also support more responsive and accurate policies and programmes".[3]

In terms of the workplace, a 2022 report for the European Parliament suggested that, accelerated by the COVID-19 pandemic, digital technologies were playing an important part in shaping what the

1 Data Reportal, 'Digital Around the World' (July 2025) <https://datareportal.com/global-digital-overview>, accessed 20 August 2025.

2 Ibid.

3 United Nations, 'The Impact of Digital Technologies 6' (2025) <https://www.un.org/en/un75/impact-digital-technologies> accessed 20 August 2025.

future of work will be.[4] A 2023 report by Future.Now (a coalition of UK industry leaders) argues that building a workforce with appropriate digital skills and confidence is vital to enhance productivity, promote economic prosperity, and position the UK as a "global technology and science superpower".[5] A 2024 Organisation for Economic Co-operation and Development report mirrors this emphasis on the importance of technology, highlighting mixed levels of uptake amongst firms and again emphasising its importance for productivity.[6] Overall, the crucial role of technology is demonstrated by the way the term "Fourth Industrial Revolution" is now commonly used to refer to the way in which new technologies are currently reshaping industries, professions, and society generally.

Technology has become an integral part of our working lives, and it features in many jobs. Digital technologies enabled many people to work from home during the COVID-19 pandemic, which allowed many businesses to keep functioning. The pandemic demonstrated that flexible working is possible and that productivity is not lost. As a result, we are seeing significant shifts in patterns of work, with flexible and remote working becoming commonplace and workers splitting their time between home and the office. Companies are readjusting to new ways of working, and this will change how businesses operate and evolve in the future. All this demonstrates that technology is now firmly embedded in our lives.

However, not everyone is able to participate in the digital world. Many people struggle to access and use the internet. Many parts of our society lack the skills, knowledge, or access to be able to engage effectively with technology. Economically disadvantaged groups cannot afford a computer or a smartphone, or the cost of mobile data or Wi-Fi. Low levels of digital literacy make engaging online very challenging. A lack

4 Regina Konle-Seidl and Sara Danes, 'Digitalisation and Changes in the World of Work' (September 2022). <https://www.europarl.europa.eu/RegData/etudes/STUD/2022/733986/IPOL_STU(2022)733986_EN.pdf>, accessed 20 August 2025.

5 Future.Now, 'The UK Workforce Digital Skills Gap: Why Closing It Matters and a Roadmap for Action' (July 2023) <https://futuredotnow.uk/wp-content/uploads/2023/07/FutureDotNow-roadmap_final-digital.pdf>, accessed 20 August 2025.

6 Organisation for Economic Co-operation and Development, *OECD Digital Economy Outlook 2024* (OECD 14 May 2024) Vol. 1 <https://www.oecd.org/en/publications/oecd-digital-economy-outlook-2024-volume-1_a1689dc5-en/full-report.html>, accessed 20 August 2025.

of confidence or people to ask for help makes many people reluctant to use technology. These issues are discussed further in Chapter 4. The global digital divide is even greater, with 2.6 billion people still offline.[7] There are also clear inequalities internationally, with only 27% of the population of low-income countries having internet access, compared to 93% of those in high-income countries.[8] Of the 100 companies who funded 40% of research and development into AI in 2022, none were in developing countries, other than China.[9] Policies on investment infrastructure, improved regulation and skills development are required to close the digital divide, because if not addressed it will lead to further inequality and exclusion of marginalised and vulnerable groups.

WHAT IS DIGITAL TECHNOLOGY?

Technology can be understood as the practice of making and using tools to achieve specific practical goals. Writing implements—from a stylus for inscribing a stone tablet with the Code of Hammurabi, to the quills used to draft and sign the Magna Carta, to the gel ink rollerball pens of today—are all examples of the slow evolution of writing technology. A field of continuous and discrete marks can be put on a writing surface. Incisions, shades of tone or smooth, curved lines can be seen by human eyes, processed in the language centres of human brains, and recognised as writing, representing items of information. These can be referred to as analogue technology. This term defines technology that does not involve processing letters, numbers, or other information electronically. Another common example of analogue technology you may have come across is a watch or clock with a numbered clock face and two hands that show and measure the passage of time.

In contrast, digital technology entails the use of electricity and electronic devices to create, process, transmit, and store information. It is distinct from analogue technology in that it uses a discrete, regular

7 Italian Institute for International Political Studies, 'The Digital Divide: A Barrier to Social, Economic and Political Equity' (4 April 2025) <https://www.ispionline.it/en/publication/the-digital-divide-a-barrier-to-social-economic-and-political-equity-204564>, accessed 20 August 2025.

8 Ibid.

9 UN Trade & Development, '2025 Technology and Innovation Report' (7 April 2025) <https://unctad.org/publication/technology-and-innovation-report-2025>, accessed 20 August 2025.

representation of information in sequences of binary values (ones or zeros). Unlike with analogue technology, there are absolutely no in-between values or states, no shades or tones or gradations; there are only two values in the base unit of expression. Using our example of a watch or clock, if you read the time from your smartphone or tablet, it is represented by a set of numbers, such as 19:00, rather than as a form of continuous measurement.

The fact there are no in-between values or states may seem like an impediment to building anything useful. In fact, as we will see in this textbook, this constraint is the basis of computing systems that exploit the physical properties of certain electrical devices. These devices are connected in specific combinations and configurations that yield the results of concrete calculations, or operations that manipulate data represented in ones and zeros. Layering these fundamental building blocks over time in assemblies, and advances in materials, processes and miniaturisation, have led to the complex web of high-speed computation and high-resolution media and communication that we experience in our daily environment, powered by digital technology.

You should note that throughout this book the terms "technology" and "digital technology" may be used interchangeably, depending on the context.

WHAT IS DIGITAL LAWYERING?

There is no single simple definition of digital lawyering, and it is likely that you will develop your own definition as you work through the textbook. Overall, digital lawyering is a broad term encompassing both practical and theoretical elements. It can be used to refer to the practical ways in which individual lawyers, and the legal profession more generally, have begun to use and adapt to digital technologies. It also refers to a body of theory which begins to identify and explain the sorts of learning that are required for law students and future professionals to thrive in a digital age. It encapsulates an understanding of some of the complex and disruptive changes brought about by technologically mediated practices, including:

- Their impact on current and future legal practice, questioning what is required for a law graduate, trainee, or lawyer to thrive in contemporary practice.

- Their impact on the sorts of knowledge that make up a law degree, exploring what interdisciplinary knowledge and awareness can equip a law student to be future-ready.

Professor Richard Susskind, Special Envoy for Justice and AI to the Secretary-General of the Commonwealth, has discussed the impact that digitalisation and technology have had on legal services. In his book *The End of Lawyers? Rethinking the Nature of Legal Services*,[10] he advised that enhancements in technology leading to improved, sustained, and advanced methods of legal services delivery are inevitable and that, consequently, lawyers should change the way they work. As the legal profession undergoes its digital transformation, reshaping how we practise as lawyers and the nature of how legal services are delivered, learning about digital lawyering can help in developing a necessary understanding of core technologies, their features and functionalities, how they are being utilised and the impact of these technologies on the role of legal professionals. Digital lawyering theory also assists in highlighting gaps within the profession and demonstrating the opportunities to merge law with technology to create hybrid roles within the legal sector. It can be used to explore limitations and gaps in the existing law and how it can be interpreted more broadly to capture both the physical and digital worlds. This raises much wider questions about the intersection between technology, law, and society. For example, as a society, how should we balance the sharing of information online with people's right to privacy? How can we protect the right to privacy while preserving the right to free speech? How can we protect the more vulnerable members of society?

Looking at these aspects of digital lawyering encourages law students and existing legal professionals to prepare for the changing legal profession. Examples of legal practice embracing digital technologies include advances in the use of Big Data and artificial intelligence (AI) for legal research and predicting outcomes of matters, the automation of a range of previously manual processes including document disclosure, the use of blockchain technologies for executing contractual agreements, the practice of law through virtual law firms, and the use of online court systems for dispute resolution. As the legal profession and the delivery of legal services undergo a journey of digital

10 Richard Susskind, *The End of Lawyers? Rethinking the Nature of Legal Services* (OUP 2010).

transformation, this creates new opportunities for lawyers and law students to explore new areas of practice. All these topics are discussed within subsequent chapters of this textbook.

The use of these types of technology, while novel in many respects, still requires lawyers to exercise the traditionally required knowledge, skills, and aptitude for the purpose of collaborating, advising clients, undertaking dispute resolution and other forms of advocacy, and processing legal transactions. The technologies used in legal practice are not, as yet, capable of replacing our human and intellectual faculties, such as legal reasoning, the art of persuasion, and the process of interpreting information in the context of the realities of our world today. However, other transformative changes, such as the emergence of alternative business structures, unbundling of services, digitalisation of services through legal platforms, off-the-shelf solutions, automation of procedural work, and machine learning impacting technical legal expertise, are all affecting the identity of the legal professional. Looking at digital lawyering provides an awareness of the relevance of this digital transformation of the profession and its linkage with our own digital understanding, and raises questions around the intersection of law, legal theory, legal practice, and technology. Our exploration of digital lawyering will highlight that digital lawyers must not only be aware of emerging technologies but also have an understanding of the way in which technology works in order to appreciate the impact that technology has on the practice of law. It will also emphasise that digital lawyering is not about requiring lawyers to be IT professionals. Instead, it is about having enough knowledge to understand where law and technology intersect, being aware of the implications of technology and becoming digitally literate so that you can leverage the benefits of technology in your work.

With the seamless integration of the digital and physical worlds in so many aspects of our lives, clients will also require advice on regulations governing the use of technology and associated issues such as digital assets, digital evidence, property ownership, privacy, and intellectual property protection. There is a significant body of writing and research upon these issues (often referred to as "law and technology" issues), and it is important to be aware of such topics. However, we will not explore these in detail in this textbook. Instead, our particular focus is on the relationship between digital technology and the legal profession. In other words, this is about the ways in which lawyers can appropriately, safely, and effectively use online technological innovations and techniques within the delivery of legal services, often through secure and authentic online law platforms. It is not a technology or law and technology textbook.

DIGITAL LAWYERING AND ETHICS

This textbook explores how we can prepare for the practice of law in a technologically enhanced world, and it considers some of the knowledge, skills, and competencies that digital lawyers require. However, as referred to previously, digital lawyering is not separate from the conventional practice of law, and we cannot consider it in isolation. The role of a lawyer is changing, and with the emergence of new technologies, the legal sector is being challenged to rethink how legal services are delivered. When we think about the future of legal practice, technology will be harnessed further to support innovation. Although online communications, paperless offices, and cloud services are all integral features of digital lawyering, technology only serves to facilitate the practice of law. We want to instil an understanding of how technology impacts on legal practice and give you the opportunity to reflect on this new reality. Ethical issues are varied, and exposing you to some of these potential issues will help you develop your own approach to the use of technology within law.

An understanding of ethics is an essential component of legal education and legal practice. Throughout your law degree you will have opportunities to explore ethics in many different contexts and engage in ethical debates. Many fundamental ethical issues arise with the development of new technologies, legal practice, and the delivery of legal services in a digital environment. In this textbook, we discuss ethics through the lens of technology to give you a flavour of some of the ethical issues that technology may raise. If you understand technology and become tech-savvy, then you will be able to consider some of the potential ethical dilemmas that arise at the intersection of law and technology. If you are advanced digitally, you will have an awareness of technology-related ethical issues, and this will enable you to leverage that knowledge and understanding in your career.

In this textbook we discuss some specific technologies, such as AI in Chapter 7, and some of the ethical issues which can arise from it. For example, there are increasing concerns about the ethical implications of the use of predictive analytics in relation to judicial decision-making (using technology to predict the likely decision of a judge in a case). In addition, the use of AI does not just impact on the administration of law; it is also changing the way lawyers practise law. The examples given in this chapter raise a myriad of ethical issues, from questions of the competence of individual lawyers, to issues of liability for automated legal tasks, to concerns over social media usage, to issues of data privacy and confidentiality online.

Technology can also reduce the need for lawyers in some instances. For example, in Chapter 4 we discuss legal chatbots, which use AI to automate interactions between the user and the chatbot. They are being developed by law firms and in the not-for-profit sector to help people who would otherwise struggle to access legal information and advice. All of this can create additional ethical issues, from ensuring individual lawyers understand the bot's use sufficiently to meet their professional obligations to act competently, to meeting their requirements to supervise its use appropriately.

In addition to thinking about ethical issues which may arise for you personally, it is important that you are aware of the ethical implications of technology because you may be in a position in the future where you have to advise on ethical challenges that face your client and your law firm. If you have a greater understanding of how technology is transforming the practice of law, then you will be better prepared to enter the workplace. You need to be ethically driven from the start and have the confidence to be able to recognise ethical issues, evaluate the options, and make sound decisions.

DIGITAL LAWYERING AND LEGAL EDUCATION

Now is an exciting time in the legal profession as it adapts to and leverages the affordances of digital transformation in its delivery of services. This means it is equally an exciting time to be a law student who is preparing to embark on this digital transformation journey and work in new and creative ways with the law and in the practice of law. For legal academics, this is also an important time to consider how to create opportunities for learning and to prepare students for the digital change in the profession.

Although not all law students will go on to (or want to go on to) become legal professionals, a significant number do so. Often law schools work with law firms and other stakeholders within the legal profession to develop their offerings and provide extracurricular activities for their students. This means that changes within the legal profession will usually also filter through to legal education. More generally, most law schools and universities are keen that their students should be able to gain employment after they graduate, so they will try to equip their students with skills they feel are necessary or desirable within the workplace.

As a result of this, digital lawyering has already begun to impact upon legal education. This will be explored further in Chapters 11 and 13, but one example is the increased number of law schools that offer modules, courses, or programmes with a focus on digital lawyering. Other students will be given extracurricular opportunities involving digital technology, such as volunteering to develop a smartphone app or online legal resources. More broadly, all students have to develop their digital skills to ensure that they can cope with the demands of the law degree, from completing word processed assignments and submitting them online to using online databases for legal research.

Digital lawyering is multifaceted in that it encompasses knowledge, skills, attributes, and professional rules into a mindset and professional way of being. As such, it asks students to consider and develop their own impressions on how they can contribute to influencing digital transformation of the legal workplace. Digital lawyering cannot be studied as a single discipline. It impacts all knowledge and skills and extends its boundaries beyond the components of subjects and modules that make up a law degree, drawing on a broad range of knowledge and awareness that can equip a law student to be future-ready. This may sound daunting, as an understanding of digital lawyering cannot be easily learnt or acquired simply through a series of lectures or a one-off project. However, it also means that students can draw upon their own existing knowledge, experience, skills, and attributes to develop their understanding and insight. We hope this textbook will help you in identifying and developing how you can best do this.

HOW TO USE THIS TEXTBOOK

Each chapter in this textbook can stand alone, or they can be read in order, cover to cover. If you are using this textbook to accompany a course or module, your instructor may ask you to read specific chapters, depending on the focus. In all cases, Chapters 1–3 are recommended as core readings.

Each chapter will have a number of features that students and instructors will find helpful:

- *Hot spots.* At the beginning of each chapter are a number of key questions that you should keep in mind as you read the chapter text. When you have completed a chapter, you should return to those questions and review them to see if you feel able to provide an answer to each one. If there are any questions you find difficult to answer, you may want to reread sections of the chapter or undertake some wider reading on the topics. Underneath the key questions for each chapter there is also space for you to write some additional questions. These may be focused on queries or issues that you think of when you read the chapter title, or ones which arise during your reading of the chapter. At the end of the chapter, you should check whether these have been answered or consider undertaking some wider research and reading.
- *Mind maps.* Each chapter contains a mind map summarising its key themes to help you navigate the content. These are also summarised in Chapter 14 of the textbook.
- *Syncs.* Each chapter includes a number of syncs, interactive exercises of varying length and complexity. These are designed to help you think about and understand what you have read, for example, by asking you to apply some of the concepts presented in the chapter or to perform a limited amount of research on a topic to see real-life illustrations.
- *Skills boxes.* Most chapters highlight key skills that a digital lawyer should be sure to acquire and practise.
- *Additional resources.* Each chapter lists a number of additional resources for learning, to enrich the information presented, or to highlight additional paths for skills and knowledge acquisition relevant to the topic at hand.
- *Glossary.* Legal and technological terms that are important for you to understand are listed and defined in the glossary included at the end of the textbook.

We recommend that you read actively, using your favourite note-taking method, whether it be outlining, mind mapping, or a more structured method. Traditional annotation in the margins of the purchased paper edition, or using note-taking features of your reader application in the case of an e-book edition, is warmly recommended, if possible, given the density and range of topics we will present.

As you read, try to take occasional breaks during reading or after your sync activities to summarise your impressions in note form and write down any questions that occur based on your work in that chapter to that point. Being active in your reading, pausing, and taking stock of questions are practices that serve the traditional lawyer well and will surely bear fruit for the rising digital lawyer.

A NOTE ON SOURCES

One of the reasons we chose to write this textbook was because there was a lack of books, particularly aimed at students, which explored digital lawyering. Although there are a range of academic articles on the topic, these are often very jurisdiction-specific; for example, some focus on the specific requirements placed on lawyers in the United States when dealing with technology. They can also appear dated quite quickly; for example, you will find older articles which discuss the implications of introducing computerised databases or email systems into law firms! Although these are interesting historical snapshots of the development of digital lawyering, they are unlikely to be very helpful to a contemporary researcher.

As a result of this, you may find that you are relying more heavily upon non-academic sources than you would usually do when studying law. For example, a wide range of websites, blogs, and podcasts are devoted to digital lawyering and related issues. The benefit of this is that you can access a diverse range of perspectives on relevant topics. You can also read commentary on very recent innovations or challenges that have arisen. However, it also means that you have to be very careful to assess the validity and persuasiveness of your sources. A good starting point is to check who the author is: Are they known for a particular viewpoint? Do they have a vested interest in the topic? For example, someone who works for a company developing AI for law firms is unlikely to argue that AI is a danger to the future of the legal profession! You will also need to check the date to ensure technological developments have not overtaken its content.

In terms of the content itself, think about whether the points the author makes are supported by evidence. What sources have they used? How reliable are they? It is important to try to separate out personal opinion from factual information and well-evidenced arguments. You should also try to think about any counterarguments that the author has ignored or disregarded to assess their validity for yourself.

This may sound like extra work, but approaching your research and reading in this way will in itself assist you in developing valuable skills. You will be practising active reading and applying critical thinking, both of which are crucial for digital lawyers.

OUR JOURNEYS INTO DIGITAL LAWYERING

Having introduced you to digital lawyering and the structure of this book, we now want to introduce you to ourselves as authors. The previous section emphasised that when reading a piece of writing, you should think about the position of the author and how that may affect their perspective. Hearing a little about our journeys will help you to understand and evaluate our perspectives as you read through the subsequent chapters. In Chapter 14, we will also give you our personal visions of digital lawyering 30 years into the future, which are again influenced by our experiences to date.

EMMA JONES

Image 1.1 Emma Jones

I began my working life as a solicitor, specialising in construction law. During my training in the late 1990s, at a large firm in London, I spent a lot of time photocopying paperwork and hand-delivering documents to the nearby court and sets of barristers' chambers. Although we did have access to email, it was not particularly well used, and there was still a large emphasis on speaking to the clients by telephone or sending documents via the direct exchange system (a kind of postal service for law firms). When I qualified as a solicitor, I worked at two large regional firms in Manchester, and during that time there was definitely a growing focus on digital technology, for example, using electronic templates when drafting construction contracts and conducting legal research using electronic databases. However, a lot of the work was still conducted fairly traditionally, and there was an emphasis on face-to-face and telephone interactions with clients.

From working as a solicitor, I eventually moved into academia via owning a bookshop, being a baby massage instructor and teaching 16- to 18-year-olds! At that point I became very interested in the role of emotions and wellbeing in legal education and the legal profession. It seemed to me to be something that had never really been discussed at my law school or during my time in legal practice. As a result, I began researching that area. During my research, digital technology was quite often referred to in relation to legal professionals as something that could potentially impact negatively on their wellbeing. In particular, the sense of emails and mobile telephones meant that clients assumed they were available 24/7. Of course, some positives also were mentioned. In particular, my research around wellbeing during the COVID-19 pandemic suggested that legal professionals really valued the opportunities which digital technology gave them to work from home and in a flexible manner.

My research has also led me to study concepts like professional identity and professionalism in detail. When doing so, it has become clear that digital technology is impacting many facets of legal life. It is not simply about making processes faster and/or more effective; it also influences how people perceive themselves and their work and has the potential to alter key concepts which define who and what a legal professional is.

In addition to my research, I have recently been studying AI safety. This has emphasised to me the need for law students and lawyers to reflect upon how broader issues around safety and ethics apply within the legal sphere.

FRANCINE RYAN

Image 1.2 Francine Ryan

I qualified as a solicitor in 1996 at a large law firm in Manchester and specialised in complex disease litigation. When I started as a trainee there were no computers and no email, and mobile phones looked like bricks! In those days, lawyers dictated letters which were typed by secretaries; the telephone and the fax machine were the other main forms of communication. During my career, technology started transforming the practice of law. Law firms introduced case management systems, along with access to the internet, email, and smartphones, and over time the practice of law was redesigned. I developed new skills to help me navigate these changes, and when I left legal practice, it had been changed beyond recognition.

In 2010, I moved from legal practice into academia, and became a law academic at The Open University, the UK's largest university, which has pioneered distance learning for over 50 years. Technology and pedagogy are symbiotic at The Open University: They go hand in hand to deliver the learning experience to our students. In the law school we innovate and are adopting new and emerging technologies to develop practical legal activities for our students. I am passionate about access to justice and how we can leverage technology to provide information and advice to people via smartphones and the internet.[11] I lead a digital justice project where students design chatbots to give legal information and advice on a variety of different areas of law. I have

11 Hugh McFaul, Elizabeth FitzGerald, David Byrne and Francine Ryan, 'A Mobile App for Public Legal Education: A Case Study of Co-designing with Students' (2020) 28 *Research in Learning Technology*.

developed a virtual reality courtroom and have designed educational resources to support the knowledge and confidence in the use of Generative AI. There is a link in the footnotes and at the end of this chapter to the free Open Learn resources on Generative AI. There are eight courses, which you can study at your own pace, and they have been designed to support an understanding of what GenAI is, and how to use it ethically and responsibly.[12] My research interests focus on bridging legal education and practice, with an emphasis on advancing access to justice through innovative teaching and research. I am interested in the intersection between law and technology and in particular technology-enhanced learning and innovation. I am also exploring how Generative AI is shaping the future of legal education and practice. I think it is an exciting time to study law and there are many new opportunities emerging that go beyond a career as a lawyer.

ANN THANARAJ

Image 1.3 Ann Thanaraj

I started teaching law at the University of Cumbria. I specialised in land law, equity and trusts, and employment law. I always created opportunities that encouraged curiosity and inspired students to learn. Eager to expand the learning ecosystem into courtrooms, I developed a new module which I called Lawyers' Skills. It focused on preparing students for the real world of legal practice, coaching, and mentoring them with

12 OLCreate: AI Law and Legal Training | OLCreate.

the confidence to thrive in the professional world of practice, combining a sense of adventure and realism. The craft of advocacy, courtroom skills, and client interviews featured heavily in this module, supported by a body of professional and legal ethics.

In 2014, as I took on the role of head of a law school, industries and professions began to embark on a digital transformation journey, I wondered what the direction of the legal profession would be: Would technology be of interest to the way the profession operated? Would it change what we do? What would that mean for my students? My reflections led to some scholarly work which has been at the epicentre of developing my future-focused thinking of how curricula can be shaped to address the changing legal profession. To me it was more than just skills to use pieces of technologies; beyond that, it involved developing the art and craft of creativity in learners, to become resilient, become adaptable and communicate in a variety of novel ways using digital solutions and other ways that are accessible. It was also about reimagining law modules so that they captured learning that seamlessly integrated the physical and digital worlds and the adequacy of laws to protect and regulate.

I set out to invest time to support students in developing digital literacies within the law curriculum through this module. I designed the Virtual Law Clinic (VLC), a novel approach that allows real-world legal transactions to take place online in partnership between students, supervising tutors and pro bono solicitors in practice. Shifting to a virtual clinic allowed me to take practical learning to a digital landscape, giving students a realistic view of the impact of technologies redefining the role of legal professionals. As a learning and teaching tool, the VLC was showcased in several countries, profiled by the Higher Education Academy in its *Handbook of Teaching and Learning: Teaching in the Disciplines* and identified as a best practice in learning and teaching (L+T) by the Solicitors Regulation Authority for its transformation of practical legal education. To accompany the practical hands-on digital lawyering experiences in the VLC, I began to build "digital lawyering" as a new body of theory within legal education. The impact on learning comes through the redesign of how students study law. I passionately advocate for an interdisciplinary law curriculum, weaving subjects from humanities, science, ethics, technology, and philosophy into the study of law to bring to life and prepare students to address societal, technological, and regulatory challenges in a technologically mediated world. This puts students at the forefront of shaping innovation and thinking beyond legal doctrine—as real-world problems are multidimensional—and futureproofing themselves for the reshaping of the world of work.

To spearhead a growing field of tech law in legal education, I founded Lawyering in a Digital Age, an international conference (now an annual event) born out of my conviction that committed and enthusiastic people interested in legal education could contribute to global excellence in L+T in the discipline. It has led to an extensive reach of a collaborative interdisciplinary and global audience sharing the value in preparing students with the creativity, digital skill set, design concepts, and systems thinking through interdisciplinarity.

As I continue to advocate strongly for modern models of legal education that encompasses digital literacies and interdisciplinary learning, I now lead the digital transformation of learning and teaching across Teesside University in my present role as Associate Professor & Head of Digital and AI Innovations. The past few years of research, curriculum design and advocacy on digital lawyering has been a catalyst for me to commence Teesside University's Education 4.0 ambitions and setting the sector standard for driving excellence in university-wide course design and delivery. There is much more for me to learn, and much more I'd love to share. I continue my search to understand how best students learn, particularly in becoming future-ready for dynamic technology-mediated practices and how teaching practitioners from across disciplines can be better supported to design excellent learning experiences to educate law students and others for the Fourth Industrial Revolution. I am also a principal fellow of the Higher Education Academy.

TERRY WONG

Image 1.4 Terry Wong

I remember vividly the day I arrived at secondary school in a quiet town in central Connecticut in the United States. I walked into our campus computing centre and sat down at a terminal, beginning a journey that has taken me through most of my education and professional life to the present. It was a privilege in those days to access and use without limitation what was a then state-of-the-art minicomputer, the Digital Equipment VAX 11–750 running the BSD 4.2 release of UNIX. It was a large, powerful, versatile machine occupying most of the floor space in a constantly air-conditioned room of nine square metres with specialised electrical outlets and fail-safes. This sort of power was usually reserved for university research or running advanced automated operations in manufacturing plants, *not* the study tool and occasional playground of a little gang of curious teenagers with a predilection for hacking. As we will see, the same computer power can be found today in the widely popular education and maker computer platform, the Raspberry Pi from the UK's Raspberry Pi foundation.

Graphics-rich word processors like today's Microsoft Word were not widely available. Most publishing was still done with analogue tools like phototypesetting systems. One of the tasks that the minicomputer class of UNIX computers I had at my disposal did better than nearly any other was text processing and digital typesetting. Precursors to the programs that now produce the Portable Document Format (PDF) files all lawyers and businesspeople handle every day were first created and used on those machines. Working not only on our school news publications but also on reports and personal publishing projects, I learned the concepts and intricacies of document structure, indexing, typesetting software, and other foundation knowledge needed to support large-scale creation and management of electronic documents at a young age.

My early professional life was as a consultant working in Boston with Andersen Consulting LLP, the firm that would become Accenture. I was chosen by the firm's leadership to be the technology lead in a specially formed unit that took emerging internet technologies and made them understandable and, more importantly, strategically useful to our clients and consultants. This role led naturally to my ongoing involvement since then in a continuous series of roles in new technology-enabled ventures, with a focus on leading teams to integrate promising new technologies in the construction of innovative, scalable systems for consumers and the companies that serve them.

A group of investors and entrepreneurs in Hong Kong approached me in 2014 to serve as the chief technology officer (CTO) on the founding team of a legal technology venture dedicated to making the process of drafting legal documents more consistent, reliable and, most importantly, accessible and affordable for the everyday small businessperson. My team did so with a novel combination of automation, expert systems technology, and an innovative online subscription service delivery model that had not yet been attempted in Asia—or indeed, in many parts of the world. Interest in the venture and in our technology led to speaking and lecturing opportunities for me, and wonderful opportunities to engage practising lawyers and firm leaders, other entrepreneurs and, perhaps most rewarding, students who always asked tough questions I could not have anticipated.

Today I continue with Cydeas, my current software development and investment business. I lead a team of professionals developing and operating a portfolio of technology-enabled businesses serving needs in a range of industries, including human resources, financial technology and, of course, legal technology. In the process I have had the good fortune to be introduced by a good friend and former colleague, Chris Sykes, to my co-authors, who all impressed upon me the need and important opportunity to share a legal technologist's views as we offer this text on digital lawyering. I hope my presentation of some of the more involved technology concepts is accessible and useful, and that it might help some of you along your path in the legal profession, but perhaps in this exciting interdisciplinary area of digital lawyering, where there is sure to be much action and new directions in the coming decades.

CONCLUSION

As you read this book you will see there are many ways students can get involved in digital lawyering and start to develop the skills required for a transforming workplace. It is also important to remember that the whole world of work is changing. The future of work is going to look different across all industries and professions. It will revolve around how we use technology to remove boundaries, connect securely and collaborate to achieve productive and meaningful interactions. Whatever your career plans, you need to be open to learning because as new digital technology is adopted, the skills required will change. This means you will need to become a lifelong learner, continuing to invest the time in building the skills that will be required for the next stage of your career.

ADDITIONAL RESOURCES

To start or continue your digital lawyering learning journey, here are some useful additional resources:

AI Safety <https://safe.ai/>
Cisco Academy <https://www.netacad.com>
Future Learn <https://www.futurelearn.com/subjects/it-and-computer-science-courses>
Hackathons <https://www.openhackathons.org/s/>
LawTech UK <https://lawtechuk.io/>
LinkedIn <https://www.linkedin.com> Join one of the many legal technology groups including Legal Hackers, Legal Design Special Interest Group, and Legal Innovation and Technology.
Society for Computers and Law <https://www.scl.org>
Eight free online courses that explore Generative AI designed for beginners: <https://www.open.edu/openlearncreate/course/index.php?categoryid=2150>

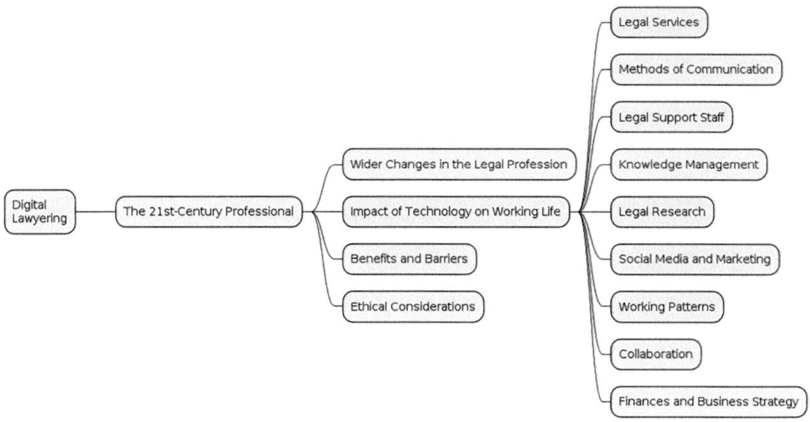

Mind Map 2.1 Chapter topics

2 The 21st-Century Legal Professional

Emma Jones

Introduction

This chapter begins by considering the various developments and changes which have shaped the contemporary role and work of the legal profession. It looks at the ways in which digital technology is impacting on, and in some cases transforming, everyday legal practice. It explores the opportunities and challenges that arise, with a particular emphasis on day-to-day workings of law firms and other legal providers. It concludes by considering how this will shape the lawyer of the future.

Chapter hot spots

When reading this chapter, questions to think about include:

- To what extent has (and is) digital technology driving change in the legal profession?
- How does digital technology interact with other factors influencing the legal profession?
- How is digital technology changing the relationships between legal professionals and their clients?
- What does the lawyer of the future do?

Having read the title and introduction, you can add any other questions you want to explore here:

DOI: 10.4324/9781003602323-2

THE CHANGING LEGAL PROFESSION

In recent years, the legal profession has experienced a significant level of transformation. It is important to understand the key changes involved to put the role of digital technology in context (Figure 2.1). These include the following:

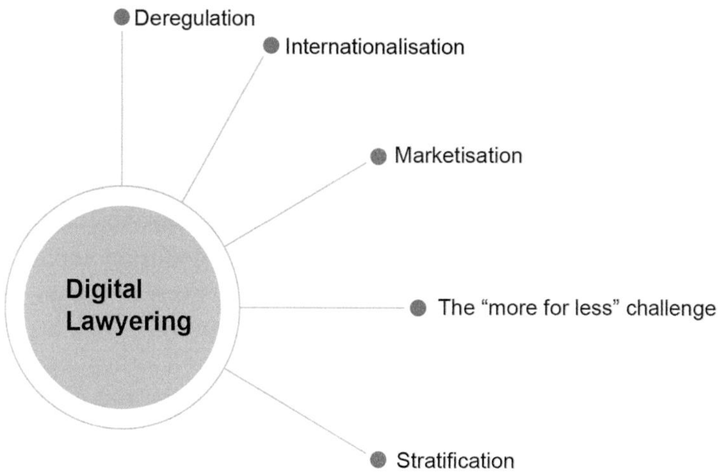

Figure 2.1 Key changes in the legal profession

- *Marketisation.* A majority of lawyers work in private practice, obtaining their work from individuals or businesses who require legal services. This could range from a person seeking to increase their contact with their children to an international company looking to acquire a potential competitor. Such clients can instruct legal professionals directly (e.g. when someone goes to see a chartered legal executive or solicitor) or indirectly (e.g. when a solicitor instructs a barrister on behalf of a client). Being in private practice means that lawyers are operating in a commercial environment where they need to compete to obtain and retain clients and generate profits in order for their firm to survive. In other words, law becomes a type of business. This is in contrast to traditional ideas of lawyers as working for the public good rather than for profits. Another word often used to describe parts of this process is commodification. This reflects the idea that law and legal advice have become a commodity, used for economic gain, rather than being viewed as having wider societal functions, such as maintaining the rule of law and promoting democracy.

- *The "more for less" challenge.* This is a phrase coined by the author Richard Susskind[1] which has links to the marketisation of the legal profession. It refers to the way in which wider economic pressures lead to businesses seeking to spend less money on legal services. However, at the same time they increasingly need specialist legal advice to assist them in their work. Individuals too are facing cuts in the public funding of legal services (such as legal aid) despite the massive impact legal issues can have on their lives (e.g. in relation to housing, employment, and family issues). Therefore, the difficulty for the legal profession is how to provide more legal assistance at a time where there is less funding and fewer resources available to do so. In addition, businesses and individuals may have expectations that their disputes will be resolved faster and more effectively through the use of modern technology, but this may not always be the case. For example, despite the increasing use of online court hearings (see Chapter 9), there can still be significant delays in procedures.
- *Diversification.* The profession has shifted (at least in part) from being largely male, white, and middle class. For example, the Law Society of England and Wales has identified that more women than men now hold practising certificates (enabling them to work as solicitors).[2] Although there are still barriers to progression within the legal profession, there is increasing recognition of these issues, and a number of schemes have been developed to promote equality, diversity, and inclusivity. For example, in the United States, the American Bar Association Commission on Sexual Orientation and Gender Identity and the National LGBT+ Bar Association are both working to ensure that lesbian, gay, bisexual, and transgender persons participate fully in the profession.
- *Stratification.* Traditionally, the legal profession consisted of a (relatively small) number of professionals and law firms that would deal with a wide range of disputes. However, over time different groups of professionals and firms have emerged, often specialising in par-

1 Richard Susskind, *Tomorrow's Lawyers: An Introduction to Your Future* (OUP 2023) 2–4.

2 The Law Society of England and Wales, 'Entry Trends' (28 January 2025) <https://www.lawsociety.org.uk/support-services/research-trends/annual-statistics-report-201>, accessed 13 August 2025.

ticular areas. As a result, today's legal profession includes a wide range of different roles, types of firms and businesses, and categories of clients spread across many geographical locations. For example, solicitors' firms range from a sole practitioner in a small town who largely does conveyancing work (buying and selling houses) to a global chain of law offices that works with international organisations on corporate deals. Many large businesses will also have in-house legal departments, and there is an increasing number of entrepreneurial lawyers creating new ways of practising law. Such a broad and diverse spread means that it is difficult to refer to the legal profession as a single, homogenous group. Even within one particular sector, or firm, individuals now often specialise in a particular area of law, such as housing or shipping law, making it even more fragmented.

- *Internationalisation.* The legal profession has reflected the broader globalisation of society in often working across borders on international disputes. Many law firms also offer legal services in a range of countries.
- *Deregulation.* Another term sometimes used to describe this is liberalisation. Traditionally, legal services have been offered by only a relatively small group of people. To protect the public and to retain the status of the legal profession, the way in which these services have been offered has been tightly regulated. For example, the type of business structure used to provide a specific legal service would be tightly prescribed.

In England and Wales, the Legal Services Act 2007 has resulted in the removal of a range of restrictions that previously governed where, how and by whom different legal services are offered. In particular, it allowed the use of alternative business structures (ABSs).

ABSs: Doing business differently

ABSs were created to generate competition in the legal services market. They do this by making it easier for non-lawyers to own and invest in law firms. This means that a wide range of organisations, including charities, trade unions, insurance companies, estate agents, and many more, now offer legal services. This has contributed significantly to the stratification of the legal profession referred to previously.

In England and Wales, a number of bodies, including the Solicitor Regulation Authority (SRA) and the Bar Standards Board (BSB), have the power to grant licences to ABSs. In October 2019, the SRA's records showed that 1025 ABSs had been licensed in total. The first to become an ABS was The Co-operative Legal Services, part of the Co-op Group, who are a large food retailer, and also offer funeral and insurance services.

It is not only England and Wales which allow these structures (also sometimes referred to as "Alternative Legal Service Providers" or "ALSPs"). The first common-law jurisdiction to do so was New South Wales in Australia in 2001, with other Australian states following its example. However, ABSs are not generally permitted in the United States, although some states are beginning to pilot such schemes.

Although the introduction of ABSs opened up the market for legal services, it would be wrong to think that this meant regulation of the sector has been abolished entirely. The Legal Services Act 2007 also created a new regulator to oversee the whole of the legal services market in England and Wales (the Legal Services Board) and introduced the Office for Legal Complaints, which in turn set up the Legal Ombudsman for England and Wales to deal with consumer complaints against lawyers.

Sync 1: The legal profession today

You should allow around 20 minutes for this activity.

Choose one of the key changes discussed in this section and think about:

1 Whether this change has been influenced by the growing use of digital technology in the legal profession.

2 Whether this change could influence the future use of digital technology within the legal profession.

Using an internet search engine, find at least one example to support your answer.

Depending on which change you selected, you may have come up with a variety of answers. If you chose to consider deregulation and ABSs, you probably found a range of articles indicating that these are promoting technological innovation within the legal sector. A recent

Legal Services Board survey of 1310 organisations offering legal services in England and Wales found that ABSs were consistently more engaged with technology and innovation than non-ABS organisations, for example, through investment in digital services, partnership with lawtech firms and appropriate written strategies and policies.[3] It could also be argued that the growth in technology was one of many factors which prompted the change in regulation. The Clementi Review of the Regulatory Framework for Legal Services in England and Wales (which preceded the Legal Services Act 2007) referred to individuals such as information technology (IT) professionals who were involved in the management of law firms but were not at that time able to be the principal (the individual with executive authority) of the firm.[4]

THE IMPACT OF DIGITAL TECHNOLOGY ON DAY-TO-DAY LEGAL PRACTICE

This section will consider what impact digital technology is having upon contemporary legal practice. This is a very broad question and, to some extent at least, the answer will vary depending on jurisdiction, type of legal service, and many other factors. The next activity is designed to assist you in breaking down some of the key issues to think about.

Sync 2: How to explore the impact of digital technology

You should allow around 10 minutes for this activity.

You are a trainee in a law firm and have been asked to write a report assessing "what is the impact of digital technology upon the legal profession". Identify the key issues to look at, or further questions to ask, to help you write this report.

3 Legal Services Board, 'Technology and Innovation in Legal Services' (May 2023) <https://legalservicesboard.org.uk/wp-content/uploads/2023/06/20230425-Tech-and-Innov-survey-2022-Designed.pdf>, accessed 13 August 2025.

4 David Clementi, 'Review of the Regulatory Framework for Legal Services in England and Wales' (December 2004) <https://www.legal-services-review.org.uk/content/report/foreword> accessed 13 August 2013.

When considering this question, you may have identified a range of issues, ranging from questioning how you define terms such as "digital technology" and "legal profession" to pinpointing large topics such as artificial intelligence or the impact of technology on legal ethics. When asking herself this question, the author of this chapter realised that one way to consider this was to divide it into two questions, as follows:

- What is the impact of technology on the day-to-day work of legal professionals?
- What is the impact on the legal profession as a whole?

For the purposes of this chapter, she decided to focus on the former question (the other question will be discussed in subsequent chapters). This led her to the following further questions:

- What impact does digital technology have on the day-to-day tasks which legal professionals perform?
- What impact does digital technology have on the ways in which legal professionals interact with their clients?
- What impact does digital technology have on the ways in which legal professionals interact with other colleagues?
- What impact does digital technology have on the ways in which legal professionals interact with the courts?

To think about the questions just raised, it is useful to compare a lawyers' office from the 1980s with a lawyers' office today. So, let's start with a look at the firm of Glossop, Charlesworth & Co Solicitors in around 1986. Figure 2.2 offers a reminder of some of the technology available at that time!

The firm is based in a large town and has eight partners, ten assistant solicitors, two trainee solicitors, and 13 legal secretaries. They deal with a wide range of work, from transactions between businesses to conveyancing and family disputes. Each partner has their own office. Assistant and trainee solicitors share offices in pairs. The working hours are 9 am to 5.30 pm with a break for lunch, but most solicitors will be in the office from around 8.30 am to 6.30 pm.

The firm conducts most of its correspondence with individual clients through the postal system. Letters to clients are typed out on typewriters by the legal secretaries. Where possible, they send post second class to save on expense (meaning it takes around three days before it is received by the client). The firm will also ring clients on

Figure 2.2 Lawtech in the 1980s!

their home or work telephone lines if there is an urgent matter to discuss. None of their clients has a mobile telephone, but a number do have answering machines on their landlines.

For business clients, the firm will also send facsimiles (known as faxes). This involves an original document being scanned through an optical scanner and then transmitted to another fax machine, where a copy appears. The firm has a dedicated fax number to avoid their landline being tied up. Other law firms are communicated with via fax or the direct exchange system, which is a form of internal postal system within the legal profession for the sending of hard-copy letters.

The firm has a file for each client, stored on shelves and in filing cabinets. There is a sheet on the front of each file on which employees record their time whenever they work on the file. Inside the file are copies of all correspondence and other documents relating to the case.

Court documents are either typed on a typewriter or completed by hand by the legal secretaries; documents are taken to the nearest court in large bundles by the trainee solicitor three times a week. A significant number of matters involve litigation, although often they are settled via negotiation between legal representatives.

Most legal research is undertaken by the trainee and assistant solicitors using the volumes of *Halsbury's Laws of England* and other large law books which are kept in the partners' offices. Occasionally they will need to travel to the larger law library in the nearest city. No one in the firm has an internet connection.

The firm has recently invested in a new word processor, but only one legal secretary is confident in using it. The aim in the next couple of years is to create a number of precedent documents to use and store on floppy disks.

The firm markets its services through a double-page advertisement in the weekly local newspaper and on two billboards which are located on the major roads in and out of the town.

Now, let's move on to the present day, when the original Glossop, Charlesworth & Co Solicitors has evolved into Glossop Law. Figure 2.3 provides some clues to the changes that have occurred.

Figure 2.3 Contemporary digital lawyering

The firm is still based in the same large town and now has eight partners, six assistant solicitors, one trainee solicitor, four paralegals, five legal secretaries, an office manager, an IT manager, and a finance manager.

They continue to deal with a wide range of work, from transactions between businesses to conveyancing and family disputes. However, in recent years they have received fewer instructions on straightforward conveyancing issues. They are beginning to receive some queries relating to digital technology, including a potential copyright dispute over online material and assisting a start-up company who are designing an AI tool. Several of its partners are trained mediators and their services are advertised on the firm's web page.

Each staff member has a computer in their office. The office arrangements remain the same, but several solicitors also have firm laptops and work from home one or two days a week. Some of the partners, assistant solicitors and paralegals use voice-to-text software. Client correspondence is usually emailed, unless a client has specified a preference for postal copies. Phone calls are still made to clients on urgent matters, often to their mobile phones. A couple of the solicitors use WhatsApp to communicate with regular clients too. Other solicitors are commonly contacted using email, and the fax machine was removed a while ago.

The firm uses an online case management system licensed from an international software company. It enables employees to record their time, make notes of conversations with clients and set reminders for key deadlines (e.g. for the return of court documents). Most client documents and correspondence are also now stored on computer, freeing up space for an additional office.

Court correspondence is regularly dealt with via email, and for some claims documents are submitted via the Money Claims Online system. Overall, significantly fewer cases result in litigation, and the firm now advises on methods of alternative dispute resolution.

The majority of legal research is undertaken by the trainee, assistant solicitors, and paralegals. It is all now conducted online, and the firm subscribes to several major online legal databases, as well as to an online database of forms and precedents which the secretaries use to generate documents as needed. It has recently subscribed to a Generative AI tool provided by a large legal publisher to speed up the research and drafting process.

In addition to a bespoke website, the firm also has a LinkedIn account and is considering expanding its social media presence. Several solicitors regularly write short articles on recent developments in the law, which are then posted on the firm's website.

Sync 3: Looking back

You should allow around 45 minutes for this activity.

1 Comparing the snapshots of Glossop, Charlesworth & Co Solicitors and Glossop Law, what do you think are the key differences in terms of the day-to-day work of the firm's employees?

2 Write a similar pair of scenarios for either (a) a sole practitioner, (b) the London office of a large law firm with offices globally or (c) a barrister in private practice.

3 Thinking about the new pair of scenarios you have written, to what extent do you think the impact of digital technology differs between different parts of the legal profession?

Your answers to Sync 3 have probably demonstrated that different types of legal professionals and firms will have been impacted in different ways, but it is clear that all parts of the legal profession have significantly evolved in technological terms.

Some of the key differences between the two eras are explored under the following subsections.

THE TYPES OF SERVICES BEING OFFERED

The example of Glossop, Charlesworth & Co Solicitors stated that the firm dealt with a wide range of work. The example of Glossop Law mentioned that the firm was dealing with less routine conveyancing matters. This is likely to be because of the rise in online conveyancing firms offering such services, often at a reduced rate. Other types of services may well be affected by competition from online alternatives, such as complaining about a consumer product or applying for a patent. The increased amount of legal information available online may also encourage some clients to research and deal with minor issues without involving a third party.

It is also likely that new areas of work have emerged, or become more significant, as the law develops to regulate the use of digital technology itself and new legal issues emerge. Several examples of this are given in the scenario.

The Legal Services Consumer Panel's 2025 Tracker Report on consumers' use of legal services found that the number of legal services users accessing online legal services (via the internet or email) rose from 21% in 2011 to 33% in 2019 to 34% in 2025. Its findings show that conducting legal services by post is in decline, falling to 3% in 2025 from 8% in 2019 and 16% in 2012. However, face-to-face delivery remains most common at 46%, and the number of users accessing these in-person services has remained fairly static in recent years.[5]

5 Legal Services Consumer Panel, 'Tracker Survey 2025: How Consumers Are Using Legal Services' <https://www.legalservicesconsumerpanel.org.uk/wp-content/uploads/2025/07/25.07.07-How-consumers-are-using-legal-services-report-2025.pdf> accessed 13 August 2025.

The use of technology has also encouraged the "unbundling" of legal services. Previously, a client would instruct a solicitor (or other legal professional) on a legal matter, and their retainer would cover all issues arising from that matter. Nowadays, a client may instead retain control over the matter and instead buy-in advice or assistance only as needed.[6] For example, an individual with a small claim against a builder for faulty workmanship may pay for a legal professional to draft a claim form, but then conduct the rest of the litigation themselves. A landlord may purchase a template lease online and seek to adapt it to their own needs. A company may pay for assistance to draft a defence to a supplier's claim against them, but then focus on negotiating a solution themselves. The 2025 Tracker Report referred to previously found that 21% of legal services consumers were choosing to use such an "unbundled" service.[7]

THE GROWTH OF ELECTRONIC METHODS OF COMMUNICATION

The example of Glossop, Charlesworth & Co Solicitors noted that most correspondence was through the postal system, supplemented by calls to landlines. The example of Glossop Law noted that emails and telephone calls to clients (including to mobile telephones) are now a routine part of their work. Further examples of the use of these communications within legal practice generally are also given in Chapter 3. The shift from paper communications to electronic communications has a range of consequences. A number of these can be beneficial, for example, in saving on paper waste and ensuring that answers and information are provided promptly without letters getting lost or delayed.

However, there can also be some potentially negative impacts. Some of these are technology focused, as electronic communications

6 The Law Society of England and Wales, 'Unbundling Civil Legal Services' (12 April 2022) <https://www.lawsociety.org.uk/topics/civil-litigation/unbundling-civil-legal-services/> accessed 13 August 2025.

7 Legal Services Consumer Panel, 'Tracker Survey 2025: How Consumers Are Using Legal Services' <https://www.legalservicesconsumerpanel.org.uk/wp-content/uploads/2025/07/25.07.07-How-consumers-are-using-legal-services-report-2025.pdf> accessed 13 August 2025. See also 'Tracker Survey 2019. Briefing Note: How Consumers Are Using Legal Services" <https://www.legalservicesconsumerpanel.org.uk/wp-content/uploads/2019/07/2019-07-25-How-consumers-are-using-2019-FINAL.pdf> accessed 13 August 2025.

do not always reach their destination. They can still get accidentally deleted or misdirected. There is the risk of viruses and malware being passed on, with ransomware becoming an increasing problem.[8] Firms and their clients can also be the victims of phishing, where emails appear to be sent from a trusted body in an attempt to obtain financial and other information. A 2024 Australasian survey found that 81% of law firms surveyed had experienced phishing.[9] There may also be issues around confidentiality if apps such as WhatsApp are used. For example, the international law firm Linklaters lists on its websites a range of attempted scams involving WhatsApp messages purporting to be sent from one of their employees.[10]

The use of electronic communications can also have other, human consequences. Lawyers may feel under pressure to be available 24/7 and to provide immediate responses to emails and other electronic communications. As solicitors usually draft and send their own emails rather than dictating them to be typed, sometimes they may send them before taking the time to reflect on the content. This may be particularly problematic when dealing with another party's lawyer, as demonstrated by a case before the Solicitors Disciplinary Tribunal, where a solicitor was reprimanded for calling his opponent's solicitor a "plonker" and making other abusive comments in emails sent during afternoons when (it was argued) a medical condition made him angrier.[11]

In addition, there may be an impact on the relationship between a lawyer and clients. If lawyers are communicating more electronically, it may result in less face-to-face client meetings. This may mean it is harder to build a rapport and establish an effective professional relationship in some situations. Without being able to read the body language

8 Rebecca Moody, 'Law Firms Hit with Average Ransom Demand of $2.5 Million' (1 August 2024) <https://www.comparitech.com/blog/information-security/ransomware-attacks-law-firms/> accessed 13 August 2025.

9 AUCyber, LexVeritas and Australasian Legal Practice Management Associations, '2024 State of Cyber Security in Law' (September 2024) <https://www.ft.com/content/4da1117e-756c-11e9-be7d-6d846537acab> accessed 18 October 2019. <https://aucyber.com.au/events/alpma-2024/report/> accessed 13 August 2025.

10 Linklaters, 'Scam and Fraudulent Communications' <https://www.linklaters.com/en/legal-notices/fraudulent-emails> accessed 13 August 2025.

11 Dan Bindman, 'The Danger of Instant E-mail Replies as SDT Reprimands Solicitor Who Called Opponent "a Plonker"' (20 July 2015) <https://www.legalfutures.co.uk/latest-news/the-danger-of-instant-email-replies-as-sdt-reprimands-solicitor-who-called-opponent-a-plonker> accessed 13 August 2025.

of the person in front of you or see their facial expressions, it may be more challenging to interpret what they are saying and gauge their reactions to situations.

Such electronic communications can also lead to issues with record-keeping. If you are sitting at your desk speaking to a client, whether by telephone or in person, it is relatively easy to make notes of the discussion. If you take a quick call from your client on your mobile phone when travelling in between meetings, it can be harder to remember to record the details.

THE CHANGING ROLE OF LEGAL SUPPORT STAFF

The example of Glossop, Charlesworth & Co Solicitors stated that the firm has 13 legal secretaries. The example of Glossop Law noted that the number of legal secretaries has been reduced to five but that there was now an office manager as well as IT and finance managers.

The increasing use of technology has impacted on the type of support which lawyers now require. While the focus may previously have been on clerical and administrative tasks, support staff now are more likely to be involved in aspects of work such as implementing and managing online systems for recording chargeable hours and billing clients. Even within a particular role, such as that of a legal secretary, there are likely to be significant changes in the type of work being carried out. For example, as legal research becomes easier to conduct online, a lawyer may ask a secretary to log on to a legal database and find a particular case or article rather than going to the law books themselves.

Although in our example the firm has had IT and finance managers for around ten years, their role has changed significantly too. The IT side of their work has expanded significantly, as now not only do they need to support the hardware and software needs in the office and maintain firm-issued equipment, but they must also have the skills to manage and interact with a wide range of cloud-based services. They must understand the nuances of managing data and communications, particularly relating to the different devices that solicitors now use when on the move or working from home.

The types of technology being used also have changed significantly; for example, it is probable that lawyers' diaries will now be managed online, with a secretary having access to all calendars to manage appointments. This is likely to require new skills, which may in turn require additional training to upskill employees. It may also require a review of the firm's standard contracts of employment to ensure they reflect the new ways of working for legal support staff.

THE DIGITALISATION OF KNOWLEDGE MANAGEMENT

Knowledge management is about handling documents and information in the most effective manner possible. The example of Glossop, Charlesworth & Co Solicitors stated that the firm had large files stored on shelves and in filing cabinets. The example of Glossop Law noted that a large number of documents were now stored online instead. One academic article has termed such a digitalisation of documents the "digital advantage" because it enables information to be "instantaneously stored, copied, organised, tagged, searched, transmitted, modified, quantified, annotated, linked, etc."[12]

One simple example of the way technology can be utilised in knowledge management during the routine work of lawyers is note-taking. Traditionally, notes would be written by hand during a client interview, conference (meeting) with counsel, or any other significant discussion or meeting. They would then be stored in hard copy in the client's file afterwards. However, it is now possible for notes to be typed up and stored online or even (with appropriate permissions) for the interview or meeting to be recorded and transcribed.

In their 2022 survey of the use of technology and innovation among legal service providers, the Legal Services Board found that over half (54%) of the 1302 participants used the cloud or similar types of data storage.[13] The term "cloud" refers to data being stored in a separate online location, hosted by a third-party provider, which is accessed online. This made it the most frequently used form of technology. An example of drafting a document using the cloud is given in Chapter 3.

Using forms of electronic data storage not only reduces the need for physical storage space but also potentially makes retrieving and managing information easier and simpler and also ensures it can be accessed remotely. At the same time, it opens firms up to a range of

12 Conrad A. Johnson and Brian Donnelly, 'If Only We Knew What We Know' (2013) 88 *Chicago-Kent Law Review* 729, 735.

13 Legal Services Board, 'Technology and Innovation in Legal Services' (May 2023) <https://legalservicesboard.org.uk/wp-content/uploads/2023/06/20230425-Tech-and-Innov-survey-2022-Designed.pdf> accessed 13 August 2025.

security risks, from deliberate hacking with malicious intent to accidental downloads by employees.[14]

Problems with storing data on third-party systems: An example

In 2023 it was reported that international law firm Proskauer Rose had experienced a data breach involving approximately 184,000 files containing highly confidential legal and financial information. It was claimed that the source of the breach was an error on the part of a third party engaged by the law firm to work on a cloud-based storage system. The report suggested that the files had been publicly available for over six months and raised questions over what information the law firm had provided to clients over the breach.[15]

It is also important for lawyers to be aware of the rights and responsibilities of the third-party providers of such storage, something which requires careful study of their privacy and data protection policies. These issues will be discussed further in Chapters 3, 6 and 7.

Another aspect to knowledge management is the way that legal documents are created and drafted. The Legal Services Board's survey also found that 14% of participants used automated document assembly.[16] This could include using electronic precedents (as in the case of Glossop Law) or by using other electronic systems, such as decision trees, to create documents such as contracts or wills (for further discussion, see Chapter 3).

Using such systems can make the process faster and more effective for everyone involved. However, there are arguments that such automation will eventually make it unprofitable for law firms to offer drafting services for documents that clients may increasingly be able to assemble themselves utilising technology, once again impacting on the types of services offered by law firms and possibly their financial

14 Cheryl B. Preston, 'Lawyers' Abuse of Technology' (2018) 118 *Cornell Law Review* 881, 923.

15 Carly Page, 'Legal Powerhouse Proskauer Exposed Clients' Confidential M&A Data' (*TechCrunch*, 6 April 2023) <https://techcrunch.com/2023/04/06/proskauer-confidential-client-data/> accessed 13 August 2025. For another useful discussion, see Eliu Mendez, 'Dropping Dropbox in Your Law Practice to Maintain Your Duty of Confidentiality' (2013) 36 *Campbell Law Review* 175.

16 Legal Services Board, 'Technology and Innovation in Legal Services' (May 2023) <https://legalservicesboard.org.uk/wp-content/uploads/2023/06/20230425-Tech-and-Innov-survey-2022-Designed.pdf> accessed 13 August 2025.

survival.[17] It could also potentially lead to fewer opportunities for lawyers working in some areas and impact on the type and level of support staff involvement required. Despite this, at present the limitations of such systems mean that less routine, more complex or nuanced forms of documents will still require a lawyer's involvement.

A GREATER FOCUS ON ONLINE LEGAL RESEARCH

In the example of Glossop, Charlesworth & Co Solicitors, the junior members of the firm spent much time and effort researching points of law using hard copies of legal books and journals. Law firms would commonly have shelves of books or (in the larger firms) libraries devoted to printed material, and these would form the basis of all the legal research conducted. Some hard copies would come in binder-style covers so that updates could be posted out by the publishers and inserted into these volumes as the law developed and changed.

In contrast, at Glossop Law the legal research required is now conducted online. If you are studying law, you are probably already familiar with online databases such as Lexis Library, Westlaw and Lawtel, which allow quick access to primary (and some secondary) sources of law. There are also online databases of journal articles (e.g. HeinOnline), and e-book versions of law books are now commonplace. Legal publishers are also launching AI tools to assist lawyers in searching their databases and conducting research more efficiently, such as LexisNexis's Lexis+ AI. Other examples of the impact of digital technology on legal research are given in Chapter 3.

Many legal professionals are still required to have the more traditional skills of legal research, such as identifying key legal principles within a court judgment or being able to interpret and summarise the wording of a piece of law accurately. Even if they use Generative AI in the process, they still need to be able to check the accuracy of the results. However, in order to effectively carry out research online they also need various digital skills, including being able to formulate keywords for searches and prompts, identifying and verifying appropriate sources, organising and filtering digital search results and storing the results.

17 Eduardo Reyes, 'Who's Afraid of Computer Generation?' (*Law Society Gazette*, 28 October 2010) <https://www.lawgazette.co.uk/analysis/whos-afraid-of-computer-generation-/57836.article> accessed 12 November 2019.

INCREASES IN SOCIAL MEDIA USE AND DIGITAL MARKETING STRATEGIES

The example of Glossop, Charlesworth & Co Solicitors states that their advertising is done via the local newspaper and billboard advertisements. The example of Glossop Law mentions the firm has a bespoke website and a LinkedIn account and is considering expanding its social media presence. This change in marketing methods mirrors the rapid expansion of digital advertising and social media in recent years. The internet (via the World Wide Web) became publicly available only in 1991, and popular social media platform Facebook was founded only in 2004, with Twitter (now X) beginning in 2006 and Instagram following in 2010. In contrast, sales of local newspapers and the use of billboard advertising have both been steadily declining in recent years. It appears businesses, including law firms, view digital advertising and social media as potentially cheaper and more interactive ways to market themselves to a wider audience.

The use of different marketing methods does require people with relevant expertise to ensure they are used effectively. Glossop Law uses a local marketing agency to run twice-yearly online marketing campaigns for them. Larger firms may have one or more individuals to focus on marketing.

The use of social media by individual lawyers and law firms also raises new ethical questions and dilemmas; for example, should an individual lawyer accept a client's offer to connect on a platform such as Facebook? Should a law firm take into account an individual's social media presence when deciding whether to hire them for a particular job? These questions will be considered further in Chapter 5.

THE GROWTH OF FLEXIBLE WORKING PATTERNS

The example of Glossop, Charlesworth & Co Solicitors states that the solicitors work long hours in their offices. The example of Glossop Law noted that some solicitors now have laptops and regularly work from home. The use of email and a variety of online systems and resources means that there are increasing opportunities to work remotely, although it is likely most clients will require some face-to-face contact. Lawyers can also manage their time using software and project management tools (see Chapter 3).

Many law firms now have arrangements in place to allow individuals to work from home at least some of the time. There are many advantages in homeworking for individuals, including:

- Greater flexibility in managing your work and time.
- Better work-life balance (e.g. spending more time with family).
- Avoiding the time and money involved in commuting.
- Avoiding the environmental costs involved in commuting.

At the same time, there can be disadvantages for individuals, including:

- Finding it hard to separate out work from other areas of their lives.
- Feeling lonely and/or isolated from colleagues.
- Dealing with domestic interruptions and distractions.

Junior professionals having less opportunity to observe and learn from senior colleagues. For employers, the advantages to individuals working from home include having staff who are well-motivated, work independently and are committed to the firm. On the other hand, it may make it harder to foster a sense of collegiality, coordinate teamwork and manage individuals. It may also involve firms having to undertake health and safety assessments to ensure their employees are working in safe and appropriate environments.

Many of these advantages and disadvantages were demonstrated by the increase in flexible working patterns, homeworking and virtual meetings necessitated by the COVID-19 pandemic. Since then, a number of law firms have retained these working arrangements, but others have reverted to pre-pandemic patterns.

In terms of technology, allowing staff to work from home requires employers to invest in the equipment and software required for successfully working at a distance. This will include providing individuals with the right equipment, such as laptops, chargers and perhaps even mobile telephones. It could also involve purchasing and setting up new software and ways to manage the transfer of information. For example, it may be necessary to establish a virtual private network (VPN), an encrypted internet connection that individuals connect to remotely in order to assist in the safe transfer of data.

Another way in which technology allows lawyers to work flexibly is through allowing forms of communication that can take place at different times in different ways. For example, it would not be possible to telephone a client at midnight, but it is possible for someone to send an email at any time of the day or night. Some of the issues that arise with working remotely are discussed further in Chapter 3.

CHANGING FORMS OF COLLABORATION

Changes in terms of collaboration have occurred both within law firms and between law firms and other individuals/organisations. Traditionally, it might have been assumed that the large majority of employees working within a law firm had a legal background and training (as is the case in Glossop, Charlesworth & Co Solicitors). As such, they were more likely to share a common understanding on various issues. Changes in the skills required from employees mean that in many law firms there is now likely to be more individuals from non-legal backgrounds (e.g. the office and IT and finance managers who work for Glossop Law). This can be challenging, as such individuals may not be used to legal terminology or legal processes and procedures. However, it can also lead to positive forms of collaboration, with new insights and ideas being generated. For example, the IT and finance managers may be able to suggest a new way of recording billable hours and invoicing clients which would make timekeeping more efficient.

Internal forms of collaboration are also likely to change as a result in the growth of flexible working patterns discussed earlier. For example, face-to-face team meetings and discussions may be replaced by virtual meetings and chats via email or instant messaging.

External forms of collaboration are also likely now to rely more heavily on digital means, from emails to virtual meetings. Documents may be shared via online links rather than in hard copy. For example, contract amendments could be carried out via a shared storage area such as OneDrive or Google Drive.

These shifts may mean that collaborations can progress more quickly and efficiently. However, they may also mean that it is harder to build up a rapport and shared understanding with the other parties involved when there is less opportunity to read body language and have more casual conversations in person.

CHANGING APPROACHES TO DISPUTE RESOLUTION

The example of Glossop Law states that several of its partners are now trained mediators. Alternative dispute resolution, including mediation, conciliation, arbitration and adjudication, is increasingly a part of contemporary legal practice (and encouraged by the courts in civil cases). Technological changes have contributed to shifts in dispute resolution, with an increasing focus on online dispute resolution both within and outside the court system. This will be explored in more detail in Chapter 9.

CHANGES IN FINANCES AND BUSINESS STRATEGY

This section has identified a number of key changes which have taken place in law firms as a result of technological developments. However, it is also important to appreciate that any one of these changes cannot be viewed in isolation. The different changes are often linked; for example, developments in the forms of digital technology used will require either additional training for existing employees or potentially the creation of new roles, which in turn will require investment and possibly impact on individuals' working patterns. It may also mean physical changes (e.g. in terms of office layout) and changes in recruitment, employment and training.

Ultimately, such changes will have an impact on the overall finances and strategy of a law firm. In terms of finances, any form of new digital technology will require investment in software and/or hardware as well as training for users. It is also likely to require some form of ongoing maintenance and updating. In terms of strategy, when considering making such financial investments, law firms will have to consider how they want to position their firm in the legal services market and what their plans are for the future. A global survey of general counsels (who run corporate legal departments within organisations) found that there was a growing interest in and use of technical solutions, but that some common digital technologies were not being utilised:

> This paradox suggests many legal departments may be investing piecemeal in a variety of disparate point solutions. This disjointed approach creates functional gaps and knowledge silos while trapping data in multiple, stand-alone applications. As a result, information and activities are not integrated, information is not easily shared, data cannot be effectively analysed, and efficiency wanes.[18]

In other words, without a strategic approach to digital lawyering which takes an overview of its different uses, there is a danger that a range of individual solutions will be implemented for various issues which do not join up or connect with each other, generating further problems.

18 Thomson Reuters, 'Digital General Counsel Are Transforming the Corporate Legal Department' (2020) 3 <https://legalsolutions.thomsonreuters.co.uk/content/dam/ewp-m/documents/legal-uk/en/pdf/reports/tr1135788-transforming-the-corporate.pdf> accessed 13 August 2025.

Sometimes these financial and strategic considerations will be driven by external factors. For example, as digital technology means some legal services can be outsourced more cheaply to others or done in-house by clients, there will inevitably be changes in the type of work potential clients require. New areas of law, such as fintech and cyber-crime, will also require new forms of legal expertise. Sometimes such decisions will also be influenced by internal factors; for example, the way in which senior leaders in a law firm view digital technology and the level of resources and skills they have to adapt to changing circumstances.

Daniel Acosta has referred to the question of whether or not law firms embrace digital lawyering as the "lawyer's dilemma".[19] In other words, law firms have to make a choice whether to continue with their existing (and often profitable) model of business or whether to risk innovating and seeking to transform their business model. Retaining a well tried-and-tested business model may be attractive as it does not require significant change or investment. However, it could result in the firm being overtaken by more innovative competitors. Seeking to transform their business model offers the potential for greater profits and success, but also holds greater risks in terms of the amount of investment and training required and the need to make more significant changes.

THE IMPACT OF TECHNOLOGY

Sync 4: Analysing the impact of digital technology

You should allow around one hour for this activity.

The discussion following Sync 3 identified four questions to explore:

- What impact does digital technology have on the day-to-day tasks which legal professionals perform?
- What impact does digital technology have on the ways in which legal professionals interact with their clients?

19 Daniel Acosta, 'The Lawyer's Dilemma: Challenges for Law Firms Adopting Legal Tech' (*Legal Technologist*, September 2020) <https://www.legaltechnologist.co.uk/TheLegalTechnologistSept20.pdf> accessed 13 August 2025.

- What impact does digital technology have on the ways in which legal professionals interact with other colleagues?
- What impact does digital technology have on the ways in which legal professionals interact with the courts?

Based on the preceding discussion, select one of these questions. You should also undertake some further independent reading and research. Write a blog post of 800–1000 words, aimed at an audience of law students or lawyers, answering your selected question.

Regardless of which question you chose to answer, your answer to Sync 4 has probably identified that digital technology has had a significant impact.

In terms of day-to-day tasks, digital technology has impacted in myriad ways ranging from how legal research is conducted to the make-up of the staff within law firms. With regard to interactions between lawyers and clients, the format of these has shifted from letters and faxes to electronic communications. This can ensure quicker and more effective contact; however, it may potentially impact on the human aspects of the relationship by removing elements of personal contact. In terms of interactions between legal professionals, more flexible working patterns may once again lead to less face-to-face contact and greater emphasis on communicating by other means, although it could also aid new forms of collaboration (e.g. via online meetings). The ways in which disputes are resolved is also evolving, with online dispute resolution and the digitalisation of the courts, and this will be considered further in subsequent chapters. All of these changes require law firms to make difficult financial and strategic decisions around whether and to what extent to embrace digital lawyering.

Digital lawyering skills: Traditional skills and legal research

Despite the transformative nature of digital technologies within law, digital lawyers still need to apply a number of more traditional legal skills in their work. These are often skills that law students are encouraged to develop during their time at law school, including:

- Reading documents for different purposes (e.g. skimming and close reading).

- Taking notes of information or discussions.
- Undertaking legal research.

Conducting legal research itself involves a variety of skills, including being able to take a research topic or question, analyse the key issues and break it down into manageable parts.

As discussed previously, there have already been significant changes in the way law students and lawyers undertake their research, with online databases of cases, legislation and journal articles becoming commonplace. Issues around law and technology tend to be fast-moving, meaning sources that are rarely used in academic law, such as web pages, blogs and social media, can all be useful sources of information.

As a law student, getting into the habit of evaluating your sources as you conduct your research is very important. You need to check that the information is:

- Up to date.
- Accurate.
- Trustworthy.
- Using appropriate evidence and/or research methodology.

Becoming competent in such evaluation at an early stage will assist you in conducting research effectively and accurately within legal practice.

TECHNOLOGY AND THE LARGE LAW FIRM

So far, this chapter has largely focused upon a type of typical high street law firm (a small- or medium-sized firm based in a town). The changes within legal practice at such firms has been significant (as the example of Glossop Law demonstrates). However, the changes at many larger firms have been even more far-reaching. A number of firms offer trainee solicitors a seat (period of training) focused upon law and technology. For example, some firms offer a six-month lawtech seat. One example is Addleshaw Goddard, which allows trainees to work alongside lawyers and technologists to develop products for use in other parts of the firm; for example, building a system for a major property transaction to produce automated documents and encode aspects of the process.[20] Other firms, such as Norton Rose Fulbright, now offer graduate career schemes specifically in lawtech and legal operations.[21]

Some firms have created large teams or labs dedicated to lawtech and innovation. For example, the international law firm A&O Shearman has a learning lab called Fuse, where legal professionals, technical providers and clients work together to devise innovative technological solutions to legal and commercial issues.[22]

THE RISE OF DISTRIBUTED AND VIRTUAL LAW FIRMS

A number of organisations have made a more radical shift to become distributed or virtual law firms. These types of firms are sometimes referred to as NewLaw. A distributed law firm is more likely to have a number of physical office locations but also have employees or consultants working remotely. The first such distributed law firm, FisherBroyles, was founded in the United States in 2002. It currently operates in 28 jurisdictions and has hundreds of partners. Its website argues that its model allows it to avoid expensive investment in offices and ensure that it can hire the best lawyers, regardless of their physical location.[23]

Are all virtual lawyers happy and healthy?

Champions of distributed and virtual law firms often refer to the flexibility involved—the idea that lawyers can work when and where they want. This can be seen as a significant benefit; for example, if you have children or other caring responsibilities, you can fit your work in around your caring

20 Addleshaw Goddard, 'Rev Up Your Legal Career with an Innovation and Legal Technology Seat: Accelerate Your Future' (22 June 2023) <https://www.addleshawgoddard.com/en/insights/insights-briefings/tech-talks/what-is-a-lawyer/> accessed 13 August 2023.

21 Norton Rose Fulbright, 'Business and Legal Operations Graduate Scheme' (2025) <https://www.nortonrosefulbright.com/en-gb/graduates/opportunities/business-and-legal-operations-graduate-scheme> accessed 13 August 2025.

22 A&O Shearman, 'Fuse' (2020) <https://www.aoshearman.com/en/expertise/fuse> accessed 13 August 2025.

23 FisherBroyles, 'Law Firm 2.0®' (2025) <https://fisherbroyles.com/> accessed 13 August 2025.

routines. However, it is important not to assume that such flexibility is wholly positive.

Such flexibility can make it harder for lawyers to establish healthy work-life boundaries; for example, they may end up answering client calls and emails during mealtimes or late at night. It could also lead to clients expecting you to be available 24/7, increasing the pressures upon you. Anecdotally, a number of legal professionals noted experiencing these issues when working at home during COVID-19.

A virtual law firm is likely to have no physical premises and to work entirely online. They often market themselves to potential clients on the basis that clients' fees are spent upon communicating and carrying out legal work, with very little spent on administrative tasks and overheads. They encourage lawyers to join them by referring to the benefits of being able to work flexibly, reduce costs, be more easily available to clients, improve wellbeing, and be more eco-friendly by reducing office waste.

Benefits of, and barriers to, the use of digital technology

When considering the impact of digital technology, you may have begun to think about a range of advantages and disadvantages arising from its application in legal practice. Often both benefits and challenges arise.

A good example of this is the issue of accessibility. On the one hand, technology can improve accessibility for clients. For example, a client in a remote location may be able to access advice online or communicate with their lawyer electronically rather than having to spend time and costs on travel. On the other hand, it cannot be assumed that all clients are comfortable and experienced with technology. Globally, a third of the population do not have internet access.[24] In the UK, 95% of households have internet access, but not all of those will have the

24 UK International Development, 'Digital Development Strategy 2024–2030' (2024) <https://assets.publishing.service.gov.uk/media/6613e7f7c4c84d4b31346a68/FCDO-Digital-Development-Strategy-2024-2030.pdf> accessed 13 August 2023.

levels of digital literacy required to access legal services online.[25] For lawyers to meet their ethical obligations and provide an appropriate quality of service, they must keep clients properly informed and ensure they understand the advice and guidance they are given. Therefore, it is vital for them to be aware of their clients' capabilities.

Another example is that of data protection. Using a cloud-based system to store documents can prevent important information from being lost if files are accidentally deleted from a law firm's computer system or if it is attacked by a virus or hacked into. It may mean documents can be accessed quickly and more efficiently, even if a member of the team is on leave or ill. At the same time, to move to using such a system, a firm will need to check the terms and conditions of the service provider it chooses to use for data storage. It will also need to ensure it is complying with the law on data protection in its jurisdiction. It will have to carefully review its regulatory body's rules and/or guidelines on data protection. It likely will also have to review, or even rewrite, its internal policies on data protection. Staff will then need to be trained to use the relevant system in accordance with these rules, policies, and guidelines.

Therefore, making what may seem like a simple change can involve a number of benefits and barriers and have a range of wider impacts and effects which will need to be anticipated in advance.

Sync 5: Analysing the benefits and barriers

You should allow around 30 minutes for this activity.

Read the lilac text boxes on pages 49 and 63 of the Legal Service Board's *Technology and Innovation in Legal Services 2022* main report (available at <https://www.legalservicesboard.org.uk> under "Research"). If this is unavailable, or to expand on your answers, you may wish to search for other reports and articles around the use of technology in the legal profession.

Based on your reading in this chapter and elsewhere, think about the potential benefits and barriers to the following proposals:

- You are a junior lawyer in a law firm. The partners in the firm have proposed removing individual offices and replacing them with an open plan

25 Statista, 'Internet Usage in the United Kingdom' (13 June 2025) <https://www.statista.com/topics/3246/internet-usage-in-the-uk/#topicOverview> accessed 12 November 2019.

area with lots of communal desks. They will issue everyone with laptops so they can work at whichever desk they choose.

- You are a partner in a law firm. The team whom you manage has presented you with a plan in which they all work from their homes at least three days per week and keep in touch using email and virtual meetings.
- You are a self-employed lawyer, and you want to advertise the legal services you offer in your local community. You are thinking about setting up accounts on social media to help you obtain more clients.

You may wish to make some notes on the key benefits and barriers you identify, to refer back to them or add to them as you work through other chapters in this textbook.

In Sync 5 you probably identified a wide range of benefits and barriers. You may have also noted that some of these would depend upon specific details, including the size of the firm, its current specialisms and client base, its financial position and its style of management.

In the first scenario, there would potentially be benefits to people being able to work whenever and wherever they wanted, possibly making them more productive. However, individuals may be resistant to the idea of losing their own personal space or to feeling less of a sense of belonging. In the second scenario, flexible working may be very useful for members of the team with caring and other responsibilities. It could also make people more productive, as they no longer have to spend time commuting to work. However, it could make it harder to communicate quickly and effectively with each other (e.g. if someone does not answer their email). It could also make it harder to access any files and other information that is in paper form rather than online. In both scenarios, issues could arise in relation to identifying the most suitable systems to use to communicate and store data in a safe but accessible manner.

The third scenario raises issues that will be returned to in Chapter 5 of this textbook around the use of social media. It would be necessary to check what rules or guidance your regulatory body had on the use of social media as a starting point. Benefits could include having a free and quick way to connect with members of the local community and market your services. Barriers could include the need to be familiar with how to use the social media platform in question, the time required to keep it updated and the need to avoid inadvertently breaching client confidentiality when adding news stories.

TECHNOLOGY AND ETHICS IN THE LEGAL PROFESSION

> Lawyers are highly educated and, allegedly, of higher than average intelligence, but sometimes individual lawyers demonstrate colossal errors in judgment, especially when insufficiently trained in the new and emerging risks involved with the technological age.[26]

The example of social media discussed earlier raises potential ethical issues. What can and should be shared on social media? What is the distinction between writing in a business and private capacity online? Such ethical issues are not restricted to social media but arise in relation to all aspects of digital lawyering. This can include seemingly minor everyday issues which lawyers may fail to recognise as potential ethical issues. Examples include stepping away from your computer screen for a few minutes and leaving a confidential document open, sending an email to the wrong address, using a weak and easily guessable password to protect important information, or inadvertently signing up to the terms and conditions of a website or social media platform which enables it to access private data. The very human issues involved in communicating by email or online can also have consequences, from informality and unprofessional writing styles to misinterpreting responses and reacting inappropriately.

The contemporary digital lawyer has to be aware of these issues and proactive in thinking of ways to avoid such potential ethical pitfalls. Similar issues may also arise for law students; for example, if they share lecture and seminar notes provided by the university more widely online or use so-called essay mills which provide ready-written answers to assignments. The importance of such ethical issues is a theme that will be returned to throughout this textbook given its importance at all stages of a legal career.

26 Cheryl B. Preston, 'Lawyers' Abuse of Technology' (2018) 118 *Cornell Law Review* 879, 881.

CONCLUSION: THE 21ST-CENTURY LAWYER

This chapter has demonstrated that the 21st-century lawyer is working in a very different environment than the 20th-century lawyer. Although the law itself evolves relatively slowly in many areas, the processes and procedures surrounding it have been changing rapidly in recent years. The results of this on individual legal professionals can be significant. Technological changes affect much more than the digital technology itself: From different career paths to different types of colleagues; from new skills and training to new ways of researching, resolving disputes and collaborating with others; and from challenging ethical issues to challenging client demands. The impacts of all these changes will not just stay within the legal workplace. They will also have consequences for the personal lives of lawyers, from the benefits of flexible working to the challenges of managing client expectations and being pushed out of your comfort zone through being required to upskill and adapt new digital tools.

Although this chapter has largely focused upon lawyers working in what could be termed a "traditional" legal workplace, it is also important to acknowledge that digital technologies are making wider changes within the legal profession so that such "traditional" career pathways and environments may eventually become obsolete. NewLaw is one example of this, and others will be discussed in Chapter 12.

For aspiring lawyers, it is important to reflect upon what digital lawyering will mean for their career, their personal life, and their professional identity. Some of these issues will be discussed further in subsequent chapters, in particular Chapter 13. As you read through this textbook, it is worth spending some time beginning this process of reflection and asking yourself, what does it really mean to be a 21st-century lawyer?

ADDITIONAL RESOURCES

For more information on contemporary opportunities and challenges facing the legal profession, see <https://www.ibanet.org/Future-of-Legal-Services-Commission>

For more information on ABSs, see McMorrow JA, 'UK Alternative Business Structures for Legal Practice: Emerging Models and Lessons for the US' (2016) 47(2) *Georgetown Journal of International Law* 665–711.

For a timeline on the development of email, see <https://www.theguardian.com/technology/2002/mar/13/internetnews>

For a discussion of social media and professional conduct, see <https://www.ibanet.org/Committees/Divisions/Legal_Practice/Impact_of_OSN_on_LegalPractice/Impact_of_OSN_Home.aspx>

For more details on NewLaw firms, see <https://lawflex.com/top-global-newlaw-companies-2025-edition/>

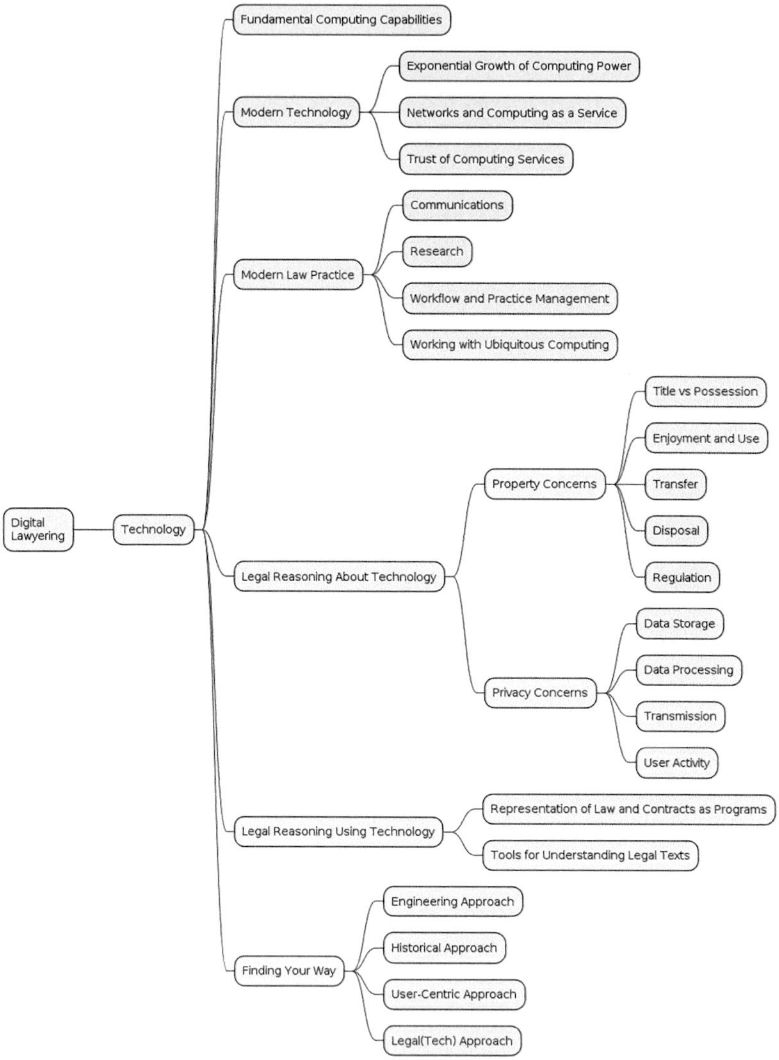

Mind Map 3.1 Chapter topics

3 A GUIDE TO TECHNOLOGY

Terry Wong

INTRODUCTION

This chapter introduces several central concepts underpinning modern computing and communications technologies. An active lawyer must be aware of a widening range of relevant technologies and their use, not only in the practice of law, but in the ways these technologies impact the rights, obligations, and options open to their clients. We take the opportunity to explore the background and implications of those technologies for lawyers, to suggest ways to learn more about specific areas and to outline ways to remain knowledgeable in a space characterised by continuous, accelerating change.

Chapter hot spots

When reading this chapter, questions to think about include:

- How does the interconnected, dynamic nature of computing and communications technologies affect their use in legal practice?
- Trust is a concept with many facets and central to the rule of law, legal practice (critically with respect to lawyer–client privilege), and the smooth conduct of commerce. How do the complexities of digital technology, with its many interacting layers, affect the various spheres of trust one might expect in certain legal and commercial contexts?
- In what ways might a lawyer stay current with the rapid evolution of digital technology to employ technologies effectively in the practice of

DOI: 10.4324/9781003602323-3

law, and to advise clients using new technologies to work in their daily business?

Having read the title and introduction, you can add any other questions you want to explore here:

ILLUSTRATION: A RIDESHARING APP

Consider a ridesharing application (an "app"), such as Uber, Lyft, or Grab. These are three examples of a widely used class of applications that has seen rapid development and adoption, quickly moving beyond being a novel, convenient alternative to become a relied-upon transportation experience, challenging long-entrenched models of mobility in urban and suburban areas around the world. Interaction with a smartphone to reserve a ride involves many of the capabilities of modern computing and communications technology:

1 Selecting the app (by tapping on the app icon on the home screen of the smartphone) and entering the destination (by tapping on the input fields and typing with the on-screen keyboard) are two *input* actions supported by the device.
2 Automatic suggestions (or auto-complete) of the destination as you type involve *processing* of your inputs and *communications* with location services (GPS) and the ridesharing service to determine known addresses nearby and at the desired destination.
3 The lists of possible location matches being displayed as the user types are an example of real-time *output.*
4 Later, when the ride is completed and payment is taken, securely stored payment credentials are retrieved from *storage*, unlocked through the *input* of a password or a facial image via a camera, and used to enable that payment to be completed.

Figure 3.1 shows these capabilities in action, together with the various interactions and infrastructure needed to deliver the service through the application.

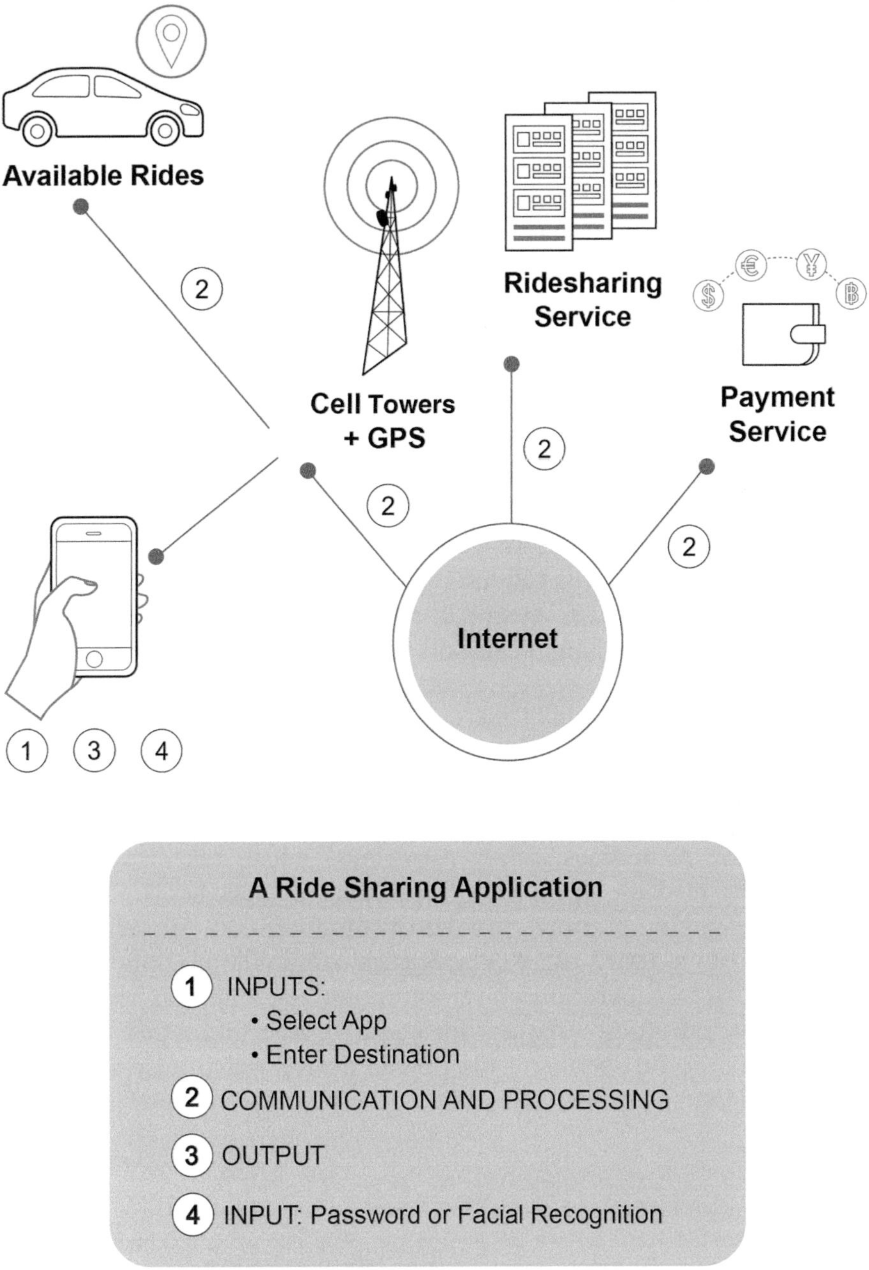

Figure 3.1 Ridesharing application example

In the following section, we will define the terms we have highlighted in this illustration to clarify their meaning and application.

UNDERSTANDING MODERN TECHNOLOGY

We experience most of our digital life through a small number of personal electronic devices—three to four, on average.[1] There is almost always a smartphone and then a portable laptop or desktop computer both at home and in the workplace. In addition, there may be a tablet device, an electronic book reader and perhaps a connected smartwatch. Each of these devices contains a few crucial capabilities that all modern computing devices share:

- *Input.* A way to enter information or to direct a device's activity, through a physical or on-screen keyboard, using gestures such as tapping, holding, dragging, pinching, or rotating with multiple fingers on a screen or touchpad, physical movement of the device, or moving an attached or wirelessly connected accessory such as a mouse or pen. Inputs can also be readers for media such as a magnetic or optical disk, magnetic tape, a memory card, scanners of various forms, an array of sensors in a factory or, increasingly, high-resolution cameras.
- *Processing.* A device will take information supplied to it and reorganise it for better user comprehension or to support itself or the user in the accomplishment of a given task. It might perform calculations or summarise the data using understood and documented methods, sometimes called algorithms, which take real form in machine-readable specifications written in specific languages or encoding. One or more modules of computer code are packaged by advanced "power" users or specialist computer programmers into programs or applications, now commonly referred to as apps.
- *Output.* Inputting a request for a search, selecting a link to a page on the web or opening a file on the device will trigger a series of processing steps that will result in the retrieval and possible trans-

1 Statista, a global data and business intelligence concern, placed the average number of connected devices per person in 2023 at 3.6, observing the highest growth from developed markets in North America and Western Europe. Statista, 'Average Number Devices and Connections per Person Worldwide in 2018 and 2023' <https://www.statista.com/statistics/1190270/number-of-devices-and-connections-per-person-worldwide/> accessed 1 January 2026.

formation of some information that can then be delivered to the user, usually on a screen or, in the case of other forms of media, through an audio output such as speakers or on paper via a printer.

- *Storage.* Computing devices must have a way to store information in varying levels of permanence, depending on the need. Memory, in temporary (RAM, or random-access memory) or permanent (ROM, or read-only memory) forms, is found in hardware components that supply the working areas (think of scratch pads when working mathematical figures by hand) and permanent programs required by the computer to supply basic functions. Data, files, and media are held in semi-permanent storage, either in optical (e.g. DVDs or CDs), magnetic (hard disks), or solid state (e.g. memory cards or solid-state drives).
- *Communications.* The ability to send data over interconnected links (or networks) to other devices is vital to modern computing, since it is impossible to store all the data that one would normally need to access locally (e.g. for practical physical reasons like limited space on devices), or in central locations (in the cloud). Modern communications networks allow instant access to remote data, dramatically increasing the power and information a person has at their command at a given instant, wherever they are in the world, so long as they have a device capable of interacting with those networks. The largest and most powerful network, the one we all know and use today, is the internet.

Together, these capabilities allow modern digital devices to deliver the information-rich, interactive, and productive experiences to which our society has grown accustomed and reliant. In Chapter 8 you will go on to think about the role such digital devices can also play in providing digital evidence through digital forensics.

Sync 1: Thinking about digital devices

You should allow around 10 minutes for this activity.

Examine a digital device you currently own (if you do not have any on hand, think about a common device such as a smartphone). Using the list of capabilities just discussed in the text, identify the specific capabilities of your chosen device: For example, how do you input information? What are the outputs? What form of storage does it use? How does it communicate?

Depending upon the device you chose, you may have identified a range of different capabilities. For example, a smartphone involves inputting information via a touchscreen keypad and by swiping left or right. There are audio outputs (when speaking to others or listening to music) but also visual outputs (when using the internet or watching a video). Information is stored in a microchip known as an SD (Secure Digital memory) card and there is a range of communication methods, from text messages to streaming data over an internet connection.

BEGINNINGS: THE AFFORDABLE COMPUTER

Histories of computing describe early digital computers that filled large rooms and drew great quantities of electricity during their operation. They were expensive, scarce resources, with every attempt made on the part of their owners and operators—typically military, government, or well-funded corporate entities—to ensure that they were operated with maximum possible usage for a given period. To ensure that the machines were idle for as little time as possible, programmers or users were required to submit their programs or requested computations as jobs, to be run in batches by operators, with the results returned in printouts.

Timesharing, together with interactive input- and output-capable devices called terminals, were innovations introduced to allow a programmer or user to interact with a computer directly, while others could also use the same machine, at the same time, in a similar manner. System designers realised that interactive users would not be taxing a machine with heavy loads while they were reading results and thinking about the next action to take. The machine would be able to handle other tasks in the intervening period. This allowed a degree of (what appeared to users as) simultaneous interactive use of a large computer (Figure 3.2). Direct interaction with computing resources in a timesharing setting was transformative for the development of software and the use of computers as tools for everyday tasks in the workplace.

As microcomputers emerged in the 1970s and early 1980s, their affordable pricing[2] (relative to larger miniframe and mainframe

2 Just a few months after its introduction in August 1981, a review in *BYTE*, a widely read computer magazine, listed the price of the IBM PC (Model 5150), with one floppy disk drive, adapter card, and DOS operating system software, at USD 2575. This amount was substantial, but within the reach of small business and office users with budgets for automation.

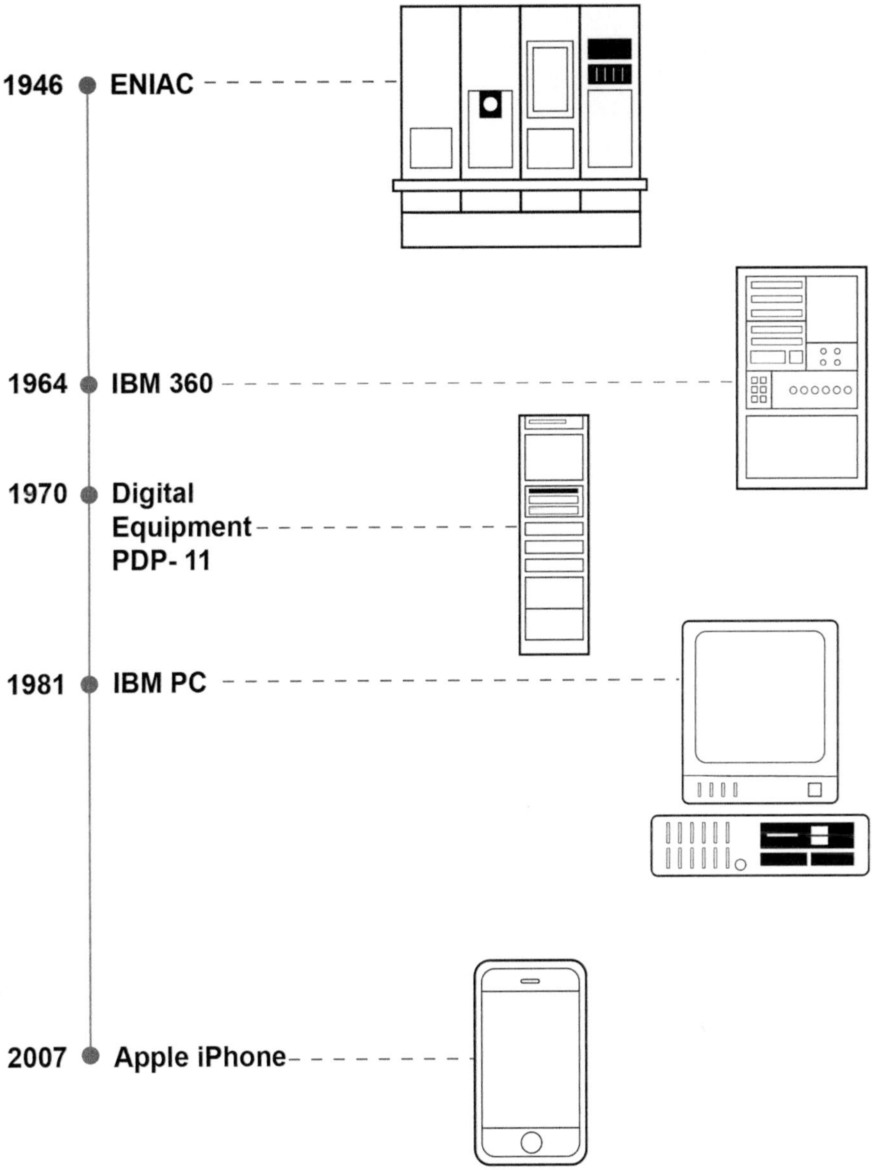

Figure 3.2 Timeline of technology evolution and miniaturisation

computers) meant that a single person could be the sole user of a computer with exclusive access to all the resources built into it. Given the early stage in the development of hardware technologies, especially in microchip fabrication, early microcomputers were not high in either processing speed or storage.[3] However, their availability paved the way for an explosion in individual learning about computer programming and the creative application of that learning in the development of applications for those early microcomputing platforms.

The downward direction of prices that made computers affordable and accessible was driven in part by improvements in research and development that enabled the doubling of transistor component density on microchips and the halving of computer prices every two years, described by an observation known as Moore's law.[4] The continued exponential rise of computing power and its accompanying exponential fall in prices allowed a consumer in 2015 to carry a smartphone in his or her pocket that was already 120 million times more powerful than the computer that guided the Apollo Lunar Modules in their landings on the surface of the Earth's moon.[5]

Computing and communication: the importance of the network and Metcalfe's law

Since the mid-1980s, the period that saw the growing mainstream adoption of affordable personal computers, emphasis has been placed on the word "personal" in the term "personal computer" or "PC". First-person physical ownership of devices and data has been the dominant relationship between individual users and their computing resources. Perhaps reflecting the nature of their human users, economic observers noted that the value of connected computer networks increased as the square of the number of members in each network. This observation, formulated as Metcalfe's law by the economist and

3 An IBM PC (Model 5150) for sale in 1981 had a single Intel 8088 processor core with a clock speed of 4.77 MHz and a maximum of 640 kilobytes of memory. By way of comparison, an iPhone 17 available in 2026 featured six processor cores, including two running at 4.26 GHz and four running at 2.60 GHz, in addition to 12 gigabytes of memory.

4 G. E. Moore, 'The Future of Integrated Electronics' (1965) 38 *Electronics* 4.

5 Tibi Puiu, 'Smartphone Is Millions of Times Faster Than NASA's 1960s Computers' (*ZME Science*, 13 October 2015, updated 11 May 2023) <http://www.zmescience.com/science/news-science/smartphone-power-compared-to-apollo-432/> accessed 1 January 2026.

investor George Gilder, described and promoted the advantage of computer networking with Ethernet, the dominant form of hardware technology for local area networks (LANs).[6]

To understand the importance of networks as described by Metcalfe's law, consider that a network with two computers or devices can make at most one connection between them, while four devices could make six connections and eight devices could make up to 28 connections. As the number of devices on the network increases, the total number of connections *c* for a network of *n* devices is described by the mathematical equation $c = n(n - 1)/2$. This property of network growth and connectivity is illustrated in Figure 3.3.

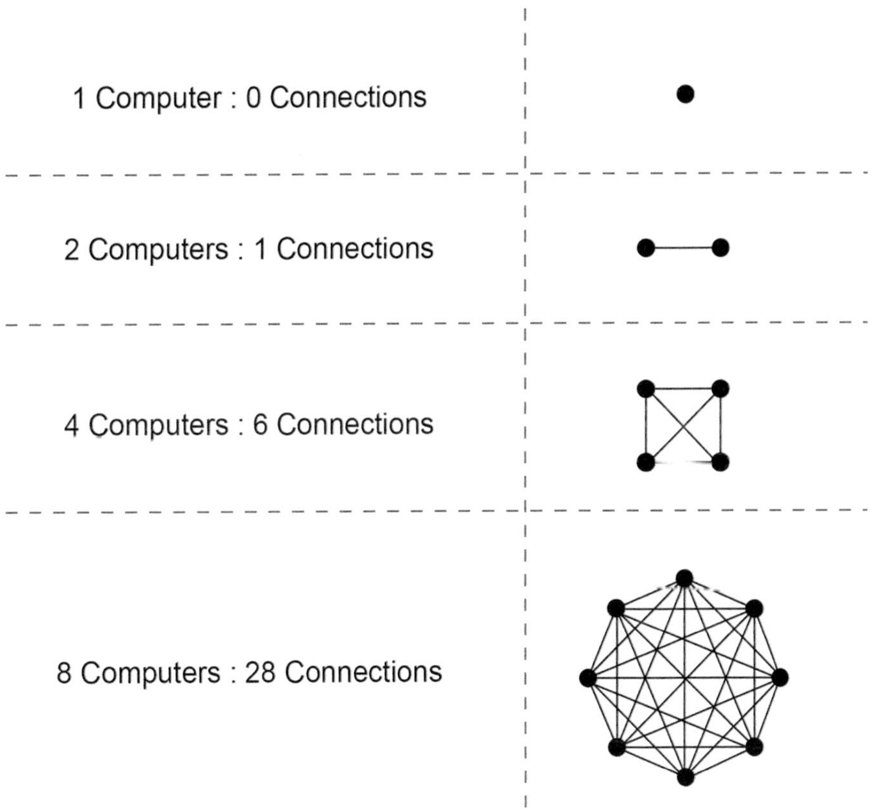

Figure 3.3 Increase of connections and growth of network

6 A local area network (LAN) is a computer network installed in offices and homes for the purpose of connecting the devices on that network to each other, and possibly for the purpose of sharing an internet connection.

As each connection would support the transfer of a file containing a document or the data necessary to deliver a specific app, one can see that the value of the network increases dramatically as the number of devices connected to it increases, and data flows freely between an ever-increasing number of nodes on the network.

Local networks, whether in separate offices on different floors of the same building, across the street, or on the other side of the globe, and belonging to the same or different organisations, can be connected using wide area network technologies (WANs) in inter-connected networks, or internets. Multiple internets, connected to each other through enough layers of intermediate networks, eventually developed the ability to route and deliver data traffic in reliable and resilient ways. They also became speedy enough to support interactive use of applications running on a digital device directly in front of a user, accessing data and supporting computing resources over very large distances in a seamless manner. The global internet is the current largest example of an internet, serving as the indispensable infrastructure of most modern connected applications we use today.

The Age of Ubiquitous Computing

As both networks and connected computing devices became more capable and more economical to own and operate, the use of connected computing devices became a fact of daily working life, no longer a novelty but rather an expectation. This is referred to as "ubiquitous computing".

Computing as a Service

Shortly after the beginning of the 21st century, Amazon Web Services began offering infrastructure as a service (IaaS). No longer were businesses required to manage physical infrastructure to support the development and operation of online computing services. With technical personnel now mostly freed from the need to devote resources to the fundamental aspects of technology installation and operations, more efforts could be deployed in the design and implementation of new and innovative services. Google Workspace, Microsoft Office 365, Dropbox, Slack, and a host of other well-known services that we now consider indispensable parts of daily working life online appeared and gained adoption as users became more comfortable with the safety, reliability, and ease of online services in the cloud. In Chapter 2 we explained that the term "cloud" refers to data being stored in a separate online location, hosted by a third-party provider, which is accessed online.

Illustration: Drafting a document

Consider using a cloud office suite, such as Office 365 or Google Workspace, to draft a document. This process can be used to illustrate how computing services are now delivered to support the task at hand:

1 Entering the URL of the cloud service, or using your mouse or trackpad to click on the bookmark in your browser, is an *input*.

2 The browser looking up the address of, and requesting the page from, the cloud service is a *communication* activity.

3 The cloud service verifies your access to the service, through *processing* passwords and cryptographic credentials, and sets up resources to allow your creation and editing of documents through further *processing* (on its network-connected server computers), *input* (from its storage facilities in the data centre), *output* (formatting and preparing the web pages), and further *communication* as the web page and the web application components are sent to the browser on your computer.

4 Your computer, receiving the resources over the network, *processes* them and draws the web page and application components (the document, editing toolbar, buttons, etc.) in your browser as *output*.

5 As you edit the document, typing at the keyboard and selecting and clicking text and buttons on the screen are *input* that will be *processed* by your computer. Occasional updates will be sent to the cloud service as it *communicates* and coordinates the state of the document and the web application with the services in the cloud that support it.

6 As the document is input and updates arrive at the cloud service's data centre, the state of the document is *processed* and saved as *output*, enabling you to close the application and browser and resume working in exactly the same place when you return to the document by repeating step 1. It should be noted that, with many cloud services, resuming work on a document in a different location and on a separate computer is entirely possible, with only the need to validate identity and authorised use by logging in on the device at the other location. Thus, one can start drafting a document on a desktop computer in a firm's office and complete the document at one's home office on a laptop computer.

7 When you have finished drafting the document, the formatted results from further *processing* can be downloaded (a *communication* activity) and printed (as *output*), or be sent in a *communication* via your email program to your client or another party for further review.

It can be seen from this illustration that a cloud-based application provides users with several key benefits:

- *Location independence.* A person using a cloud-based service usually has access to the service on all devices on which the service is available, subject to having a valid login and possible limits on the number of simultaneous logins imposed by the operators of the service.
- *Timeliness.* Location independence and a good range of device support ensures that needs for the service are satisfied sooner and closer to the point of identified need, allowing more immediate fulfilment and possibly resulting in a greater speed of task completion.
- *Backup, recovery and security.* Cloud services tend to save their data using storage facilities in data centres, generally providing mechanisms for preventing data loss, from physical failure, from accident, or from malicious intent resulting in physical theft of devices or physical media such as disks or flash drives. A range of issues related to custody of data, including its location, the means of storance, and its stored state (e.g. encrypted or not encrypted at rest) arise using cloud services, which we will explore further in Chapters 5 and 6.

MODERN TECHNOLOGY AND EVERYDAY LAW PRACTICE

Applying the concepts discussed in the previous sections, we can now examine the applications of modern networked computing technologies to three critical areas of the practice of law; namely, communications, research, and drafting. The impact on workflow and practice management will also be considered.

COMMUNICATIONS

One may say that a lawyer is the communicator of the first and last resort. A lawyer is often the person sent by a client to explore ways to initiate dialogue with another party, or the lawyer is the person who is sent to attempt to save a negotiation or to begin to mitigate the harms in an unresolved dispute. Through informed dialogue with all the parties involved, a lawyer can help understand the particulars of a matter, the goals and constraints for the client, and the concerns and requirements of possible other parties in transactions or opponents in a dispute. In all cases, effective communication leading to greater understanding is a prerequisite to achieving good outcomes.

Technology-mediated communication today takes many forms:

- *Voice.* Once limited to traditional fixed telephone lines in the home, in the office or at pay telephone locations, voice communications can now be found on mobile handsets, and with the growth of internet penetration and bandwidth, any device with an internet connection may be a point for voice communications, at a low cost that was once unthinkable. One notable fact of internet telephony (voice communications supplied using telephone network numbers but transmitted over the internet) has been the location independence of numbers using VOIP (Voice Over Internet Protocol) technologies. It is now possible for a telephone number originally allocated for a telephone exchange in one city to ring in a city on the opposite side of the planet. For example, a number originally allocated to the City of London may now ring in the central business district of Christchurch, New Zealand, if a firm supplying services in London but based in Christchurch had a need and had purchased and set up such service. It should be noted that the costs for basic implementation of such service could be had for under £10 per month at the time the first edition of this textbook was written.

- *Video.* Video conferencing was once the exclusive province of well-funded large companies with dedicated facilities and possibly additional staff to support the sophisticated audio-visual equipment needed to support even rudimentary video conferencing activity. Today, the average mobile handset is capable of video conferencing, even with large numbers of simultaneous participants. During the COVID-19 pandemic, video conferencing took on a new central role in not only facilitating meetings between remote participants but serving as a key enabler of continuity and cohesion for business meetings, classroom instruction, and social gatherings as lockdown measures and social distancing rules were put in force to contain the spread of the virus.
- *Email.* More formal online communications are now done via email, almost entirely replacing the paper memorandum and letter. In many jurisdictions, email is considered an acceptable form of notice for certain contracts and even government notices from different departments and levels of agencies, from local town councils to national departments and bureaus. Email has long operated with varying forms of validation and security. In some cases, email users may be vulnerable to attack from abusers sending spam (unsolicited, irrelevant messages often selling or trying to bait recipients into illicit activities or attempting to defraud them) and from malicious operators leading to phishing attacks, identity theft, and even extortion.
- *Short messages.* Short messages sent on mobile handsets and using text messaging applications fill a wide-ranging set of roles, from casual streams of communication between friends and family to formal notification of important events such as deliveries or bank transfers. Once limited to standard messaging protocols provided by telecommunications carriers, a range of messaging applications now exist, including WhatsApp, WeChat, Facebook Messenger, LINE, and others. In practice, lawyers will often use short messages to coordinate meetings, exchange documents, and conduct workflow.
- *Multimedia messages.* Extensions to short messaging applications allow the sending of attachments and embedded images, videos, and other multimedia content. Drafts or sections of text are often sent as attachments for immediate review and feedback using multimedia messaging (e.g. attaching a PDF draft to a WhatsApp message to a counter party for rapid, informal review).
- *Forums and social media.* Online forums and social media platforms allow participants to communicate with others in various com-

munities using postings of text and other media, in settings of varying formality. For example, X, a popular social network formerly known as Twitter, started with an offering originally based on the length of a short message (280 characters). It grew into a leading social network, with participants ranging from casual groups of friends to online influencers to global brands and public figures. The use of forums and social media for legal communication is limited but not unknown, and will be discussed further in Chapter 5.

Each of these forms of communication depends on access to connectivity and resources available on traditional telecommunications networks or, more likely, the internet.

RESEARCH

The lawyer in a law firm working diligently in the library deep into the night remains a central image of the legal profession. While many texts are still available only in traditional paper, microfilm, or microfiche form (sheets or reels to store highly miniaturised images of texts for reading on magnification devices), many important texts, including recent statutes, regulations, and court proceedings can now be found in electronic form, indexed and searchable using modern search engine technology. The tools can resemble popular internet search engines such as Google or Bing, but they often incorporate more advanced tools to refine searches. Depending on the area of legal practice, various resources now exist to make the research process more efficient and comprehensive. Some examples include:

- *Intellectual property.* Many governments now make patent, service mark, and trademark applications and grants searchable, significantly reducing the time and risks associated with searches for the purpose of ascertaining existing protections and potential liabilities, making the preparation of applications or actions to assert rights more efficient, safe, and complete.
- *Regulatory compliance.* Businesses contemplating investment in areas that are heavily regulated (e.g. exploration for oil and gas, heavy manufacturing) will need to ensure that the particulars of the given investment are compliant with relevant, current regulations and those to come into force in the investment period—or if not, that the range and severity of exposure can be understood and managed before approaching regulators for approval. Similarly,

when a business is found to have breached a regulation, it may look for ways in the regulatory texts to argue for more favourable terms, whether by citing precedents, emerging regulatory regimes, or approved practice in similar situations.

- *Civil litigation.* When bringing civil actions, relevant statutes and codes vary depending on jurisdiction and on the complexity of the matter. The relevant contracts and supporting documentation are also likely to be relevant for building a case. Complex matters may see rooms full of documentation, mostly irrelevant to a particular point in question. Search engines and agents built with artificial intelligence (AI) applied to documents scanned and converted to electronic form make easy work of sifting through large volumes of text.

In the context of a global law firm with many offices spread around the globe, internal search engines linked with client management systems not only support more integrated service across geographies and jurisdictions, but they also allow the firm's relationship managers and partners to recognise and seize opportunities to offer more advantageous advice in potentially strategic, cross-border, company-wide matters, delivering greater value, and promoting greater client loyalty. Client management systems linked to and monitored by advanced analytics systems can warn partners of potential conflicts of interest or regulatory impediments to taking on specific items of client work.

DRAFTING

The core activity of document drafting changed dramatically with the spread of word processing software such as WordPerfect and Microsoft Word in the 1980s and 1990s, allowing significantly greater flexibility in editing and formatting as well as incorporating tools such as spell checking, grammar suggestions, and reference management, both internal and external to a document.

Cloud-based office productivity suites such as Microsoft Office 365 have increased the flexibility for lawyers to work on drafting not only in their offices but also while at client sites or in their home offices, on a number of devices including their office computer, their tablet device and, when the need arises, even on a mobile handset. They do so with the same word processor software, with current changes synchronised and made available for work on any registered device. All this has to be done safely with secure logins and sharing controls, so that only the authoring lawyer and specified collaborators and counterparties will have access and at only the right times in the process.

In recent years, legal technology entrepreneurs have developed online services that specialise in the delivery of document drafting capabilities, offering standardised libraries of high-quality document templates that not only lawyers but, in some cases, clients themselves use to draft documents for routine matters and transactions.

WORKFLOW AND PRACTICE MANAGEMENT

Even in a small legal practice, as workloads increase, the complexity of managing work between different clients and matters for each client can easily get overwhelming. Legal practice requires a level of organisation and punctuality that can best be termed as exacting, indeed, challenging and distracting for a lawyer needing to focus on billable work. Lawyers often resort to to-do lists in paper or electronic planners, while others turn to task managers in office suite software, and more sophisticated practices have turned to project management tools like Microsoft Project or online process coordination and collaboration tools like Basecamp, Smartsheet, or Monday.com.

Practice management software purpose-built for legal practice combines communications, process, drafting, and filing, often operating in tandem with familiar office software tools like word processing and email software.

WORKING WITH UBIQUITOUS COMPUTING

During the COVID-19 pandemic, the legal profession faced significant challenges in settings where presence in an office was considered a necessary condition for work. Many partners and principals (individuals with executive authority) in firms had previously invested heavily in prestigious offices in central business district locations, both to project an image of success and to make it easier to arrange and conduct meetings with clients. In the early months of 2020, as the scope and gravity of the pandemic became clear and governments began to impose lockdown and social distancing measures, firms scrambled to articulate policies for personnel to work from their homes, aided by the full range of online tools we have discussed in this chapter.

Our purpose here is not to examine or advance opinions on the effectiveness of remote working arrangements in legal practice, but rather to highlight three important issues that arise when ubiquitous computing technologies are used in legal practice. All these issues were thrown into sharp relief when firms had to adapt, often reluctantly, to work enabled and mediated with these technologies. In brief, they are:

- *Trust.* How can legal practitioners ensure client confidentiality when working with a wide range of technologies and tools that rely on the internet, inherently open and (in some people's perception) insecure by nature?
- *Ownership of property.* When it is not only possible but even expected that personnel will use both firm-owned and personal devices to interact with online resources belonging either to the firm or to clients, how can the control of the information on the various devices that make up a given user's digital footprint be ensured, such that firm or client rights to intellectual property and information are not compromised, and indeed are handled in a context of trust? The issues that arise when an individual is working for a firm using their personal devices are sometimes referred to as "bring your own device" (BYOD) issues.
- *Ownership of time.* Ubiquitous computing now makes it possible for personnel to complete substantive, valuable work outside of the traditional office on schedules that better suit their individual needs and situations. Communications technologies can also be abused, and there are many stories of employers encroaching on time outside of normal business hours, to the extent that some employees feel that they must be available around the clock, even during appointed personal time, weekends, and holidays.

An issue often raised in the age of always-connected digital work is the fluidity of the online environment, with devices that encourage multitasking and constant consumption of often unrelated, disjointed content that arrives and demands attention, often through notifications that interrupt the flow of work or intrude on personal activities. As the current time-billing model continues in the legal profession, the management and accounting for billable time will remain paramount to one's practice of law. The potential impact of this upon wellbeing was raised in Chapter 2. It also raises further questions, including:

- How can a lawyer manage their technology tools in such a way that they can maximise the effectiveness of the time spent using those tools?

- What concrete steps might they take to minimise interruptions in the flow of work, while also ensuring that they are responsible to the legitimate demands of their clients or colleagues in the firm for time and support?

Unexpected events and ubiquitous computing

During the COVID-19 pandemic, several jurisdictions, including Hong Kong, experienced at least two working days when severe weather necessitated the declaration and hoisting of tropical cyclone warning signals. Under such conditions, employees are not expected to report for work at their offices. With lockdown and social distancing measures driving work-from-home arrangements, many knowledge workers, including lawyers, found themselves in a grey zone with respect to the application of this regulation. It is perhaps instructive to consider what points about the realities of always-connected work you would raise if asked by an employer for advice in this scenario, bearing in mind that they may already be struggling with productivity and cash flow under the serious restrictions and economic conditions imposed by the pandemic response. For a lawyer, it is possible that tensions may arise between their personal needs and those of their clients in such scenarios.

Sync 2: BYOD issues in the workplace

You should allow around 20 minutes for this activity.

Consider a lawyer who is a specialist in an area of practice working as a consultant to a small firm. Her arrangement is such that she is not issued a computer belonging to the firm but instead is allocated an account in the firm's online office services, which includes email and productivity software, as well as practice management and workflow tools. The consultant will log into those services and use them to complete and deliver her work using her own laptop computer and use her smartphone to access the firm's email and calendar services. Consider the following questions relevant to this and many other BYOD scenarios:

- What are some of the issues with client confidentiality that arise in this situation?

- What would be a consultant's express or implied duties to the firm and the client regarding the safeguarding of data and information related to any client- and firm-related matters?
- What rights does the firm have with respect to the information on the consultant's devices, and the devices themselves?
- How might policies be framed and enforced, such that the property and privacy rights of all parties concerned in a BYOD scenario would be protected, and what might be an equitable and/or legal basis for prioritising such rights?
- While some firms and clients may not generally have provisions in their policies for remote or work-from-home (WFH) scenarios, unexpected contingencies such as COVID-19 made the immediate adoption of such scenarios not only a precondition of productivity but a strict necessity for the mere survival of many organisations. In such cases, even when the principals of a firm were normally not receptive to such arrangements, they found themselves acquiescing, scrambling (and sometimes failing) to put in place robust policies. What steps could you take, while advising a client or the managing partner of your firm, to ensure that you frame a set of working criteria with which to evaluate such measures, to protect your clients and balance the rights of your employees to privacy and control of their devices?
- Clients in many cases prefer to communicate using bursts of text or chat application messages. These exchanges often take place on personally owned smartphone devices. Given such preferences and the advantages realised, what steps can a lawyer take to ensure that such messages are protected, especially in the event of theft or accidental loss of the device? How might a lawyer recover from such a loss, assuming the use of a major messaging service that provides seamless backup and recovery procedures? Are such services in fact always desirable in legal work?

When answering Sync 2, you needed to be mindful of the fact that this is an emerging area in business and employment law, with wide variations among jurisdictions. Awareness of the range of controls that online software products provide, the already established precedents in a particular jurisdiction, and existing individual company policies will be instrumental in your formulation of guidelines and advice for clients in the future.

LEGAL REASONING AND TECHNOLOGY

With a firm grasp of technological concepts, we can now turn to the ways in which we can think critically about two related, equally important, though in practice quite different views of technology as lawyers:

1 How do we reason about technology, not only about its use but also its creation and management as it affects the legal positions and options open to clients?
2 How do we think about using technology in the practice of law? What concepts can we apply to evaluate new tools? How does one stay abreast of and apply new technologies at the right time in the technology evolution cycle to balance the benefits against possible risks and costs?

LEGAL REASONING ABOUT TECHNOLOGY

As we have seen, ubiquitous computing has transformed the nature of media and its consumption, not just limited to print, video, and music forms, but also the software that enables these experiences. The next part of this chapter will demonstrate the importance of legal reasoning about technology by discussing property concerns and privacy concerns.

PROPERTY CONCERNS

Legal frameworks of thinking about property are relevant, as they are seeing varying levels of application and transformation as case law develops and technology trends continue their ongoing rapid evolution. When thinking about technology in a legal context, it is often helpful to consider a few aspects of the law of property:

1 *Title*. As with physical property, digital property (of which video, music, or software are but a few representative examples) has relationships with individuals or entities defined by law. It is important to understand who has title to (owns and controls) the digital property in question.

2 *Possession.* Having physical possession of a piece of digital property, on physical media such as an optical disk or in the memory of an electronic device, does not necessarily mean having control of that piece of digital property. Digital rights management, licensing, and service entitlements are important aspects to consider.
3 *Enjoyment and use.* The extent to which a person may use a piece of digital property may be limited by certain licensing or service agreements.
4 *Transfer.* Delivering a piece of digital property may be done with physical media, although it might just as easily be done over the internet, using a range of schemes for conveying the location and procedure for delivery.
5 *Disposal.* In some contexts, particularly in work involving intellectual property, most of the assets in question are now in digital form. This means that obligations to safeguard and (when possession is no longer necessary or permitted by agreement) to dispose of such digital property are incurred.
6 *Regulation.* While many regulations apply to the people, property, and activities within the borders of a legal jurisdiction, the global reach of the internet has made enforcement of such regulations and even relevant law difficult to interpret, let alone enforce in relation to digital property.

Let us explore each of these aspects of reasoning, informed by our recent reading about the fundamentals of technology in earlier parts of this chapter. For the remainder of this section, we will use the term "digital property" to refer to consumable media (texts, images, and audio and video recordings) as well as software.

Title versus possession

The distinction between title to digital property and physical possession of a copy of the digital representation of that property is extremely important in reasoning about technology. For digital media and for software, it is understood that the creator of the software, or the employer or commissioning entity in the case of work for hire, has ownership of that property. This means that copies that are distributed on media or via download, either as complete files or streamed and managed by specialised apps (such as music or movie players on modern devices), are merely licensed for limited uses, limited audiences or limited sets of users (a certain number of users at a specified location, or certain named individuals in some cases).

Possession of the digital asset, therefore, does not necessarily entitle one to unlimited use; instead, it obligates the holder of the physical media containing the asset to comply with the terms of the licence. To enforce compliance with licence terms, creators of digital assets have long relied on encryption, wherein a mathematical equation takes a digital file and scrambles the contents according to a well-known algorithm. The complexity of the bits of information contained in the digital file, together with large random numbers known as keys, is used by a program implementing encryption algorithms to scramble the contents of the file such that they are not readable unless decoded. The decoding operation is the reverse operation of the same algorithm, enabled through the possession of an appropriate key, sometimes combined with a process to check the validity of an applicable licence, a paid-up subscription, or some other indicator of a valid entitlement. Such validations can be done on the device, but more often now, they require at least intermittent network connectivity so that access to the digital asset may be controlled by the owner of the digital asset from a central location.[7]

This method of using digital rights management (DRM) systems, wherein a person who pays for a digital licence receives not possession of the asset but rather limited access increasingly mediated through the use of network-based verification, is a subject of intense, sometimes impassioned cultural and political debate. It goes beyond the content of the law, with deep implications for culture and the preservation of what is becoming a digital heritage. The fact that companies who distribute these assets are also in sole possession of the legally sanctioned means to access those assets, even beyond the period of what would be considered the normal term for copyright, has profound yet untested implications. One might ask what would occur if the business owning the rights to a significant work protected by DRM goes out of business, and enough time passes during which not only the creators of the work but also the distributors and the software vendors for the DRM all cease to exist, and in many cases do not have successors or heirs.

7 A glimpse at some of the complexity in digital rights management is found in Krishna Rao Vijayanagar, 'EME, CDM, AES, CENC, and Keys—The Essential Building Blocks of DRM' (*OTTverse*, 28 August 2020) <https://ottverse.com/eme-cenc-cdm-aes-keys-drm-digital-rights-management/> accessed 1 January 2026.

Publicly available, but not public domain

In 2002, Marcel Proust's famous novel series *In Search of Lost Time* was published in a translation by Penguin UK. However, at the time, because of the copyright regulations in the United States under the Sonny Bono Copyright Act of 1998, only the first four of the six volumes could be published in the United States.[8]

Readers who wanted to read the books in other earlier translations could find them online at public domain book sites like Project Gutenberg,[9] but again could find only the first four volumes, as the Project Gutenberg servers were located in the United States at the University of North Carolina at Chapel Hill. Readers who wanted the last two volumes as electronic books could buy the previous translations from online booksellers such as Amazon.com, or could find them available for download from Project Gutenberg Australia,[10] a sister site to Project Gutenberg but not formally affiliated in any way. Only in 2020 would the remaining three volumes in the Penguin translation series begin to be released for sale in print and electronically in the United States, finishing with the final Volume 7, *Finding Time Again*, in January 2023.

This is a good point to pause and think about the implications of a file being available on the internet from a jurisdiction in which copyright protection has expired, and whether a person in a jurisdiction in which such protections are still in force would commit an act of copyright infringement or piracy if they were to download and save that file for personal use. What regulations would possibly be applicable if they were then to distribute and share that file?

Consider that in many jurisdictions, online privacy laws do not allow the monitoring of user traffic without investigators meeting a certain standard showing reasonable suspicion of a crime being committed. Law enforcement are much more active in targeting illegal distribution and file sharing than individuals downloading, simply because of the practical considerations and sheer effort in gathering evidence.

So far, we have discussed ownership and licensing of online content and software. Consider the reverse situation for content

8 Aaron Matz, 'In Pursuit of Proust' (*Slate*, 3 March 2005) <https://slate.com/culture/2005/03/the-new-proust-translation.html> accessed 1 January 2026.

9 <https://www.gutenberg.org/ebooks/search/?query=proust> accessed 1 January 2026.

10 <https://gutenberg.net.au/plusfifty-n-z.html#proust> accessed 1 January 2026.

creation, where users generate content and post it on a social media platform. This sync gives you the opportunity to read and review some facts regarding two popular services that manage and offer a considerable amount of user-generated content.

It may come as a surprise to see the broad scope of usage rights granted to service providers by service agreements for the purpose of

Sync 3: Who owns user-generated content?

You should allow around 30 minutes for this activity.

Examine Facebook's terms of service, as described and summarised in this FindLaw blog post: <https://blogs.findlaw.com/law_and_life/2014/10/who-legally-owns-your-facebook-posts.html>

Also consider the copyright selection features of Flickr, a large, long-established photo-sharing service, which recognises its users' needs to control the licences granted for photos shared on the service: <https://blog.flickr.net/en/2011/05/13/at-flickr-your-photos-are-always-yours/>

What are the limitations of the service provider's use of that content to promote use of its service?

marketing their service offering and in generating engaging feeds of user content. A substantial amount of value is given to the service provider in exchange for engaging user experiences, not least the ability to see the activities and photos of friends. Substantial debate has been generated around the fairness of this exchange and whether service providers of social media offerings do enough to protect their users from malicious actors on their service, from misinformation, data leaks, and a range of other online perils.

ENJOYMENT AND USE: OPEN SOURCE, CREATIVE COMMONS, AND PUBLIC DOMAIN

As we have seen, in addition to legal, not always practicable means of enforcement, DRM mechanisms allow digital asset owners direct ways to enforce restrictions on the use of those assets. When considering the enjoyment and use of digital property, it is important to consider other models, ones that many technologists and industry observers have identified as critical to the accelerated development of the computing environment we have today.

Another widespread approach for managing the legal ownership and licensing of digital assets entails the use of sharing models, wherein licences are granted for digital assets that include the right to inspect and change the asset (as in the end user directly modifying the source code of a program or an artist remixing an audio track of music). Some licences may go further in allowing the redistribution of the original or derivative works, usually with some stipulations on the preservation of copyright notices and attribution, whether fees for distributions may be charged and whether subsequent recipients also enjoy rights to modify and redistribute the original and intermediate derivative works.

Sync 4: What does free software really mean?

You should allow around 60 minutes for this activity.

Download and read the three most commonly used licences for open source software:

1 The GNU General Public Licence v3.0 (GPLv3) <https://www.gnu.org/licenses/gpl–3.0.en.html>

2 The MIT Licence <https://opensource.org/licenses/MIT>

3 The Apache Licence, Version 2 <https://www.apache.org/licenses/LICENSE–2.0>

These licences grant rights to use and modify the software to which they are attached (usually significant bodies of software used as infrastructure for services delivered over the internet) and in some cases stipulate requirements for attribution, permissions to modify and redistribute original or derivative versions, and (in the case of GPLv3) to transfer the same rights in the case of derivative works.

Consider the following questions:

1 What are the differences between these licences and the terms for an actively developed piece of software in the public domain like SQLite? <https://sqlite.org/copyright.html>

2 In the case of GPLv3, where the protection of user rights is paramount, what possible steps must the developer and operator of an online service using pieces of source code to build a commercial service take to ensure compliance?

You will have seen in Sync 4 that the intention of many open source software licences is to protect the rights of the user to access and use software. This is in tension with the interests of those who wish to incorporate open source software in proprietary commercial software services. The GPLv3 licence does not discourage this act per se, but it requires that software incorporating GPLv3 components also fall under the same licence and that the resulting source code be made available to all users on demand.

Transfer

Because of the limitations of networks in the past, digital assets were originally distributed—and to some extent, for very large assets (e.g. high-definition, movie-length videos, and large data sets), continue to be distributed—on physical media such as optical disks (e.g. Blu-ray, DVD). Smaller assets, such as music tracks, many electronic books, and documents, can all be provided for download using a wide range of now-proven internet tools and protocols, the most common of which are of course the World Wide Web and the HTTP protocol.

Improved network infrastructure and availability, even over the air to mobile devices, have enabled many owners of digital assets to provide controlled access to their assets only over the network on demand, optimising delivery by sending small chunks of the asset to the device in near real time as it is being consumed, in what is known as streaming.

Streaming began with music, with implementations of digital radio on the early internet, and gradually evolved with increasingly capable network infrastructure to the streaming of on-demand music and on-demand, full-length movies with popular global services such as Spotify and Netflix. Streaming access also applies to software in situations where the physical copies of even the user interface are operated in a remote infrastructure. A remote-control view of the interface is provided to the user, much like fly-by-wire controls in a large airplane, where the electronic control signals in a cockpit are conveyed by wire to computers that do the work of mechanically controlling flight, embedded deep in the body of the plane or in the wings. Banks, health care organisations, research and development organisations, and even some law firms requiring ways to assure clients of strong controls over copies of legal documents and other digital assets will resort to using streaming access to software as another layer of protection in desktop-as-a-service configurations, made possible with networks and ubiquitous computing resources.[11]

11 A good example of streaming application services in use at the time of this writing is Amazon Workspaces: <https://aws.amazon.com/workspaces/>

Disposal

Licences for digital assets are now often enforced with DRM schemes, which prevent access before the start and after the expiration of a subscription or rental term. The problem of disposal becomes one of deleting the encrypted bytes (units of digital information), a generally safe and reliable experience. In the workplace, however, data files and other digital assets are exchanged between parties or disseminated to employees while doing everyday business. Some of these files may contain information of a confidential or proprietary nature, and in government may even include matters of state security. It is therefore imperative, depending on the sensitivity of the information contained in those files, that individuals, and especially lawyers advising them, understand and can state clearly the obligations for disposal that are attached to physical possession of those files, whether in a non-disclosure agreement, provisions in an employment contract or service agreement, regulatory publications, or other applicable documents.

Regulation

The regulation of online technologies and digital assets can be understood from two perspectives:

1 The sale, distribution, and use of digital assets within a given jurisdiction.
2 The use of digital assets and services, based on the location of the computing infrastructure elements providing those assets and services over the network and the location in which they are used.

It is our purpose here to introduce the key concepts to consider when reviewing regulations and legislation in consideration of a given matter.

In many cases, with or without DRM, digital assets are licensed for use in a single jurisdiction. The use of those assets by residents of that jurisdiction while travelling outside the jurisdiction is currently an area of ambiguity, unless applicable treaties are in place. Physical enforcement of such regulations usually takes the form of checking the location of a user using his network location[12] and then permitting access based on certain rules. The implementation of mechanisms for such

12 A practice known as reverse IP address lookup.

enforcement is far from uniform or reliable, a frequent source of rights owner frustration and deplorable user experience.

In addition to user access, regulations may affect the required practices of service providers and publishers. The country in which a service provider is domiciled may affect the practices it must adopt regarding user identity and data privacy as well as the nature of the services it may provide to those users. We will consider identity and privacy concerns in a subsequent section. First, let us consider aspects of regulation applied to the provision of services.

Certain services, such as electronic marketplaces (including those that deal in the sale of goods and commodities such as drugs, pornography, and food sourced from rare or endangered plants and animals) or services for online gambling, have fallen under the scope of legislation and regulations in many jurisdictions seeking to extend policies and norms in those societies to the online activities of their citizens.

While certain activities such as the sale and delivery of physical goods can still be controlled and taxed within and between jurisdictions through existing trade and customs laws, the sale and delivery of digital goods is not so easily controlled, even when the exchange is legitimate and permitted, in part due to the varying levels of political will to enforce existing laws, and in some cases because of the magnitude of the resources required for such enforcement.

The practice of place-shifting[13] allows a user in one jurisdiction that prohibits certain activities online to engage in those activities in another jurisdiction where they are permitted or even encouraged, provided they have adequate access via the network to those services. Depending on the jurisdiction in which the services are hosted or offered, there may or may not be agreements to regulate users from other jurisdictions. Two examples of place-shifting are particularly relevant when studying the effects of law and regulation on digital activities and assets:

1 *Online gambling*. Using virtual private networks (VPNs), citizens in countries where gambling is banned may connect to services hosted in countries promoting online gambling, such as Gibraltar or

13 To be compared with time-shifting, enabled with video cassette recorder (VCR) and digital video recorder (DVR) technologies that allow users to record broadcast television programmes for viewing at a time convenient to the user, simultaneously supporting the skipping of advertisements and multiple viewings and archiving at the user's discretion. Ted Johnson, 'Dish, NBCUniversal Settle AutoHop Ad-Skipping Lawsuit' (*Variety*, 17 June 2016) <https://variety.com/2016/biz/news/dish-nbc-autohop-lawsuit-settled-1201797895/> accessed 1 January 2026.

Denmark. The legal implications of such services and their use are beyond the scope of this discussion, but this example is raised to make you aware of just one of the many situations where legislation, regulation, and inter-jurisdiction cooperation vary greatly. These can either limit or create opportunities for clients and their lawyers, depending on the context.

2 *Electronic signatures.* Many jurisdictions now consider an electronic signature as valid for many transactions up to certain value limits, often stopping at matters involving the conveyance of real property or articles above a certain value to exclude adjudication in a small claims process. Electronic signatures may take the form of hand-drawn signatures on a document using a pen, trackpad, or mobile device; pasting an uploaded signature; or a more sophisticated process involving secure signatures that validate the user's identity and the contents of the document being signed.

Sync 5: In what contexts are electronic signatures legally binding?

You should allow around 40 minutes for this activity.

Research and familiarise yourself with the requirements for electronic signatures in your jurisdiction, taking note of the limits for validity and use of such signatures. Are there fixed values for transactions, above which only traditional (so-called wet signatures) are required? Are there specific classes of transactions that require wet signatures, such as probate matters or the conveyance of real property or moving vehicles?

Depending upon where you are based, you may have found a variety of different requirements relating to electronic signatures. Considering the rationale behind these requirements may well demonstrate the wider approach taken within a jurisdiction to technological developments, i.e. whether they are embraced or treated with suspicion.

Privacy concerns

When computers were stand-alone devices, physical security measures were, in most cases, sufficient to ensure the safety of the data stored on removable media and hard disks. Computing services delivered via the internet now require users concerned with safety and legal position to evaluate services and service providers on four critical aspects:

- *Data storage.* How and where data is stored has a direct impact on the expectations of privacy a user may rely upon. Is the data stored in encrypted form (a storage practice known as "encrypted at rest")? Under what conditions is the physical media kept? Is it always available on a network-connected device, or must someone physically connect it to a device on the network for the data to become available?
- *Data processing.* The way data is processed for various services and for what purpose, whether used for marketing purposes (with or without consent) or for influencing opinions, affects whether a person may be targeted for advertisements or certain communications that, if not desired or perhaps even embarrassing when seen out of context by third parties, may constitute a breach of privacy.
- *Transmission.* The means and methods by which data is prepared and transmitted from each machine involved in the delivery of a service may affect a user's privacy, especially if networks are compromised and unauthorised access to data is obtained by an untrusted or malicious third party.
- *Identity and user activity.* Users of online services will not necessarily want records of their online activities to be made available to unknown third parties. Identification of a user in a setting outside the interactions in question may be inappropriate or compromising to the user, who will often expect and demand control over such information.

PRIVACY IN DATA STORAGE

If a service provider follows prescribed best practices for securing access to physical computing assets and networks (physical security), a factor that is often important is the state of the data when it is stored on a medium such as a disk, whether accessible via the network or not. Users of sensitive services such as financial or government services will expect that their data is stored in encrypted form, a condition known as "encrypted at rest", requiring some sort of encrypting software and key to decrypt the data for access and processing. Sophisticated service providers will also employ algorithms requiring user input, such as a password or encryption key generated by a security application, so that only an authorised user can unlock the data stored on the service's infrastructure.

PRIVACY IN DATA PROCESSING

In some cases, data processing produces by-products, such as logs (electronic records), intermediate results, and copies of data stored within a running app's allocated or assigned memory on a device. While data processing professionals should be trusted to apply good practices to the management and disposal of intermediate data and to ensure that data is used only for the purposes under relevant terms of service and privacy policies, it is incumbent on lawyers advising clients in particularly sensitive situations or those running online businesses to be aware of the specific regulations related to the processing of data and the duties of the service operator with regard to privacy in data processing.

PRIVACY FOR TRANSMISSION

Because networks like the internet are public networks, safety of data transmission from source to destination is of greatest concern. This is to ensure that unauthorised third parties may not access that data in transit. Encryption technology is employed to ensure safe transmission in ways transparent to the user and (for the most part) to the software developer and system operators, using such technologies as SSL (Secure Sockets Layer) or TLS (Transport Layer Security). As a lawyer, it is important to ensure that the technologies and services one uses for professional work all use some scheme for securing transmission of data.

PRIVACY FOR USER ACTIVITY

The tracking of user activity for various purposes, whether to improve a physical device, online service, or app, to profile the user to target content for marketing or influence campaigns, or to ascertain compliance to laws and regulations are all matters of concern. Jurisdictions have varying levels of completeness in their treatment of activity tracking and privacy, ranging from no regulation to a presumption that all activity is at least tracked and reported to operators, and perhaps authorities.

This is a developing area of law. Societies are beginning to recognise the importance of user consent for tracking, the need for explicit mandates for opting out of tracking and use of that data, and more comprehensive policies such as ensuring the right to be forgotten, wherein all data pertinent to a person's usage history must be expunged from a system according to law. Of particular concern are regulations requiring the complete expunging of data from systems, and the complexity of compliance when there are multiple backup copies and information technology (IT) organisations, overwhelmed with workloads and limited in their ability to comply fully with the letter of the law.

Sync 6: Where is data stored?

You should allow approximately 15 minutes for this activity.

Consider the modern use of cloud-based services. As you use online services to handle client matters, you may have a copy of a document stored in a cloud storage area or cloud drive, a local copy of that same document synchronised with the copy in the cloud, and one downloaded when you had a few minutes to spare in a taxi travelling between client meetings. What steps must you take to ensure that those copies remain in control and confidential?

The proliferation of forgotten downloads on every device is a common condition in modern digital life. Perhaps you thought that a practice that restricted downloads to a single download directory that is periodically purged, or a strict practice of filing downloads immediately in an appropriate folder for each client or matter, would work well for you. Some might minimise downloads and use a synchronisation function found with some cloud-based services that allows a user to work in offline mode when travelling or for whatever reason. There is no universal solution, but you now have a starting point to develop your own method for managing this critical practice.

Case study: Health care app security leaks

Health care applications on connected mobile devices are indispensable for providing a bridge for exercise and personal body measurement and telemetry data (such as pulse rate) as part of fitness and health improvement regimes. All such devices require the support of online services in the cloud, and thus face the challenges to user privacy we have examined in this section. Three high-profile data breach incidents occurred over the two-year period from 2018 to 2019 for three prominent apps:

- MyFitnessPal, owned by Under Armour. Attackers[14] accessed personal data for over 150 million users, taking names, addresses, email addresses, and location information.

14 We use the term "attackers" here, instead of "hackers", more accurately conveying the malicious or felonious intent of the individuals. Mass media will often refer to

- PumpUp, an online fitness community, had the data of over six million users stolen, including contact information, photographs, and health data.
- Strava, an online shared fitness map service, had data openly shared for users who engaged in fitness activities like running and cycling. The community-sourced map and routing information was valued for its richness and currency. It also, however, had the unintended characteristic of being widely used by military personnel, whose open sharing of location data allowed some people examining the openly available data set to deduce the location of secret military installations where those personnel were stationed.

More detail on these three incidents can be found in an article by a design firm exploring ways to prevent such incidents <https://www.ego-cms.com/post/most-expensive-healthcare-app-security-fails-in-2018-2019>

You may want to spend some time reviewing these incidents and identifying the issues that come to mind related to the elements of privacy we have discussed in this section; namely, data storage, data processing, transmission, and user activity.

LEGAL REASONING USING TECHNOLOGY

In this section we examine some ways in which technology can be used to enhance legal reasoning and the practice of law. Legal texts generally pose two problems in which technology can be of service and sometimes of great utility.

First, there is the problem of representation of legal constructs, specifically in the way the substance and intent of a legal construct such as a law or contract is communicated. The analogy of a legal text as a program—more concretely, a declarative program specifying the constraints placed upon actors, whether they be individuals or legal parties under the law, or whether they be parties to an agreement, and whether they must act under pain of some specified penalty or

individuals obtaining illicit access to systems and data as "hackers", ignoring and inaccurately co-opting the long-held positive use of the term in technology and computing culture, celebrating hackers and hacking as the ingenious developers of know-how to solve problems, particularly in software development or in prankster tomfoolery at engineering schools.

liability—is often employed to illustrate the notion of the representation of the law for purposes of explanation or discussion. We examine in this section some techniques in representation and semantic analysis that have emerged as technology has evolved to help the understanding of natural language texts.

The second problem relates to surveying and comprehension of legal texts. While lawyers may rightly or not take pride in their drafting and syntactic prowess, the typical non-lawyer is often challenged to understand any legal language. Even trained lawyers with many years of practice will have widely divergent readings of complex texts, a reality that often figures as a condition for eventual litigation to settle the meaning of particular points in laws or contracts. In the need for precision and comprehensive specification, texts can grow, resulting not only in verbose and sometimes tortuous language but also in sheer volume and complexity, such that legal texts rival engineering endeavours for complexity. Just as in software engineering, where a single person will have difficulty understanding the full scope of a complex software system, so a single person may have difficulty understanding fully a body of legal text.

Note that we will omit discussion in this section of applications in which AI or machine learning techniques are applied to simulate or implement machine understanding of law, or in which they are used to aid or replace decision-making on the part of a human judge or lawmaker. You will find an introduction to those topics in Chapter 7.

REPRESENTATION OF LAW AND CONTRACTS AS PROGRAMS

Since the late 1950s, researchers have looked for ways to apply rigorous mathematical reasoning, specifically tools such as symbolic logic and logic programming, to the modelling and interpretation of laws and, to a limited extent, to commercial contracts. An academic paper published in 1957, titled “Symbolic Logic: A Razor-Edged Tool for Drafting and Interpreting Legal Documents”,[15] is an example of such efforts. By applying a technique of linguistic analysis and decomposition, author Layman E. Allen advanced the concept of “systematic pulverization”, in which language constructs are reduced to concise statements

15 Layman E. Allen, ‘Symbolic Logic: A Razor-Edged Tool for Drafting and Interpreting Legal Documents’ (May 1957) 66(6) *Yale Law Journal* <https://doi.org/10.2307/794073> accessed 1 January 2026.

that can be sequenced and represented as logical assertions suitable for evaluation by humans (and, as technology advanced, machines). Thus, clauses in legal texts can be restated in more precise terms, reducing or eliminating ambiguity, while also serving as an aid in the drafting of those texts.

The use of computing tools to aid in evaluation and understanding of legal texts was largely out of the realm of practicality, until gains in commodity computing power and data handling in the 2000s matched the computing needs that came with theoretical advances made earlier in the 1980s and 1990s. These advances came as methods for the systematic representation of knowledge in text, such as ontologies and rhetorical structure theory,[16] and methods to discern and disambiguate the meaning of words and texts.[17] Growing use of ontologies allowed the identification of discrete concepts (such as actors, objects, requirements, and constraints) and the delineation of the relationships between those concepts, while rhetorical structure theory supports, as its name suggests, the identification of conceptual representations in text and the pieces of text that relate to specific representations. Between ontological methods and rhetorical structure theory, concepts in their idealised, abstract forms can be rendered comprehensible with the former, and concepts in their textual representation can be understood and evaluated with the latter.

Investigation into the use of symbolic logic continued, with a notable 1986 paper examining the British Nationality Act 1948 as the specification of an algorithm for determining the eligibility of an individual to be classified as a British national. This was a rich study, illustrating, with non-trivial cases of legal reasoning, the difficulty of various approaches to encoding the application of law as a system of rules in an expert system or as other unspecified AI applications.[18] One can imagine efforts to encode the semantics of a given statute or regulation in an attempt to build an impartial "weighing machine" or "automatic

16 William C. Mann and Sandra A. Thompson, 'Rhetorical Structure Theory: Toward a Functional Theory of Text Organization' (January 1981) 8(3) *Text & Talk*.

17 Michael Lesk, 'Automatic Sense Disambiguation Using Machine Readable Dictionaries: How to Tell a Pine Cone from an Ice Cream Cone' (June 1986) *SIGDOC 86: Proceedings of the 5th Annual International Conference on Systems Documentation* 24–6 <https://doi.org/10.1145/318723.318728> accessed 1 January 2026.

18 M. J. Sergot et al., 'The British Nationality Act as a Logic Program' (May 1986) 29(5) *Communications of the ACM* <https://doi.org/10.1145/5689.5920> accessed 1 January 2026.

judge" to be used in case of a dispute. Such a tool would, in theory, remove the fallibility, imprecision, and arbitrary bias of a human interpreting a given legal text and matter.

A class of applications known as expert systems emerged as IT systems analysts took knowledge of certain laws and regulations, derived using the techniques described in this section, and developed specifications—intermediate representations of the legal constructs—that computer software developers could translate into runnable representations as computer programs or, in the parlance of the field of expert systems, *rules.* These rules could be evaluated by expert system *kernels* or *rule engines*—programs purpose-built to take rules as inputs and operational instructions—to answer specific applications of law. Examples of expert systems used in legal applications might include the determination of a person's eligibility to acquire British nationality, or whether to recommend to a judge that an accused criminal should be granted bail while awaiting trial. Note that these applications are representations of law translated by direct human effort, sometimes in multiple steps, from a text in a natural language such as English into a machine-runnable representation as software.

Expert systems applications are distinct from AI or machine learning applications, which will take data representing the range of conditions that may be embodied in or describe the subjects of the law, together with the desired outcomes of applying the law, and train a machine by building a mathematical model mapping such conditions to known correct outcomes. The resulting mathematical model, trained on a set of known inputs, enables the machine to evaluate previously unseen combinations from the same domain of possibilities and to render a specific application of that law as a determination or recommendation.

Machine learning systems can be classified as supervised (requiring measurement and human input and tuning after each iterative attempt to improve the model through training) or unsupervised (fully automated, improving using algorithmic techniques such as randomisation, or programmatic limiting of inputs based on specified measurements). A comparison of supervised and unsupervised machine learning systems is seen in Figure 3.4. Both types of systems are in wide use. The choice of one type over the other is highly dependent on the problem to be solved, the available data and the other components of the approach selected by the engineers building and operating the system.

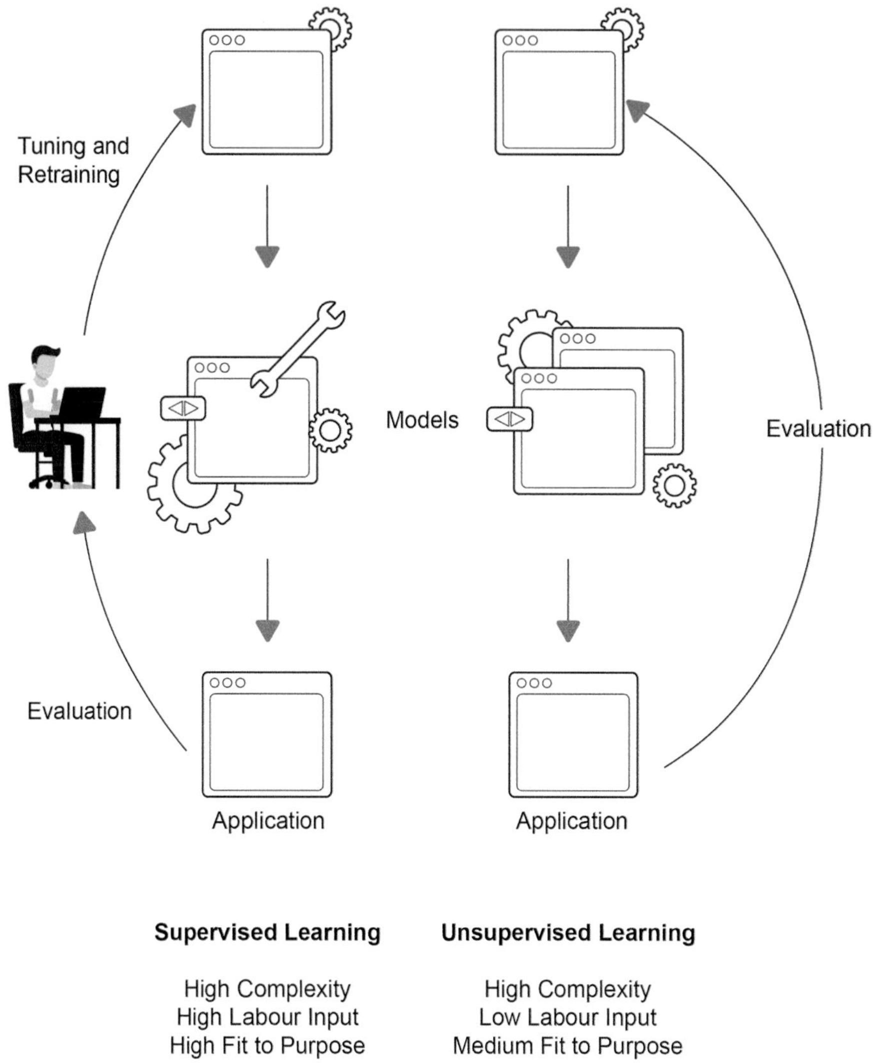

Figure 3.4 Supervised versus unsupervised machine learning

TOOLS FOR UNDERSTANDING LEGAL TEXTS

So far, we have examined ways in which people have begun to use symbolic logic and related forms of systematic modelling and semantic analysis to build machine-readable, "computable" representations of legal constructs. While these techniques do support the development of some levels of understanding of the legal texts they represent, and in some cases can be used to build systems attempting to apply the same texts as law or contracts, they may not contribute to a lawyer's everyday ability to understand a text for the purposes of serving a client, providing an opinion or building a case for action. Tools normally used by software engineers to manage and process large bodies of source code (the components of a computer program) have proven useful to lawyers and legal scholars approaching larger bodies of legal text or complex regulations, by supporting the finding of facts about the text itself, of what is known as the metadata related to the text.

A 2015 study[19] by researchers at the Massachusetts Institute of Technology (MIT) and Harvard University examined ways in which software engineering tools and techniques can be applied to legal text analysis, using multiple major revisions of the US Code as the study subject. The team explored the analogy between legal code and software code, asserting that four key principles and practices from good software design (conciseness, change, coupling, and complexity) all matter in the drafting of law for comprehension as much as they do in software engineering. They reasoned that just as software engineers strive to communicate their rationale for future maintainers of their code and to work to make the code comprehensible for others joining the team, so lawyers could benefit from the practices and tools in the application to legal drafting.

- *Conciseness.* Software engineers, as a matter of best practice, strive for compact expression, as less code means less code to understand, debug and maintain over the long term. In a similar way, well-written prose will display compactness and clarity in expression. Software engineers often employ tools to count lines of code, check for correct syntax, and use tooling to achieve compact expression. Lawyers have similar tools built into modern word processing software, as well as online services for grammar correction, word choice, and usage enhancement, but there are few tools currently in mainstream use to assess textual complexity and structure, let alone assist in improving clarity or conciseness.
- *Change.* Managing, tracking, and controlling the release of changes to a body of code is a critical skill to permit software developers to have confidence in the changes they are making. While many

19 William Li, Pablo Azar, David Larochelle, Phil Hill and Andrew W. Lo, 'Law Is Code: A Software Engineering Approach to Analyzing the United States Code' (2015) 10 *Journal of Business & Technology Law* 297 <http://digitalcommons.law.umaryland.edu/jbtl/vol10/iss2/6> accessed 1 January 2026.

lawyers may use a change tracking function in their word processing software to manage a single document, doing so across a collection of documents is not a common practice, nor is it supported by generally accessible office productivity tools. Change management tools also allow the assessment of percentage of change, highlighting for lawyers the texts that may need the most attention for review.

- *Coupling.* In software, dependencies between modules directly affect the functions a system can provide. The presence and ordering of those modules in some systems affect the way functions are manifested in the running code. In law, a sufficient understanding of interdependencies between bills and related laws is necessary to ensure that the desired outcomes for legislation are achieved. Software engineering tools build reference tables of significant entities in a code base, as well as relationship maps. The same types of tools can be used to build indexes, summaries and cross-reference tables, as well as text network diagrams, to show relationships between significant portions of a legal text and, in some cases, reveal relationships that may otherwise be overlooked in the absence of such tools.
- *Complexity.* Software engineers use discovery tools that can generate diagrams to provide overviews of bodies of code. Similar tools exist to provide semantic structure analysis and diagrams that provide overviews of significant bodies of text.[20]

In addition to using code management tools, software developers have begun applying natural language processing (NLP) techniques that involve the construction of mathematical models to describe the structure of texts, permitting functions such as search, analytics, discovery, and redaction. These are also referred to in Chapter 6, but here we give some examples of how these tools might be used:

- *Search.* Indexing strategies developed through years of investment in search engine technologies now allow easy location of words or phrases of interest and documents containing such fragments. Summarisation algorithms and Large Language Models support more efficient overview processing of large bodies of documents, such

20 M. Abdeen, R. El-Sahan, A. Ismaeil, S. El-Harouny and M. Shalaby, 'Automatic Generation of Mind Maps from Text with M2Gen' (2009) *Science and Technology for Humanity (TIC-STH)*, IEEE Toronto International Conference.

that painstaking examination of boxes of documents can now be done with significantly greater speed and accuracy from a connected device's browser.

- *Analytics.* Lawyers looking to build a case on publicly available records may use analytic tools to confirm assertions of complaint frequency and build quantitative evidence quickly and cost-effectively before approaching a regulator with a claim or request.
- *Discovery.* Computing statistics showing frequently or (as the case may be) infrequently used terms in context in legal documents sometimes reveal unusual conditions, previously unknown persons who may have interest in a specific matter, and other facts that might be overlooked when reading large bodies of text for other purposes.
- *Redaction.* When releasing certain documents to comply with discovery requirements or other lawful requirements for visibility, organisations may be required to redact certain sensitive items of information, such as personally identifiable information (PII) of individuals, trade secrets, and so forth. A suitably trained set of tools using NLP techniques or Large Language Models can automatically redact sensitive documents prior to final review and release.

The state of tools being developed for understanding and reasoning about the law evolves as rapidly as software techniques and data processing capacity, and it is expected to continue to accelerate in the coming years. A digital lawyer will need to keep abreast of developments in technology, looking for ways to experiment and apply such developments that are reasonable in terms of protecting the client and one's firm or practice from risk and that can take advantage of tools and techniques that provide significant advantage in finding solutions for the range of matters a digital lawyer may encounter.

Digital lawyering skills: Interdisciplinary working

The need for digital lawyers to follow and understand developments in technology demonstrates the interdisciplinary nature of digital lawyering. Today's legal professional will find themselves working and communicating with specialists in other areas, particularly IT, digital technologies, legal design, and project management as they apply such developments and provide advice and guidance to clients.

As a law student, it is easy to become immersed in legal terminology and jargon. However, as a digital lawyer you may well find yourself having to use technical terms which fall outside the usual language of law. You may also find yourself having to explain complex legal concepts and issues in a way which is accessible to colleagues working in other disciplines. Conversely, you may need to explain unfamiliar technical concepts to clients when identifying solutions to problems.

There are some simple ways that students can begin to develop the skills required for interdisciplinary working, including:

- Reading books, articles, blogs, and websites from different disciplines to acquaint yourself with frequently used terminology and key issues.
- Looking at whether your law school offers any non-legal optional modules or any voluntary opportunities to work with students from other disciplines.
- Attending events and conferences which have an interdisciplinary focus.
- Seeking out opportunities for work experience or internships in different industries and sectors to gain valuable transferable skills.

All of these are methods of familiarising yourself with different disciplines in a way that will help you to work and communicate with others clearly and effectively.

FINDING YOUR WAY

In this section, we offer some general pointers for you to learn more about the intersection of technologies and the law, to build on the foundations that we have laid down in this chapter.

ENGINEERING APPROACH

In this chapter, we have attempted to avoid extensive detail behind the technologies that underpin devices, networks and services that are now indispensable for the digital lawyer. Those so inclined may benefit from learning some fundamentals of technology implementation, for instance, by learning to write software code in a modern programming language. A hands-on understanding of the process and techniques, even at a beginning level, would help a lawyer to appreciate the issues and complexities faced by software developers building the tools and services users rely upon in everyday work.

HISTORICAL APPROACH

In parts of this chapter, we have taken the historical approach to give a sense of the evolution of technology from its simpler roots to the complex, multilayered networks we have in use today. The historical approach to learning about technology will become more important as we continue using computing and communications technology in everyday life, if just to set technologies in context when we encounter them. The historical approach is certainly useful in understanding how, for example, copying and pasting entered conceptually into user interaction design, or, more concretely, to know that some organisations use magnetic tapes as their primary backup and archiving medium and will continue to do so because of the sheer volume of data to be handled. Such knowledge will help a lawyer advising clients in the transfer of certain digital assets to specify the transfer of all backup media as well, and possibly to require means to ensure the ability to read potentially discontinued recording formats.

USER-CENTRIC APPROACH

A user-centric approach to learning about technology considers a user's goals while examining only those technologies that are needed to serve those goals. User centricity frequently incorporates aspects of design thinking and user experience design, ensuring that the elements that directly affect the user—in this case a client or a fellow lawyer, counterparty or even oneself—are understood. This means that the focus is on whatever technologies are needed for the user goals, and only those technologies are considered.

LEGAL(TECH) APPROACH

Learning about technology from a legislative and regulatory perspective is perhaps the more traditional way for lawyers to encounter technologies in everyday practice, and then conceptually rather than in practice. The legal approach is of course useful to stay abreast of one's peers and colleagues and to ensure a common vocabulary for discourse with peers and other parties.

As more technology-minded lawyers and technologist-lawyers have been building legal technology (legaltech) businesses that become going concerns, general awareness of technology and technology-related issues in the profession has grown, leading to events, community organisations, media outlets and conferences. In addition, there are legaltech-focused funding programmes with hackathons and incubation schemes to support and advance innovation.

STAYING CURRENT

As with any field, staying current with technology involves keeping abreast of developments through reliable mainstream media, but more importantly, also through profession-oriented news sources and media. For lawyers interested in technology, the legaltech sections of popular professional sites such as Law.com's LegalTech News[21] and Stanford University's CodeX Techindex[22] are good places to start, as are the legaltech groups at local law society or bar association organisations.

ADDITIONAL RESOURCES

Ford P, 'What Is Code? If You Don't Know, You Need to Read This' (*Bloomberg.com*) <https://www.bloomberg.com/graphics/2015-paul-ford-what-is-code/>

Kernighan BW, *Understanding the Digital World: What You Need to Know About Computers, the Internet, Privacy, and Security* (Princeton UP 2017).

Lessig L, 'Code Is Law' (*Harvard Magazine*, 1 January 2000) <https://harvardmagazine.com/2000/01/code-is-law-html>

21 <https://www.law.com/legaltechnews/>
22 <https://techindex.law.stanford.edu/>

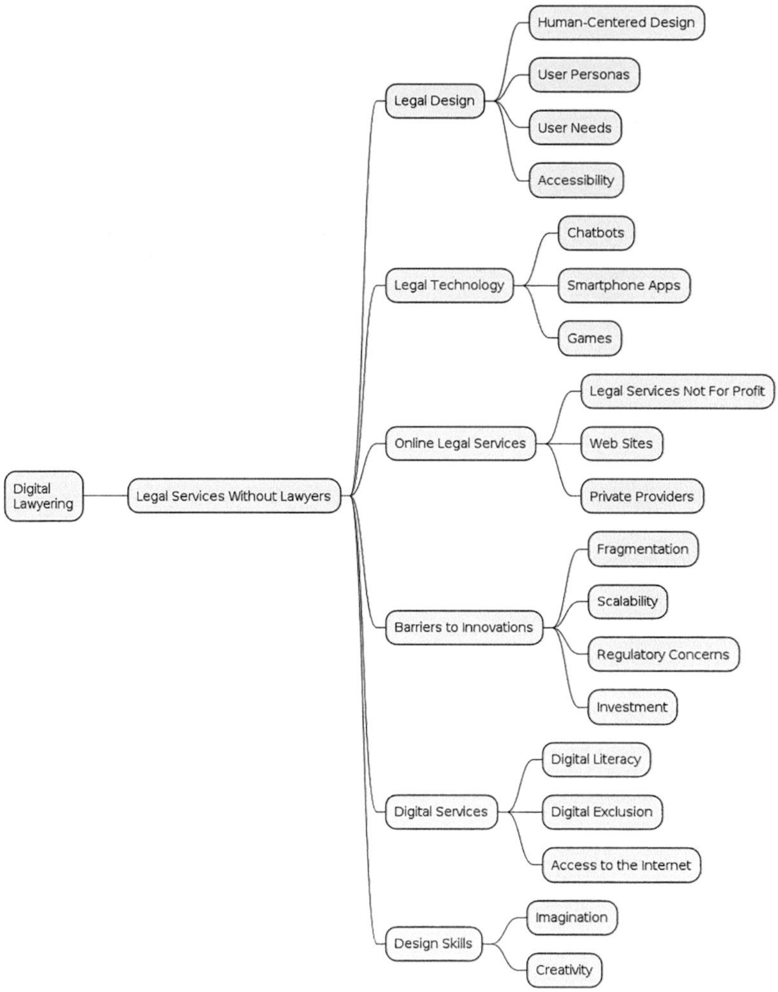

Mind Map 4.1 Chapter topics

4 DELIVERING LEGAL SERVICES WITHOUT LAWYERS

Francine Ryan

INTRODUCTION

This chapter will consider the delivery of legal services without the use of lawyers. It will examine this issue through an exploration of how we can improve access to justice using digital technologies. You will be encouraged to think about how technology can be used to support individuals to resolve disputes without the need for lawyers. It will consider ways in which technology is developing to provide innovative solutions; for example, chatbots like DoNotPay (see Chapter 3), digital platforms to store and archive legal documents, and legal docs companies that allow individuals to create personalised contracts online. It will analyse the emerging legaltech market, highlight the impact of GenAI, and discuss the potential and concerns of using technology to transform access to justice.

Chapter hot spots

When reading this chapter, questions to think about include:

- What types of online services exist?
- How is technology being developed to widen legal access?
- What opportunities and challenges are presented by GenAI?
- What is design thinking?
- Why is understanding users' needs important?

DOI: 10.4324/9781003602323-4

- What are the risks associated with the proliferation of technological tools?

Having read the title and introduction, you can add any other questions you want to explore here:

Technology is having a profound impact on business and the provision of legal services. The cloud, cybersecurity, the Internet of Things, mobile technology, GenAI, and legal design are all important aspects of digital transformation. The pace of change is rapid, and it can feel overwhelming trying to keep abreast of and understand the emerging technology trends. This chapter attempts to demystify how technology is impacting on the delivery of legal services. This is an exciting time to study law. Technology is changing the legal landscape, and there are lots of opportunities to think creatively about how we use technology to democratise the public understanding of law and improve access to justice. Understanding the intersection between law and technology will ensure you are able to thrive in the new digital age.

Writing in *Tomorrow's Lawyers*[1] in 2013, Richard Susskind argued that technology would radically change the provision of legal services and the legal profession. Susskind has long been an advocate for technology and, although the pace of change has perhaps not been as radical as he has predicted, it is clear that new technologies are affecting the legal landscape. The COVID-19 pandemic had a significant impact on the delivery of legal services. The launch of ChatGPT in November 2022 changed the technological landscape presenting both significant opportunities and challenges in addressing the access to justice gap. In Chapter 2 you began to explore how technological innovation impacts upon those who provide legal services. You will return to this theme in subsequent chapters. However, the focus of this chapter is upon how technological innovation is relevant to the ways in which we deliver legal services.

1 Richard Susskind, *Tomorrow's Lawyers* (OUP 2013).

WHY IS THERE A NEED TO DESIGN LEGAL SERVICES WITHOUT LAWYERS?

Why are so many people turning to the internet to help them resolve their legal problems? The challenge is that most people cannot afford to pay for legal advice, and the availability of legal aid has been restricted. In the UK in 2013, the Legal Aid, Sentencing, and Punishment of Offenders Act 2012 (LASPO 2012) came into force. This legislation introduced significant funding cuts to legal aid, meaning that fewer people had access to legal advice in the areas of family, immigration, employment, and welfare benefits law. In other jurisdictions legal aid is also restricted from the very poorest in our society.

There are some types of cases, such as personal injury claims, where, if the case is successful, the legal costs are recovered from the opposing party. Under a conditional fee agreement (sometimes referred to as a "no win, no fee agreement") the law firm agrees with the client that they only have to pay the legal costs if their case is won, and they receive compensation. If the claim is not successful, the client does not have to pay legal costs to their solicitors, but they are likely to be ordered to pay the other side's costs under the costs rules. There are insurance policies that can be purchased to cover these risks. The law firm can charge a success fee for this type of arrangement, and this is deducted from the compensation the client receives if their case is successful. Another way of funding a case is through a damages-based agreement where the law firm takes a percentage of any compensation awarded as payment for their services.

However, in many instances clients want advice on legal issues where there will be no recovery of damages (e.g. in the case of a divorce). In those cases, unless a client qualifies for legal aid they will have to pay for the legal advice. Instructing a lawyer can be very expensive, and many people cannot afford to pay privately. They therefore turn to other sources of help to assist them with their legal issue.

WHAT IS LEGALTECH?

Lawtech and legaltech are interchangeable ways of describing "technologies that aim to support, supplement or replace traditional methods for delivering legal services, or that improve the way the justice system operates".[2] Lawtech refers to a range of different technological tools

2 The Law Society, 'Introduction to LawTech 2019' <https://tlsprdsitecore.azureedge.net/-/media/files/campaigns/lawtech/introduction-to-lawtech-october-

including chatbots, legal document drafting automation and knowledge and research tools, some of which were described in Chapter 3. Technology is being leveraged to provide resources to enhance the public understanding of law and to provide legal advice through chatbots and triage tools. There are now examples of technology tools that are being used by the free advice sector to help support those who cannot afford to pay for legal advice. Throughout this chapter we will explore some of the different ways technology is being used to improve access to justice.

The increasing range of online help has been fuelled by the growth of lawtech start-ups. The organisation Legal Geek publishes a startup map each year, which showcases lawtech start-ups and scale-ups. The start-ups focus on different areas of law and different types of services; some are more business orientated, providing ways to support the legal profession to become more efficient. One example is Made In Law,[3] which is an online service for incorporating a business in Europe. Other start-ups are around Law for Good, designing solutions to support access to justice.

Sync 1: Legaltech start-ups

You should allow around 15 minutes for this activity.

1 Access the Legal Geek start-up map <https://www.legalgeek.co/startup-map/>
2 Click on the link to three start-ups to find out more about what they do.

As you will have seen from the map, it is divided into sections including managing the business, managing and/or performing, performing work, and consumer services.

TYPES OF ONLINE LEGAL SERVICES

Digital legal tools are being developed in the form of websites and applications that can be downloaded onto a smartphone to provide

2019.pdf?rev=fc0013791e0c474198daaabd648a304d&hash=F030B90541BF66B22233A9702F4B22A5>

3 <https://madeinlaw.com/en/>

legal information and services to support non-lawyers in resolving legal problems. In 2019, Sandefur[4] carried out the Survey of US Legal Technologies to find out what kind of digital technologies exist to support non-lawyers in resolving their legal problems. The main findings of the survey were:

- Over 320 digital tools exist in the United States to assist non-lawyers in areas of law including civil, criminal, and employment.
- Fifty-two percent of the tools facilitated the user being able to take some form of action (e.g. diagnosing a legal issue, creating a form).
- The legal design of many of the tools was out of date; often there was too much reliance on text; and many were a collection of information about the law.
- Often there was not a correlation between the digital tools created and the types of problems non-lawyers required help with.
- As yet, there is no single tool that offers a complete solution to a legal problem.
- Some of the tools were free but quite a number charged the user.

In the UK, there are an increasing number of internet sites offering free legal information and services to the public. The market is changing, with new providers emerging offering paid legal services that in the past would have been provided by legal professionals. Hagan[5] classifies the different types of online help as shown in the following sections.

Government help

These are online sites where the law and legal procedure are explained. For example, the UK government website has a section on crime, justice, and the law. It provides information on a wide range of issues including prisons and probation, reporting crimes and getting compensation, young people and the law, and your rights and the law. It provides sources of information and provides links to other organisations.

4 Rebecca L. Sandefur, 'Legal Tech for Non-Lawyers: Report on the Survey of US Legal Technologies' (2019) <https://www.americanbarfoundation.org/wp-content/uploads/2023/04/report_us_digital_legal_tech_for_nonlawyers.pdf> accessed 12 January 2026.

5 M. Hagan, 'The User Experience of the Internet as a Legal Help Service' (2016) 20(2) *Virginia Journal of Law & Technology* 394–465.

Non-profit referrals/information

These are online sites where individuals can find out information about their legal issue and use the information to help them to try to resolve their legal problem. For example, AdviceNow[6] has a selection of legal information on a range of legal issues and links to other trusted sources of help. They also provide a help directory to signpost users to other organisations that may be able to offer legal assistance. Citizens Advice[7] provides extensive legal information on a range of topics including benefits, work, housing, immigration, and much more.

Legal services/not for profit

These are online sites that provide a mix of legal information and paid-for legal assistance. For example, Which Legal[8] is owned by the Consumer Association, which is a registered charity. Which Legal provides legal advice on consumer issues, employment law, and small claims. The guidance is provided by email and telephone. There is a joining fee and then a monthly charge.

Private legal information sites

These are online sites where individuals can access personalised legal information for free; for example, Ask A Lawyer[9] and Free Legal Advice.[10] These sites offer to answer legal questions for free on a range of topics, but they do not guarantee they will answer every question. They also provide legal information and post answers to questions that have been asked by other users. Although it is not completely apparent, these sites are often linked to law firms and probably serve as a way of generating new business to the firm.

Private legal self-help tools

These sites share similarities with the private legal information sites, but they charge for their services. For example, Just Answer[11] and Expert Answers[12] offer services where they charge for answering legal ques-

6 <https://www.advicenow.org.uk/categories>
7 <https://www.citizensadvice.org.uk/>
8 <https://legalservice.which.co.uk/>
9 <https://www.askalawyer.co.uk/>
10 <https://www.free-legal-advice.co.uk/>
11 <https://www.justanswer.co.uk/>
12 <https://www.expertanswers.co.uk/>

tions. Legal Zoom[13] is an online legal service provider that offers legal advice on conveyancing, wills and supporting small businesses. Rocket Lawyer[14] provides a range of services, offering free legal guides and paid-for services including legal advice and legal documents. GenAI tools are now being developed to provide the public with access to legal information. One example is Contend Legal,[15] which uses a Large Language Model to answer legal questions.

One of the issues to consider with the development of these types of sites is reliability and trustworthiness. These platforms are often not subject to the same regulation as lawyers, but people accessing these sites might be unaware of this. An increase in the provision of legal services delivered online raises questions about how we protect users of these services. Although there has been growth in the number of digital tools available to help non-lawyers, there are regulatory challenges in the adoption of such technology.

UNDERSTANDING USER NEEDS

Both Sandefur and Hagan agree that many of the digital tools developed do not meet the need of the users. Defining what is a "legal need" has been problematic, and what constitutes the definition of legal need is subject to much debate.

> "Legal need" arises when citizens (or businesses) require support from legal services (broadly defined) in order to resolve problems, which have a legal definition.[16]

Research[17] has found that many people struggle to recognise their problem as a legal issue. Over many years, legal needs surveys have been conducted which have demonstrated that many UK citizens have been

13 <https://www.legalzoom.com/uk/>
14 <https://www.rocketlawyer.com/gb/en>
15 Contend Legal | Your AI Legal Assistant.
16 Pascoe Pleasance, *"Legal Need" and Legal Needs Surveys: A Background Paper* (Open Society Foundations, 2016) <https://namati.org/wp-content/uploads/2016/11/OSJI-Legal-Needs-Surveys-Background-Materials-1-An-Introduction-to-Legal-Needs-Surveys-1-v3.6-2016-06-22-web_Pascoe.pdf> accessed 2 October 2019.
17 Rebecca Sandefur, *Accessing Justice in the Contemporary USA: Findings from the Community Needs and Services Study* (American Bar Foundation 2014).

denied access to justice because they do not have sufficient legal knowledge or capability to navigate their legal problems.[18] However, many of the digital tools that have been created assume that a person already knows they have a legal problem for which there is a legal remedy. Let's take an example of a tenant who has a problem with their hot water. Do they fix it themselves or recognise the situation as legally actionable because their landlord has failed to repair the property under the tenancy agreement? Although many websites provide legal information on tenancy issues, without some form of diagnosis tool a non-lawyer may struggle to recognise the legal aspects of their problem.

Although the internet offers the potential to help people resolve their legal issues, the current provision is not always effective because it is not user-friendly, and often it is designed in ways that replicate how lawyers think and operate.[19] Therefore, to understand how to use technology to support individuals dealing with legal problems, it is important to think about the design of legal information to ensure that it is user-friendly.

Hagan[20] conducted a study in the United States to better understand how people use online services. She found that:

- Google search was used first when people wanted to better understand their legal issue, and the highest-ranking search engines were where the information was drawn from.
- The internet searches and sites visited gave users basic information on how to resolve their problem.
- Users wanted free help that was clear, had interactive navigation and included case studies and some form of marker to demonstrate that the information provided was authoritative and legitimate.

Hagan then looked at the features users wanted from online services. She found that these included:

- The site must be easy to use and navigate, with information presented in small segments so that it does not overwhelm the user.

18 The Civil and Social Justice Panel Survey (CSJPS) 2010, 2012. See also <https://www.lawforlife.org.uk/wp-content/uploads/LASPO-Implementation-Review-Consultation-Law-for-Life-Advicenow-response-Final-Sept-2018.pdf>

19 Queensland Association of Independent Legal Services Inc., *Queensland Community Legal Centres Use of Technology Literature Review and Discussion Paper* (Queensland Association of Independent Legal Services Inc. 2014) 18.

20 *Supra* n. 5, p. 413.

- A site that is authoritative and legitimate, and so ideally affiliated or linked in some way to an official organisation.
- When in the initial stages of finding out information about their legal problem, users do not want advertising, marketing, or paywalls.
- Ideally users prefer all the information in one place or on one site.
- The site needs to be designed well with interactive features, search facilities and menu choices.
- The visual look of the site has to meet modern design standards.
- There was a preference for case studies, narratives, and stories that reflected similar situations to the user's experience.
- The ideal site would take the user through each step of the legal process to navigate their legal problem. It would include assistance in helping the user identify their legal problem, develop a strategy to tackle the issue, and allow them to complete any forms/documents to resolve the problem.

HOW IS THIS ACHIEVED?

To help non-lawyers use online platforms, developers need to think about their design and navigation and ensure that search tools are easy to use. There should be menus, headings, and icons to orientate the user to easily find the information that is relevant to them. In designing content, it should be framed around how a non-lawyer experiences a problem rather than around legal topics. Platforms should include text, video, and images to engage different types of users. Interactive tools that allow users to customise the information to the specifics of their case should also be included. Online sites should be as comprehensive as possible to avoid the user having to visit multiple sites. It is helpful to provide links to other sites to guide the user through their legal journey. For example, if the online site provides legal information, it should provide a clear link to a court site to complete court forms and file them electronically if possible. Overall, the site needs to have an interactive design that supports non-lawyers to navigate their legal journey efficiently and effectively.

There are several different ways that technology is being used to support access to justice. One way is through the improvement of processes to make the operation of the service more efficient and more accessible; this is highlighted through the examples of Justice Connect and Access to Justice Author.

Justice Connect

In most jurisdictions, significant levels of unmet legal need exist. There is the potential to revolutionise access to justice by leveraging technology to build systems and digital tools that deliver legal assistance directly to people who require help. Justice Connect is an Australian not-for-profit organisation that combines pro bono legal support and digital innovation to increase access to justice. It connects individuals and not-for-profit organisations who have a legal issue with a network of law firms and pro bono lawyers who provide free legal assistance. It also has developed a range of digital tools to provide additional legal support, including Justice Connect Answers, a self-help resources hub and a Dear Landlord self-help tool. To find out more about Justice Connect, visit their website.[21]

Access to Justice Author (A2J Author)

In the United States, A2J Author software has been developed to support self-represented litigants to complete court paperwork and documents. It facilitates this process through the development of guided interviews which allow end users to create web-based documents. The software is available free to organisations such as courts, law schools, and legal aid providers. There is also a portal that matches law schools and legal aid organisations so they can work together on a project. Many law schools in the United States use the tool as part of classes in legal technology and access to justice.

Both of these projects use design thinking in conjunction with user testing to develop the digital tools and build the systems to deliver legal assistance. This will be explored in greater detail later in the chapter.

Developing legaltech tools

Another way in which technology is being used to support access to justice is through the development of chatbots.

21 <www.justiceconnect.org.au>

WHAT IS A CHATBOT?

A chatbot is a piece of software that allows you to perform an automated task. There are different definitions of a chatbot, but the most capable form of chatbot is one that can have a conversation with a human. If you ask the chatbot questions, it can respond with an answer.

There are three different types of chatbots: scripted, intelligent, and application.

- *Scripted.* The interactions within a scripted chatbot are determined by a set path. The user will pick from various options to move on to the next step. The bot can be programmed to respond to text, voice, or touch.
- *Intelligent.* These chatbots use artificial intelligence (AI) to allow the user to put in a free-form response, and with AI, the more they are used, the better they perform.
- *Application.* These chatbots allow for interaction via a graphical user interface (a visual way of interaction, for example, via menus and icons). This can form part of an intelligent and scripted chatbot.

The integration of GenAI has significantly improved chatbots, moving them from tools that answered basic questions to much more sophisticated systems capable of having more human-like conversations that produce contextually relevant responses. As AI capability improves, we will see AI chatbots handling more complex interactions.

THE LEGAL ACCESS CHALLENGE

The UK's Legal Access Challenge[22] was run in collaboration with the Solicitors Regulation Authority (SRA) and the innovation foundation Nesta.[23] The £500,000 challenge was to encourage and support innovation to help individuals and small businesses access legal information and advice. In April 2020, the two winners were CourtNav and FLOWS by RCJ Advice and Rights of Women and Mencap and Access to Social Care.

22 <https://www.legalaccesschallenge.org>
23 <https://www.nesta.org.uk/>

The Mencap and Access to Social Care project provides free legal information about social care law, helps users navigate their situation and generates letters to resolve specific issues.[24]

Sync 2: Flows

You should allow around 15 minutes for this activity.

1 Access the FLOWS website. <https://www.flows.org.uk>

2 Have a look around the website to see what help it provides.

3 Click on "Browse safely" and reflect on why this is an important element of the design of this website.

The FLOWS website offers a variety of different sources of help for anyone who is experiencing domestic violence. One of the most interesting features of the website is the ability to apply for a court order online. CourtNav is an online decision tree tool which helps the users to automatically create an application for a court order, which is then checked by a legal advisor.[25] These projects are examples of technology being leveraged to support access to justice and demonstrate the potential of digital technologies to help meet unmet legal need.

In addition to innovation in the not-for-profit sector, there are developments in the commercial sector to develop legaltech to support non-lawyers accessing legal services.

Case study: DoNotPay

Joshua Browder was born in London in 1997 and graduated from Stanford University in America. He taught himself to code at age 12, and at 18 he created a chatbot called DoNotPay. DoNotPay allows users to challenge disputed parking tickets. Joshua Browder used technology to disrupt the traditional way in which legal services are delivered. When he came up with this idea, many lawyers were dismissive of the idea that technology could be used to resolve legal issues.

24 <www.accesscharity.org.uk/chatbot-information?t#section1>
25 <https://www.courtnav.org.uk>

DoNotPay originally used Browder's own natural language processing (NLP) algorithms, but in 2016 he teamed up with IBM and started building bots on IBM Watson. DoNotPay first launched in London, and within six months it was reported that it had been successful in 160,000 cases.[26] The bot works by asking a series of questions to determine whether you are entitled to appeal your parking fine. If it determines you qualify, it generates an appeal letter.

DoNotPay expanded in 2017, launching new bots across the UK and the United States. However, in the United States, DoNotPay has faced significant legal challenges, including being fined by the Federal Trade Commission (FTC) and being subject to several class action lawsuits.[27] Despite these challenges, the DoNotPay website states that it is "your AI consumer champion" and suggests it can assist consumers with a myriad of different issues.

BARRIERS TO IMPROVING ACCESS TO JUSTICE THROUGH TECHNOLOGY

The not-for-profit sector does face barriers to technological innovation. It is more challenging to secure investment and harder to encourage start-ups to develop legaltech for non-profit than for commercial ventures, and there are issues of resourcing, fragmentation, and scalability that must be overcome. GenAI offers both opportunities and challenges in addressing the access to justice gap. GenAI tools such as chatbots like ChatGPT can explain legal rights in plain English, help people conduct legal research and democratise access to legal resources. But there are challenges. These tools can hallucinate and provide inaccurate or misleading advice. Legal systems are different, GenAI tools

26 Cheyenne Macdonald and Stacey Liberatore, 'The Robot that Could Get You Off a Parking Ticket: DoNotPay System Has Won 160,000 Disputes in London and New York' (*Daily Mail*, 28 June 2016) <https://www.dailymail.co.uk/sciencetech/article-3664413/The-Robot-parking-ticket-DoNotPay-created-student-won-160-000-disputes-London-New-York.html> accessed 26 April 2021.

27 Federal Trade Commission, 'FTC Finalizes Order with DoNotPay That Prohibits Deceptive "AI Lawyer" Claims, Imposes Monetary Relief, and Requires Notice to Past Subscribers" (11 February 2025) <www.ftc.gov/news-events/news/press-releases/2025/02/ftc-finalizes-order-donotpay-prohibits-deceptive-ai-lawyer-claims-imposes-monetary-relief-requires> accessed 12 January 2026.

may not provide advice related to the specific jurisdiction and members of the public might not be aware they need to verify the reliability of an AI output.[28] Furthermore, better-performing GenAI tools often require a subscription, potentially reinforcing structural inequalities.

The development of legaltech and AI tools also raises regulatory concerns. The legislation governing data protection can be a barrier to innovation, and this issue is explored further in relation to Big Data in Chapter 6. Digital solutions that collect any form of data must comply with data protection regulations. If the solution provides legal advice, then in some circumstances the advice given may also be subject to professional indemnity rules. In England and Wales, the SRA recognise that the development of new technologies can widen access to legal services, and they state they are committed to simplifying regulatory rules to enable growth and innovation. SRA Innovate is a space that has been created to support innovation in legal services.[29] The regulatory framework is an important consideration for the development of technological tools and will differ depending on the jurisdiction.

Although there is potential to explore how technology can help non-lawyers with their legal problems, it is also important to recognise that some people struggle to access or use technology. There needs to be careful consideration of the implications of using technology to widen access to legal advice and information. A lot of work is happening within the free advice sector to consider how technology can be leveraged to support access to justice. Citizens Advice's Future of Advice: Strategic Framework 2019–22 sets out its vision for using technology to test out new ideas around machine learning and automation.[30] One of the key points in the strategy concerns the risks of digital exclusion.

28 Francine Ryan and Elizabeth Hardie, 'We Asked ChatGPT for Legal Advice—Here Are Five Reasons Why You Shouldn't' (*The Conversation*, 31 May 2024) <https://theconversation.com/we-asked-chatgpt-for-legal-advice-here-are-five-reasons-why-you-shouldnt-229147> accessed 5 January 2026.

29 <https://www.sra.org.uk/resources/innovate/sra-innovate>

30 Citizens Advice, 'Future of Advice: Our Strategic Framework 2019–22' <https://www.citizensadvice.org.uk/about-us/future-of-advice-our-strategic-framework-2019-22/> accessed 7 January 2025. At the time of writing, a new Framework has not been updated or replaced.

DIGITAL EXCLUSION

Technology may offer innovative ways to address access to justice, but it is not without its challenges. One of the other major problems with the proliferation of technological tools is digital exclusion. There is a risk that sections of society who do not have access to technology and/or do not have the required digital skills to engage with technology will be excluded. Chapter 9 discusses the digitalisation of the court system. There are concerns that many parts of our society may become further excluded from the justice system with greater use of technology because they will be required to use technology to communicate with the courts and to enforce their legal rights. As more and more services move online, it is essential that everyone has the required digital skills to access and use these platforms.

This is a useful opportunity to consider the essential digital skills that people require to successfully navigate and use online sites. We need to be clear about the skills and level of skills we expect people to have. We need to consider whether people require only basic skills such as how to use email, access the internet, navigate websites and complete documents online, or whether there is a requirement for more advanced skills. Many of us probably feel reasonably confident about our own digital skills; we might not recognise that other people might struggle, and we may underestimate the scale of digital exclusion. Can you recall a time when your Wi-Fi or mobile data did not work? How did that make you feel? You might have felt frustrated or a bit panicky that you were suddenly cut off from the digital world; if you are digitally excluded you might feel that a lot of the time, especially as more services move online.

Sync 3: How do you rate your digital skills?

You should allow around 30 minutes for this activity.

1 What digital skills do you think are important to effectively engage online?

2 Complete the following table.

Skill	**Essential skill**	**Desirable skill**	**Rate your confidence 0–10**
Creating and editing events in calendars (Outlook, Google, etc.)			
Sending an email			
Filling in an online form			
Creating a spreadsheet			
Setting up and using online banking			
Creating a strong password			
Setting up an email account and an email address			
Understanding the difference between mobile data and Wi-Fi			
Creating a digital signature			
Creating a witness statement in Word			
Using WordPress to create a blog or a website			
Using webchat			
Taking and editing photos on a mobile device			
Making a Gantt chart in Excel			
Knowing the risks of using public Wi-Fi			
Inserting a digital signature into a form or a document			
Attaching a document to an email			
Creating a letter in Word			
Searching and accessing websites			
Converting a Word document to PDF format			
Evaluating an output from a GenAI tool			

3 Thinking about your own skills, how confident would you feel about using technology to resolve a legal problem?

4 What are the consequences for the rule of law if parts of our society feel digitally excluded?

Hopefully, you feel confident that you have the skills to engage online and use Large Language Models such as ChatGPT. Access to justice and the rule of law are connected, and it is essential that lack of digital skills do not preclude people from exercising their legal rights. You will go on to consider the type of skills which a digital lawyer requires in Chapter 11 and have further opportunities to reflect upon your own skills in Chapter 13.

Digital skills: Digital literacy and digital competence

Sync 3 demonstrates the importance of digital literacy to enable you to carry out relatively routine and everyday tasks. For students who are aspiring digital lawyers, it is important to focus upon developing your digital literacy and also your digital competence (in other words, your abilities to use your digital skills) within legal practice in appropriate and effective ways to meet the needs of clients.

As a student there are many ways you can develop your digital literacy and digital competence. These range from doing your own research online (e.g. watching a YouTube video on how to use a different application or piece of software) to looking out for courses at your university (e.g. many university libraries offer helpful courses on using legal search engines). You may want to use any spare time you have to experiment with using technologies in different ways, from creating a website or podcast to developing a program or application. These can be great ways to have fun while developing your digital skills.

THE SCALE OF THE DIGITAL DIVIDE

The Lloyds Bank Consumer Digital Index report in 2023 identified 96% of UK adults as having accessed the internet, but there are 13 million people with very low digital capability.[31]

The Essential Digital Skills Framework was created in 2018. It has 26 Life tasks and 20 Work tasks across five skills areas:

- *Handling information and content.* Use a search engine to look for information online; find a website that they have visited before; download and save a photo found online.
- *Communicating.* Send a personal message via email or online messaging service; carefully make comments and share information online.
- *Transacting.* Buy items or services from a website; buy apps and install on a device.
- *Problem-solving.* Verify sources of information found online; solve a problem with a device/digital service using online help.
- *Being safe and legal online.* Be careful about sharing information online and how to keep online content secure; recognise suspicious links; understand about not sharing other people's data or intellectual property without consent.

In 2023, 44.7 million UK adults (84%) have the Foundational Level compared with 80% in 2022, 8.5 million (16%) do not have the Foundational Level and 1.3 million (2%) are digitally disadvantaged. Although more people have the digital skills required to thrive in a digital world, there are still 1.5 million people with zero digital Life skills, they are most likely to be female, be over 65, and have no formal qualifications.[32]

The data suggests that there is a relationship between education and level of skill, and that a social and economic divide exists. Furthermore, while more people are online, a significant number of people still lack the skills to navigate the digital world effectively, and this exacerbates issues like financial exclusion. Digital exclusion is an issue for many groups in society, but certain people and groups are

31 Lloyds Bank UK Customer Digital Index, 2023 <https://lloyds-consumer-digital-index-2023-report.pdf> accessed 23 September 2025.

32 Ibid., p. 47.

disproportionally affected. The ability to resolve legal problems without the need for lawyers is possible only if people have more than basic digital skills. There is a risk of a deepening social justice crisis if digital exclusion is not addressed. It is important to ensure that everyone has the same opportunities to benefit from technological transformation, and part of that challenge is to think about how we design legal services to be digitally inclusive. This is an issue for everyone connected to the administration of justice and the delivery of legal services. It is essential that law students understand and recognise these issues, because as future digital lawyers you have a key role in helping to ensure that legal technology and design meet the needs of all users.

One important way to tackle these issues is through innovation and design. In the next section we will explore design thinking and the importance of human-centred design in helping to develop technological solutions to support the delivery of legal services without lawyers.

DESIGN THINKING

Design thinking is an iterative process that provides a framework to help solve complex problems. It involves seeking to understand the user, challenging any existing ideas and beliefs to generate innovative solutions to problems. There are many different versions of design thinking; the one outlined here was developed by the Hasso-Plattner Institute of Design at Stanford, which is also known as the d.school.[33] According to the d.school, there are five phases of design thinking (Figure 4.1):

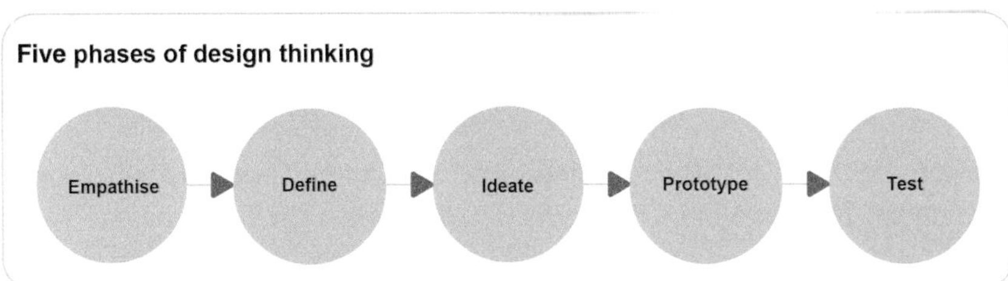

Figure 4.1 Five phases of design thinking

33 <https://dschool.stanford.edu/>

- *Empathise* with your users.
- *Define* your user's needs, their issues and your thoughts.
- *Ideate* challenge any pre-existing ideas and think about innovative solutions.
- *Prototype* start the process of creating the solutions.
- *Test* the solution created.

The steps in the process are not necessarily sequential. They do not have to be followed in a specific order, they can occur together, and they can be repeated. It is important to involve the user at each stage of the process to understand their needs. This is an iterative process, which means you may need to go back to refine and retest your ideas. Through the testing process you learn more about users, which might lead to you redefining the problem.

The next part explains the process you might adopt to apply design thinking in the creation of a digital tool.

INITIAL PROCESS MAPPING

The first stage in designing any digital tool is to create a process map that identifies how a person will use the tool. Using a series of sticky notes is a helpful way of doing this, because they can easily be moved around to reflect changes in the design process. It is important to map out each stage of the user journey and clearly understand how the user will navigate through each part of the tool.

UNDERSTANDING THE USERS

The next stage involves understanding the experiences of the user. In this process it is essential to think about how they identify their problem, how they look for help and how they would use the tool. This could involve journey mapping, storytelling, reflecting on their experiences of using other services, and testing the tool. It is important to engage with a range of different users because they will have a variety of experiences and may use the tool in different ways. A digital tool will be successful only if it reflects the needs of the users, and the user must be at the heart of the design process. It is therefore essential to have a clear understanding of what users want before finalising the design of the prototype tool.

USER PERSONAS

To really understand your users, it is a good idea to create user personas. To do this you need to choose a person to be the persona. This can be a real-life person or a mix of people that you know. You should give the person a name and then think about their experiences, values, and ideas. As you create your solution, you think about how your user would respond to the tool and put the user's needs at the forefront of the design. It is recommended that you create several different personas to inform your design and solution. The types of information you might want to capture are detailed in Figure 4.2.

Figure 4.3 provides a completed user persona.

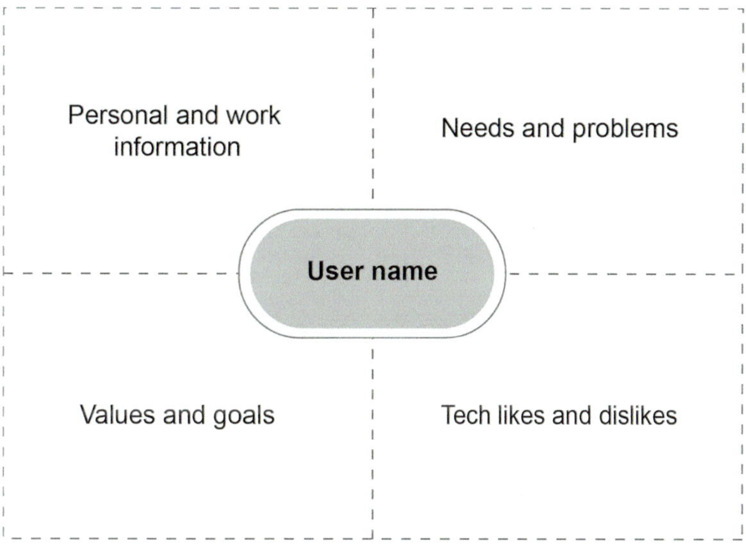

Figure 4.2 User persona

Sync 4: Creating a user persona

You should allow around 20 minutes for this activity.

1 You are designing a smartphone application to provide information and support to people who have experienced domestic violence.

2 Using the matrix displayed in Figure 4.2, create a user persona for someone who you think might use the smartphone application.

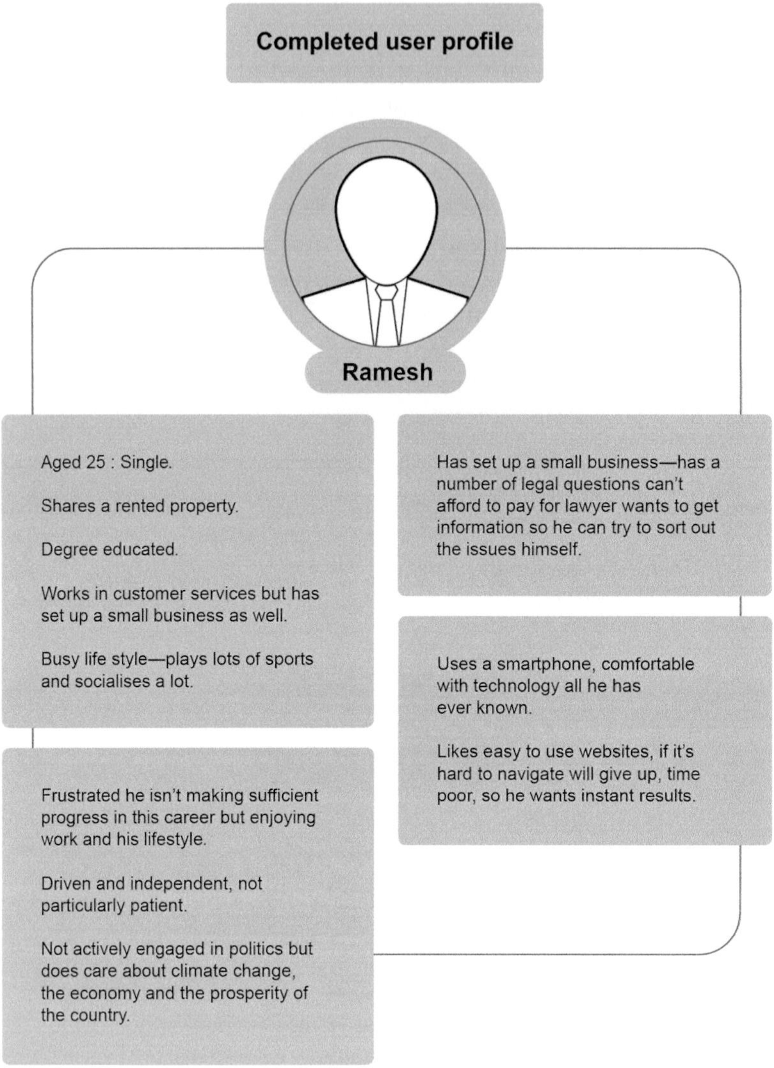

Figure 4.3 Completed user persona

If you were designing a smartphone application to support survivors of domestic violence, you would create several user personas to incorporate the different categories of people who are likely to use the application; for example, you might create male and female personas. Although it is predominantly women who experience domestic violence, it does also happen to men. Women and men may use the application differently. It might be important to capture those differences to ensure the tool is effective if you are designing it to be used more widely.

Initial design and prototypes

The tool should be mapped out before it is built. It is essential to create an initial design that supports the development of the prototype tool. Once the mapping process has been done and there is an initial design, then the prototype is built. It is important to remember that the initial design does not need to be perfect; what is important is to have a prototype that can be tested.

Testing the prototype

This involves user testing of the prototype and gathering feedback on how the user experiences the digital tool. A list of criteria should be developed to determine the minimum viability of the project. The feedback can then be mapped onto the criterion.

Refining the prototype

The feedback from the user testing should then be applied to the next iteration of the tool. Depending on the complexity of the tool and the period for development, it may be appropriate to conduct further testing before finalising the tool.

Finalising the design and content

Once user testing has been completed, the tool can be finalised for first release. First release may be restricted to a group of users to ensure that the tool works appropriately, and then released more widely. Consideration needs to be given to how the tool will be marketed and promoted.

Evaluation

Once the tool has been released and used for a set period of time, an evaluation should take place. It could comprise:

- *Data collection and analysis.* Usage data, Google Analytics, data within the tool.

- *User testing and user surveys.* Focus groups, interviews, surveys to collect feedback from the users on their experience of using the tool.

The evaluation should inform further iterations of the tool. In designing and developing legaltech it is important to accept that the perfect version of the tool will not be created straight away. The purpose of the design process is to refine the tool several times. It is not uncommon to want to spend too much time trying to perfect ideas in the initial design stage. Often there is a reluctance to move on to the creation of the prototype before perfecting the initial design. Creating a digital tool is a fluid process, so it is important to embrace the uncertainty and messiness of the project. It is also not a linear process, and there is no requirement to proceed through each stage sequentially. The testing of the prototype is critical because the collection of data provides more information on how the digital tool performs, a greater understanding of the user and how much refinement will be required to move on to the next stage.

The process of developing legaltech requires being able to work iteratively, embracing an experimental approach and becoming comfortable with uncertainty. The process can be frustrating when what might appear to be a well-designed tool does not work effectively with users. Several bugs and glitches may be found in the testing process that need to be addressed. Each part of the process is a learning opportunity and provides a deeper understanding of how the tool might work with larger groups of users.

To find out more about evaluation of a digital technology, read the evaluation report from Justice Connect[34] on their Gateway project. Points to think about include:

- How will users respond to the tool?
- Is the tool easy to navigate?
- Is the tool visually appealing?
- Is legal terminology explained clearly?

Design principles

Understanding legal language is complex and can be baffling to non-lawyers.

34 <https://justiceconnect.org.au/about/our-approach/digital-innovation/gateway-project/our-intake-tool/>

If you have studied law, it is easy to forget that non-lawyers might struggle to understand words such as estoppel, liability, or breach. A digital tool should use plain English to ensure the information is accessible by a non-lawyer. For example, if you were thinking about designing a digital tool that provides information on contract law, the first question might be: Is there a contract in place? This seems a reasonable question to ask, but how many non-lawyers will be familiar with the elements that make up a valid contract? The phrasing of the questions is important to prevent errors and misunderstandings. An alternative approach might be to ask whether the parties have an agreement and then follow up with questions to establish whether there is a legally binding contract. Failing to understand legal language puts non-lawyers at a disadvantage; therefore it is essential in the design of a digital tool that we do not inadvertently build in that disadvantage.

Margaret Hagan argues that "design, put shortly is the practice of making things that are useful, usable, and engaging. It is domain agnostic—it is about methods and outcomes, not about a particular subject matter".[35] A human-centred approach to design and innovation is about understanding the user needs and to creatively think about how technology can be used to solve a problem. Designing a digital tool that helps a non-lawyer with their legal problem is effective only if it connects with and meets the needs of its users. Technology by itself will not support non-lawyers in resolving their legal problems, but if technology is designed in such a way that it addresses the needs of its users, then there is a stronger possibility it will be "useful, usable, and engaging".[36]

Organisations are now encouraging designers to put people at the centre of the design process. Earlier in this chapter we discussed user personas; these are important when thinking about a human-centred design and innovation approach. The Design Justice Network has an agreed set of principles to help support collaborative and creative practices. The principles include putting at the centre the voices of those who are directly impacted by the outcomes of the design process. The principles link to the human-centred approach and emphasise the importance of the collaborative process in design. You can find out more about the principles by visiting their website: <https://designjustice.org/read-the-principles>

35 M. Hagan, 'Design Thinking About Law: A Perfect Match' (*Legal Practice Today*, January 2014).

36 <https://www.lawbydesign.co/en/home/>

DESIGNING TECHNOLOGY WITH ACCESSIBILITY IN MIND

Haben Girma[37] became the first deaf-blind graduate of Harvard Law School; she works as a disability rights advocate and is passionate about the power of technology to improve inclusivity. She argues that when technology is being designed, inclusion and accessibility should be considered from the start. She also advocates for engaging users from the initial design stage through to when the technology is updated. There are universal benefits to designing with accessibility in mind from the outset. Technology has enormous potential to help all users to understand and access their legal rights, but as part of the development of digital tools, designers need to ensure they have considered inclusion and accessibility. Apple produces human interface guidelines that explain the accessibility features that can be incorporated into an accessible app; these include VoiceOver and increased text size.[38] Google also has a platform which helps developers build more accessible apps for Android devices.[39]

Universal design is not about designing for users with disabilities, but about designing for everyone irrespective of their ability, experience, or capability. Designers need to think about a number of elements, but particularly simplicity and perceivability.

- *Simplicity.* Making tasks simple and easy to perform.
- *Perceivability.* To ensure that the content can be perceived regardless of whether users are using sight, hearing, or touch.

There are a range of resources and tools to help design and build digital tools that are accessible. According to Google there are one billion digital users in the world with some form of disability; therefore, when we think about designing technology tools, it is imperative to prioritise accessibility and inclusion.[40] There are many factors to consider when

37 <https://habengirma.com/>

38 <https://developer.apple.com/design/human-interface-guidelines/accessibility/overview/introduction/>

39 <https://developer.android.com/guide/topics/ui/accessibility/index.html>

40 Channing Ritter, 'Reach More Users: 4 Tips for Designing Accessible Apps and Websites' (2018) <https://www.thinkwithgoogle.com/marketing-strategies/app-and-mobile/website-app-accessibility-guidelines/> accessed 28 April 2021.

creating digital solutions to help non-lawyers resolve their legal problems, and it is not a straightforward process. More research needs to be done to understand how we improve the ways in which we communicate legal information. The next activity gives you an opportunity to reflect on some of these issues and consider how you might design a digital tool.

Sync 5: Designing a digital tool

You should allow around 90 minutes for this activity.

You have just signed up for a law and tech module, and part of the course involves the creation of a smartphone application. One aspect of the smartphone application is the creation of smart answers (sometimes called decision trees) which allow you to present complex information in a quick and accessible way. Smart answers work by taking the user through a series of questions until they reach the answer to a legal question. The information is tailored to their specific circumstances.

1 Go to <https://www.gov.uk/pay-leave-for-parents>

2 Use the calculator to see an example of how smart answers work.

3 Then look at the Guides to Statutory Maternity Pay and Maternity Allowance on the Government website. You can compare how the information is presented through smart answers and then in the guide. Make a list of the benefits to users of each approach.

4 Then think of a legal question; for example, who is a worker? Map out (using sticky notes) a series of questions to allow someone to arrive at the answer to the question.

5 You might want to show a friend what you have done to see if they understand the questions you are asking.

Distilling complex legal information is not easy. Designing digital tools requires you to work hard to simplify the law to help a non-lawyer understand how it applies to them. Developing digital tools requires creative and innovative solutions to help people understand their legal rights and responsibilities. It requires imagination to think how technology can be used to develop new solutions, meaning you need to be creative and innovative to design digital tools. These are essential skills for a digital lawyer, and they are highly valued by law firms. If you move into legal practice and have the opportunity to work with developers to create more complex legaltech tools, your experiences of designing even a very simple tool will help you think about the opportunities and risks that should be addressed when designing technological solutions.

SKILLS FOR THE FUTURE LAWYER

The UK Government's Future Skills Projections research identified six core transferable skills that will be most in demand by 2035:[41]

- Communication
- Collaboration
- Problem-solving
- Organising, planning, and prioritising work
- Creative thinking
- Information literacy

The Future of Jobs Report 2023 from the World Economic Forum[42] suggests that while analytical and creative thinking are the most important skills for workers, AI and Big Data are increasing in importance.

IMAGINATIVE LAWYERS

Designing digital tools provides an opportunity to experiment and to come up with imaginative solutions that use technology to disrupt how things have traditionally been done. AI and machine learning are now impacting legal design and the creation of technology solutions. We face complex challenges, and there are benefits and risks of using technology to address legal issues. Having the opportunity to engage

41 A. Dickerson et al., 'The Skills Imperative 2035: An Analysis of the Demand for Skills in the Labour Market in 2035' (National Foundation for Educational Research 2023) <https://www.nfer.ac.uk/media/utwf2grb/the_skills_imperative_2035_working_paper_3_an_analysis_of_the_demand_for_skills_in_the_labour_market_in_2035.pdf> accessed 2 January 2026.

42 World Economic Forum, 'The Future of Jobs Report' (2023) <https://www.weforum.org/publications/the-future-of-jobs-report-2023/> accessed 19 August 2025.

with digital tools and understand the process of legal design allows you to explore your creative side and offers insights into the relationship between law and technology.

Traditionally, lawyers have required deep knowledge of the law and legal skills such as drafting, communication, and advocacy. Although knowledge and these skills are important, other skills such as teamwork, collaboration, creativity, and an understanding of technology are now highly prized. In 2014, R. Amani Smathers introduced the idea of a T-shaped lawyer.[43] The top of the T represented the multidisciplinary skills lawyers required as a result of the impact of technology, and the changing market for legal services. The model was then developed further by Natalie Runyon, Alyson Carrel, and Shellie Reid, who created the Delta Model, and we also have the O Shaped Lawyer.[44] You will find out more about these models and the changing nature of skills in Chapter 11. What these models highlight is how the profession is changing, and that lawyers now require a much broader skill set. If you are prepared to develop these skills, then you will be in a good position as you start your career.

HOW TO KICK-START CREATIVITY

Sync 6: The daily drawing

You should allow around 1 minute for this activity.

Ozenc and Hagan[45] suggest that you can use daily rituals to encourage a creative mindset. One exercise they suggest is a daily drawing task. You spend one minute doodling anything, but it must be a drawing and must take exactly one minute! It does not have to be good: There is no requirement for you to be Picasso or Banksy! They suggest that you should do this activity at the start of each day, as it helps to encourage creativity.

Try it for a week and see if you feel a little more creative.

43 R. Amani Smathers, 'T Shaped Lawyer' (September 2019) <https://www.amanismathers.com/technolawgic/2014/2/21/t-shaped-lawyer> accessed 13 January 2026.

44 O Shaped <https://oshaped.com>

45 K. Ozenc and M. Hagan, *Rituals for Work* (John Wiley & Sons 2019).

The previous section discussed the skills that lawyers will require to practise in a changing legal market, and we have focused on the importance of innovation, imagination, and creativity. Lawyers in the future will need to take ideas and methods from other fields and apply them in a legal context. It is important to remember that creativity is a mindset: It is a way of thinking about new solutions to existing problems. It is about being open to ideas and challenging yourself to be curious.

LEGAL GAMES

One of the ways to make the law more accessible and engaging is through the creation of legal games. Legal games offer an innovative and creative solution to educating people on their legal rights and responsibilities.

Sync 7: Let's play a game

You should allow around 15 minutes for this activity.

1 Go to <https://lawdojo.co/> and select one of the games to play.

2 Rate the game from 1 to 10 based on how useful you think the legal game is in educating people on their legal rights and responsibilities.

You might want to engage your imagination and creativity to devise your own legal game. The earlier example of Joshua Browder illustrates how a pre-existing problem can be tackled in an innovative way using technology.

WHERE DO WE GO FROM HERE?

This chapter has explored how technology is impacting on the delivery of legal services. Currently there are no fully enabled technology solutions that support non-lawyers in addressing legal issues, but we are seeing pockets of innovation that are making a difference. We have seen from examples such as DoNotPay how members of the public can use technology to navigate legal systems to resolve their legal problems. It is likely that with the advent of GenAI, we will see more tools being developed. There has been recognition that technology can be leveraged to assist non-lawyers, but as this chapter has identified, there are challenges in designing legal services for non-lawyers. There are barriers to overcome, and there are valid concerns around the reliability and trustworthiness of online sites, GenAI tools and the implications for the regulation of these services.

Technology alone will not solve access to justice or facilitate the delivery of legal services without lawyers. In fact it is legal design, not technology, that is critical. Legal design focuses on the needs of users and empowers people to understand and resolve their legal problem. Developers must think carefully about the importance of legal design and accessibility. We must also be aware of the digital divide and think carefully about how we develop solutions that do not further exclude the most vulnerable parts of our society. It is important to understand the potential of legaltech, but also to be aware of how we ensure trust and confidence in the tools that are designed. Throughout this textbook, you also need to consider the broader relationship between law and technology. The future digital lawyer needs to be creative, open to new ideas, and able to recognise the potential of and challenges of technology.

CONCLUSION

This chapter has considered the delivery of legal services without the use of lawyers. It has examined this issue through an exploration of how we can improve access to justice using digital technologies. You have been encouraged to think about how technology can be used to support individuals to resolve disputes without the need for lawyers. The chapter has considered ways in which technology is developing to provide innovative solutions to support non-lawyers as they resolve their legal problems. The problems associated with digital exclusion have been discussed, and also how the lack of digital skills impacts on the way in which technology can transform access to justice.

ADDITIONAL RESOURCES

If you want to improve your digital skills, there are lots of free courses available. You may want to visit <https://makeitclick.learnmyway.com/directory/search>

A2J Access to Justice Author System <https://www.a2jauthor.org>

Haben Girma—Designing Technology with Accessibility in Mind <https://www.youtube.com/watch?v=44VEwsBfux0>

Law by Design (Margaret Hagan) <https://www.lawbydesign.co>

The Legal Design Alliance <https://www.legaldesignalliance.org>

The Legal Design Lab (Stanford University) <https://law.stanford.edu/organizations/pages/legal-design-lab/>

If you want to find out more about GenAI and access to justice:

Generative AI: Redefining Access to Justice, Society for Computers & Law

'Unboxing Generative AI for the Legal Professions: Functions, Impacts and Governance', *International Journal for Court Administration*

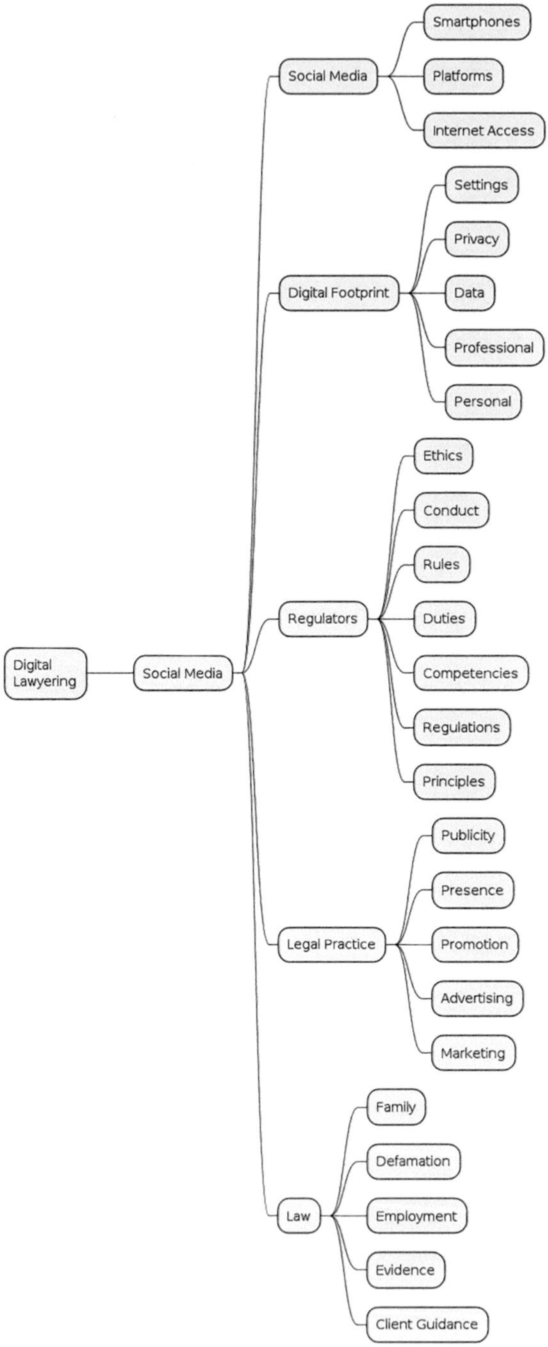

Mind Map 5.1 Chapter topics

5 THE USE AND PRACTICE OF SOCIAL MEDIA

Francine Ryan

INTRODUCTION

This chapter will apply the principles of digital lawyering within the practical context of social media. It will begin by asking you to reflect upon your own existing digital footprint and think about the implications of your online presence for you. It moves on to consider the wider use of social media within law and the legal profession. The chapter explores some of the relevant professional conduct rules and considers some examples where lawyers have been in breach of those rules. It refers to the topic of privacy and confidentiality, which is also discussed in Chapter 6, in the context of the marketing and promotion of legal practices. It then allows you to consider how changes in law and practice associated with technology have become an essential element of a lawyer's role and to think about the skills you need to be a digital lawyer. Following on from this, there are several case studies on the ethical implications of using social media platforms both as individual practitioners and within legal practice. It is important for future lawyers to understand the risks and benefits of social media use.

Chapter hot spots

When reading this chapter, questions to think about include:

- What does my digital footprint say about me?
- How can I effectively manage my social media presence?
- What are the professional rules on the use of social media?
- How is social media impacting the practice of law?

DOI: 10.4324/9781003602323-5

- What are the ethical and professional considerations of law firms using GenAI within social media marketing?
- What are the ethical implications of using social media platforms both as an individual practitioner and within legal practice?

Having read the title and introduction, you can add any other questions you want to explore here:

WHAT IS SOCIAL MEDIA?

Social media refers to the collective term for online communication channels that facilitate the interaction and sharing of information. Social media is defined broadly. It comprises a variety of different communication tools, with social media channels sharing some common features including profile pages, newsfeeds, friends, followers, like buttons, notifications, and rating features. Social media allows users to connect and share information. There is no legal definition of social media, but the first time it was referred to in an English court was in 2011 by the Lord Chief Justice dealing with the case involving Facebook and the riots that took place in London.[1] Although it may appear that social networking platforms have been around forever, Facebook launched only in 2004. Mobile technology has fundamentally changed social networking, and the capabilities of the smartphone have facilitated the experiential growth of social media platforms. There are 5.22 billion people in the world who use a mobile phone.[2] The interaction with different social media platforms shapes our online presence

1 *R v. Blackshaw and others* [2011] EWCA Crim 2312.

2 Simon Kemp, 'Digital 2021: Global Overview Report' (*Datareportal*, 27 January 2021) <https://datareportal.com/reports/digital-2021-global-overview-report> accessed 14 April 2021.

Sync 1: Social media platforms

You should allow around 5 minutes for this activity.

1 Make a list of all the social media sites you are familiar with.

2 Circle the ones you use regularly.

Internet penetration has allowed social networking sites to create online communities connecting all aspects of our lives and offering new opportunities in both the personal and professional space. There are a variety of different types of social media platforms such as Instagram, Pinterest, TikTok, and VKontakte. We have categorised some of the current social media platforms in Figure 5.1.

The increasing popularity of social media means that new platforms launch regularly, and you may be aware of other sites which are not listed here. It is worth exploring the popularity of different platforms by examining the statistics for certain demographics, locations, and markets.

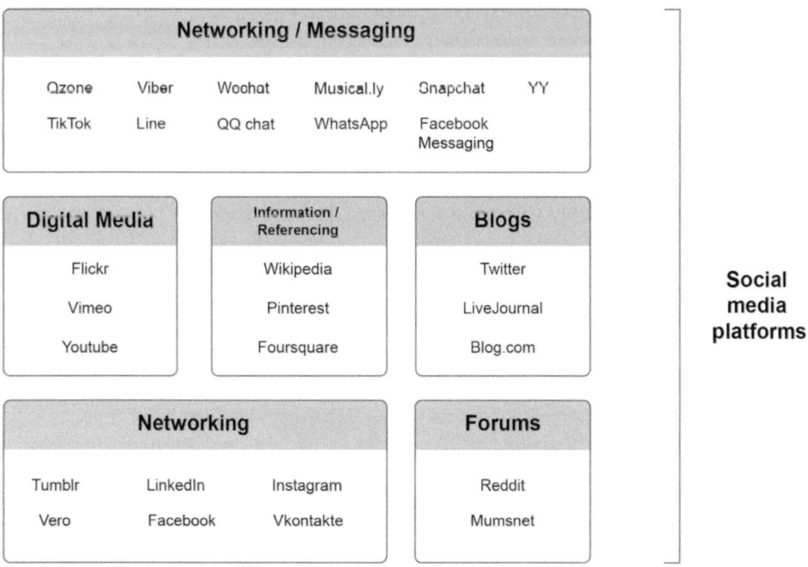

Figure 5.1 Social media platforms

The rise of mobile technology has increased the popularity of social networking. In 2025, 5.17 billion people actively use social media, equating to approximately 63.7% of the global population.[3] Typical social media users spend around 2 hours and 20 minutes per day on social media and engage with an average of 6.7 platforms per month.[4]

Facebook still remains the most popular social media platform, followed by YouTube, Instagram, and WhatsApp.[5] In America, there have been concerns around TikTok, and as a result of discussions with the US government and the Chinese parent company ByteDance, US and global investors will run TikTok in the United States. There have been ongoing calls from organisations such as Amnesty International for greater regulation of tech companies.[6]

Organisations are also using social media tools to engage with their employees through channels such as Yammer, Huddle, Chatter, and Facebook's Workplace. These platforms facilitate the formation of groups, offer useful ways for communications, and promote engagement within the workplace.

Social media platforms have had a significant impact on our lives, allowing people to connect across borders, and thus bringing many benefits, but there are concerns around some of the harmful aspects of increased use of social media. There are growing calls for governments to properly regulate tech companies to address data privacy, content moderation, and transparency. Social media platforms collect extensive user data, and there needs to be greater awareness of the importance of protecting personal information.

DIGITAL FOOTPRINT

A data trail is formed from our interactions with the internet and social networking sites, creating a body of data that represents our online

3 Backlinko, 'Social Media Usage & Growth Statistics' (19 November 2025) <https://backlinko.com/social-media-users?t> accessed 2 January 2026.

4 Ibid.

5 Kemp, *supra* n. 2.

6 Amnesty International, 'US: TikTok Ban Won't Solve Big Tech Harms' (17 January 2025) <https://www.amnesty.org/en/latest/news/2025/01/us-tiktok-ban-wont-solve-big-tech-harms/?t> accessed 2 January 2026.

presence. It comprises a range of actions such as identifying visited websites, Facebook posts, emails sent, or photographs uploaded. There are two types of digital footprints: Active and passive. A passive digital footprint occurs when data is collected from the user without their knowledge. An active digital footprint happens when the user chooses to share information via the internet and social media sites.

Sync 2: Digital footprint

You should allow around 15 minutes for this activity.

'Google' yourself. Search using Google.co.uk or Google.com. Start with just your name and then your name and where you went to school or university. Then choose another search engine and make the same searches. Did you get different results? What did you find out about yourself? Were there any surprises?

A person's digital footprint is not just what they have posted online, but also what others have published about them, which might include information shared with or without their knowledge. It might be important to curate a separate public and private online presence and actively manage how that presence is shaped.

PRIVACY AND DATA

Technology governs so many aspects of our lives, and we no longer remain in control of how our data is used, distributed, and stored. A tension exists between our increasing reliance on technology and retaining control of our data self. Several incidents have happened involving large breaches of data, causing individuals to be hacked or exploited. When thinking about data privacy and protection, it is important to recognise our vulnerability. Social media platforms are a permanent and public reminder of everything we do. Even if you can remove a post, it could still be screenshotted and reshared. There is quite an involved process to delete a social media account. Anyone using social media sites has a personal responsibility to review their privacy settings and understand how they work.

Sync 3: Whose data is it?

You should allow around 10 minutes for this activity.

Go to YouTube and watch "Who Owns Your Data? (Hint: It's Not You)" <https://www.youtube.com/watch?v=y1txYjoSQQc> Then reflect on the implications for you in your professional life from the data trail you have created.

Juan Enriquez suggests we should think of our online life as a digital tattoo.[7] We should be aware of how we use social media platforms and the creation of our digital footprint. Our online presence represents our personal brand: It tells people who we are, and our values. A brand is a very powerful asset, so it is important to protect it. In 2013, the youth and crime commissioner, Paris Brown, resigned because of tweets that she had sent between the ages of 14 and 16.[8]

Social media spaces are used for different purposes, and the audience and the message will not be the same for Facebook and LinkedIn. However, we cannot ignore the unintended audience—someone who likes, shares, retweets, or finds us online. Therefore, regardless of what site we are using, we must be confident that the posts, pictures, and comments reflect who we are.

Think about these two examples and reflect on their implications from a personal and professional viewpoint.

Instagram or Facebook

Posting pictures of you on holiday are looking a little worse for wear. Would you be happy and/or would it be acceptable for your employer to see your photographs and your posts?

7 Juan Enriquez, 'Your Online Life, Permanent as a Tattoo' (*Ted2013*, February 2013) <https://www.ted.com/talks/juan_enriquez_how_to_think_about_digital_tattoos#t-338590> accessed 3 February 2021.

8 BBC, 'Paris Brown: Kent Youth PCC Resigns after Twitter Row' (*BBC News*, 9 April 2013) <https://www.bbc.co.uk/news/uk-england-22083032> accessed 14 April 2021.

LinkedIn "specialties" and "skills"

Exaggerating your skills and experiences on your LinkedIn profile, or getting your friends to endorse you for a skill that you do not have. Is LinkedIn the equivalent of an online CV? Do you need to ensure that what you write about yourself is not misleading or untrue?

USING SOCIAL MEDIA IN A PERSONAL CAPACITY

Recruitment companies and prospective employers check candidates' social media profiles. You might have an impressive curriculum vitae or résumé, but if your Bluesky feed contains comments that do not represent a prospective employer's values, you may find yourself in difficulties. Having a positive profile may improve your prospects of being offered an interview or getting a job. Having a profile that does not reflect the image you want to portray may have a negative impact on your prospects. Understanding how privacy settings work is important to ensure that you protect your online appearance. Turning on your privacy settings to make your profile entirely private may appear an attractive option. However, if your social media site portrays a positive image, allowing some restricted access may be beneficial. It is important to prioritise active management of your social media platforms, and you should regularly check your digital footprint to manage how you appear online. It is an important skill to curate and manage an effective online presence. The boundaries between professional and personal are blurring, so you should consider your online presence from both perspectives.

USING SOCIAL MEDIA IN A PROFESSIONAL CAPACITY

In England and Wales, solicitors are regulated by the Solicitors Regulation Authority,[9] and barristers by the Bar Standards Board.[10] It is

9 <https://www.sra.org.uk>
10 <https://www.barstandardsboard.org.uk>

important you familiarise yourself with the relevant professional regulations that apply in your jurisdiction. The Australian Solicitors' conduct rules include similar duties to those that govern solicitors in England and Wales.[11] Lawyers have special responsibilities to ensure that they do not act in a way that damages the reputation of the profession and are held to very high standards of honesty and integrity. The Bar Standards Board Handbook has published guidance for barristers on how they should conduct themselves when using social media and some of the issues that can arise.[12] The Solicitors Regulation Authority has set out the requirements for how solicitors must act when using social media.[13]

The boundaries between our private and professional lives are increasingly blurring, especially in our use of social media platforms. Therefore, it is important to be aware that, when lawyers interact with social media networks, professional conduct rules apply. This means that any inappropriate social media posts, regardless of whether they are in a personal or professional capacity, are subject to professional conduct rules. The profession expects the highest standards of behaviour from its lawyers, and inappropriate conduct may result in disciplinary action from the relevant professional body. The rules apply to posting material online, sharing content, networking, and liking or commenting on posts. This applies in both a personal and professional capacity, as something posted on a social media site in a personal capacity may still be considered to diminish the trust and confidence of the public and would be subject to the rules. The rules remind us of the importance of being careful when posting in both public and in private and to think through the implications of our actions.

BREACHING PROFESSIONAL CONDUCT RULES

The following case studies illustrate breaches of the professional conduct rules, all of which relate to different aspects of social media.

11 <https://www.lawcouncil.asn.au/policy-agenda/regulation-of-the-profession-and-ethics/australian-solicitors-conduct-rules>

12 The Bar Standards Board Handbook, 'Social Media Guidance' (2023) <https://www.barstandardsboard.org.uk/static/61d13750-880c-4423-a4bf80cf96d3f06c/4590471b-3272-4f66-ad8684a76315cdd0/BSB-social-media-guidance-September–2023.pdf>

13 Solicitors Regulation Authority, 'Use of Social Media and Offensive Communications' (25 November 2019) <https://www.sra.org.uk/sra/corporate-strategy/sra enforcement-strategy/enforcement-practice/social-media-offensive-communications/> accessed 29 April 2021.

Case study 1[14]

Social media posts

A solicitor working as a sole practitioner was rebuked, fined £1500 and ordered to pay £600 in costs for a series of social media posts where he had posted inappropriate comments or emoji icons following visits to the police station, prison, or court, including:

- "From Attempted Murder at Smethwick", followed by two emoji icons to show crying with laughter.
- "DV (Domestic violence) . . . Christmas Coming Up . . . . What you Expect".
- "Drugs". When another person responded "What kind? Lol x" He responded, "Not From the Pharmacy That's For Sure pms", with emoji icons to showing crying with laughter.
- "Sexual Assault", with two emoji icons showing a sad face and a tear.
- In two social media posts he disclosed specific confidential information about a client matter.

The SRA found he was in breach of Principle 6 of the SRA Principles 2011 and failed to achieve Outcome 4.1 of the SRA Code of Conduct 2011. (The SRA Code has been updated since this decision.)

Case study 2[15]

LinkedIn

A barrister was suspended from practice in relation to three charges. It involved him broadcasting serious allegations made by a third party (A) against a barrister (M) in the robing room of a Crown Court. The third charge involved the barrister contacting M's partner (L) via a professional networking site and making references to issues relating to M. M invited L to connect with him via LinkedIn (there had been no previous contact between the two

14 You can read the full decision in this case: Solicitors Regulation Authority, 'Decision: Harmal Singh Paul' (*SRA.org*, 13 August 2009) <https://www.sra.org.uk/consumers/solicitor-check/339008/> accessed 14 April 2021.

15 *Forz Khan v. Bar Standards Board* [2018] EWHC 2184 (Admin).

prior to this) and then sent a message to L when L started work at a new firm of solicitors:

M: "Congratulations. Glad to see you are doing well considering everything".

L replied, asking the barrister to explain what he meant.

M's response was "Oops, I have heard your husband has a personal difficulty. I hope I am in error".

L replied: "I don't know what you mean".

The BSB found he was in breach of: Core Duty 3 and 5 of the Bar Standards Handbook.

Case study 3[16]

Blogging

The complaint involved a lawyer in the US state of Illinois who published a blog relating to her legal work. The blog contained confidential information about her cases and derogatory comments about judges. In her blog, the lawyer had attempted to protect client confidentiality by anonymising the clients, but from the facts provided it was possible using public records to identify the clients and judges the lawyer was referring to.

The lawyer received a 60-day suspension from the two state bars she was admitted to.

Case study 4[17]

A solicitor was fined for a series of tweets made over an 18-month period. The Solicitors Disciplinary Tribunal (SDT) fined him £2500 because "he used his Twitter account which publicly identified him as a solicitor to publicly

16 *Office of Lawyer Regulation Complainant v. Kristine A Peshek* [2011] WI 47 <https://www.wicourts.gov/sc/opinion/DisplayDocument.pdf?content=pdf&seqNo=66464>

17 Neil Rose, 'Lewis Case: "Wishing Death on Neo-Nazis" Went Too Far' (*Legal Futures*, 17 December 2018) <https://www.legalfutures.co.uk/latest-news/lewis-case-wishing-death-on-neo-nazis-went-too-far> accessed 29 April 2021.

post offensive and profane communications". The solicitor had been subject to a series of offensive tweets, but the fact he had responded meant that "he had not behaved in a way that maintained the trust that the public placed in him and in the provision of legal services".

Are you surprised by the conduct and behaviour of the lawyers? These cases demonstrate the risks lawyers face when using social media. There can be significant consequences for a lawyer's career if their social media activity breaches professional regulations. The lawyers received sanctions from their professional bodies, but there are also implications for their future practice of law. The examples highlight the need to think before you act when using social media platforms, otherwise there are risks of breaching professional standards.

Digital lawyering skills: Understanding ethics and values

The preceding case studies demonstrate the importance of ethical issues when using social media as a legal professional. However, this is broader than simply complying with a particular code of conduct. Ethics is also about acting in a manner which accords with your own personal values and beliefs. As a digital lawyer, you may need to navigate complex ethical issues which are not covered in codes of conduct but which will impact on your actions (and potentially have consequences for other people). For example, to what extent would it be appropriate to explain a legal rule around divorce to people seeking help via a wholly anonymous online forum on parenting? How should you deal with a request to connect on social media from your colleague or line manager?

Of course, as a student you are already developing ideas around ethics and values. For example, most students choose not to use so-called essay mills (websites selling essays to students) or GenAI tools such as ChatGPT because they feel it would be an unethical way in which to approach their assignments. As you work through topics within your studies, you may also find yourself formulating opinions on ethically controversial subjects which are informed by your personal ethical perspective and values.

For aspiring digital lawyers, it is important to have an awareness of your ethics and values, how these inform your actions and how these may apply when you move into the legal workplace. Sometimes this can involve questioning any assumptions or unconscious bias that lies behind them. Sometimes it can involve working out your boundaries and how you will apply them. This is a challenging and ongoing process, but one that will inform your professional development going forward.

SOCIAL MEDIA TIPS

Even though social media has been a feature of our lives for a long period of time, the preceding examples illustrate the risks of a lack of self-awareness and the implications for lawyers if they make mistakes. The consequences of making inappropriate posts could end or significantly impact on your career. It is easy to think we are immune from doing something stupid, but the spontaneity and reach of social media does pose a risk. Saying something inappropriate in a tweet or posting something late at night to a few friends can be shared and read by many other people and have far-reaching consequences.

Here are some tips that you might find helpful to reflect on when managing your online presence:

1. Think before you post! Social media platforms can be a permanent and public reminder of everything we do.
2. Understand and check your privacy settings. Decide on how much access you want to give and carefully monitor who has access. Check your privacy settings on a regular basis because the terms and conditions are continually updated.
3. Social media changes all the time, so it is critical to keep up to date with the development of the platforms and optimise your use of the tools.
4. Keep your personal and professional online lives separate. If you integrate your social media accounts with other apps, this will allow other apps to see your connections. If, for example, you have connected with a client on LinkedIn through an application that integrates different accounts, you may have revealed that connection without the client's permission.
5. Never comment or discuss clients, cases, other lawyers, law firms, chambers, or judges on social media.
6. Never send confidential information via social media.
7. Think very carefully about whether to discuss politics or religion on social media. If you want to engage in debate this article has some

useful tips on how to argue more effectively on social media <https://www.theguardian.com/media/2017/jan/28/how-to-stop-arguing-and-actually-change-someones-mind-on-social-media?CMP=oth_b-aplnews_d-1>

8. It is important to consider not just what you post but also the tone of your post. You might post something that you think is reasonable, but other people might not consider it to be in good taste. Always think carefully about whether your regulatory body would consider your comments to undermine the profession in any way.
9. Do not use location services when you meet clients, attend chambers, or court hearings because your location could risk unintentionally revealing that you are acting for a client.
10. Think about who you follow on social media, what you share and what you like because all those activities are associated with approving of the person, organisation and content.
11. Employers are concerned about the reputational risks from social media. Make sure you read and abide by your workplace social media policy and ensure your online behaviour is in line with the requirements of the organisation.

Lawyers are required to understand how social media platforms operate to be able to identify potential issues that may arise for themselves and their clients. Having an awareness and an understanding of social media platforms can prevent you from making any mistakes when using social media. Understanding your ethical obligations and the professional conduct rules that apply will ensure that you engage with social media appropriately and maximise the opportunities social media provides to develop both your personal and professional profiles.

The first part of this chapter has considered individual use of social media. It will now explore how social media can be used in the context of the marketing and promotion of legal practices.

MARKETING AND PROMOTION OF LEGAL PRACTICES

Chapter 2 introduced the ways in which social media has changed how law firms communicate with their clients and potential clients. An online presence offers law firms the opportunity to market their practice, raise their profile, and create awareness of the law firm. A social media strategy provides a way for a law firm to build and curate its brand. Through different social media channels, it can manage its reputation, demonstrate its values, recruit new staff, and develop and maintain client relationships. It can help establish the expertise and visibility of their lawyers and provide accessible and engaging content that can build the firm's brand.

A firm's social media presence needs to be actively managed in terms of content and frequency, and it needs to be active to attract and maintain followers. A social media strategy forms part of a law firm's overall communication strategy that includes marketing and business development. It is an important tool for relationship building, marketing, reputation management and maintaining a competitive edge in the legal market.

ADVERTISING AND PUBLICITY

Social media is categorised as a form of publicity, and therefore both the individual lawyer and the law firm in England and Wales must adhere to the SRA Code of Conduct. There are similar rules across other jurisdictions.

Social media content must be accurate and not misleading in accordance with outcome 8.8 of the SRA Code of Conduct.[18]

A law firm must ensure that it keeps clients' affairs confidential. This means it must avoid developing content such as case studies which potentially risk breaching client confidentiality. Outcome 6.6 of the SRA Code of Conduct sets out the duties on confidentiality and disclosure.[19]

A law firm should ensure it has systems and controls in place to manage its online presence and its social media engagement. Outcome 2.1 of the SRA Code of Conduct sets out responsibilities for compliance that law firms must have in place.[20] These duties include having the appropriate governance processes in place.

Law firms also need to be aware of the risk of creating lawyer–client relationships through their use of social media. For example, if a

18 Solicitors Regulation Authority, 'SRA Code of Conduct for Solicitors, RELs, RFLs and RSLs' <https://www.sra.org.uk/solicitors/standards-regulations/code-conduct-solicitors/> accessed 2 January 2026.

19 Solicitors Regulation Authority, 'SRA Code of Conduct for Solicitors, RELs, RFLs and RSLs' <https://www.sra.org.uk/solicitors/standards-regulations/code-conduct-solicitors/> accessed 2 January 2026.

20 Solicitors Regulation Authority, 'SRA Code of Conduct for Firms' <https://www.sra.org.uk/solicitors/standards-regulations/code-conduct-firms/> accessed 2 January 2026.

law firm answers a legal question via a social media platform, it could be inadvertently creating a retainer by implication. The SRA recommends that law firms avoid any discussion on a potential matter with a client via a social media channel and ensure this is done at the first meeting.

SOCIAL MEDIA IN LAW FIRMS

A law firm should regularly review its social media strategy, and consider:

- Who is the target audience?
- Which social media platforms are currently being used, and which ones should be considered?
- What content should be created and shared?
- What are the goals of the strategy, and how will they be measured?
- What policies are in place to respond to negative comments?

Firms are now investing significantly in digital marketing because they recognise the importance of developing their brand, and it is an essential part of their business strategy. You may be asked to comment on a law firm's social media presence at an interview; therefore, it is essential that you understand how social media is being used within the profession.

Sync 4: Researching social media presence

You should allow 30 minutes for this activity.

Go to the websites of Clifford Chance <https://www.cliffordchance.com> and Tuckers Solicitors <https://www.tuckerssolicitors.com>

1 Identify how many and which social media platforms each firm uses.

2 Choose one of the platforms and review the content. You might want to consider who is the target audience; what is the engagement rate; how many comments, likes and followers the firm has; and how you would rate the social media presence of the firm.

3 What similarities and differences did you identify in relation to their social media presence?

If you are in a different jurisdiction, you may want to choose other law firms to review.

AI-GENERATED CONTENT AND CREDIBILITY

GenAI tools can be used in social media marketing such as writing website content, social media posts, and blogs. The ability to use GenAI in this way can improve efficiency and productivity, but law firms need to consider whether they should disclose they are using GenAI-generated content in public-facing content and consider the implications for the brand's authenticity and maintaining trust.

Lawyers are responsible for their published content, and it is essential they ensure AI-generated text does not misrepresent or breach confidentiality. AI-generated marketing content can raise issues of copyright and ownership; therefore, the tools have to be used responsibly, and checks should be in place to ensure that content does not infringe any third-party rights. All content should have human oversight to ensure both legal and ethical compliance.

The SRA has produced several reports exploring the use of AI within legal practice. In its 2022 document, "Compliance Tips for Solicitors Regarding the Use of AI and Technology"[21] it states that lawyers are free to use any technology, but they must ensure compliance with SRA principles and standards, and they must understand the legal framework of the underlying technology. The focus for all legal professionals is to ensure they are maintaining ethical standards, client confidentiality, transparency, and accountability.

AI is potentially a powerful tool to enhance social media marketing for law firms, but it must be done ethically and responsibly to ensure that risks are mitigated.

21 Solicitors Regulation Authority, 'Compliance Tips for Solicitors Regarding the Use of AI and Technology' <https://www.sra.org.uk/solicitors/resources/innovate/compliance-tips-for-solicitors/> and 'Risk Outlook Report: The Use of Artificial Intelligence in the Legal Market' (November 2023) <https://www.sra.org.uk/sra/research-publications/artificial-intelligence-legal-market/> accessed 23 September 2025. Also see Bar Standards Board, 'Updated Guidance on Generative AI for the Bar' (26 November 2025) <https://www.barcouncil.org.uk//resource/updated-guidance-on-generative-ai-for-the-bar.html>; Courts and Tribunals Judiciary, 'Artificial Intelligence (AI) Judicial Guidance' (October 2025) <https://www.judiciary.uk/guidance-and-resources/artificial-intelligence-ai-judicial-guidance-october-2025/> and The Law Society, 'Generative AI: The Essentials' (October 2025) <https://www.lawsociety.org.uk/topics/ai-and-lawtech/generative-ai-the-essentials> accessed 12 January 2026.

DIGITAL LAWYERING AND SOCIAL MEDIA

Lawyers need to understand how social media platforms work and how information is shared to be able to effectively practise in the digital age. In the United States, the American Bar Association (ABA) includes within their professional conduct rules a duty of technology competence. ABA Rule 1.1 Competence, comment 8, states that a "lawyer should keep abreast of changes in the law and its practice, including the benefits and risks associated with relevant technology".[22] At the time of writing, 40 US states have adopted the duty of technology competence.[23] The rule has been discussed in case law:

***Womack v. Yeoman*, 2011 WL 9330606 (Cir. Ct. Va. 2011).**

A case in Virginia discusses the danger for lawyers of not being conversant in technology.

***James v. Natl. Fin. LLC*, No. 8931-VCL 2014 WL 6845560 (Del. Ch., Dec. 5, 2014)**

Counsel: "I have to confess to this Court, I am not computer literate. I have not found presence in the cybernetic revolution. I need a secretary to help me turn on the computer. This was out of my bailiwick".

The Delaware court stated: "Professed technological incompetence is not an excuse for discovery misconduct".

Lawyers are required to effectively represent their clients, and to do that they must understand social networking platforms and keep up to date about changes in law and practice associated with technology. Technology impacts on every aspect of legal practice, and being

22 American Bar Association, 'Model Rules of Professional Conduct, Rule 1.1. Competence' <https://www.americanbar.org/groups/professional_responsibility/publications/model_rules_of_professional_conduct/rule_1_1_competence/comment_on_rule_1_1/>

23 Bob Ambrogi, 'Another State Adopts Duty of Technology Competence for Lawyers Brining Total to 40, LawSites' (24 March 2022) <https://www.lawnext.com/2022/03/another-state-adopts-duty-of-technology-competence-for-lawyers-bringing-total-to-40.html>

proficient in technology extends not just to an area of practice, but also to how law firms develop their services. Ethics opinions from the US states of New York, Pennsylvania, North Carolina, Florida, West Virginia, and the District of Columbia have said that to properly advise clients, lawyers must understand social media. Technology competence is a requirement for all lawyers.

Social media posts have increasingly become a source of evidence in legal proceedings. Earlier parts of the chapter have already identified some of the potential pitfalls of social media, but lawyers also need to be aware of ethical issues that may occur when dealing with social media, including:

- Unethical information gathering.
- Failing to assert client control.
- Evidence preservation and spoliation.

UNETHICAL INFORMATION GATHERING

Lawyers need to advise clients on their use of social media prior to, during and after legal proceedings. It is important for lawyers to advise clients not to discuss their case on social media and the requirements to preserve evidence.

Case example: family law

Using evidence from social networking sites in a family law case is becoming increasingly common. Social media posts, photos, or videos can provide evidence of a new job, an affair or the purchase of new items such as a car.

What might you advise your client?

- What social media evidence to gather.
- How to gather social media evidence to ensure they are not contravening the law.
- How social media can be used in their case.
- What social media evidence is likely to be admissible.
- How to address negative social media evidence in their case.

What practical matters might you advise your client on?

- To deactivate their social media accounts, but that they are prohibited from deleting posts in anticipation of proceedings.
- To reset their profile settings so that mutual friends cannot share posts with their spouse.
- Public posts can be used as evidence, but they cannot hack into another account and use those posts as evidence.

A study from Australia showed that social media evidence was adduced in 136 first-instance decisions in family law cases between 2009 and 2014.[24] The examples included evidence of the financial circumstances of the parties, the suitability of one party's ability to be an effective parent, and evidence supporting or denying another relationship. The study found that in 36% of cases the social media evidence was weighted heavily in the proceedings and Facebook private messages had probative value. The study shows the importance of the lawyer knowing about their client's social media activity. The fact that so many people are active users of social media means that what a client uploads or posts can have an impact on their case.

FAILING TO ASSERT CLIENT CONTROL

The rapper 50 Cent

The rapper 50 Cent was ordered by a bankruptcy court judge to explain why he was posting photos on Instagram during the bankruptcy proceedings—pictures of him surrounded by money. One post spelt out "I'm Broke" in piles of $100 bills.

Advising a client on how they engage with social media also applies after the case has concluded.

24 Victoria Blakeley, Patricia Easteal, Emma Fitch and Jessica Kennedy, 'Social Media Evidence in Family Law: What Can Be Used and Its Probative Value' (2015) 5 *Family Law Review* 81–101.

***Gulliver Schools, Inc. v. Snay* (Fla. Dist. Ct. App. 2014)**

The daughter of the winning plaintiff posted on Facebook:

> Mama and Papa Snay won the case against Gulliver. Gulliver is now officially paying for my vacation to Europe this summer. SUCK IT.

The Facebook post breached the confidential agreement and the settlement was successfully appealed.

The cases of Snay and 50 Cent demonstrate why it is important that lawyers understand social media and manage their clients' usage.

Social media is being used in many different types of cases. The following examples show how social media can be used to challenge the credibility of a claimant in a personal injury case.

***Saunderson and Others v. Sonae Industria* (UK) Ltd [2015] EWHC QB**

One of the claimants was cross-examined over a Twitter conversation which could have suggested that his claims may be fraudulent.

Cirencester Friendly Society v. Parkin *[2015] EWHC 1750 QB*

Judge Seymour said:

> Nemesis overtook from Mr Parkin most dramatically because like so many people nowadays, in particular those who seem minded to perpetrate frauds, he seemed incapable of keeping off the internet and sharing the true nature of his activities through social media.

Mr Parkin made a series of representations to say he was incapacitated from working. There was a video on YouTube showing him refurbishing and racing a sports car.

EVIDENCE PRESERVATION AND SPOLIATION

A lawyer has a responsibility to advise their client about the implications of their social media activity. This includes advising a client on the consequences of altering or destroying social media posts, pages, or messages, known as spoliation. The advice needs to be clear and unambiguous because there are serious consequences for both lawyers and clients if social media evidence is compromised. Lawyers may use social media to gather evidence, but they also are required to have effective protocols in place to ensure the preservation of evidence.

It is important to understand the data collection process, such as screenshots, web capture tools, time stamps, and social discovery tools, to ensure the evidence from social media platforms is collected properly and can be authenticated. Facebook allows you to download your data. You can download a copy of your Facebook information over specified date ranges and by type, including posts, photos, comments, likes, friends, stories, following and followers, messages, groups, events, profile information, pages, and places. You can also retrieve a history of your searches, location, and security and login information, which includes periods of time you have been active on Facebook. It is available in HTML or JSON format and allows data to be preserved electronically. Issues around digital evidence will be discussed further in Chapter 8.

Social media platforms have tabs and expandable comment sections that may not be immediately visible. Locating those will allow the full archived conversation to be revealed. To ensure the authenticity of the data, it is important to collect key metadata such as IP addresses, timestamps, and URLs. If web content is collected as part of any litigation, it has to be saved in a format that is exactly how it appears online. Metadata and expert analysis can be used to prove authenticity. Understanding how to capture and preserve social media data is essential to ensure that evidence is collected appropriately. Lawyers also need to address with their clients any inconsistencies between the client's social media presence and their legal claim, and to be vigilant about their client's social media activity. Ultimately, lawyers have a duty to uphold the law and the administration of justice.

SOCIAL MEDIA RISKS: LEGAL PERSPECTIVE

Having an awareness and understanding of social media is a key part of being a lawyer, and understanding the best practices for collecting and presenting social media evidence is critical. The pervasiveness of social media means it is relevant across legal practice, and social media posts are becoming a critical part of legal cases. GenAI presents further risks, as it can create realistic but false content including AI-generated, manipulated images and deepfakes which can show people saying or doing things they never said or did.[25] The purpose of this textbook is to raise your awareness of the intersection between law and technology so you can apply your skills of critical thinking and analysis to the emerging legal issues.

EMPLOYMENT LAW

The cases of *Weeks* and *Creighton* illustrate the employment law consequences for inappropriate postings on social media. *Creighton* demonstrates how actions on social media can have long lasting implications.

***Weeks v. Everything Everywhere Ltd* [2012] ET/2503016/2012**

Mr. Weeks posted on social media that his work was like "Dante's inferno". His employer had a social media policy that applied to postings in their own time and a requirement not to criticise the employer. He was dismissed for gross misconduct, and the decision was upheld by the Employment Tribunal.

Creighton v. Together Housing Association Ltd *[2016] ET/2400978/2016*

Mr. Creighton was a long-standing employee who had three years earlier made some derogatory comments about his colleagues and his employer on Twitter. The comments came to light only following an investigation into another employee for bullying.

He argued that he thought his tweets were private, that he had posted them two or three years prior and that he "deserved to be treated sympathetically" after nearly 30 years' service.

He was dismissed, and the decision was upheld by the Employment Tribunal.

25 K. C. Yang, D. Singh and F. Menczer, 'Characteristics and Prevalence of Fake Social Media Profiles with AI-Generated Faces' *arXiv preprint* arXiv:2401.02627.2024

DEFAMATION

Social media has significantly impacted defamation cases; there are now an increasing number of cases involving statements made online through social media platforms. For example, in *Miller v Peake*,[26] a parish clerk was awarded £20,000 in damages after defamatory social media posts were made by a parish councillor on Facebook.

Vardy v. Rooney [2022] EWHC 2017 (QB) 29 July 2022

This case is often referred to as the "Wagatha Christie" trial. Rebekah Vardy issued a libel claim against Colleen Rooney because she named her in social media posts as the person sending information to a newspaper from her private Instagram account. The claim was unsuccessful, with Mrs Justice Steyn ruling in favour of Colleen Rooney.

In the United States, the case of *Depp v. Heard* was one of the most publicised libel trials. The jury found that Amber Heard had defamed Johnny Depp over an article she wrote for the *Washington Post* in which she said she was a victim of domestic abuse, without naming Depp. The couple have an extensive legal history.[27]

These cases highlight some of the social media risks that lawyers will be required to advise on. There are also similar examples in other jurisdictions. In the next sync, you will research an area of law to explore the impact of social media.

Sync 5: Social media and the law

You should allow around 15 minutes for this activity.

Choose an area of law and consider some of the issues that might arise in relation to social media. You can choose from the following:

- Employment law
- Defamation
- Data protection and confidentiality

26 *Miller v. Peake* [2025] EWHC 453(KB) (28 February 2025).
27 Clemence Michallon, 'Johnny Depp and Amber Heard: A Timeline of Their Relationship, Allegations and Court Battles, Depp v. Heard: A Timeline of Their Relationship and Who Won' (*The Independent*, 2023) accessed 6 August 2025.

- Online advertising and marketing communications
- Third-party intellectual property (IP) rights
- Criminal law

This list does not represent all the areas of law that social media might be relevant to, but it does demonstrate how the use of social media crosses many areas of legal practice. If you considered third-party IP rights, you may have thought about issues relating to counterfeiting or how you would advise a client if their IP rights had been infringed on Facebook.

There are a number of issues you could have considered relating to employment law. You may have thought about how you would advise a client on its social media policy or what clauses should be contained in an employment contract that relate to social media. Social media is a high-risk area for defamation and, as we have seen from examples in this chapter, people do not always consider the consequences of their actions when posting online.

Online advertising includes social media advertising. To find out more about how it is governed, you can look at the UK Code of Non-Broadcast Advertising and Direct and Promotional Marketing (CAP Code). The UK's Financial Conduct Authority has rules on advertising when it is capable of being a financial promotion on social media. There are numerous examples of criminal offences relating to social media, including cyberbullying, sexting, revenge porn, trolling, and virtual mobbing. The UK's Crown Prosecution Service has produced guidelines on prosecuting cases involving communications sent via social media; the guidelines are available on the CPS website.

Governments around the world are increasingly concerned about how social media platforms protect their users. In the UK, the Online Safety Act 2023[28] is a set of laws that protects children and adults online. It places duties on social media companies for users' safety when they are using their platforms. OFCOM is the independent regulator of Online Safety in the UK.[29] There have been some criticisms of the Act,

28 Online Safety Act 2023.

29 OFCOM, 'Ofcom's Approach to Implementing the Online Safety Act' (2023) <https://www.ofcom.org.uk/online-safety/illegal-and-harmful-content/roadmap-to-regulation> accessed 2 January 2026.

suggesting that it erodes individual privacy and freedom of expression.[30] It is important to be aware of future trends in social media law and online regulation and consider how that may impact on lawyers and the delivery of legal services.

SOCIAL MEDIA RISKS: BRINGING IT TOGETHER

This chapter has discussed the implications of our social media use in personal and professional capacities, explained the relevant professional conduct rules and considered some examples where lawyers have breached the codes. The impact of social media is profound: It affects the law and is relevant to legal proceedings. To practise in a digital age, lawyers are required to understand how social media works and keep up to date with changes to social media platforms.

To bring this all together, these case studies give you the opportunity to apply what you have learned and to think about the practical implications of social media.

Sync 6: Social media case studies

You should allow around 60 minutes for this activity.

Read each case study and consider the related question before reading the comment. These comments draw upon the law and the professional regulation of solicitors in England and Wales. If you are based in another jurisdiction or are interested in a different legal role, you might like to consider whether similar laws and regulations would apply.

Case study 1

Law firm A has Bluesky, Instagram, and TikTok with lots of content and regular postings, but the firm does not have an overall social media strategy, and messaging from their online presence is confusing. The firm has a social media policy, but it is vague and poorly drafted, and it appears that anyone

30 Aidan Clifford, 'Does the Online Safety Act Violate Privacy Over Security Concerns Too Harshly' in *Does the Online Safety Act Violate Privacy Too Harshly Over Security Concerns?* (Lancaster University 2024) accessed 6 August 2025.

with access to the accounts can post. Some of the firm's lawyers have posted showing them attending conference dinners and events.

What are the implications for law firm A?

A law firm should have a social media policy which is clear, unambiguous, and easily accessible. The policy should set out the firm's expectations on social media use, what obligations are placed on lawyers, and what lawyers can and cannot do in their personal and professional capacities. The policy should restrict who is authorised to post on behalf of the firm. There should be procedures in place to make sure those with access to social media accounts are properly trained. Training explaining the social media policy should be provided to new starters, and regular refresher training should be offered.

In this case study, the law firm should consider how their social media posts may appear to the outside world, and what message they convey about the law firm. If there are posts and photographs of lawyers attending conferences, it is important to think about how that may be perceived by clients. It is important to consider any reputational damage that might result from what might appear to be quite an innocuous post. This is also relevant to your own individual social media accounts; always think about why you are posting and what could be the potential impact of your posts.

Case study 2

Law student B has just completed his law degree, and he is starting to apply for training contracts. At university he was a regular user of social media; he enjoyed an active and fulfilling university experience, a lot of which he documented on social media.

What issues do you think law student B may have when applying for a training contract?

It is important to be aware of the risks of putting public posts on social media. We should all consider what information an employer might find if they conduct an online search and to what extent that could convey a negative impression. This example illustrates the problem of habitually sharing information. It is incumbent on all of us to regularly check privacy settings, to review our data trail and critically reflect on our online presence to ensure it does not impact on any future jobs and careers. Self-awareness is imperative: We have the tools to control and actively manage our online presence. It is also important to remember that social media can be helpful in developing your networks and securing opportunities. LinkedIn is a good example of how social media can be used to help build your profile and connect with people who may assist you in your career.

Case study 3

Lawyer C is searching the internet one day and comes across a chat room for families and victims of a recent fire at a chemical plant. The chat room home page states that the purpose of the chat room is to provide emotional and practical support for the victims and their families. Lawyer C enters the chat room and posts a message to say that she is really sorry to hear about the disaster, that she is a lawyer and that she is happy to answer any legal questions. The family of one of the victims posts a message back with a series of questions on their legal right to compensation, and lawyer C answers the questions.

What issues do you think arise from lawyer C's conduct?

The SRA Principles state that a lawyer must behave in a way that maintains the trust the public places in them and in the provision of legal services. There is a risk that entering a chat room that has been created to provide emotional and practical support for the victims and their families risks exploiting vulnerable people and may damage the trust that the public places in the profession. A lawyer must act with integrity, and these interactions may be considered a breach of integrity. There is also potential here for the inadvertent creation of a lawyer–client relationship which contravenes requirements of the SRA Code in terms of confidentiality, conflict of interests, and publicity.

Case study 4

Lawyer D has recently joined a new law firm as a partner. The marketing team are keen to raise the profile of lawyer D and want her to do some public engagement and provide some hypothetical examples of her recent cases to share her knowledge, opinions, and experiences. The firm has asked her to write a blog post about a recent case she has been involved in: the blog post will feature on the firm's website; they will also share it via LinkedIn. She is concerned to make sure that she does not breach any of the rules on confidentiality, but she hopes she will be fine if she makes it all hypothetical.

What advice would you give lawyer D?

Social media is an effective tool to engage new audiences, but lawyers need to be aware of the risks and understand the professional conduct rules that apply to their conduct online. The SRA Code covers confidentiality, conflict of interests and publicity; a lawyer must ensure they act with integrity and ensure the public trust and confidence in the legal profession. Lawyers also have duties of confidentiality, and even hypothetical examples may still risk breaching those duties if there is a reasonable likelihood that a third party could identify the client or legal situation.

Case study 5

Lawyer E is meeting his client about her personal injury case. He asks about her social media activity. She explains that she is a prolific user of Facebook; laughingly, she tells him there are a lot of pictures from her holidays "a little worse for wear!", but she tells him not to worry because she has deleted a lot of her pictures and posts recently. Lawyer E asks her about her privacy settings, and she explains she has no idea. He recommends that she check and ensure that her account is private.

What advice do you think lawyer E should give to his client?

Lawyer E should advise his client about the implications of her social media activity, including advising her on the consequences of altering or destroying social media posts, pages, or messages if they are likely to be relevant to the personal injury claim. Deleting her pictures and posts could constitute spoliation if they are related to her legal claim. Relevance is a prerequisite for spoliation, but what is deemed relevant is not always easy to determine. The advice needs to be clear and unambiguous because there could be serious consequences for both lawyer E and the client if social media evidence is compromised. It is not enough to advise the client on her privacy settings; lawyer E would also need to consider the relevance of social media posts to her personal injury claim to ensure upholding the rule of law and the proper administration of justice, and that they are acting with integrity and not allowing their independence to be compromised or breached. These same obligations apply in other jurisdictions. The ABA advises lawyers in the United States that they must advise clients on the content of their social media sites, including their responsibility to preserve information and the restrictions on not removing or destroying information.[31]

Case study 6

Lawyer F is representing Miss Mahmood, a former employee of ABC Industries, in an unfair dismissal claim. Miss Mahmood provides him with a list of employees who are unhappy with the company. The lawyer sends Facebook friend requests to two of the employees in the list in the hope that he can find out some information on the employer to help him with his case. He goes into a local cafe, logs on to his computer using the public access Wi-Fi and sends a tweet from his firm's X account: "In a café outside ABC Industries if anyone can provide any help to Miss M, please message me back". He is waiting for his client to arrive, so he decides to update his LinkedIn profile. He adds some information on the areas of law he has expertise in; he thinks he might have slightly exaggerated his experience, but he is confident that everyone does this, so he figures it will be fine.

What potential breaches of the professional conduct rules can you identify?

In this case study there are several potential breaches of professional conduct rules. Have a look at the rules that govern lawyers in your jurisdiction.

- Was it appropriate to send the Facebook requests?
- What are the implications of using public access Wi-Fi?
- Does the tweet breach client confidentiality?
- Have there been any breaches of the firm's social media policy?
- Is it appropriate to exaggerate your experience on LinkedIn?

31 Daniel J. Siegel, 'Ethics Corner: 12 Rules for Ethically Dealing with Social Media' (*ABA*, 16 February 2017) <https://www.americanbar.org/groups/business_law/publications/blt/2017/02/ethics_corner/> accessed 11 April 2021.

These cases illustrate some of the issues that need to be considered in practice and the importance of understanding your ethical obligations when using social media platforms.

Conclusion

This chapter has applied the principles of digital lawyering within the practical context of social media. It began by asking you to reflect upon your own existing digital footprint and think about the implications for you of your online presence. It then considered the wider use of social media within law and the legal profession, exploring the relevant professional conduct rules and considering some examples of where lawyers have been in breach of those rules. It has also considered some of the risks that are emerging from the use of GenAI within law and legal practice. Aspiring lawyers need to have a rounded skill set that is more than just knowledge of the law. Firms expect lawyers to understand the legal ramifications of social media use. The ability to use social media and understand its potential is an important aspect of legal practice, particularly in the context of the marketing and promotion of legal services. In this chapter we have considered how changes in law and practice associated with technology are now an essential element of a lawyer's role, and you had the opportunity to think about the skills you need as a digital lawyer. Finally, you considered a number of case studies on the ethical implications of using online social networking both as individual practitioners and within digital lawyering practices.

Additional resources

Committee on Culture, Science and Education, 'Regulating Content Moderation on Social Media to Safeguard Freedom of Expression' (2024) <https://rm.coe.int/as-cult-regulating-content-moderation-on-social-media-to-safeguard-fre/1680b2b162?t>

'Digital Skills: Social Media' <https://www.futurelearn.com/courses/digital-skills-social-media>

Social Media Risk and the Law <https://www.routledge.com/Social-Media-Risk-and-the-Law-A-Guide-for-Global-Communicators/Grantham-Pearson/p/book/9781032017990>

Tims B, *Unguided: Social Media Usage in the Legal Profession and the Need for Practical Guidance* (24 January 2021) <https://ssrn.com/abstract=3772116>

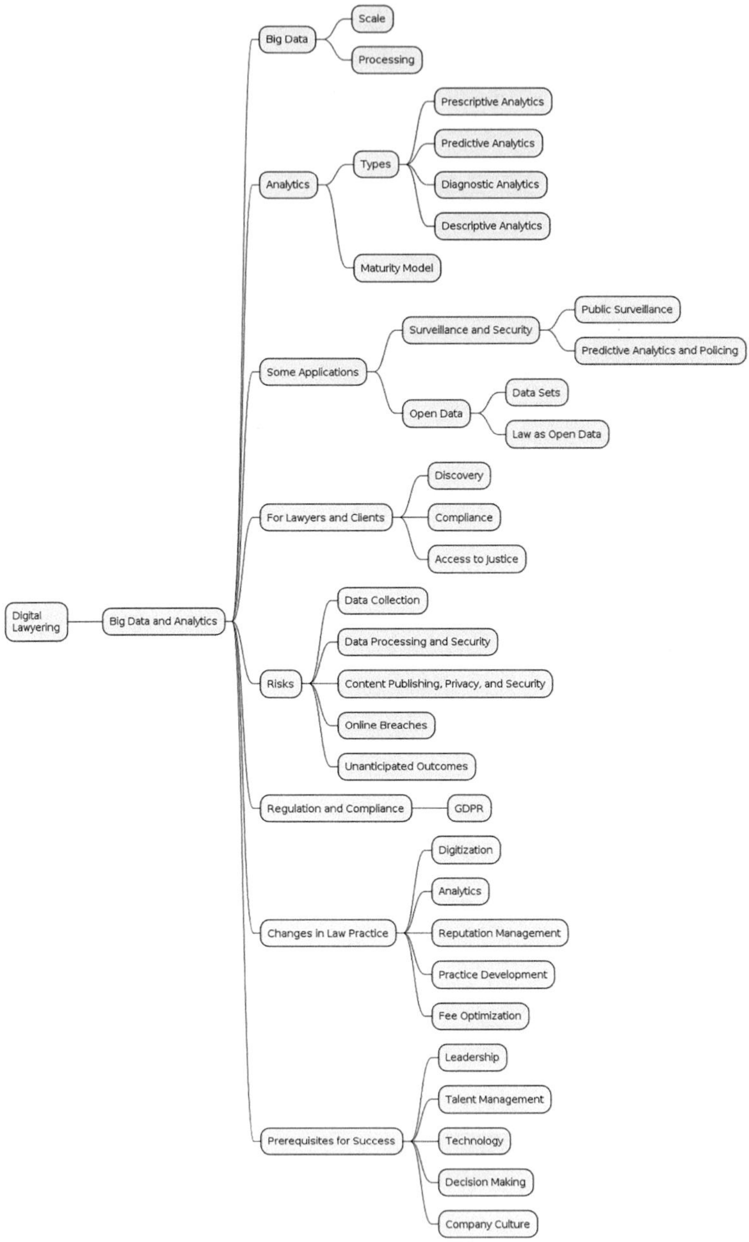

Mind Map 6.1 Chapter topics

6 Big Data and Analytics

Terry Wong

Introduction

This chapter will introduce the concepts and applications of Big Data, with illustrations in both legally oriented and general contexts. It will go on to identify important considerations for data protection in light of legislation, revealing risks that lawyers will need to bear in mind, whether as users or when advising clients in legal practice.

Chapter hot spots

When reading this chapter, questions to think about include:

- What are the opportunities and benefits that large data sets and analytic techniques present to clients, lawyers, governments, and society?
- What are the risks in trusting analytic models, and how might lawyers mitigate those risks in daily practice?
- How might a lawyer maintain a balanced perspective of openness and scepticism when examining the opportunities and risks presented by Big Data, especially when advising clients?
- What challenges and opportunities does the legal profession face as it encounters Big Data, a technology that requires ways of thinking and decision-making that are fundamentally different to critical aspects of its traditional culture?

Having read the title and introduction, you can add any other questions you want to explore here:

DOI: 10.4324/9781003602323-6

ILLUSTRATION: FRAUD DETECTION

Every day, as a shopper makes an online purchase with a debit or credit card, the authorisation process for the transaction initiates a series of checks that occur automatically, unobtrusively, on the systems of the card processor. The purchase is compared to previously known patterns of spending from the shopper, derived from data collected from previous transactions. This data may include the spending amounts, types of products purchased and the locations of retailers, among other items. If activity identified by algorithms trained to detect anomalous spending appears, the shopper will receive a communication from the card issuer asking for verification of the transaction, in some cases refusing further transactions until such verification takes place. This process of fraud detection is shown in Figure 6.1.

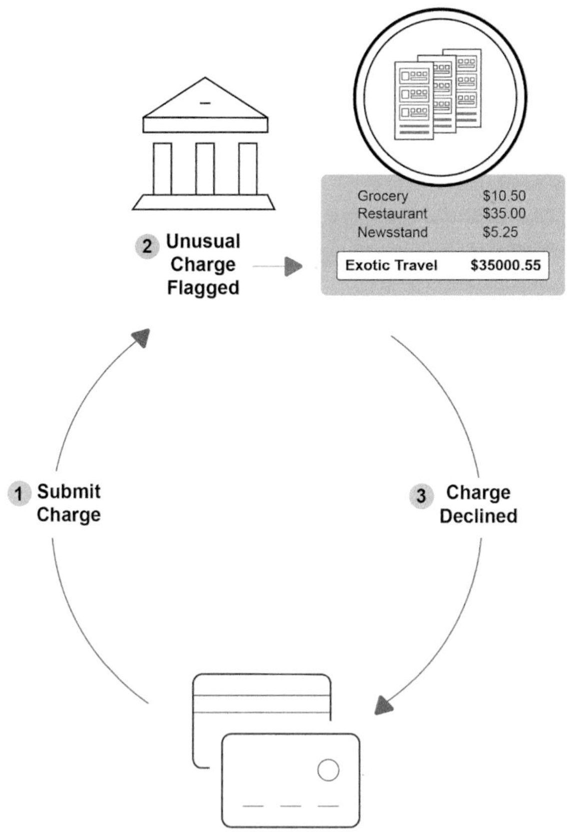

Figure 6.1 Credit card fraud detection

Payment card transactions occur every day in significant volumes, with 75.7 million payments occurring per day in the UK in June 2025, according to a report published by UK Finance in September 2025.[1] Fraud detection systems are a classic example of a mature Big Data application, having evolved from early applications of data warehousing and analytics.

WHAT IS BIG DATA?

Big Data can initially be understood to involve collections of data sufficiently large as to be difficult, if not impossible, to store in files or databases and to process using traditional computing systems. The data may be what is termed "effluent" from processing, meaning data that results as a by-product from the processing of everyday activities and transactions at a large scale—for example, as might be recorded in conducting and servicing individual electronic transactions, web browsing activity and telephone call records. Other examples of Big Data sources include, but certainly are not limited to, security cameras, sensors in factories, utility meters in homes, connected household appliances and assistants, and any number of other devices in an emerging network of devices sometimes termed the "Internet of Things" (IoT).

Organisations providing goods and services, from governments to multinational companies to small entrepreneurial ventures, amass significant volumes of data which, when processed and analysed, can enable a wide array of innovative applications of high utility. A frequently cited example of large-scale Big Data investment is that of Walmart, one of the largest retailers in the world, which generates over 40 petabytes[2] of data per day in its over 20,000 stores worldwide. According to a report published in 2017, the company at that time was processing at least 2.5 petabytes of that data per day.[3] Two well-known and often-cited examples of government Big Data applications include the email metadata mining conducted by the US National Security Agency (NSA) with

1 'Card Spending Update' (*UK Finance*, June 2025) <https://www.ukfinance.org.uk/system/files/2025-09/Card%20Spending%20Update%20-%20June%202025.pdf> accessed 26 September 2025.

2 For a sense of scale, consider that a petabyte is one billion megabytes.

3 'Big Data at Walmart Is All About Big Numbers; 40 Petabytes a Day!' (*Data-floq*, n.d.) <https://datafloq.com/read/big-data-walmart-big-numbers-40-petabytes/1175> accessed 2 January 2021.

data sourced from telecommunications providers, and China's Social Credit System, in which the activities of citizens across a wide range of domains are recorded and mixed with law enforcement and financial data in a state-built application to establish a score for the trustworthiness of an individual. Later in this chapter, we will highlight some points to consider when looking at issues of government data and citizen privacy.

WHAT ARE ANALYTICS?

No matter the volume of data available, it does not become useful information until it is organised, processed, and interpreted while considering a specific goal. The process involves using tools and techniques requiring a level of mathematical transformation and calculations with some level of systematic process formalisation, known in a general sense as *analytics*.

Analytics can be more concretely broken down into several types, rising in complexity and in the risks involved in their implementation and application (Figure 6.2):

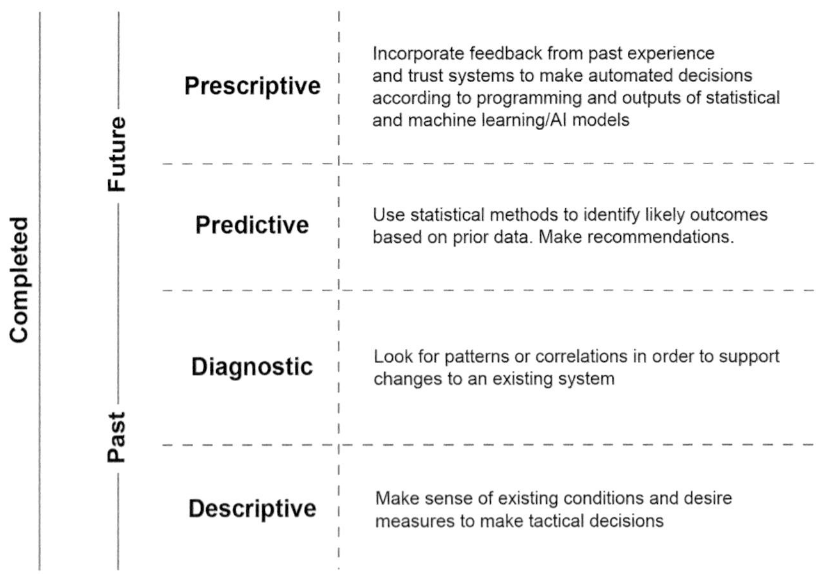

Figure 6.2 The types of analytics

- *Descriptive analytics.* These are what have been traditionally thought of as analytics in business contexts, providing measurements, descriptive statistics (such as averages), and visualisations of activity in the form of graphs and dashboards. The term "dashboard" refers to an application that collects frequently viewed information around a specific activity, such as the key performance metrics of a business. The power of such analytics to inform is sometimes strained or even impeded by overlaying an inappropriate automobile dashboard-like concept with many gauges and dials, as a business dashboard merely presents information and does not offer switches or levers to control the underlying machine.
- *Diagnostic analytics.* These are tools that support inquiry and exploration of data sets, allowing an analyst to look for patterns and discover paths of inquiry to apply in solving a given problem. They also support analysts in efforts to uncover yet-unrealised opportunity in user activity data. Developers of online software products rely upon "click stream data" (logs showing how people navigate through a website) and diagnostic analytic tools (investigating why something happened) in efforts to understand user behaviour and uncover opportunities to optimise existing functions or develop new ones.
- *Predictive analytics.* These analytics take data and apply certain statistical techniques such as linear or logistic regression and attempt to construct models that enable an analyst to develop options for a decision maker. Predictive analytics drive recommendations that are presented in online electronic stores and commerce platforms as well as marketing campaigns and promotions.
- *Prescriptive analytics.* These advance the work done with predictive analytics, feeding experience data from applying certain options and training a system to recommend courses of action in response to new incident data based on results from previous data driven decisions with known outcomes. Examples include material requirements planning (MRP) applications in manufacturing and routing applications for logistics or ridesharing driver applications.

Król and Zdonek[4] examined several maturity models, which measure an organisation's capacity for improvement, that are used in industry and academia to describe analytics practices. They saw in common among those maturity models a continuum starting from descriptive analytics,

4 Karol Król and Dariusz Zdonek, 'Analytics Maturity Models: An Overview' (March 2020) 11 *Information* 142 <https://doi.org/10.3390/info11030142>

building up to prescriptive analytics, continuing through to the introduction of artificial intelligence (AI) applications in what are termed "cognitive analytics".

Experts also view the evolution of analytics in three waves:

- *Analytics 1.0.* Data was stored using traditional databases, and analysis was possible using snapshots of daily operational data.
- *Analytics 2.0.* Large data sets required advanced storage and processing techniques as well as flexibility in the definition of structures to hold data. Technologies such as cloud storage and large processing clusters as well as NoSQL databases marked the arrival of Big Data as we now know it.
- *Analytics 3.0.* The introduction of advanced, optimised processing techniques as well as machine learning and AI techniques defines Analytics 3.0 as a stage of rapid evolution and innovation, with potential to revolutionise operations and practice in the business domains where applied.

Sync 1: Everyday Big Data

You should allow around 20 minutes for this activity.

List some recent interactions you may have had with an online buying experience, or after clicking on an advertisement while browsing a website.

Recall how the specific items you clicked on informed the advertisements or product recommendations you were shown on websites you browsed later that day or for several days afterwards. What related items were shown to you?

You probably identified that the advertisements and recommendations you were shown were closely linked to your initial purchase. These effects which occur based on browsing behaviour are well known but perhaps are no longer noted in everyday experience as novel. They are, however, ubiquitous and a feature of Analytics 2.0 and the predictive analytics applications behind modern digital marketing.

Technology enabling Analytics 3.0

A few key developments that have enabled the rise of Analytics 3.0 include:

1 *Increasingly bigger data.* Sensor data from home devices and other IoT devices such as voice-driven assistants, as well as rich, real-time location data, are but a few examples of rising technologies that contribute to burgeoning volumes of raw data as Big Data sources.
2 *Mature statistical techniques and pattern recognition.* These allow the data itself to embody what is normal and to classify new examples as normal or not according to the definition derived from "experience" (i.e. large volumes of samples from Big Data sets or the data itself).
3 *Computer vision.* This term refers to the way computers understand and interpret the visual world (such as pictures and videos). Growing mainstream knowledge and application of AI techniques in computer vision have supported the derivation of data from photos and video streamed from continuous live feeds, as well as in more complex text recognition and visual conversion applications,[5] increasing the size of available data in Big Data sets by orders of magnitude and with greater speed of data acquisition.
4 *Natural language processing and text mining.* Natural language processing (NLP) techniques have allowed technologists to build useful tools from simple foundations like word frequency counts, word groupings, and significant word identification. NLP techniques also allow spelling and grammar correction, concept mapping, and the creation of fast search techniques. NLP works best when there are large bodies of text data to use in the building and training of models. Because of the text-intensive nature of law and legal texts, NLP becomes the keystone of technologies applied to the practice of law with Big Data. We will further discuss the applications of NLP as applied using AI in Chapter 7.

BIG DATA IN ACTION

In this section we examine several examples of mainstream applications built with analytics and Big Data, with emphasis on applications that may have implications for lawyers advising or representing clients.

5 Examples include invoice and expense receipt conversion to data and high-volume scanned document ingestion and conversion to text (i.e. automated transcription).

VISIBILITY OF WORKER ACTIVITY AND PRODUCTIVITY

Workplaces with timecards provided a scalable means for employers to gather attendance data for payroll functions. A tamper-resistant time clock and a policy requiring workers to clock in and out during paid work periods enabled accurate time reporting, fostered a sense of trust that employers were paying for work performed and ensured that workers would get paid for the time put in.

Updated time and attendance systems work in similar ways with key code systems and biometric inputs such as fingerprint or facial recognition scanners. Beyond the entrance to the business, technology has enabled measurement of activity inside the workplace to be significantly more detailed, with a wide range of counting tools and monitors to measure individual worker productivity and time spent on specific tasks and breaks, and even monitoring the content of the websites and other resources accessed from employees' computer workstations. The online retailer Amazon received significant amounts of mixed coverage in the press for its technology measuring every aspect of their warehouse employees' productivity and efficiency. In recent years, the company has turned that technology into a packaged product available for other businesses to buy and implement in their workplaces, with the data streamed to subscription cloud services hosted by Amazon.[6]

SURVEILLANCE AND SECURITY SYSTEMS

Security systems and surveillance systems for law enforcement generate large volumes of streaming video data, which is often fed into recognition systems for subject identification and tracking, and for counting in aggregate to assess security in venues with specific requirements (e.g. during events, protests, or visits by high-profile individuals). Figure 6.3 shows an application of a surveillance system used in a public space, identifying possible persons of interest using automated facial recognition techniques applied at scale.

The US Federal Bureau of Investigation (FBI), in cooperation with participating states, maintains a national mugshot repository for use in developing leads upon request from state and local law enforcement

6 See, for example, Jack Morse, 'Amazon Announces New Employee Tracking Tech, and Customers Are Lining Up' (Mashable UK, 2 December 2020) <https://mashable.com/article/amazon-aws-panorama-worker-customer-tracking-technology-smart-cameras/?europe=true> accessed 2 January 2026.

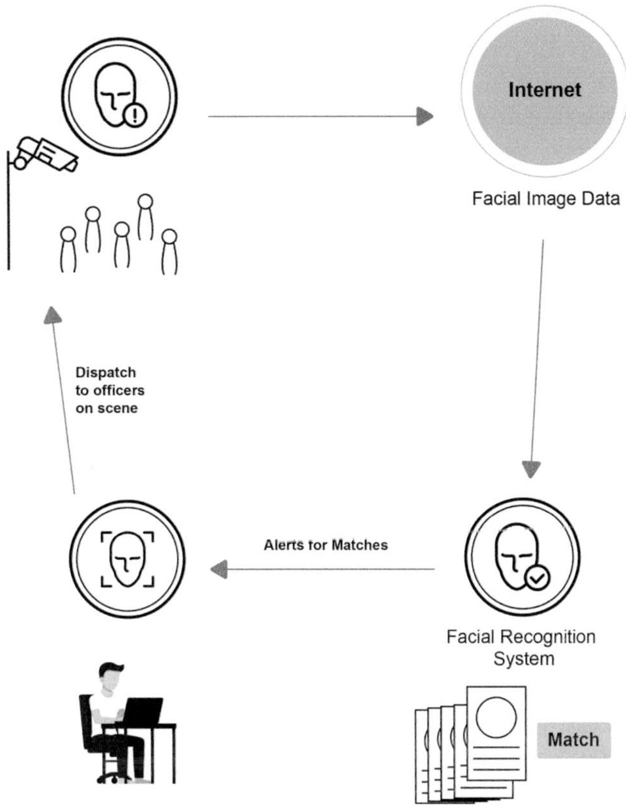

Figure 6.3 Illustration of camera surveillance apps and data

agencies. Probe images are submitted to the national database for comparison and facial recognition, not to generate a positive identification—a recognition of the limitations of facial recognition models—but to generate a lead for local law enforcement to follow, possibly leading to a subsequent positive identification through additional means. The FBI operates the database and analytic tools for facial recognition under congressional oversight[7] and makes explicit policy on the handling of the requests and disposal of the request images and materials, detailed in Privacy Impact Assessments. Similar programs in the UK also have publicly appointed oversight. In England and Wales, for instance, the

7 See the 2017 statement to the House Committee on Oversight and Government Reform, 'Law Enforcement's Use of Facial Recognition Technology' (FBI.gov, 2017) <https://www.fbi.gov/news/testimony/law-enforcements-use-of-facial-recognition-technology> accessed 2 January 2026.

programs fall under the oversight of a Surveillance Camera Commissioner appointed by the Secretary of State.

It is worth noting that facial recognition, gait recognition (identifying people by how they walk), and other technologies are in an evolving zone in the law, where gains in effective investigation must be balanced, sometimes in conflict with the rights guaranteed in a civil society under the rule of law.

You may find after this sync that the stated goals of mass surveillance in public spaces in both jurisdictions are the same; that is, to preserve public safety and support law enforcement. You may generally find that the outcomes for law-abiding citizens do not differ, at least not in the short run. The methods in both systems use cameras and video processing technology. In the case of suspected wrongdoing, where facial recognition is applied, the technologies and methods are in fact the same. The differences in law enforcement methods when infractions are detected and the processes for redress afforded to offenders may seem to be different, prima facie, but are they? Did you find yourself asking whether having points deducted from a social credit score differs from being issued a speeding ticket or traffic fine from an automated video record processing system, which we accept without question, or at least as a matter of settled law?

Sync 2: Public surveillance

You should allow around 30 minutes for this activity.

Undertake some independent research to explore the use of mass surveillance in China and the UK, noting especially its use in China for its Social Credit System. You should also note the comprehensive scope of the data gathered by the Chinese government. While avoiding political judgement, contrast the approach of China with that of the UK regarding access to justice for susptected offenders, individual freedons, the role of government, and the possible benefits and dangers involved in the continuum of trust in complex organisational and technological systems.

PREDICTIVE ANALYTICS IN POLICING

Crime incident data has been used to build predictive models for the times and conditions under which crimes have been known to occur. The Los Angeles Police Department in the US state of California and the Police Department of Kent in the UK ran trials of such a model, implementing epidemic-type aftershock sequence forecasting originally used to predict the spatial distribution and timings of earthquake aftershocks. The models allowed dynamic adjustment of parameters using various methods, including randomising inputs, to support the generation of predictions for crime occurrence. The predictions enabled the police departments involved to achieve up to a 7.4% reduction in crime volume as a function of patrol time.[8] Such results enabled more effective deployment of limited personnel, held as an indication of the promise of predictive analytics in improving law enforcement effectiveness.

OPEN DATA

The availability of large data sets for the public to access, develop applications, and re-publish is commonly known as Open Data. While a single data set may be a small silo of data, complex applications involving the mixing and cross-referencing of multiple data sets rise to a level of complexity to be called Big Data applications.

Big Data as Open Data

One example of a successful Big Data initiative, referred to in Chapter 4, is DoNotPay,[9] a company started by Stanford University law student Joshua Browder. Originally more of an expert system type of AI application, DoNotPay expanded into travel fare optimisation, in which subscribers could register for real-time monitoring of price fluctuations for already-booked tickets, and have the option to be notified and instantly accept an automatic rebooking to a lower-priced ticket with a refund of the difference if available and if booking rules permit. DoNotPay's technology, monitoring real-time feeds, applying a set of relatively complex rules and regulations and then passing on savings to the customer,[10] is held up as a case study of using Open Data to deliver value to consumers in an area with complex laws and regulations.

8 G. O. Mohler, M. B. Short, Sean Malinowski, Mark Johnson, G. E. Tita, Andrea L. Bertozzi and P. J. Brantingham, 'Randomized Controlled Field Trials of Predictive Policing' (2016) *Journal of the American Statistical Association* <https://amstat.tandfonline.com/doi/full/10.1080/01621459.2015.1077710>

9 DoNotPay website <https://donotpay.com/about/> accessed 26 September 2025.

10 'When Big Data Meets Big Law' (*Legal Insights Europe*, 20 September 2019) <https://blogs.thomsonreuters.com/legal-uk/2019/09/20/when-big-data-meets-big-law/> accessed 2 January 2026.

Open Data is also concerned with the availability of legal texts to the public, in particular codes, statutes, regulations, edicts, and judicial rulings. Article 2(4) of the Bern Convention for the Protection of Literary and Artistic Works[11] places the status of such texts at the discretion of the signatories to the Convention. Most have placed them in the public domain, while the UK has them under Crown Copyright, and some Commonwealth countries have similar regimes in place, with latitude for use while respecting the copyrights.

Attempts have been made in certain jurisdictions to make it illegal for texts to be republished by individuals as a means of ensuring access to those texts and equal access to justice, conflicting sometimes with the interests of legal publishers. If you are interested in this topic, you might want to read the ruling by the US Supreme Court in *Georgia v. Public.Resource.Org, Inc.*[12]

There are ongoing initiatives in many jurisdictions by citizens and non-profits, in cooperation with government, to digitise legislation and the proceedings of legislative bodies (known as Hansard in Commonwealth jurisdictions) that are not already in electronic form. While apparently a simple task, only the texts from recent decades are available, often converted from word processing formats and Adobe Portable Document Format (PDF). These formats, while optimised for the purpose of printing on paper, are poor starting places in practice for making those texts accessible in Big Data and NLP contexts, as they are created not with the structure of the text as the primary objective, but rather with the appearance of the text. Workers must often spend significant time manually cleaning such texts or must rely on the help of programmers to write text-filtering software that will not inadvertently destroy content during conversion.

Sync 3: Law as Open Data

You should allow around 30 minutes for this activity.

Briefly examine the online Hansard systems of the UK Parliament at Westminster, and then of a Commonwealth or former Commonwealth jurisdiction like Singapore or Hong Kong. Note the available downloadable text

11 'Berne Convention Texts at the World Intellectual Property Organization' <https://www.wipo.int/treaties/en/ip/berne/>

12 *Georgia v. Public.Resource.Org, Inc.* <https://www.supremecourt.gov/opinions/19pdf/18-1150_7m58.pdf> accessed 2 January 2026.

formats, search facilities, and the presence or absence of tools like an API (application programming interface) for software developers to use in building automated interactions and applications to interact with the Hansard system.

You will be able to recognise an API where there is documentation in a section possibly titled "For Developers", with terms such as REST and references to toolkits compatible with common programming languages such as JavaScript, Java, Python, and PHP.[13]

Consider the following:

- How far back in time do the Hansard texts online reach?
- Do the downloads or searches yield formats suitable for computer systems and software developers to work with in developing new applications—for instance, XML, JSON, and plain text formats—or do they exclusively provide word processing files like Word or formatted print formats like PDF?
- What challenges can you see with limited availability of texts when attempting to build certain applications?

Your answers to this sync will vary depending upon which jurisdictions you have researched. In terms of the challenges faced, it may help you to draw an analogy with the situation of physically working in a legal library when most of the texts are not available.

LAWYERS AND CLIENTS

Tools in legal practice for tracking work and time can vary from a collection of spreadsheets and isolated pockets of automation to integrated practice management suites with linkages to office automation tools, specialised time reporting, and client portal software. More sophisticated, cloud-enabled offerings allow clients to access specific project details and documents, and see time spent, offering the client control in managing the expense in collaboration with the lawyer(s) working with them on specific matters.

In larger firms, tools to automate and collect practice data can support multiple objectives related to law firm competitiveness; for

13 See the 'UK's Hansard API' <https://api.parliament.uk/historic-hansard/api> accessed 25 September 2025.

example, ensuring teams meet their targets for billable hours or ensuring the firm is achieving the right mix of client work in designated practice areas. More sophisticated tools help law firm partners manage their contacts; for example, to build wider relationships across different parts of the same client organisation, and to deliver higher-value service when practice management tools highlight cross-region client relationships and work being done in other locales. The same tools also support knowledge exchange and access to expertise in larger and/ or national and international law firms beyond the one department or office, when practice management data is processed with the right analytic tools. For example, a partner in a law firm may receive instructions on a new matter from the marketing department of a large international manufacturing firm. They may then be able to use analytical tools to identify that another partner is working with a different part of the firm based in a different jurisdiction on an issue where there is the opportunity to share relevant information.

USE OF ANALYTICS IN DISCOVERY AND COMPLIANCE

Large bodies of documentation can be instrumental in determining the path a lawyer may take when handling a matter. If the documentation is in a machine-readable form and formatted to allow human-supported annotation and possible enrichment with additional data sources, NLP and machine learning techniques can be applied using analytic tools that are now becoming more available and accessible to smaller firms and individual practitioners.

Language-based analytic tools consuming text as Big Data can, for instance, identify parties of interest or those affected by specific events. Visualisation tools showing connections or common occurrence of certain parties, concepts, or items across a large body of documents can cut down discovery time drastically, sometimes limited only by the amount of computing resources available.

For organisations with an obligation to protect consumers from certain harms, analytic tools monitoring news and court claims may alert them to a possible issue with their products or services and prevent possibly costly liability claims that could result. An illustrative case can be found in a case concerning Fosamax, by the pharmaceutical company Merck. There were, according to the case history, a substantial number of reports of adverse drug interactions, such that the company had an obligation to issue a warning. The ruling against

Merck was based on testimony from a data scientist noting the presence of the reports, and the ability to have known of those reports had Merck used certain Big Data sources and descriptive analytic tools to process and deliver reports on those interactions.[14]

BIG DATA AND ANALYTICS TO INCREASE ACCESS TO JUSTICE

In a society that espouses the rule of law, access to means by which to settle disputes, whether through litigation or arbitration or other procedures mandated under the law, is of primary importance for the functioning of the system. This problem of access to justice is characterised by three conditions:

1. *Complex processes involve significant paperwork* to file for even the simplest of complaints at the lowest levels of the justice system, making necessary the services of legal professionals and increasing the expense for small claims. It clearly can be seen that in some cases, the expense to take action may exceed the value of the possible remedy, effectively subordinating justice to a purely economic calculation for the parties. The aggrieved party must decide whether it is worth pursuing the matter. The defendant in some cases will not be deterred from acting badly or contrary to the law.
2. *The process of adjudication is complex*, designed to ensure correctness and adherence to the letter of the law, if not the spirit. The process involves in many cases several steps from beginning a claim through perhaps multiple hearings before a trial or mandatory mediation. Again, the economic costs associated with the time come into the calculus applied by the parties.
3. *The reality in the justice system is one of increasing caseloads*, such that the complex process as discussed in point 2 are drawn out, in some cases creating additional hardship for those seeking justice.

A proposal for the use of predictive analytics as one possible way to address this problem has been made, described in popular media[15] and

14 'How Big Data is Impacting the Legal World' <https://e27.co/how-big-data-is-impacting-the-legal-world-20190408/> accessed 27 September 2025.

15 Bernard Marr, 'The Future of Lawyers: Legal Tech, AI, Big Data and Online Courts' (*Forbes*, 17 January 2020) <https://www.forbes.com/sites/bernardmarr/2020/01/17/the-future-of-lawyers-legal-tech-ai-big-data-and-online-courts/> accessed 2 January 2026.

the writings of Richard Susskind,[16] a leading thinker on the digital transformation of law. In the proposal, complaints may be filed using online tools, which will take the facts of the complaint as a set of data that may be assessed using predictive analytics. The analytics will have access to a set of judgments and settlements data from similar cases, making a prediction as to the likely outcome if the complaint were to proceed as usual through the judicial system to its conclusion. The parties, if they accept the recommended result, agree to be bound by the predicted outcome as the terms of the settlement, and the matter is thus closed.

It can be argued that such a system, if implemented, would speed claims through the system, reducing or eliminating the economic burden that the existing process imposes in terms of required funds, advice, and time, making access to justice more equal for all under the law.

The risks of Big Data

As with many technology developments, Big Data offers attractive benefits when supporting advanced analytics as we have described. We can also look forward to further innovations as applications built on the foundations of Big Data sets gain sophistication and reliability. However, Big Data also entails risks, as we will explore in this section.

DATA COLLECTION

It is now possible for anyone with the inclination and some basic investment to collect rapidly significant volumes of data. There are already diminishingly low barriers to entry in getting started with the necessary tools. Indiscriminate collection is indeed possible, creating volumes of data that can easily exceed any organisation's aspirations to manage with intention and care. While some may argue that such an approach may lead to serendipitous opportunities, it can also lead to exceeding the boundaries of granted authority or permission, especially when gathering data from persons giving explicit consent in terms of service agreements and other legal contracts, or when granting authority to the entity collecting data under regulations or statute.

16 Richard Susskind, *Online Courts and the Future of Justice* (OUP 2019).

Lawyers working with organisations collecting Big Data can serve their clients well by offering guidelines and reviewing data collection agreements to confirm that they comply with relevant laws, ensuring that clients are aware of the limits and consequences of non-compliance in the relevant jurisdictions.

DATA CUSTODY, CLOUD COMPUTING RESOURCES AND REGULATORY RISK

Big Data necessarily is large in volume, can grow rapidly and may in some cases be exploited for a range of unspecified purposes different from those originally intended during collection. It is imperative, therefore, that data containing confidential facts and personally identifiable information (PII) be handled with adequate care from the moment of acquisition, with clear procedures and safeguards for its lifetime in the organisation's care, from transport, storage, retrieval, processing, delivery, and use to disposal.

Aspects of network and physical computing infrastructure security that apply to computing environments also apply to those hosting Big Data operations. Given the favourable economics of cloud computing, much Big Data is stored in online, on-demand infrastructure, prompting concerns over agreements with cloud computing providers to ensure compliance with regulations, adequate security, and safe handling of data in those environments.

Major cloud computing providers such as Amazon Web Services, Google Cloud Platform, and Microsoft Azure have developed detailed understandings of the requirements for effective, safe computing operations in cloud environments. Each provider, as a competitive act, fields a range of features and tools to ensure compliance by default for regulatory standards such as the US Health Insurance Portability and Accountability Act (HIPAA), the UK Data Protection Act 2018, and the EU General Data Privacy Regulation (GDPR). We will examine some of these regulations in a later section of this chapter.

Smaller providers, chosen for specific advantages of service level, features or price, are building similar programs as the hosting space matures. Their stated policies and practices for protections may require more detailed review and advice from lawyers depending on client goals, risk profiles, and jurisdictional requirements.

You should have found a nearly uniform set of statements in various forms respecting customer ownership of data and the undertaking of the hosting providers not to disclose or expose customer data

Sync 4: Cloud provider data privacy and compliance

You should allow around 30 minutes for this activity.

Perform an internet search for the data privacy and compliance pages for the major cloud hosting providers. Familiarise yourself with the policies and technical support offerings of each provider, noting similarities and differences. Consider the following questions:

- What are the positions each provider takes with respect to ownership of data stored in the respective cloud environments?
- What responsibilities are outlined for the cloud provider with regard to security of data stored in the cloud, and what are those of the customer?
- What items would you take as starting points for discussing data privacy compliance with a client who approaches you for advice in looking to manage the risk for a cloud-hosted online service offering?

under any circumstances unless compelled to do so to comply with applicable law or investigations by law enforcement. Certain cloud providers go on to state the general compliance and support in their infrastructure offerings for customers needing to run applications in certain domains such as financial services or healthcare, having to comply with additional regulations such as PCI (Payment Card Industry Data Security Standard) or HIPAA. It is important to note that these offerings are merely tools, and they require active selection, setup, and review by competent technologists and reviewers in real-world applications.

DATA PROCESSING AND SECURITY

The analytic tools that are developed to process Big Data sets, together with the policies and procedures used to manage operation of those tools, are clear areas of concern for security during processing. Both internal and third-party suppliers of tools and services should be required to define, together with the client, a set of actionable, auditable processes to ensure not only the satisfaction of business objectives but also that those processes do not violate regulatory requirements or ethical standards in the relevant jurisdictions.

Another concern in data processing is the safeguards put in place around intermediate forms of data as they are transformed from raw input into working forms that may involve enriching the original data with lookups from reference sources like databases of names, addresses, or product catalogue data. To understand this concept of intermediate forms, consider a website that tracks its visitors with a website cookie, a code unique to that web browser that is generated and stored on the browser at a website provider's request. The cookie is to be made accessible to that same website's provider in the user's future interactions using that web browser. With anonymous visitors, repeat visitors consenting to cookie use are tracked, but not necessarily identifiable using this mechanism. Cookies, with their limitations, form the basis for digital marketing and targeted online advertisements as well as product recommendations. Because of website cookies, these capabilities are available even in the absence of a user account on a given website.

When a visitor finally registers or logs into that website with specific credentials and consents to creating and completing a user record, the activity information prior to that registration or login already collected on the web server platform is now available to the provider together with the PII provided during registration, significantly enhancing the ability of the website provider to analyse the behaviour of the individual and to tailor interaction with the site and its services. The cookie data can be linked using simple data processing tools to the PII provided by the user, and it is typically held in that intermediate form in memory on a running system. Meant to be purged once a specific processing activity is completed, it is safe as long as it is protected against unauthorised outside access and is not stored in unencrypted form on a disk or other storage medium.

Some operations are computationally expensive and may involve large amounts of intermediate data that needs to be retrieved and held in working storage. Although most of these operations are detailed procedures in the IT and data management domain of expertise, a lawyer may serve a client engaging in such activities by ensuring awareness of these issues. They may also need to offer guidance to ensure that the organisation is taking sufficient actions to ensure compliance with privacy and data protection regulations even during complex processing protocols.

CONTENT PUBLISHING, PRIVACY, AND SECURITY

Cloud computing services with a heavy content delivery component in their offerings, notably websites and social media networks, often rely on a large body of user-contributed, user-owned content (e.g. blog posts, videos, comments on online forums). As these services have grown and matured, privacy and content ownership considerations have come to the fore, with users demanding significant control and accountability from providers for content visibility, sharing policies, and the permitted uses of the content.

Following the 2016 US presidential election, with the growing debate over truth in media and the posts of elected public officials, came calls on one side to regulate the social media posts of figures like the US president, who was notorious for posts that could be deemed inflammatory and misleading. When the president disputed the 2020 elections, this raised arguments over the merits of his efforts and those of his legal team and his supporters on social media, with those with more extreme views choosing alternative platforms. A riot at the US Capitol on 6 January 2021 and the subsequent activities of the president and his supporters led to the deactivation of his primary social media accounts on the social media service Twitter,[17] and the social media network Parler being taken offline by Amazon Web Services, Parler's hosting provider.[18]

News accounts and blog posts in the days after the takedown of Parler showed that technically skilled individuals were able to exploit a fundamental security flaw in Parler's login system to save a large portion of the user content posted to the service. Included in this body of content were videos and images posted by the insurrectionists who entered the US Capitol illegally, boasting of their exploits, and attempting to rally others in the attempt to overturn the results of the 2020 presidential election.[19]

The incident illustrates several key points regarding privacy and data in these contexts:

- *Service providers have obligations to protect user data.* Operators of such services must take care to ensure that their system implemen-

17 N. Tiku, T. Romm and C. Timberg, 'Twitter Bans Trump's Account, Citing Risk of Further Violence' (*Washington Post*, 8 January 2021) <https://www.washingtonpost.com/technology/2021/01/08/twitter-trump-dorsey/> accessed 2 January 2026.

18 T. Romm and R. Lerman, 'Amazon Suspends Parler, Taking Pro-Trump Site Offline Indefinitely' (*Washington Post*, 11 January 2021) <https://www.washingtonpost.com/technology/2021/01/09/amazon-parler-suspension/> accessed 2 January 2026.

19 WIRED, 'This Site Posted Every Face from Parler's Capitol Hill Insurrection Videos' (*Ars Technica*, 23 January 2021) <https://arstechnica.com/tech-policy/2021/01/this-site-posted-every-face-from-parlers-capitol-hill-insurrection-videos/> accessed 30 April 2021.

tations are fit for purpose and tested for safety. Although the individuals who compromised protected data and engaged in downloading it may have been violating terms of service and possibly copyright regulations, there was also an apparent failure on the part of the service provider to put in place basic protections.

- *Hosting providers exercise wide discretion when service providers and end users engage in activities violating service terms.* Hosting providers have terms of service that often provide them with a wide latitude in deciding whether to continue or terminate services in matters involving law enforcement. There is limited recourse for the individuals using those hosting services in the case of a dispute.
- *Media posted on content services and social networks may be used for unintended purposes if safety controls fail.* Concerned individuals who downloaded the Parler data applied Big Data analytic techniques to isolate images of the rioters' faces and subsequently posted them to websites in efforts to support investigators' efforts to identify and charge those who participated in the riot. Other individuals who came into possession of the data applied NLP techniques to identify topics of concern and possible targets for further violence in the discussion data.

Sync 5: Conflicting concerns in online breaches of Big Data

You should allow around 30 minutes for this activity.

Consider the case of Parler and its role as an online service and unintended source of data for concerned citizens and law enforcement attempting to bring rioters to justice following the US Capitol riot and insurrection of 6 January 2021. Consider the following questions:

- What possible liabilities with misuse of customer data might Parler have faced, assuming its terms of service (no longer online as of the writing of this text) maintained ownership of user content with its users?
- What possible actions for violations of user data regulations did the concerned citizens potentially face because of their possible use of the data set from Parler?
- What are the ethical considerations when there is data that is unwittingly made publicly available for download, distributed through third-party hosts, of disputable provenance, when there are legitimate law enforcement aims, concerned citizens technically capable and willing to help, and content owners and service providers who exercise varying degrees

of discretion, interpretations of personal responsibility, and physical control of the data in question?

- What considerations would you need to raise if you were advising investigators or prosecution teams gathering evidence to prosecute the Capitol insurrectionists, given the means by which some of these items of evidence were obtained?

Given the politically and culturally charged nature of this incident, you may have found yourself in the first moments of the exercise applying your personal reaction to the questions. Perhaps you reacted positively to the ingenuity and application of skills on the part of the concerned citizens to exploit the data for a subjectively judged positive outcome. Perhaps you jumped straight to the question about the ethics and legality of downloading a publicly accessible but not licensed data set. These are all questions you may encounter as a digital lawyer. Always challenge yourself to clarify your reasoning as you examine the facts surrounding every question, seeing especially the many grey areas where technology makes things possible, but not always lawful nor ethical.

UNANTICIPATED OUTCOMES APPLYING ANALYTICS TO BIG DATA

One of the benefits of Big Data with the analytic tools and practices that have developed is the uncovering of unforeseen facts, often reverently termed "insights" in popular parlance. Insights gained and applied, in the right context, are the precursors for good decisions and the resulting activities that convey advantage to the individuals and organisations that acquire them.

An unanticipated arrival

At the intersection of online and offline commerce, combining online browsing records with in-store buying behaviours revealed through loyalty and rewards card incentive programmes, retailers have built some of the largest data collection, management, and analysis programmes, starting with data warehouses in the 1990s. Those systems have evolved in complexity from descriptive analytics built on large (for the time) data snapshots to prescriptive analytics built on Big Data today. We have already remarked on the scale of the data operations at the retailer Walmart. It should be understood as a matter of course that competitors engage in similar efforts, with similar goals, challenges, and risks.

An incident that received substantial media attention involved Target, a major global retailer headquartered in the United States. As described in detailed accounts published in the *New York Times*[20] and *Forbes*,[21] the marketing group at Target, working with in-house analytics teams, developed a predictive analytic model that identified customers who had a high probably of having entered the second trimester of pregnancy, based solely on their recent purchasing behaviour in Target stores and online at Target.com, their e-commerce website. The model was robust enough in its predictions that the marketing organisation incorporated it into a program to send coupons to such customers to establish and reinforce a habit of buying. According to the account, the buying of certain items in the second trimester of pregnancy also predicted continued purchasing following delivery of the child and beyond.

Although Target took steps to prevent what would appear to the customer to be an invasion of privacy by sending coupons for other, unrelated items and never using messages revealing its purpose, a father made a complaint in person to a manager in a Target store when his teenage daughter was sent coupons for maternity wear and nursery accoutrements. The news accounts concluded by reporting that following a string of apologetic communications from the father, it came to light that the daughter was, in fact, pregnant.

Together with frequently occurring news accounts of online tracking by technology and advertising firms, and calls for the regulation of tracking, data custody, and the permitted applications of such data with powerful analytic tools, it is easy to see the wide range of legal and ethical concerns around customer privacy that follow.

This is an evolving area of law where technology innovation, commercial opportunity, and user appetite far outpace collective understanding in society. To appeal to societal norms that either do not exist

20 Charles Duhigg, 'How Companies Learn Your Secrets' (*New York Times Magazine*, 16 February 2012) <https://www.nytimes.com/2012/02/19/magazine/shopping-habits.html> accessed 2 January 2026.

21 Kashmir Hill, 'How Target Figured Out a Teen Girl Was Pregnant before Her Father Did' (*Forbes*, 16 February 2012) <https://www.forbes.com/sites/kashmirhill/2012/02/16/how-target-figured-out-a-teen-girl-was-pregnant-before-her-father-did/> accessed 2 January 2026.

or which are being shattered by the continued evolution of technology would be premature and certainly an exercise in futility. A lawyer fielding calls for advice in this area would certainly be well-served to read widely regarding emerging privacy issues and legislation and to cultivate working relationships with technical experts who may be consulted for understanding in this fluid area.

BIAS IN ANALYTIC MODELS

Facial recognition systems are often used to identify possible suspects in law enforcement incidents. These systems use algorithms trained on Big Data sets consisting of faces that allow the algorithm to develop its model for identifying a person and expressing a level of probability that the identification is correct. Researchers at the Massachusetts Institute of Technology and Microsoft Research showed that the under-representation of Black and Asian faces in training sets caused systems trained with those data to be less capable of correctly identifying persons or indicating their genders. A report by the US National Institute of Standards and Technology (NIST) also indicated that algorithms by vendors submitted for testing had significant difficulty identifying individuals of Asian and African descent, and least difficulty with faces from individuals of Eastern European descent.[22]

In June 2020, the *New York Times* reported the first documented and publicised case in which a person was arrested for a crime he did not commit, due to a false positive identification made by a facial recognition system.[23] According to the account from Wayne County, Michigan (US), despite the fact that photos taken from surveillance footage at the scene of a theft did not appear to match the face of the suspect, law enforcement officers decided to arrest the suspect, who was a Black man. Observers noted that a possible escalation in the situation, compounded by distrust of law enforcement[24] and mistaken identity,

22 Patrick Grother, Mei Ngan and Kayee Hanaoka, 'Face Recognition Vendor Test (FRVT) Part 3: Demographic Effects', *NISTIR 8280* (National Institute of Standards and Technology, 2019) <https://doi.org/10.6028/NIST.IR.8280>

23 Kashmir Hill, 'Wrongfully Accused by an Algorithm' (*New York Times*, 24 June 2020) <https://www.nytimes.com/2020/06/24/technology/facial-recognition-arrest.html> accessed 2 January 2026.

24 The incident in Wayne County occurred just weeks after the death of George Floyd, an incident which triggered massive, sometimes violent protests alleging systemic racism in law enforcement around the United States that lasted for weeks, making racial inequality and justice under the law a critical issue in the 2020 national election in that country.

could have resulted in highly undesirable (if not fatal) outcomes had the suspect not yielded and cooperated.

Sync 6: Tools in criminal justice

You should allow around 15 minutes for this activity.

Some jurisdictions currently use tools to assist judges in assessing the eligibility of alleged criminals for bail based on several criteria, including an assessment of flight risk (how likely the individual is to attempt to leave the country before their hearing). These tools provide judges struggling with increasingly large caseloads with consistent guidelines for evaluating bail eligibility, which are intended to remove bias and support impartiality. While such tools might be programmed with a reasonable freedom from bias, the data used to train an algorithm implementing such an evaluation might reflect the fact that minority groups are more likely to be arrested, leaving those groups at a disadvantage when requesting bail.[25]

- What are the possible sources of bias that could be found in data sets used to train systems recommending decisions for bail granted to alleged criminals?
- What precautions must be taken by legislatures and courts to ensure that the effects of bias in such automated tools can be recognised, and what guidelines must be issued to give judges necessary latitude when deciding courses of action prior to trial?

You may have found yourself laying the onus of ensuring freedom from bias in training data squarely on the technology provider. While technologists have methods and tools for ensuring that their tools and models are checked and reasonably guard against certain forms of bias, those tools and models are only as good as the information and knowledge (especially of bias) available to their creators. A fruitful dialogue between technologists and jurists evaluating or designing such tools would also seek actively for and incorporate knowledge from a wider range of experts and expertise, going beyond crime and criminal court statistics to take in and give weight to the findings of social scientists, specialists in corrections, and advocates for access to justice.

25 Justia, 'Bail Algorithms' (n.d.) <https://www.justia.com/criminal/bail-bonds/bail-algorithms/> accessed 2 January 2026.

Digital lawyering skills: problem-finding and problem-solving

In this chapter you have considered a range of scenarios and issues, including those discussed in Sync 5. All of these require a digital lawyer to be able to both problem-find and problem-solve. The term "problem-finding" refers to having the vision and insight to be able to anticipate and identify potential problems before going on to frame them in a way which enables you to seek appropriate and workable preventive solutions.

Law students usually spend a considerable amount of time preparing answers to problem-style questions, replicating the types of scenarios that may arise when advising a client in practice. These are very helpful in assisting you to think about and apply the content of the law. However, they are often very focused on a specific topic and do not factor in the many variables that arise in reality.

Other ways to develop your abilities to problem-find and problem-solve could include looking for volunteer opportunities with law clinics or similar organisations, becoming involved in events such as hackathons, and even playing board games and puzzles.

Regulation and Compliance for Big Data

Having examined in brief a few of the possibilities of Big Data in application and the risks that its use and misuse with modern analytics technology may raise, we now turn to an introduction of the characteristics of regulatory regimes for data, data processing, and privacy.

GDPR

Regulation (EU) 2016/679 of the European Parliament, known commonly as the General Data Protection Regulation (GDPR), provides for the protection of rights related to the data concerning individuals. We provide here only a summary of the regulatory points sufficient to further our discussion of Big Data. You are, of course, warmly invited to download and read the regulation for deeper understanding.[26]

26 The text of the GDPR can be found at <https://eur-lex.europa.eu/eli/reg/2016/679/oj>

Rights of the individual

The GDPR first defines and mandates protection of specific rights of the data subject; that is, of the person identifiable from the data or to whom the data pertains. These rights include:

- *Right of information.* Individuals must be informed about data collection activities, the purposes for which the data is collected and processed, and the ways and duration of time the data will be kept and shared with other parties.
- *Right of access.* A person must be given access to their personal data and information regarding how that data is processed, including how it is obtained, the purpose of the processing, and to whom the data is shared.
- *Right of rectification.* Individuals have the right to have inaccurate personal data rectified, or completed if it is incomplete.
- *Right of erasure.* Individuals can request that organisations erase data pertaining to them, on any number of grounds defined in the GDPR. This was originally more broadly defined in a "Right to Be Forgotten", but that provision was changed to the Right of Erasure in the version of the GDPR adopted by the EU Parliament in 2016.
- *Right of portability.* To comply, data controllers (e.g. online services) must provide data to individuals when requested in structured, commonly used electronic formats. It would not, therefore, be acceptable to comply with a request for personal information by sending a bulky set of paper printouts, thereby placing a burden on the individual requester to have to input the information into a computer, whether for further personal use or to audit the activities of the online service provider.
- *Right to restrict processing.* The GDPR provides that individuals must be able to restrict the ways in which data controllers process their personal information, whether for sales, marketing or non-service-related activities. Exceptions include situations where the processing is necessary in order to provide the service in question, legal compliance, or activities required in the public interest.
- *Right to object.* Individuals must be informed of processing activities undertaken with their data and to be given methods to object with reasonable timeliness and practicability.

Obligations of the data controller and processor

The GDPR also defines specific responsibilities for the content provider, hosting provider, or other entity providing services with custody of data pertaining to individuals. This individual or organisation is known as the data controller or, in the case of someone providing processing services (in-house or outsourced), the processor.

- *Pseudonymisation.* Data that is to be on a disk, tape, or other storage medium (i.e. stored "at rest") must have PII modified so that it is not readable without a separate piece of data that is not stored together with the data in question, such as an encryption key. This is to ensure that records are not readily able to be connected to individuals. Instead of scrambling records with encryption, some implementations of this measure issue a string of letters and numbers, known as a token, with a secure lookup facility to provide the corresponding, de-tokenised data from another system that stores the PII in a securely encrypted form.
- *Records of processing.* Data processors are required to document the procedures for processing personal data, as well as the identifying information for all those involved in processing and delivering processed information. Depending on the EU country implementing the GDPR, other items, such as the effective and end dates of the documented procedures, safeguards and security measures to be taken, must also be documented.
- *Personal data security.* Controllers and processors of personal information must notify the individuals or controllers, respectively, within 72 hours after detecting a security breach in which readable personally identifying data is leaked.
- *Data protection officer.* Every organisation involved in controlling or processing data must appoint a member of staff or a qualified contractor who can assist the controller or processor in their compliance with the regulation.

It can be seen from the foregoing description of the GDPR stipulations (also summarised in Figure 6.4) that a comprehensive effort to understand the scope of data under the control and processing of an organisation is necessary to be fully compliant with the regulation.

Other jurisdictions have varying levels of data privacy regulation, sometimes very limited in scope. As students and new lawyers advance in training, they should take care to familiarise themselves with the

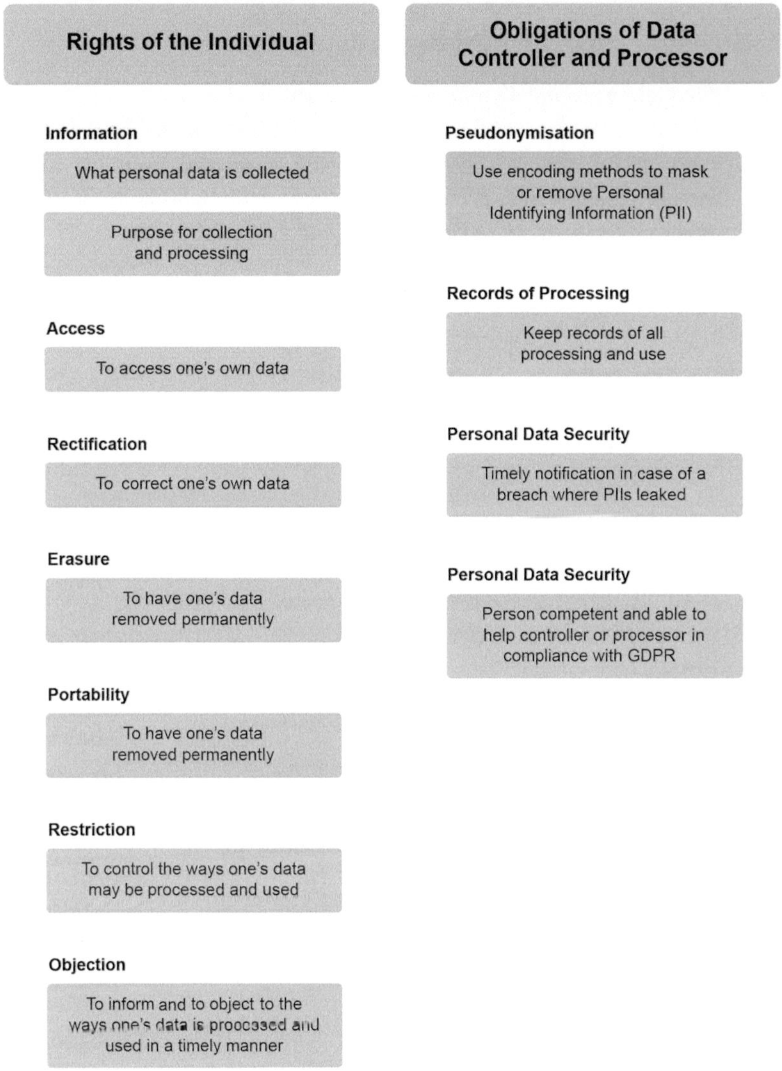

Figure 6.4 Diagram of individual rights under GDPR

relevant privacy regulations and existing enforcement practices in the jurisdictions where they practise. Some, like certain US states, do not necessarily have the same level of protections. California has regulations based on opting out of practices, as opposed to the mandated regulation of the GDPR. At a national level, only health-related records are protected under HIPAA.

Sync 7: Post-Brexit data protection

You should allow around 45 minutes for this activity.

With the completion of the UK's withdrawal from the European Union, the question of the applicability of the GDPR is important for those operating online services and data-driven businesses in the now-separated UK and those serving customers and subscribers in the European Union.

Review the UK GDPR guidelines at the Information Commissioner's Office website: <https://ico.org.uk/for-organisations/guide-to-data-protection/guide-to-the-general-data-protection-regulation-gdpr/>

Note the similarities between the UK GDPR and the EU version, including the differences for law enforcement and intelligence services processing in the UK, as well as the considerations for data flowing over networks in either direction between the UK and EU.

You will likely find that the similarities between the two GDPR versions make them in principle the same, but that terms for extraterritorial application of the regulation complicate understanding when they do differ. Another area where you may have some difficulty is with personal data inextricably linked or embedded in other application data. There are yet to be cases to settle the definition under law of inextricable data in processing. Processors and custodians may not in practice remove or obfuscate personal data in cases where it is not economically feasible, or simply impossible in some physical way; for example, when doing so will corrupt or destroy the files containing the PII and data in question.

Big Data driving changes in law practice

Law practice has been traditionally slow to adopt digital technology beyond local office and network productivity tools, such as an electronic system for organising information about clients. In an article titled "Why Is Law So Slow to Use Data?", Mark Cohen, a lawyer and leader of a global non-profit exploring and promoting digital lawyering, discussed the prevalence of an attitude of exceptionalism in the legal profession which leaves the legal profession, in his words, "a data wasteland in the digital era".[27] Professional exceptionalism in law asserts that the accumulated experience of a single legal mind transcends mere mechanical actions by technology, leaning on vaguely defined notions of the "superiority" of the human mind, dismissing the need to embrace the change that technology brings. Contrary to its normal practice of demanding evidence, perhaps best exemplified in other disciplines like the sciences or entrepreneurship, some members of the legal profession have taken such positions without a basis in evidence and data.

As we have seen, Big Data, using well-chosen, well-implemented and well-fitted[28] models, allow many sectors and even certain aspects of the legal system to realise and deliver benefits to individuals and to society as a whole. The notion that data is the oil of the digital era, first introduced in an influential article in the *Economist*,[29] has even been borne out in the legal profession. Cloud computing, as we have seen in Chapter 3, has started to change the way lawyers can collaborate with colleagues and counterparties. Firms are now looking at ways to adopt and exploit Big Data management and analytic practices as they begin to see the possibilities and look to use them as competitive tools. It is not our purpose to judge whether such adoption is voluntary and advantage-seeking or, as the case may be, a shrewd act of self-preservation. A lawyer leading a practice certainly faces such a choice if they are not already an adopter.

In this section we will examine a few of the ways that Big Data is having significant impact on the practice of law.

DIGITISATION

As discussed in Chapter 2, the traditional image of a lawyer hard at work finds her at a desk amid stacked boxes of documents, poring over

27 M. A. Cohen, 'Why Is Law So Slow to Use Data?' (*Forbes*, 24 June 2019) <https://www.forbes.com/sites/markcohen1/2019/06/24/why-is-law-so-slow-to-use-data/> accessed 2 January 2026.

28 Machine learning techniques operate on computations that generate a function that when applied to inputs, matches, as close as possible, the data points that make up the example data in a training set. In these applications, there is allowance for a level of variance from the model, which still defines examples that are correct and accomplishes the goals for the model. When models are too specific, and become inaccurate because of extreme conditions in the data, the model is said to be over-fitted.

29 The Economist, 'The World's Most Valuable Resource Is No Longer Oil, but Data' (*The Economist*, 6 May 2017) <https://www.economist.com/leaders/2017/05/06/the-worlds-most-valuable-resource-is-no-longer-oil-but-data> accessed 2 January 2026.

casebooks, searching for precedents to use in forming an argument. The ability of larger firms, with the sheer size and wherewithal to keep deep benches of junior staff and associates, conferred on those organisations great practical advantages when competing for client business, conducting discovery, or assessing the risk at various stages of litigation. Digitisation of documents, through scanning, optical character recognition (OCR), and automated transcription, makes large bodies of documents available as data for NLP tools built with models suited for specific purposes, commonly employed in tools for technology assisted review (TAR), with functions including but not limited to search, classification, semantic analysis, and ontology construction.

ANALYTICS IN THE MODERN LAW FIRM PRACTICE

As firms collect data internally from past records, combining them with external sources both publicly and privately sourced, opportunities arise to ensure better outcomes through the judicious use of Big Data sets and analytics.

Big Data practices and maturing analytics offered as products now give lawyers access to case history data compiled from public sources. This data is sometimes enriched with the vendor's proprietary data offerings, together with a firm's own performance data, to assess the probability of success in acting on a matter; for example, whether a specific course of action in litigation based on the presiding judge or opposing counsel's track records in similar cases would indicate a reasonable probability of success. Naturally, such indicators could highlight unacceptable risks in litigation and would thus inform the firm to counsel the client to accept a negotiated settlement that would, in this data-driven assessment, be the best result.

Internally, firms may choose specific lawyers to handle certain types of cases based on recommendations or scoring based on past performance in similar matters. Other firms may combine risk assessments with the need to train junior lawyers to handle certain matters, ensuring that opportunities to develop experience can be taken and ensuring better outcomes for the client and the firm.

REPUTATION MANAGEMENT

With access to large bodies of case data aggregated and processed by legal data providers, firms can develop analyses of their performance in their specialty areas of practice, in some cases creating opportunities to highlight the firm's superior performance in marketing efforts, giving prospective clients greater confidence in their choice of representation. Reputation data and surveys are also useful for highlighting areas of improvement for a firm, whether in practice, client business development, or recruiting new talent for a firm's practice.

PRACTICE DEVELOPMENT

In the past, leaders in law firms focused efforts on new business development based on relationships and what their immediate networks showed for "market signal" (pieces of information indicating which way the market is heading). This practice was based on anecdotal information—arguably far from data-driven in the systematic sense. The same data sources that can be used for reputation management can also give indications of emerging new areas of business or areas in which a firm may invest more to support the needs of clients, anticipated with data.

FEE OPTIMISATION

Applications of Big Data and analytics in the modern law firm provide numerous opportunities to augment the value delivered to clients in the practice of fee optimisation:

- *Lower costs and efficiency.* Machine learning tools supported with Big Data can dramatically reduce the personnel and time required to conduct discovery, search and other traditionally labour-intensive tasks done by junior staff, associates, and paralegal personnel. Firms with large databases of practice metrics also can highlight the efficiencies in the execution of tasks together with the cost savings realised.
- *Focus on higher-value service.* Far from reducing billing, the efficiencies realised with Big Data and analytic tools support the application of fees to higher-value service, elevating the practice overall and enhancing experience, reputation and future ability to win, and service higher-value client business.
- *Visibility into billings and demonstrated value.* Modern practice management systems support a client portal with visibility into lawyer billings, updated at least daily, if not more frequently. When combined with reports tailored to the concerns of individual clients showing the increases in value realised with the firm through

judicious application of technology, firms not only can service higher-value business but can also demonstrate concretely to cost-conscious clients their effectiveness in doing so. This means they can address multiple concerns of cost, value of time billed, overall legal position, and business outcomes.

PREREQUISITES FOR SUCCESS

In this chapter we have introduced the concepts of Big Data and its interrelationship with analytics. We have examined general applications and more specialised applications in the legal profession and justice systems, as well as the risks, regulatory requirements, and ethical considerations that follow. It is important that we conclude with some points that a new digital lawyer should bear in mind in encountering and navigating the opportunities and challenges of Big Data.

Andrew McAffee and Erik Brynjolfsson, researchers from the Initiative on the Digital Economy at the MIT Sloan School of Management, discussed the challenges to effective use of Big Data and analytics in their *Harvard Business Review* piece "Big Data: The Management Revolution". They found that while technical challenges that come with the increasing volume, variety, and velocity of data were non-trivial, the way organisations made decisions, starting with the senior executive team, needed critical examination as a prerequisite in the transformation to data-driven practice. While not discounting the value of experience and intuition, they stressed the need for leaders to develop an ability to look at data with objectivity—the same objectivity that a lawyer would bring to evidence—and to develop a willingness to subordinate their experience and intuition to possible conclusions revealed in data. The willingness is best put into practice in a removal of what they termed the primacy of the HiPPO: the highest-paid person's opinion.[30]

Most legal firms believe that data-driven understanding and methods for managing legal issues are valuable, though the culture in the profession, education, and training have not matched that belief. Instead, prevalent attitudes and mindsets dividing the world into

30 Andrew McAffee and Erik Brynjolfsson, 'Big Data: The Management Revolution' (*Harvard Business Review*, 1 October 2012) <https://hbr.org/2012/10/big-data-the-management-revolution> accessed 2 January 2026.

"lawyers" and "non-lawyers", with clear distinctions in hierarchy and influence on firm policy and practices, have had profound effects on the profession's understanding and pursuit of data-driven practice.

McAffee and Brynjolfsson identify five key challenges for organisations seeking to transform themselves and benefit from data-driven practices.

- *Leadership.* For a data-driven practice to take root, leaders in a firm must not only have a vision for how to develop and grow their firm, a way to blend creative thought with action, but also a clear commitment to decision-making with data that takes best advantage of the new combination of objective results from data, experience, and intuition. For the legal profession, this type of organisational transformation at the level of the individual firm may well be the most difficult, testing leaders and their structures of governance.
- *Talent management.* Firms seeking to gain a competitive advantage with data will compete not only with peers in the legal profession for competent and talented professionals skilled in data science, but with the entire business sector, as the adoption of Big Data applications accelerates.[31]
- *Technology.* The volume, variety, and velocity of Big Data that we have highlighted several times as its defining characteristic poses unique challenges to IT departments. Law firms have not treated IT investments as strategic investments. Leaders in these firms must recognise the enablement that comes with strategic IT investment. They will benefit from study and consultation with professionals in other sectors who have gone through the process of digital transformation, developing frameworks and, more important, cultures for strategic IT investment and stewardship.
- *Decision-making.* Successful leaders effecting change will locate decision-making closest to problems in the organisation while supplying the broadest range of resources possible. They will encourage their colleagues to be problem-solvers with an openness to the information and experience across the organisation. A data-driven culture of decision-making will enhance such efforts, considering evidence objectively, alleviating scepticism and "not invented here"

31 Thomas H. Davenport and D. J. Patil, 'Data Scientist: The Sexiest Job of the 21st Century' (*Harvard Business Review*, 1 October 2012) <https://hbr.org/2012/10/data-scientist-the-sexiest-job-of-the-21st-century> accessed 2 January 2026.

behaviours (which do not value external ideas and influences) when confronted with approaches from far-flung colleagues in the firm who are effective strangers.
- *Company culture.* Asking the right questions and letting the data offer possibilities before asking for opinions may produce superior results to starting with advancing opinions or a HiPPO and then sending colleagues forth to gather supporting evidence.

The digital lawyer who has a clear understanding of the range of issues and concerns surrounding Big Data and its applications will be well-positioned to advise clients and to lead in data-driven legal practice. Operation based on information revealed in data is in direct line with the legal profession's tradition of objectivity and considered action based on interpretation of facts under the rule of law.

ADDITIONAL RESOURCES

Davenport TH, 'Analytics 3.0' (*Harvard Business Review*, 2013) <https://hbr.org/2013/12/analytics-30> accessed 1 December 2013.

'The Dictatorship of Data' (*MIT Technology Review*, n.d.) <https://www.technologyreview.com/2013/05/31/178263/the-dictatorship-of-data/> accessed 31 January 2021.

Duhigg C, 'How Companies Learn Your Secrets' (*New York Times Magazine*, 16 February 2012) <https://www.nytimes.com/2012/02/19/magazine/shopping-habits.html> accessed 2 January 2026.

Economist, 'The World's Most Valuable Resource Is No Longer Oil, but Data' (*Economist*, 6 May 2017) <https://www.economist.com/leaders/2017/05/06/the-worlds-most-valuable-resource-is-no-longer-oil-but-data> accessed 2 January 2026.

Gurin J, *Open Data Now* (McGraw-Hill Education 2014).

Król K and Zdonek D, 'Analytics Maturity Models: An Overview' (2020) 11(3) *Information* 142 <https://doi.org/10.3390/info11030142>

Manyika J and others, *Big Data: The Next Frontier for Innovation, Competition, and Productivity* (McKinsey Global Institute 2011).

Marr B, 'Really Big Data at Walmart: Real-Time Insights from Their 40+ Petabyte Data Cloud' (*Forbes*, n.d.) <https://www.forbes.com/

sites/bernardmarr/2017/01/23/really-big-data-at-walmart-real-time-insights-from-their-40-petabyte-data-cloud/> accessed 2 January 2021.

Mohler GO and others, 'Randomized Controlled Field Trials of Predictive Policing' (January 2016) *Journal of the American Statistical Association* <https://amstat.tandfonline.com/doi/full/10.1080/01621459.2015.1077710>

Staff CACM, 'Big Data' (2017) 60(6) *Commun. ACM* 24–5 <https://doi.org/10.1145/3079064>

Susskind R, *Online Courts and the Future of Justice* (OUP 2019).

'What Is China's Social Credit System and Why Is It Controversial?' (*South China Morning Post*, 2020) <https://www.scmp.com/economy/china-economy/article/3096090/what-chinas-social-credit-system-and-why-it-controversial> accessed 9 August 2020.

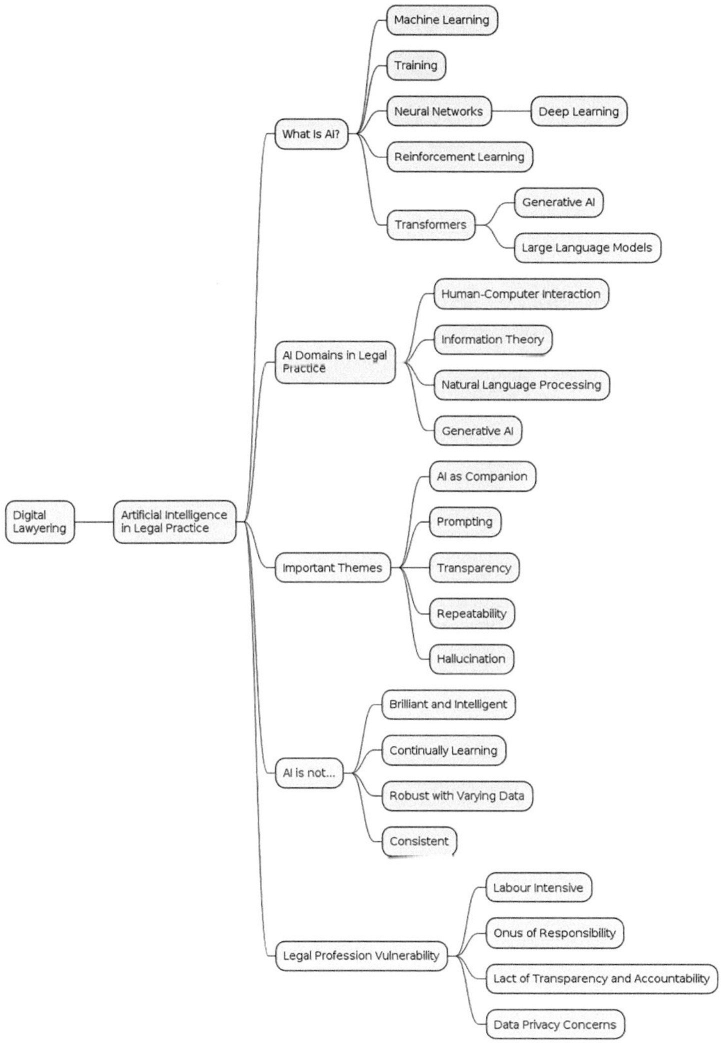

Mind Map 7.1a Chapter topics

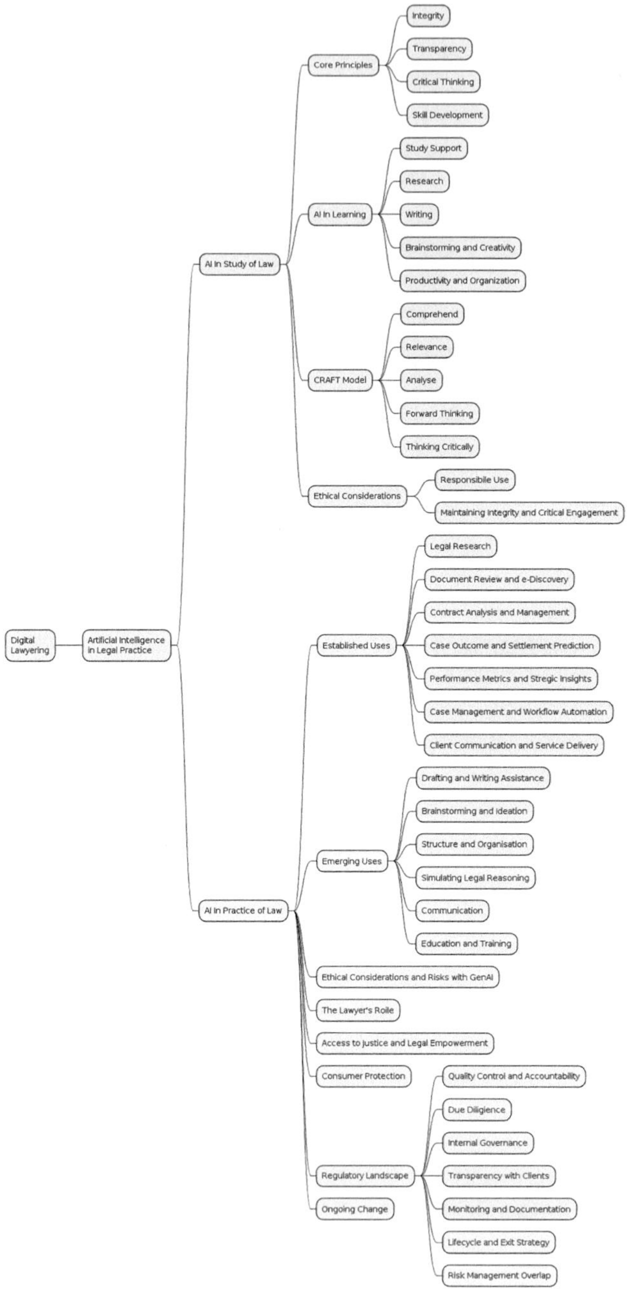

Mind Map 7.1b Chapter topics

7 Artificial Intelligence and Legal Practice

Ann Thanaraj and Terry Wong

Introduction

Human society approaches artificial intelligence (AI) with a combination of exuberant expectation, jaded disappointment and, in some quarters, paralysing existential fear. For over 50 years, since the early days of AI research, early pioneers and science fiction writers have alternately touted the imminent emergence of artificial general intelligence (AGI), or laughed at the seemingly quixotic efforts of dedicated technologists playing creator. In recent years, investors and marketing departments have joined the ongoing fray, sensing tremendous opportunity. Still others have continued serious, long-standing speculative inquiries and debates on frameworks for controlling AI development before it is too late to prevent an apocalyptic event fuelled by overabundant optimism and negligence. In the midst of this back-and-forth, with real promise emerging in the landscape of AI-powered tools, legal professionals must chart for themselves a forward-looking course, pragmatic yet open to possibility.

In this chapter, we examine ongoing developments in AI in the context of the legal profession and offer some perspectives and guidance that we have developed as educators and practitioners, both in law and technology.

Chapter hot spots

When reading this chapter, questions to think about include:

- What is the role of a human lawyer in the future, where systems built with AI undertake the basic discovery and retrieval of information that once kept lawyers gainfully employed in the hourly fee-for-service model?

DOI: 10.4324/9781003602323-7

- Can and should AI-driven systems do the work of negotiating and memorialising agreements between parties, eliminating the once-fundamental role of lawyers in concluding contracts?
- What are the duties of a lawyer when employing AI-powered systems in daily practice?
- Has the practice of law finally become an "industry"? Is it wise to invest in studying to become a lawyer, given that the already-high standards of achievement one must meet in traditional practice will only increase with the competitive capabilities promised by AI, while at the same time making obsolete many of the traditional tasks for lawyers that represented much of the demand for trained professionals?
- What skills must one cultivate to work effectively with technologists, together developing innovations that further the beneficial application of AI to delivering valuable client service and improving the quality of life for legal professionals?

Having read the title and introduction, you can add any other questions you want to explore here:

AN INTRODUCTION TO AI

WHAT IS ARTIFICIAL INTELLIGENCE?

Artificial intelligence is the field of technology that seeks to replicate the rational decisions and actions of humans performing specific tasks. These tasks may range from the simple, such as setting a thermostat, to finding and recommending texts meeting certain criteria, to driving a car safely at highway speeds without human intervention.

To accomplish these goals, technologists use a range of techniques, drawing from such disciplines as statistics, neuroscience, and linguistics. Along the way, they developed methods to represent and implement these algorithms in software. In time, these programs benefitted from hardware that advanced exponentially in speed and capability, as we have already discussed in Chapter 3.

HOW AI WORKS: STATISTICAL METHODS, MACHINE LEARNING, AND AI

In the early years of AI research and development, mathematical methods such as descriptive statistics and others with names such as linear regression, logistic regression, and linear algebra formed the basis for many of the advances in the field. This first branch of AI we will discuss, known as machine learning, built upon some of the analytic techniques we described in Chapter 6, such as fitting a line to points of observed data, or computing the relative distances between points in two or three dimensions.

These mathematical methods can, for example, permit one to determine the degree of similarity between two subjects. One can do so in a manner likened to visually examining points plotted on a graph or a map. If one is looking for the most similar neighbour to a subject in a specific location, one might guess that its nearest neighbour in terms of distance might also exhibit similar, sought-after characteristics.

Concretely, these characteristics might be as disparate as one's manner of speech, monthly income, food preferences, or measured level of tooth decay. If the characteristic of interest can be measured or somehow reliably reduced to a numeric value, these methods might be applied. They are known as *similarity measures*, with names such as K-means and least squares.

If one can quantify similarity, one can also do the same for *dissimilarity*. In either case, a threshold value is chosen that determines, in the context of the application, a minimum degree of similarity or dissimilarity. Calculating and evaluating that value for each subject in a set of observations will permit the determination of a given subject's membership in a set or class. Figure 7.2 illustrates high versus low similarity.

Using our graph analogy as before, a subject earning more than USD 500,000 and who likes to cook with organic vegetables might be considered a member of the class "Target Customers" for a marketing research exercise using this method. This process is known as *classification*, while software that implements such methods is known as a *classifier*. In legal settings, classifiers have been used since the early 2010s for such tasks as determining the relevance of a document to a given matter.

TRAINING WITH DATA

Machine learning models, including our classifier example, are generally built with a set of controlling inputs. Like the switches and knobs on a control panel, these inputs can be used to change the behaviours

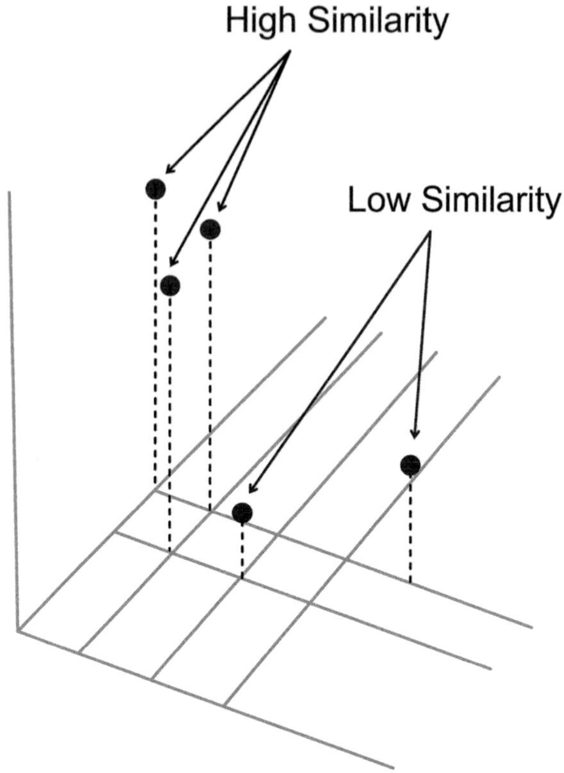

Figure 7.1 Similarity measures

and sensitivity of models to certain aspects of the data sent to them by modifying the calculations running in the model. With appropriate adjustments, the model might fit the objectives of a particular application. For example, the settings might sharpen the model's response to the presence of a certain colour in a photo. They might allow the model to identify, with a reliable measure of probability, a certain type of document displaying required content characteristics, e.g. a transcript of a deposition specifically related to a criminal matter.

In the process of developing an application using a machine learning model, a critical step called *training* is undertaken, in which the inputs and settings in a model are varied and tested with randomly drawn samples from a body of data representative of that which will be processed using the finished application. For a document classifier model, sample documents would be selected at random from a collection of similar documents. As part of preparing the *training data*, each sample is evaluated in advance by a human, who annotates or *labels* the sample with the correct value that should be expected from the model. Each sample for our document classifier example would be labelled TRUE or FALSE, to indicate the condition RELEVANT or NOT_RELEVANT.

During training, a model's parameters are initialized either to specific values selected by a practitioner or to values drawn randomly, depending on the goals of the implementation. The model is then run in iterations across the entire training data set. Each of the model's responses to the training data are recorded and examined, while practitioners tune the model's settings after each iteration or set of iterations, until the model responds in a way sufficiently close to that which the practitioners intend. At that point, the model is considered "trained".

The trained model is then tested using the previously prepared test data, to evaluate the effectiveness of the training. If the model passes thresholds for accuracy and reliability set by the designers, they may proceed to incorporate the model into a full-fledged application, or they might go back and continue in a repeated cycle to train, test, and evaluate the model again until they are satisfied.

This iterative model of development and training usually involves evaluation of results considering a real or theoretical penalty, a "cost function" calculated and assigned to errors in the model's operation. This cost function is the heart of the machine learning practice called *supervised machine learning*, which seeks to minimise the value of such a cost function. One could take the view that the "supervision" involves the critical human intervention of measurement, evaluation and iterative improvement of the model, eventually minimising the variation from a set of expected responses as labelled by a human. Figure 7.2 demonstrates the annotation of a data set.

There are also *reinforcement machine learning* methods, which involve semi-automated and fully automated techniques with supporting software to train, test, and evaluate models in continuous feedback loops. While such models can do more with less human intervention, the current state of development still requires human intervention in most cases to operate and maintain such systems, and to determine if they can continue in operation at any given stage.

NEURAL NETWORKS

Neural networks are a branch of AI that build upon mathematical models mimicking the structure of a human neuron. These artificial neuron models, originally simulated in isolation on a computer,

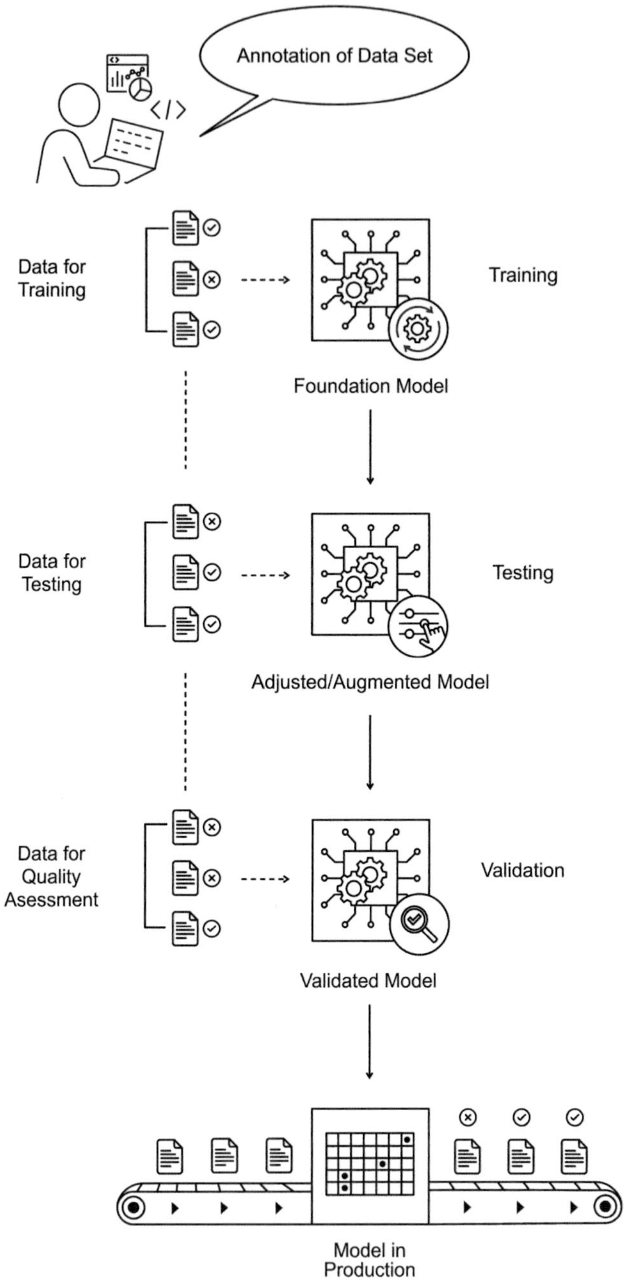

Figure 7.2 Preparing data and models for AI applications

take on promising characteristics when programmed into layered networks linking the outputs of one layer to the inputs of others. When first introduced, these neural networks proved astonishingly effective in solving previously difficult non-linear problems such as shape recognition.

Small neural networks were used in early commercial machine learning applications to identify letterforms for text recognition and transcription. Pen and touch-screen gesture inputs were also handled in like manner for handwriting input applications.[1] Voice recognition applications also appeared, allowing voice input in place of keyboards and number pads, greatly enhancing the usability of Interactive Voice Response (IVR) systems for telephone-based customer service applications.

Despite such promising beginnings, two limiting factors impeded increased early adoption of neural networks into more significant applications in the 1990s into the 2000s: Computing resources and data for training. Let us examine each of these factors more closely.

- *Training and operating neural networks are computing resource intensive.* Until the mid-2010s, generally available hardware had been neither powerful enough nor economical enough to operate at sufficient scales to make commercial applications of AI based on neural networks feasible. After initial enthusiasm for pen-oriented Personal Digital Assistants (PDAs), most commercial applications involving neural networks were limited to carefully scripted, extensively tested interactions involving voice input via telephone interactions on customer service hotlines—the so-called IVR systems.[2] IVRs once revolutionized customer service by delivering valuable automated customer service at scale, but they remain limited in their capabilities to scripted interactions. They have not fully supplanted the human service representative but now serve the additional role of gatekeeper and flow regulator to scarce human support personnel.
- *To train neural networks for more complex applications, large bodies of data are required.* A gradually building wave of digital conversion applied over time to printed texts through scanning and text recog-

1 'System and Method of Handwritten Character Recognition' <https://patents.google.com/patent/US20030048948A1/en> accessed 30 September 2025.

2 'Neural Nets Create Natural Speech Interaction' <https://www.eetimes.com/neural-nets-create-natural-speech-interaction/> accessed 30 September 2025.

nition made large bodies of text available. As those texts became available in digital form, a substantial body of them had to be prepared to train more powerful text recognition applications used to turn images of the printed word into computer-readable text. Given time, the efforts of commercial and university-based research groups combined with the efforts of independent open source software development teams gradually built the data sets now available for use in training AI models.[3]

DEEP LEARNING, LARGE LANGUAGE MODELS, AND GENERATIVE AI

In the early 2010s, as hardware became sufficiently capable, and substantial bodies of digitally readable text appeared, researchers and entrepreneurs realised the opportunity to experiment with more complex neural networks. At that time, they were able to build and train deep neural networks with significant numbers of layers. While, strictly speaking, a neural network with three or more layers qualifies as a deep neural network, the term has come to be applied to instances with over a thousand layers. These increasingly massive networks require specialised computational hardware and programming techniques to train and run. Figure 7.3 illustrates such neural networks and deep neural networks.

Three critical developments building on the successful implementation and routine use of deep neural networks led to the emergence of modern AI applications:

- Reinforcement learning
- Transformers and Generative AI
- Large Language Models

REINFORCEMENT LEARNING

Models that have high levels of self-directed learning capabilities oriented to maximising specific measurable outcomes are in this category. These systems are engineered to improve as they become exposed to more data and gain experience in their operating contexts. Examples

3 One prominent example of such a dataset is the massive dataset known as 'The Pile' <https://pile.eleuther.ai/> accessed 30 September 2025.

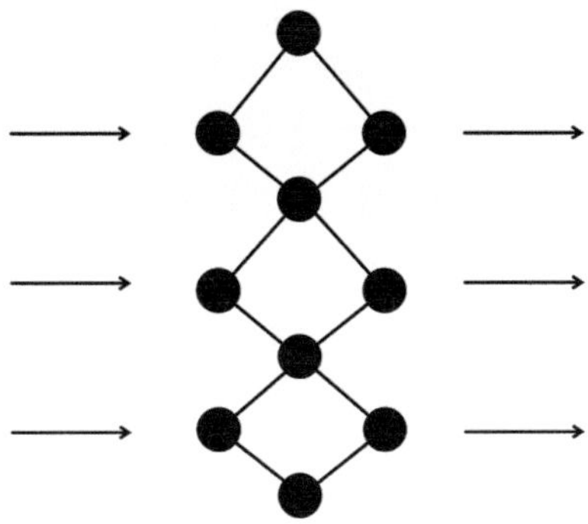

A Neural Network

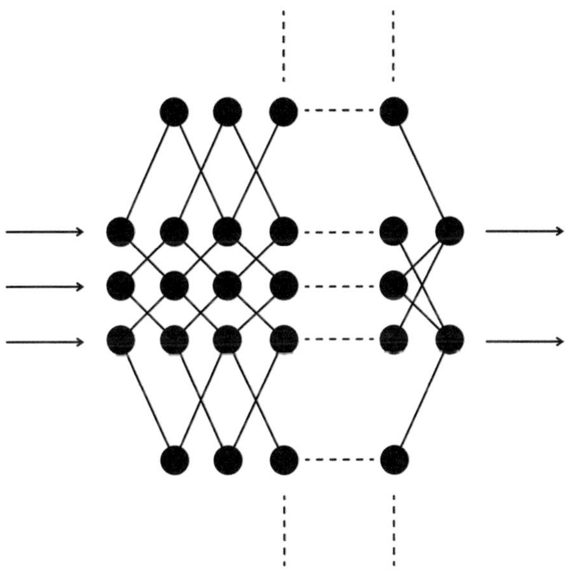

A Deep Neural Network

Figure 7.3 Neural networks and deep neural networks

include goal-seeking systems that learn to play board games or video games, growing in skill with more play. Some of these systems can surpass the performance of human players. A widely publicised example of a reinforcement learning system in game play was Google

DeepMind's AlphaGo, which was the first system playing the game of Go to beat a human expert player.[4]

TRANSFORMERS AND GENERATIVE AI

Deep learning networks, with certain processing enhancements, excel at predicting common patterns in input, and at extrapolating patterns that could occur in outputs that are relevant in each context. Transformers as improved deep learning models incorporate mechanisms that model the concept of human attention, the ability of humans to keep concepts in appropriate context as they are embedded in long chains of words as we find in complex language constructions. Applications of transformers on capable modern hardware in the mid-2010s and early 2020s led to a boom in text and image generation with the application of transformers and generative functions.

Generative functions are a powerful statistical method that allow the generation of samples that fit a distribution of data and can be plausibly drawn from a set in that distribution. Without further explanation and mathematical background, one might infer from the terms that the models "generate" text in some leap of intelligent volition. In fact, the generative functions in Generative AI are mathematical functions whose outputs are values that can be said to be plausibly generated from a mathematical description of a domain or set of values. The outputs for text can in many cases appear random and nonsensical, but the use of transformers permit the filtering and selection of generated word sequences and sentences that not only are correct grammatically but make sense in context. In this way, AI systems began to acquire the apparent ability to write, speak, and draw in ways that in some cases are hard to distinguish from those of a human.[5]

LARGE LANGUAGE MODELS

Large Language Models (LLMs) take the advances with transformers and attention and layer them in progressively deeper assemblies

4 Choe Sang-Hun and John Markoff, 'Master of Go Board Game is Walloped by Google Computer Program' (*New York Times*, 9 March 2016) <https://www.nytimes.com/2016/03/10/world/asia/google-alphago-lee-se-dol.html> accessed 30 September 2025.

5 It is critical in understanding AI to keep in mind that until proven otherwise, these are prudently considered as the appearances of ability and not actual abilities possessed by a sentient being with agency.

supported with massive computational resources, train them on massive datasets of text, supported by humans who evaluate the models' operation and provide feedback in Reinforcement Learning with Human Feedback (RLHF) techniques. LLMs have the capability to take large bodies of text not seen before and not only digest that text and answer questions about those texts with reasonable accuracy, but also compose usable summaries and analyses derived from those texts. The primary form of interaction with LLMs is in a text chat form known as *prompting*, which we will discuss further in this chapter.

The rapid proliferation of LLMs in the mid-2020s and what has come to be termed the thawing of the AI Winter is in large part due to the ability LLMs have to recognise patterns in natural language inputs and to produce plausible outputs in fluent language, of such quality that some AI promoters have gone so far as to herald a coming breakthrough in artificial general intelligence (AGI). AGI is the goal of human-level intelligence, which can learn and think autonomously.

The debate over the emergence of AGI is centred around the apparent abilities of LLMs and Generative AI systems. The apparent ability to understand and respond convincingly to unstructured conversational inputs with intelligent-sounding, grammatically correct and, in most cases, factually correct text has led many to believe that AGI has either already been achieved or is near. Critics and sceptics point to the fact that the same models fail at basic arithmetic or word problems requiring a balance of reasoning, common knowledge, and common sense.[6]

It is not our purpose here to advance a view as to when or if AGI will be ultimately achieved. It is important to note, however, that the increased capabilities and rapid adoption of AI in the form of LLMs such as the popular ChatGPT and Gemini offerings in the mid-2020s has led to substantial changes in legal education and legal practice. We counsel students to maintain an open attitude grounded in critical thinking and examination of verifiable facts as they see claims of intelligence and even real-world demonstrations.

It is instructive to read more general introductions to the technology and the phenomenon of its adoption. Some references are suggested in the *Recommendations for Further Reading* at the end of this chapter.

6 Ernest Davis, 'Mathematics, Word Problems, Common Sense, and Artificial Intelligence' (25 January 2023) <https://arxiv.org/abs/2301.09723> accessed 30 September 2025.

AI DOMAINS RELEVANT TO LEGAL PRACTICE

With some background in AI and its development, we can examine four areas of AI with specific impact on legal practice:

- Human–computer interaction
- Information theory
- Natural language processing
- Generative AI

HUMAN–COMPUTER INTERACTION (HCI)

Using a chat interface to interact with an AI-supported application has become commonplace. This originated in 1966 with the development of the ELIZA program to simulate conversation with a psychotherapist. This showed with some novelty the possibilities and the then-current limitations in creating programs to enable fluid, natural language interaction with computers of the time.[7] ELIZA focused on a specific set of interactions that could elicit follow-up questions that appeared contextually relevant for the first few rounds of interaction, but soon revealed the scripted and repetitive, "unaware" nature of the underlying program.

After an intervening period of over 40 years, Apple Computer introduced Siri, its voice-powered assistant. The company did so first on its iOS mobile devices and later as a core feature across all its supported platforms. The introduction marked the transformation of interaction with computing devices using speech into a more widespread, usable, and thus more accepted mode of daily technology use. Apple competitors followed suit, with companies such as Google and Samsung introducing similar support on their competing Android platforms with their wide range of supported devices.

While conversational interfaces are still not yet used for extended interactions with primary computing devices—users are not yet having extended conversational working sessions with their computers—the length and complexity of the interactions have gradually increased as devices have gained more usable and more responsive voice recognition and text processing capabilities. Software developers have surmounted

7 J. Weizenbaum, 'ELIZA—a Computer Program for the Study of Natural Language Communication between Man and Machine' (1966) 9 *Communications of the ACM* 36.

many of the obstacles in interactions between subsystems designed to handle language interaction with the underlying information technology traditionally operated directly by humans using web pages or screens.

These problems have often been a limiting factor in constructing effective *agents* with AI technology. Agents are programs that act, often autonomously, in a limited domain, causing real-world changes for users or other programs. The techniques have been embodied in reusable frameworks of software, allowing developers and AI-savvy users to develop richer, focused, agent-based solutions.[8]

INFORMATION THEORY

Methods to represent and encode information compactly and efficiently for storage, transmission and recovery led, as computing power continued to increase exponentially in the 1990s, to powerful search engines that are now ubiquitous and indispensable on the internet. Originally emerging as a discipline to surmount physical challenges in storage, transmission and information retrieval, information theory is replete with complex mathematics. Further extensions of research building on information theory led to fundamental work in transformer and LLM technologies that underpin the AI of the 2020s.

NATURAL LANGUAGE PROCESSING

Algorithmic methods in natural language processing draw on fundamental insights from the field of linguistics and focus on identifying and quantifying fundamental structures and patterns in both written texts and spoken language. Systematic analysis of the grammars of languages, statistics describing common sequences and orderings of words occurring in large bodies of texts, and techniques of measuring the occurrences and conformance of texts to patterns and the similarity of different texts allowed such feats as rating texts for readability and reading level, establishing probability of authorship, plagiarism detection, and the recommendation of similar content. All these solutions were possible with techniques developed in the 1990s through 2010, before the later emphasis on text processing, manipulation, and

8 Andrew Ng, 'Why Agentic AI Is the Smart Bet for Most Enterprises' <https://www.insightpartners.com/ideas/andrew-ng-why-agentic-ai-is-the-smart-bet-for-most-enterprises/> accessed 30 September 2025.

generation using more advanced tools involving advanced machine learning techniques and neural networks.

GENERATIVE AI

Generative AI has built upon and revolutionised the application of each of these key areas of AI, in the sense that long-held goals for the use of computing devices are at least now partially realised:

Interactions with computing devices to accomplish significant tasks can now take place using fluent natural language in a chat format. One no longer inputs cryptic search terms into a box and is no longer limited to pointing and clicking through multiple layers of application menus to accomplish parts of a complex task. Instead, one can specify in fluent prose not only the information one is seeking, but the outcome to be accomplished with that information, and provide guidance for the system to find data and complete the task or tasks needed on the way to achieving the desired outcome.

AI has demonstrated the potential to reduce significantly the toil in everyday research. LLMs can now ingest and summarise large bodies of text and answer detailed questions with impressive levels of usability. While not perfect, and sometimes prone to shockingly poor performance and error (sometimes termed hallucinations), AI used as a tool to survey and build summaries as a precursor to detailed study of a body of texts is effective, provided adequate precautions are taken in checking the outputs at various stages in the process.

In preparing summaries and generating text in general, Generative AI has shown its capabilities to produce text that is not only fluent, but context aware and, in most cases, appropriate and usable if accurate. Generative AI is also used to generate graphics, video, and computer source code.

Successive iterations of models trained on more data and tuned for specific application domains have fuelled enthusiastic adoption among investors, marketing departments, and users. Real utility in the automation of certain tasks and reduction of toil using AI has reinforced this adoption. Nearly every substantial organisation must now articulate its approach to using AI.

Education institutions have had to respond to the use of AI in academic work, forced to promulgate policies regarding academic integrity and appropriate use of AI-generated outputs as original work. Although many academic journals require the declaration of use of AI in preparing manuscript submissions, a survey noted that compliance to such policies is inconsistent, with many papers in a surveyed corpus of works displaying markers of AI use in writing, or cited as generated by a hallucinating AI.[9]

These incidents demonstrate that AI-generated work products have at least the appearance of accuracy and utility. When they are in fact accurate and useful, they can represent significant value in productivity and time savings for the user or the organisation.

As with each wave of technology promising increased productivity, predictions of the demise of the knowledge worker were pronounced by both media commentators and some enthusiastic practitioners in the field, eager to see and reap benefits from hype brewing around the emerging developments. In 2025, reports of unemployment due to job loss or worker replacement by AI were published but were countered with predictions and views from economists predicting that Generative AI would unleash, in the long term, a wave of productivity and job creation similar to that which occurred with the commercial adoption of the internet. For some, the emergence of AI supports the notion of a Fourth Industrial Revolution.[10]

It is unnecessary and unproductive for us to speculate here on the future of the job market in response to AI. In our opinion, however, any person will do well to focus on the core skills of his or her chosen profession. Actively seeking education in other disciplines, learning diverse skills for the sake of understanding, broadening of interests and, more important, risk reduction, will leave that person in good stead, whatever the future holds.

IMPORTANT THEMES WITH AI

The following section offers some underlying themes emerging from experience with the use and development of AI in the past decade. Rising legal professionals should find these points useful to keep in mind as they complete their studies and enter practice.

9 'Suspected Undeclared Use of Artificial Intelligence in the Academic Literature: An analysis of the Academ-AI Dataset' <https://arxiv.org/abs/2411.15218v1> accessed 30 September 2025.

10 Klaus Schwab, 'The Fourth Industrial Revolution: What It Means, How to Respond' (World Economic Forum, 14 January 2016) <https://www.weforum.org/stories/2016/01/the-fourth-industrial-revolution-what-it-means-and-how-to-respond/> accessed 30 September 2025.

AI AS A COMPANION

AI models are often used to generate ideas and conduct initial, sometimes speculative investigations in various topics in the early stages of a project. The broad exposure to content many AI models have in the training process may prove useful in the early stages of a project in helping generate options for further study.

PROMPTING

The primary means of interaction and specification of desired outcomes with modern Generative AI tools is the prompt. A great deal of emphasis is placed on the act of *prompt engineering*, a way of writing inputs for LLMs that is specific enough, and prescriptive enough, to allow the underlying model to take appropriate actions to effect specific outcomes or produce desired work products. As with many human endeavours, including the practice of law, honed skills in writing will prove invaluable. We will develop a view of AI prompting later in this chapter.

STRIVING FOR TRANSPARENCY AND REPEATABILITY IN AI

In most computing applications, human users expect the system to "just work". Put more precisely, human users expect the system to work in ways that, given sufficient time and resources, can be explained to a person with sufficient background knowledge. Such a system should be expected to behave in the same way, consistently, from use to use. Such an assumption assumes, of course, control over the variables that may affect the operation of the system.

Because of their scale and mathematical complexity, and the scale of the data on which many AI models have been trained, it is impossible to explain with any degree of certainty the behaviour of a model in any given instance. Furthermore, because of the nature of some of the algorithms that implement underlying components of some models —heavily reliant on probability—it is not possible to predict the behaviour of the model beyond certain mathematical approximations.

Put plainly, a model cannot be guaranteed to "just work" the same way on each use, nor even after a countless number of uses.

Models have been known to work consistently for dozens or hundreds or even thousands of runs, but then will "drift" and cease, with no apparent cause, to function consistently with the same prompts and inputs. This issue of unpredictability and inconsistency, despite extensive investment in training, tuning, and prompting, is often ignored or does not enter the consciousness of enthusiastic users and businesspeople looking for success with a full-scale product or application implementation.

AI Hallucinations

Current AI models are at their core pattern recognisers and generators, having little to no machinery to validate the veracity or quality of their outputs. AI systems in various applications have been known to hallucinate; that is, to generate untrue or nonsensical responses to queries or instructions, packaging them in perfectly reasonable responses to the user. AI models in software development contexts often generate code that is incorrect, sometimes in subtle ways, not manifesting their errors unless tested extensively, or worse, when a user encounters them in a critical production operations scenario.

The problem of hallucinations is a complex one, affecting the training process, the data used to train, feedback and monitoring methods, and quality assurance processes. In none of these areas is the state of practice mature enough to ensure that hallucinations can be prevented. Hallucinations pose a danger in the academic setting when AI-produced results are accepted without critical evaluation, or worse, when used without verification by students as time savings or coping strategies, or worse, in academically dishonest activities. The dangers in professional practice are apparent, exposing the legal professional, the firm, and the client to risks and liability. We will explore these dangers further in this chapter when we explore the use of AI in education and practice.

Bursting the Bubble on AI

Much of the hype in AI focuses on sometimes uninformed impressions of inexplicable and therefore "magic", "superhuman" abilities found in AI, playing on the worst fears associated with technological change. It is important to evaluate AI claims while keeping in mind its limitations.

- *Machines are as limited as their creators.* We have seen that AI is prone to bias in training data. It may hallucinate and fabricate plausible-sounding but inaccurate or outright nonsensical results. AI models are sometimes good, even superlative beyond human performance in one specific area, but do not perform as well in others or generally.
- *Loose prompting can lead to undesirable outcomes.* While LLMs can generally interpret a prompt, they often can misinterpret an insufficiently precise or vaguely written one. Much like a vaguely worded clause in a contract can cause great harm, so a model's confusion can lead to undesirable outcomes.
- *Wrong goal seeking.* When developed in isolation, goal-seeking models will optimise their functions for whatever has been defined as its goal or cost function. A well-known example occurred in the training of a model to play a boat racing game. A model set to maximise its score focused on traversing the game's course instead of on winning the race, and never completed the race, but had the highest overall score. While instructive and entertaining to observe, the implications on real-world systems cannot be ignored, especially if one intends to deploy such systems, fully automated, with limited controls. The need to put sufficient safeguards around the operation of more sophisticated models, balancing the need to further innovation and accomplish real goals of users, stands out as a critical challenge in the further safe and productive use of AI.
- *Exposure to liability by premature reliance on AI.* Law firms are rushing to articulate their strategies and incorporate AI tools into their practice, fearing the consequences of being left behind by faster-moving peers. In the process, some have failed to evaluate their approaches to staffing, tools evaluation, and operational safety, let alone promulgating clear policies on professional responsibility with AI. Such firms risk exposure to errors and professional liability, as well as severe damage to client relationships in the event of a significant negative event involving use of AI in practice and giving advice.

WHAT IS NOT ARTIFICIAL INTELLIGENCE?

While it is easy to become alarmed at predictions of massive job losses with each successive wave of technological advancement, a few key points are worth keeping in mind. These points emphasise what AI is *not*.

1 *AI is NOT brilliant and intelligent.* It does not demonstrate those qualities, or the potential for them across the board. AI is only able to recognise and assemble patterns in text, images, and other media to which it has been exposed. In many cases with current general knowledge, speaking about current events, or about subjects that can be found in general encyclopaedia texts like Wikipedia, AI can provide usable and, in most cases, useful results. In areas requiring more specialised knowledge, AI often fails or provides incorrect answers packaged in believable presentation.

2 *AI is NOT continually learning.* AI implementations do not have reliable mechanisms with which to develop solutions to new problems they encounter while in continual operation. Though it is possible to train an AI model to beat the best of human players in specific complex games like Chess and Go, the same AI system is not, in this stage of AI development, similarly adaptable to play a first-person shooter video game or pilot a drone, let alone write a convincing manual on how to play Go at an expert level. Each of these activities requires significant computing resources and processes to set up the training and data support necessary to make the AI model perform at such high levels. Such capabilities might allow the approximation of *general* intelligence as in AGI, though they are not yet solved.

3 *AI performance is NOT robust in the slight rephrasing of prompts in many scenarios.* The need to write with a kind of precision that hinges on the shades of meanings of certain words that a particular model emphasises in its formulation can sometimes make for a troubling lack of reliability and breakdown in trust of an otherwise functional and adequate AI solution. This is a hurdle to adoption of AI tools and an active area of research.

4 *AI does NOT yield results with the same data consistently.* Using the same prompt with only slight changes in data yields inconsistent outputs. The changes can be unintuitive to human users and hint at the complexity and lack of transparency in the behaviour of many models.

While many tasks can be automated with greater success using AI support, it should be instructive, if not comforting to those apprehensive about the future, to bear in mind the observations earlier in the chapter on the nature of successful AI implementations. A single AI implementation matching the superlative performance of a human in a specific area is likely to have been trained and developed in such a way that it is not currently adaptable to other settings. Such an AI tool simply cannot be expected to perform with superlative results in a separate unrelated area, if it is functional at all.

One can examine the descriptions and guidelines for using the widely available commercial and open source models. General purpose LLMs commonly available now for use in application development, called foundation models, excel in a specific area of text recognition, generation of images, or other generative tasks. Rarely do they attempt to address more than a specific area, and none of the general-purpose foundation models are used in applications without either retraining or significant enhancement and augmentation with supporting tools and subsystems in the development of a production-grade solution.

While many organisations have even announced sweeping job cuts, replacing certain workers performing tasks amenable to automation with the current generation of AI, many are finding difficulty in achieving truly robust replacement with AI. The Finnish fintech company Klarna is one widely reported example of a firm that attempted to replace workers with AI systems. Difficulties in delivering quality customer service following substantial layoffs led Klarna executives to reevaluate their approach, leading to efforts to rehire workers, especially for customer-facing service roles.[11,12]

Staff cuts resulting from attempts to gain savings and efficiency with AI have been like previous waves of technology adoption and organisational transformation, with workers finding new employment in roles that emerge in transformed organisations and economies. An optimistic view holds that the long term increased productivity and employment opportunities that will come to economies adopting AI systems will far outweigh the interim job losses and costs of worker displacement in the short term.

Some global thinkers are right to worry about fully automated AI systems given free rein in military conflict scenarios that could lead to catastrophic loss of life and even unintended existential threats if AI systems are given control over weapons of mass destruction without sufficient safeguards and ultimate override capability in the hands of

11 Noam Scheiber, 'Why Is This C.E.O. Bragging About Replacing Humans With A.I.?' (*New York Times*, 2 February 2025) <https://www.nytimes.com/2025/02/02/business/klarna-ceo-ai.html> accessed 27 September 2025.

12 Joe Wilkins, 'Company Replaces Customer Support With AI, Then Panics and Forces Engineers to Work the Phones as the AI Fails' (*Futurism*, 4 September 2025) <https://futurism.com/klarna-ai-automation-engineers> accessed 27 September 2025.

responsible humans. In industry and in the realm of small and medium enterprises as well as in the practice of law, ill-considered programmes focus on replacing less experienced personnel with AI on a permanent basis.

In time, as organisations fail to train members to take over intermediate and senior roles, gaps in organisational memory are expected to become manifest. Such organisations may already have encountered the issues in consistency and reliability experienced with the current generation of Generative AI solutions, and a growing scarcity of personnel experienced in solving the problems unique to that organisation and its domains. Given sufficient time, they will of course also suffer from a lack of personnel experienced in the organisation's methods and certain aspects of culture and processes that differentiated that organisation.

These observations suggest the need for a measured approach to AI adoption, one grounded in organisational culture, long-term mission, and growing the ability of personnel at all levels to take advantage of working with AI-powered systems and agents as tools and working assistants. One helpful analogy is to view AI for knowledge work as like an exoskeleton for a worker in a physical work scenario, for instance on a shop floor, or in a warehouse. A trained worker can wear an exoskeleton to augment his or her physical abilities, permitting the lifting and moving of objects many times the worker's weight.

THE VULNERABLE LEGAL PROFESSION

Perhaps more than other occupations, the legal profession finds itself uniquely vulnerable to artificial intelligence. Let us examine some aspects of this assertion.

- *It is labour intensive.* The tasks associated with legal discovery, legal research, drafting, and negotiating agreements are time intensive and therefore expensive. AI promises to provide legal professionals with ways to reduce toil and provide speed to complete complex tasks at speeds unheard of just years before. Time and cost savings are always attractive. As such tools proliferate, professionals feel pressure to adopt and incorporate them into their workflows, changing the way they practise, upending in some cases decades of accustomed habits. Some are scrambling to adapt, while others fear for their job security in firms adopting tools wholesale. As clients learn about firms adopting and using AI tools, the calculus for determining the value of legal services changes. What took a firm deploying associates with a large allocation of hours becomes different when an AI tool can accomplish the same basic research tasks, albeit imperfectly, and requiring quality assurance, for far less time and money. The profession and its clients have yet to settle on general notions of fairness and value in these cases.

- *One cannot blame errors on "the computer"*. Even with the adoption of AI tools, the responsibility remains with the lawyer to ensure correct and appropriate advice is rendered to the client. AI can compress the time required to reach solutions, but the risks associated with inaccuracy and hallucinations are real, and lawyers must review work products as they always have. In the US State of Utah, the case of *Garner v. Kadince* illustrates the emerging risks attorneys face as they incorporate general purpose AI tools in their practice, and their binding duty for due diligence and candour to the court when submitting filings so prepared.[13] Similar cases have also occurred in the UK High Court.[14]
- *Lack of transparency and accountability*. It may be necessary to trace the provenance of information collected using AI tools. It may also be necessary to understand the detailed reasoning behind certain statements. LLMs, as we have noted elsewhere in this chapter, are not transparent, nor are they necessarily able to provide results repeatably, notwithstanding the correctness of a given solution they produce. The nature of these tools in their current state of development indicates a need for additional care on the part of legal professionals when incorporating their use in practice, documenting their use at each step of a given task if possible.
- *Privacy and data*. Online AI models commonly available do not necessarily provide guarantees or clear explanations of the ways in which data input to those models is held and disposed after each interaction. To varying degrees, some providers may dispose of data immediately but are more likely to hold the prompts and supporting data for analysis and further improvement of their models over time, whether for testing or retraining. The possibility of user data

13 *Garner v. Kandice*, Court of Appeals of Utah <https://caselaw.findlaw.com/court/ut-court-of-appeals/117297291.html> accessed 30 September 2025.

14 Robert Booth, 'High Court Tells Lawyers to Stop Misuse of AI After Fake Case-Law Citations' (*The Guardian*, 6 June 2025) <https://www.theguardian.com/technology/2025/jun/06/high-court-tells-uk-lawyers-to-urgently-stop-misuse-of-ai-in-legal-work> accessed 30 September 2025.

being incorporated unknowingly into training data would expose a lawyer and their client to significant risk. Such a possibility would be a clear breach of confidentiality and pose a threat to the client-attorney relationship. Lawyers must be particularly aware of a vendor's data handling and data disposition policies when using online AI models in their practice.

The legal profession will certainly undergo an extensive transformation in the coming decades, as the technology continues to mature and gains adoption, while mistakes are made and experience gained. One area should be given specific attention: That of the effects on new lawyers entering practice, who may face greater difficulties in securing training positions, and who have fewer opportunities to take on the tasks their seniors took on earlier in their careers. Some firms dispensing with the hiring of junior personnel because of yet-untested beliefs that AI is sufficiently capable of replacing junior members of firms may find themselves in time with fewer experienced personnel who can rise to fill senior positions as those positions become vacant through the normal course of time, attrition, and retirement.

The effects on organisational memory—an aspect not often discussed, but critical to organisation culture and the strength of organisations' ability to deliver differentiated service—may put firms at risk in the long term. The trade-off for short-term gains in labour cost savings must be viewed in a longer-term context of the organisation and its longevity. Tools, not even AI tools, cannot yet solve the problem of maintaining the human experience that time growing through a career in legal practice gives to firms in the professionals they cultivate and retain over the long term. AI currently provides point solutions and single-task accelerants. It cannot yet replace integrated experience and intuition, qualities that are difficult to quantify and perhaps even more difficult to replace.[15]

Using AI in the study of law

As AI becomes increasingly integrated into professional environments, university students must learn to navigate its use with both confidence

15 Brinda Sarathy and Rajeshwari Ganesan, 'Why AI Efficiency May Be Making Your Organization More Fragile' (*O'Reilly Radar*, 25 September 2025) <https://www.oreilly.com/radar/why-ai-efficiency-may-be-making-your-organization-more-fragile/> accessed 30 September 2025.

and integrity. While AI tools can boost creativity, streamline research, and support productivity, academic work still demands the development and demonstration of your own knowledge, critical thinking, and original ideas. The responsible use of AI in university is not about rejecting new technology, but about learning how to use it ethically, transparently, and thoughtfully. This means engaging with AI as a tool to enhance, not replace, your intellectual work. Your use of AI must reflect the academic maturity and professional readiness expected of a graduate. Responsible AI use is not just about avoiding plagiarism; it is about upholding the values of scholarship: integrity, independence, originality, and critical inquiry. Striking this balance will not only protect the value of your academic achievements but also prepare you to enter the workforce with the skills and judgement needed to use AI effectively and responsibly in your future career.

CORE PRINCIPLES FOR RESPONSIBLE USE OF AI IN LEARNING

Before turning to AI for help with your studies, take a moment to reflect on why you are attending university in the first place. You are here not to submit perfect work, but to learn, think critically, and grow into a capable, independent thinker. These principles are not about limiting your use of AI; they are about helping you use it well, in ways that strengthen your voice, not silence it. Fundamental knowledge plays a vital role in this process. It gives you the foundation to understand how AI tools work, what their limitations are, and how to engage with them ethically and responsibly. Without that understanding, it is easy to misinterpret outputs or become overly reliant on technology. At the same time, experimenting with AI is key to developing practical skills and confidence. By combining critical thinking with hands-on exploration, you'll be better prepared to use AI thoughtfully and effectively, both in your studies and in the professional world beyond university.

INTEGRITY

AI can be a powerful support tool, but it should never do the thinking for you. There's a big difference between using AI to enhance your ideas and letting it take over your work. Your lecturers are not expecting perfection; rather, they are looking for evidence of your learning, your process, and your unique perspective, even if it is still developing. That's where meaningful growth happens.

Using AI to brainstorm, get feedback, or clarify your thinking is not only acceptable, it can be smart. But integrity means being transparent. If AI helped shape your expression, structure, or ideas in a significant way, cite it—not because you are in trouble, but because acknowledging your sources is a core part of academic honesty.

Ultimately, assessments are about showing what you understand and how you are progressing. Passing off AI-generated content as your own undermines that purpose and your development. Use AI to support your learning, not shortcut it.

Key points

- Do not present AI-generated content as your own.
- Use AI to support, not replace, your thinking.
- Be transparent and cite AI tools when they influence your work (always check your institution's guidelines).
- Academic integrity means owning your learning journey, even the messy parts.

TRANSPARENCY

Being honest about your use of AI is not a weakness, but a strength. In a space where AI tools are still new and evolving, transparency takes courage, but it also builds trust. It shows that you are thinking critically, using tools responsibly, and taking ownership of your learning.

Ask yourself: Did AI help you structure your thoughts? Rephrase a paragraph? Provide feedback on clarity or tone? That's okay—just be upfront about it. Transparency does not diminish the value of your work; it highlights your integrity, your self-awareness, and your readiness to engage with new technologies in a mature and ethical way. These are qualities that academics respect and employers actively seek.

Whether in your coursework or future career, being clear about how you've used AI promotes trust and credibility. It shows that you are not just using the tool—you understand your role in using it well.

Key points

- Be honest with yourself, your peers, and your educators about how you've used AI.
- If asked, be able to clearly explain the role AI played in your process.
- Transparency is not just academic; it is a professional standard that builds trust and demonstrates ethical thinking.

CRITICAL THINKING

AI can be a useful tool, but it does not understand context, nuance, or truth the way you do. It can generate ideas, suggest structures, or summarise information, but it cannot tell you what's relevant, reliable, or meaningful in your specific context. That's your job.

Using AI responsibly means thinking critically about its outputs. Do not just accept what it gives you—question it, test it, improve it. Ask yourself: Does this make sense? Is it accurate? Does it align with the task, and with my voice and values? You should feel confident saying: "That doesn't sound quite right, I'll check the source myself", or "This structure is useful, but I want to add my own interpretation".

AI can assist, but it cannot replace your judgment, creativity, or insight. Think of it as one tool in your academic toolbox: helpful in some situations, but not a substitute for the depth and rigour of human thinking—your thinking.

Key points

- AI lacks deep understanding, context, and reasoning—you do not.
- Always verify information, challenge assumptions, and refine what AI gives you.
- Use AI to support your thinking, not to replace critical engagement or decision-making.

SKILL DEVELOPMENT

Here's something worth remembering: struggle is not a setback; it is part of how real learning happens. When you wrestle with a difficult concept, revise a messy draft or rethink an argument that's not quite working, you are developing the skills that matter most—critical thinking, creativity, and resilience. These moments of effort are where your academic voice begins to take shape.

AI can make certain tasks easier, but do not let it take away the challenges that help you grow. Use it to clarify your ideas, test your reasoning, or experiment with different ways of expressing your thoughts, but stay in control of the process. That struggle, however uncomfortable, is what builds confidence, independence, and genuine capability.

The goal is not to produce perfect work or finish faster; it is to become someone who can think, create, and adapt, with or without AI. Your ideas, your insights, and your intellectual voice are the foundation of your learning journey.

Key points

- Your voice, not AI's, should drive your work.
- Use AI to support your learning, not to skip the thinking that builds skill and confidence.
- Embrace the process, even when it is messy; that's where growth happens.

Skill development means staying actively engaged, not outsourcing effort. You are capable. Your thinking matters. Even imperfect work, when it is truly yours, is more meaningful and more powerful than anything AI can produce. AI is here to support your journey, not to walk it for you. Use it wisely, use it transparently, and, above all, trust in the value of your own learning.

USING AI IN YOUR LEARNING

AI IN LEARNING AND STUDY SUPPORT

AI can be a valuable companion in your learning journey when used thoughtfully and purposefully. One of its strengths lies in helping you engage with content more efficiently. For instance, AI can summarise lecture notes or readings, allowing you to grasp key points quickly and revisit material in a more manageable form. If you are grappling with a complex concept, AI can act like a virtual tutor—offering explanations, breaking down ideas into simpler terms, or translating technical language into something more accessible.

It can also support active learning strategies. You might use AI to generate quiz questions for self-testing, identify counterarguments in a debate, or simulate a Socratic-style dialogue to explore your topic more deeply. These approaches encourage critical thinking and help solidify your understanding.

Beyond content, AI can assist with organisation and time management. It can help you create a study schedule, prioritise tasks, or organise material for revision. For students doing research, it might even suggest relevant case studies or further readings to explore.

Used in these ways, AI becomes a supportive tool—not a replacement for learning, but a means to enhance it. The key is to remain curious, questioning, and in control of your process, so that the learning remains yours.

Responsible use tips

- Revisit original sources to confirm and deepen understanding.
- Use explanations as a jumping-off point, not a final answer.
- Avoid becoming dependent on AI for understanding—try to explain concepts in your own words.
- Treat AI as an academic aide, not a final authority.
- Push AI outputs further; ask for more nuance, complexity, or alternative views.

AI IN RESEARCH

When used carefully, AI can be a helpful tool throughout the research process, offering support at different stages of planning, organising, and refining your work. At the beginning of a project, it can assist with brainstorming research questions or hypotheses, helping you explore possible directions and clarify your focus. It can also support the early stages of a literature review by suggesting relevant keywords, databases, or themes to investigate, as well as helping you map out a potential structure.

As you dive deeper into your topic, AI can help identify possible gaps in the existing literature or propose new angles for exploration. It might also suggest appropriate methodological approaches or analytical frameworks based on your research goals, or explain unfamiliar research methods in clearer terms—acting almost like a virtual guide as you refine your understanding.

AI can even help summarise key themes across multiple sources, although this should always be done with caution and followed up by your own critical reading and verification. Remember: While AI can assist in surfacing ideas and organising information, it does not replace the depth of engagement, ethical judgment, and critical thinking that real research requires.

Used responsibly, AI becomes a tool that supports your development as a researcher—not by doing the work for you, but by enhancing your ability to think deeply, plan effectively, and work with greater confidence and clarity.

Responsible use tips

- Do your own reading—do not let AI summaries substitute for primary sources.
- Always trace facts and citations to original, peer-reviewed sources.
- Never rely on AI for factual accuracy or source reliability.
- Use AI to generate leads, not conclusions.
- Verify all references—hallucinated citations are common.
- Keep a clear record of AI contributions in your research log or methodology section if required.

AI IN WRITING

AI can be a useful companion in the writing process, offering support from the earliest stages of idea development through to final editing. Whether you are staring at a blank page or refining a near-complete draft, AI can help ease the process and strengthen your writing.

At the start, it can assist with brainstorming essay topics or generating potential titles, helping you clarify your focus and explore different angles. It can also help you outline and structure your essay, offering suggestions for logical flow and cohesion between sections. For more complex assignments, such as research papers or dissertations, AI can support you in organising arguments, outlining sections, and developing a clear framework for your work.

During the drafting stage, AI can generate sample paragraphs or help craft smooth transitions between ideas, giving you a model to work from—not something to copy, but something to build on. It can also help with revising tone, structure, and clarity, especially for non-native English speakers who may want to polish their language without losing their original voice.

In the final stages, AI can assist with editing for grammar, flow, and consistency, acting like a digital writing assistant to help ensure your work is clear and professional. Used thoughtfully, AI can enhance your writing skills—not by replacing your ideas, but by helping you express them more effectively.

Responsible use tips

- Your writing must reflect your voice and ideas.
- Do not copy-paste AI-generated content without modifying and citing appropriately.
- Use AI suggestions as a scaffold, not a crutch.
- AI is not a shortcut to avoid doing the reading, research, or writing yourself.
- Never outsource entire sections of your argument to AI.
- Let AI help you refine expression, not generate content.

- When using AI for language editing, ensure that disciplinary terminology and nuance are preserved.
- If AI shaped the phrasing or structure, cite it appropriately.

AI IN BRAINSTORMING AND CREATIVITY

AI can also be a valuable tool for expanding your thinking and exploring new directions in your academic work. It can help you consider different perspectives or approach a topic from an interdisciplinary angle—encouraging you to make connections across fields or challenge your initial assumptions. This kind of exploration can deepen your understanding and lead to more original, well-rounded arguments.

If you are working with hypotheses or conceptual questions, AI can support creative thinking by helping you test out "what if" scenarios or explore the implications of different viewpoints. It can also suggest analogies, metaphors or real-world examples to help clarify complex ideas or strengthen your explanations, which is particularly useful in writing or presentations.

When you are in the early stages of a major project, such as an essay, dissertation, or capstone assignment, AI can help generate preliminary ideas or offer prompts to get your thinking started. While these ideas should always be developed and refined through your own research and critical analysis, AI can be a helpful catalyst for getting unstuck and moving forward.

Responsible use tips

- Let AI spark ideas, but develop and refine them independently.
- Do not just stop at what AI suggests—interrogate it, challenge it, remix it. AI does not understand context or nuance like you do
- Use AI to escape creative ruts, but return to your own analytical lens.

AI IN PRODUCTIVITY AND ORGANISATION

AI can be a practical tool to help you stay organised and manage your academic and professional responsibilities more effectively. It can assist with writing to-do lists or creating study plans that break larger goals into manageable, actionable tasks, making it easier to stay on track, and avoid feeling overwhelmed.

In addition to helping organise your workload, AI can support your communication skills by drafting polite and professional academic emails, cover letters, or CVs—providing templates and suggestions that you can personalise to fit your voice and purpose. This can be especially valuable if you are unsure where to start or want to ensure your writing is clear and respectful. AI can also help you develop time management strategies, creating study or revision schedules tailored to your needs and deadlines. When preparing for interviews or presentations, AI can generate mock questions to practice with, helping you build confidence, and polish your responses. Used thoughtfully, AI becomes a versatile assistant—helping you plan, communicate, and prepare so you can focus more fully on learning and professional growth.

Responsible use tips

- Use tools like AI as a guide, not a taskmaster.
- Do not let it add complexity, keep your systems simple and suited to your learning style.
- Refine all AI-generated materials to reflect your personal voice and values.
- Use AI to simulate feedback, then critically evaluate that feedback.
- Begin developing your own ethical stance on AI use; many industries now expect it.

INTRODUCING THE CRAFT MODEL FOR RESPONSIBLE USE

We take the opportunity to offer a model for thinking about working with AI, considering Comprehension, Relevance, Analysis, Forward Thinking, and Thinking Critically (CRAFT).

C—COMPREHEND

Start by making sure you understand what the AI is saying.

- What is the main message or idea in the response?
- Does it clearly answer your question or task?
- Are there any parts that are confusing or unclear?
- What assumptions is the AI making?

Tip: Do not just skim—read closely to understand what's being said and why.

R—RELEVANCE

Check whether the response is useful and appropriate for your assignment or learning goals.

- Is the content relevant to your topic, subject area, and level of study?
- Does it meet your assignment brief or learning outcomes?
- Is the information too basic, too complex, or just right?
- What new ideas or insights did you gain?
- How does the AI's response build on what you already know?
- Are there any unfamiliar terms or concepts that you need to research further?
- How could you apply this information to your own understanding and development of your existing knowledge?

Tip: *Not everything AI generates will fit your task—use your judgement.*

A—ANALYSE

Take a step back and evaluate the quality and accuracy of the response.

- Does it seem factually correct and well-reasoned?
- Are there gaps, vague claims, or errors?
- How trustworthy are the sources it relies on?
- Is the reasoning logical and well-supported?
- How does it compare with other credible sources or your existing knowledge?
- Does the response rely on assumptions or generalisations?

- Does it support or challenge your current thinking?
- What needs deeper research or checking?
- How can you expand on it in your own voice?

Tip: *Do not take AI at face value—dig into the details and verify the claims.*

F—FORWARD THINKING

Now decide what to do next with the AI's response.

- What can you *do* with this information next?
- How will it inform your next step in producing your assessment—more research, writing, decision-making?
- What follow-up questions do you now have?
- What needs verifying, refining, or expanding?
- Are you using this response responsibly? Submitting the output from AI is academic misconduct.
- What action will you take to either verify, refine, or expand upon the AI's answer?
- Is your use of AI responsible and within academic integrity guidelines?
- Remember: Submitting AI output as your own work is academic misconduct.
- Make sure you are making your own decisions, not just copying what AI says.

Tip: *You are in control. AI can help, but the final thinking and work must be yours.*

T—THINK CRITICALLY AND REFLECT

Finally, pause and reflect on the experience of using AI.

- What ideas or questions has this sparked for further exploration?
- What have you learned or seen differently through this interaction?
- How has it deepened your understanding or challenged your thinking?
- How effective was the AI as a learning support tool in this instance?
- Did it give you new ideas or perspectives?
- What was helpful—and what was not helpful?

- How will you approach AI differently next time?
- Have you clearly shown how you've upheld academic standards?
- Did you properly attribute any AI content you included?

Tip: AI is a tool, not a substitute for your learning. Growth comes from thinking, questioning, and doing the work.

ETHICAL CONSIDERATIONS AND BOUNDARIES IN USING AI

As you integrate AI into your academic work, it is crucial to navigate ethical considerations and respect important boundaries. One key aspect is privacy: Always be cautious about sharing personal information, unpublished research, or sensitive academic data when using AI tools. These platforms are not designed to securely handle confidential material, so protecting your privacy must be a priority.

Another important factor is equity. Not everyone has equal access to AI tools, and this imbalance can affect fairness in group work and classroom discussions. Be mindful of how AI use might impact others and strive to maintain an inclusive learning environment.

AI tools can also reproduce existing biases, stereotypes, or misinformation. This means you must apply critical judgment at every step, questioning outputs rather than accepting them at face value. Remember that your university and future employers highly value your originality; your unique ideas and contributions are what truly matter.

When it comes to citing AI use, transparency is essential. If AI has influenced the structure, phrasing, or core ideas of your work, or if you quote or paraphrase AI-generated content directly, you should acknowledge this clearly according to your institution's guidelines.

USING AI RESPONSIBLY TO ENHANCE LEARNING

You are entering a world where AI literacy is expected, but independent thinking remains invaluable. AI can make you a more effective learner, thinker, and writer—if you use it wisely. Here are some guiding principles for responsible AI use:

- Use AI to enhance, not replace, your capabilities.
- Let AI help you learn faster, not lazier.

- Use it to think deeper, not narrower.
- Always start with your own questions and engage actively with your material.
- Treat AI like a tutor or brainstorming partner, not a source of finished answers.
- Stay grounded in ethical academic practices throughout your work.

It is important that you do not copy and paste AI-generated content directly into your assignments unless explicitly permitted. Instead, use AI to support your research and thinking, for example, by brainstorming ideas or exploring different perspectives. But your own ideas, analysis, and academic voice must remain the core of your work.

If you use AI for language assistance, such as grammar or spelling, keep it limited to basic corrections unless your institution allows otherwise. Over-reliance on AI can flatten or dilute your thinking, so use these tools thoughtfully and with care.

AI-generated content is not reliable, traceable, or recoverable, so it should never be cited as a formal source. Instead, treat AI responses as a starting point, guiding you to consult credible, scholarly sources you can verify and cite appropriately.

MAINTAINING INTEGRITY AND CRITICAL ENGAGEMENT

Your academic integrity depends on submitting work that reflects your own thinking and voice. Always be confident that what you submit is your own creation, supported but not replaced by AI tools.

Use models like CRAFT to evaluate and integrate AI outputs meaningfully. Remember that independent research, reflection, and review remain central to university-level work. Consult a wide range of credible sources, cross-check facts, and do not rely too heavily on AI, which can limit creativity and curiosity.

Before using AI, consider whether it will enhance or hinder your learning and development. Your degree should represent not just what you know, but how you've learned to think, inquire, and create.

AI is a tool—not a teacher, not a textbook, and not a shortcut. Your learning depends on your engagement, judgment, and integrity. Use AI wisely, transparently, and ethically to support your academic journey and personal growth.

THE IMPORTANCE OF FOUNDATIONAL KNOWLEDGE AND ETHICAL AI USE

As AI becomes more integrated into higher education and professional practice, it is tempting to rely on it for speed and convenience. But the reality is, if you do not build a strong foundation of knowledge in your subject—especially in a discipline like law—you will not have the skills to check or verify what AI gives you. And that's a serious risk.

AI tools are not experts. They generate plausible-sounding responses based on patterns in data, not genuine understanding. Without the underpinning legal knowledge and critical reasoning skills that your degree is designed to develop, you will not be able to spot errors, challenge assumptions, or assess the reliability of AI-generated content. And in a field like legal practice, where accuracy, clarity, and ethical judgment are essential, that kind of unchecked reliance could have real consequences.

Learning how to use AI ethically and responsibly is not just about meeting academic integrity standards—it is about preparing yourself for professional practice. If you do not understand the legal principles, frameworks or methods you are working with, you will not be equipped to use AI as anything more than a surface-level tool. Worse, you may reproduce incorrect information, violate confidentiality boundaries, or fail to meet the expectations of clients, colleagues, or courts.

Employers, particularly in the legal field, are looking for graduates who can think independently, assess information critically, and communicate with precision. AI can support your growth in these areas, but only if *you* are in control. That means starting with your own understanding, using AI to explore and test ideas, and always verifying and refining outputs based on your own expertise.

In short: You cannot outsource learning. AI can assist, but it cannot replace the core academic and ethical skills required for professional competence. If you want to move into legal practice with confidence and credibility, you must do the hard work of learning the law—and learning how to use AI tools wisely, transparently, and with sound judgment.

USING AI IN THE PRACTICE OF LAW

AI is revolutionising the legal profession by enhancing efficiency, accuracy, and client service through a wide range of applications. This overview explores how AI is integrated into various aspects of legal practice, from predictive analytics and case management to ethical considerations and access to justice.

Legal practice has long made use of AI—through tools for legal research, contract review, predictive analytics, document review, and case management. What's new with *Generative AI*, however, is its ability not only to retrieve or organise existing material but to *produce* novel text, simulate arguments, generate drafts, and help craft legal strategy in more fluid, creative ways. In this section, we discuss key areas where Generative AI adds value, alongside more established uses.

ESTABLISHED USES OF AI IN LEGAL PRACTICE

Traditional AI tools have helped legal professionals manage information, reduce administrative burdens, and improve decision-making with speed and accuracy. These established applications continue to play a crucial role across legal workflows.

Legal research and case law analysis

AI-powered legal databases like Westlaw, LexisNexis, Casetext, and others allow lawyers to:

- Rapidly search and summarise case law, statutes, and regulations across jurisdictions.
- Identify precedents and key legal principles with far greater speed than manual methods.
- Predict legal trends or uncover novel arguments by analysing patterns in case law.
- Access real-time updates on legal developments, ensuring arguments are based on the most current law.

Document review and e-discovery

AI automates the time-intensive task of reviewing large volumes of documents in litigation, investigations, or due diligence:

- E-discovery platforms like Relativity and Everlaw can identify, categorise, and flag relevant materials from millions of documents.

- Natural language processing helps tools understand context and highlight key evidence or legal issues.
- This drastically reduces the cost and time associated with manual review, while also lowering the risk of missing critical data.

Contract analysis and management

AI assists with contract-heavy workflows by:

- Extracting, categorising, and reviewing clauses for risk, compliance or litigation exposure.
- Highlighting non-standard or high-risk language that could lead to disputes.
- Automating reminders for renewal dates, performance obligations, and key deadlines.
- Tools like Kira Systems and Luminance are used extensively in mergers, acquisitions, and commercial transactions to review thousands of contracts efficiently.

Case outcome and settlement prediction

Predictive analytics tools use historical data to:

- Assess likely case outcomes based on judge behaviour, jurisdiction, and case specifics.
- Forecast settlement probabilities, helping lawyers decide whether to negotiate or proceed to trial.
- Anticipate sentencing ranges or recidivism risk in criminal matters.
- Support litigation strategy by simulating negotiation outcomes or alternative scenarios.

Performance metrics and strategic insights

Firms use AI to monitor and evaluate:

- Success rates of specific motions, appeals, or trial strategies.
- Case durations and workflow bottlenecks to improve efficiency.
- Performance of opposing counsel to tailor litigation tactics.
- Judge-specific preferences and tendencies (e.g., common rulings, procedural preferences).

Case management and workflow automation

AI enhances day-to-day practice management by:

- Automating document filing, deadline tracking, and calendar management.
- Integrating with court databases to avoid missed hearings or procedural missteps.
- Monitoring ongoing cases across jurisdictions and adjusting strategies based on developments.
- Freeing up legal teams to focus on higher-value tasks by handling administrative processes.

Client communication and service delivery

Traditional AI tools have also transformed the client experience:

- AI chatbots and virtual assistants streamline client intake and FAQs.
- Real-time translation and transcription tools bridge language barriers during consultations or court appearances.
- AI can personalise communication, suggest proactive updates, and track sentiment, creating more responsive, accessible, and inclusive services.

EMERGING USES ENABLED BY GENERATIVE AI

While traditional AI has long supported legal research, document review, and workflow optimisation, the rise of Generative AI tools which can produce original content like text, summaries, arguments, and even strategy suggestions represents a significant shift in how lawyers interact with legal information and perform their work.

Generative AI tools are still evolving and must be used with caution, critical thinking, and oversight, especially in a legal context. However, their potential to augment legal practice is rapidly expanding across a number of domains.

Drafting legal content and writing assistance

Generative AI can significantly accelerate legal drafting processes by:

- Producing first drafts of legal briefs, memos, letters, or pleadings based on case facts or legal questions.

- Rewriting or improving grammar, clarity, tone, and style—particularly useful for junior lawyers or non-native English speakers.
- Suggesting alternative clause phrasing or language tailored to specific jurisdictions or regulatory requirements.
- Helping lawyers align tone and structure with the intended audience (judges, clients, opposing counsel).
- Enhancing clarity and persuasion by refining argument structure or simplifying complex legal language

However, AI-generated legal writing must always be reviewed by a qualified practitioner. Generative AI cannot reliably understand legal nuance, ensure factual accuracy, or meet jurisdictional requirements on its own.

BRAINSTORMING AND IDEATION

Generative AI is becoming a useful tool in the early stages of legal work, supporting:

- Brainstorming research questions, hypotheses, or lines of legal inquiry.
- Generating counterarguments in litigation or regulatory matters.
- Exploring interdisciplinary or comparative perspectives on legal problems.
- Offering examples, analogies, or metaphors to explain complex legal ideas in plain language—useful in both advocacy and client-facing work.
- Identifying emerging issues or unexplored angles in areas like tech law, privacy, or AI regulation.

These capabilities encourage legal professionals to explore more diverse, innovative, and user-centred ways of thinking about legal challenges.

Structuring and organising legal work

Generative AI can assist with:

- Outlining complex opinions, reports, or legal documents such as literature reviews, court submissions, or opinion letters.
- Structuring arguments logically by suggesting how to sequence points or connect legal authorities.

- Developing work/study schedules or task plans for junior lawyers, trainees, or students learning legal skills.
- Generating checklists or procedural guides for areas like litigation preparation, contract review, or regulatory compliance.

These tools support better time management, improved workflows, and a more strategic approach to legal tasks.

Simulating legal reasoning and scenarios

One of the more advanced applications of Generative AI is its ability to simulate reasoning and anticipate how legal ideas might play out:

- Mimicking Socratic questioning or prompting deeper exploration of legal principles.
- Running "What if . . ." scenarios to test legal theories, negotiation strategies, or hypothetical legal changes.
- Simulating jury reactions or the tone and framing of opening/closing statements.
- Testing negotiation tactics by generating possible counteroffers or settlement framing.
- Identifying potential flaws or gaps in legal arguments, enabling lawyers to strengthen their case proactively.

While this does not replace expert judgment, it helps lawyers think through options more efficiently and creatively.

Supporting professional communication and client interaction

Generative AI tools can:

- Draft professional emails, memos, CVs, or cover letters.
- Translate legal content or client communication to/from other languages.
- Prepare clients for interviews, depositions, or hearings by simulating Q&A.
- Generate simplified summaries of legal documents for clients.
- Tailor communications based on client tone, needs, or background, supporting better client experience.

By enhancing day-to-day communication, Generative AI improves service delivery and accessibility, especially for international or multilingual clients.

Enhancing legal education and training

For law students and early-career professionals, Generative AI offers valuable learning support:

- Clarifying complex legal theories (like a tutor might).
- Summarising lecture notes, judgments, or statutes.
- Generating self-test questions or multiple-choice quizzes.
- Rewriting or simplifying technical legal language for study or comprehension.
- Suggesting relevant readings, case law, or legal commentary.

Used responsibly, Generative AI can help learners build foundational knowledge, reflect on their reasoning, and improve academic performance—provided they remain the primary thinkers and evaluators of their own work.

Ethical Considerations and Risks with Generative AI

Generative AI is not a shortcut to legal expertise, but it is a powerful tool for thinking, drafting, learning, and developing strategy. When used thoughtfully, it can help legal professionals work more efficiently, develop stronger arguments, and better serve their clients. But without critical thinking, foundational legal knowledge, and ethical awareness, its misuse could undermine both credibility and compliance.

While legal-specific AI tools like Lexis+ AI or Westlaw Precision are often marketed as more reliable than general-purpose models such as ChatGPT, it is essential to understand that no AI system is infallible. For instance, research by Magesh et al. in 2024 found that Lexis AI had an overall accuracy rate of just 65%, even when responding to legal queries within its domain. This highlights a crucial point: specialisation does not guarantee precision. While these tools are becoming increasingly sophisticated, they still make mistakes, overlook nuances or produce outdated or jurisdictionally incorrect results. As such, students and legal professionals must approach AI outputs with a critical, questioning mindset.

Trusting the tool unquestioningly—even if it is purpose-built for legal practice—risks introducing errors, omissions, or ethical missteps into client work. Checking, verifying, and interpreting AI-generated content remains a core professional responsibility, and developing these habits now is essential preparation for ethical legal practice in an AI-augmented profession. Legal professionals must verify AI-generated content against authoritative sources to ensure accuracy and uphold ethical standards. While these tools can enhance efficiency, they should not replace the lawyer's judgment, which remains central to legal practice.[16]

Generative AI raises new ethical, verification, and professional responsibility issues:

- Outputs must be checked carefully; AI does not "know" the law.
- Unique legal reasoning, interpretation, and domain knowledge are essential for quality and liability.
- Transparency and originality become more complex but even more important.

While Generative AI offers great potential, its use must remain firmly grounded in legal ethics, professional responsibility, and academic integrity. Users must:

- Never submit AI-generated text as original legal advice or academic work unless clearly allowed and cited.
- Always review AI outputs critically, for factual accuracy, legal validity, and ethical risks.
- Never input confidential client data or sensitive legal information into public GenAI tools.
- Be aware of bias, misinformation, or overconfidence in AI responses.
- Understand that Generative AI is not a legal authority and cannot replace professional legal reasoning or citation to primary sources.

16 V. Magesh, F. Surani, M. Dahl, M. Suzgun, C. Manning and D. Ho, 'Hallucination-Free? Assessing the Reliability of Leading AI Legal Research Tools' (2025) *Journal of Empirical Legal Studies* 1–27. <https://dho.stanford.edu/wp-content/uploads/Legal_RAG_Hallucinations.pdf> accessed 30 September 2025.

AI has long supported law in more mechanical, retrieval-oriented tasks. Generative AI layers on creative, generative, and predictive power—but only those who have mastered core legal knowledge and ethical use can safely and effectively use that power in professional practice.

PUTTING THE CRAFT MODEL INTO PRACTICE

We have developed a scenario in which we show you how AI can augment legal practice, but the lawyer remains the architect, advocate, and ethical compass throughout.

The client matter here is a simple commercial contract dispute.

INITIAL CONTACT AND CLIENT ONBOARDING

A small business owner, Jane, contacts a mid-sized law firm through its website, concerned about a breach of contract by one of her suppliers.

AI's role:

- AI-enabled chatbot on the website responds in real time, asks relevant triage questions, and identifies that Jane may need commercial litigation support.
- The bot schedules an appointment and pre-fills an intelligent intake form, including a brief case summary, key dates, and contract upload.
- AI streamlines client onboarding, improves responsiveness, and allows early issue spotting.

Lawyer's role:

- Professional responsibility begins immediately. The lawyer must review the AI-gathered information critically and verify its accuracy.
- Empathetic engagement: The initial meeting is still handled by a qualified lawyer to build rapport and assess risks. During the first consultation, the lawyer listens to the client's concerns, clarifies facts, explains legal options, and establishes trust—things AI cannot do.
- Early risk assessment and duty of care rest firmly with the lawyer, especially if the client is emotionally distressed or legally vulnerable.

CRAFT model focus: Comprehend, Think Critically, Forward-Thinking

Comprehend: What types of information did the AI gather during Jane's initial contact? Why is this information useful to the lawyer?

1 Think Critically: What risks arise if the lawyer relies solely on AI-generated intake data without verifying it? Consider issues such as accuracy, empathy, or potential legal complexity.

2 Forward-Thinking: How might over-reliance on AI at this early stage impact the client relationship or the case strategy later on?

CONFLICT CHECKS AND MATTER OPENING

AI's role:

- AI runs conflict checks across the firm's database in seconds, flagging potential issues for human review.
- The system uses natural language processing and text classification to auto-categorise the matter type and suggest appropriate billing models.
- Administrative efficiencies free up time for higher-value client interaction.

Lawyer's role:

- Final conflict clearance is a legal and ethical duty; the lawyer must review flagged conflicts carefully and assess materiality.
- Billing discussions must be handled with transparency and tailored to the client's situation, ensuring informed consent.

CRAFT model focus: Relevance, Analyse, Think Critically

1 Relevance: Why must final conflict clearance remain a human responsibility even if AI flags potential conflicts efficiently?

2 Analyse: If the AI system miscategorises the matter or suggests the wrong billing model, what could the consequences be for the client and firm?

3 Think Critically: Should clients be told that AI tools are being used to help open their matter? Why or why not?

DOCUMENT REVIEW AND CASE ANALYSIS

The lawyer uploads the supplier contract and related correspondence.

AI's role:

- AI analyses contracts and correspondence to extract clauses and timelines, and to identify key issues.
- AI conducts clause extraction and comparison to standard commercial terms.
- AI identifies potential breach points.
- AI generates a timeline of key events.
- AI suggests relevant legal precedents and jurisprudence, which the lawyer reviews for accuracy and relevance.
- AI accelerates early analysis but does not make legal judgements. Human interpretation remains critical.

Lawyer's role:

- Interpretation and strategic analysis remain the lawyer's domain. AI can spot patterns, but it cannot determine legal relevance or assess credibility.
- The lawyer verifies every AI-generated insight, ensuring it aligns with the facts and jurisdictional nuances.
- Professional competence requires lawyers to understand the limits of the tool and to avoid over-reliance.

CRAFT Focus: Comprehend, Analyse, Think Critically

1 Comprehend: What specific tasks did AI assist with during the document review stage? How do these tasks support early case analysis?

2 Analyse: How can a lawyer assess whether AI-suggested precedents or clause interpretations are jurisdictionally accurate?

3 Think Critically: What professional risks arise if the lawyer accepts the AI's breach analysis without reviewing the correspondence in detail?

CLIENT COMMUNICATION

AI's role:

- AI generates a draft client memo summarising the legal position, risks, and possible remedies.
- AI-assisted tools help prepare a client-facing litigation roadmap with projected timelines and cost estimates.
- Client understanding is enhanced by clear, AI-generated visualisations, but trust is built through personal engagement.

Lawyer's role:

- Translates legal complexity into clear, tailored advice the client can act on.
- Customises it with strategic advice tailored to Jane's business priorities.
- Strategic judgment—weighing risks, costs, commercial context, and client priorities—is the lawyer's core responsibility.
- The lawyer maintains ongoing informed consent, ensuring the client understands each stage and decision point.

CRAFT model focus: Relevance, Analyse, Forward-Thinking

1. Relevance: How does AI improve the client's understanding of the legal process? Where might it fall short?
2. Analyse: What are the ethical implications of using AI-generated client memos or litigation timelines in real client communication?
3. Forward-Thinking: How might future Generative AI tools be designed to better support personalised legal advice while preserving the lawyer's ethical duties?

DRAFTING LEGAL DOCUMENTS

AI's role:

- AI assists in drafting a letter before action, pulling language from similar successful cases.

- If litigation proceeds, the system can help generate:
  - Draft pleadings
  - Initial disclosure lists
  - Skeleton arguments (based on a library of prior submissions)

Lawyer's role and responsibilities:

- Drafting is a critical professional activity. The lawyer reviews and refines all outputs, ensuring accuracy, tone, and compliance with procedural rules.
- The lawyer ensures legal accuracy, tone, and compliance with court rules—AI handles the groundwork, not the final product.
- The lawyer ensures that documents reflect the client's specific situation and goals, not just a generic output.
- The lawyer maintains confidentiality and data security when using AI tools—a key professional obligation.

CRAFT model focus: Analyse, Think Critically, Comprehend

1. Analyse: How can a lawyer balance the efficiency gains of AI drafting with the need to maintain professional standards?
2. Think Critically: What risks exist if AI-drafted documents are submitted without proper legal review? Consider both technical (e.g. court rules) and ethical (e.g. client interests) aspects.
3. Comprehend: What professional obligations must the lawyer meet when using AI tools to generate or edit legal documents?

NEGOTIATION AND SETTLEMENT SUPPORT

AI's role:

- During pre-trial negotiations, AI tools model settlement scenarios, factoring in potential costs, success probabilities, and case timelines.
- Chat-based tools simulate potential counterparty arguments, helping lawyers anticipate and prepare responses.

Lawyer's role:

- Negotiation is a human skill requiring judgement, persuasion, and flexibility—no AI can replicate that in real time.
- The lawyer uses AI data cautiously, aware that risk modelling is probabilistic, not predictive.
- Advises the client on the legal, commercial, and personal implications of any settlement.
- AI supports decision-making, but strategic calls and client counselling remain human responsibilities.

CRAFT model focus: Forward-Thinking, Think Critically, Analyse

1. Forward-Thinking: How might AI change the way lawyers prepare for negotiations in the future? What new skills might become essential?
2. Think Critically: If AI models suggest an early settlement that the client dislikes, how should the lawyer manage the discussion?
3. Analyse: What is the difference between data-informed and data-driven negotiation? Why does this distinction matter?

OUTCOME, BILLING, AND POST-MATTER REVIEW

AI's role:

- AI prepares a case summary for internal knowledge sharing.
- AI updates the firm's precedent database with anonymised insights.
- AI analyses time-recording data for billing optimisation.
- The client receives an automated feedback request, and AI analyses responses across the firm to improve service quality.
- AI helps turn one matter into institutional learning while enhancing client service continuity.

Lawyer's role:

- The lawyer conducts a final review of billing for fairness, transparency, and compliance with client agreements.

- The lawyer reflects on the matter—not just outcomes, but processes to improve practice.
- The lawyer ensures client feedback is considered professionally, especially if any complaints arise.

CRAFT Focus: Analyse, Think Critically, Forward-Thinking

1 Analyse: What benefits can AI bring to post-matter analysis and firm knowledge management? What are the potential risks?

2 Think Critically: Should AI-generated client feedback analysis be relied upon to evaluate a lawyer's performance? Why or why not?

3 Forward-Thinking: What ethical or reputational considerations might arise if law firms over-automate billing and feedback processes?

Map each stage of the client matter (from onboarding to outcome) to relevant parts of the CRAFT model:

- Which stages rely most heavily on comprehension and critical thinking?
- Where does forward-thinking become especially important?
- Where is the boundary between AI support and professional responsibility most clearly tested?

THE LAWYER'S ROLE

At each stage of the client care lifecycle, AI offers speed, structure, and support, but it must be the lawyer who:

- Exercises legal and ethical judgment
- Builds and sustains the client relationship
- Maintains professional responsibility and confidentiality
- Tailors legal strategy to unique facts and goals
- Stands accountable to the client, the court, and the profession

In this new era of augmented legal practice, AI is a powerful tool. AI can support nearly every stage of a client matter, from intake and research to drafting, negotiation, and review, but always under the direction and ethical oversight of qualified legal professionals. The technology enhances efficiency, consistency, and insight. But it is not, and must never become, a replacement for the lawyer's role as trusted advisor, ethical guardian, and strategic thinker. The human lawyer remains central: advising, interpreting, and advocating with nuance and empathy. The future of law lies not in resisting technology, but in mastering it with integrity, always in service of justice, client care, and professional excellence.

Because legal work involves highly sensitive client information, it is essential to use AI tools that meet strict data protection and privacy standards.

Tips:

- Prioritise data security: Always consider the privacy and confidentiality of client information when using AI tools.
- Vet AI providers carefully: Research and select vendors with proven, robust security measures.
- Stay current on regulations: Keep informed about data privacy laws that impact legal practice.
- Advocate for ethical AI use: Understand the importance of responsible data governance and compliance in the deployment of AI.
- Develop a privacy-first mindset: Recognise that protecting client data is not just legal compliance but a core part of ethical legal practice.

As discussed earlier in this chapter, artificial intelligence can sometimes produce false or misleading information, an issue commonly referred to as "hallucination". These inaccuracies are not intentional; rather, they occur when AI tries to fill in informational gaps by drawing from patterns it has learned. The result may sound plausible, but it can be completely incorrect, much like a human confidently guessing or inventing facts.

In the legal profession, the consequences of AI hallucinations can be particularly serious. For example, an AI-based legal research tool might generate a fictitious case or misquote a legal precedent. If a lawyer relies on such faulty information, it could lead to weak legal arguments, negative rulings, and broader harm to the integrity of the legal process. To mitigate these risks, cross-checking AI-generated content against trusted legal databases like Westlaw or LexisNexis is crucial. AI tools should be treated as starting points, not final sources.

Careful verification and a critical mindset are essential to uphold professional standards and prevent the spread of misinformation within legal practice.[17]

Sync 1

The practice of law remains deeply human. In its current stage of development, AI cannot replace critical qualities like nuanced judgment, empathy, and creativity that human lawyers bring.

You should allow around 45–60 minutes to reflect on the following questions:

- How can lawyers balance reliance on AI with their own professional judgment to avoid potential pitfalls?
- In what ways might AI's inability to understand human emotions or ethical considerations impact legal decision-making?
- What steps should a lawyer take to verify and validate AI-generated recommendations in their practice?
- How might overreliance on AI affect the quality and fairness of legal services?
- What are the ethical responsibilities of lawyers when using AI tools in their work?
- How might the collaboration between AI and human lawyers reshape the role of legal professionals? Could AI enhance or hinder critical thinking and creativity in legal practice?
- If AI begins to outperform lawyers in research and argumentation, what challenges and opportunities might arise for the legal profession?
- What measures should be in place to ensure that AI-driven legal strategies uphold ethical standards and contribute to justice rather than undermine it?
- How can lawyers identify and address biases in the data that AI systems are trained on to avoid unfair or flawed legal recommendations?

17 D. Charlotin, 'AI Hallucination Cases' <https://www.damiencharlotin.com/hallucinations/> accessed 30 September 2025.

- Given that AI can sometimes produce incorrect or misleading information, how should legal professionals balance reliance on AI tools with their own critical thinking and professional judgment?
- In what ways can AI be used as a powerful assistant without replacing the essential role of due diligence and human expertise in legal work?

ACCESS TO JUSTICE AND LEGAL EMPOWERMENT

Around the globe, millions struggle to resolve legal issues due to high costs, limited legal aid, complex procedures, and geographic isolation. In many regions, even simple disputes, like those involving housing, employment, or small claims, go unresolved because individuals either cannot afford a lawyer or find the legal system too difficult to navigate alone. These issues are discussed further in Chapter 4. Responsibly developed artificial intelligence offers a promising way to close this justice gap. Beyond just improving current legal processes, AI has the potential to fundamentally reshape how people access, understand, and interact with the law, especially those historically excluded from the system.

One of the most enduring barriers to justice is financial. According to the World Justice Project (2023), more than 5 billion people globally lack meaningful access to justice.[18] A Law Society report (2024) reveals that civil legal aid fees have stalled for nearly three decades, resulting in widespread "legal aid deserts" outside urban centres.[19] The National Audit Office found that in 2022–3, over half of the

18 World Justice Project, 'Global Insights on Access to Justice' (2023) <https://worldjusticeproject.org>; also see HiiL, Understanding Justice Needs—The Elephant in the Courtroom, The Hague; Justice for All: The Report of the Task Force on Justice April 2019' (2018) <chrome-extension://efaidnbmnnnibpcajpcglclefindmkaj/https://www.hiil.org/wp-content/uploads/2019/06/Justice-for-All-report-1.pdf>

19 Law Society of England and Wales, 'Civil Legal Aid: Millions Still without Access to Justice' (21 February 2024) <https://www.lawsociety.org.uk/contact-or-visit-us/press-office/press-releases/civil-legal-aid-millions-still-without-access-to-justice>; Law Society of England and Wales, 'Access to Justice Crisis: Millions Left without Legal Aid' (21 February 2024) <https://www.solicitorsjournal.com/sjarticle/access-to-justice-crisis-millions-left-without-legal-aid> accessed 30 September 2025.

population lived more than 10 kilometres from a legal aid provider.[20] These shortfalls disproportionately affect women, especially those dealing with domestic abuse or maternity discrimination, with 85% reporting difficulty accessing civil legal aid.

AI-driven platforms can dramatically reduce the cost of delivering legal assistance by automating routine tasks like document preparation, legal triage, and information retrieval. But cost is only part of the problem. Legal systems are often inaccessible by design, full of procedural hurdles, obscure language, and systems that presume legal literacy. For non-lawyers, this complexity can be overwhelming. AI, particularly in the form of natural language processing tools, can decode legal jargon and translate it into plain, understandable language. This alone can empower users to better comprehend their rights and responsibilities. AI offers a route forward through cost reduction, streamlined guidance, and expanded reach. Automated platforms can:

- Lower costs by handling routine tasks like legal triage, document drafting, and information retrieval.
- Simplify complexity through natural language explanations and step-by-step guidance.
- Increase availability, offering 24/7 support via virtual assistants or a "one-stop legal entry point" akin to an "NHS 111 for law".

Professor Rebecca Sandefur is an American sociologist and legal scholar known for her influential work on access to justice, civil legal needs, and the role of legal services in society. She is recipient of a MacArthur "Genius" Fellowship in 2018 for her work on how people resolve their civil justice problems and how legal systems can be more responsive and equitable. Sandefur challenges the traditional assumption that access to justice equals access to lawyers. She instead argues for a people-centred metric, measuring success based on whether people can resolve their legal issues fairly, efficiently, and with dignity. This shifts the focus from legal infrastructure to legal outcomes and capabilities. AI, in this context, becomes a facilitator of legal capability, not merely legal information. It also supports the argument that AI should aim not to replace lawyers, but instead to increase people's ability to resolve

20 Committee of Public Accounts, 'Value for Money from Legal Aid (NAO Findings on Legal Aid Deserts)' (2023) <https://publications.parliament.uk/pa/cm5804/cmselect/cmpubacc/481/report.html> accessed 30 September 2025.

problems, especially for those traditionally underserved by the legal system.[21]

We are already seeing the emergence of AI-powered legal assistance platforms that can help individuals complete forms, generate documents, and receive tailored legal advice. For example:

- Document automation tools can guide users through step-by-step questionnaires to create simple legal documents such as wills, leases, small claims filings or protection orders, at little or no cost.
- Conversational AI chatbots, such as those piloted by DoNotPay or LawDroid, offer 24/7 support to answer common legal questions, suggest next steps, and refer users to human support when needed.[22]
- Guided pathways provide interactive, logic-based routes through common legal problems, offering checklists, deadlines, and procedural advice tailored to individual circumstances.

The UK Ministry of Justice's AI Action Plan (2025) envisions citizen-facing tools to help people navigate legal options, resolve disputes without court, and file claims more equitably.[23] This government-led vision reflects a commitment to integrating AI across the justice system in a fair and scalable manner. Meanwhile, in its final 21st Century Justice report (2025), the Law Society has called for the creation of an AI-backed "one-stop shop" platform to provide a single digital entry point into the civil justice system.[24] The goal is to help individuals better understand their legal problems and connect them with appropriate support, whether it be legal advice, online dispute resolution (ODR), or litigation, guiding users through civil legal problems

21 R. Sandefur, 'Access to What?' (2019) 148(1) *Daedalus* 49–59 <https://direct.mit.edu/daed/article/148/1/49/27247/Access-to-What> accessed 30 September 2025.

22 DoNotPay, 'The World's First Robot Lawyer' (2023) <https://donotpay.com> accessed 30 September 2025.

23 Ministry of Justice, 'AI Action Plan for Justice' (2025) <https://www.gov.uk/government/publications/ai-action-plan-for-justice/ai-action-plan-for-justice> accessed 30 September 2025.

24 Law Society of England and Wales, 'Law Society Calls for "One-Stop Shop" AI Platform for Civil Justice' (24 June 2025) <https://www.legalfutures.co.uk/latest-news/law-society-calls-for-one-stop-shop-ai-platform-for-civil-justice> accessed 30 September 2025. Also see: Solicitors Regulation Authority, 'Improving Access—Tackling Unmet Legal Needs' (2023) <https://www.sra.org.uk/sra/research-publications/improving-access---tackling-unmet-legal-needs/> accessed 2 January 2026.

and directing them to appropriate dispute resolution options. The then Law Society president Richard Atkinson reinforced the message that justice is a public service, and that modernising it through AI and digital innovation must ensure inclusivity and fairness for all, regardless of background or means.[25]

AI can also support virtual legal clinics that operate beyond office hours, staffed by hybrid teams of AI assistants and remote lawyers. These models are particularly impactful in rural or underserved communities where physical legal services may be unavailable.

One of AI's most powerful features is its scalability and adaptability. It can be programmed to provide services in multiple languages, helping to break down linguistic barriers that often prevent refugees and minority communities from seeking legal assistance. It can also offer accessible formats for people with disabilities, ensuring that information is delivered in ways that match individual needs, whether that is via voice, text, or visual aids.

AI can also be proactive, identifying legal risks and flagging potential problems before they escalate. For example, predictive analytics might help tenants understand if they are at risk of eviction or assist consumers in identifying unfair contract terms. This kind of pre-emptive support has the potential to shift justice systems from being reactive to truly preventative.

The future of access to justice also lies in how disputes are resolved. AI is playing a growing role in online dispute resolution (ODR) platforms, which allow parties to mediate and settle disputes virtually. Courts in the UK are exploring AI-supported virtual hearings, case triage, and digital filing systems, creating faster, more accessible alternatives to traditional litigation.[26] These systems can particularly benefit those with mobility challenges, caregiving responsibilities, or jobs that prevent them from attending court during working hours.

The UK's Ministry of Justice is piloting AI chatbots to help users navigate complex legal processes, especially in areas like child arrangement disputes.[27] These tools, adapted from the GOV.UK Chat

25 'Redefining 21st Century Justice as a Vital Public Service' (The Law Society, 25 June 2025) <https://www.lawsociety.org.uk/contact-or-visit-us/press-office/press-releases/redefining-21st-century-justice-as-a-vital-public-service> accessed 3 January 2026.

26 R. Susskind, *Online Courts and the Future of Justice* (OUP 2019).

27 Ministry of Justice, 'AI Action Plan for Justice' (2025) <https://www.gov.uk/government/publications/ai-action-plan-for-justice/ai-action-plan-for-justice> accessed 30 September 2025.

interface, can deliver real-time advice and suggest alternative dispute resolution pathways, reducing unnecessary court applications.

According to the Master of the Rolls (2023), following COVID-19 pandemic adaptations, the business and property courts transitioned from in-person to full remote hearings almost overnight.[28] This shift demonstrated the feasibility of online court proceedings and paved the way for a broader digital transformation. The Online Procedure Rule Committee (OPRC), established under the Judicial Review and Courts Act 2022, oversees rulemaking for fully digital case handling in civil, family, and tribunal matters. It facilitates pre-action triage, ODR integration, and smart case management via a unified online portal.

Lord Briggs's proposal for an Online Civil Money Claims system, inspired by Canada's Civil Resolution Tribunal, has received significant investment—up to £1.4 billion—to roll out a digital-first approach across courts and tribunals in England and Wales.[29] ODR is being progressively embedded across UK sectors, especially with the HMCTS Online Civil Money Claims (OCMC) platform for filing and resolving small claims entirely online. Platforms like Resolve Disputes Online (RDO) offer court-grade features—automated intake, mediation tools, video hearings, and digital case management, demonstrating how digital infrastructure can reshape case handling.

AI's role in improving access to justice is not about replacing human expertise; it is about scaling compassion, capability, and clarity in a system that too often leaves people behind. When responsibly integrated, AI can democratise legal support, making it cheaper, easier to understand, and available to all, regardless of geography, income, or background. It is important to clarify: AI is here not to replace lawyers, but to augment their capabilities and allow them to focus on more complex, high-value work. By offloading repetitive tasks like intake, triage, and document review, AI allows legal professionals to devote more time to human advocacy, negotiation, and judgment. This human-AI collaboration is especially important in legal aid contexts where demand far outstrips capacity. AI offers a practical way to

28 'Speech by the Master of the Rolls: AI—Transforming the Work of Lawyers and Judges' (11 March 2024) <https://www.judiciary.uk/speech-by-the-master-of-the-rolls-ai-transforming-the-work-of-lawyers-and-judges/> accessed 3 January 2026.

29 'Speech by Lord Justice Colin Briggs: Online Dispute Resolution Forum' (7 June 2022) <https://www.judiciary.uk/speech-by-lord-justice-colin-birss-online-dispute-resolution-forum/> accessed 3 January 2026.

scale legal support without compromising on quality or professional oversight. Lawyers, policymakers, technologists, and justice advocates have a shared responsibility to lead this transformation ethically. That means designing systems that put people first, investing in digital public infrastructure, and ensuring that AI enhances, not erodes, our commitment to fairness and equality. The future of justice is not just more efficient—it is more inclusive, transparent, and human. AI, when applied with purpose and care, can help get us there.

CONSUMER PROTECTION

The increasing availability of AI-driven legal advice platforms—such as Contend Legal and similar services—raises important consumer protection issues. These platforms often operate outside the scope of traditional legal regulation, creating risks for individuals who rely on AI-generated advice without the benefit of professional legal oversight. The Law Society's 21st Century Justice report highlights concerns that unregulated AI legal tools could lead to misunderstandings, misapplication of the law or reliance on inaccurate information, ultimately exposing consumers to potential harm. Unlike regulated lawyers, these AI services may lack accountability, confidentiality safeguards, and the ethical duties lawyers owe clients, such as ensuring informed consent and assessing vulnerability. Therefore, it is essential to develop clear regulatory frameworks and ethical guidelines to protect consumers, ensuring AI complements rather than replaces professional legal advice, and that clients understand AI's limitations and risks.[30]

30 Law Society of England and Wales—21st Century Justice Report, 'Discusses the Challenges and Opportunities of Digital Technology in Justice, Highlighting Consumer Protection Concerns Around Unregulated AI Legal Services' (2021) <https://www.lawsociety.org.uk/topics/research/21st-century-justice-report> 'Contend Legal is a Real-World Example of an AI-Based Legal Services Platform That Provides Automated Legal Documents and Advice But Operates Outside Traditional Lawyer Regulation, Raising Questions about Consumer Protection' <https://www.law.com/legaltechnews/2021/06/10/contend-legal-raises-new-questions-about-ai-and-legal-regulation/> accessed 30 September 2025.

THE REGULATORY LANDSCAPE

The Law Society of England and Wales published detailed guidance titled "Generative AI: The Essentials" (2025).[31] The guidance advises that if you use Generative AI (GenAI) in your legal services, you are fully responsible for its outputs and must take rigorous steps to manage the ethical, legal, and operational risks. There is no specific AI regulation yet, so legal professionals must proactively safeguard clients, data, and their practice. It urges legal professionals to use Generative AI carefully, take ownership of all outputs, be transparent with clients, stay in control of procurement and exit, and treat AI as part of a broader risk-managed legal practice.

As such, solicitors retain full professional responsibility over AI-generated outputs and they must understand regulatory obligations, secure output accuracy, and manage the risk of misleading or incorrect content. The burden falls on them and on law firms to apply good governance, clear documentation, and ethical judgement when using these tools. Misuse or over-reliance on GenAI could lead to client harm, regulatory breach, reputational damage, or litigation.[32]

In October 2023, Lord Justice Briggs, a judge in the Court of Appeal of England and Wales, publicly acknowledged using ChatGPT to help draft a judgment.[33] In a speech given in September 2023 at The Law Society's Dispute Resolution Conference, Lord Justice Briggs said he asked the AI to summarise an area of law and confirmed that the summary was accurate enough to include directly in the judgment. Importantly, he reviewed and verified the AI's output himself before using it. This marked the first known use of ChatGPT by a UK judge, making it a high-profile example of AI-assisted legal writing. Lord Justice Briggs emphasised that human oversight was key; rather than wholly relying on the tool, he treated it like a "useful assistant". The example reflects a cautious, responsible model for AI use in judicial or

31 The Law Society of England and Wales, 'Generative AI: The Essentials' (20 May 2025) <https://www.lawsociety.org.uk/topics/ai-and-lawtech/generative-ai-the-essentials> accessed 30 September 2025.

32 The Law Society of England and Wales, 'Generative AI: The Essentials' (20 May 2025) <https://www.lawsociety.org.uk/topics/ai-and-lawtech/generative-ai-the-essentials> accessed 30 September 2025.

33 'Speech by the Master of the Rolls: AI—Transforming the Work of Lawyers and Judges' (11 March 2024) <https://www.judiciary.uk/speech-by-the-master-of-the-rolls-ai-transforming-the-work-of-lawyers-and-judges/> accessed 3 January 2026.

legal decision-making. It set a precedent for how legal professionals might use AI safely: as a tool to assist, not replace, judgement, and triggered broader discussion about the role of AI in courtrooms, including its benefits and limitations.

In "Bridging the Gap: A Practical Guide to Generative AI in Legal Disclosure" (2025), the Law Society emphasised explainability, validation, and human oversight, ensuring that AI augments—but does not replace—legal judgment. Its recommendations include structured prompt testing, audit-ready workflows, and transparency in AI-assisted disclosure processes.[34]

In a UK tax tribunal case, a self-represented litigant (litigant-in-person) used a generative AI tool (likely ChatGPT) to prepare their case.[35] They submitted legal arguments supported by fictitious case law citations entirely invented by the AI. The tribunal discovered that the cited cases did not exist, undermining the credibility of the submission. This case is a textbook example of AI "hallucination"—when generative AI produces false or fictional information. The litigant likely did not realise the AI's outputs needed to be verified, highlighting risks for non-experts using these tools without legal training. It reinforced warnings from regulators and courts that AI cannot be wholly relied on, especially in formal legal settings. And it prompted calls from judges and legal bodies for greater education, safeguards, and possibly even regulation around AI use in legal submissions. In June 2025, the High Court issued a warning to all lawyers in England and Wales to stop the misuse of AI tools, particularly when it leads to false or unverified content in legal documents.

The Law Society advises that the following guidance should be followed:[36]

34 The Law Society of England and Wales, 'Dispute Resolution Bridging the Gap: A Practical Guide to Generative AI in Legal Disclosure' (2 June 2025) <https://communities.lawsociety.org.uk/dispute-resolution/bridging-the-gap-a-practical-guide-to-generative-ai-in-legal-disclosure/6003339.article> accessed 30 September 2025.

35 Society of Computers and Law, 'False Citations: AI and "Hallucination"' (26 February2024)<https://www.scl.org/uk-litigant-found-to-have-cited-false-judgments-hallucinated-by-ai/> accessed 3 January 2026.

36 The Law Society of England and Wales, 'Generative AI: The Essentials' (20 May 2025) <https://www.lawsociety.org.uk/topics/ai-and-lawtech/generative-ai-the-essentials> accessed 30 September 2025. Other useful readings include: OECD, *OECD Principles on Artificial Intelligence* (2019) <https://www.oecd.org/going-digital/ai/principles/> accessed 30 September 2025; American Bar Association, 'The Future is Now: Artificial Intelligence and the Legal Profession' (2024)

Quality control and accountability

- You must fact-check everything generated by AI before using it in legal work.
- Do not rely wholly on AI—it can produce convincing but inaccurate or misleading content ("hallucinations").
- Even though AI companies are not required to audit accuracy, you are still professionally accountable for any wrong advice given to clients.

Due diligence on tools and suppliers

- Investigate the AI tool's capabilities, limitations, provider claims, and warranties.
- Do proper supplier due diligence—this includes negotiating contracts that protect you (warranties, indemnities, exit terms, IP access, source code if needed).
- Consider the sustainability of the vendor. (What happens if they shut down?)

Internal governance

- Set up clear internal policies on how AI is used by your staff.
- Provide training and usage protocols to avoid improper use.
- Integrate AI planning into existing risk management frameworks.

Transparency with clients

- Although not legally required, it is best practice to tell clients if and how Generative AI is used.

<https://www.ibanet.org/document?id=The-future-is%20now-AI-and-the-legal-profession-report> accessed 30 September 2025; Ministry of Justice & The Alan Turing Institute, 'AI and Data Science Ethics Framework' (*GOV.UK.*, 2021) <https://www.gov.uk/government/publications/ministry-of-justice-ai-and-data-science-ethics-framework> accessed 30 September 2025; The House of Lords Library, 'AI Technology and the Justice System: Lords Committee Report' (2023) <https://lordslibrary.parliament.uk/ai-technology-and-the-justice-system-lords-committee-report/> accessed 30 September 2025; Crown Prosecution Service, 'How the CPS Will Use Artificial Intelligence' (*CPS.gov.uk*, 2023) <https://www.cps.gov.uk/how-cps-will-use-artificial-intelligence> accessed 30 September 2025; The Law Society of England and Wales, 'Ethics and Artificial Intelligence in the Justice System' (2020) <https://www.lawsociety.org.uk/topics/research/ethics-and-artificial-intelligence-in-the-justice-system> accessed 30 September 2025.

- This ensures trust and avoids confusion over how legal outputs are created.

Monitoring and documentation

- Document all inputs, outputs, and any errors—especially if the AI system does not retain usage history.
- Continuously assess whether the AI tool still meets your needs.
- Evaluate performance using clear, outcome-led metrics.
- Be ready to transition away if the AI tool underperforms or becomes non-compliant.

Lifecycle and exit strategy

- Take a full lifecycle view of the AI tool: from adoption to eventual decommissioning.
- Plan for data extraction/deletion, source code access, and termination logistics.

Overlap with existing risk management

- Generative AI creates new risks, but many cybersecurity and insurance practices already in place may help mitigate them.
- You should integrate AI-specific risks into existing frameworks rather than treat them as separate.

The Law Society provides tools to help law firms evaluate AI adoption,[37] covering:

- Cybersecurity considerations
- GDPR and data protection
- Ethical and regulatory compliance
- Cost–benefit analysis and training requirements
- Guidance for SMEs seeking to collaborate on AI procurement and adoption

37 The Law Society of England and Wales, 'How Can My Firm Use AI to Benefit Our Business?' (27 January 2025) <https://www.lawsociety.org.uk/contact-or-visit-us/helplines/practice-advice-service/q-and-as/how-can-my-firm-use-ai-to-benefit-our-business> accessed 30 September 2025.

Similarly, the American Bar Association's Standing Committee on Ethics and Professional Responsibility released a Formal Opinion about lawyers and AI dated 29 July 2024, which begins as follows:

> Generative Artificial Intelligence Tools: To ensure clients are protected, lawyers using generative artificial intelligence tools must fully consider their applicable ethical obligations, including their duties to provide competent legal representation, to protect client information, to communicate with clients, to supervise their employees and agents, to advance only meritorious claims and contentions, to ensure candor toward the tribunal, and to charge reasonable fees.[38]

Key takeaways for AI use in legal practice

- *Embrace AI as a tool, not a threat.* Use AI to handle repetitive, time-consuming tasks, freeing yourself to engage with the higher-level thinking, strategy, and human interaction that define legal practice.
- *Maintain human judgment.* A qualified legal mind must always verify outputs. Always critically evaluate AI-generated insights, predictions, and recommendations rather than accepting them at face value.
- *Be transparent.* Keep clients informed about when and how AI is used in their cases, including its benefits and limitations.
- *Practise ethical responsibility.* Use AI tools responsibly to support fairness in the legal process, ensuring technology enhances rather than undermines justice.
- *Stay curious and adaptable.* Recognise that AI is driving changes in legal and ethical frameworks, and be prepared to engage with these evolving challenges thoughtfully.

Artificial intelligence is rapidly transforming the legal profession by enhancing efficiency, reshaping workflows, and redefining the role

38 American Bar Association, 'Standing Committee on Ethics and Professional Responsibility' in *Formal Opinion on Generative Artificial Intelligence Tools* (29 July 2024) <https://www.americanbar.org/content/dam/aba/administrative/professional_responsibility/ethics-opinions/aba-formal-opinion-512.pdf>

of lawyers. This technology not only automates complex tasks but also enables a more proactive, inclusive, and ethical legal system. The future of legal practice will be characterised by collaboration between AI and human judgement, fostering innovation while upholding core professional values. Viewing AI as a partner, not a threat, will allow legal professionals to build a more human-centred, ethical, and inclusive legal system that meets society's changing needs.

- *AI reshapes legal practice.* AI processes vast data, supports decision-making, and transforms tasks from contract drafting to litigation strategy, redefining legal work itself. In legal practice, AI should be evaluated based on its reliability for specific tasks, with proper oversight, verification, and lawyer review. Responsible use depends on sound judgement. This involves aligning AI tools with specific tasks, implementing oversight and verification protocols and having qualified lawyers review key outputs. AI should be assessed based on its suitability for the task, not on flawless performance.[39]
- *Future roles for lawyers.* It is not to replace the human element, but to elevate it. Lawyers will focus on strategic oversight, creative problem-solving, and client relationships as AI handles routine legal tasks, making services more accessible globally. Lawyers who thoughtfully integrate AI will lead the evolution of legal services, combining AI's analytical power with human empathy, ethics, and expertise to create a more efficient, inclusive, and responsive legal system.
- *Proactive legal systems.* AI enables predictive and preventative approaches by analysing trends to recommend early interventions, shifting legal systems from reactive to proactive models. AI can enhance client engagement and broaden access to legal services through tools like chatbots and personalised communication. When used thoughtfully, these technologies improve responsiveness and inclusivity, helping make legal services more human-centred and accessible.
- *Human-centred legal design.* AI offers a chance to redesign the legal system to be more intuitive, transparent, and user-friendly. By incorporating human-centred design and insights from other disciplines, AI can make legal processes more empathetic and accessible. This approach empowers individuals, improves understanding of

39 Stephen Embry, 'Gen AI and Law: Perfection Is Not the Point' (*TechLaw Crossroads*, 20 July 2024) <https://www.techlawcrossroads.com/2024/07/gen-ai-and-law-perfection-is-not-the-point/> accessed 30 September 2025.

legal rights, and helps prevent conflicts through clearer, more personalised support.

- *Ethics as foundation.* AI systems in law must promote fairness, transparency, and accountability. Lawyers are responsible for ensuring AI tools protect confidentiality, avoid bias, are used transparently, and remain accountable for all outcomes. AI can assist, but it cannot replace the lawyer's ethical and professional responsibilities.
- *Continuous learning is imperative.* Legal professionals must pursue ongoing education in AI technology and ethics to adapt and lead confidently in an evolving landscape. This includes staying informed, engaging in industry events, and gaining skills in both technology and ethics. The goal is to build digital literacy that empowers lawyers to adapt, evaluate, and lead confidently.
- *Human–AI collaboration and partnership.* AI acts as an amplifier for lawyers' creativity and judgement, supporting analysis and strategic thinking without replacing human decision-making. When used wisely, AI can serve as a thinking partner for lawyers, enhancing rather than replacing their reasoning. It helps uncover patterns, spark creativity, and support strategic decisions. However, human judgement must remain central, as only legal professionals can provide the necessary interpretation and context. AI expands the lawyer's mind but does not replace it.

Sync 2

You should allow around 15 minutes for this activity.

Consider the following questions:

- How do we embrace these advancements in a way that strengthens, rather than compromises, our core values?
- What characteristics form a future-oriented mindset?

LOOKING FORWARD TO ONGOING CHANGE

AI is already a powerful, transformative technology reshaping the legal profession, but we are still only witnessing the early stages of its development. We present this chapter as a mere introduction to understanding and applying AI in legal practice, warmly encouraging readers to stay curious, informed, and open as the technology rapidly evolves, and unlocks new possibilities. Legal professionals must proactively ensure AI tools are used responsibly and ethically by focusing on data quality and diversity, maintaining transparency about AI usage, and supporting policies that promote ethical AI in law. They should choose AI systems that offer explainable results, thoroughly document the AI's data sources and decision processes, and keep clients informed about AI's role and limitations. Accountability remains with lawyers; they must take responsibility for AI-driven decisions and ensure human oversight, exercising due diligence in reviewing AI outputs before acting on them.

The coming years will see continued expansion of AI capabilities, with great promise in augmenting productivity and opening new fields of endeavour perhaps previously not possible with human activity alone, but now possible with the help of AI. Emerging advances in reasoning and agentic AI systems will allow researchers and practitioners, working together with informed legal domain experts, to build new, practical, and immediately viable solutions to further the pursuit of a more equitable and insightful legal system. While this future holds tremendous promise, it also demands vigilance and ethical oversight to ensure that these powerful tools continue moving forward, always aligned with human values and justice.

Recommendations for Further Reading

Brynjolfsson E, Chandar B and Chen R, 'Canaries in the Coal Mine? Six Facts about the Recent Employment Effects of Artificial Intelligence'

Huyen C, *AI Engineering: Building Applications with Foundation Models* (O'Reilly Media, Inc 2024)

Lewis M and Mitchell M, 'Evaluating the Robustness of Analogical Reasoning in Large Language Models' [2024] CoRR <https://openreview.net/forum?id=iJgjBSN2XT> accessed 8 March 2025

Phoenix J and Taylor M, *Prompt Engineering for Generative AI* (O'Reilly Media, Inc 2024)

Raaijmakers S, *Large Language Models* (MIT Press 2025)

Tredennick J and Webber DW, 'An Introduction to Large Language Models for Ediscovery Professionals' [2024] MIT Computational Law Report <https://law.mit.edu/pub/anintroductiontolargelanguagemodelsforediscoveryprofessionals/release/1> accessed 5 December 2024

'Ethics of Artificial Intelligence | UNESCO' <https://www.unesco.org/en/artificial-intelligence/recommendation-ethics> accessed 9 August 2023

Mind Map 8.1 Chapter topics

8

Digital evidence and its admissibility in the courtroom

Ann Thanaraj

Introduction

Evidence is fundamental to the outcome of establishing the certainty of facts in civil litigation, criminal litigation, corporate matters, and settlements outside of court. With the seamless integration of the physical and digital worlds brought on by the rapid developments in technology, digital technologies provide indispensable evidence in the investigation process and where they are admissible in courts. In order to administer justice, the court requires reliable, trustworthy, and authentic evidence. The digital forensics practitioner plays a vital role in this: Their qualifications, competencies, and integrity along with their duty to present evidence in an objective and factual way support the court in determining the weight given to digital evidence. Therefore, lawyers and judges require a deep understanding of the important questions they need to ask regarding digital evidence, whether it is to identify digital evidence that is missing in cases or to analyse digital evidence which is presented in court. Lawyers must also be capable of handling digital evidence regardless of its volume and complexity. Whilst digital evidence may be presented to the court by expert witnesses such as professional digital forensic investigators during the court proceedings, a lawyer must be fully equipped to form an opinion of the witness and the evidence itself. This will involve considering its authenticity and integrity, accuracy, facts, acquisition, recovery process and analysis, and the impact of all of this to the case in hand.

By developing an awareness of the digital forensics process and forms of digital evidence, a digitally proficient lawyer will be able to determine for themselves what sorts of evidence they should ask for from a digital forensics investigator and what is discoverable. They

DOI: 10.4324/9781003602323-8

should be able to determine its relevance, understand the contents of a forensics report, determine their examination and cross-examination strategies towards the expert witness, their own client and other witnesses, and be able to explain the evidence to the judge and (where applicable) jury. By developing a solid understanding of the processes and capabilities of modern digital forensics, informed legal professionals can generate a distinct advantage for their clients and cases. Lawyers should also be able to understand the specific practices which investigators may deploy in order to recover, exhibit, and produce digital evidence and the regimes of disclosure around this, which may also have an impact on key arguments within the case.

Chapter hot spots

When reading this chapter, questions to think about include:

- What is the relevance of the digital forensics processes and the retrieval of authentic evidence in determining the strengths and weaknesses of a client's case?
- What types of evidence are discoverable from digital sources and devices?
- What digital forensics evidence is admissible in court?
- What sort of framework would be most useful to guide digital forensics professionals to ensure that their processes and evidence are admissible in court?

Having read the title and introduction, you can add any other questions you want to explore here:

AN EXPLORATION OF DEFINITIONS

Digital forensics is a discipline borne out of the need to support law enforcement in investigating acts of suspected crime, where a digital device may contain relevant data that may describe such events. Digital evidence can provide an insight into the behaviour of an individual, for example, via communication records or location information. Device interrogation may in some cases be the only source of evidence regarding an event.[1]

A digitally proficient lawyer must realise that digital evidence is a dominant form of evidence in courts. In addition, they must be able to determine the credibility and integrity of the digital evidence for use in legal proceedings. They should also be able to understand the story that the digital forensics process tells and the impact on this on the case. Guidance[2] sets out how investigators should also deal with volumes of digital evidence, and this may have an impact on how the case has been progressed. Lawyers should be familiar with the specific "chain of custody" requirements around digital evidence and should robustly test this to ensure that any digital evidence has been handled following the correct procedures, and that there is no break in the chain of custody which may offer a different explanation to the data. This is an area, through disclosure, where evidence if handled incorrectly may become inadmissible.[3]

Digital evidence is straightforward to define. The Scientific Working Group on Digital Evidence defines digital evidence as being "any information of probative value that is either stored, received or transmitted in digital form".[4] In other words, digital evidence is digital information that can be used to prove a fact or facts within a case. The sources of digital evidence go beyond information that is stored in electronic devices such as computers and mobile phones. It extends to associated networks and cloud technologies, including data, that can be retrieved from the Internet of Things (referred to in Chapter 6).[5] One's digital footprint across any device or digital platform can be used as digital evidence such as photographs, log files, instant message chats,

1 The Police Foundation, 'Digital Forensics: The Next Steps' (2020) <https://www.police-foundation.org.uk/project/the-next-steps-for-digital-forensics/> accessed 3 January 2026.

2 Attorney General's Guidelines on Disclosure (2024). Attorney General's Office, Paragraph 55 & Annex A.

3 S.78 PACE 1984, the courts' discretional power to exclude inadmissible evidence.

4 Scientific Working Group on Digital Evidence, 'SWGDE Multimedia and Digital Evidence Glossary Ver 3.0' (June 2016) 6 <https://swgde.org/documents/Current%20Documents/SWGDE%20Digital%20and%20Multimedia%20Evidence%20Glossary>

5 This is a term used to describe devices connected to the internet which consequently connect with other devices and sync and talk to each other sharing data. The connections form networks of devices which collect, share and analyse the data to produce context-specific and user-specific solutions to tasks and processes.

chats on various digital media platforms, photos, chats, log files, and emails. Digital evidence can be fragile and fleeting.

Digital evidence can play both a primary role in the investigation of a suspect or provide supplementary context in other cases. Perhaps one of the most prominent recent cases is that of Mitesh Patel,[6] who murdered his wife. In this case, in addition to traditional physical trace forensic science evidence (which typically includes things like hair or fibres from clothing), a combination of closed-circuit television (CCTV) and mobile phone evidence—in particular Apple Health data—provided evidence refuting the defendant's description of events.

Digital forensics is more complex to define. When characterising the forensic investigation of digital technologies, terms such as "digital forensic science" or "digital forensics" best capture the subject discipline, and this goes beyond computer forensics. Figure 8.1 depicts digital forensics as a subdiscipline of forensic science. Contained within digital forensics are a number of specialist areas, typically defined by a technology, service, or operating system variant. Each specialist area can contain multiple components due to the number of technology types which exist within it. For example, there are occasions when a mobile phone may be subject to a mobile forensic examination. Mobile forensics is a

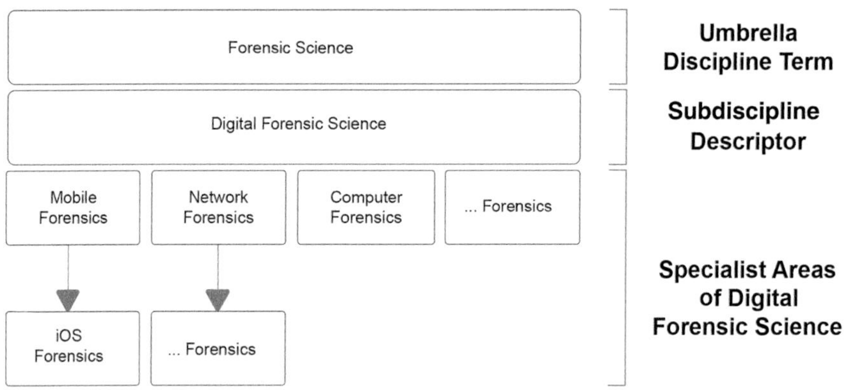

Figure 8.1 Discipline terminology

6 V. N. Franqueira and G. Horsman, 'Towards Sound Forensic Arguments: Structured Argumentation Applied to Digital Forensics Practice' (2020) 32 *Forensic Science International: Digital Investigation* 300923; Sky News, 'Mitesh Patel: Gay Pharmacist Jailed for Murdering Wife to Be with Boyfriend' (*Sky News*, 2018) <https://news.sky.com/story/mitesh-patel-pharmacist-who-murdered-wife-jailed-for-30-years-11572248> accessed 3 January 2026.

specialist area of digital forensics, where a practitioner may be a specialist in examining specific device types (e.g. Apple iPhones running iOS). Additionally, the Forensic Science Regulator (FSR) has mandated that all forensic examinations, which includes digital forensics, are accredited in accordance with the Forensic Science Regulators Code of Practice (April 2023) which was issued under the Forensic Science Regulator Act 2021.[7] In practice Police Forces may have various levels of 'in-scope' practices which are accredited, and some which are yet to be accredited. It is worth remembering that in accredited processes, there are likely to be more defined procedures which need to be followed in order for the process to be described as compliant.

The Forensics Capabilities Network of England and Wales defines digital forensics as "the examination of digital evidence to support investigations and prosecutions, formally defined as 'the systematic and coherent study of digital traces to address questions of authentication, identification, classification, reconstruction, and evaluation for a legal context'".[8] Another definition is from the Forensic Science Regulator for England and Wales, which defines digital forensics as "the process by which information is extracted from data storage media, rendered into a useable form, processed and interpreted for the purpose of obtaining intelligence for use in investigations, or evidence for use in criminal proceedings".[9]

In breaking down the definitions that form the components of digital forensics, let's begin with its two fundamental components, "digital" and "forensic science".

- *Digital.* The focus of digital forensics is digital data; binary code utilised by digital technologies in order to function; sometimes colloquially referred to as ones and zeros. Digital technologies process binary code in order to perform functions and store data.[10] Whilst

7 G. Tully, N. Cohen, D. Compton, G. Davies, R. Isbell and T. Watson, 'Quality Standards for Digital Forensics: Learning from Experience in England & Wales' (2020) 32 *Forensic Science International: Digital Investigation* 200905.

8 Forensic Capability Network, 'Digital Forensic Science Strategy' (2020) 12 <https://www.fcn.police.uk/sites/default/files/2020-07/Digital%20Forensic%20Science%20Strategy%20EMAIL%20VERSION%20ONLY.pdf>

9 Forensic Science Regulator, 'Newsletter' (2015), 3 <https://assets.publishing.service.gov.uk/government/uploads/system/uploads/attachment_data/file/470526/FSR_Newsletter_26__October_2015.pdf> accessed 3 January 2026.

10 TechTerms, 'Binary' (2020) <https://techterms.com/definition/binary> accessed 3 January 2026.

binary content is not easily readable in its native form, software programs translate it into more accessible forms such as the files users commonly see on their device, like word processing documents, pictures or, in some cases, communication data like chat messages. To increase simplicity, the term "digital" encompasses all the contents of a digital device, or in some cases, assessing the capability and function of the device to ensure it is functioning properly. The device itself may give rise to an offence.
- *Forensic science.* Simply put, the *Oxford English Dictionary* defines forensic science as "the application of scientific methods and techniques to matters under investigation by a court of law".[11]

The field of digital forensics is a hybrid of fundamental computer science and investigation, supporting the justice system through the examination of digital devices and the digital data they contain in order to identify and interpret the presence of any digital evidence. In turn, drawing on the Scientific Working Group on Digital Evidence definition of digital evidence as valuable information that is stored "stored or transmitted in digital form" (discussed earlier).[12] The results of the investigation will be used to help indicate whether or not a belief or proposition relating to the case in question is true or valid.[13] As such, the digital forensics examination and process take place on digital artefacts such as computers, mobile phones, hard drives, cloud-hosted applications, software, apps, internet browsers, servers or any endpoint networks, or infrastructures. The activity also includes collecting information from emails, texts and images, deleted files, and much more to determine the digital footprint.

Digital forensics occurs post-mortem, after an alleged crime or event has taken place which is in need of investigation. As a result, digital forensics is reactive, serving the purpose of attempting to reconstruct behaviours from digital traces and information left on relevant digital devices. In that sense, digital forensics interprets digital information which may be stored upon a device to assess whether it may help an investigation. It tells a story and the origins of the digital evidence.

11 Oxford English Dictionary, 'Forensic Science' (2020) <https://languages.oup.com/google-dictionary-en>

12 *Supra* n. 2.

13 Oxford English Dictionary, 'Evidence' (2020b) <https://languages.oup.com/google-dictionary-en>

It can explain the conduct of parties and helps to contextualise facts of a case with evidence.[14]

In 2020, the Forensic Capability Network's Digital Forensic Science Strategy noted that "over 90% of all crime is recognized as having a digital element, and society's accelerating use of technology means the critical role Digital Forensic Science plays will only grow".[15] As such, digital forensics is somewhat driven by trends in technology development and use, and the need to investigate these potential evidence sources,[16] leading to it becoming one of the most prominent branches of forensic science in use. The importance of the field of digital forensics cannot be understated, and it is necessary to ensure that the public at large understand what the field of digital forensics is and the role it plays within the justice sphere.[17] Doing so encourages societal trust in digital forensics which in turn shapes best practice, facilitates an understanding of this service, and raises an awareness of capability—supporting witnesses and victims to determine when it may be necessary to come forward and engage these services through the reporting of an offence. This not only improves the chance of a positive outcome for those subject to a form of crime where digital evidence may exist, but also for those tasked with investigating such instances.

14 The Crown Prosecution Service of England and Wales (2020) define the following two categories of cyber crime into which an incident will fall:

- *Cyber-dependent crimes*: Crimes that can be committed only through the use of information and communications technology (ICT) devices, where the devices are both the tool for committing the crime and the target of the crime (e.g. developing and propagating malware for financial gain, hacking to steal, damage, distort or destroy data and/or network or activity).
- *Cyber-enabled crimes*: Traditional crimes which can be increased in scale or reach by the use of computers, computer networks or other forms of ICT (such as cyber-enabled fraud and data theft).

Crown Prosecution Service, 'Cybercrime—Prosecution Guidance' (2020) <https://www.cps.gov.uk/legal-guidance/cybercrime-prosecution-guidance> accessed 3 January 2026; see also C. Wexler, 'The Changing Nature of Crime and Criminal Investigations' (2018) <https://www.policeforum.org/assets/ChangingNatureofCrime.pdf> accessed 30 April 2021.

15 *Supra* n. 5, p. 4.

16 G. Horsman, 'Tool Testing and Reliability Issues in the Field of Digital Forensics' (2019) 28 *Digital Investigation* 163–75.

17 *Supra* n. 5, p. 4.

THE PROCESS OF DIGITAL FORENSICS

Digital forensics can be described as the investigatory process of acquiring and retrieving digital evidence from digital sources and tools. Figure 8.2 sets out the digital forensics process. Here, it describes a process that involves identification, recovery, analysis, and presentation in court of relevant information taken from electronic devices. The information or data elucidated from the digital forensics process becomes digital evidence that is presented to court as evidence to establish the causal link between people and events and civil wrongdoings.[18]

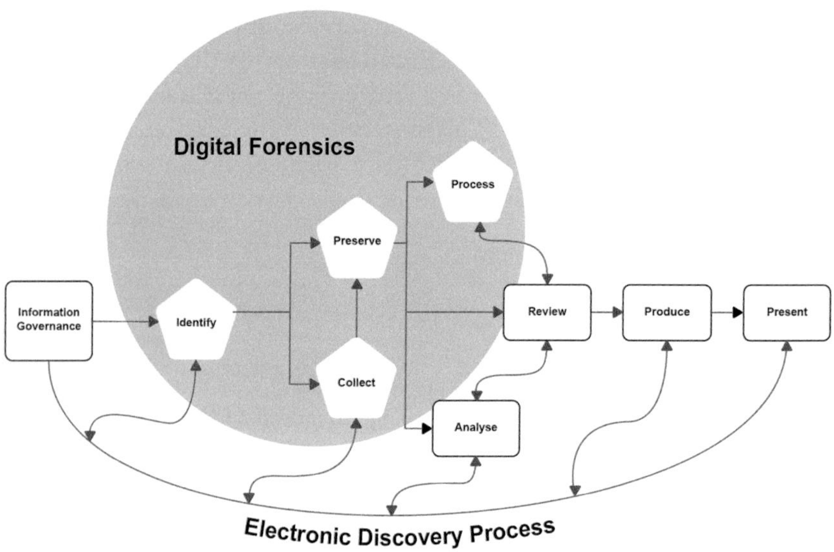

Figure 8.2 The digital discovery process

18 S. E. Goodison, R. C. Davis and B. A. Jackson, Digital Evidence and the US Criminal Justice System. Identifying Technology and Other Needs to More Effectively Acquire and Utilize Digital Evidence. Priority Criminal Justice Needs Initiative (Rand Corporation, 2015); D. Lawton, R. Stacey and G. Dodd, 'eDiscovery in Digital Forensic Investigations' (UK Home Office, 2014). 'CAST Publication Number 32/14' <https://assets.publishing.service.gov.uk/government/uploads/system/uploads/attachment_data/file/394779/ediscovery-digital-forensic-investi gations-3214.pdf>

In England and Wales, the Criminal Procedure Rules (CPR) specifically address the role of the digital forensics practitioner as a provider of expert evidence in the court process:

1 An expert must help the court to achieve the overriding objective by giving an objective, unbiased opinion on matters within their expertise.
2 This duty overrides any obligation to the person from whom the expert receives instructions or by whom the expert is paid.
3 This duty includes an obligation to inform all parties and the court if the expert's opinion changes from that contained in a report served as evidence or given in a statement.[19]

The act of searching for digital evidence may imply that such information is deemed to always exist and therefore it is simply a case of finding it, suggesting possible bias. In fact, digital forensic practitioners and those operating in a digital forensics role need to ascertain those events which are depicted by any stored digital data and interpret their meaning. In essence, the digital forensic practitioner's job is to assess whether information contained within any given seized digital device supports or refutes what is believed to have occurred. These pieces of digital information may sometimes be referred to as "digital trace evidence" or "digital artefacts".[20] Lawyers should consider the use of the term "expert" in this context, as there are distinct differences between investigators being experts in their field around gathering evidence, compared to an expert who provides an opinion on the nature of evidence and how it is formed, and how it should subsequently be interpreted. In *R v. Calland*,[21] the prosecution sought to rely on a level of detail from evidence gathered from phone masts (known as "cell site data"); the court rejected this on the basis that an expert would be needed, and this was not something a police analyst could provide evidence around. Lawyers can expect that from October 2025 onwards the FSR will subject cell site data to the forensic regulators code, and this

19 Crown Prosecution Service, 'The Criminal Procedure Rules 2020, Part 19, Expert Evidence' (Updated 10 September 2019) <https://www.cps.gov.uk/legal-guidance/expert-evidence#:~:text=The%20duty%20of%20an%20expert%20witness%20is%20to%20help%20the,to%20matters%20within%20their%20expertise> accessed 3 January 2026; and Civil Procedure Rules, Part 35.

20 G. Horsman, 'Raiders of the Lost Artefacts: Championing the Need for Digital Forensics Research' (2019) 1 *Forensic Science International: Reports* 100003.

21 *R v. Calland* [2017] EWCA Crim 2308, paragraphs 29–30.

may mean lawyers need to consider evidence from sources which are accredited and those which are not.

Digital forensics examinations go through a number of stages before reaching completion, often described as the "digital forensic process".[22] Whilst in reality this process is complex and multifaceted, shaped in part by case-specific variables, a digitally proficient lawyer will need to understand a few of the high-level concepts designed to be informative of the general process, but not exhaustive.

- *Identification.* Before any digital forensics device examination can take place, all digital devices and data sources which are of potential relevance to an investigation must be identified and collected appropriately by a first responder (such as a police officer).[23] This activity is often part of any search and seizure process undertaken, which may involve the methodological processing of a particular crime scene to ascertain any "digital presence" and the collection of electronic devices containing the digital evidence. Those conducting these tasks must adhere to any relevant jurisdictional requirements, whilst also considering the impact that such activities may have on those subject to these processes (e.g. intrusion into an individual's privacy).[24]
- *Acquisition.* Acquisition is the process of extracting data from a device in a way which best preserves the device's original state—meaning that where possible, no changes to the device's digital content should have occurred. The result of the acquisition process is the creation of a "forensic image or extraction",[25] which could be thought of as a clone of the data which was present on a device, either in full or part. This will involve a meticulous and diligent

22 M. Reith, C. Carr and G. Gunsch, 'An Examination of Digital Forensic Models' (2002) 1(3) *International Journal of Digital Evidence* 1–12; W. J. Tilstone, K. A. Savage and L. A. Clark, *Forensic Science: An Encyclopedia of History, Methods, and Techniques* (ABC-CLIO, 2006); C. Roux, B. Talbot-Wright, J. Robertson, F. Crispino and O. Ribaux, 'The End of the (Forensic Science) World as We Know It? The Example of Trace Evidence' (2015) 370(1674) *Philosophical Transactions of the Royal Society B: Biological Sciences* 20140260.

23 G. Horsman, 'The COLLECTORS Ranking Scale for "At-scene" Digital Device Triage' (2021) 66(1) *Journal of Forensic Sciences* 179–89.

24 G. Horsman, 'Can We Continue to Effectively Police Digital Crime?' (2017) 57(6) *Science & Justice* 448–54.

25 The Association of Chief Police Officers, 'ACPO Good Practice Guide for Digital Evidence' (2012) <https://www.digital-detective.net/digital-forensics-documents/ACPO_Good_Practice_Guide_for_Digital_Evidence_v5.pdf> accessed 30 April 2021.

review of information available electronically. There are two purposes for device acquisition. The first purpose is to preserve the existing state of any device being examined to maintain its integrity and prevent any contamination of the evidence. This is noted by the UK's National Police Chiefs Council, who state that "the onus is on the prosecution to show to the court that the evidence produced is no more and no less now than when it was first taken into the possession of law enforcement".[26] The second purpose is that acquiring data from a device allows the examination of it as part of any investigation.

- *Examination and interpretation.* Any acquired digital data is then examined by the digital forensics practitioner in order to identify any available information which may be of evidential value. The practitioner will interpret the meaning of this information in line with any case propositions (facts of and issues of particular relevance to the case). Given that many devices maintain large volumes of storage media, in many cases there is the potential for millions of files and pieces of digital data to be sifted and examined. To do this, practitioners will define an appropriate investigative strategy, taking into account the type of device being examined and the suspected type of offence. As part of the examination of data, practitioners will deploy specialist tools to identify, recover, and interpret any relevant digital data present whilst also utilising techniques like keyword searching, log parsing, and known-file matching.
- *Reporting.* All relevant information identified as part of the examination and interpretation process will be communicated to the digital forensics practitioner's client (e.g. a law enforcement officer), typically in report form. Whilst digital evidence can be complex, all efforts are made to convey its meaning in a way which is accessible to the layperson.

A digital forensics practitioner will need to provide a robust and unimpeachable audit trail so that their digital forensics process, from collection and retrieval to examination, analysis, and preservation methods, demonstrates sufficient authenticity, reliability, accuracy, and integrity to become admissible in court. All aspects of the digital forensics process should be governed, from oversight and assurances of lawful device search and seizure to lawful device examination and reporting. Practitioners conducting digital forensics should utilise examination techniques which are reliable, ensuring any findings offered are valid.

26 Ibid.

This often includes the use of specialist tools which search, parse, and display digital content for their review. Verification techniques should be in place to prevent data from being added or removed maliciously from any examination scenario, which could lead to misinterpretation or an incorrect outcome. In England and Wales, the Forensic Science Regulator helps to define and develop relevant standards.[27]

Lawyers should be familiar with the 'examination requirements' set by either the Officer in Case (OIC) or the Senior Investigating Officer (SIO). These requirements are designed to direct an examiner to digital evidence. Lawyers should carefully examine these from the outset and determine if these requirements are sufficiently extensive to satisfy their handling of the case, and their client's defence. This early engagement should come at the outset of the case, even at the point of any interview and in the phases of pre-interview briefings at police stations. Lawyers should examine with their clients any aspects of digital evidence they might seek to preserve or have examined and consider that some digital evidence may diminish over time if it is not preserved. A Disclosure Management Document (DMD) may be produced to outline the digital evidence strategy, and this may contain specific details about the examination request.[28] Whilst prosecuting lawyers should be driving the initial stages of disclosure about digital evidence,[29] those defending should offer significant interest in the issue at the earliest stage in the case to establish if reasonable lines of inquiry have been adequately considered and address any elements of the digital evidence which may need to be additionally examined.[30]

THE ROLE OF DIGITAL DEVICES

With widespread technology uptake in society comes an inherent increased risk of technology misuse. However, there is also the potential that these devices themselves may help to describe specific events of interest to any investigating authority; in essence, a device may become

27 Forensic Science Regulator, 'Newsletter' (2015), 3 <https://assets.publishing.service.gov.uk/government/uploads/system/uploads/attachment_data/file/470526/FSR_Newsletter_26__October_2015.pdf> accessed 3 January 2026.

28 Attorney General's Guidelines on Disclosure (2024) paragraphs 52, 96 and Annex A.

29 *R v. R* [2016] 1 W.L.R. 1872 paragraph 34.

30 G. Horsman, 'When Is a Line of Inquiry "Reasonable"?—A Focus on Digital Devices' (2023) 55(4) *Australian Journal of Forensic Sciences* 560–71.

a “witness” to an event, recording information about it in digital form.[31] Information found on digital devices now supports the investigation of many traditional physical offences; for example, where recorded footage of incidents has been captured.[32] It is not just those devices seized from a suspect who may be subject to investigation that may be forensically examined; in some cases victim and/or witness devices may also be required in order to ascertain available relevant information. This may be required where a victim or witness's device possesses the only available records of an event, which are needed in order to further an investigation; for example, victim and/or witness data is required to corroborate the details of an event.

The term “digital devices” may make individuals think of computers and mobile phones, meaning that, when digital forensics is discussed, some may gravitate towards defining this field as for use in examining these device types alone. Whilst computing and mobile devices are prolific among society, digital forensics concerns itself with all digital devices which may be of value to a given investigation. Where a device maintains some form of storage capacity (memory in which digital data can be retained by a device), then if its functionality may mean it could offer potential value to an investigation, it may subsequently be submitted for forensic examination.

Sync 1: Uses and abuses of digital devices

You should allow around 15 minutes for this activity.

A lawyer will require a meticulous eye for detail and clear understanding of what data (digital evidence) is required and an ability to check whether it has retained its authenticity during the digital forensics process so that it can be relied on in court.

31 A. Nieto, R. Rios and J. Lopez, ‘IoT-Forensics Meets Privacy: Towards Cooperative Digital Investigations’ (2018) 18(2) *Sensors* 492; The Open University, ‘Digital Forensics’ (2020) <https://www.open.edu/openlearn/science-maths-technology/digital-forensics/content-section–4.2#:~:text=Until%20the%20late%201990s%2C%20what,and%20Response%20Team%20(CART)>

32 Home Office, ‘Forensic Science Strategy’ (2016) <https://assets.publishing.service.gov.uk/government/uploads/system/uploads/attachment_data/file/506683/54493_Cm_9217_Forensic_Science_Strategy_Print_ready.pdf> accessed 3 January 2026; D. Lawton, R. Stacey and G. Dodd, ‘eDiscovery in Digital Forensic Investigations’ (UK Home Office, 2014), CAST Publication Number 32/14 <https://assets.publishing.service.gov.uk/government/uploads/system/uploads/attachment_data/file/394779/ediscovery-digital-forensic-investigations-3214.pdf> accessed 3 January 2026.

Develop a list of device types which you might expect to be present in a standard dwelling. From this list, identify:

1 The types of digital offences that they could be involved in.

2 The potential types of digital evidence which they may retain.

You may have identified a wide range of digital devices, including some of the following:

- *Computer hard drives.* A digital forensics process will be able to tell the story of how a file was located in a particular place, when the file was last viewed or opened, who has had control over the file, and the activities which took place within the file. Files can be encrypted to prevent unauthorised access to contents. Microsoft applications, such as Word and Excel, and Adobe Acrobat have options to password-protect their files. However, it is still possible to access a version of the file or decode the password as part of the digital forensics process. It should also be considered as to the nature of any accredited process and if this has been followed.
- *Smartphones.* Mobile phones, especially those with internet access built into them, provide an extensive amount of information about an individual and their preferences, behaviours and conduct, and can help to form a timeline of events. They are capable of providing a detailed account of one's location and activities at a given moment in time because they have become indispensable to our daily lives, going along with us to almost every place and situation. They contain a wealth of information and metadata about the individual and their social network and frequency of engagement with the social network through internet browsers, apps which store frequency and exchange of information, calls, emails, texts, and other forms of data. Smartphones have become one of the most powerful devices in digital forensics investigations. For example, forensics from mobile phones can provide crucial information about the conduct of a motorist at the time of an accident. Social media sites and internet browser histories can provide a timeline of activities and behaviour of others.
- *Ephemeral applications on mobile devices or desktops.* These are messaging applications that cause the sent message or video to disappear in the recipient's device a short while after viewing. Snapchat

introduced the concept, and Instagram later added that feature. These apps are built around the premise of privacy and freedom to communicate without leaving a permanent trace of information. However, this is not a foolproof system. There is the possibility to screenshot a message as soon as it is viewed and therefore hold on to a copy of the message before its automatic deletion. There is also the ability to track and retrieve these messages through tools and techniques used in digital forensics. Information in texts, emails, and messaging services can provide valuable evidence to support the construction of a case. A number of prominent examples of retrieving information from Snapchat are available online in the UK and abroad, where they have been used in court as evidence of a person's involvement in a crime. An exception to ephemeral applications is messaging applications that offer end-to-end encryption for text, video, and voice messaging, which means the information exchange cannot be decoded.

- *Internet of Things* (IoT). This was referred to in Chapter 6. It is a terminology used to describe devices connected to the internet that subsequently connect with other devices, sync and talk to each other, sharing data. The connections form networks of devices. Each network then collects, shares, and analyses data to produce context-specific and user-specific solutions to tasks and processes. For example, a smartphone and a TV can be synced, showing viewers' preferences of programmes, a timestamp of what programmes were watched and when. The same smartphone can be linked to one's Amazon or Google home assistant and/or smartwatch, collecting information around movement, characteristics of one's voice or eye movements, location, temperature, and so forth.[33] All of these are items of digital evidence that provide a considerable amount of invaluable information about our daily lives. Moving beyond investigating individual devices, a digitally proficient lawyer should enquire about smart technologies and the networks in which they function. Wearable technologies are another example of IoT, where data gathered from wearable devices can sync with mobile phones and other applications, leaving traces of information that can be linked to persons and locations. An issue

33 Anjelica Cappellino, 'The Amazon Echo: Expert Witness in a Murder Trial?' (Expert Institute, 17 February 2021) <https://www.expertinstitute.com/resources/insights/amazon-echo-expert-witness-murder-trial/> accessed 3 January 2026.

with the IoT, when being used as a source of evidence, is data diffusion (the merging together of a range of data from different sources). The nature of IoT technology is the variety of networks which talk to each other and share information. Networks can be shared, and determining whose data it is can be challenging.

TYPES OF DIGITAL EVIDENCE

Legal professionals must possess a working knowledge of specific digital files and information and their potential relevance to an investigation in order to assess when to interrogate this information and in what contexts it may provide investigative support.

Sync 2: Exploring digital evidence

You should allow around 45 minutes for this activity.

1 Consider JPEG picture files. These can often contain additional information called EXIF, which describe additional metadata about the picture including the make and model of the device which took the photo, timestamp information, and potentially coordinate information relating to the place where the image was taken. This also allows investigation of possible manipulation (digital forgery) of pictures, video, and audio content.

- In what types of crime might JPEG picture files be relevant to examine?
- In what contexts may embedded EXIF data be of value to an investigation?
- What are the sorts of questions a digital lawyer may want to ask a digital forensics practitioner to establish the reliability and authenticity of the evidence being presented in court?

2 Consider the sorts of evidence gathered from electronic storage devices such as desktops, laptops, servers, hard drives, and hard disks.

- What sorts of information are you likely to find on electronic storage devices?
- What are the scenarios in which metadata from internet browsers become useful?

- What sorts of digital evidence may be helpful in creating a description of someone's digital behaviour?
- How would a digital lawyer establish the authenticity of the information presented in court?

3 When an investigation of a digital device takes place, those examining this content must consider relevant content which may exist as a result of any third-party applications which a user has downloaded. They will also need to consider any data retained by the operating system installed upon that device (for example, Microsoft Windows 10, iOS). Often operating systems contain a range of functions designed to provide the user with a "good user experience". Achieving this experience usually means making use of the device as easy as possible. This includes ensuring that many functions remember what files a user has interacted with and what activities they may have carried out on the system. Whilst this information is helpful for a user, these retained records also provide insight into the user's behaviour for a digital forensic practitioner and can often support an interpretation of how a device has been used and by whom. Consider:

- When would evidence from an operating system be valuable?
- Is data from recently wiped devices retrievable?
- How would a digital lawyer establish the re-creation of evidence from a device that has been wiped, and is an expert required to explain this to a court?

At the end of this activity, you should start to question the sorts of digital evidence that is useful and the risks associated with digital evidence, including the questions that may be useful for a digitally proficient lawyer to consider.

DIGITAL LAWYERING AND DIGITAL FORENSICS

In common law jurisdictions such as England and Wales, criminal cases are established on the standard of proof that is beyond reasonable doubt. In civil disputes, the standard of proof is the balance of probabilities. Philosophical, ethical, and legal constructs of fairness and justice are applied over the entirety of the case as a whole, whilst scientific and technical evidence is a particular aspect of the whole matter.[34]

Why do you, as a law student and potentially a future digital lawyer, need to know about digital forensics? The answer is simple: To determine the admissibility of evidence and the weight that is to be given to that evidence.

Digital evidence is vital in court proceedings. However, it can be utilised only if it is deemed to be admissible by the courts. A digital lawyer will benefit from being aware of the rules and guidance governing the admissibility of digital evidence. These will help to determine the accuracy, authenticity, and integrity of the evidence in any particular case. They will also assist the lawyer to ask the right questions to determine its effectiveness during the court proceedings.

The process of determining the admissibility of evidence is complex. There is a legal set of requirements and a procedural set of requirements.

Evidence is generally legally admissible when:

- It is offered to prove the facts of a case.
- The manner in which it was obtained meets the legal requirements of searches and seizure of information.
- It does not violate other laws.
- The process in which it was collected, examined, and analysed are forensically sound and can be justified.

The judge in a case determines the admissibility of the evidence. Considerations include the following.

THE EXAMINATION OF AUTHORISATION TO LEGALLY CONDUCT A SEARCH AND SEIZURE OF DEVICES AND INFORMATION

The digital forensics investigator has the responsibility for ensuring that the evidence-gathering process, and the evidence gathered through it, adhere to any relevant guidelines and best practice protocol. This is to ensure it will be admissible in court. Prior to commencing any form

34 J. I. Thornton, 'The General Assumptions and Rationale of Forensic Identification' in D. L. Faigman, D. H. Kaye, M. J. Saks and J. Sanders (eds), *Modern Scientific Evidence: The Law and Science of Expert Testimony* (Vol. 2, West Publishing Company 1997).

of investigation, collection or retrieval of digital evidence, it must be established by the digital forensics practitioner that the means used to achieve the evidence are in fact legal. It must be legally obtained with authorisation and a search warrant, or obtained following the arrest of a suspect and PACE search powers exist.[35] The most common reason why digital evidence becomes inadmissible is because it has been obtained without the necessary legal authorisation, such as a warrant to carry out the search and seizure. The challenge within the digital sphere is the nature of networks and infrastructures which are interlinked with each other. A warrant with specificity may not always allow for the wide span of networks, such as where the IoT comes into play.

As a lawyer you may also need to consider the appropriateness of a Digital Processing Notice (DPN). The DPN system was introduced in September 2020 following the judgment in *R v. Bater-James and Mohammed*.[36] The DPN system is designed to offer safeguards against excessive intrusion into victim and witness devices and offer information to those suspected of offences about the seizure of their device. These notices are required to be signed by a police inspector in the same way that warrants are ratified. The notices often exist alongside submissions procedures and offer such information as the reasonable grounds for seizing the device and what information will be searched. Investigators may ultimately separate this information into either evidence, unused material or sensitive material.[37] Notices and authorities should be in compliance with Chapter 3 of the Police, Crime, Sentencing, and Courts Act 2022 which establishes the legal framework for the extraction of information from electronic devices.

Many criminal investigations are multidisciplinary, requiring input not just from multiple forensic areas (e.g. a crime scene where physical trace and digital evidence is present), but also from investigatory and legal contexts. As a result, all those involved in the criminal investigation process must understand the value that specific evidence types can bring to an inquiry, including any digital evidence involved. However, it is not simply about understanding the value of the evidence; it is also important to understand the evidential chain and the legal and professional challenges which exist around it.

35 Also note that in addition to PACE, S.23(2) MDA 1971 will permit seizure of a phone and or the recording of an IMEI number which may be used by an investigator to determine the seizure of a device for further investigation.
36 [2020] EWCA Crim 790.
37 CPIA 1996 disclosure.

Sync 3: Examining the evidential chain and authority of digital evidence

You should allow around 45 minutes for this activity.

A person was arrested for a criminal offence at 1300hrs, they were conveyed to a police station and arrived at 1330hrs. Their mobile device was seized at 1345hrs and was placed into the evidential store at 1348hrs. At 1400hrs the device was removed from the store and examined by an investigator, who neither documented this process nor completed the DPN paperwork nor made any notes about the examination. At 1500hrs the arrested person was interviewed and information from the mobile phone used to explain his involvement in a criminal offence. At 1700hrs the same mobile device was authorised for examination by a police inspector and entered a forensic examination process at 1730hrs.

- What authority should the digital lawyer search for in relation to the first examination?
- What could be identified about the chain of custody and what are the gaps in this?
- What are the future limitations of this evidence if the forensic examination finds further evidence on the device?
- How could the digital lawyer explore the examination requirements presented within the application to employ the further forensic process?

The Authorised Professional Practice Extraction of material from digital devices (2021) indicates that manual examination, including screenshots or other images or record of what is on screen, should be considered only when: (a) there is minimal material that would be of significant evidential value; (b) material on devices may be lost if not captured immediately; (c) volatile material is present, such as data that might be lost if the device is turned off; (d) if, after seeking to reassure the device user, persuading them of the strict necessity of acquiring their device, and explaining the potential consequences of refusing to provide it, the device user does not agree to hand over the device, but will agree to screenshots as an option to secure a record of the material.[38] The digital

38 College of Policing, 'Authorised Professional Practice Extraction of Material from Digital Devices' (2021) <https://library.college.police.uk/docs/college-of-policing/

lawyer may need to assess if mobile device evidence, which has been obtained through manual examination, meets these requirements and if the evidence obtained is sufficient to provide the case with a sufficient extent of material. An expert may be required to explain the nature of the state of the device and if any manual examination has been carried out on the device which has changed the nature of the evidence itself or caused it to be deleted in the case of time and action sensitive data—i.e. items received via Snapchat.

In England and Wales, Rule 19.2 of the CPR confirms that an expert's duty is to "help the court to achieve the overriding objective" that criminal cases be dealt with justly, through providing objective, unbiased opinion within the expert's area of expertise, regardless of who they are being instructed by. Therefore, digital forensics experts are not "hired to support a particular belief" by any given party; instead, they are required by law to remain independent, producing findings which may support the court in their overriding objective under Rule 1.1 of acquitting the innocent and convicting the guilty.

One of the preliminary challenges for law enforcement lies with recognising the value that any digital device may have to an investigation by acknowledging their capability, capacity and relationship to an offence. Whilst this may seem straightforward, the pace of technological change now means that any one individual is unlikely to recognise all available devices and their abilities. An issue of paramount importance is that much cloud-based data can transcend different jurisdictions, with data hosted outside of the jurisdiction that the digital forensics practitioner and the court may operate in. This may make it difficult to obtain access to the data, and its use may be governed by different legal rules.

A full description of the legal obligations placed upon forensic science experts in England and Wales is provided by the Forensic Science Regulator (2020); however, it should be stressed that experts are required to assess and pursue all avenues which lead both to and away from any suspect in question.[39] In 2020, the Criminal Procedure and Investigations Act 1996 (Code of Practice) Order 2020 introduced

APP-the-extraction-of-material-from-digital-devices-2021.pdf> accessed 13 January 2026.

39 Forensic Science Regulator, 'Legal Obligations' (2020) <https://assets.publishing.service.gov.uk/government/uploads/system/uploads/attachment_data/file/882074/FSR_Legal_Obligations_-_Issue_8.pdf> accessed 3 January 2026.

a revised code of practice under the Criminal Procedure and Investigations Act 1996.[40] Further key sources of best practice guidelines come from the Scientific Working Group on Digital Evidence, the UK National Police Chiefs Council and the US National Institute of Justice. These best practice guidelines set out principles based upon which digital forensics practitioners and investigators undertake the process and procedure of establishing digital evidence.

In Sync 4 you will be able to spend some time considering the rights of those from whom digital forensics practitioners may retrieve data for evidence from personal artefacts such as personal computers, mobile devices and other forms of digital devices where personal data is stored. In some jurisdictions, this gives rise to a potential conflict between Article 6 of the European Convention on Human Rights (the absolute right to a fair trial, confirmed by the Criminal Procedure and Investigations Act 1996 (Code of Practice) Order 2020 in England and Wales) and Article 8 of the European Convention on Human Rights (the right to respect for private and family life, home, and correspondence).

Sync 4: The challenge of creating a code of ethics

You should allow around 30 minutes for this activity.

Taking into consideration the balance between the right to a fair trial and the right to respect for privacy, make some notes on what you would include if you were creating a code of ethics for digital forensic practitioners who are undertaking the collection and retrieval of data from electronic devices.

In developing your initial thoughts, consider the following:

- What specific behaviours would be covered?
- What themes would the code address?
- What agency or organisation would enforce the code?
- To whom would the code apply—all practitioners involved with digital evidence, or just those processing it?

40 The House of Lords Library, 'The Criminal Procedure and Investigations Act 1996' (*Code of Practice, Order 2020*, October 2020) <https://lordslibrary.parliament.uk/the-criminal-procedure-and-investigations-act-1996-code-of-practice-order-2020/> accessed 3 January 2026.

- How do you balance the principles of trust, justice, freedom, privacy, and fairness?
- What other principles will you include in your framework?

At the end of this sync, you should start developing some critical thinking around the ethical issues that surround digital forensics process and examination. You should be able to make a strong case towards the fine and fair balance between the right to a fair trial and the right to respect for privacy in this process, including how privacy can be balanced and protected at the same time as carrying out the absolute right to a fair trial.

Digital lawyering skills: critical thinking

The reference to "critical thinking" in relation to Sync 4 is no accident. Critical thinking is an important skill for all lawyers, including digital lawyers, to possess. Indeed, there is evidence that law firms are increasingly testing for critical thinking within their recruitment processes.[41] These tests commonly look for a number of abilities, including:

- Being able to deduce whether a conclusion follows on logically from a statement.
- Being able to infer a conclusion from a set of statements.
- Being able to interpret statements to justify whether or not a conclusion is accurate.
- Being able to recognise assumptions and whether or not there is evidence to support them.
- Being able to evaluate arguments to assess their strengths and weaknesses.

All of these are skills which law schools commonly encourage their students to develop. For example, when discussing a topic in an essay, you are encouraged not just to describe the viewpoints of academics, but also to critique them and evaluate their validity and strength for yourself. Avoiding

41 The Lawyer, 'The Watson Glaser and BCAT Critical Thinking Tests' (*The Lawyer*, 28 April 2015) <https://www.thelawyer.com/watson-glaser-test/> accessed 29 April 2021.

simply accepting facts and information, and instead questioning the thinking behind them, is an important way of thinking for an aspiring digital lawyer to develop.

THE EXAMINATION OF THE TECHNICAL AND SCIENTIFIC PROCESS, TOOLS, TECHNIQUES, AND PROCEDURE TO CONDUCT DIGITAL FORENSICS

Understanding the process, tools, techniques, and procedure to conduct digital forensics is a key element of a proficient digital lawyer's toolkit. Figure 8.3 summarises the essentials. In this section, we explore in greater detail how the digital lawyering process and digital forensics process become vital in establishing admissible evidence in court. During the investigation, collection, examination, and analysis of digital evidence, the evidence should never be altered, deleted, or tampered with. It should be a complete and accurate copy of the digital evidence and remain unchanged since its collection. There are no exceptions to this guideline. Furthermore, the digital forensics process will be questioned by lawyers during court proceedings to ascertain whether there were probabilities of any alteration to the evidence from its original form and the form in which it is presented at court. Some of the questions a digital lawyer will be keen to find out answers to include the manner in which any deleted data was reconstructed, whether there was any manipulation of the data during the reconstruction phase, the security of the equipment that contained the data to avoid tampering, and any contamination of information in safeguarding the data and establishing its authenticity. It is also useful to establish whether the digital artefact from which the evidence was collected was functioning in the way it should. Errors within the digital artefacts and devices could lead to mistakes in date stamps, timestamps, and locations as examples. As such, further evidence to support the examination and conclusion of the digital forensics process would be useful. In the absence of any evidence to the contrary, the courts will automatically presume that the digital artefacts and devices were in proper working condition at the time of the digital forensics collection and retrieval of evidence.[42]

42 Law Commission, 'Evidence in Criminal Proceedings: Hearsay and Related Topics' (1997) *Law Commission Report* 245.

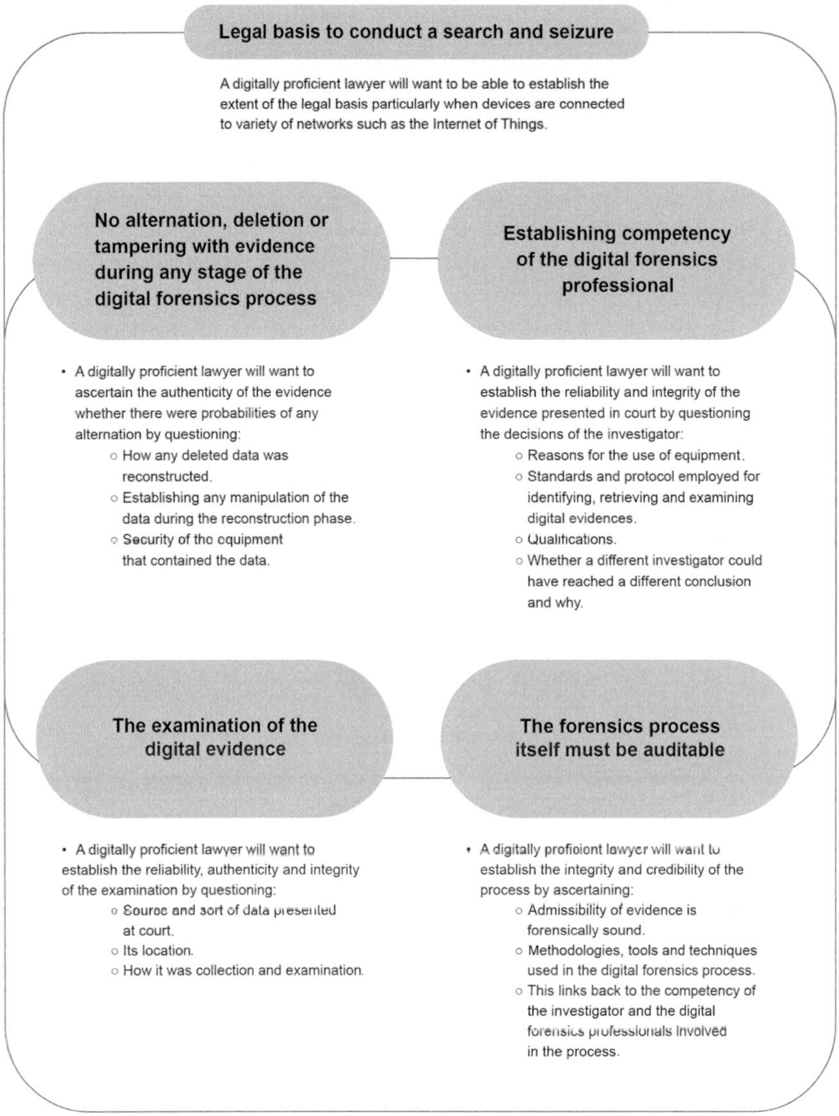

Figure 8.3 Key points about the digital forensics process

The competency of the investigator of the digital evidence could be questioned in court proceedings. Therefore, it must be someone who is a qualified digital forensics practitioner. Again, no exceptions are available to this guideline even if the process and evidence collection and analysis were time constrained. Challenges here could include use of equipment which may be outdated and the lack of national and international standards for identifying, retrieving, and examining digital evidence. As such, two different investigators might reach different conclusions about a particular piece of evidence because they used different equipment or had divergent training. An awareness of these challenges is crucial for a digital lawyer, as they can cause evidentiary issues around the reliability and integrity of the evidence presented in court. The examination of the digital evidence will be of interest to a digital lawyer. To pre-empt questioning by the court or the other party's lawyer and to establish reliability, authenticity, and integrity of the examination, the lawyer may want clarification around the sort of data that is being presented at court, its location, and its manner of collection and examination. This again helps to establish that the data could not have been changed or modified. If another party in a case is using digital evidence, a digital lawyer may well want to ask their legal representatives similar questions. The digital lawyer will also ensure that any keyword searches applied to any search within digital material have been recorded and made available for inspection. This may also be accompanied by a record of the 'hits' found when certain keywords have been applied and if these have been limited to a particular date range or filtered on a certain application or section of the device.

The process of the investigation and the process of obtaining digital forensics must be auditable so that the process can be evaluated. Another expert digital forensics practitioner should be able to repeat the process documented in the hope of replicating the result to demonstrate the integrity and credibility of the process where necessary. This means that its reliability and validity can be peer-reviewed where necessary.[43] The audit trail will also help the investigator to justify the use of the technical and scientific aspects of the admissibility of evidence and demonstrate that these aspects are forensically sound and can be used by another investigator to establish and corroborate the reliability and integrity of the evidence.[44] The audit trail is particularly beneficial to

43 European Network of Forensic Science Institute, 'Best Practice Manual for the Forensic Examination of Digital Technology' (*ENFSI-BPM-FIT-01*, 2015) <https://enfsi.eu/wp-content/uploads/2016/09/1._forensic_examination_of_digital_technology_0.pdf> accessed 3 January 2026; US National Institute of Justice, 'Digital Evidence in the Courtroom: A Guide for Law Enforcement and Prosecutors' (2004) <https://www.ojp.gov/pdffiles1/nij/211314.pdf> accessed 30 April 2021.

44 A. Antwi-Boasiako and H. Venter, 'A Model for Digital Evidence Admissibility Assessment' in G. Peterson and S. Shenoi (eds), *Advances in Digital Forensics* (Springer 2017) 23–38.

review the methodologies, tools, and techniques used in the digital forensics process to help determine the reliability of digital evidence and the strength of the analysis and conclusion. Limitations to the process, procedure, tools, and techniques used must be disclosed, including any factors which could have contributed to any potential bias.

A digitally proficient lawyer may want to understand how evidence has been produced for the court. Documentation provided by digital forensics professionals helps to demonstrate the authenticity of the evidence presented in court, such as how and where the evidence was collected and retrieved from and establishing the reliability and integrity of the evidence including its original form. In many forensic processes a streamlined forensic report (SFR) is produced to provide a simple overview of the evidence, and this may explain some features of the evidence.[45] Given the persuasiveness of some digital evidence the language used within the reporting and documentation is critical, as this could cause certainty or doubt over the way in which the evidence is being presented. The real issues around some digital evidence may not be who the evidence originates from but how the evidence arrived on the device or in its current location.[46] Therefore, a digitally proficient lawyer should question the documentations to establish the level of certainty in the conclusion of the reporting, establishing different possibilities and scenarios through questioning. A question which may arise is the ability of the court, and lawyers, to determine and explain the evidence:

> The probative value of scientific findings depends on the propositions that they are taken to be addressing. If scientists were always to restrict their interpretations to source level issues and propositions, they would effectively be trusting other criminal justice professionals, or factfinder's themselves, to contextualise the scientific findings and interpret them correctly.[47]

It is therefore imperative that no misunderstanding is drawn from scientific reports which have been produced using a streamlined report,

45 CrimPR 3.2(a); to identify the issues in the case as early as possible.

46 See also the discussion on similar issues in DNA evidence in *R v. Reed, Reed & Garmson* [2009] EWCA Crim LR 2698.

47 G. Jackson, C. Aitken and P. Roberts, 'Case Assessment and Interpretation of Expert Evidence: Guidance for Judges, Lawyers, Forensic Scientists and Expert Witnesses' (2015) <https://www.researchgate.net/publication/273698920_Case_Assessment_and_Interpretation_of_Expert_Evidence_Guidance_for_Judges_Lawyers_Forensic_Scientists_and_Expert_Witnesses> accessed 15 January 2026.

and as required any further reports are required to assist the courts understanding of key forensic positions in the case.

Examples of situations where digital evidence were used in determining the conduct of the parties involved include the following.

Using internet search history

Lusha was arrested based on his internet search pattern. Activities on his laptop showed that he had downloaded a substantial amount of information on how to make detonators, explosives, and associated belts from online sources. Searching his apartment, the police found large volumes of products to make explosives and associated devices. He had also been corresponding online through chat sites such as MSN, and these conversations were retrieved from his computer and used as digital evidence in the court. Lusha was found guilty based on this evidence of terrorist offences.[48]

Using internet search history

In a distressing case, the internet search history of Mikayla Munn gave substantial evidence to support a conviction of neglect and homicide and she was subsequently convicted. According to her internet history, she had searched for "at-home abortions" and "ways to cut the umbilical cord of a baby" prior to giving birth to and immediately drowning her baby in a bathtub, which helped to establish evidence around how the child had died.[49]

Using data from a pacemaker[50]

Data from a pacemaker served as evidence in court. The data consisted of information such as heart rate and corresponding pacer demand. This information helped the courts establish that in fact the information provided

48 *R v. Lusha (Krenar)* [2010] EWCA Crim 1761; 'Man Jailed Over Suicide Bomb Book' (*BBC News*, 15 December 2009) <https://news.bbc.co.uk/2/hi/uk_news/england/derbyshire/8414527.stm> accessed 3 January 2026.

49 'The Indiana Lawyer' <https://www.theindianalawyer.com/tags/mikayla-munn?__cf_chl_jschl_tk__=pmd_3a38ebf9bc89d30130627ffa18fc85682499f3ef-1627493748-0-gqNtZGzNAeKjcnBszQji> accessed 3 January 2026.

50 *State of Ohio v. Ross Compton*, 153 Ohio App.3d 512; Lauren Pack, 'Arson Suspect in Unique Case Featuring Pacemaker Data Is Back in Custody' (*Journal-News*, Hamilton, Ohio, 24 July 2018) <https://www.journal-news.com/news/arson-suspect-unique-case-featuring-pacemaker-data-back-custody/dn6JyzsOemZovpayJMZLNJ/> accessed 3 January 2026.

by the defendant included fake medical documentations and that he had committed insurance fraud and arson of his home. The defendant had claimed that he was asleep when his house caught fire. He quickly packed some essentials and leapt from his bedroom window to safety. However, the data from his pacemaker before, during and after the fire took place were inconsistent with his account of events.

In this case, whilst the defence argued that the search and seizure violated the defendant's privacy around medical information collected and used to provide medical care, the courts allowed the data from the pacemaker to be submitted as evidence against his testimonial. This in turn raises wider questions within the forensics and law enforcement disciplines around wearable and health technologies and when data can be collected and used in legal proceedings.

Using data from a Fitbit

Wearable technology information was used in court to determine the truth in the defendant's testimony. A Fitbit device is capable of establishing the wearer's heart rate, sleep patterns, steps taken, distance travelled, and location via GPS tracking. Data from Fitbits and most wearable technologies can be synchronised with other digital artefacts and platforms, and data can be collected from the device itself or the platforms which contain the data.[51] In establishing the truth of the defendant's claim and the time of death of the victim, evidence collected from Connie Debate's Fitbit showed that she had been in the house at the time the defendant, her husband, had claimed that she was out of the house. When he sounded the alarm, which he claimed was caused by an intruder, the Fitbit data showed that Connie had already stopped moving before the alarm went off.

Using network data

Analysis of data from servers and other networking infrastructures such as routers can help to trace and monitor network activity and investigate user

51 NBC News, 'Fitbit Murder Case: Richard Dabate Pleads Not Guilty in Wife's Death' (29 April 2017) <https://www.nbcnews.com/news/us-news/fitbit-murder-case-richard-dabate-pleads-not-guilty-wife-s-n752526> accessed 3 January 2026; In a similar case where Fitbit data was used to establish murder, the BBC Tech News Reports, 'Fitbit Data Used to Charge US Man with Murder' (4 October 2018) <https://www.bbc.co.uk/news/technology-45745366> accessed 3 January 2026.

activity.[52] An engineer who worked for Apple's autonomous car division had been downloading vast amounts of company information, design blueprints, and trade secrets from databases which held secret and sensitive information, according to network forensics which led to him being indicted for theft of trade secrets.

Conclusion

Drawing on the legal requirements and technical and scientific requirements to establish the admissibility of evidence produced for a digital forensics' investigation, this conclusion sets out some key principles to ensure the ethical and admissible collection, retrieval, examination and analysis of evidence from electronic devices.

Whilst there are no competency definitions for digital forensics and no standardisation and framework to demonstrate competency, the court must establish that the investigator is competent to report on their investigation and to be able to give evidence explaining the process and decisions they have made, the relevance of the evidence and the implications of their actions. Therefore, as you read each of the principles in the following table, consider carefully, as a digital lawyer, what sorts of questions you would ask the digital forensics practitioner to establish the reliability, authenticity, accuracy, and integrity of the digital evidence and the procedures and process conducted prior to the evidence being presented at court.

Principles	**Ethical considerations and reflections**
In any investigation, an investigator is expected to pursue all reasonable lines of inquiry, whether they favour the case or not, and whether they point towards the existing suspect or not.	This is an area of utmost concern in the digital forensics sector right now. Considerations include: • Does the investigator understand that they are under this obligation?

52 Sean O'Kane, 'A Second Apple Employee Was Charged with Stealing Self-Driving Car Project' (*The Verge*, 30 January 2019) <https://www.theverge.com/2019/1/30/18203718/apple-self-driving-trade-secrets-china-titan> accessed 3 January 2026.

The investigator's role is neutral. They have a particular responsibility to perform, one that is unbiased throughout the digital forensics process.	• Is it typical practice for the digital forensics investigator to overlook this duty and side with the party who requested the investigation? • How does the lawyer in a trial determine whether relevant content has been missed or whether there was a deliberate overlooking of lines of inquiry, where the burden of proof lies, and how this issue can be determined? • How do digital forensic investigators evidence that they have considered inculpatory/exculpatory evidence? • How does the lawyer determine if elements from the investigation could be missed? • How does the investigator know where to being their investigation and follow-up? • What happens if you get a poor evidence examiner? No two examiners are equal. There is a real risk that the same case examined in two different police forces might not come up with the same results.
During the collection and retrieval phase, the investigator is responsible for deciding which material it is reasonable to inquire into, in what manner, and to what extent.	Considerations here include: • What is the extent of the legal permission for search and seizure? • Has the extent of the permission been explained clearly to the investigators so that they understand the parameters of the search? • What were the sorts of explanation and documentation that led to someone consenting to a search? • How has the investigator managed the balance between privacy and search? Recent mobile device examination recommendations published in 2020 by the Information Commissioner's Office[53] and the College of Policing also have a consultation out for making sure that devices and their data is not "over-processed".

(Continued)

53 Information Commissioner's Office, 'Mobile Phone Data Extraction by Police Forces in England and Wales Investigation Report' (June 2020) <https://ico.org.

The investigator should comprehensively record all information.	Case notes are also an issue. Courts in England and Wales have mandated the need for robust case notes as part of the admissibility procedures of digital evidence. Comprehensive notes should be seen as a support mechanism for the practitioner: They record what they have done, when they have done it, and why they have done it. Also, this should allow a third party to repeat their processes and get the same result.[54] The lawyer should determine that the notes presented in court have been written with the necessary attention to detail and account for all elements of the process and decision-making. The investigator is expected to investigate all relevant persons linked to the chain of evidence if there is a belief that persons may be in possession of material that may be relevant to the investigation. Investigative decision-making is key.[55]
All information gathered must be marked accurately. Sensitive material should be recorded but marked as such, warning others of the nature of the content.	Some content must be viewed only in controlled environments under the right conditions—for example, indecent images of children,[56] where a digital forensics practitioner has legal protections in some instances but must not stray beyond them.

uk/media/about-the-ico/documents/2617838/ico-report-on-mpe-in-england-and-wales-v1_1.pdf>

54 *R v. Smith* [2011] EWCA Crim 1296. See discussion by D. H. Kaye, 'R. v. Smith: Court of Appeal Rebukes Latent Fingerprint Identification in Britain for Being Out of Step with Modern Forensic Science' (June 2011) <https://for-sci-law.blogspot.com/2011/06/displaying-grave-dissatisfaction-with.html> accessed 3 January 2026; Forensic Science Regulator, 'His Honour Judge Andrew Goymer, The Importance of Forensic Science to the Courts' (March 2014) <https://www.gov.uk/government/publications/his-honor-judge-andrew-goymer-oral-transcript> accessed 3 January 2026.

55 *Supra* n. 19.

56 Protection of Children Act 1978.

An audit trail of all the processes followed and decisions applied to the digital evidence should be recorded.	Considerations here include: • An exploration of the digital forensic practitioner's digital evidence strategy and how it was formed prior to the examination of evidence. A digital evidence strategy would help to show their methodological approach to a case and also evidence the work that has been undertaken to others who may wish to evaluate it. It also helps to determine what the examiner has done and whether it is sufficient to address all lines of inquiry. • How was it evaluated? • How was information integrity maintained throughout the process?
The audit trail should enable another investigator to undertake the same process and use the same decisions to arrive at the same outcome and result.	Considerations here include: • Sufficient details provided in the audit trail so that method validation can take place. Method validation is vital if results are to be relied upon. The complexity of cases is so great that it should be transparent to all involved what a practitioner has done and has not done as a quality assurance and control mechanism. • Has the digital evidence strategy been sufficiently articulated with a clear audit trail to bring it to life?

ADDITIONAL RESOURCES

'The European Network of Forensic Science Institutes (ENFSI)' <https://enfsi.eu/>

'The European Union Agency for Cybersecurity (ENISA)' <https://www.enisa.europa.eu/>

'The Forensic Science Regulator' <https://www.gov.uk/government/organisations/forensic-science-regulator>

Horsman G, 'ACPO Principles for Digital Evidence: Time for an Update?' (2020) 2 *Forensic Science International: Reports* 100076.

Horsman G, 'Raiders of the Lost Artefacts: Championing the Need for Digital Forensics Research' (2019) 1 *Forensic Science International: Reports* 100003.

Horsman G and Sunde N, 'Part 1: The Need for Peer Review in Digital Forensics' (2020) 35 *Forensic Science International: Digital Investigation* 301062.

'National Institute for Standards and Technology' <https://www.nist.gov/programs-projects/digital-forensics>

'Scientific Working Group on Digital Evidence' <https://www.swgde.org/>

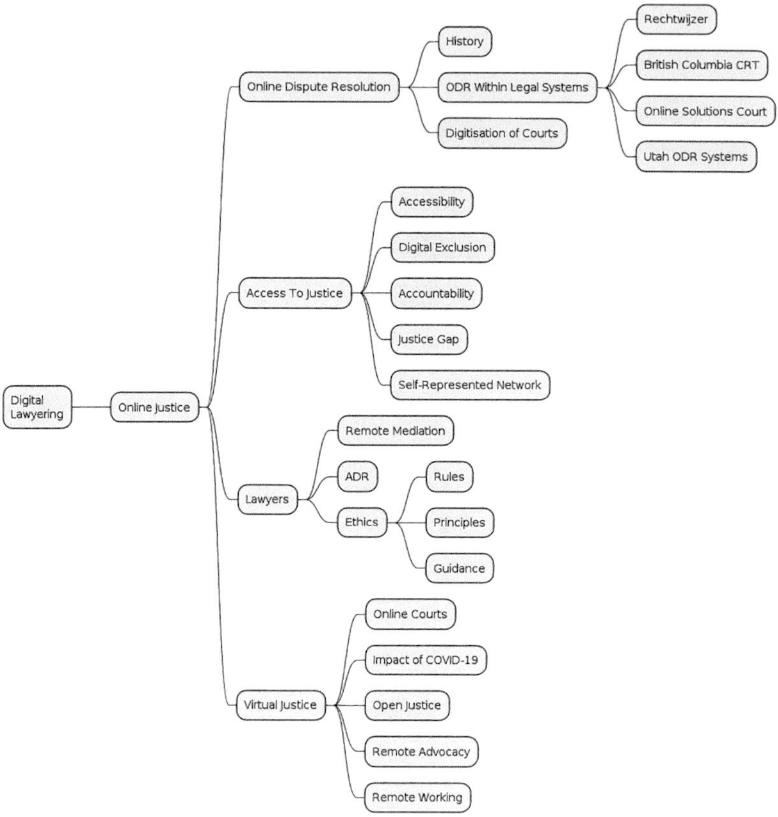

Mind Map 9.1 Chapter topics

9 ONLINE JUSTICE

Francine Ryan

INTRODUCTION

Technology is driving the administration of justice. Online dispute resolution (ODR) provides an alternative method of resolving legal issues, and virtual courts are now an integral part of the legal system. This chapter will consider how legal disputes are resolved via web-based systems and examine a variety of different ODR systems. It will discuss the development of online and virtual courts and consider the legacy of the COVID-19 pandemic on the use of remote hearings. You will consider the opportunities and challenges that arise from delivering justice online and reflect on how, as technology is adopted, there are increasing opportunities to increase access to justice without creating a digital divide.

Chapter hot spots

When reading this chapter, questions to think about include:

- What is online dispute resolution?
- How is technology transforming the administration of justice?
- How will online courts work?
- What lessons have been learned from the COVID-19 pandemic on the use of remote courts?
- What is the role of GenAI in online courts and online dispute resolution?
- How do we ensure there is not a digital divide?

Having read the title and introduction, you can add any other questions you want to explore here:

DOI: 10.4324/9781003602323-9

ONLINE COURTS

In his book *Online Courts and the Future of Justice*, Richard Susskind argues that online courts will become an essential element of our legal system.[1] There is some confusion over what is meant by the term "online court" because there is no agreed definition. It may refer to online procedures for resolving disputes provided by the state, or it may be an online service where the case is resolved through the system by a judge without any form of hearing.[2] As you will discover, different forms of online courts already exist in different jurisdictions.

WHAT IS ODR?

> Eventually ODR may be the way we resolve most of the problems in our lives, with algorithmic approaches even more trusted than human powered resolutions.[3]

If there is a greater use of technology to resolve disputes, then we need to understand what constitutes ODR. This is the settlement of disputes between the parties through the use of technology. It is a concept that has emerged over a number of years from alternative dispute resolution (ADR) and involves elements of negotiation, mediation, and arbitration. It has been described as "technologically assisted dispute resolution".[4] In order to mediate disputes, it uses different forms of technology such as chat, email, online forms, automated decision-making tools, and video conferencing. ODR can resolve disputes entirely or partly online, and it concerns disputes that arise both online and offline. It is used both formally and informally. This means that what is considered to be ODR is very broad and can include a wide range of processes for resolving disputes, including online debt collection, online tribunals, and automated decision-making systems where the computer is the adjudicator. ODR is used in different legal systems and across different areas of

1 Richard Susskind, *Online Courts and the Future of Justice* (OUP 2019).
2 Ibid., p. 6.
3 Ethan Katsh and Colin Rule, 'What We Know and Need to Know about Online Dispute Resolution' (2016) 67 *S.C.L. Rev.* 329, 343.
4 Colin Rule, 'Is ODR ADR?' (2016) 8 *Online Dispute Resolution* 8.

law to resolve consumer, family, civil, and commercial disputes. One of the interesting aspects of ODR is that it is being used outside of legal systems to resolve complaints before they become legal problems.

There are many examples of ODR, and each one works slightly differently and incorporates a variety of different tools. In this chapter we will explore some examples of ODR to get a better understanding of how it works and how it can assist parties to resolve their disputes. We need to consider what types of disputes are most suitable for ODR and how processes can be developed to improve the use of ODR. ODR systems are evolving, so we need to think carefully about the expansion of ODR and make sure it is being used for the right types of cases. ODR systems are developing, and different platforms have strengths and weaknesses. Although there are benefits of ODR, we need to decide whether they apply equally across all forms of ODR.

The range of technology solutions for resolving disputes is growing, but it is essential to critically analyse these changes to ensure that technology is developed in a way that improves the resolution of disputes for everyone. It is important to question the use of technology so we are not blinded to the potential issues and challenges that might emerge with the growth and expansion of technology solutions. A digital lawyer is a critical thinker who can evaluate and challenge the different narratives around technology.

Sync 1: Online dispute resolution: opportunity or threat?

You should allow around 15 minutes for this activity.

1 What are the benefits to ordinary citizens with the increased use of ODR?

2 What are the barriers to the adoption of ODR within legal systems?

Several reports have been published arguing that ODR can improve access to justice for ordinary citizens. The costs of instructing a lawyer and issuing court proceedings are very expensive and prevent many people from enforcing their legal rights. ODR could be designed to be more affordable and accessible for people who would ordinarily find it difficult to engage with the court process. A well-designed ODR system that is simple to use could allow people to represent themselves at no disadvantage and make the process of resolving disputes quicker and more efficient.

Although public bodies such as courts and governments are more open to the idea of ODR, there are barriers to adopting technology within current legal systems. In most jurisdictions, current court rules and procedures are not designed to support ODR. A significant investment from the state is required to develop and introduce ODR into the administration of justice. Lawyers are naturally conservative, and many of them are concerned about the risks of making such significant changes to the court system. Many lawyers worry that a lack of sufficient investment from the state will result in ODR systems not being fit for purpose and not delivering on improved benefits such as access to justice. Although some lawyers view ODR as an opportunity to deliver new legal services, other lawyers, such as litigators, may be concerned that ODR will reduce the need for their specialist skills.

ODR: THE BEGINNING

In 1995, eBay[5] launched; its original name was AuctionWeb. Most people are familiar with how eBay works: It is a platform that brings buyers and sellers together to trade goods. By 1997 eBay had over 700,000 users, and many of them had disputes over their transactions. At first the company attempted to resolve complaints via email, but with the growing number of users, it was evident that was not going to be feasible, and they needed to develop a more cost-effective and efficient system. eBay contracted SquareTrade to develop an ODR system that could help them address a significant number of disputes. The first stage of the SquareTrade system was an online form where the user could make an initial claim that set out their demands. Then, if a settlement could not be reached, a human mediator would become involved to resolve the dispute. The system was revolutionary because the software replaced the functions of humans. In 2003, eBay started developing the system internally, and by 2011 they were handling over 60 million disputes a year.

The way in which eBay chose to resolve disputes was the beginning of the journey for ODR. eBay demonstrated it was possible to resolve disputes at scale using specialist software systems. It was and still is an informal and voluntary system that sits outside the legal system. The intention of eBay's system is to resolve problems before they escalate

5 <http://www.ebay.co.uk>

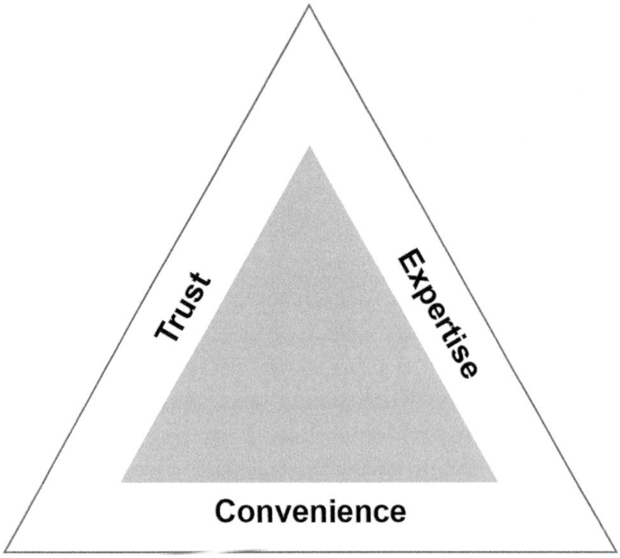

Figure 9.1 Essential elements of the ODR system

into legal disputes, and it is perhaps the most widely known ODR system. Other companies such as Amazon, Airbnb, and Uber have all adopted similar processes for resolving consumer complaints. The eBay system pioneered the development of ODR. The success of ecommerce providers utilising ODR systems encouraged public bodies such as governments and courts to explore the potential for ODR within their legal systems.

Figure 9.1 represents the essential elements of an ODR system which are required to ensure that it works and persuades users to sign up.[6]

RECHTWIJZER: ODR WITHIN A LEGAL SYSTEM

The first example of an ODR within a legal system was Rechtwijzer. *Rechtwijzer* ("signpost" in Dutch) which was developed by a group from the Dutch Legal Aid Board, the software company Modria, and the Hague Institute for the Internationalism of Law (HIIL) to support people with the legal process of divorce. It was dissolved in July 2017 after three years in operation. There were two versions of Rechtwijzer.

6 Ethan Katsh and Orna Rabinovich-Einy, *Digital Justice* (OUP 2017).

Version 1 was an interactive pathway designed to meet the individual needs of the user; it helped the parties work out agreements on issues connected to their divorce (e.g. children, housing, money). Version 2 incorporated ODR to allow the parties to negotiate agreements.

The major challenge for Rechtwijzer was that it was funded through social investment and could not be made financially viable. Nevertheless, it was an innovative project that demonstrated the potential of digital solutions to provide interactive advice coupled with ODR integration. The learning from Rechtwijzer influenced the development of other systems around the world, and it demonstrated the importance of having government support to succeed. Although it was disappointing for many that Rechtwijzer was dissolved, it has now been replaced by Uitelkaar.nl, which is based on the original platform and offers a paid service that provides customised divorce plans. The learning and innovation that was pioneered with Rechtwijzer was built on in the next iteration of an ODR system developed in British Columbia (Canada) called the Civil Resolution Tribunal.

BRITISH COLUMBIA CIVIL RESOLUTION TRIBUNAL

In July 2016, British Columbia launched the Civil Resolution Tribunal (CRT),[7] an online tribunal that resolves motor claims (up to $50,000), small claims (up to $5000), property (condominium) disputes of any amount, intimate images, and society and co-operative disputes of any amount. The CRT was established by the Civil Resolution Tribunal Act [SBC] 2012. One of the interesting features of the CRT is that it sits outside the court structure in British Columbia. There is a four-stage process (Figure 9.2).

The first stage of the process is the solution explorer, which is very important because it allows the parties to ask questions about their dispute and, based on their answers, provides free legal information and tools to assist the user. It allows the user to understand their legal issues, guides them through the process, and provides them with options to help them resolve their problems. After receiving information and guidance about their legal problem, if the user still wants to continue, the next stage allows them to make a claim with CRT. The parties are encouraged to negotiate to try to resolve their issues, but if that is not possible, a case manager attempts to facilitate an agreement;

7 <https://www.civilresolutionbc.ca>

Figure 9.2 The four-stage process

if that is not possible, then an independent decision is made by an adjudicator. Agreements can be made into orders which can be enforced in a similar way to a court order. The role of lawyers is limited to allow parties to represent themselves.

The five principles that underpin the CRT are timeliness, flexibility, accessibility, affordability, and efficiency. The CRT was designed in collaboration with and continues to work with community partnership organisations in British Columbia. Since its creation, the number of people using CRT has increased, and the feedback from users appears positive. CRT has demonstrated that ODR systems work and have the potential to resolve small claims.

The success of CRT has led to other jurisdictions exploring ideas to incorporate ODR into their legal systems, and new models of ODR are being developed. In 2016, there was a proposal to develop an Online Solutions Court for England and Wales. This was different from CRT because it would incorporate ODR into the court and tribunal structure rather than be developed separately to the court system.

MODELS OF ONLINE DISPUTE RESOLUTION: ENGLAND AND WALES

In 2016, the Lord Chancellor, the Lord Chief Justice, and the Senior President of Tribunals published a report titled *Transforming Our Justice System*, which set out a new vision for the justice system.[8] The report proposed an online system for starting and managing cases with the use of virtual hearings and, more controversially, some cases being resolved entirely online. It offered a radical vision for the justice system in England and Wales, bringing together ODR, and virtual hearings to resolve civil cases. Lord Briggs suggested that it should be called the Online Solutions Court, and not the Online Court, because there were plans for aspects of all court processes to be conducted online. However, most people still refer to it as the "online court". The plan was that the online court would deal with civil claims up to a value of £25,000 through a three-stage process (Figure 9.3).

8 Lord Chancellor, the Lord Chief Justice and the Senior President of Tribunals, 'Transforming Our Justice System' (2016) <https://assets.publishing.service.gov.uk/government/uploads/system/uploads/attachment_data/file/553261/joint-vision-statement.pdf> accessed 19 April 2021.

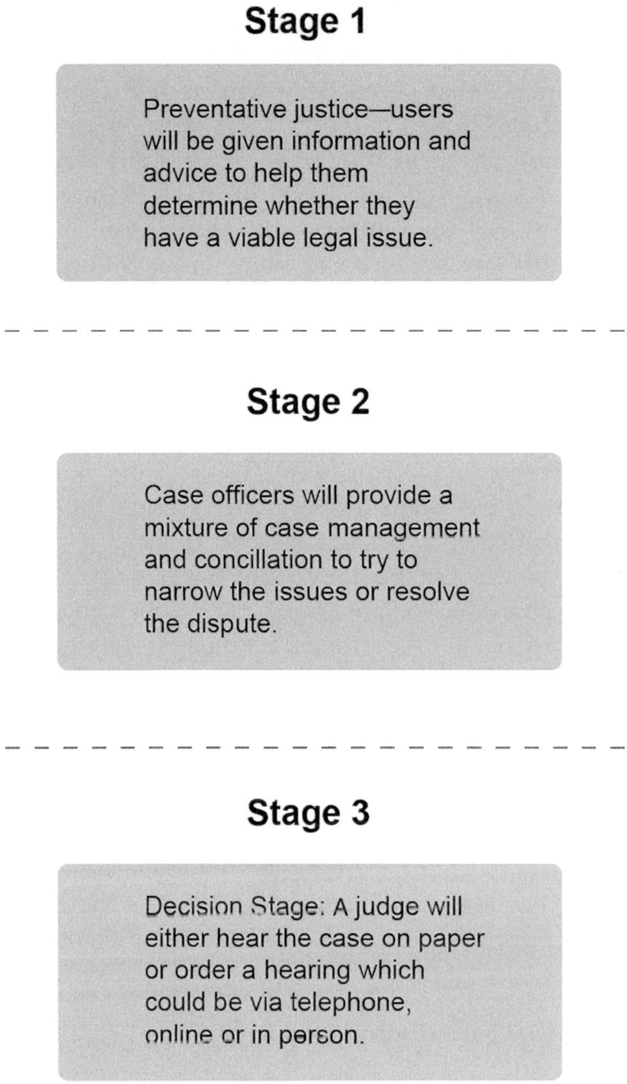

Figure 9.3 The three-stage process

Stage 1 of the process is similar to CRT. Its purpose is to help users better understand their legal problems to help them decide whether they should start court proceedings. The provision of information and guidance at the first stage is meant to try to filter out spurious cases. The use of case officers is designed to reduce the number of cases that need to proceed to the decision stage, as it is hoped they will be able to resolve a significant number of the disputes. One of the overriding factors in the design of the online court is to create a process that removes the need for lawyers. The vision was to create an efficient and simplified system that could deal with straightforward civil claims and improve access to justice.

The legislation to create the online civil court was contained in the Prison and Courts Bill published in 2017. However, the legislative process was not straightforward. The Prison and Courts Bill never made it into law because the then Prime Minister Teresa May called a general election and the bill lapsed. In the Queen's Speech in June 2017, the government said it intended to bring in legislation to modernise the court system, and it was thought this would include the online court. However, it was not until May 2018 that the Courts and Tribunals (Judiciary and Functions of Staff) Bill was published. It became law in December 2018, but it did not contain most of the provisions in the original Prison and Courts Bill, including the online court. In 2022, the Judicial Review and Courts Act 2022[9] led to the creation of the Online Procedure Rules Committee (OPRC). The OPRC is responsible for governing the practice and procedure for online court and tribunal proceedings. Its mission statement is:

> The aim of the Online Procedure Rule Committee is to improve access to justice for all by harnessing the power of modern digital technology in the pre-action space, in the civil and family courts and in the tribunals.[10]
>
> The OPRC is responsible for simplifying Online Procedure Rules to ensure that they are accessible and fair, support quick and efficient resolution of disputes and allow for innovative methods of dispute resolution.[11]

The aim of OPRC is to make legal processes more accessible because the HMCTS £1 billion court reform project closed and centralised the court estate and digitalised the process for civil, family, and probate cases. The streamlining of court processes has led to, for example, the Online Civil Money Claims, the Damages Claim Portal, Possession Claims Online, and online applications for grant of probate and

9 Judicial Review and Courts Act 2022

10 Online Procedure Rule Committee <https://www.gov.uk/government/organisations/online-procedure-rule-committee/about>

11 Ibid.

divorce. However, a combination of digital and nondigital processes remains, and there is still a long way to go to a fully digitalised system.

DIGITISATION OF COURTS

The digitalisation process has led to the ability to start court proceedings online.

Case study: Money Claim Online[12]

Money Claim Online (MCOL) is an HMCTS online service in England and Wales. It can be used by those bringing a claim (claimant) and those defending a claim (defendant). The service is designed to allow a claimant to bring an action online in the county court for a fixed amount of money that is less than £100,000. There are two platforms: Money Claims Online and Civil Money Claims. Once the claim has been issued, the defendant can file a response online. If the defendant admits the claim, then the claimant can make a request for judgment online; if the defendant makes a payment straight away, then the claimant can mark the claim as settled online. If the claimant has a judgment against the defendant but the defendant does not pay, a warrant for payment can also be issued online. If the case is defended, and it is less than £10,000, the parties must attend mediation, which the court will organise. If the claim is for more than £10,000, the court may still arrange mediation. If an agreement is not reached at mediation, then the parties need to attend a court hearing.

The online service works well for straightforward cases that are not disputed and demonstrates the potential for resolving claims online.

The court system in England and Wales is centralised, but in other jurisdictions they have state or federal systems, which means the digitalisation of the court system is not necessarily the same across the country. There are a growing number of examples worldwide of technology being used in different courts to assist with the resolution of legal disputes.

12 HMCTS is piloting a new service called Online Civil Money Claims which is in addition to MCOL. This is an online service for members of the public to issue claims of up to £10,000. HMCTS is currently piloting a number of other services in the County Court. <https://www.moneyclaim.gov.uk>

THE WORLDWIDE DEVELOPMENT OF ODR

Other jurisdictions are incorporating online platforms into their legal systems, for example, courts in New South Wales (NSW, Australia) use online systems for interlocutory hearings and messaging between lawyers and judges. In the supreme and district courts, the judge can decide to resolve civil law matters that are not contested in an online courtroom.[13] Singapore has an online system that allows for virtual negotiation to resolve small claims matters.[14] The court website contains information to support court users, including a chat function. China has been at the forefront of technological innovation; it has incorporated ODR platforms, internet courts, and emerging technologies within its justice system. The West Lake Court in Hangzhou uses virtual courtrooms, and a robot provides support for court users. Several regions in China have internet courts that have been created specifically to resolve internet disputes, such as domain name or copyright infringements.[15] China is also developing AI tools to help litigants draft court proceedings and understand their legal issues.

UTAH ODR SYSTEM

In 2018, the US state of Utah launched the first version of an ODR platform created by the Utah Administrative Office of the Court (AOC). The platform is available for use in some jurisdictions within Utah. A report was prepared by the Innovation for Justice programme, which stated:[16]

> [Online dispute resolution] is this emerging approach to access to justice that is at the intersection of law and technology and has so much hope and promise.

13 <https://courts.nsw.gov.au/>
14 <https://www.statecourts.gov.sg/cws/Pages/default.aspx>
15 <https://www.netcourt.gov.cn/>
16 Stacy Butler, Sarah Mauet, Christopher L. Griffin Jr and Mackenzie S. Pish, 'The Utah Online Dispute Resolution Platform: A Usability Evaluation, and Report' (September 2020), Arizona Legal Studies Discussion Paper no. 21-06 <https://law.arizona.edu/sites/default/files/i4J_Utah_ODR_Report.pdf> accessed 19 April 2021.

One of the important lessons from this project is the importance of user testing in the design of these platforms, which we explored in Chapter 4. Stacey Butler said:

> But I was fascinated that no one has run a [user experience] test on an online dispute resolution platform in the U.S. to evaluate whether it was going to work for the people who use it.[17]

Research from Butler et al. (2020)[18] suggests that users do not always find engaging with an ODR process straightforward. If there is to be an expansion of new platforms, there must be more research and engagement with stakeholders into the design and development of ODR to ensure that it meets the needs of end users. The Filing Fairness Project[19] is a multi-jurisdictional endeavour to modernise the court filling system in the US being led by Stanford University to improve the process of going to court for self-represented litigants.

Case study: Self-represented litigation network[20]

In the United States, each state has its own procedures for dealing with civil legal issues. The Self-Represented Litigation Network (SRLN) estimates that three out of five people in civil cases go to court without a lawyer. The growing number of self-represented litigants led to the creation of SRLN in 2005. It brings together judges, court managers, lawyers, librarians, academics, and community organisations to develop resources, education and training to help support people navigating the court system alone.

17 Emma Cueto, 'Online Court Pilot Gets Low Marks Ahead of Wider Launch' (Law 360, 13 September 2020) <https://www.law360.com/access-to-justice/articles/1309437/online-court-pilot-gets-low-marks-ahead-of-wider-launch?nl_pk=77322a31-1bbc-4e35-8532-8a4ef2d22451&utm_source=newsletter&utm_medium=email&utm_campaign=access-to-justice&read_more=1> accessed 19 April 2021.

18 Stacy Butler, Sarah Mauet, Christopher L. Griffin Jr and Mackenzie S. Pish, 'The Utah Online Dispute Resolution Platform: A Usability Evaluation, and Report' (September 2020), Arizona Legal Studies Discussion Paper no. 21-06 <https://law.arizona.edu/sites/default/files/i4J_Utah_ODR_Report.pdf> accessed 19 April 2021.

19 <https://filingfairnessproject.law.stanford.edu/#slsnav-history-and-theory-of-change>

20 <http://www.srln.org>

Sync 2: Self-help resources

You should allow around 20 minutes for this activity.

1 Go to <http://www.lawhelp.org/find-help>

2 You will see a map of the United States. Click on the state of New York and have a look around the website, in particular the self-help tools.

The LawHelp.org website contains a wide range of resources and information. When you looked at the resources, did you check when they were last reviewed? Some of the reviews were in 2022 and 2023; one of the issues with online resources is whether they are regularly updated, because if they are not updated this can cause problems for self-represented litigants. There was a link to the NYCourts.gov website that allowed someone to use the do-it-yourself forms to process their case if they did not have a lawyer. A HP Action could be started in New York City through an app called JustFix, which was a free and confidential service to force a landlord to make repairs.[21] But since June 2021 the Housing Court has not allowed tenants to use the tool. Although there is the potential to expand the use of ODR and self-help resources, there is work to be done to enable technology solutions to effectively support access to justice.

ACCESS TO JUSTICE

One of the main drivers for ODR has been the need to improve access to justice for ordinary citizens. In Chapter 4 you learned about the impact of cuts to funding for legal advice and how many people cannot afford the services of lawyers. Despite the lack of access to specialist advice, many people have to navigate the court system alone, which means that the process can be distressing and confusing. Many parts of the justice system are making the case that access to courts must be more accessible and more affordable. There is an expectation that ODR will be a part of the solution, but that will be possible only if the platforms are accessible and easy to navigate.

21 A tenant can bring a case against their landlord to require them to take action or perform repairs; this is called an HP action. <https://app.justfix.nyc/en/ehp/splash>

Sync 3: Justice gap

You should allow around 20 minutes for this activity.

Consider the strengths, weaknesses, opportunities, and threats (SWOT) of ODR systems in relation to addressing the justice gap by completing the SWOT analysis (Figure 9.4).

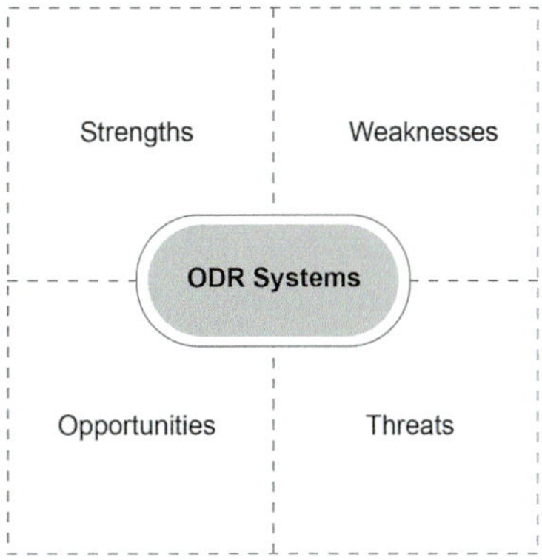

Figure 9.4 ODR systems SWOT analysis

You may have included some of these points in your SWOT analysis.

Strengths

- To provide faster and cheaper options than those currently existing.
- To provide a more flexible system to resolve legal disputes by negotiation and through online hearings rather than having to attend court in person.

Weaknesses

- A perception that ODR platforms provide second-rate justice which is not comparable to current systems.
- It requires users to have access to and be able to engage with technology.

Opportunities

- To engage more users in the legal system.
- To improve court efficiency.

Threats

- A lack of investment that will impact on the viability and performance of the platforms.
- Government or state support is required, the current economic situation is challenging and modernising court systems may not be an investment priority.

Although there is considerable potential for ODR, it is important to recognise the challenges of developing and incorporating these platforms into existing legal systems. There are significant barriers to overcome before they can become widely adopted. ODR is gaining acceptance and there is a growing infrastructure around these platforms, which may lead to a greater desire to leverage the benefits ODR can offer.

THE ROLE OF LAWYERS

ODR originally was considered for low-value claims, but since COVID-19, aspects of ODR have been explored for use more widely and, in particular, in complex commercial claims. In these types of cases, the term "ODR" has been replaced with "remote or online mediation", and more substantial disputes are being resolved online. There has been an increased level of acceptance and confidence in using remote mediation. Remote mediation replicates face-to-face mediation through video conferencing platforms such as Zoom.

A mediator hosts the meeting and uses breakout rooms for each of the parties. The mediator visits the breakout rooms and has private discussions with each of the parties. The parties then come together in a joint session and, through a collaborative process, come to a resolution and agreement on the issues. There is already a trend towards ADR from court-based litigation. Future lawyers will need an understanding of remote mediation and the skills to successfully support clients through the process. It is important to have a practical understanding of how remote mediations are conducted because there are a number of technology-related issues that need to be considered in advance of a remote mediation.

REMOTE MEDIATION TIPS

- Agree with your client in advance how you will communicate in a joint session.
- Have the bundle on a second device so you have the documents you need readily available.
- Check your hardware and make sure you have good connectivity before the meeting starts.
- Do not leave your client in the breakout room; use the time you have with your client during the mediation effectively.
- If there is a chat function, ensure that it is used only for non-confidential and non-private messages.
- Have a video pre-meeting discussion with the mediator to make sure everyone fully understands the process.
- Make sure there is good lighting: It is more challenging to read non-verbal clues online and even more difficult when there is poor lighting.

It is important to be aware of the changes that are happening within legal practice. Lawyers will increasingly participate in mediations rather than in trials. Many law schools are now offering training in advanced negotiation and mediation, providing students with the opportunity to acquire the practical skills and techniques required for facilitating negotiations. Mediation training can support the development of effective listening, conflict management, and negotiation skills. Mediation is becoming a preferred approach to conflict resolution in many jurisdictions. Many lawyers are now also trained mediators. The range of disputes mediated online is also expanding, including complex commercial cases, employment, and family law disputes, so it is therefore relevant to all parts of the legal profession.

ETHICAL PRINCIPLES

As the potential for ODR increases, we need to consider the ethical principles that underpin the design and developments of ODR systems. There needs to be an awareness of both the positive and negative benefits that emerging technologies can bring. Although ODR may have the potential to increase access to justice, there are risks in relation to data security, privacy, and (as discussed later) lack of access and power imbalances with the adoption of more technology-enhanced solutions. We need to consider whether there are appropriate standards and regulations governing ODR platforms now and in the future. The National Center for Technology and Dispute Resolution has developed Ethical Principles for Online Dispute Resolution.[22] These are not enforceable rules but act as guidance around the shared values that should be incorporated into the design and development of ODR systems. The purpose of these principles is to assist ODR designers, practitioners, and public bodies to respond more effectively to some of the ethical issues and challenges that arise with the development and implementation of ODR systems.

In the United States, the International Council for Online Dispute Regulation promotes standards for worldwide adoption of ODR systems.[23] It builds on the previous work of the National Center for Technology and Dispute Resolution and has a simplified set of standards. ODR systems should be:

- Accessible
- Accountable
- Competent
- Confidential
- Equal
- Fair/impartial/neutral
- Legal
- Secure
- Transparent

There is a recognition that with the expansion of ODR, more robust forms of regulation will be required. Lawyers and future lawyers must work towards ensuring that ethical principles of confidentiality, fairness, transparency, and accountability are central tenets of the regulation of ODR systems. Lawyers are going to be required to understand these issues from a global perspective because the increase in technologically enhanced dispute resolution will be across borders. The globalisation of dispute resolution is going to have a significant impact on the way in which digital lawyers of the future practice law.

22 National Center for Technology and Dispute Resolution, 'Ethical Principles for ODR Initiative' (2016) <https://odr.info/ethics-and-odr/> accessed 20 August 2025.

23 International Council for Online Dispute Regulation, 'ICODR Standards' <https://icodr.org/standards/> accessed 18 April 2021.

WHAT IS THE FUTURE FOR ODR?

The expansion of ODR systems is becoming possible through developments in machine learning and artificial intelligence (AI). You learned about AI in Chapter 7. The increased use of ODR in the private sector and improvements in technology will drive the expansion of ODR in the next few years in the public sphere. We may see ODR platforms moving from handling low-value claims to more complex disputes. There are an increasing number of AI tools and systems being developed which are likely going to be linked to the further development of ODR systems. It is important to be aware of the implications of algorithms, AI, and decision making. ODR also has the advantage that it can be used to resolve cross-border disputes, and this is a significant selling point in an increasingly globalised world. Technology can be leveraged to ensure that ODR is an effective dispute resolution mechanism, but it is no panacea. There are still significant challenges to the future development of ODR systems, and significant investment is required in order to realise the benefits of ODR.

In the first part of this chapter, we considered the relationship between online courts and ODR systems. The next part of this chapter will explore virtual justice and online hearings.

VIRTUAL JUSTICE

The introduction of online hearings is having a significant impact on the way in which millions of people engage with the justice system, not just in the UK but across many jurisdictions. Virtual hearings are now commonplace with either all parties online or some parties in a physical courtroom and some joining virtually. In bail hearings, a defendant joins from prison via a video link.

In England and Wales, the modernisation programme led to significant court closures. One of the aims of the modernisation programme is to improve the court system by moving to digital services and to recoup the investment by selling court buildings. As a result of the court closures, many people have to travel much further to attend court, and there is concern about the impact on access to justice. The impact of this policy on court users who have a disability, are on low incomes, live in rural areas, rely on public transport or have caring responsibilities is more significant. There is also another interesting issue about whether the lack of physical court buildings undermines public confidence and diminishes the rule of law.

However, proponents of online courts argue that courts are intimidating places for non-lawyers and that the provision of virtual courts means that it will be easier and cheaper for people to access courts and legal services. It is argued that this will improve access to justice, particularly for those people who cannot afford the services of a lawyer. The increasing capability that technology can deliver will result in a more seamless journey for the court user through the justice system.

Research has examined the impact of the pandemic on the court users and the court system which provide important insights into some of the opportunities and challenges of remote hearings.[24]

The findings suggest that lawyers using remote hearings were broadly satisfied with their experience but believe that some types of hearings, such as interlocutory hearings[25] and where both sides are legally represented, are more suited to being heard remotely.

Lay users face a number of barriers to accessing remote hearings:

- The inability to access the technology and participate fully in the hearing.
- The challenge of creating bundles to be submitted online.
- The use of technology coupled with an unfamiliar process causes anxiety that may exacerbate issues of participation.

At the height of the pandemic, many cases were adjourned and the number of new claims being issued was reduced; this meant that the participation of laypeople in remote hearings may have been lower than in "normal" times. It is therefore important to recognise that these studies may not present a complete picture on how laypeople engage

24 Dr Natalie Byrom, Sarah Beardon and Dr Abby Kendrick, 'Rapid Review: The Impact of COVID-19 on the Civil Justice System' (2020) <http://www.judiciary.uk/wp-content/uploads/2020/06/FINAL-REPORT-CJC-4-June-2020.v2-accessible.pdf> accessed 4 January 2026.

25 Interlocutory hearings are those that take place in the course of the legal proceedings but before the trial takes place, and may include a directions hearing, for example. For more information on different types of hearings, see <https://www.gov.uk/guidance/designs-disputes-resolution-hearings>

with remote hearings. The pandemic exacerbated welfare, housing and employment issues and as a result led to an increased need for legal services. There is a lack of access to free legal advice because of cuts to legal aid, and increasingly people are representing themselves in legal proceedings.

The research indicated that there were some issues with remote hearings:[26]

- Technical issues, such as people not being able to access the hearing.
- Poor connections, causing people to drop out of the hearing or lose video or sound or experience a delay in sound.
- A lack of technical support, so there was no one to try to resolve technical issues.
- Time wasted at the start of hearings: A lot of time was spent trying to deal with technical and connection issues.
- Interruptions: During COVID-19 more people were working from home, so hearings could be interrupted by children, animals, or the doorbell.
- Difficulties using e-bundles.
- Lack of process: There were no agreed standards of what would happen if connections were lost or what the ground rules for the hearing would be.
- Difficulty of lawyers being able to communicate with their clients during the hearing.
- Multitasking was challenging: Laptops were often used to access the hearing; another screen was needed to view the documents as well as a mobile phone to communicate with the client.

The research investigated how remote hearings compared with physical hearings. In relation to interlocutory hearings and fast-track trials where there were no witnesses, remote hearings were seen as helpful, as they have brought benefits including reducing travel and waiting time, improved efficiency and improved work/life balance. In complex cases that were contested and involved laypeople, remote hearings were considered not to be suitable.

26 *Supra* n. 25, p. 22.

Sync 4: Article 6(1) European Convention on Human Rights

You should allow around 15 minutes for this activity.

The right to a fair trial is enshrined in law, and this includes the right for a party to be heard "either in person or through his/her own legal representative with whom s/he can freely communicate".

1 What impact might remote hearings have on laypeople being able to communicate freely with their legal representative?

2 What are the implications for access to justice?

One of the difficulties that laypeople have is accessing suitable technology to connect to a remote hearing. There is often a presumption that everyone has access to a computer or a tablet, but many people may only have a mobile telephone. If they use their mobile telephone to access the hearing, they have no other way of communicating with their representatives during the court proceedings. Interpreters are often required in court hearings, and this may complicate matters further if there are challenges in translating what is happening. There is also a perception problem: One of the dangers of remote hearings is that they may be seen as a poor substitute to a physical hearing, and laypeople may feel that justice was compromised. It is important that these issues are addressed in the future design of online courts to ensure they do not undermine the faith in our justice system and the rule of law.

As a result of COVID-19, remote hearings are now an integral feature of legal proceedings, and they are more prominent in the court system. The remote hearings website[27] encourages discussion around remote hearings and shares good practice. The site includes experiences from around the world that demonstrate how different jurisdictions have adapted their court system, and they are conducting research to explore the use of remote hearings on a worldwide basis.

COMMON LAW AND CIVIL LAW JURISDICTIONS

The adoption and use of virtual hearings varies around the world but can also differ between common law and civil law countries, reflecting

27 <https://remotecourts.org>

the differences in legal traditions and technology infrastructure. In the inquisitorial system, which is typical in countries such as Italy and France, the court is actively involved in directing the investigation of the case. The judge plays a key role in the trial, cases often rely more on written submissions than oral advocacy, and evidentiary hearings in civil law systems are often shorter. In comparison, the adversarial nature of the common law system means that hearings are often longer and involve much more oral argument and cross-examination. The adversarial system has theatrical aspects which are not easily replicated online.

Conducting more substantive hearings virtually may cause issues with cross-examination of witnesses and the parties' ability to challenge more complex aspects of the case. Both common and civil law systems need to think carefully about the role virtual hearings will play in the future of court systems. Irrespective of the legal system, it is important to ensure that the public understand the processes that underpin the justice system, and when decisions are taken, all court users are heard. We need to understand the implications of moving from face-to-face to online and factor in the impact of digital exclusion on our justice system.

CRIMINAL TRIALS

During the pandemic, the non-governmental organisation JUSTICE[28] started testing the idea of fully remote jury trials. In a fully remote jury trial, all participants join the virtual court via video link and the case is live-streamed to a virtual public gallery.

Sync 5: Virtual Crown Court

You should allow around 20 minutes for this activity.

1. Go to <https://justice.org.uk/justice-pilots-first-ever-worldwide-virtual-mock-jury-trial/>
2. Read pages 3–7 of the evaluation report of the study <https://files.justice.org.uk/wp-content/uploads/2020/04/06165956/Mulcahy-Rowden-Virtual-trials-final.pdf>
3. Write down your reflections on your thoughts on the benefits and challenges to virtual jury trials.

28 <https://www.justice.org.uk>

You can read the full report, but it is 32 pages long. You might want to consider whether, as a practising lawyer, you need different skills to conduct advocacy in a virtual hearing compared with a physical hearing. Do you think you need to take a different approach to planning and conducting the case? What do you think are the differences between building rapport with the jury in a virtual hearing compared with a physical hearing?

OPEN JUSTICE

The principle of open justice is fundamental to the rule of law, and it is one of the mechanisms that ensures accountability, scrutiny, and the adherence to professional standards in the administration of justice. Lord Shaw of Dunfermline quoted Jeremy Bentham in *Scott v. Scott* [1913] AC 417, 477: "Publicity is the very soul of justice. It is the keenest spur to exertion and the surest of all guards against improbity. It keeps the judge himself while trying under trial". Open justice allows the public and the press to participate in the justice process and ensures that there is public oversight of court proceedings.

The use of remote hearings for court cases poses challenges for the principle of providing open access to courts for the public. With physical courts, the public and the media can sit in the public gallery and watch the proceedings. Access to virtual courtrooms often requires the permission of the court. One of the complexities of remote hearing is balancing openness and confidentiality. Family courts allow accredited journalists carrying press cards to access hearings. In those hearings, restricted material may be discussed which the press is not allowed to report on, but which does not prevent their attendance. The courtroom is therefore a protected space where complex issues can be explored freely in the knowledge that those discussions will not leave the room. The difficulty is how to achieve this in a remote courtroom and still protect open justice. This is an issue that courts and tribunals around the world will need to consider if there is an increased use of remote hearings. In 2023, the Ministry of Justice started a call for evidence on the way forward for Open Justice,[29] and you can read the summary of

29 Ministry of Justice, 'Open Justice: The Way Forward' (2023) <https://assets.publishing.service.gov.uk/government/uploads/system/uploads/attachment_data/file/1155744/open-justice-cfe.pdf> accessed 23 September 2021.

the responses.[30] Respondents noted that there was much more work to be done to ensure open justice.

Digital lawyering skills: remote advocacy

Legal professionals need to be able conduct in-person and remote advocacy. The skills required may overlap, but will include learning to use electronic documents and working with Acrobat or PDF Expert to mark up the documents. It is important to understand data protection legislation, which is explored in Chapter 6. All documents have to be stored remotely (compliant with the General Data Privacy Regulation), not directly on your device. In a remote hearing, face-to-face communication is reduced, and you will not be able to pick up the same verbal clues you would see in a face-to-face hearing. In a hearing it is important to be able to identify whether the witness is following the line of questioning or whether you are "losing" the judge. Advocates might be required to adapt their style of advocacy in remote hearings, so questions might need to be shorter and arguments made clearer and more concise; this is especially critical if there are issues with sound and video quality. The professional skills in communication and persuasion that advocates develop in the course of their practice remain the same, but they need to be adapted to be effective in remote hearings. These skills will be essential for law students as they move into legal practice, as there will be more opportunities to work in geographically dispersed teams on virtual hearings. Lawyers will need to have remote collaboration skills to be able to discuss strategy, develop arguments, and prepare documents.

Sync 6: I am not a cat!

You should allow 20 minutes for this activity

1 Watch these videos: <https://www.youtube.com/watch?v=qcnnl6HD6DU> and <https://www.ncsc.org/newsroom/public-health-emergency/tiny-chats>

2 What checks should you have in place before you start a remote hearing?

3 What did we learn about access to justice from the chat?

30 Ministry of Justice, 'Call for Evidence: Open Justice: The Way Forward' (2025) <https://assets.publishing.service.gov.uk/media/679a5a5161c295e9331f789a/open-justice-call-evidence-summary-responses.pdf> accessed 4 January 2026.

In the chat, Judge Roy Ferguson (394th Judicial District, Texas) discusses some of the benefits of remote hearings for improving access to justice. However, there are also challenges to moving hearings online.

DIGITAL EXCLUSION OR DIGITAL POVERTY?

Although there are many benefits of ODR and virtual courts, the efforts to move legal services online does risk impacting disadvantaged income groups, older people, or those with disabilities. As discussed in Chapter 4, there are parts of our society that either are unable to operate online or struggle to do so. As more of our legal services are digitally transformed, it is important to consider how digital exclusion impacts on people and also more broadly on the rule of law.

INTERNET ACCESS

According to OFCOM (the UK's regulator of communication services), 5% of individuals over 16+ have no access to the internet at home.[31] While internet access in the UK is now comprehensive, there are disparities around quality and speed of connections that impact lower-income households and those in rural areas. Digital exclusion is compounded if households lack access to a computer. Online access to a computer is required to engage effectively with court services, but many people have only a mobile phone. It is very challenging to navigate court services or attend remote hearings with a small screen and mobile data. The increase in technological transformation risks making it harder for those who are digitally excluded.

DIGITAL LITERACY

Chapter 4 discussed the importance of digital skills because to navigate digital services, people need the necessary skills and levels of digital literacy. This concept will also be discussed further in Chapter 11. The way in which online platforms and services are designed is an essential

31 OFCOM, 'Online Nation 2024 Report' (2024) <https://www.ofcom.org.uk/siteassets/resources/documents/research-and-data/online-research/online-nation/2024/online-nation-2024-report.pdf?v=386238&t> accessed 23 September 2025.

part of ensuring that users can easily navigate websites and find accessible information. Chapter 4 explored the importance of human-centred design which is critical with more services moving online.

Case study: Good Things Foundation

The work of the Good Things Foundation[32] is to promote digital inclusion. They have a network of centres in the UK, providing community-based learning to support the development of digital skills. As discussed earlier in the chapter, many courts and tribunal services are moving online as part of the reform programme. They provide support to help people in accessing digital services and to help people improve their digital skills. The people they support are often in the most vulnerable and socially excluded groups in our society. Their strategy has three aspects:

- The National DataBank: It provides free mobile data for those who cannot afford to connect.
- The National Device Bank: It receives refurbished donations of used tech and ensures that people who cannot afford a device have access.
- The National Digital Inclusion Network: It comprises community-based hubs where people can access digital inclusion services.[33]

They also have a free online learning platform, "Learn My Way", that covers beginners' skills topics.

AI JUSTICE

In July 2025, the government launched the AI action plan for justice.[34] Part of the plan includes embedding AI across the justice system with the development of a range of AI tools; at the current time of writing, there is limited information contained within the plan to assess the impact of AI on the justice system. However, it is clear that the government believes that AI has the potential to improve productivity, efficiency, and decision-making within the justice system. It is recognised that staff within the justice system need training and skills development

32 <https://www.goodthingsfoundation.org>
33 <https://www.goodthingsfoundation.org/about/our-strategy>
34 Ministry of Justice, 'AI Action Plan for Justice' in *AI Action Plan for Justice* <gov.uk>

to understand the benefits from the advances in technology and to become more confident in using AI systems. As a future lawyer, it is critical that you keep up to date with these changes and that you understand both the opportunities and limitations of embedding AI within the justice system. The potential of AI to impact on all aspects of our lives means that AI literacy is essential across society. In order for ordinary people to be aware of the implications of AI, we need to ensure that AI literacy is addressed; otherwise, we risk compounding further structural inequality.

CONCLUSION

This chapter has explored the development of ODR both outside and inside the legal system. As law firms face more global competition, the cost savings and improvements in productivity that can be achieved through digital transformation are increasingly becoming even more important. The justice system and lawyers responded well to the changes brought about by the pandemic. There will be increased use in ODR platforms to resolve disputes and use of AI more widely in court systems. It is also necessary to ensure that everyone has the digital skills to navigate legal processes. Law students need to understand the importance of online dispute resolution across all areas of legal practice and have the skills to confidently work in remote teams and understand the impact of AI on law and legal practice.

ADDITIONAL RESOURCES

Remote Courts Worldwide <https://remotecourts.org>

Susskind R, *Online Courts and the Future of Justice* (OUP 2019).

Wing L, Martinez J, Katsh E and Rule C, 'Designing Ethical Online Dispute Resolution Systems: The Rise of the Fourth Party' (2021) <https://doi.org/10.1111/nejo.12350>

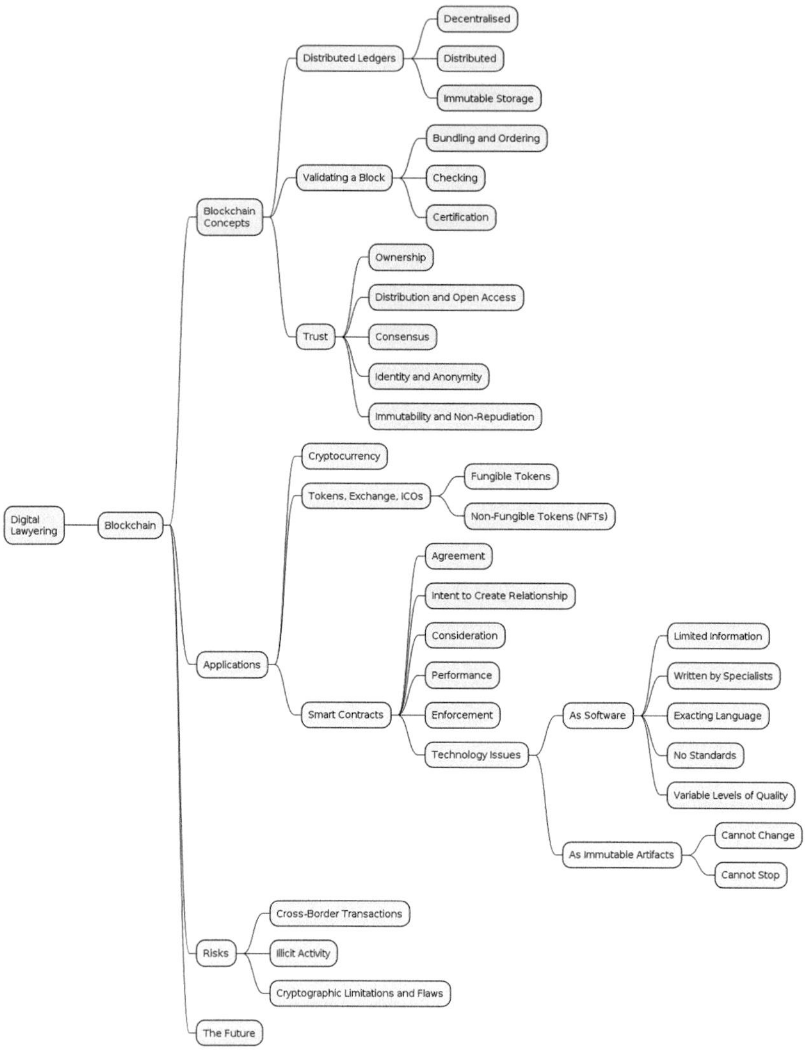

Mind Map 10.1 Chapter topics

10 BLOCKCHAIN

Terry Wong

INTRODUCTION

This chapter will introduce blockchain technology, highlighting key characteristics that make it the foundation of trust for a growing variety of commercial and legal applications. Going beyond the use of blockchain as the basis for various forms of digital currency, we explore these applications and the options the technology offers for anonymity, privacy protection, and legal positioning. Questions of regulation, jurisdiction, and compliance applicable to the use of the technology will be considered together with the implications of increasingly important features like smart contracts and distributed execution.

Chapter hot spots

When reading this chapter, questions to think about include:

- As a vehicle for conducting commerce and legal exchange, what are the characteristics of blockchain (beyond currency) that are most important for a lawyer to keep in mind?
- What are the challenges facing governments with blockchain applications, who cannot fully control the operation of distributed blockchains beyond their borders, even as their citizens increasingly use such technologies? What is the role of international cooperation in such cases?
- How might a lawyer advise clients seeking legal protections for activity conducted using blockchain technologies, where the basis of trust is primarily technological and is legal in nature only when legal regimes are current and practicable?

Having read the title and introduction, you can add any other questions you want to explore here:

DOI: 10.4324/9781003602323-10

ILLUSTRATION: AN URBAN POWER MICROGRID

The New York City (US) borough of Brooklyn has a community project for electricity generation by homeowners with solar panels, and the sale and transfer of excess power to other participating members of the community. An electronic marketplace for community power facilitates the bidding process for power, tabulates the flows of electricity from producers to consumers on the community grid, and allows payment in the form of exchange credits purchased with US dollars. Users start participating by downloading a mobile application and registering. To sell power, one must have or install solar panels meeting a minimum generation capacity and install a smart meter that also serves as a node on the marketplace network.

Local generation and peer-to-peer provision of power is a significant break with power delivery through traditional, centralised public utility monopolies, made possible using blockchain technology. Whereas traditional marketplace approaches would rely on a centralised authority for setting prices, accepting bids, matching counterparties, and finally clearing transactions, a blockchain supporting applications that implement each of those steps allows the decentralised marketplace to function, addressing a number of key concerns:

- *Timely gathering and processing of marketplace information.* If this was done by a central authority, it would introduce significant communications delays between parties. The data flows made possible by blockchain technology will include real-time power capacity and demand from each of the participants as well as bid and ask prices.
- *Fair pricing.* A central authority could change the prices of electricity for its own benefit. Open and auditable pricing data ensures transparency and fairness in marketplace pricing.
- *Cost-effective transaction processing.* Processing exchanges through a central authority would require additional payment infrastructure, with the possible involvement of financial intermediaries and the introduction of additional costs for processing and handling. Direct value exchange between participants in the network using credits not only speeds transactions, but also lowers costs. The availability of transaction data on the blockchain ensures that participants can audit and trust the chains of transactions recorded on the network.

A key theme with blockchains in operation is trust. The trust assurance mechanisms built into blockchain technology and its applications make such marketplaces possible, as we will see in other examples to follow.

A BLOCKCHAIN PRIMER

Sync 1: What is blockchain?

You should allow around 10 minutes for this activity.

Make some initial notes on what you understand by the term "blockchain". You can review these at the end of this chapter to see how your understanding has changed and developed.

What is blockchain? Is it currency? Is it a database? Is it a replacement for the internet? These are the questions that arise when considering the technology or supporting those doing so in a lawyerly capacity, trying to make sense of its varied applications and the incomplete explanations of its nature.

Blockchain technology has, in mainstream media, been primarily associated with cryptocurrencies[1] like Bitcoin and, to a lesser extent, with application-oriented hybrid implementations like Ethereum and Solana.[2] The technology represents a significant advance in the decoupling of applications and control, to a decentralised model combining high trust, resilience, and privacy. As we will see, these characteristics give blockchain technology and its applications both great appeal and a risk profile that business, regulators, and lawyers will be challenged to understand, harness, and manage in the years to come.

1 In this book, we will always refer to cryptographic currency applications on blockchain, such as Bitcoin, as "cryptocurrency" rather than the imprecise and sometimes incorrect usage "crypto" popularised in mass media. We feel that "crypto" is vague, conflating two very broad and important concepts: cryptography with cryptocurrency. The former is a more mature but still-evolving foundation technology with exceedingly broader application in communications, commerce, and so forth, while the latter is a narrower application of exchange enabled by the former.

2 J. Ito, N. Narula and R. Ali, 'The Blockchain Will Do to the Financial System What the Internet Did to Media' (*Harvard Business Review*, 2017) <https://hbr.org/2017/03/the-blockchain-will-do-to-banks-and-law-firms-what-the-internet-did-to-media> accessed 4 January 2026; John Naughton, 'Is Blockchain the Most Important IT Invention of Our Age?' (*Guardian*, 24 January 2016) <https://www.theguardian.com/commentisfree/2016/jan/24/blockchainbitcoin-technology-most-important-tech-invention-of-our-age-sir-mark-walport> accessed 4 January 2026.

Blockchain technology serves as the basis for many new decentralised applications in commerce, finance, utilities, manufacturing, law, and other sectors of the economy. A blockchain can be thought of, in the fundamental sense, as a decentralised, distributed data storage technology. The term "distributed ledger" is also used when describing blockchain. Indeed, blockchain is now the most used type of distributed ledger. Let us examine each of these important aspects of the technology:

- *Decentralised.* The network of participants in a blockchain-based application act without a single central point of control. Central points of control generally provide the function of ordering and recording information, serving as the reference or source of truth for application data. Blockchains are designed to operate with multiple points of activity, sharing control through consensus, achieved through several operations relying on rigorous, provable algorithmic methods.
- *Distributed.* Multiple points of activity operating through consensus each have a full copy of the application's data. This redundant distribution means that the data on the application network is resilient, highly available, and very difficult to destroy. Because members have access to all the application data, the data is open to inspection and validation, offering opportunities for greater trust.
- *Storage.* Many blockchains can store application data of varying size, though a balance must be struck between storing rich application data and processing speed and data size, affecting the willingness of participants to join the network.

The word "blockchain" conjures an image of a linked sequence of blocks, which is in fact an effective way to visualise its structure. Blockchain is thus, technologically speaking, a sequential block implementation of a distributed ledger (Figure 10.1).

The basic unit in a blockchain is a parcel of application data, the block, containing the details of a transaction, such as the transfer of value, goods, or real property. In cryptocurrency applications, the block would concretely contain records of transfer transactions in the cryptocurrency. In addition, the block would contain coordinating information which members of the network would need to treat the data as part of the blockchain. Most important is a cryptographic signature of the previous block that it proposes to follow. In blockchain applications, members on the network running applications that conduct

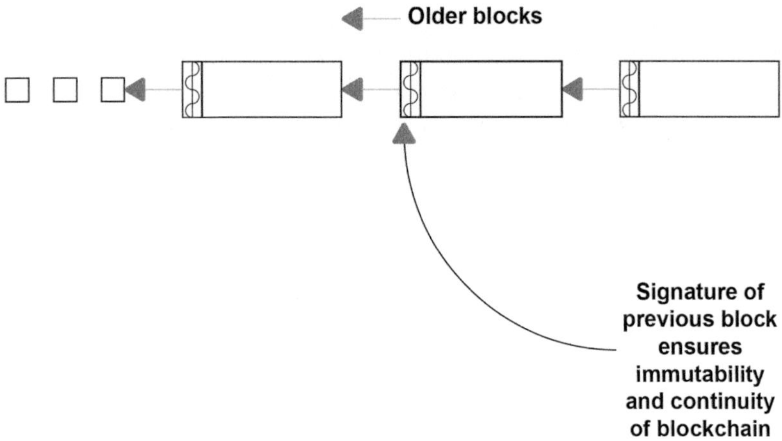

Figure 10.1 Illustration of a blockchain

transactions would submit transaction data to the network, to be received by members engaged in transaction validation.

Validating a block (in cryptocurrency applications, the process is called "mining") involves several steps:

1 *Bundling and ordering.* The records submitted to the network within a given time window are bundled together and sorted into submission-time order.
2 *Checking for consistency and conformity to application rules.* Individual records are checked for consistency; for example, transfer quantities between cryptocurrency wallets are in balance, or only the power that is currently available and stored at a node on a microgrid network may be transferred to a consuming member.
3 *Certification.* Correct—in other words, consistent and conforming—blocks are certified by computing a cryptographic hash function whose result can be used at any later time to ensure the integrity of the contents of the block (in other words, that the records cannot and have not been altered in any way once accepted). Specific applications have additional rules that are validated during the certification process (e.g. the hash must meet certain conditions set by the network for cryptocurrencies like Bitcoin).

You will note that the cryptographic hash value—a very large, unique number computed for certifying a block—is also used as part of the contents of the following block. That following block is thus able to assert its own order in the chain, ensuring the ordering of other blocks in the blockchain and ensuring immutability by precluding the alteration of blocks already accepted and committed. In other words, they cannot be changed. Arbitrary reordering and alteration of any committed correct block is not known to be possible in a blockchain, hence the technology's name.

By design, the computation of cryptographic hash functions used in certifying blocks in a blockchain is an expensive operation involving substantial calculations that consume time and energy in the form of electricity. In early 2021, the BBC reported that Bitcoin mining alone consumed over 121.36 TWh (terawatt-hours) a year, greater than the power consumption of a country like Argentina or the United Arab Emirates for the same period.[3] Power consumption, and the results of the calculations themselves used in ensuring the integrity of the blockchain, represent some of the economic value rewarded in turn to members who validate transactions or are said to "mine" cryptocurrency.

Members of the network performing validation or mining who successfully complete the operation on a block will submit the result to the network. The first member who successfully submits a correct and conforming result according to the rules of the application will, in the case of cryptocurrencies, be awarded a certain quantity of that cryptocurrency as a reward, representing the incentive for participating and expending the time and resources needed to validate transactions. This process is illustrated in Figure 10.2.

TRUST IN BLOCKCHAIN

Research in the early 1980s combining cryptographic techniques in contexts of mutual distrust led to explorations that would come to fruition with the emergence of Bitcoin. This was the first widespread blockchain application and first successful decentralised cryptocurrency, created in the aftermath of the 2008 global financial crisis. Many observers assert that Bitcoin was developed as a direct response to the loss of trust in the world financial system, combining in its blockchain desirable characteristics that build trust:

3 Cristina Criddle, 'Bitcoin Consumes "More Electricity than Argentina"' (*BBC News*, 10 February 2021) <https://www.bbc.com/news/technology-56012952> accessed 4 January 2006.

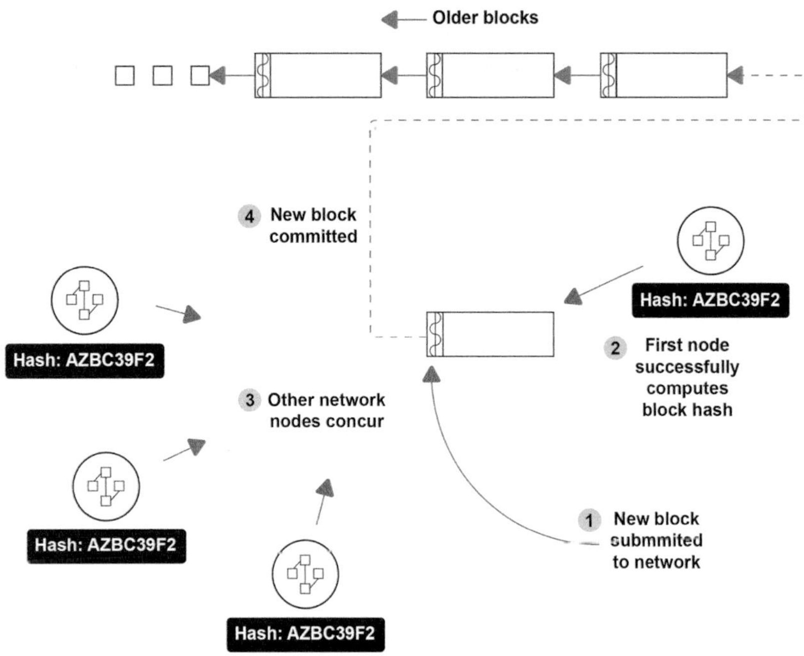

Figure 10.2 Validation by consensus/proof of work

- *Decentralised.* No longer could a financial institution, central bank, or network of banks act individually or in concert against the interests of individuals.
- *Distributed.* Members and actors on the network contribute to its operation and are rewarded for doing so.
- *Immutable storage.* The unchangeable, redundant storage of transaction data open for inspection allows members to realise a level of transparency and reliability heretofore unknown with traditional banking and exchange.

Other views assert that Bitcoin's enigmatic creator, Satoshi Nakamoto, had been developing the technology for some time, simply choosing an opportune time for its release and the publication of the seminal paper describing its theory of operation.[4]

While it may be debatable whether Bitcoin was a response to the great loss of public trust in the financial system in 2008, its characteristics

4 Satoshi Nakamoto, 'Bitcoin: A Peer-to-Peer Electronic Cash System' (31 October 2008) <https://bitcoin.org/en/bitcoin-paper> accessed 4 January 2026.

by virtue of being a blockchain application were critical to its early success. Let us examine some aspects of trust and the ways blockchains address those aspects in various contexts and with operational methods that do not of themselves engender trust among parties. These include:

- Ownership
- Distribution and open access
- Consensus
- Identity and anonymity
- Trust across borders
- Immutability and non-repudiation.

OWNERSHIP

A particularly difficult characteristic of some blockchain applications is the nature of ownership of the data and the network on which the application runs. For some applications like the Bitcoin cryptocurrency, there is no single operator or central authority controlling the network. There is likewise no privileged member who has the ability on the network to approve or "correct" transactions. This lack of a single operator or central authority controlling the network is critical for the success of a cryptocurrency serving as a decentralised means of exchange. By design, it provides strong protections against a possibly corrupt central authority manipulating volumes and prices.

DISTRIBUTION AND OPEN ACCESS

A common criticism levelled by detractors[5] of blockchain technologies is the common understanding from anecdotes and experience with Bitcoin that all blockchain data is open and publicly available, and therefore inherently insecure and not suitable for storing confidential and personally identifying information. One must unpack the concerns and assumptions embedded in those objections:

1. *That a lack of a trusted intermediary like a bank, government, or some similar organisation is an indicator of less than 100% trustworthiness.*

5 A healthy, substantial population of sceptics is necessary. Sceptics open to new facts and information ensure that a technology trend garnering such an enormous level of hype and interest, with such far-reaching implications on commerce and on society overall, is adopted or, as the eventual case may be, put aside for better alternatives.

This assumes that a trusted intermediary is 100% trustworthy, which is not true. Centralised intermediaries are not 100% reliable in practice, as it has been seen that actors in banks and governments can and sometimes do alter and withhold information for their own benefit.

2 *That distributed copies of data in a blockchain are inherently insecure.* While it is true that all application data is openly available for inspection by participants on the blockchain network, it is also true that a large number of full copies of the data distributed to all participants, updated by consensus, ensures that attempts to tamper with, falsify, or destroy application data will in all likelihood be unsuccessful.

While it is true that participants on public blockchains can read the bytes committed to those blockchains, it is also true that in practice only the critical metadata necessary to verify the transaction and the integrity of supporting documents and data are committed and made publicly readable from the blockchain. Many applications will store the supporting data—which may be non-trivial in size—in privately controlled cloud storage, with encrypted storage and access control suitable for their particular use cases. Cryptographic signatures taken of the data must match those stored on the blockchain, thus ensuring the integrity of the off-blockchain-supporting data. Figure 10.3 illustrates this transaction recording and data storage strategy.

Blockchains will tend to have several, if not countless more copies of their data on their networks, ensuring that data and metadata committed to them cannot change, sometimes even with the computing resources of state actors. The distributed, decentralised data of blockchains is thus a significant assurance of trust.

CONSENSUS: THE ENABLER OF TRUST

The assumption built into consensus-based decision-making is that the consensus (agreement) of a larger group is more reliable than that of a single individual or smaller group of individuals. While this mode of decision-making and ascertainment of truth is not always desirable (e.g. for abstract problem-solving), some systematic ways of computing by consensus work on a large scale for blockchains.

Blockchain applications use one of the numerous commonly accepted protocols (sets of rules and procedures) to achieve consensus on their networks, examples of which include:

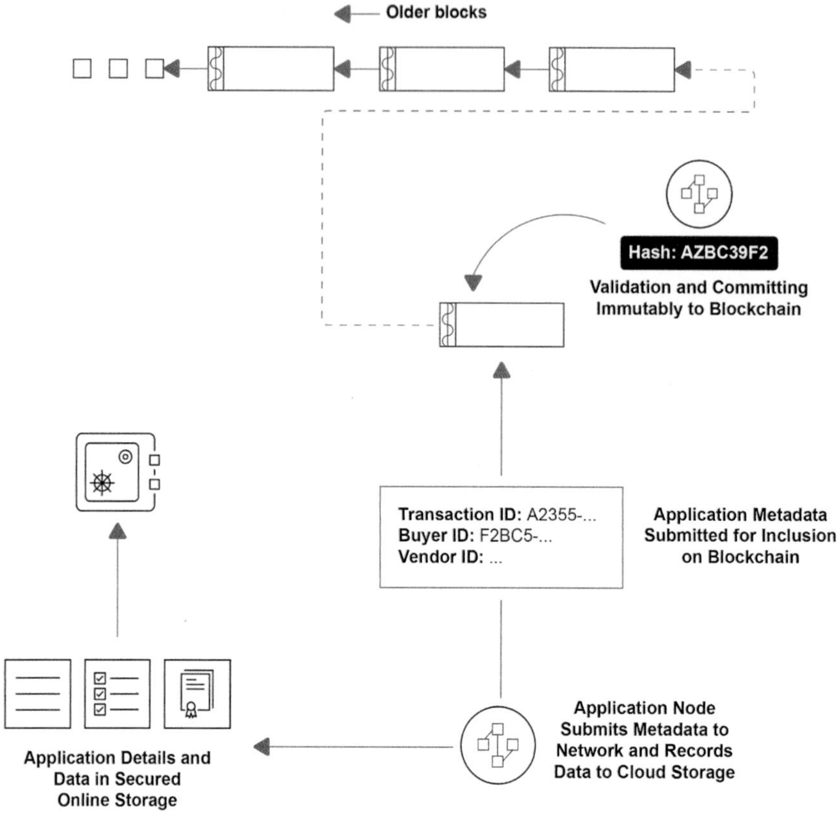

Figure 10.3 Recording transactions with blockchain

1 *Proof of work* (PoW). Certain cryptographic functions take large amounts of time and resources to execute, thereby obtaining a result that is usually a large number (a very long sequence of digits), mathematically proven to conform to certain specifications. It is considerably less expensive, if not trivial, to validate the correctness of such a number than to compute it. Because of this property, it is possible to present PoW to ensure that, for example, a Bitcoin transaction is valid and complete. This is because it is necessary to present a valid PoW in order to assert that a specific block of transactions is valid in the act of mining.
2 *Proof of stake* (PoS). Participants on a network must prove that they are invested in a network for a certain period of time prior to being able to operate in validation or mining operations on a cryptocurrency network. Members must hold a certain amount of an asset of value on

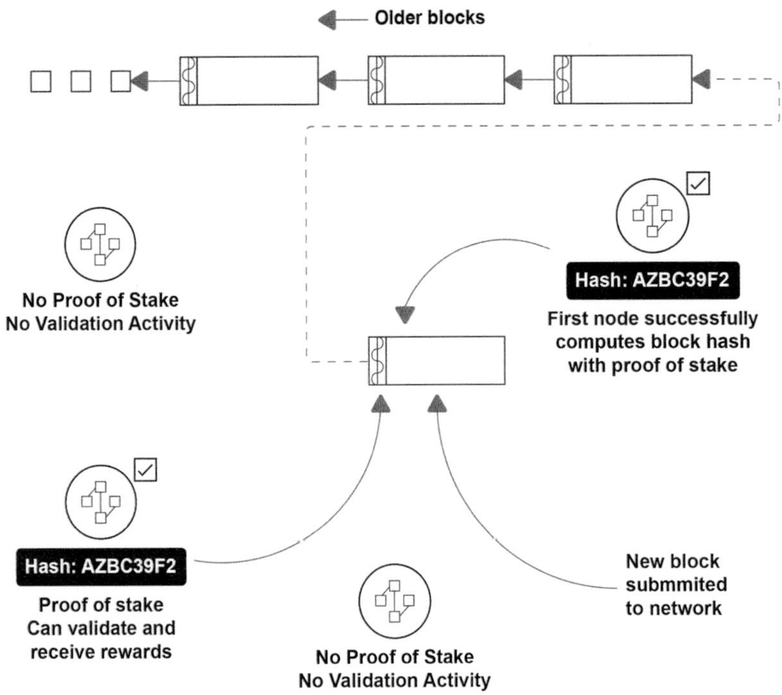

Figure 10.4 Proof of stake

the network, such as a cryptocurrency, for a verifiable period to be considered for selection to create the next block on the blockchain. In this way, actors have an incentive to participate as reliable actors, since the stake is put up as collateral, with penalties for behaviour detrimental to the system ranging from the loss of the stake to rejection of the block or replacement of the block (Figure 10.4).

3 *Practical Byzantine fault tolerance* (PBFT). The Byzantine Generals Problem is a well-known systems problem, the solution to which specifies an upper bound to the number of bad actors that a system can withstand. The example in a seminal paper describing the problem involves a number of Byzantine generals besieging a city who may communicate only via messenger. An indeterminate number of the generals are disloyal, possibly issuing misleading or malicious instructions to betray the army laying siege.[6] The solution is also directly applicable to blockchain applications, in which the

6 L. Lamport, R. Shostak and M. Pease, 'The Byzantine Generals Problem' (1982) 4 *ACM Transactions on Programming Languages and Systems* 382.

actors are not trusted by design. Using Byzantine fault tolerance, a network can have up to one-third of its actors be unreliable, go missing because of hardware or communications failure, or have malicious intent and still be able to function reliably. The two-thirds majority will allow consensus to be reached.

The foregoing is by no means a comprehensive list of all the consensus mechanisms being used. Innovation in this area continues, with new methods being developed and tested regularly, as both speed of computation and reliable means of achieving consensus are sought-after characteristics in blockchain development and operations. The former characteristic (speed) enables higher throughput and volumes, while the latter (reliability) maintains the critical factor of trust.

IDENTITY AND ANONYMITY

When conducting a transaction, the ability to trust that we are dealing with a counterparty on whom we can rely to complete the transaction is a prerequisite to successful exchange. In traditional transaction contexts, legal traditions, legislation, and case law establish penalties for the breach of an agreement. A generally necessary part of the contract is ascertaining the identities of the parties to an agreement such that their obligations and performance may be ensured and penalties for breaching the agreement enforced. What happens, however, when one or both parties wish to remain anonymous, even to one another, yet still enjoy strong protections against each other as to performance under their agreement? As we will soon see, the distributed, decentralised, cryptography-reliant nature of blockchains provide the way such requirements may be fulfilled.

How can one establish the identity of another party for the purpose of conducting a transaction, while omitting all other identifying data (personally identifiable information [PII]), such that it would be impossible to connect that transaction with a natural person? Blockchain-mediated transactions offer a viable solution for such transactions, reliant as they are on strong cryptographic methods. Such methods involve the exchange of cryptographic public keys, which are large, unique numbers generated through the computation of functions. These public keys support two important capabilities:

1 *Security of transmission*, whether of a message or a unit of cryptocurrency. Only the owner of the private key matching a given public key can decode a message encrypted with that public key.

2 *Validation of transmission.* A message signed with a user's private key can be authenticated using a published public key, again ensuring that the message was sent from the owner of the private key. There is an assumption that the owner follows good practice in physically securing copies of his or her keys, limiting access to them with passwords or biometric locking mechanisms such as facial recognition or fingerprint locking.

An example of an anonymous transaction

Let us consider an example where a freelance marketing analyst offers services with a blockchain-based matching service. A buyer looking for research to support evaluation of a possible market opportunity will pay a certain amount of cryptocurrency for a report quantifying the demand for a specific class of products in the freelancer's country, together with a list of key brands and the distributors of those brands. Because the buyer is considering entering that market and does not wish to disclose its plans, it withholds its identity when posting the brief and requirements for the job on the matching service's online platform. In addition to protecting its identity, the buyer hopes to minimise possible bias in its research results, which may result if the freelancer were to know for whom the research is being conducted.

Under the terms of the matching service, half of the full amount is to be paid by the buyer and held in escrow in the researcher's cryptocurrency wallet on the matching service until the final deliverables are posted to the service's online document sharing area. At that time, pending a verification of the general nature of the deliverables by the service, the initial payment is released. Upon final payment, the deliverables are released to the buyer, and the balance of the funds less the online service's fees is released to the freelancer's wallet, available for conversion to traditional currencies, to other cryptocurrencies or for use by the freelancer in another transaction but in the role of a buyer.

TRUST ACROSS BORDERS

In our previous example, we saw how a blockchain-based work-matching service could facilitate a successful transaction involving substantial contracting of work and exchange of value in cryptocurrency. In many traditional transaction contexts, the exchange is governed by a set of regulations in the jurisdictions hosting the service. Such regulations are applicable and enforceable not only because of geography, but especially because payment is made in the local currency or in commonly used hard currencies such as the US dollar or British pound. This provides mechanisms and pathways that traditional banking providers can use to track and mediate the exchange.

As the basis of transaction is in the end the means of payment, which in the traditional case is in the ultimate control of the banks licensed by the jurisdiction's regulator, a government has a range of highly effective tools to regulate these exchanges if it so chooses or requires to do so in order to meet policy objectives. The use of cryptocurrencies that does not require government-sanctioned banking services for transmission and clearing of payment could raise some concerns, especially when transactions occur across borders.

Some users may view the complete removal of government and banking involvement in the conduct of commerce as a beneficial feature, but in the end, there is a need to establish trust in some way so that exchange may take place. There are two options:

1 *Rely on other intermediaries.* These include exchanges or other third-party services who offer mechanisms for establishing trust. Some services are built using certain blockchain technologies that rely on cryptographic key and identity management tools managed by trusted authorities that issue certificates, known as certificate authorities (CAs), which serve as the source of trust in a given application network.[7] These parties take the place of governments and banks, and in some contexts, particularly in developing countries or countries with corruption and weak banking systems, may be preferable.
2 *Rely on technological features.* These are built into certain blockchain technology implementations. They allow the technology itself to supply and operate the mechanisms for trust. Smart contracts are the best known of these approaches, allowing application operators ways to execute programs that run in the context of blockchain operations themselves. Some of these programs can even perform gatekeeping and payment release functions when those conditions are met, as specified by the application or the particular transaction. We will examine smart contracts in more detail later in this chapter.

In general, the use of government-sanctioned means of exchange is preferable not only for compliance with local laws but also for recourse

7 At the time of this textbook's writing, the most prominent example of such an implementation in general use is Hyperledger Fabric.

in case of problems or disputes. Resolution mechanisms and existing legal processes provide at least some levels of protection and established process for seeking redress when transactions go awry.

We might, with some optimism, anticipate the eventual development of international trade agreements covering exchange and commerce using cryptocurrency and blockchain-mediated transactions as local and international law catches up with the rapid developments in technology.

IMMUTABILITY AND NON-REPUDIATION

A significant feature of blockchains is their immutability. This is to say that records committed and accepted through consensus mechanisms onto a blockchain may never be altered, thus providing a permanent, reliable record of activity and exchange. Unlike with traditional data storage mechanisms, such as databases or file-sharing mechanisms, there is no privileged mechanism that would allow some party to "correct" or in any way alter records committed to a blockchain.

A distributed asset exchange application built with a blockchain would provide a significant assurance of reliability, even in the absence of a regulator or trusted exchange operator or clearing entity. The exchange can be trusted because not one of its transactions can be altered in any way without being detected. It is impossible to give the privileged with access on a centralised network the ability to alter results in favour of certain parties retroactively after market close. In the blockchain application context, many objections to the privilege of a central authority and its manipulative potential simply do not exist.

The property of immutability also prevents participants on a network from denying or retroactively trying to cover up their participation in specific transactions. Reliable recording with consensus and the strong encryption protocols used to sign network requests for blockchain applications assure the validity of even anonymous transactions. It is a small irony that while regulators and would-be detractors of blockchain applications decry the ability of blockchains to operate without government oversight, the non-repudiation (inability to challenge the validity of a signature) built into blockchain technology ensures reliable attribution of transactions if identity can be established through other means, as might happen in far-reaching criminal investigations.

The immutable and distributed nature of blockchain transactions, with their numerous cryptographically signed copies of application data, ensures that non-repudiation is also a survivable fact, so long as there is a sufficiently large enough number of participants on the network. It would be extremely difficult, if not physically impossible, for a well-funded actor or even a state operator to eliminate all traces of a transaction from a large enough blockchain network.

Sync 2: Blockchain and trust

You should allow around 15 minutes for this activity.

Select one of the features discussed earlier (ownership, distribution and open access, consensus, identity and anonymity, and immutability and non-repudiation). In your own words, write a paragraph explaining its importance.

For lawyers dealing with sometimes complicated technological concepts, it is important that they can explain information in a clear and accessible way. This is vital to ensure that clients, colleagues, and third parties who are less familiar with such ideas can understand the relevance of such concepts and any advice based upon them.

APPLICATIONS OF BLOCKCHAIN

In this section we present several blockchain applications to offer a general sense for the student of the range of possibilities. This exploration is by no means exhaustive but provides a sense of scope and scale.

CRYPTOCURRENCY

It is inevitable in an introductory discussion of blockchain that we have already gone into some detail about Bitcoin and its underlying technology, uses, and regulation. In the years since its introduction, an explosion in innovation has occurred, with cryptocurrencies emerging to fit into every conceivable space and application. In March 2021, during the writing of the first edition of this text, CoinMarketCap, a website tracking cryptocurrency capitalisation, listed over 8795 cryptocurrencies in its directory.[8] As this second edition was being prepared, the same

8 'Cryptocurrency Prices, Charts and Market Capitalizations' (*CoinMarketCap*) <https://coinmarketcap.com/> accessed 22 March 2021 and 4 August 2025.

site tracked over 19 million cryptocurrencies. You are recommended to visit the CoinMarketCap site, or find a similar listing in an internet search, to see the range of cryptocurrencies that continue to emerge.

Some governments hastened to prohibit certain cryptocurrency-related activities within their borders. China did so in 2017, originally to address energy consumption concerns with transactions and mining activities.[9] Since 2019 the Chinese government has banned the first public sale of several new cryptocurrencies (known as initial coin offerings [ICOs]) and cryptocurrency exchange activities that could, in the eyes of the government, result in speculative and economically destabilising activities.[10] In 2021, the government imposed a complete ban on cryptocurrency ownership and trading, in anticipation of a nationalised stable coin offering tied to the Chinese yuan.

In contrast to the situation in China, many jurisdictions, including the United States, UK, and EU, have not prohibited financial institutions from handling cryptocurrencies. In those jurisdictions, cryptocurrencies are not legal tender, but are legal assets.[11] The Bitcoin boom of the late 2010s and early 2020s saw many online financial technology start-ups and established banks all offering services related to the cryptocurrency, adding momentum to the meteoric rise in the market value of a single Bitcoin. The United States, under the second Trump administration, continued down a path of adopting cryptocurrency, with the passage of the GENIUS Act and by executive order began the creation of a Strategic Bitcoin Reserve.[12]

Not all cryptocurrency is used for pure exchange. The second cryptocurrency in widest use, Ether (ETH), is used with Ethereum, a decentralised, open source blockchain used for general applications requiring the execution of smart contracts. The execution of the code in a smart contract requires payment from the parties in the form of Gas, a fractional portion of a unit of Ether, whose value is determined by the supply

9 'Bitcoin Mining in Northern Chinese Province to Be Halted amid Energy-Saving Push' (*South China Morning Post*) <https://www.scmp.com/economy/china-economy/article/3123633/bitcoin-mining-northern-chinese-province-be-halted-amid> accessed 22 March 2021.

10 L. Zhang, 'Regulation of Cryptocurrency' (June 2018) <https://www.loc.gov/law/help/cryptocurrency/china.php> accessed 14 March 2021.

11 UK Government Press Release: New Cryptoasset Rules to Drive Growth and Protect Consumers <https://www.gov.uk/government/news/new-cryptoasset-rules-to-drive-growth-and-protect-consumers> accessed 13 August 2025.

12 S.1582—Genius Act (*Congress.gov*, 2025) <https://www.congress.gov/bill/119th-congress/senate-bill/1582> accessed 4 January 2026.

and demand relationship in time between contracts to be executed on the Ethereum network and the computing resources available.

TOKENS, EXCHANGE, AND ICOS

Cryptographic tokens, or simply tokens,[13] are a type of cryptocurrency that are used, as their name implies, to represent an asset. Often the asset is a physical asset, such as a piece of art or other item of property. The token can be used to accomplish the exchange for payment or other value, whether in tokens representing other assets or other cryptocurrency acceptable in the context of a transaction.

Some use cases for blockchain

Provenance of Goods for Human Consumption

Outbreaks of disease resulting from the consumption of contaminated raw vegetables can be costly in terms of lost goods, lost consumer confidence, and exposure to liability. Agricultural producers, from vegetable growers to winemakers, are turning to blockchain to ensure quality in their products and to provide the means to trace the production and supply chain for those products. The retailer Walmart implemented a blockchain application for suppliers of leafy green vegetables to record every step of production, harvesting, processing, packaging, and delivery. Instead of discarding every package of produce on its shelves, as it has done in previous outbreaks, the application supplies enough information to pinpoint the location of contaminated packages for removal. The system allows Walmart to work more closely with public health officials to contain outbreaks caused by contaminated produce while providing greater control over loss.

Know Your Customer

Know Your Customer (KYC) verifications required by financial and legal organisations before taking on clients are time-consuming and expensive to conduct. A common application of blockchain is KYC, taking advantage of distribution and non-repudiation to firmly establish a person's identity and their key financial and legal profile information. Some scenarios have customers unlocking access to their data stored on a public blockchain, with the requesting institutions paying the network for accessing the released data.

13 Sometimes also called crypto tokens, though we also discourage the use of "crypto", as it is vague, and it is especially imprecise when discussing tokens.

Diamond Provenance Certification

The provenance of diamonds is of great concern to consumers and the commercial members of the diamond trade. There are particular concerns over the trade in blood diamonds, stones mined in war-torn countries in Africa and often obtained with modern slave labour and sold to finance war efforts, insurrection, and terrorism. Their trade raises not only ethical questions but also serious issues of legal compliance at every step in the supply chain. Given the high stakes and risk, it follows that solutions to address the issue of diamond provenance have emerged. It also follows that blockchain-based solutions should figure prominently in a solution, considering the key benefits of the technology and the objectives:

- *Distribution.* Multiple industry partners cooperating on a network provide more trust than a single, possibly corrupt central authority or clearing organisation. Cooperation of key players in the trade lays a core of trust in the network, leading smaller players to join and participate as well. The increasing activity in the network further strengthens its acceptance as growing numbers use it. Instead of relying on a mandated standard or central authority, cooperation and convention may yet lead to an even stronger, more trusted, decentralised network as a positive collective foundation for the future of the trade.

- *Auditable.* Open accessibility of data to all network participants, not just a central authority, supports transparency in reporting, while security protocols allow protections of proprietary information related to sourcing and pricing.

- *Immutability.* Strong guarantees that records cannot be altered support trust in the system's information, guaranteeing compliance to ethics and law in the trade and supporting the confidence of the final purchaser.

- *Non-repudiation.* Should there arise questions or issues, players cannot deny transactions, and thus they have the incentive to comply with and ensure good practices in trade.

It is illustrative to note that multiple efforts have emerged in the industry, one from the dominant diamond supplier DeBeers and another spearheaded by IBM and backed by a consortium of mining, distribution, and retail players. The two solutions reflect contrasting approaches and, in some respects, the dynamics of the diamond trade.

SMART CONTRACTS

Perhaps the application of blockchain technology that is most associated with the legal profession, and which attracts the most attention from it (if just for the name), are so-called smart contracts. Building upon blockchain technology and its key features of decentralisation, distribution, immutability, and non-repudiation, smart contracts offer lawyers and technologists working together many options to implement structures for agreement and exchange. These new structures represent new approaches that are simpler, faster, and in some cases more trustworthy than those implemented using traditional contracts.

One illustration of this is in the field of media licensing. Publishers working in print and online media often have the need to obtain licences to use images and illustrations in their works. The process is sometimes managed using paper forms mailed, faxed, or more often emailed or uploaded to an intermediary organisation such as a clearing house or stock agency, depending on the intermediary's preferred or supported mechanisms for conducting business. Intermediaries often have websites that support the purchase of licences, but in fact the websites are merely e-commerce mechanisms, offering little in the way of certification of ownership, certification of licence, or access control and metering of access.

Using an existing website to initiate a transaction and support the creation of a smart contract, intermediaries or media owners may use the smart contract to receive confirmation of payment from a banking system or directly from a cryptocurrency's blockchain, following which access to the media would be granted. The media would contain watermarks or have their digital fingerprint recorded on a public blockchain to prove ownership. The media may be delivered to end users from a web service that counts digital impressions or views, much like an online advertising server. The smart contract may be written in such a way as to demand payment from the licensee at certain view count levels, allowing licence use, compliance and payment to take place all at once, without intervention from either party.

A SMART CONTRACT PRIMER FOR LAWYERS

A critical question that arises when considering smart contracts is whether they are, in fact, legal contracts. Let us examine their qualities in greater detail, considering the elements of contracts.

AGREEMENT

While traditional contracts may be memorialised in writing, and in many cases, use language open to human interpretation, such as "the parties undertake to . . .", smart contracts encode the conditions of an agreement using software code evaluated by a computer with specific inputs that represent conditions expected by the parties to yield a specific, deterministic result. Because of the specificity of computer code, it is often difficult, if not impossible, to render an agreement made between humans with the level of flexibility that a computer may take and operate upon, much less interpret. Smart contracts have been used to express contracts that have a limited set of conditions and interpretations, in contexts with high volumes of transactions, such as financial transactions or low-unit-value, high-volume settings such as automated consumer sales.

A middle ground is often taken with smart contracts, in which an external, traditional contract is made between parties, sometimes called a wrapper, that either defines the terms of the agreement in its entirety (in which case the smart contract is a mere accessory to performance, and not the contract itself), or which defines certain terms, and the outcome of executing the smart contract's code as the balance of the terms of the agreement. The parties may or may not place limitations on the smart contract, in some cases defining terms of recourse, should there prove to be errors in the execution of the smart contract's code.

INTENTION TO CREATE A RELATIONSHIP

Many have argued that, given the nature of blockchains and the use of encryption keys in the control of the parties, smart contracts do in fact capture the intention to create a relationship. Where traditional contracts use verbal agreement, handshakes and, in the case of contracts in writing, wet signatures and notarisation to certify the creation of the relationship, a smart contract comes into force (becomes legally binding) when the smart contract is committed to a blockchain with submissions signed using the encryption keys of the parties involved. Many of the precedents established in earlier generations of technological change with electronic signature have been applied to the use of cryptographic keys and signatures in smart contracts.

CONSIDERATION

Whether using cryptocurrency or tokens representing virtual or real assets, smart contracts display the characteristics of an exchange of assets or value. Legal scholarship has asserted the validity of the element of consideration, given that the automated nature of smart contract exchange resembles other online transaction methods in traditional electronic commerce resulting in the formation of contracts.[14]

PERFORMANCE

Whereas traditional contracts leave the matter of performance to the parties to a contract, a smart contract's code may be delegated the task of execution, ensuring that both parties fulfil their part of the agreement. The code may execute and fully complete in the same unit of time in which it is recorded on a blockchain, particularly if it is created to facilitate an exchange of virtual assets.

Other smart contracts will need inputs from outside sources, called "oracles" in technological terms. These inputs may be provided by the parties or other automated applications at the time of contracting or at points during the lifetime of the contract. The data is evaluated by the systems running the smart contract code on the network hosting the blockchain application. An application on a blockchain network incorporating a smart contract is sometimes termed a decentralised application ("DApp"), executed by numerous members of the network in duplicate, as the transaction records are committed to the blockchain in the act of mining or committing blocks. As we have mentioned, certain blockchains, such as Ethereum, may charge a certain amount of cryptocurrency as payment (Gas, in the case of Ethereum) for the processing of the source code in the smart contract and the recording of the result to the blockchain.

It is in the performance of a contract that many find significant, even compelling, value in smart contracts. If written correctly and trusted by all parties, the exchange may happen frictionlessly, with little attention from human principals. Whereas traditional contracts may involve numerous third parties to certify and validate a transaction, the secured automation provided by the smart contract and the blockchain offer the potential to streamline the transaction while maintaining trust, unlocking value in one transaction, and more as others conduct similar transactions at scale.

14 M. Giancaspro, 'The Consideration Myth about Smart Contracts' (2020) 1 *ANU Journal of Law and Technology* 11.

ENFORCEMENT

The complexity embodied in the full scope of a non-trivial traditional contract can be considerable. The need for arbitration and litigation in the case of disputes that are not resolved through negotiation is indicative of the level of difficulty in drafting contracts that can withstand the rigors of the real world. The complexity is not reduced in the transformation of contracts from natural language to computer languages. It can be argued that this reality is a testament to the enduring indispensability of human lawyers.

A common concern raised when considering smart contracts is the recourse parties to a smart contract may have in the event that the results of executing the contract code are not what some or all of the parties intended. This area of law is evolving. Some legal scholars have argued that the need for a traditional contract continues to exist,[15] and that smart contracts as they currently exist should be trusted only as a way of automating the performance of a contract. Wrapper contracts sometimes include terms to override the results of a smart contract under certain conditions, acknowledging that it is currently difficult to ensure complete reliability in the code of certain smart contracts.

Technologists sometimes argue that, especially in cross-border transactions or in transactions occurring outside the borders of a jurisdiction, the smart contract is the law, in an expansion of a new subset of law recalling the early days of the internet called *Lex Cryptographia*.[16] Such assertions may in time be tested. Perhaps simpler questions regarding the legality of smart contracts used in the exchange of property will ground much of the near- to medium-term discussion of smart contract legality.

The conveyancing of property is an area where much activity and speculation has occurred. Proponents of property applications with blockchains and smart contracts hope for a simplification through the use of technology, while incumbent interests assert the reliability and resilience of processes based on traditional contracts, open to negotiation and adjustment. The important point to consider with the introduction of smart contracts as tools or outright replacements for

15 M. K. Woebbeking, 'The Impact of Smart Contracts on Traditional Concepts of Contract Law' (2019) 10 *JIPITEC* 8.

16 A. Wright and P. De Filippi, 'Decentralized Blockchain Technology and the Rise of Lex Cryptographia' (Social Science Research Network 2015) SSRN Scholarly Paper ID 2580664 <https://papers.ssrn.com/abstract=2580664> accessed 21 March 2021.

traditional contracts is that the matter of those contracts must themselves be legal. In other words, it must be legal for that contract to be formed and executed under the law, regardless of whether it is done with a traditional contract, or a smart contract with the exchange of cryptocurrency and a non-fungible token representing ownership of a piece of land. A title that cannot be recognised by a court would not be recognised, regardless of the form of the contract used in the transaction.

In November 2019, the LawtechUK Panel, established by the UK's Ministry of Justice, published a *Legal Statement on Cryptoassets and Smart Contracts* through its UK Jurisdiction Taskforce. It offers a more detailed set of guidance and points for lawyers to consider as they work with clients and technologists to navigate the selection and guide the implementation of blockchain applications, with particular attention to smart contracts and their consequences in application. The publication was put out as a proactive action by the government, recognising the importance of this rapidly growing area of technology and the need for government to have robust frameworks for understanding, negotiating, and promulgating guidance and policy.

Sync 3: Smart contract legal concepts

You should allow around 90 minutes for this activity.

Download and carefully read the *Legal Statement on Cryptoassets and Smart Contracts* from the UK Jurisdiction Taskforce[17] to familiarise yourself with the task force's thinking on the issues likely to arise at law when applying blockchain technologies. This is an opportunity for exposure to some critical points for understanding blockchain, cryptocurrency, tokens, and smart contracts in the context of legal thinking by leading members of the UK legal community.

Consider the following questions:

1 Are cryptocurrencies, tokens, and other virtual assets, which have no physical form and are distributed in sometimes countless copies in a blockchain application network, to be treated as property?

17 'The LawtechUK Panel' (*Tech Nation*) <https://technation.io/wp-content/uploads/2019/11/6.6056_JO_Cryptocurrencies_Statement_FINAL_WEB_111119-1.pdf> accessed 16 August 2025.

2 Is it legal to use blockchain applications in the conveyancing of property? What are the various approaches to answering this question in England and Wales?

3 If a transaction carried out by smart contract on a blockchain takes place on a network in jurisdiction A, conducted between parties in two separate jurisdictions B and C, exchanging property in a fourth jurisdiction D, what laws apply to the transaction? What reasons do you give for your assertion?

As you read through the *Legal Statement*, and examined some of the cases in the sync, you should have found that in near-term practice as smart contracts are adopted, people will rely on hybrid arrangements using traditional contracts as wrappers or catch-all solutions until more experience is gained in mainstream use of smart contracts. We hope that you will have noted that English law is capable of supporting the view of smart contracts as enforceable contracts, provided the subject of the contracts is legal matter for a contract (i.e. a traditional contract on equivalent terms would be enforceable).

TECHNOLOGICAL ISSUES WITH SMART CONTRACTS

As computer programs, smart contracts present all the challenges associated with developing, running, and maintaining software:

1 *Limited information.* It is developed according to certain specifications made by persons working with the knowledge at hand.
2 *Written by specialists often removed one or two degrees from the business.* Software is written by persons knowledgeable in the practice of computer programming. The software engineer writing the code is not necessarily the person who gathered and documented the requirements, who in turn is not a party using the smart contract.
3 *Require languages demanding high precision.* Computer software code must be written in highly constrained languages and must express the intended process steps or desired result with great precision, allowing for little ambiguity if strict correctness is required.

4 *No standards mandated by law.* As we noted in Chapter 3, software engineering is a relatively young discipline and is yet to develop codified standards for quality and practice, enforced by regulations. While good software practice and high-performing software development and operations organisations exist, there is no single applicable standard.

5 *Highly variable levels of testing for quality and reliability.* Software is tested to varying degrees and to varying levels of certainty, as a function of the skills available in the organisation developing the software, and the time and resources allocated to the task.

Smart contracts, recorded immutably on a blockchain at the time of creation, present two additional problems:

1 *They may not be changed.* Software code executing the smart contract must be correct and capture the intent of the parties perfectly, unless the parties have made provisions in a wrapper agreement in case of error.

2 *They may not be stopped.* When a smart contract begins execution on a blockchain application network, there is no way to terminate or reverse its execution. If the parties to the contract intend the contract to be the only memorial and means of executing and enforcing the contract, then any fail-safe mechanisms must be built into the code and tested to the satisfaction of the parties, or the intention of the contracting parties is not in fact realised.

Lawyers working with clients and software developers building applications with blockchains and smart contracts will be well-served to keep these challenges in mind when giving guidance and advice.

Sync 4: Developing a blockchain concept

You should allow around 60 minutes for this activity.

Consider pairing up with a classmate for this exercise. Identify an existing process in commerce, legal procedure, or property transfer that requires a trusted third party such as a government or clearing organisation to complete.

Drawing on some of the examples we have presented in the chapter so far for background knowledge, sketch two diagrams on a piece of paper:

1. Draw a diagram showing the existing process, and the steps to complete the process, highlighting the steps requiring trust and trusted intermediaries, such as a government, bank, or service operator.
2. Draw a diagram imagining a transformed process, identifying one or more opportunities for the application of blockchain technology, where its use may enhance trust, reliability, processing speed, user adoption, or other factors.

Assess your two diagrams and consider the following questions:

- What were the difficulties you had in drawing the diagrams? Was it difficult to choose the level of detail of the diagram, such that you could draw it to communicate to your classmates?
- Why did you choose a particular step for transformation with blockchain technology?
- What regulatory or cross-border legal concerns might be raised by your transformed process? What options might you suggest in order to address those concerns, or how would you go about learning what you need in order to come up with options?

As an additional, advanced step, consider finding a technologist friend and discussing this exercise! This activity is a brief version of the type of work that participants in legal technology hackathons and ideation sessions go through, to learn more and to develop new, innovative solutions, advancing the state of the art.

Digital lawyering skills: creativity

Sync 4 is a good example of the importance of creativity to a digital lawyer. You are creating a transformed process in a way which requires new and innovative thinking. Although this is a skill which you may not be expressly taught in law school, it is a skill that can be developed in a huge variety of different ways. Many hobbies, from writing stories and poetry to drama, from dance to sewing and knitting, and from painting to playing a musical instrument all require creativity. Although you may be used to being creative in areas seemingly far removed from the law, this skill can be transferred to all different types of settings.

Even if you do not feel you are creative in an artistic sense, it is still possible to be creative intellectually and with technology. Writing a piece for a law and/or technology journal or blog, setting up your own website or podcast or simply answering the syncs within this textbook are all ways to develop your creative flair!

Risks of blockchain

As with many promising technologies approaching mainstream adoption, there are risks to bear in mind with blockchain, especially as a lawyer advising clients or working with technologists to develop innovative new legal applications. We have already discussed issues of enforceability and technology risks with smart contract applications. The following risks also apply to smart contracts and more generally to blockchains and distributed ledger applications:

- *Cross-border and extraterritorial transactions.* While the UK and many Commonwealth jurisdictions that may follow its lead will develop legal frameworks and reasoning applicable within their borders, much similar work will have to be done in jurisdictions from other legal traditions, and protocols and treaties developed to regulate trade and transactions between jurisdictions. The directions recommended by the UK task force regarding the treatment of virtual assets and the application of existing law to activities taken with blockchain-enabled applications should inform the policies eventually promulgated.
- *Illicit activity.* The anonymity that is possible with blockchain applications may allow them to support illicit activities in plain sight or hidden away in DApps deployed on dark web nodes. Outlawed activities, trade in illicit goods such as drugs or endangered animals, human trafficking, and other activities may be supported through the use of blockchain technology.
- *Cryptographic limitations and flaws.* Blockchains rely on cryptographic suites that can be proven mathematically to be extremely difficult to break. History has shown that cryptographic suites either have flaws that are revealed through persistent analysis by motivated, skilled cryptographers or are made obsolete by technological advances. In the latter case, increases in computational speed have

made some previously strong cryptography obsolete. Advances in quantum computing or other computation methods yet to be discovered may render the current generation of blockchain technologies vulnerable and possibly unusable.

A digital lawyer will take the risks we have highlighted and work with technologists to develop guidance for clients seeking advice that balances technological and legal realities, offering the balance that best meets the client's risk tolerance, and optimising compliance with applicable law.

Sync 5: Challenges to law enforcement

You should allow around 30 minutes for this activity. Please note that this activity contains a reference to images of child sexual abuse.

Blockchain technologies enable a class of highly distributed computer applications with network participants spread around the globe, operating at the fringes of regulation or even beyond it. They are often deployed and operating in jurisdictions that have widely varying regulatory regimes, in some cases trading between two jurisdictions whose governments have poor or non-existent diplomatic relations, let alone treaty frameworks for negotiating solutions.

Consider a scenario where there is exchange in illicit digital property, such as the exchange of images of child sexual abuse, conducted using multiple cryptocurrencies. While the material itself is not committed to a blockchain, the anonymous sales and purchase transactions are. Illicit vendors operating on the dark web monitor these transactions to provide one-time access for downloading the material.

Governments around the globe have enacted legislation prohibiting the creation, sale, and consumption of such material, while international efforts have resulted in a number of protocols in various stages of implementation and enforcement. Given the challenges in legislation and international cooperation, what other challenges does government face in enforcing such legislation and protecting minors with its jurisdiction, given the additional nuances of blockchain technology?

Consider the following questions:

1 How could a law enforcement agency establish possession of illicit digital material, given there are few publicly visible records of the material itself?

2 What necessary steps would agents and police need to take in order to establish a chain of custody?

3 How would a publicly visible blockchain help or hinder such efforts?

Despite the technical and legal challenges of enforcement across borders, it is possible to start with vigorous enforcement within a jurisdiction, with the cooperation of international law enforcement partners and digital forensics practitioners who can develop protocols for evidence gathering in these contexts. As you completed this activity, you may have found that there are views that blockchain-based exchange with cryptocurrency are a boon to law enforcement, in as much as all transactions are immutable and there is a quality of non-repudiation, making it much more difficult to destroy evidence.

THE FUTURE OF BLOCKCHAIN

ENVIRONMENTAL IMPACT AND SUSTAINABILITY

A common criticism of blockchain applications focuses on the substantial consumption of computing power and the electrical energy required to operated PoW consensus mechanisms needed by many of those applications. As we saw earlier in this chapter, consumption of energy for a PoW-reliant cryptocurrency such as blockchain will only grow as more coins are mined and more users conduct transactions. While some players have located themselves in areas where there are lower-cost power sources for the sake of economic viability,[18] few have explicitly addressed operations with renewable or carbon-neutral sources. Certain blockchain technology implementations already contribute in substantial ways to global warming.

18 'Soaring Bitcoin Prices Put Central Washington Electrical Utilities on Alert' (*The Seattle Times*, 9 January 2021) <https://www.seattletimes.com/business/technology/sunday-buzz-soaring-bitcoin-prices-put-central-washington-electrical-utilities-on-alert/> accessed 22 March 2021.

GROWTH OF SMART CONTRACT USE AND STALE, IRREVOCABLE CONTRACTS

It is possible to write smart contract templates without specifying time limits for the execution of the code pertaining to instances of smart contracts created from those templates. Such contracts may live on and either pose risks for economic loss or lead to enforcement issues requiring adjudication. Old, still-running software from previous eras, possibly no longer maintained because the original software developers or vendors have retired or gone out of business, may in the coming decades pose challenges to businesses reliant upon so-called legacy code. Smart contracts may become the legacy code of the future, with all the business, technological, and legal challenges that come with aging technology with no means of replacement. Well-reasoned legal frameworks for handling such situations fall outside of the highly regulated parts of the financial sector. The precedents set there may prove useful but perhaps not completely prescriptive for what forms of regulation may be required for aging blockchain solutions.

BREAKDOWN OF EXPENSIVE COMPUTING MODEL WITH QUANTUM COMPUTING

We have mentioned briefly the possible vulnerability of cryptographic software suites used to build blockchain technology. Advances and upgrades in cryptographic technology based on new computing capabilities like quantum computing may bring enhanced features to future blockchain implementations, including real-time, high-performance execution beyond the minute or multiple minutes required for current solutions, enhancing adoption, and enabling applications yet to be conceived.

CRIMINALISATION AND REGULATION

The near-term future will likely bring regulation or criminalisation of certain blockchain applications in many jurisdictions, particularly involving cryptocurrencies and tokenised assets. Other applications may be deployed and see widespread adoption with little regulation until a major incident involving a data breach or a catastrophic event involving major loss of value or life spurs policymakers into reacting, or in some unfortunate cases, over-reacting. Digital lawyers who have advised clients and technologists as the technology matures will be well-positioned accordingly to act for their clients or to influence policy.

ADDITIONAL RESOURCES

'Beeple's Masterwork: The First Purely Digital Artwork Offered at Christie's'. *Christie's* <https://www.christies.com/features/Monumental-collage-by-Beeple-is-first-purely-digital-artwork-NFT-to-come-to-auction-11510-7.aspx>

'China's Courts Use Data Analytics and Blockchain Evidence Storage on the Way to First AI-Integrated Legal System' (*South China Morning Post*) <https://www.scmp.com/news/china/politics/article/3124815/chinas-courts-use-data-analytics-and-blockchain-evidence>

Corkery M and Popper N, 'From Farm to Blockchain: Walmart Tracks Its Lettuce' (*New York Times*, 24 September 2018) <https://www.nytimes.com/2018/09/24/business/walmart-blockchain-lettuce.html>

'Distributed Ledger Technology: Blackett Review' (*GOV.UK*) <https://www.gov.uk/government/publications/distributed-ledger-technology-blackett-review>

Kolb J and others, 'Core Concepts, Challenges, and Future Directions in Blockchain: A Centralized Tutorial' (2020) *53 ACM Computing Surveys* <https://doi.org/10.1145/3366370>

Lipton A and Levi S, 'An Introduction to Smart Contracts and Their Potential and Inherent Limitations' (*The Harvard Law School Forum on Corporate Governance*, 26 May 2018) <https://corpgov.law.harvard.edu/2018/05/26/an-introduction-to-smart-contracts-and-their-potential-and-inherent-limitations/>

Nakamoto S, 'Bitcoin: A Peer-to-Peer Electronic Cash System' (31 October 2008) <https://bitcoin.org/en/bitcoin-paper>

Ramamurthy B, 'Blockchain in Action' (*Manning*, 2020) <https://www.manning.com/books/blockchain-in-action>

Reyburn S, 'The $69 Million Beeple NFT Was Bought with Cryptocurrency' (*New York Times*, 12 March 2021) <https://www.nytimes.com/2021/03/12/arts/beeple-nft-buyer-ether.html>

'What Is an NFT and Why Should Photographers Care?' <https://petapixel.com/2021/03/12/what-is-an-nft-and-why-should-photographers-care/>

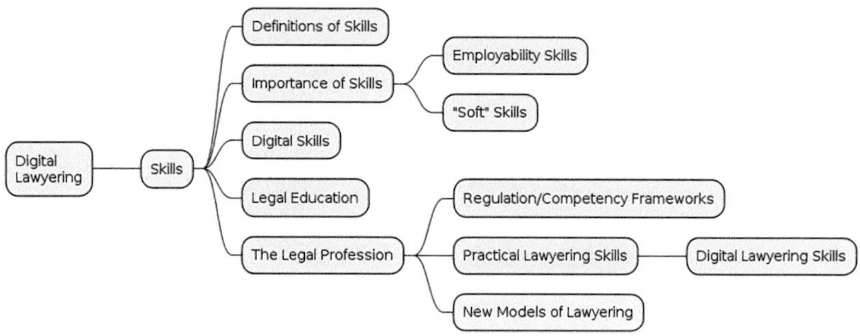

Mind Map 11.1 Chapter topics

11 DIGITAL LAWYERING SKILLS

Emma Jones

INTRODUCTION

This chapter will begin by exploring the importance of skills and the idea of "digital skills". It will discuss the extent to which these skills are acknowledged and developed in legal education. The chapter will then consider the key skills currently valued within the legal profession and contrast these with the skills required to become a successful digital lawyer. It will conclude by considering a number of models of lawyering which encompass a broad range of skills.

Chapter hot spots

When reading this chapter, questions to think about include:

- Do the skills legal professionals are currently required to demonstrate equip them for digital lawyering?
- What skills are necessary to be a successful digital lawyer?
- Can and should legal education include digital lawyering skills?
- How can you develop your own digital lawyering skills?

Having read the title and introduction, you can add any other questions you want to explore here:

DOI: 10.4324/9781003602323-11

THE IMPORTANCE OF SKILLS

The term "skills" is frequently used, but it can be difficult to define. It is often used interchangeably with terms such as "attributes", "abilities", or "competencies". One way to define it is as an ability to perform or execute a job or task well. This could range from knitting a scarf to coding a computer program to memorising a very long piece of poetry. In this chapter we will be using the term broadly to capture all of the aforementioned terms as appropriate.

In today's society, skills are increasingly viewed as important and valuable. It is often not enough to simply know something; it is about being able to apply that knowledge in practical settings. In universities, the focus has traditionally been on cognitive (or thinking) skills. For example, when you are asked to write an essay, it is not enough simply to know lots of facts about a topic; you also need to be able to understand what the question is asking, select the most relevant points to include, synthesise information from different sources, and analyse and evaluate arguments made in articles and books.

However, in recent years, there has also been an increasing focus on employability skills within universities—in other words, developing the skills that are required within the workplace. A number of employers have criticised universities for not producing graduates who are prepared for the world of work. In a recent UK survey of employers, only 49% "agreed" or "strongly agreed" that graduates were "career ready" when beginning work.[1] Similar concerns have also been raised in other countries, including the United States, Australia, and Hong Kong.

Government policies often emphasise the importance of universities producing skilled graduates who can contribute to the economy and assist in future economic growth. Such skills are important for economic growth and productivity. For example, according to estimates, 61% of the UK workforce needs to hold a higher education qualification by 2035 for government goals to be achieved.[2] However, empha-

1 Institute of Student Employers, 'ISE's Student Development Survey Shows a Widening Gap between Student Education and Employer Skills Needs' (1 May 2024) <https://universitybusiness.co.uk/news/graduate-employability/> accessed 13 August 2025.

2 Universities UK, 'New Analysis Shows that Graduates Will be Key to Government's Industrial Strategy' (11March 2025) <https://www.universitiesuk.ac.uk/latest/news/new-analysis-shows-graduates-will-be-key> accessed 19 August 2025.

sis on employability skills can be controversial, as many people would argue that learning is a good in itself and should not be about the eventual economic outcomes. They also argue that developing strong cognitive skills is important training for any form of employment.[3]

Despite this controversy, in reality there is now a significant focus on employability and more practical skills within universities. For law students, one example of this is the common use of problem questions, where you are given a scenario and asked to apply legal principles to that particular set of facts. By doing so, you are applying your legal knowledge in a way which demonstrates a number of skills, such as identifying key facts, analysing how the law will apply to these and writing in an accessible and concise manner. Often the idea is that these problem questions mirror the situation where a legal professional has a new client and has to try to unpack their issues and give appropriate advice. Other examples include the increase in clinical legal education provision, where students gain opportunities to provide legal advice in law clinics, produce resources and/or presentations to schools and community groups, and undertake other "real-life" legal work.

In addition to the focus on skills within university education, there is a growing emphasis on lifelong learning and the idea of people developing new skills or transferable skills to assist them in adapting to changes in the labour market or to aid them in moving into new areas of employment when they need to (e.g. due to a downturn in the economy). A 2023 report from the World Economic Forum explains: "Providing access to skills-based learning, upskilling and reskilling opportunities is essential for individuals and organizations to remain competitive and adapt to changes in the labour market".[4] Technology is one of the factors driving these changes, with the automation of tasks and the use of artificial intelligence (AI) removing some job roles and creating demand for others.

3 See, for example, Anthony Bradney, *Conversations, Choices and Chances: The Liberal Law School in the Twenty-First Century* (Hart Publishing 2003).

4 World Economic Forum, 'Putting Skills First: A Framework for Action' (May 2023) <https://www3.weforum.org/docs/WEF_CNES_Putting_Skills_First_2023.pdf> accessed 19 August 2025.

Sync 1: Key employability skills

You should allow around 15 minutes for this activity.

Using your university's website (or, if you are not a current university student, the web page of your local university), find out what information it includes on employability skills. It may well have a list of graduate attributes or details of the employability skills your degree will assist in developing. Based on these, think about the following:

1 What does the website suggest are the key employability skills a degree will assist in developing?

2 How many (if any) involve digital technology?

You may have identified a number of different employability skills. A 2025 World Economic Forum report, based on a global survey of large companies, identified the most important skills as analytical thinking; resilience, flexibility, and agility; leadership and social influence; creative thinking; motivation and self-awareness; technological literacy; empathy and active listening; curiosity and lifelong learning; talent management; and service orientation and customer service.[5] Different subject areas may also refer to specific skills (and we will consider these in relation to legal education further on in this chapter). What is clear is that the range of skills which graduates are required to display is becoming far more diverse than traditional cognitive skills and often now refers to skills more commonly associated with the workplace, such as oral communication, teamwork, and collaboration. In addition, there is an increasing awareness of the need for graduates to be digitally literate and have the skills to thrive in a digital workplace. Figure 11.1 presents a word cloud illustrating a number of the skills often identified as key attributes for graduates.

5 World Economic Forum, 'The Future of Jobs Report 2025' (11 January 2025) <https://www.weforum.org/publications/the-future-of-jobs-report-2025/in-full/3-skills-outlook/#3-skills-outlook> accessed 19 August 2025.

Figure 11.1 Key skills and attributes for graduates

THE RISE OF DIGITAL SKILLS

In Chapter 4 you were introduced to the term "digital literacy". Describing this term in 1997, Paul Gilster argued that it was "the ability to both understand and use digitised information".[6] A range of other terms such as "information literacy" and "computer literacy" also developed in the same period. The focus was largely upon the use and management of digital information in an appropriate manner.

Around the same time, it also became common to find the idea that the younger generation (born after 1980) were "digital natives"—in other words, people who had grown up with digital technology and whose work and personal lives were all heavily influenced by technology, from socialising online to using the internet for research to the way they access news stories and music. As one book put it: "They all have access to networked digital technologies. And they all have the skills to use those technologies".[7] This was often contrasted with older generations who were perceived as struggling to adjust to digital technologies. The notion of 'digital natives' could

6 Paul Gilster, *Digital Literacy* (Wiley 1997), 2.
7 John Gorham Palfrey and Urs Gasser Born Digital, *Understanding the First Generation of Digital Natives* (Basic Books 2008), ii.

lead to the assumption that younger lawyers would find it easier to adapt to technological advances, whereas older lawyers would struggle with the transition.

However, since then it has been recognised that it is too simplistic to divide people between so-called "digital natives" and those of older generations. A range of other factors also influence levels of digital literacy, including socio-economic status and geographic location. In 2024 the Lloyds Bank UK Consumer Digital Index (referred to in Chapter 4) estimated that 16.8 million people in the UK had low or very low digital capability with 3% of the population (1.6 million people) remaining offline. Age was found to be the most important factor in determining digital capability, with almost nine out of ten of the people with very low digital literacy being aged 50 or over. However, other relevant factors were found to be living alone, having lower levels of education and/or having an impairment.[8] Research by the New Zealand government found that, not only age, but also socio-economic circumstances, disability, educational levels, geographic location and ethnicity all influenced levels of access to the internet.[9] Globally, levels of digital literacy do appear to be increasing; for example, an Australian survey found that, in 2023, 9.4% of the Australian population was highly digitally excluded, a reduction of 1.2% from 2021 (10.6%).[10] However, issues with digital literacy remain.

Alongside the evolution of a more nuanced approach to the question of who is digitally literate, a more pluralistic way of looking at the skills involved has also developed. This means that the term "digital literacies" or "digital capabilities" is now sometimes used to illustrate the wide range of different skills encompassed. It is also recognised that which skills are included within this definition may vary depending on the context the term is used in; for example, a law student may need a very different set of digital skills from someone

8 Lloyds Bank, 'Lloyds Bank UK Consumer Digital Index 2024' <https://www.lloydsbank.com/assets/media/pdfs/banking_with_us/whats-happening/lb-consumer-digital-index-2024-report.pdf> accessed 19 August 2025.

9 Digital Government, 'Digital Inclusion and Wellbeing in New Zealand' (2025) <https://www.digital.govt.nz/dmsdocument/161~digital-inclusion-and-wellbeing-in-new-zealand/html#executive-summary> accessed 19 August 2025.

10 Australian Digital Inclusion Index, 'Key Findings and Next Steps' (2025) <https://www.digitalinclusionindex.org.au/key-findings-and-next-steps/> accessed 19 August 2025.

employed by a business selling goods online. It may also be that some people struggle to transfer their digital skills from one setting to another; for example, someone may use social media frequently but may have little or no experience with word processing programs.

The notion of digital literacy now implies that digitally literate individuals will have the skills needed to use technology in an appropriate and effective manner in settings which are relevant to them. For digital lawyers, this means being able to use technology within their legal practice in a way which enhances their work and their service to clients whilst taking account of practical and ethical issues.

Equality, diversity, and inclusion and digital literacy

The preceding discussion demonstrates that the level of digital literacy you have can be influenced by socio-economic status and geographic location. For example, if you have a low income or live in a rural area, you may not be able to afford or access an internet connection at all. If you are able to obtain a connection, it may not be able to run at a high enough speed or quality to enable you to use online services or information effectively.

Other personal and practical factors may also be relevant; for example, if you experience social anxiety or are working from home in a very crowded household, you may not be able or willing to put on your webcam, or even to use the microphone, in meetings or workshops. There may also be cultural and legal issues; for example, some countries have strict censorship policies in relation to internet usage.

Individuals with disabilities may be unable to access certain types of technology. Conversely, they may have different skills in using specialist software. For example, an individual may be unable to use a keyboard to type into word processing programs, but may instead be skilled at using voice recognition software to input information.

When considering digital literacy, it is therefore important to think about how this relates to issues of equality, diversity, and inclusion. Such issues can have negative impacts, as in some instances people may not be able to develop certain digital skills or may not be able to apply them in certain settings. However, they can also have positive impacts; for example, a client with physical disabilities may be able to receive legal advice online, making it more accessible.

MODELS OF DIGITAL LITERACY

A number of different models have developed to try to capture the core skills involved within being digitally literate. One of these, developed by Jisc for use in higher education, refers to six different digital capabilities. At its centre is "digital proficiency and productivity" with the other elements including "digital creation, problem-solving and innovation", "digital learning and development", "digital identity and wellbeing", "information data and media literacies", "digital communication, collaboration and participation".[11] Another, developed by Doug Belshaw, has eight "C" elements, including cultural, cognitive, constructive, communicative, confident, creative, critical, and civic.[12] For the cultural element, Belshaw uses the example of "digital natives", suggesting that although they may be confident using their smartphones to socialise, they may not be comfortable using technology in other settings, such as the classroom and workplace. This is because they may not have developed the skills allowing them to move easily between the application of technology in different environments. It is therefore necessary to be able to adapt the use of technology to different cultural contexts. The cognitive element refers to the need to have a broad perspective, enabling individuals to adapt to different technologies and become fluent in navigating them (e.g. the types of menus commonly used on websites). For a digital lawyer, this could involve being able to navigate the menus and files involved in a case management system.

The constructive element relates to being able to use technology in different ways, building upon what has already been done and using it in innovative ways; for example, when applying algorithms to case law to more accurately predict the likely outcome in future cases. The communicative element refers to the need to be able to communicate in a way that demonstrates an acknowledgement and use of appropriate assumptions and norms; for example, including an appropriate digital signature when using email. The confident element refers to people being able to manage their own learning and solve problems in the digital environment; for example, by lawyers adapting to new technology and seeking

11 Jisc, 'Building Digital Capabilities Framework: The Six Elements Defined' (January 2024) <https://repository.jisc.ac.uk/8846/1/2022_Jisc_BDC_Individual_Framework.pdf> accessed 19 August 2025.

12 Doug Belshaw, *The Essential Elements of Digital Literacies* [PDF] (Self-Published 2014), 11–12 <https://dougbelshaw.com/essential-elements-book.pdf> accessed 4 January 2026.

out training to assist them in using it effectively. The creative element involves doing new things in new ways to uncover and identify new problems requiring solutions; for example, creating e-discovery systems which can also deal with means of electronic communication. The critical element involves looking beyond the technologies to question their basis and assumptions; for example, a lawyer questioning how accessible new technologies are for their client base. The civic element refers to the need to use technology to support the development of society more generally. One example of this is the use of online law clinics to provide free legal advice to people in need, particularly those who may find it difficult to physically travel to access help.

Sync 2: Elements of digital literacy

You should allow around 10 minutes for this activity.

Using an internet search engine, locate two different models of digital literacy or capability. These could be models that are used within higher education, the workplace or more generally.

1 What do you think are the strengths and weaknesses of these models?

2 Based on these models and your reading so far, what would you say are the essential elements of digital literacy?

You may have found a variety of models. Some may be more focused on technical know-how and abilities (e.g. being able to code), whereas others may be broader and focus on wider elements, such as Belshaw's reference to culture. In the next part of this chapter, we will move on to consider the skills currently required from legal professionals and to what extent these include elements of digital literacy.

SKILLS AND LEGAL EDUCATION

As many digital lawyers begin their careers as law students studying within law schools, it is useful to look at which skills are currently emphasised within legal education and to what extent digital lawyering skills are included within these.

In some jurisdictions, law schools are heavily regulated (commonly by the bodies which regulate the legal profession). This can lead to specific requirements in terms of which skills are focused upon. In other jurisdictions, law schools have more freedom to choose which skills they want to emphasise. The level of regulation can also depend upon whether the law school is offering an academic or vocational qualification.

In the UK, the content of a law degree is largely at the discretion of individual law schools. However, the Quality Assurance Agency produces an influential "Benchmark Statement for Law".[13] This is regularly updated and tries to capture some of the key skills a graduate in law should have. The version in place at the time of writing refers specifically to the importance of digital skills and entrepreneurship. It requires law students to "develop an awareness of the future direction of the legal profession and its constant evolution" and indicates that law graduates should be able to "engage with a range of forms of digital technology to collate, analyse, select and present information".[14]

In the United States, the American Bar Association (ABA) is the accrediting body for law schools. It requires the law schools it accredits to establish a programme that "prepares its students, upon graduation, for admission to the bar and for effective, ethical, and responsible participation as members of the legal profession". Although digital skills are not specifically mentioned within the objectives it sets, it could be argued they are implied by this and references to students being competent in "legal analysis and reasoning, legal research, problem-solving, and written and oral communication in the legal context" as well as "other professional skills needed for competent and ethical participation as a member of the legal profession".[15]

In terms of dedicated modules and courses, several UK universities run master's (postgraduate) programmes in law and technology; for example, the University of Law offers an MSc in Legal Technology. In the United States, an example is the University of California, Berkeley, which offers a range of courses via its Center for Law and Technology.

13 Quality Assurance Agency, 'Subject Benchmark Statement Law November' (March 2023) <https://www.qaa.ac.uk/docs/qaa/sbs/sbs-law-23.pdf?sfvrsn=c271a881_6https://www.qaa.ac.uk/docs/qaa/subject-benchmark-statements/subject-benchmark-statement-law.pdf?sfvrsn=b939c881_16> accessed 30 November 2025.

14 Ibid., p. 14.

15 American Bar Association, '2025–2026 Standards and Rules of Procedure for Approval of Law Schools: Standard 301: Objectives of Program of Legal Education' <https://www.americanbar.org/content/dam/aba/administrative/legal_education_and_admissions_to_the_bar/standards/2025-2026/2025-2026-standards-chapter-3.pdf> accessed 19 August 2025.

In Australia, an example is the University of Melbourne, which offers a range of courses on digital law and technological innovation. In New Zealand, the University of Auckland offers a course on "Shaping the Law in the Tech Driven Era". However, some of these offerings are more focused on technology law (e.g. regulating cyberspace) than on digital lawyering. Such provisions are also not offered to all law students and in all law schools.

In terms of incorporating digital skills in existing modules, many examples of this now exist. These range from using quiz tools in lectures (such as Wooclap) to creating an escape room, where students enter a room and use a range of technology, including virtual reality headsets, to solve a range of puzzles and challenges.[16] Other examples include using technology to compile a digital collection of law texts, which were then used to extract law-related words and facilitating a virtual international exchange with technology.[17]

Between the first and second editions of this textbook, there have already been significant shifts in the extent to which legal education is engaging with digital technology and digital lawyering. There is now far greater explicit acknowledgement of the importance of these topics. Nevertheless, arguably, an even greater focus on technology within legal education is needed. The US legal academic Dyane O'Leary captures the argument well:

> Today's farmers use moisture sensors for soil, drones to monitor crops, self-driving GPS wielding tractors to seed, and even wearable trackers on cows to check their vitals (yes, really!)—all to make farming more profitable and efficient. But what if I told you apprentice farmers were not introduced to these things? That they were too busy being shown how to tend to oxen pulling plows. Too busy being trained to navigate crops with their handheld hoe. Too busy being taught the art of kneeling to the soil to gauge moisture. That's crazy, right? How can a student prepare for their future if instruction is based on their teacher's past? But that is the approach many law schools take in the required curriculum.[18]

16 Kirsten Maslen, 'Teaching Law with Technology Prize 2020—Finalists Announced' (*Thomson Reuters*, 6 March 2020) <https://blogs.thomsonreuters.com/legal-uk/2020/03/06/teaching-law-with-technology-prize-2020-finalists-announced/> accessed 19 August 2025.

17 Laura Charleton, Jenny Kemp and Lydia Bleasdale, 'Interview with the 2024 ALT Best Paper in Legal Technology Prize Winners' (2024) 58(4) *The Law Teacher* 626–31.

18 Dyane L. O'Leary, '"Smart Lawyering": Integrating Technology Competence into the Legal Practice Curriculum' (2021) 19 *University of New Hampshire Law Review* 197–272, 199.

O'Leary argues that, instead of being viewed as optional, technical competence should be integrated fully into the curriculum of law schools as a core professional skill and ethical requirement. This could help students prepare to enter the legal profession and also give them digital skills they can use in other careers, such as project management or marketing, and in other areas of their lives. However, it does require law schools to invest time and money to develop the curriculum in this way. It may also require hiring additional staff (or retraining current staff) with the appropriate knowledge and skills in this area.

Of course, legal education is not all focused upon training aspiring lawyers, and not all law students will go on to be lawyers. However, if (as seems likely) law schools do gradually increase their focus on digital lawyering and technical competence, then this in turn may have an impact on the legal profession. Legal employers may begin to look for a higher level of digital skills and prioritise them more when recruiting trainees. This in turn could accelerate the impact of digital technologies on the legal profession more widely. However, before considering which digital skills may become increasingly prized, the next question to consider is what skills the legal profession currently requires from its members.

Skills and the Legal Profession

Working in the legal profession requires a range of different skills, from those involved in client care to those involved in administration and management. To identify which skills are currently viewed as important within the legal profession, a good starting point is the requirements of the bodies who regulate different parts of the legal profession. They will often specify key skills or competencies which individuals are required to possess before they can obtain entry to the legal profession.

Sync 3: Skills in the legal profession

You should allow around 30 minutes for this activity.

Using the internet, research what legal skills legal professionals are currently required to display for entrance into the legal profession.

If your legal profession is divided into a number of roles, you may wish to focus on one (e.g. attorney, solicitor, barrister, or advocate), or you can compare and contrast different roles to see whether similar skills are required. You should base your research on whichever jurisdiction you are currently located within.

Make a note of your answer so that you can revisit it later in this chapter.

If you are located in England and Wales, a useful starting point is the 2013 Legal Education and Training Review.[19] This looked at what is required for a legal professional to be competent—in other words, to be able to perform their role appropriately. As part of its work, the review conducted research into the knowledge, skills, and attributes required within the legal profession at that time and what respondents thought would be required in 2020.

Based on the Legal Education and Training Review, the Solicitors Regulation Authority (SRA) and the Bar Standards Board (BSB) introduced competency statements. These set out the skills and abilities a solicitor or barrister must be able to demonstrate to work in their role.

The SRA's Statement of Solicitor Competence covers "ethics, professionalism, and judgment", "technical legal practice" (in terms of skills such as researching and drafting rather than referring to digital technology), "working with other people" and "managing themselves and their own work". Under "managing themselves and their own work", there is a requirement that solicitors make appropriate use of information management systems, both in hard copy and electronically, which includes storing and retrieving information. They must also comply with requirements relating to data protection, confidentiality, security, and file management (e.g. guidelines on how long to keep a file when a matter is concluded). The reference to electronic information management systems is the only clear reference to the use of technology in the work of solicitors. However, some of the competencies listed could arguably require solicitors to use technology. For example, solicitors must maintain an appropriate and current understanding of practice, policy and the law; adapt their practice to meet developments in legal services delivery; and communicate in a style and method that best fits the circumstances and the person receiving the communication. They must also record and present findings and information in a

19 Legal Education and Training Review, 'Setting Standards. The Future of Legal Services Education and Training Regulation in England and Wales' (2013) <https://letr.org.uk/index.html> accessed 20 August 2025.

clear and accurate way.[20] Similarly, the SRA Code of Conduct for Solicitors, Rule 3.3, requires lawyers to keep their knowledge and skills up to date, which could also be interpreted as including technical knowledge and skills.[21]

The BSB's Professional Statement for Barristers covers "legal knowledge, skills and attributes", "practical knowledge, skills and attributes", "advocacy", "professional standards", "values characteristics and behaviours" and identifies aspects of "working with others" and "management of practice". When referring to skills relating to research, it requires barristers to use appropriate and up-to-date methods and resources (including electronic resources). As with the SRA statement, there are some skills that could imply an engagement with technology; for example, a requirement to use the form of communication most suited to its content and the recipients. However, overall, there are few explicit references to technology.[22]

In contrast to the aforementioned statements, CILEx Regulation, the regulatory body of the Chartered Institute of Legal Executives (CILEx, a body of legal professionals who perform functions similar to solicitors) introduced "technical competence" as a required competency for individuals to demonstrate before being awarded membership of CILEx.[23]

In the United States, the ABA does not provide a single statement setting out the skills required from lawyers. However, in 2009 the ABA set up a Commission on Ethics 20/20 to consider the ABA's Model Rules of Professional Conduct (the rules governing the behaviour of lawyers in the United States) and the way lawyers are regulated in light of developments in technology and global changes to the way law is practised. The Commission noted that technology had changed legal practice in ways which were both fundamental and irrevocable and that,

20 Solicitors Regulation Authority, 'Statement of Solicitor Competence' <https://www.sra.org.uk/solicitors/resources/cpd/competence-statement/> accessed 20 August 2025.

21 Solicitors Regulation Authority, 'SRA Code of Conduct for Solicitors, RELs, RFLs and RSLs' <https://www.sra.org.uk/solicitors/standards-regulations/code-conduct-solicitors/> accessed 2 January 2026.

22 Bar Standards Board, 'Professional Statement for Barristers' <https://www.barstandardsboard.org.uk/uploads/assets/0279b209-dab6-40c9-a554af54994e2566/bsbprofessionalstatementandcompetences2016.pdf> accessed 20 August 2025.

23 Vicky Purtill, 'Lawtech: Standards for the Lawyers of the Future' <https://www.regulationmatters.uk/features/legal-tech-for-the-lawyers-of-the-future/> accessed 20 August 2025.

as a result, lawyers must understand its role to ensure that they can provide the client care and service that is required.[24] The notes to Rule 1.1 of the Model Rules of Professional Conduct, which set out the standards required from legal professionals, state that a lawyer must stay informed of legal changes and changes within legal practice, including the risks and benefits connected to relevant technologies.[25] This was also referred to in Chapter 5.

In Australia, one acknowledgment of the importance of technology is the creation by the Law Council of Australia (the legal profession's representative body) of a Futures Committee, which advises the Council on a range of technologies, as well as cybersecurity and risks.[26]

There are also other examples from different countries which indicate that there is a gradual acknowledgement of the increasing importance of digital technology within the legal profession. For example, the Federation of Law Societies of Canada includes in its Model Code of Conduct at 3.1.2 a requirement for lawyers to understand and use relevant technology within their practice, in order to maintain their competence.[27]

The preceding discussion demonstrates that many countries see digital skills as increasingly important within the legal profession. However, to date, the ways these skills are acknowledged and incorporated into legal education and legal practice are somewhat piecemeal and fragmented. There is no single comprehensive digital skills framework against which legal professionals (and their regulators) can judge their competency in this area. It is therefore perhaps unsurprising that a UK report on the digital lawyering landscape identified concerns over a

24 ABA Commission on Ethics 20/20, 'Introduction and Overview', 3 <https://www.americanbar.org/content/dam/aba/administrative/ethics_2020/20120508_ethics_20_20_final_hod_introdution_and_overview_report.pdf> accessed 20 August 2025.

25 'ABA Comment to the Model Rules of Professional Conduct' <https://www.americanbar.org/groups/professional_responsibility/publications/model_rules_of_professional_conduct/rule_1_1_competence/comment_on_rule_1_1.html> accessed 20 August 2025.

26 Law Council of Australia, 'Futures Committee' (19 August 2025) <https://lawcouncil.au/about-us/advisory-committees/futures-committee> accessed 20 August 2025.

27 Federation of Law Societies of Canada, 'Model Code of Professional Conduct as Amended April 2024' <https://flsc.ca/wp-content/uploads/2024/05/2024-Model-Code-of-Professional-Conduct-with-Changes-Marked.pdf?_rt=OHwxfGNvZGUgb2YgY29uZHVjdHwxNzU1Njk1MTA2&_rt_nonce=a6393033b0> accessed 20 August 2025.

skills shortage, stating "it could be difficult to find lawyers with the sufficient skills and experience to fully understand the technology".[28] The next sync asks you to consider whether having a digital skills framework for use across the legal profession could help to address some of these challenges.

Sync 4: A digital skills framework

You should allow around 10 minutes for this activity.

What would be the advantages and disadvantages of having a common digital skills framework for the legal profession?

You may find it useful to make a note of the key arguments you identify.

You may have identified a range of arguments. Some advantages could include a framework raising the legal profession's awareness of the importance of technology and digital skills and assisting aspiring lawyers to identify the digital skills required in legal practice. A framework could also be used to assess the suitability of an individual's existing skills and identify gaps where further training and development are required. Disadvantages could include the fast-moving nature of technology, meaning that skills identified now could be obsolete in a few years (or even months). It may also be that different parts of the legal profession require very different digital skills; for example, whereas a lawyer in private practice may need to be competent in using time recording and client management systems, an in-house lawyer may instead require expertise in using their company's online business systems.

WHAT DIGITAL SKILLS DO LAWYERS NEED?

The next question to consider is what digital skills lawyers actually need to have now, and what digital skills they will need to have in the future. As noted earlier, there is no single digital skills framework for the legal

28 Alan Cunningham, Andrew D. James, Paul Taylor and Bruce Tether, 'Disruptive Technologies & Legal Service Provision in the UK: A Preliminary Study' (7 December 2018) <https://ssrn.com/abstract=3297074> accessed 20 August 2025.

profession, perhaps reflecting the fact that different roles within practice will have different digital requirements (see Chapter 12 for further discussion). However, there is a wide range of suggestions over what should be considered as key digital skills within the legal profession generally. This section will consider some of these, but it is necessary first to consider an underlying debate in this area; namely, whether lawyers should learn to code.

Should lawyers learn to code?

A question that has often arisen, particularly in the legal press, is whether lawyers should actually learn to code—in other words, to be able to use computer programming language to design software. Some people have argued that lawyers should learn to code to enable them to understand the technology they are using, to give them important employability skills and to set them apart from their competitors when working with clients involved in digital businesses. An article in the *Legal Technologist* suggested that a knowledge of coding could be applied to help lawyers work out simple solutions to some issues; for example, where they had a lot of information to record and organise online. It also indicated that coding would be useful in dealing with many of the digital platforms now available for the legal profession, by assisting individuals to become familiar with digital structures and approaches, such as algorithms.[29] Therefore, it is perhaps unsurprising that a number of law firms now offer their staff training in coding.

At the same time, others have argued that lawyers learning to code is not a productive use of their time and expertise. Writers such as Richard Susskind suggest that it is more important for lawyers to understand the function and purposes of technology and how that interacts with the law rather than develop detailed technical skills themselves.[30] This is particularly the case when coding can change and evolve rapidly, so such skills could quickly become outdated. For example, it is very unlikely that a lawyer who has undertaken an introductory coding course will be able to design software sophisticated enough to assist with client issues. Instead, a better business model is for them to work as a team with software developers to ensure

29 The Legal Technologist, 'Why Lawyers Should Learn to Code, but Not for the Reasons You Think' (*The Legal Technologist*, 25 November 2020) <https://www.legaltechnologist.co.uk/article/why-lawyers-should-learn-to-code-but-not-for-the-reasons-you-think/> accessed 19 August 2025.

30 Richard E. Susskind, *Tomorrow's Lawyers an Introduction to Your Future* (OUP 2013).

solutions meet clients' technological and legal issues. A qualified software designer is likely to be able to undertake the coding work more quickly and cost-effectively and does not have the issue of having to justify chargeable hours spent on coding activities the way a lawyer would.

Of course, it is possible that there is a middle way, in which lawyers understand the basics of coding but use that to work with software developers and others to ensure they can work together productively and understand the terminology used and any issues raised. As we discuss the various digital skills which lawyers should or could develop, it is worth thinking about what your position is on this debate and whether or not you think legal professionals should learn to code.

Thinking about digital skills which lawyers require, a fundamental skill (or group of skills) is around the everyday use of technology in the legal workplace. One of my co-authors, in an article proposing a digital lawyering framework for students, describes this as "Collaborating & undertaking legal services using digital tools & software articulated by appropriate e-practice & project management".[31] Chapter 2 discussed the changing face of legal practice and the ways in which digital technology has now become an integrated part of the workplace; for example, word processing information, sending emails to colleagues and clients, recording chargeable time online, and conducting legal research using online databases. This means that any legal professional will now require a basic level of technological competence to enable them to practice effectively. It is hard to imagine a lawyer who wholly relied on handwritten letters, the postal service and a local law library being able to work efficiently and obtain and retain a large number of clients! Of course, some individual lawyers may rely upon support staff, such as legal secretaries, to undertake much of the work involving digital technology. However, this is unlikely to be cost-effective in the long term, and some level of technical competence would still be required; for example, to forward relevant emails or cope when a member of staff was on annual leave.

Understanding how to use such technology goes beyond just knowing which button to press to send an email or working out how

31 Ann Thanaraj, 'Making the Case for a Digital Lawyering Framework in Legal Education' (2017) 3 *International Review of Law* 17, 32.

to log on to a video call, for example. Part of "appropriate e-practice"[32] also includes understanding the relevant etiquette involved. You looked at a humorous illustration of this type of issue in Sync 6 of Chapter 9, which referred to the case of the so-called cat lawyer. A Texan lawyer appearing at an online court hearing had a cat filter on his screen which he could not remove. The video of him saying "I'm here live, I'm not a cat" went viral globally.[33] Although this was seen as an entertaining mistake, failures to use technology appropriately could have more serious consequences. Sending kisses at the bottom of an email to an important client or appearing in a video call in your pyjamas or during a shopping trip to the supermarket is likely to seem unprofessional and could mean you lose the confidence of clients and colleagues.

This leads to another area where digital skills are required, which is to take part in digital marketing and networking, when lawyers and law firms are looking to obtain new clients and retain existing clients. Although a range of networking is carried out face-to-face, the COVID-19 pandemic has demonstrated the importance of digital marketing and networking. Having a social media account can be an important way to connect with clients or potential clients and spread the word about your services (as discussed in Chapter 5). Running or joining in webinars, conferences, and other online workshops and discussions can also be valuable. It is also important to be aware of the wider digital environment and the broader changes advances in technology are making to the legal sector; for example, it may be more attractive to clients and profitable if your workplace moves to an alternative business structure or adopts a virtual law firm model (examples are given in Chapter 2).

The reference by Thanaraj to project management in this context also suggests a wider range of skills than just being able to master using specific forms of technology. As an individual, it is important to understand how to manage your time effectively when working with technology. This can include everything from avoiding getting distracted by googling irrelevant points, to ensuring your email inbox is well organised so you can find important messages easily, to ensuring you back up information saved on your laptop.

32 *Supra* n. 28.

33 BBC News, 'Lawyer Gets Stuck with Cat Filter During Virtual Court Case' (9 February 2021) <https://www.bbc.co.uk/news/av/world-us-canada-56005428> accessed 19 August 2025.

So far, the digital skills discussed could be largely viewed as the basic digital skills that all lawyers will now need. However, for many legal professionals, the skills needed will go beyond this. Thanaraj refers to the need to "acquire the knowledge and skills to use digital tools and software to deliver alternative forms of technology-driven legal service" as another key area.[34] For individuals, this could involve participation in online dispute resolution (see Chapter 9), developing new skills to deal with the requirements for evidence-gathering and e-discovery in the digital age (see Chapter 8) and applying generative AI as part of legal practice (see Chapter 7). When working in a team and/or incorporating digital technology into a project, there is likely to be an even wider range of skills required (digital and otherwise). The International Institute of Project Management divides such work into four stages: define, plan, deliver, and close.[35] Figure 11.2 gives some examples of the work involved in each stage (you may notice some similarities with the stages of design thinking illustrated in Chapter 4).

Sync 5: Project managing a lawtech project

You should allow around 10 minutes for this activity.

Imagine you are a lawyer working for a large firm. One of your clients is a large company that manufactures televisions. Your company wants to launch a new website selling its products online. It asks you to lead a team considering the potential legal implications. The team will consist of in-house lawyers, several of the company's directors, members of its IT department and representatives from a marketing agency, all of whom are based in different countries.

Consider each stage of the project management process. What issues might arise that you need to deal with? You may want to make some notes for your own reference.

34 Supra n. 28, p. 33.

35 International Institute of Legal Project Management, '4-Phase LPM Framework' <https://www.iilpm.com/wp-content/uploads/2020/05/IILPM-LPM-Framework-English-Version_2020.png> accessed 19 August 2025.

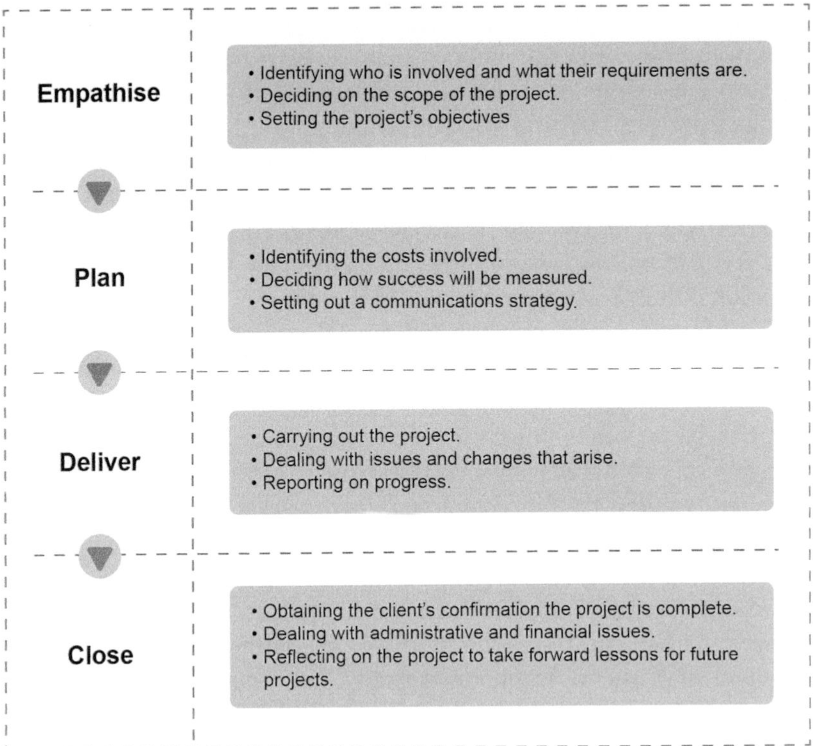

Figure 11.2 The stages of project management

You may have thought of a range of ideas. In relation to the define stage, it will be important to understand the technical side of the company's plans, such as whether the website will be a bespoke design; whether there will be an agreement with a host server; who is providing the content and images; and what system will be used, or developed, to collect payments. With so many people involved, it would be vital to know who has what role and what expectations each individual has about their involvement. It will also be important to know what the overall objectives are; for example, is it to have the website successfully launched, or simply to provide a written piece of advice on the legal implications?

Moving on to the plan stage, organising a communications strategy will be key. Even arranging a meeting can be complicated when the attendees are in different time zones, so it will be vital to agree on the best ways to communicate as a team, as well as knowing who else in the company you will need to report to (and when).

In relation to delivery, a range of potential challenges could arise; for example, the marketing agency may be keen to decide upon specific images and wording for a launch campaign before the overall design of the website has been finalised. Having such a large team also carries potential for misunderstandings and miscommunications, such as the IT team assuming the in-house lawyer is dealing with cyber-protection issues whilst the in-house lawyer believes this to be part of the IT team's role. It will also be important to identify who has the ultimate decision-making power over aspects of the project.

Finally, at the close stage, it will be valuable to gain feedback from every member of the team as well as from the company as a client. There will be a need to ensure that all records are up to date and stored appropriately and that your time and that of any others in your firm (which is likely to have been recorded using an online system) has been appropriately billed to the company.

Each of these stages will require a range of skills, from planning and organisation to communication and collaboration to an ability to respond appropriately to feedback (and possibly criticism). There will be a need to be able to understand the requirements and demands of each stage, plan ahead, think strategically, and anticipate any issues that may arise. Of course, this is alongside the more technical skills, such as being able to schedule an online meeting and record your chargeable time accurately.

Digital lawyering skills: innovation and entrepreneurship

Lawyers have often been perceived as risk-adverse and cautious. In contrast, innovators and entrepreneurs have been portrayed as forward-thinking pioneers, identifying new markets, introducing new business models and exploiting gaps and opportunities that arise.

However, in recent years a new brand of "legal entrepreneurs" has begun to emerge.[36] These are people who have recognised the opportunities arising from the developments in digital technology, the deregulation of the legal profession and the emergence of new models of legal practice such as alternative business structures (discussed in Chapter 2). Although these

36 Mark A. Cohen, 'The Golden Age of the Legal Entrepreneur—Why Now and Why It Matters' (*Forbes*, 1 June 2018) <https://www.forbes.com/sites/markcohen1/2018/06/01/the-golden-age-of-the-legal-entrepreneur-why-now-and-why-it-matters/?sh=5a4496447803> accessed 19 August 2025.

individuals often do not have a traditional legal background as lawyers, they are an increasing presence in the legal world.

For lawyers to be able to compete with such legal entrepreneurs and remain relevant in the legal market, they are increasingly having to develop their own skills of innovation and entrepreneurship; for example, partnering with other professionals to offer a more comprehensive range of services to clients, redesigning the management structures of law firms and rebranding their services.

As a student, you can begin to develop your skills of innovation and entrepreneurship in a number of ways. This could include volunteering to lead on projects, putting forward proposals for new innovations (e.g. the creation of a new student society or a new journal or magazine), starting your own part-time business (such as selling on Etsy or eBay) or perhaps finding a mentor who can offer support and guidance. All of these have the potential to assist you in transitioning into the world of digital lawyering.

Broadening the Scope

The final principle Thanaraj identifies when discussing a digital lawyering framework is "the knowledge and skills to consider the safety, security, confidentiality, privacy, appropriateness and ethical issues before using digital tools for legal practice".[37] This demonstrates once again that purely technical skills in isolation are not sufficient for a digital lawyer. Instead, it is important to be able to consider the wider issues that arise when using such technology. Thanaraj explains that this principle includes understanding the repercussions of unprofessional and unethical behaviour online, taking into consideration issues of safety, privacy, and digital footprint in online interactions. Specific to lawyering and professional skills, students will need to develop an understanding of the roles of technology, privacy, and security and how they affect the online practice of law.[38]

A number of these issues have already been discussed within this textbook; for example, Chapter 5 looked at the ethical issues that can arise as a result of lawyers' use of social media, and Chapter 6 discussed the implications of breaches of data protection laws for law firms. Being able to identify such potential issues, avoid them where possible and respond appropriately where that is not possible requires a range of skills.

37 *Supra* n. 28, p. 33.
38 Ibid.

To demonstrate this, imagine you are a trainee lawyer in a small law firm specialising in employment disputes and you are asked to create a new monthly electronic newsletter updating existing and potential clients on changes and developments in employment law. Your first thoughts might be about what content to include (such as recent cases and legislation) and also which word processing and publishing program(s) would be most suitable to use to produce the newsletter. These are both important issues, but they are not the only ones to consider. You will also need to think about points such as whether your existing clients have consented to their email addresses being used for the purposes of newsletter circulation, how you will obtain consent from prospective clients and how and where you will store the data being used for these purposes. You will also need to bear in mind ethical issues, such as how to ensure your readers understand that you are giving generic summaries of the law and not offering legal advice in your articles. If you want to write about a recent case your firm has been involved in, you will need to consider how you can do this without breaching client confidentiality in any way.

To tackle all of these potential issues, you are going to need to have a range of skills, including (but certainly not limited to):

- Organisational and administrative skills (e.g. setting up or directing the setting up of a mailing list).
- Legal research skills (e.g. to look into questions of data protection and client confidentiality and to identify relevant newsletter content).
- Commercial awareness (e.g. if your law firm intends to use the newsletter as a form of marketing, you need to be aware what type of content will be of interest to prospective clients to encourage them to use the firm's services).
- Legal writing skills (e.g. to draft a suitable disclaimer to go on the newsletter explaining that it does not contain legal advice).

Underpinning all of these will be a need for critical thinking to help you in identifying such issues in the first place.

Sync 6: Identifying relevant digital skills

You should allow around 30 minutes for this activity.

The preceding section has considered a wide range of digital skills. However, it is not intended to be comprehensive. What eight digital skills would you see as being most important for a digital lawyer, and why?

To answer this question you can use the preceding section, your wider knowledge and reading and perhaps your own experience (e.g. if you have undertaken a clinical legal education module or legal work experience). To help you narrow down your ideas, you may wish to focus upon one role or practice area, perhaps one you are interested in being involved in during your career.

There is no single right answer to Sync 6. Instead, the skills you choose are likely to be influenced by any particular role or practice area you focused upon, together with your own experiences and research. However, hopefully your list reflected the fact that digital skills are not the same as technical skills. Instead, they include a much wider range of skills, such as project management, which are adapted to and applied within the digital environment. Another illustration of the width of this range of skills is the growth of interest in what are sometimes called "soft skills".

SOFT SKILLS

The earlier discussion about digital lawyering skills demonstrates that technical skills cannot be considered in isolation. To apply technical skills effectively in the legal workplace requires a range of other skills, including organisational and time management skills, critical thinking, and communication skills. In addition, the growth of digital technology has also led to an increased emphasis on so-called soft skills within the legal profession (sometimes also known as human skills or people skills). These are non-technical skills which relate to how you regulate yourself and your relationship with others; for example, being able to understand and control your emotional responses to situations appropriately, demonstrating empathy with clients, and using patience and tact to work well within a team. As you can see from these examples, they often involve what are termed social and emotional competencies or social and emotional intelligence.[39] The term "soft skills" is used here because it is a commonly used shorthand. However, it is a

39 Daniel Goleman, *Emotional Intelligence* (Bloomsbury 1996); Peter Salovey and John D. Mayer, 'Emotional Intelligence' (1990) 9(3) *Imagination, Cognition and Personality* 185.

contentious term because there is a strong argument that such skills are equally important to "hard skills" within legal practice, such as analysing problems and evaluating courses of action. Despite this, soft skills have traditionally often been ignored or undervalued because they often involve social and emotional competencies which sometimes appear to conflict with traditional legal values of objectivity and rationality.[40]

To think about the place of soft skills in legal practice, imagine that you are a junior lawyer who has received an email from a client complaining quite aggressively that you have not responded to their last email for over 48 hours. Your first thought might be to feel cross and think that the client is being unreasonable; alternatively, it might be to apologise straight away to avoid any further complaints. Rather than respond immediately, a good starting point is to pause and think about what lies behind the wording of the email. It could be that the client is anxious and worried about their case, or that they have little understanding of the usual etiquette for email writing, or that they have low levels of literacy generally. Using empathy to put yourself in the client's shoes will help you to understand the background behind this email. In turn, this understanding will enable you to respond in a sensitive way, which can potentially enhance your relationship with the client; for example, rather than dashing off an email response, you may choose to telephone the client to reassure them that the work they require is in progress and explain the usual timescales involved.

It is also worth reflecting upon your own response. If you are angry, is it because you react defensively to criticism, or that you find it hard to build a rapport with that particular client? If you immediately want to apologise, is it because you are scared of making a mistake or just want the situation to go away? None of these responses is wrong, but understanding what lies behind them will enable you to regulate your responses and learn from them for the next time a similar situation arises.

The growth of interest in and importance of soft skills is inextricably linked to the rise of digital technology. There have been fears that the automation of a range of legal processes and the offering of cheaper online platforms for legal services will result in the traditional lawyer role becoming redundant, or at least much reduced. As a result, law firms have sought to demonstrate that they can offer personalised and responsive individual services in a way technology cannot—in other

40 Emma Jones, 'Making Practice More Affective: Emotional Intelligence as a Legal Meta-Competency' (2018) 24(1) *European Journal of Current Legal Issues*.

words, providing a human touch within legal practice. This demands a high level of skills, including "a delicate blend of empathy and detachment, approachability and boundary setting".[41] Unfortunately, there are arguments that current legal education and training has tended to ignore these types of skills or dismiss them as irrelevant to law. This means that lawyers may not always be well-equipped to demonstrate these skills in their practice. Even the different competency frameworks and statements which govern different parts of the legal profession tend largely to imply such skills (e.g. by discussing client care), rather than explicitly identifying the different skills involved and their importance. However, there is some evidence that this approach is gradually changing; for example, in England and Wales the Chartered Institute of Legal Executives has introduced the idea of emotional competence within their educational standards. Also, a range of models of lawyering have been developed to try to capture the much broader range of skills now required from legal professionals, including digital lawyering skills and soft skills (which arguably form a part of digital skills in any event).

Do lawyers come in all shapes and sizes?

The growth in importance of soft skills has contributed to a number of different models of lawyering designed to demonstrate that it is not enough for a lawyer to simply have a narrow skill set; for example, focusing on either technical skills or problem-solving abilities. Instead, they emphasise that a lawyer must have a wide range of skills and abilities. This is in contrast to the traditional "I-shaped" model, where lawyers have a narrow focus on legal expertise. Several of these more recent models are briefly described here and shown in Figures 11.3–11.5:

- The T-shaped lawyer

In this model, the vertical bar of the "T" represents traditional, in-depth legal knowledge, and the horizontal bar represents other knowledge, expertise and skills; for example, in technology, project management, leadership, and teamwork. The idea of a T-shaped professional has been used widely outside of law. It is increasingly being used within law to acknowledge the fact that

41 Emma Jones, 'Digital Lawyering and the Growing Importance of the Human Touch: Implications for Wellbeing' (October 2019) 7 *The Legal Technologist* 25 <https://www.legaltechnologist.co.uk/TheLegalTechnologistOct19.pdf> accessed 19 August 2025.

many lawyers now have to work together with a range of non-lawyers on projects, and as a result they need a much broader range of skills and abilities to enable them to adapt and work appropriately.[42]

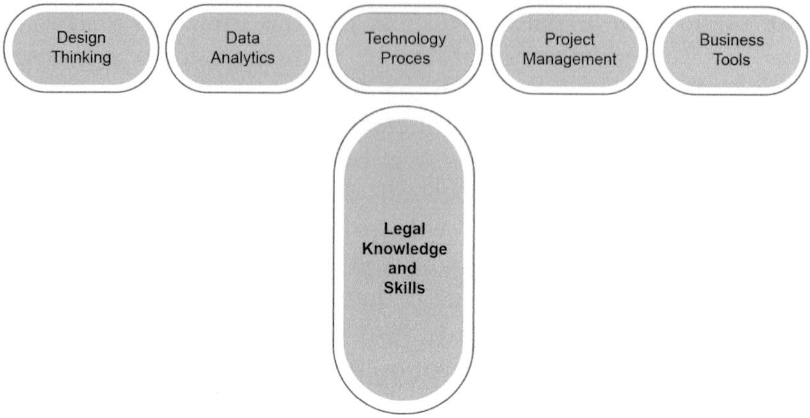

Figure 11.3 The T-shaped lawyer

- The delta model

The delta model is based on the T-shaped lawyer model and is still evolving, based on the work of a group of legal academics in the United States.[43] It conceptualises legal practice in the form of a triangle, with each side representing a different area of competency required from lawyers. Like the T-shaped lawyer, there is a need for the more traditional in-depth legal knowledge and skills ("the Practice"). However, the other areas are "the Process" and "the People". The former covers technical and commercial skills, whilst the latter is about having the self-awareness and skills to work well with others.

- The O-shaped lawyer

In this model, which was designed in the UK by an in-house lawyer, the focus is on lawyers being rounded and demonstrating a range of skills, behaviours, and mindsets.[44] These are divided into five components: optimism, owner-

42 Elaine Mak, *The T-Shaped Lawyer and Beyond: Rethinking Legal Professionalism and Legal Education for Contemporary Societies* (Eleven International Publishing 2017).
43 Design Your Delta, 'Developing the Delta Model' <https://www.designyourdelta.com/about> accessed 19 August 2025.
44 The O Shaped Lawyer, 'Mindset & Attributes' <https://oshaped.com/the-o-shaped-mindset-and-attributes> accessed 19 August 2025.

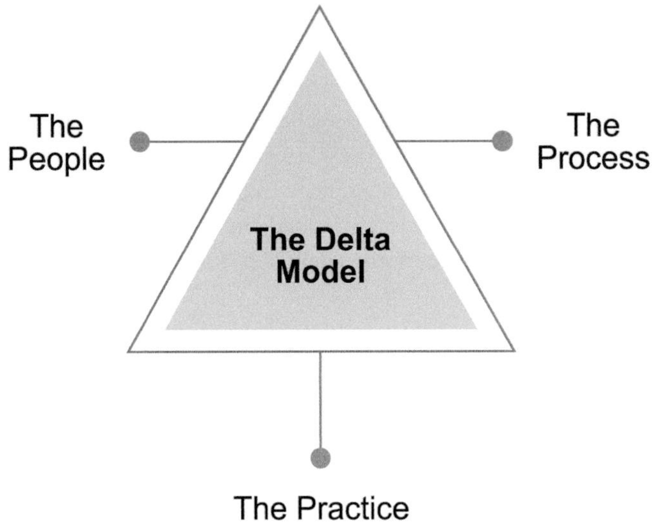

Figure 11.4 The delta model

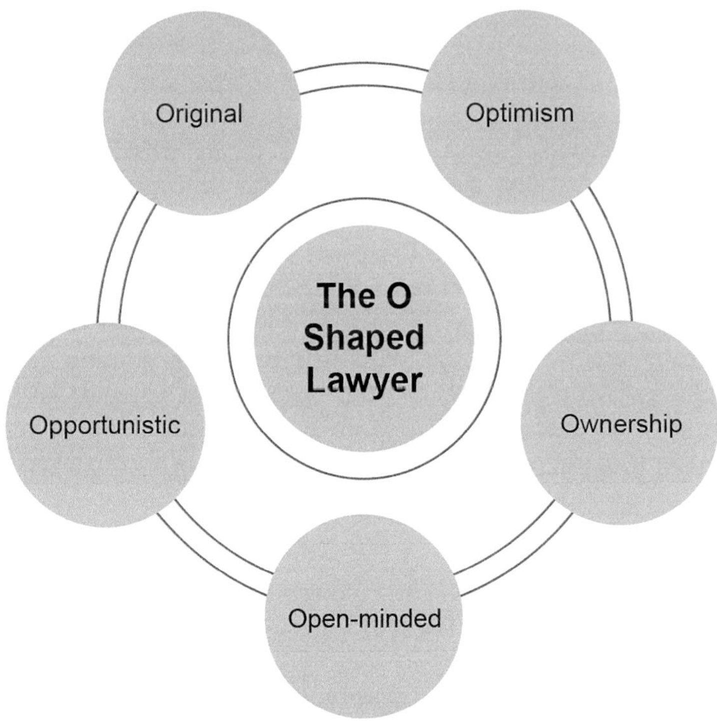

Figure 11.5 The O-shaped lawyer

ship, open-minded, opportunistic, and original. The focus of these components is on encouraging lawyers to be more positive, proactive, and creative in their approach in a way which enables them to add greater value in commercial situations. Although this model does not expressly refer to digital lawyering within it, the components it includes do mirror many of the skills required by digital lawyers; for example, being open to trying new digital solutions for issues, using opportunities to incorporate digital technology in new and innovative ways and thinking more widely about the broader implications of such technologies.

Sync 7: Evaluating the models

You should allow around 10 minutes for this activity

Consider each of the three models in the preceding box (you may also want to look at the additional information given in the Additional Resources section at the end of this chapter). Which model do you think is the most appropriate, and why?

Once again, there is no right answer to this sync, as each of the models has a range of advantages and disadvantages. You may also have questioned what "most appropriate" means in this context. For example, you could view the O-shaped lawyer as more applicable to a corporate lawyer than one who practises family or criminal law. Conversely, you may feel that the T-shaped lawyer is a simpler and more achievable model given it still has a significant focus on traditional legal knowledge as its supporting column. The important part of this question is really the "why". This demonstrates the reasoning (and critical thinking) you used to reach your decision. In Chapter 13 we will consider to what extent you feel your legal education and training has equipped you to demonstrate these different models of lawyering and how you can develop relevant skills.

CONCLUSION: DEFINING DIGITAL SKILLS

This chapter has explored the importance of skills in society generally and within higher education, the growing employability agenda and the type of skills required within legal practice. It has considered the type of digital skills which are becoming an increasingly important part of legal practice and emphasised that this is not just about being able to use certain types of technology. Instead, digital skills are much broader, encompassing project management, and more besides. As a part of this, soft skills are also increasingly acknowledged as a vital part of legal practice. This has led to the development of new models of lawyering. For the digital lawyer of the 21st century, it is crucial to be aware of the digital skills that are needed and to consider ways to develop these. In Chapter 13 we will develop this theme further.

ADDITIONAL RESOURCES

For a recent UK report on lawtech and regulation, see <https://www.legalservicesboard.org.uk/wp-content/uploads/2020/04/LSB-Technical-Perspectives-FINAL.pdf>

For resources on the T-shaped lawyer, see <https://www.researchgate.net/publication/331022253_The_T-shaped_Lawyer_and_Beyond_Rethinking_legal_professionalism_and_legal_education_for_contemporary_societies>

For resources on the delta model, see <https://www.lawdeltamodel.com/>

For resources on the O-shaped lawyer, see <https://www.oshapedlawyer.com>

For resources on lawyer wellbeing, emotional competence and professional resilience, see <https://www.lawcare.org.uk/how-we-help/fit-for-law/>

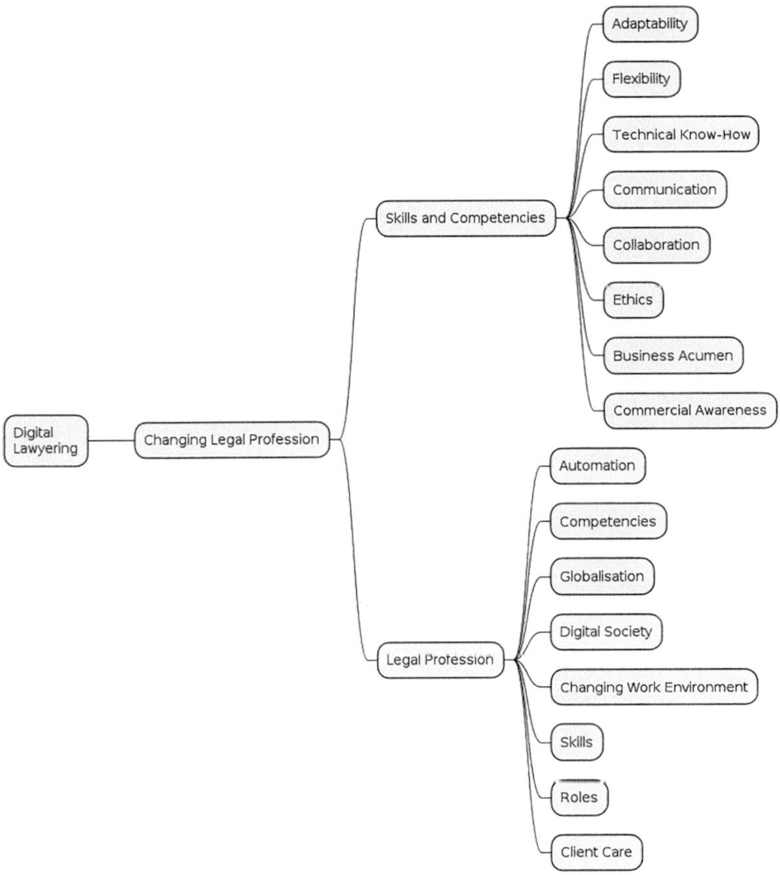

Mind Map 12.1a Chapter topics

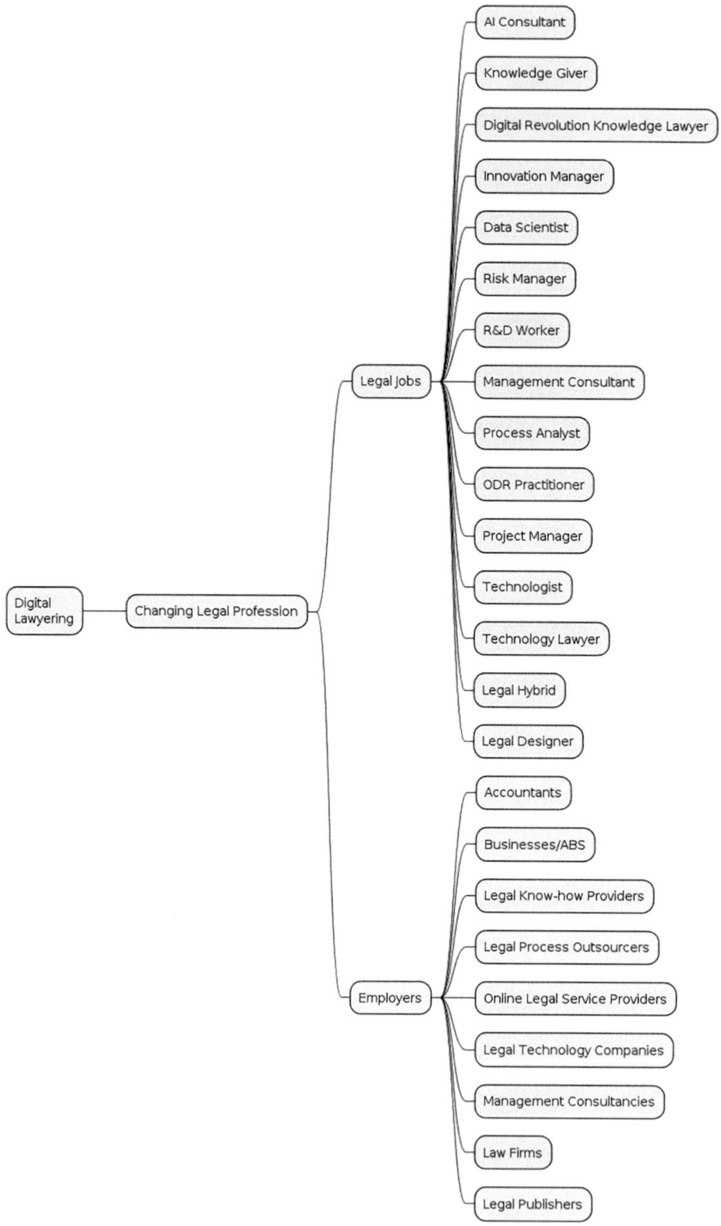

Mind Map 12.1b Chapter topics

12

The Changing Legal Profession

Francine Ryan, Ann Thanaraj, and Emma Jones

Introduction

This chapter considers how the impact of technology is changing the practice of law. It explores new careers in law and the new businesses and employment structures. It also encourages you to think about the different skills these new roles will require and ways in which you can begin to develop them. What it means to be a lawyer is changing; lawyers will have different career opportunities available to them, and some key roles for the future have probably not even been created yet. It is an exciting time to be considering a legal career, and those students who understand how legal practice is changing and can develop the skills required for a very different workplace will find themselves in demand from employers.

Chapter hot spots

When reading this chapter, questions to think about include:

- Is knowledge or skills more important?
- What will the legal profession look like in ten years?
- Who will be the key stakeholders in the future of the legal profession?
- What skills will the legal practitioner of the future require?
- When, where, and how can these skills be developed?

Having read the title and introduction, you can add any other questions you want to explore here:

DOI: 10.4324/9781003602323-12

THE CHANGING LEGAL PROFESSION

> Around 85% of the jobs that today's learners will be doing in 2030 haven't been invented yet.[1]

> We are living through a fundamental transformation in the way we work. Automation and "thinking machines" are replacing human tasks and jobs, and changing the skills that organisations are looking for in their people.[2]

If you are reading this book, you are likely a Generation Y or Generation Z. These are terms commonly used to describe people born from the early 1980s up to the mid-2000s who have grown up alongside rapid technological advances. From smartphones to smart televisions, from social media to virtual learning environments, from the World Wide Web to virtual reality, from travel apps to fitness monitors, it is likely that technology is integrated into many (if not all) aspects of your daily life. Other generations have also had to adapt to what is now commonly termed the "digital society". These developments are intertwined with other key changes around the globe, including globalisation, demographic shifts, and scarcity of resources.

As you saw in Chapter 2, the working environment is no exception to this increasing emphasis on technology, with emails, online meetings, chatbots, virtual assistants, Generative AI, and many other innovations changing how and where people work. At a more fundamental level, it is also having an increasing impact on the types of work that people do. There is clear evidence that jobs are changing and new roles are emerging, and this leads to a demand for different skills and competencies.

The legal sector is not immune from these changes, and artificial intelligence (AI) and automation now pose a threat to people's jobs. If many of the more routine tasks, such as reviewing and sorting documents, can be done electronically, this reduces the need for human

1 Institute for the Future for Dell Technologies, *The Next Era of Human Machine Partnerships* (2017) 14 <https://www.delltechnologies.com/content/dam/delltechnologies/assets/perspectives/2030/pdf/SR1940_IFTFforDellTechnologies_Human-Machine_070517_readerhigh-res.pdf> accessed 3 October 2018.

2 C. Stubbings, 'Foreword' in *Price Waterhouse Cooper*, 'The Workforce of the Future. The Competing Forces Shaping 2030' (2018) 3 <https://www.pwc.com/gx/en/services/people-organisation/workforce-of-the-future/workforce-of-the-future-the-competing-forces-shaping-2030-pwc.pdf> accessed 17 October 2018.

input and will impact jobs within law. To address this, there has been an increased emphasis on the need for law firms to provide personalised and high-quality client care with a "human touch" to ensure that services cannot be easily replaced, however, it is arguable that over the next 20 years there will be more fundamental change to the legal profession.

The market for legal services (in other words, the type of legal work being demanded by clients and employers) is shifting in light of the increased role of technology. For example, clients need lawyers who can protect their intellectual property in the digital content they create, advise on technologically innovative methods of production and delivery and deal with the consequences of potential cyberattacks. The legal profession must respond to these demands to remain relevant and competitive. Technology is disrupting legal practice by changing what is required from lawyers and the ways in which they themselves work.

The term "legal profession" has typically been defined to include solicitors and barristers (commonly termed "lawyers", depending on which jurisdiction you are in). It can also include other roles, such as that of a chartered legal executive or paralegal, which often involve performing many similar tasks to those of traditional members of the profession. However, it is questionable whether this definition of the legal profession captures the new jobs and roles beginning to emerge.

Sync 1: What is a legal professional?

Using your general knowledge, and your reading of this textbook so far, how do you define the term "legal professional"?

We will return to this question later in this chapter (in Sync 6 and Sync 7), so you may wish to make some notes to remind yourself of your ideas.

Of course, the existing legal profession covers a wide range of different types of firms and individuals, ranging from very large, international law firms to small firms offering local services to individuals in towns and villages. Therefore, the impact of technology is likely to differ greatly even within the legal sector. For example, while a number of firms have legal technology and innovation departments[3] dedicated

3 See Addleshaw Goddard as One Example: <https://www.addleshawgoddard.com/en/>

to developing advanced technological solutions, others may still rely heavily on posting out letters and sending faxes. However, as discussed in Chapter 2, even the least technologically advanced firm is likely to be using emails and online legal databases, demonstrating that no part of the legal profession is immune from change.

While thinking about the opportunities digital lawyering presents, it is important to consider the varied and broad wider impact on the legal profession. For some legal practitioners, this could be negative. For example, individuals undertaking routine legal work that can be automated may become surplus to requirements. This could particularly impact on parts of the profession where there is less protection and stability, such as the work of paralegals. If they are seen as easily expendable, then this could mean this route to entry into law becomes even more difficult. For those already working within law, the demands to "upskill" and develop new competencies could also place a heavy burden on people in terms of time, resources, and wellbeing. These points should not detract from the opportunities available, but it is important to consider them critically as you work through this chapter.

Any changes within the legal profession are also likely to impact on legal education. In the UK, although only a minority of law students actually go on to qualify as a solicitor or barrister, many law schools do try (at least to some extent) to prepare their students for these roles. In other jurisdictions, such as the United States, a large majority of law graduates go on to work as lawyers and expect to graduate "practice-ready". Therefore, law schools must think carefully about what their students will need to enter the legal profession in the future. As discussed in Chapter 11, this can mean focusing on developing skills rather than knowledge; for example, ensuring students know how to use legal databases to find cases rather than learning a large list of cases. If you are a law student, as you read this chapter you may find it interesting to reflect on how well your studies are preparing you for the world of digital lawyering.

LEGAL JOBS IN THE DIGITAL WORLD

As the market for legal services is changing, the traditional model of delivery is being disrupted by technology and globalisation. Over the past ten years, technology has altered legal practice, and these shifts will accelerate with the pace of technological change. The COVID-19 pandemic changed the legal profession. Remote working created a new and different dynamic within the culture of many law firms. Home working and virtual meetings have become more common, and the use of technology has been amplified in these new ways of working. Many larger law firms are investing in AI, which is being used to support the work of lawyers. There has been a lot of discussion around whether AI is going to take lawyers' jobs; while AI can do some incredible things, it is not yet able to replace a lawyer with years of professional training. But future lawyers will need to embrace change, be curious and be interested in learning new skills to respond to new opportunities as they emerge. The future law firm will offer alternative career paths for lawyers, and new jobs will continue to be created which reflect the shifting legal market. This will lead to opportunities but also challenges, as you will be expected to demonstrate new skills and competencies. Understanding how the job market is changing will prepare you for a competitive marketplace where innovation and technology are central to the practice of law.

Sync 2: The changing legal services market

Watch this video to learn more about how technology is changing the legal services market. <https://www.youtube.com/watch?v=vyjWIHHUXNo>

The video in Sync 2 demonstrates that the future is already here; there has been a proliferation of new technologies with law firms adopting automated legal tools.

Analysts predict the need for fewer lawyers because technology will automate many routine legal tasks.[4] However, a technology-enabled future also offers the possibility of a greater range of roles and opportunities connected to legal practice. In 2017, Richard Susskind[5]

4 A Deloitte study argued that 114,000 jobs in the legal sector are likely to be subject to automation in the next 20 years: Deloitte, 'Developing Legal Talent: Stepping into the Future Law Firm' (February 2016) <https://www2.deloitte.com/content/dam/Deloitte/uk/Documents/audit/deloitte-uk-developing-legal-talent-2016.pdf> accessed 12 October 2018.

5 R. Susskind, *Tomorrow's Lawyers* (OUP 2017) 133.

identified ten "new" jobs for lawyers, which are now jobs that exist within law firms.

THE NOT-SO-NEW JOBS!

What are these not-so-new jobs?

Sync 3: Thinking about different roles

Consider the ten jobs in Figure 12.1. In the first column, indicate whether this is a job you are familiar with, and in the second column, consider whether it is a job you may be interested in. We will revisit this later in the chapter to consider whether any of your answers have changed.

Figure 12.1 The not-so-new jobs

New jobs	Yes/no	Interested/not interested?
Legal knowledge engineer		
Legal data scientist		
Research and development worker		
Legal hybrid		
Legal technologist		
Legal project manager		
Legal process analyst		
Legal risk manager		
Legal management consultant		
Online dispute resolution practitioner		

WHAT ARE THESE JOBS?

When you are reading about these jobs, consider what relevant skills and competencies you may already have to undertake these roles, and what skills and competencies you might need to develop.

LEGAL KNOWLEDGE ENGINEER

The legal market is becoming increasingly more competitive, and law firms use technology to enhance their productivity to become more efficient. Law firms are looking at legal processes to think about ways to create new legal products and services. A legal engineer is someone with both legal knowledge and technological expertise to find creative solutions to optimise existing legal processes and find technological solutions to address the needs of clients. The role requires someone who is technologically proficient and has knowledge of legal practice to understand the problems. Most importantly, a legal engineer needs to be creative, as they need to be able to use technology to solve legal problems.

LEGAL DATA SCIENTIST

A data scientist is "someone who can bridge the raw data and the analysis—and make it accessible".[6] Predictive analytics, machine learning, and data mining are all buzzwords in data science. Law firms are using analytic tools in e-discovery. Data science is furthering our ability to predict what will happen, but this raises many legal and ethical implications around how data is stored and used. A legal data scientist needs to understand the data collection process and be able to curate and analyse it for many different purposes and consider the implications of these methods and uses. Technical knowledge is required, but communication skills are also essential to present data in a clear and usable way to lawyers. Several universities now offer a postgraduate master's degree in data science, which indicates that this is an area for growth.

RESEARCH AND DEVELOPMENT WORKER

In many sectors, research and development (R&D) departments are commonplace, but they have not featured within many law firms. Jordan Furlong[7] identifies four R&D activities law firms could engage in:

- New products and services
- New delivery mechanisms
- New pricing systems
- New management systems

Investment in R&D is going to be important to the success and competitiveness of legal practice. It will create new opportunities to develop innovative ways to shape the business of law firms. If you would like to be challenged to consider new ways of developing legal services, R&D is an interesting field to be involved in.

LEGAL HYBRID

As explained in Chapter 2, complex legal matters often require a multidisciplinary approach, and clients need lawyers to work with other

6 S. Rogers, 'What Is a Data Scientist?' (*Guardian*, 2012) <https://www.theguardian.com/news/datablog/2012/mar/02/data-scientist> accessed 12 October 2018.
7 J. Furlong, 'Why Law Firms Need R&D Investment' (*L21 Blog*, 2014) <https://www.law21.ca/2014/08/law-firms-need-rd-investment/> accessed 12 October 2018.

professionals. For example, family lawyers work with mediators, psychologists, and social workers. Corporate lawyers liaise with consultants, brokers, bankers, and accountants. Changes to the way legal services are being delivered has led to many lawyers gaining additional professional qualifications and offering a broader range of services to clients. Many family and civil lawyers are trained mediators, so they can add new services to their practice. As clients seek multifaceted support, the demand for legal hybrids will grow.

LEGAL TECHNOLOGIST

The expansion of IT and technology departments has provided new opportunities for lawyers with an interest in technology to transfer into legal technology roles. The rapid pace of change has resulted in the growing demand for legal technologists to such an extent that it is now recognised as a career in its own right.

With the development of new technologies, it is no longer a generalist role; instead, there are growing opportunities to specialise in different technological applications. Understanding how lawyers use technology, with the ability to explain it in an accessible way, is key to the role. A passion for technology with a willingness to learn about different applications and develop expertise will be important for anyone pursuing a career as a legal technologist. Technological innovation is the future of legal practice, and there are exciting opportunities to engage in developing legal services.

LEGAL PROJECT MANAGER

You were introduced to the importance of project management in Chapter 11. According to the International Institute of Legal Project Management:

> Legal Project Management is the application of project management principles and practices which enhance the delivery of legal services. In practice, our research confirmed that it also encompasses technology enablement, process improvement and the people dynamics that brings greater success to legal service delivery.[8]

8 A. Smith and T. Hutchinson, 'Building Legal Project Management Skills and Organisational Capability' (2017) <https://gallery.mailchimp.com/ef0907072acfd9dfa8857ea40/files/d4eb13ae-8896-4b27-81ca-3ad6cf48e5ad/Building_LPM_

Once the legal service has been designed, a project manager will plan, allocate resources, and prepare a budget to ensure the successful delivery of the project. These roles already exist, and there is a growing legal project management community.[9] The Institute offers certification as a legal project associate or legal project practitioner.[10] There is significant potential in legal project management, and it offers the opportunity to work in conjunction with other roles such as legal management consultants and legal process analysts.

LEGAL PROCESS ANALYST

Legal process analysts review the legal processes and systems to identify and analyse issues that limit efficiency and devise solutions to improve the central process. They may work in in-house legal departments to map the process of legal work and ensure the efficiency of the operation. They may work independently and offer their services on a consultancy basis to law firms. They will focus on making changes to strategy, operating models, and business processes to optimise the performance of the organisation and support future growth. Jobs in this field require individuals who can identify how technology can be used to innovate and shape the practice of law.

LEGAL RISK MANAGER

With increasing amounts of regulation in areas such as privacy and data protection,[11] law firms and their clients face multiple risk and compliance issues. Legal risk needs to be managed systematically with an identifiable risk management framework. It is complex and challenging work, involving the ability not only to identify legal risk but also to analyse and evaluate it. The role of a legal risk manager will involve integrating different processes using technology to proactively manage risk and add value to their law firm.

Skills_Organisational_Capability.pdf> Sourced from: <https://legalprojectmanagement.co.uk> accessed 12 October 2018.

9 See <https://www.iilpm.com>; <https://www.linkedin.com/groups/13509439>; <https://www.facebook.com/groups/legalprojectmanagement>

10 <https://www.iilpm.com>

11 See, for example, the Solicitors Regulation Authority Code of Conduct; Bribery Act 2010 c.23, and The Money Laundering, Terrorist Financing and Transfer of Funds (Information on the Payer) Regulations 2017.

LEGAL MANAGEMENT CONSULTANT

In January 2018, Deloitte Legal[12] launched its legal management consultancy, stating "LMC is a new approach and a new discipline, developed for lawyers by lawyers and other experts. . . . LMC focuses on operating models, technology, work-sourcing and cost management".[13] Legal management consultancy offers clients a range of different services, but an important aspect is to work in partnership with clients to develop strategies to respond to changes in the legal market. This is an area that will develop as law firms focus on how to use technology to contribute to their growth and will need specialist support to embed technology within their organisations.

ONLINE DISPUTE RESOLUTION PRACTITIONER

As you learned in Chapter 9, there are an increasing number of online dispute resolution (ODR) systems, particularly in civil mediation and consumer redress. ODR platforms provide an alternative to traditional court-based litigation. In the UK and elsewhere, the courts themselves are also becoming increasingly digitalised with the introduction of online court systems. Digital solutions to resolve legal problems have the potential to create new opportunities for lawyers and add value for clients. A dispute resolution professional will need to understand how to successfully support and work with clients online.

Richard Susskind originally identified ten 'new' jobs, but other roles are emerging and there might be some overlap between these jobs, or organisations may have slightly different names for similar roles (see Figure 12.2).

LEGAL INNOVATION MANAGER

Law firms with legal technology and innovation departments view these as important to ensure that the firm can respond and innovate to stay at the cutting edge of legal practice. These departments need managers who have responsibility for the strategic

12 <https://www2.deloitte.com>

13 Deloitte Legal, 'A Changing World Requires a New Approach to Law' (2017) <https://www2.deloitte.com/content/dam/Deloitte/global/Documents/Legal/dttl-legal-deloitte-approach-legal-management-consulting.pdf> accessed 12 October 2018.

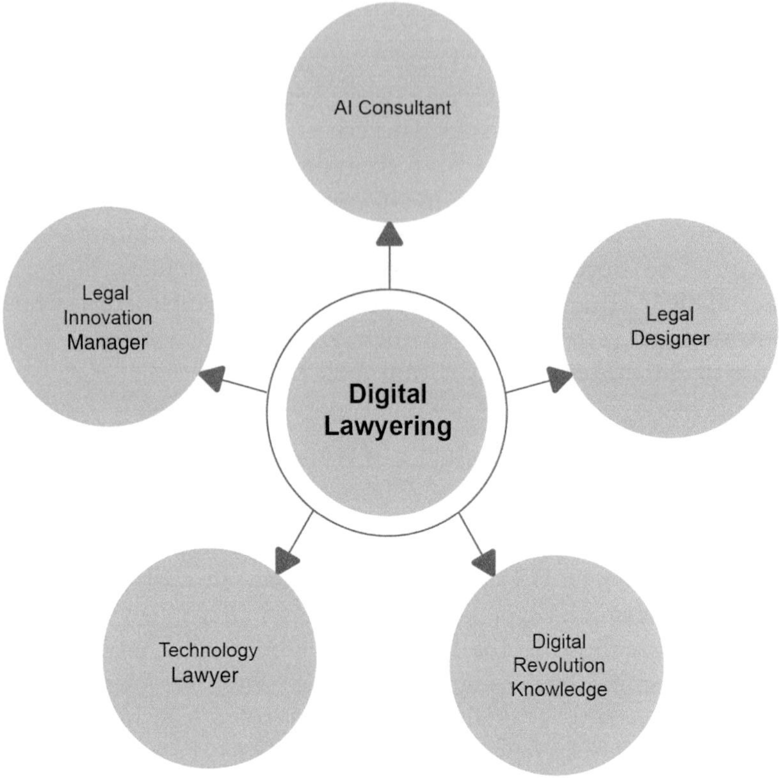

Figure 12.2 Emerging jobs

development of the team. The managers act as a bridge between the team and the rest of the organisation, sharing knowledge of new technologies and identifying and promoting the use of technological solutions.

DIGITAL REVOLUTION KNOWLEDGE LAWYER

Law firms already employ professional support lawyers (non-fee-earning positions) to support knowledge management in their practice areas. The nature of the role varies but may include research, professional development, and leading the firm's know-how activities. Lawyers are required to understand all aspects of digital transformation and the impact technological disruption has on them and their clients. A new type of professional support lawyer is required who can provide lawyers with this type of insight and support.

AI CONSULTANT

In Chapter 7 you explored AI and learned how it can automate tasks that would have been undertaken by junior lawyers. Proponents of AI argue that it will free up lawyers to focus on more complex work. AI is being used in discovery and legal contracts and provides significant benefits to clients to solve legal problems more efficiently. Law firms are incorporating platforms such as Harvey AI, which uses AI to support legal workflows. Knowledge of AI and Generative AI offers opportunities to work with law firms to incorporate AI into existing processes but also in consultancy roles to provide AI expertise.[14]

LEGAL DESIGNER

> Legal design is the application of human-centered design to the world of law, to make legal systems and services more human-centered, usable, and satisfying.[15]

The legal designer works to embed technology and innovation into an organisation through the creation of legal design maps to visualise the process of integrating technology and human interaction. A design approach starts with the end user, focusing on solving legal problems in a clear and user-friendly way. Technology is viewed as a resource to support human-centred design. In other words, the people within the system or process are at the heart of legal design. Thinking like a designer can lead to improvements in current processes and innovative new products and services.

TECHNOLOGY LAWYER

We are seeing the rise of the technology lawyer. Advice on the legal implications of specialised and emerging technologies is required by clients; for example, intellectual property protection, e-commerce, contracts, data protection, and privacy. Large law firms now often offer training seats in their legal and technology group. Law firms also offer

14 Infographic taken from <http://ai.lawgeex.com/rs/345-WGV-842/images/LawGeex%20-%20The%20In-House%20Counsel%27s%20LegalTech%20Buyer%27s%20Guide%20-%202018%20Edition.pdf> accessed 13 October 2018.

15 M. Hagan, 'Law by Design' (2014) <https://www.lawbydesign.co/en/legal-design/> accessed 5 January 2026.

secondment options for qualified lawyers to gain experience of technology platforms and develop digital skills

Sync 4: Finding out more

Now that you have had the opportunity to read more about different roles in the legal profession, would you change any of your original answers in Sync 3? Has this discussion piqued your interest in finding out more? Choose a role and search the internet to see what you can find out. Also take some time to reflect on the challenges involved in these roles. For example, accessing relevant training may take time and money, and competition for such jobs can be fierce. Weighing up the opportunities and the challenges can help you consider your future career direction.

For someone with a passion for technology and law, there are some exciting alternative career paths being offered by law firms.

Digital lawyering skills: flexibility

A few generations ago, people had a job, or at least a career, for life. It is now more common for people to have a range of careers within their working lives. Some people might have a "portfolio career", working in several different roles; for example, as a part-time professional support lawyer and part-time legal consultant, or as a part-time fee-earning lawyer and part-time life coach. Even within one profession, it is now more common for people to move between jobs, and this is likely to increase as digital technology changes and develops, leading to changes in the roles required.

These shifts mean that individuals have to be flexible to cope with and adapt to the changes that occur. This can sound daunting, but you have probably already learnt ways to be flexible; for example, by changing from school or college to university and by changing your study style according to the demands of individual modules.

Some tips to help with flexibility include:

- Distinguish between what you can change and what you cannot change. If something is outside of your control, there is no point in worrying about it. You need to focus on the things you can change.

- Be aware of your own values and ethics. This will help you to understand when and why you may find some types of change stressful.
- Take measured risks. Not all change is bad. It is important to realise that some change is positive and can lead to types of challenges that motivate or even inspire you.
- Keep your eyes on the bigger picture. Sometimes change can seem overwhelming, but if you rationalise it, usually it is only one small part of a much bigger picture. For example, even if you change jobs and find you do not enjoy it, you will still have your family, friends, and hobbies.

TYPES OF EMPLOYERS

Now that you have a better understanding of the types of roles that are available, let's consider where you might work. Alongside law firms, there are a range of other employers who will recruit for these roles; you may be familiar with some, like accountants, but less so with others, like legal publishers. Figure 12.3 summarises the range of potential employers.

ALTERNATIVE LEGAL SERVICE PROVIDERS

The legal marketplace has seen a growth of alternative legal service providers (ALSPs) offering a range of legal services. The following table[16] outlines what ALSPs offer and examples of key players. More information about these providers is explained as you progress through this chapter.

16 Adapted from 'Alternative Legal Service Providers: Understanding the Growth and Benefits of These New Legal Providers' (2017) <https://static.legalsolutions.thomsonreuters.com/static/pdf/Alternative-Legal-Service-Providers_Long.pdf> accessed 13 October 2018.

Figure 12.3 Employers past and present

ACCOUNTANTS

The Big Four global accountants in the UK[17] already employ significant numbers of lawyers in their legal practices. The Big Four are global operators and have put legal technology at the core of their business and suggest that Generative AI has the potential to transform the way in which legal services are delivered. They recruit talent across a range of different disciplines and are an attractive option for law students and lawyers who want to pursue a career outside a traditional legal practice.

17 This term refers to the four largest and most influential accounting companies globally: Deloitte, PWC, KPMG, and Ernst & Young.

	Accountants	Legal process outsourcing connected to law firms	Legal process outsourcing	Managed legal services	Contract lawyers
What do they do?	Deliver legal services; developing a wider legal consultancy service.	Owned by law firms; located in lower-cost area-volume work.	Independent of law firms; project-based work; managed by in-house departments or law firms.	Organisations that provide part or all of the legal function of an in-house department.	Provide lawyers and paralegals on a contract basis.
Examples of organisations	Deloitte EY PwC KPMG	Clifford Chance Eversheds Allen & Overy	Thomson Reuters Mindcrest Integreon LDiscovery	Thomson Reuters Axiom Riverview Law Elevate	FLEX Axiom LOD Halebury

LEGAL PUBLISHERS AND KNOW-HOW PROVIDERS

LexisNexis[18] and Thomson Reuters[19] provide news, information, software solutions, and analytic tools relating to legal, regulatory and tax changes using technology to support legal professionals. Both companies have launched AI products—Lexis AI and Thomson Reuters CoCounsel—and both are advocates of the role AI will play in legal services delivery. Thomson Reuters is working in close collaboration with Legal Geek[20] to support the tech start-up ecosystem. Both companies offer a variety of different roles, with a demand for both legal and digital skills.

18 <https://www.lexisnexis.com/en-us/home.page>
19 <https://www.thomsonreuters.com/en.html>
20 <https://www.legalgeek.co>

LEGALTECH COMPANIES

Sync 5: Legal Geek

1 Visit the Legal Geek website and access their start-up map: <https://www.legalgeek.co/startup-map/> Read in the FAQs the question 'How is the legal tech startup map categorised?'

2 Research three companies from this map to find out what they do and the positions they are recruiting for. The companies on the map are situated across many jurisdictions and therefore give you the opportunity to find out what is happening both within and outside your own jurisdiction.

It is a good idea to think about what areas of legaltech interest you and research different companies to explore what they offer to get a better understanding of how automation and workflows are impacting legal services.

Online legal services providers are also part of the legaltech revolution. For example, Rocket Lawyer[21] allows you to create legal documents, ask a lawyer and register your company online. The driver for online legal service providers is to harness technology to make legal services more affordable.

LEGAL MANAGEMENT CONSULTANCY

Consultancy firms like OMC Partners[22] offer a wide range of services to law firms, in-house legal departments, and newly formed alternative business structures (ABSs), including legal process analysis, legal spend management, legal technology advice, and alternative resourcing. Legal management consultancies will recruit for many of the new jobs identified earlier in this chapter as demand increases for these types of services.

LEGAL PROCESS OUTSOURCING

Legal process outsourcing (LPO) involves delegating work to another organisation to carry out work such as litigation support services or

21 <https://www.rocketlawyer.co.uk>
22 <https://www.omc-partners.com>

services in specialised areas such as risk and compliance. Integreon[23] is an example of a LPO provider. Other examples of LPOs were provided in the table at the start of this section. Law firms have also created LPOs which they own to offer their clients better value for the money for generally high-volume work. Ownership of the LPO allows them to retain control over the quality of the work. Freshfields[24] in Manchester, England, and Herbert Smith Freehills[25] in Belfast, Northern Ireland, are examples of law firms that have an LPO.

LAW FIRMS

Law firms are creating different opportunities within their legal practices. There are roles within innovation departments but also within specialist law firms. Digital Law[26] started in 2014 and specialises in online, data, and cyber law. Change is also happening to the way in which lawyers work. Flexible Legal Resources is a consulting business of PWC;[27] it has a bank of specialist lawyers with a range of different backgrounds including risk and compliance. Lawyers work on projects on a consultancy basis within in-house departments. As discussed in Chapter 2, virtual law firms are now part of the legal landscape; Vlaw Limited[28] is an example that offers lawyers an alternative option to traditional legal practice. Lawyers are self-employed and collaborate on matters together virtually. F-LEX[29] is an online platform which connects law students to law firms to work as paralegals. It is a lawtech start-up which is using a tech-enabled platform to disrupt traditional legal recruitment.

BUSINESSES

A range of different businesses will recruit digital lawyers, from large global corporations to high street banks. High street brands may continue to challenge traditional high street law firms by offering services such as conveyancing and wills and probate but using technology to

23 <https://www.integreon.com>
24 <https://www.freshfields.com>
25 <https://www.herbertsmithfreehills.com>
26 <https://www.digitallawuk.com>
27 <https://www.pwc.co.uk/careers/experienced-jobs/opportunities/flexible-legal-resources-html>
28 <https://www.virtuallaw.eu>
29 <https://www.flex.legal>

optimise the process of delivery. Large corporations are likely to retain in-house legal support, but with an expectation that cost efficiencies will be achieved through using technology and perhaps outsourcing some provision to other providers. There are myriad opportunities going forward to explore in this area.

Sync 6: Changes to the legal profession

Reflect on these questions:

1 What type of legaltech will most radically change the way in which lawyers will work in the next five years?

2 Do we need a new definition of the "legal profession" considering these changes?

3 What is one thing you should do to prepare for legaltech changes in the next five years?

RETURNING TO DIGITAL SKILLS

With the emerging new uses of technology in the delivery of legal services, and the way in which existing laws are being applied as solutions to digital living, you will need a variety of skills and competencies, including knowledge of substantive laws, awareness of technology and its uses and an appreciation for the changing trends in the ethics and professional responsibility for lawyers.

As Chapter 11 illustrated, a broad range of skills are required for an individual to be considered digitally competent, and this captures an important shift in thinking about competent 21st-century lawyering. Historically, competency in legal practice was very much focused on gaining and demonstrating competency in the foundations of legal knowledge and other substantive areas of law, and the ability to represent your client in accordance with the codes of conduct and professional rules.

TECHNICAL KNOW-HOW

Substantive legal knowledge is the foundation of our core competency to deliver a fit-for-purpose legal service. This also requires the

Sync 7: Which digital skills?

Based on your reading of Chapter 11, the "digital lawyering skills" boxes in each chapter and the reading you have done about jobs in this chapter, make a note of the five skills you think are essential for working as a digital lawyer. Take time to reflect on how this differs from the skills and competencies currently required within the legal profession.

We have identified several broad areas of skills and competencies we see as crucial, including:

- Technical know-how
- Communication and collaboration
- Understanding ethics and confidentiality
- Business acumen
- Commercial awareness and entrepreneurship
- Adaptability and resilience.

These are not necessarily "new", but they will need to be applied in very different ways.

continued acquisition of the types of key legal skills referred to in Chapter 2. However, the knowledge we need is also changing as technology evolves and emerges. For example, in handling contractual matters, blockchain technology, digital currencies, and smart contracts are a few relevant areas of study. Within civil procedure rules, learning about ODR and electronic discovery are necessary topics of study. In criminal law, learning about digital theft or digital ownership in property law are key foundations of our legal knowledge. As technology evolves and its use becomes ubiquitous, every aspect of legal practice will require an awareness and basic knowledge of technology's impact—in other words, as discussed in Chapter 4, a level of digital literacy and digital competence. Knowledge of how technological developments would be addressed by existing law and whether that law is adequate becomes an integral part of a future lawyer's competency.

As much as there is no expectation on lawyers to know how to code, a digitally competent professional will be confident in choosing solutions for online tasks for a particular purpose or audience. To do this you must understand what the technology does, how it functions and what it is capable and not capable of doing, whilst having a clear objective of what you are setting out to achieve and what the technology is capable of offering. Acquiring the knowledge and skills to use digital tools and software to deliver alternative forms of technology-driven legal service requires you to learn continually about the developments in technology.[30]

This means that being considered digitally competent is more than being able to source information online; it means possessing the understanding, knowledge, and skills required to enable the effective use of technology, keeping abreast of the changes in the law and its practice, the influence of technology on both domains, and acquiring knowledge continually about the benefits and risks associated with relevant technology, coupled with the necessary confidence and adaptability required to learn and utilise new technologies. This does not mean that you will need to become a technology expert, but there is an obligation to have a basic understanding of different technologies, including their affordances, limitations and potential use in legal services. As the uses of AI, blockchain technology and other innovative tools are rolled out, lawyers will be expected to know how those tools affect their clients too. Keeping yourself up to date on suitable technology for the delivery of legal services is necessary, including best practices for the use of these delivery models.

COMMUNICATION AND COLLABORATION

Working online requires excellent collaboration, communication, and the sharing of tasks and goals with each other. The knowledge and skills relevant to communicating and undertaking legal services online include the need to be flexible in communicating and listening, because each client and colleague they encounter will have a different concept of accessibility and varying levels of comfort in communicating online. You will need to be aware of acceptable etiquette when working online with clients and other professionals and how to collaborate effectively utilising an individual's strengths in an online team. As discussed in Chapter 3, legal teams will increasingly be interdisciplinary in nature,

30 Some of the legal services already using technology include automated document assembly, electronic court scheduling and file share technologies—technologies used within law practices include digital means of communicating with clients and third parties and transmitting information, electronic research and software applications for document generation, electronic calendaring, docketing, and much more.

requiring the ability to collaborate with a wide range of people, communicating clearly, and effectively.

UNDERSTANDING ETHICS AND CONFIDENTIALITY

A focus on codes of conduct, professional responsibilities, and legal ethics is important for online delivery of legal services, especially for ensuring that all forms of communication and data handling are safe and encrypted. As discussed in Chapter 5, you will require the knowledge and skills to consider the safety, security, confidentiality, privacy, digital footprint, and ethical use of digital tools for legal practice.

Further, within the practice of law, ethical, and professional responsibility are key elements of codes of conduct, and as such, data security in the form of safeguarding electronically stored client information and communications is crucial. Whilst you need not master the security rules and features of a piece of technology, as this will evolve as the technology changes, you will be expected to continuously keep abreast of digital security practices. This means being aware of the benefits and risks of emerging technologies that can be used to deliver legal services and safeguards to ensure your client's information and data are held confidentially, with the appropriate security in place to protect it from disclosure, access or acquisition. This is for both information that is privileged between the lawyer and client and any other information held about the client. Further, the obligation to competently maintain client confidentiality requires an understanding of data encryption and its purpose in transmitting data electronically; safe ways of communicating confidential data is essential, alongside being aware of the risks associated with using public wireless access to view clients' files and undertake communication.

Maintaining privacy and security over data becomes a bigger challenge when data is held in the cloud. This means that data and information relating to a client and case files will be stored on virtual servers owned by third parties outside the relevant law practice. The duty to keep information safe and confidential still remains the professional responsibility of the lawyer even if the data is stored elsewhere. In fact, this places even more of a burden on verifying and ensuring that the cloud host has an enforceable service-level agreement on how data held in the cloud will be preserved and handled, methods of data retrieval, and backup and storage of data.

Given the abundance of retrievable data online, there is a need to develop one's ability to evaluate content found online and make informed judgments on its reliability for the handling, sharing, and safe storage of data. Electronic discovery is the preservation, retrieval, review, and production of electronic information as evidence in court. Skills such as problem-solving and critical and analytical thinking skills are exercised when discussing practical e-discovery issues. You will require an understanding of the various e-discovery processes to be able to challenge or critique the results of the discovery if necessary, such as due to biases or reliance on incomplete data. Knowing about ethical sources of information is useful to ensure the quality, reliability and credibility of data gathered.

BUSINESS ACUMEN

Business acumen and an understanding of business intelligence are significant and necessary skills in our data-driven world. The practice of law remains a profession, a vocation and a business. Alongside the traditional key skills of a practising lawyer such as substantive legal knowledge, professional and practical client-facing skills and legal skills, the business world requires that a lawyer can run a legal practice business with excellent customer service and client care aided using appropriate technology. The ability to understand financing, budget handling and reporting on cost and benefit is important. In this regard, project management is becoming a fixture in many law courses. Your ability to scope, schedule, and cost legal work, accompanied by resourcing, managing, and monitoring progress on work with a view to delivering that legal work in an efficient and effective manner that balances the expectations of clients and business objectives, is deemed an essential skill in legal practice business. As discussed in Chapters 8 and 10, there is also a need for critical thinking and creativity to enable you to be proactive in both identifying and addressing client issues.

COMMERCIAL AWARENESS AND ENTREPRENEURSHIP

It is essential that you understand the environment in which law firms and clients operate. Lawyers are trusted advisors, and the legal advice they give must support the needs of their clients. Clients will expect their lawyers to use technology as part of their operating model and advise them on the legal implications of emerging technologies. This requires a digital lawyer to be both a systematic thinker and also a problem finder and problem-solver (as discussed in Chapters 6 and 7).

ADAPTABILITY AND RESILIENCE

There is a need for a competent lawyer's skill set and knowledge to evolve along with the emerging technologies being used for the delivery of legal services and in the use of technology across our personal and professional lives.

A willingness to continually learn is much needed in a disruptive and innovative fast-paced environment. The not-so-new jobs in legal services require you to develop an appreciation for a global perspective on the law and legal practice. Many disputes and transactions are more frequently giving rise to cross-border issues, particularly enabled by technology, so that a purely domestic legal practice is becoming rarer. Further, the digital age gives rise to the need for cross-disciplinary awareness as legal services become more often unbundled, requiring lawyers to work with other professions and occupations. This requires the types of flexibility referred to earlier in this chapter.

The COVID-19 pandemic is an illustration of the need to adapt and be resilient. It required legal professionals to change their ways of working almost instantly; for example, by switching to the forms of remote advocacy discussed in Chapter 9. However, this pandemic also illustrated the ways in which demands to adapt can also be stressful and sometimes harmful to wellbeing. It is important that individuals are able to adapt and show resilience in healthy ways, rather than feeling a pressure to change and succeed at all costs.

Sync 8: Analysing digital lawyering careers

Based on this chapter, and any wider reading you have undertaken, complete the following table to form a SWOT analysis which identifies the strengths, weaknesses, opportunities, and threats involved in a career as a digital lawyer. You can focus on yourself personally or on the legal profession as a whole and choose a specific role or look at digital lawyering more broadly.

Strengths	
Weaknesses	
Opportunities	
Threats	

CONCLUSION

The legal profession in 20 or 30 years' time is likely to look very different than today. There will be more career options available for qualified lawyers. Many of you will work in roles that have yet to be created. Lawyers will need to use their legal knowledge and apply it across a range of different industries. It is an exciting time to be a law student; there are myriad opportunities connected to a future legal career. It is important to think about these changes critically and reflect on both the opportunities and challenges that might be involved. Before moving on, look back at this chapter's hot spots and take time to complete Sync 8; pause and reflect on how these changes could also impact on you and your future career.

ADDITIONAL RESOURCES

Here are some ideas on how to find out more:

- Join professional associations like the Society for Computers and Law (SCL) and the International Legal Technology Association. Many offer free membership and resources, and they often have events you can attend where you can make connections.
- Educate yourself. There are lots of free courses where you can learn about technology: try Future Learn.
- Subscribe to *Legal IT Insider*,[31] which produces a free monthly legaltech newsletter.
- Use social media: Follow and engage with industry experts on Twitter and LinkedIn.
- Participate in a Tech Challenge or a Hackathon: The SCL Junior Lawyers' Group organises one each year, but there may be other ones you can participate in.
- Look for work experience: Firms are now offering placements in law and technology.[32]
- Keep up to date with legal technology: Stanford CodeX created a searchable database where you can find companies providing different legal technology to the legal market.

31 <https://www.legaltechnology.com>
32 The Lawyer Portal provides resources and links for aspiring lawyers <www.thelawyerportal.com>

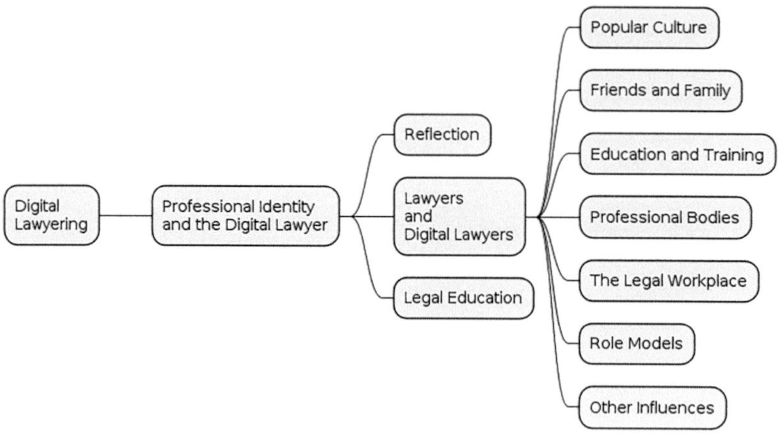

Mind Map 13.1 Chapter topics

13 Professional Identity and the Digital Lawyer

Emma Jones

Introduction

Throughout this chapter there will be an emphasis on you, as the reader, reflecting upon your own professional identity and how this can influence your future career as a digital lawyer. To assist you in this reflective process, this chapter will begin with a brief discussion of what reflection is and why it is so important for all legal professionals.

This chapter will then consider what the term "professional identity" means, and how this idea is currently applied within the legal profession. It will explore the existing tensions around professionalism in the legal profession and discuss how these may translate into the digital environment. It will identify which potential elements could be included in a new form of professional identity for digital lawyers, before concluding by discussing the possible implications for the law schools of the future.

Chapter hot spots

When reading this chapter, questions to think about include:

- What is your image of a traditional lawyer?
- What is your image of a digital lawyer?
- If these two images differ, how and why is this?
- What is your professional identity as a law student?

Having read the title and introduction, you can add any other questions you want to explore here:

DOI: 10.4324/9781003602323-13

THE REFLECTIVE PRACTITIONER

> To be prepared to face a myriad of interconnected and complex challenges, twenty-first century legal professionals need a reflective legal education that emphasizes self-assessment and self-efficacy, develops metacognition, supports and diversifies life-long learning, promotes innovative and critical thinking, strengthens legal professionalism, and builds a stronger aptitude for problem-solving and tackling "wicked problems". An increased capacity for individual, critical and collective reflection—beginning in law school—could help to ensure that the legal profession is better equipped to provide responsive leadership in the face of dire predictions of a future of unrelenting and disorienting change.[1]

Reflection is a way to process your thoughts and feelings about an incident or situation. Reflecting upon something gives the opportunity to come to terms with the experience and the actions, responses, thoughts, and feelings it has generated. For example, as a student you may receive some critical feedback on an assignment that you initially find confusing ("but I thought I had done that") or upsetting ("I did my best, but it wasn't good enough"). One approach could be to try to put the feedback behind you by putting it out of your mind and moving on to your next piece of work. However, another approach would be to spend some more time thinking about the feedback and your reaction. You may end up realising that some of the criticism was valid and raised points you can work on in future. You may realise your initial confusion was because you had skimmed the feedback comments rather than reading the full detailed explanation. You may end up making an action plan for how you are going to tackle your next piece of work. Each of these potentially positive outcomes would arise from you spending time reflecting upon the original feedback. Doing so could enable you to build on your mark in a subsequent assignment, resulting in more positive comments. It could also assist you in identifying any comments you still felt confused or unsure over, so that you could discuss those with the person who had marked your work.

Reflection is not just important for students; it is valuable in all walks of life. This means it is important for all lawyers, including digital lawyers, to be what is known as a "reflective practitioner".[2] This term

1 Michele M. Leering, 'Integrated Reflective Practice: A Critical Imperative for Enhancing Legal Education and Professionalism' (2017) 95 *The Canadian Bar Review* 47, 49.

2 Donald A. Schön, *Educating the Reflective Practitioner: Toward a New Design for Teaching and Learning in the Professions* (Jossey-Bass 1987).

was coined by Donald Schön, a professor who conducted research into the ways in which professionals think. He describes two different kinds of reflection: "Reflection-in-action" and "reflection-on-action". The first of these, reflection-in-action, refers to reflecting during a particular incident or situation. This can result in you adapting your behaviour or approach to deal with the scenario more appropriately. For example, if you are conducting an interview with a new client, you may begin to realise that the client is very emotionally invested in a particular issue, leading them to become agitated and repeat points several times and not answer your questions. Having been focused on listening patiently and building a rapport with your client, you may then wish to become more assertive about redirecting the conversation to move the client on to other topics.

The other form of reflection, reflection-on-action, refers to when you look back over a particular incident or situation to think about how you responded and what you can learn from it. This is the sort of reflection a student can engage in when they receive feedback on their assessments. Taking the example from legal practice discussed earlier, after your interview with a client you could spend some time thinking over what happened. You may realise that you omitted to set clear ground rules for what the interview would cover at the start and that you missed some indications that the client was beginning to get agitated. As a result, you may make a note of ground rules to put in place at the start of interviews in future and resolve to focus more on interpreting the client's reactions to your questions.

One important point to note is that reflection is not just about what you thought or how you acted in a particular incident or situation. You can also reflect on your emotional responses. This can help you to become more self-aware and understand your emotional responses better, which in turn can help you to regulate them appropriately in future. Returning to the client interview again, you may have felt yourself becoming cross or upset when the client did not answer your questions. On reflection, you could realise that this is not about the client but about your difficulty with the feeling of being "ignored" which stems from an experience in your past. Alternatively, it may be that you realise what you thought was anger actually stems from worry and concern that you have mishandled the interview and that the client will be unhappy with your approach. All of these realisations could help you to understand and respond appropriately to future emotional reactions and to adjust your approach to similar situations that arise.

This chapter will largely focus upon the idea of reflection-on-action. One way to incorporate this reflective process into your own

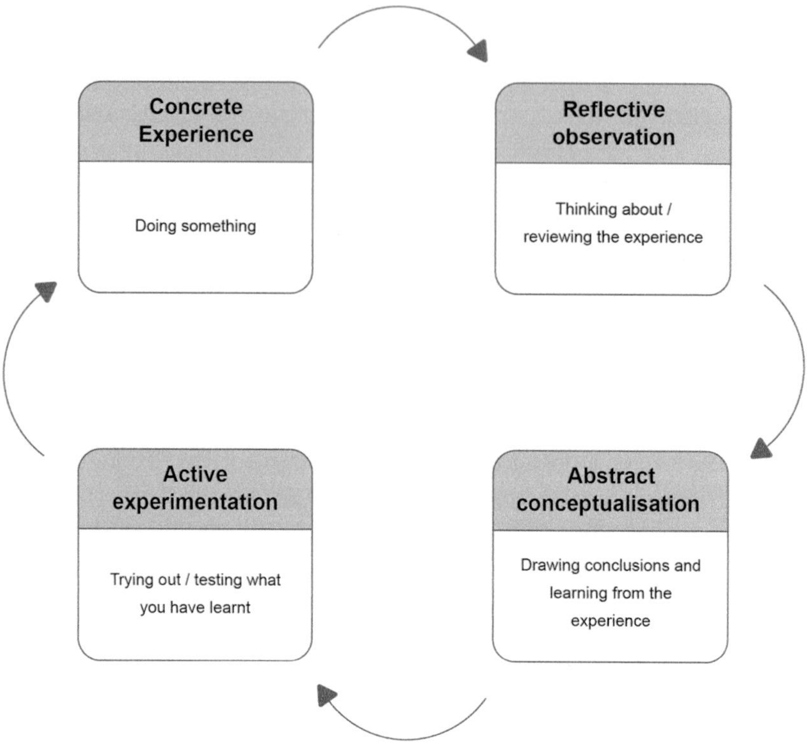

Figure 13.1 Kolb's cycle

situation is to set out in a learning cycle designed by the educational researcher David Kolb.[3] He identified four stages to work through. The first stage is "concrete experience", where you live through an incident or situation. The second stage is "reflective observation", where you think over what happened and review it. This can involve recalling what happened and how you reacted and felt during it. The third stage is "abstract conceptualisation". This is about learning from your reflections and asking yourself questions such as "Am I happy with my response?" and "Is there anything I could do differently next time?" The final stage is "active experimentation". This involves taking the lessons you learnt and applying them when another appropriate incident or situation arises. Of course, once you do that, you have another "concrete experience" and the whole cycle begins again (Figure 13.1).

3 David A. Kolb, *Experiential Learning: Experience as the Source of Learning and Development* (Vol. 1, Prentice-Hall 1984).

Sync 1: Practising reflection

You should allow around 15 minutes for this activity.

Think of a recent incident or scenario. It could be something that has happened relating to your study or work, or your personal life (e.g. a discussion with your parents, siblings, or children). Using this as your "concrete experience", spend some time in "reflective observation" and make some notes about it. Then practice "abstract conceptualisation" and write down at least three learning points you can take from the experience. This could be something you did well, something you would change next time, or anything else you think is useful.

Keep your learning points somewhere safe so that you can refer back to them in a few weeks or months and see if they were helpful when you faced a similar incident or situation.

So far this section has emphasised the importance of individual reflection and suggested that it can be divided into two types. The legal academic Michele Leering (writing in relation to legal education and legal practice) takes a somewhat different approach.[4] She refers to "reflection-on-practice" (which is similar to Schön's reflection-on-action). However, she suggests this largely focuses on reflecting upon your skills and performance. For example, in Sync 1 you thought about your reactions to a particular incident or scenario.

Leering also argues that there is a need for two other types of reflection. The first of these is "critical reflection". This involves reflecting on, and critiquing, your knowledge and questioning any underlying assumptions. For example, you may assume that digital technology is a huge benefit for the legal profession, but in doing so you could fail to acknowledge the disruption and the change it can bring, and how this may impact the wellbeing of individual legal practitioners. More broadly, you may want to reflect upon the impact of digital lawyering upon society and justice as a whole. The second additional type of reflection which Leering identifies is "self-reflection". This is about reflecting on your values and asking questions about why you are doing certain things and what meaning lies behind them. For example, for

4 Michelle M. Leering, 'Conceptualizing Reflective Practice for Legal Professionals' (2014) 23 *Journal of Law and Social Policy* 83, 94.

some people their interest in digital lawyering is driven by a desire to improve access to justice.

Leering also emphasises the need for "reflecting in community". In other words, sharing your reflections with others to open up discussions and debates and help you (and others) to develop their thinking further. You may be aware of the old proverb, "Two heads are better than one". This captures the idea that sharing thoughts and reflections can help you take on new perspectives and ideas and reframe your thinking on issues. As digital lawyers often have to work collaboratively with others, often in interdisciplinary teams, this type of reflection can be a valuable way to foster trust and closer relationships with colleagues.

Having considered the importance of reflection, and how to approach reflection, this chapter will now move on to discuss the notion of professional identity. As you work through this chapter, there will be more opportunities to develop and apply your skills of reflection in other syncs.

THINKING ABOUT PROFESSIONAL IDENTITY

When individuals join a profession, such as the legal profession, it is not just about applying their skills and knowledge in a new environment. At the same time, individuals will also develop a sense of professional identity. This refers to how you see yourself as a professional and how others see you as a professional. Individuals will have ideas about how they think about and see themselves as professionals and how they should appear to others within that particular role. This will then shape the ways in which they think and act within their role (and perhaps more generally in life). In particular, an individual's professional identity will involve certain attributes (characteristics or features), beliefs, values, motives, and experiences.[5]

Hilary Sommerlad, a legal academic, conducted an experiment a few years ago in which she asked aspiring solicitors in England and Wales who were undertaking the vocational stage of their studies to write and draw what came into their mind when they thought of solicitors.[6] Despite the participants being both male and female and from a range of backgrounds and ethnicities, the figures they drew were all

5 Herminia Ibarra, 'Provisional Selves: Experimenting with Image and Identity in Professional Adaptation' (1999) 44 *Administrative Science Quarterly* 764, 765.

6 Hilary Sommerlad, 'Researching and Theorising the Process of Professional Identity Formation' (2007) 34(2) *Journal of Law and Society* 190.

white, mostly male corporate lawyers—wealthy and powerful. This suggests that the participants had a particular view of solicitors in their mind. Given this view, it seems likely that a number of them would seek to adopt some of the attributes, beliefs, values, motives, and experiences they viewed these figures as possessing (although some did indicate they wished to challenge these stereotypes).

This experiment also shows that professional identity begins to be shaped before an individual actually enters a profession. Factors contributing to these ideas about professional identity for traditional lawyers could include (Figure 13.2):

Figure 13.2 Factors influencing professional identity

- *Legal education.* The time people spend at law school is often described as an important part of their professional identity formation.[7] Law students will absorb messages about the law and lawyers

7 See, for example, Susan L. Brooks, 'Fostering Wholehearted Lawyers: Practical Guidance for Supporting Law Students' Professional Identity Formation' (2018) 14 *University of St Thomas Law Journal* 412.

throughout their studies. Some of these may be expressly taught to them (e.g. if they undertake a course on professional ethics). However, other messages will be hidden (knowingly or unknowingly) in the ways law is taught and discussed more generally. For example, law students may discover that displaying an emotional reaction to a case they are studying is often frowned upon in the classroom. Instead, they are expected to suppress their emotional response and instead focus on a legal analysis of the principles involved.

- *Professional bodies.* Most, if not all, parts of the legal profession will be regulated and/or represented by one or more professional bodies. Regulation refers to a body having powers to grant or refuse entry into the profession, set the standards required within the profession and discipline individuals or organisations which fall below those standards. Representation refers to supporting, protecting, and advocating for the rights of a particular part of the legal profession. For example, solicitors in England and Wales are regulated by the Solicitor Regulation Authority and represented by the Law Society of England and Wales. In the United States, each state has its own body known as a bar association. In some states these both regulate and represent lawyers. In others, they may just represent lawyers. The American Bar Association is also a national association, with voluntary membership, which represents lawyers. Similarly, in Australia, different territories have their own bodies, but there are nationwide bodies such as the Law Council of Australia (who represents solicitors). An important part of the work of regulatory bodies is to set the standards required of legal professionals. This usually involves a code of conduct, or similar, setting out the ethical rules governing the work of members. For example, most will contain a provision around "conflict of interest", stating that you cannot represent a client if you already work for a client who has a potentially conflicting interest, such as a buyer and seller of a particular property. Chapter 5 included a range of examples of codes of conduct dealing with the use of social media. These codes will help determine how individuals behave and act within legal practice, assisting in forming their professional identity. It is likely that professional bodies will also contribute to professional identity formation in other ways; for example, by holding workshops, discussions, and webinars on specific topics, by showcasing the work of specific organisations or individuals and by setting the agenda for debate on key topics within legal practice.

- *The legal workplace.* There is evidence that a lawyer's professional identity will be significantly influenced by their workplace.[8] Each individual workplace is likely to have its own working practices and culture—a set of ways of working and behaving—which a new entrant will be expected to adhere to in order to fit in. It has been identified that there are certain aspects of culture which are common in many law firms and other organisations, including a competitive atmosphere and an emphasis on long working hours.[9] In a traditional law firm, it is likely that the partners who lead the firm will have a significant influence on the working practices and culture within it. This may be by having express policies and rules on various issues (e.g. not using the internet for personal purposes) but also by the ways in which they behave (for example, not leaving the office until 9 pm). However, it is also likely that the behaviour and attitudes of those you work most closely with, such as your line manager, will also influence your professional identity. In other legal settings (e.g. barristers' chambers, which are groups of self-employed barristers who work together), the approach of colleagues is likely to be even more influential.
- *Popular culture.* From watching *Suits* on television to reading John Grisham books and following law firms on social media, lawyers are often portrayed in popular culture using a range of stereotypes; for example, as somewhat dull and bland individuals with no sense of humour surrounded by piles of old law books, or as rich, successful and glamorous people working in the corporate world, or as passionate campaigners fighting for a specific cause.
- *Role models.* If you have friends or family members in the legal profession, you are likely to have developed some of your ideas around professional identity through speaking to and observing them. However, you may also have had a range of other role models, from a lawyer in your local town to a legal author whose work you find inspiring to a professor at law school who you admire.

By contributing to peoples' ideas around professional identity, these factors also help shape what is seen as "professionalism"—in other

8 See, for example, Stephen Tang, Vivien Holmes and Tony Foley, 'Ethical Climate, Job Satisfaction and Wellbeing: Observations from an Empirical Study of New Australian Lawyers' (2020) 33 *Geo. J. Legal Ethics* 1035.

9 Emma Jones, Neil Graffin, Rajvinder Samra and Mathijs Lucassen, *Mental Health and Wellbeing in the Legal Profession* (Bristol UP 2020).

words, the conduct, behaviour, and attributes that are viewed as part of being a professional. However, it is important to be aware that other broader factors also contribute to notions of professional identity and professionalism. This includes the range of factors identified in Chapter 2 as impacting upon the legal profession more generally. For example, Chapter 2 referred to the marketisation of the legal profession with a move towards seeing practising law as less of a public service and more as a form of business. This could contribute towards lawyers viewing themselves as businesspeople rather than as public servants, potentially encouraging them to measure their success more in terms of chargeable hours rather than whether they have helped someone.

In fact, there have long been tensions between different, often seemingly opposing, visions of lawyers. For example, in the novel *Bleak House*, author Charles Dickens portrays the legal profession as greedy and grasping, using their knowledge of the law purely for financial gain.[10] However, some contemporary authors such as the academic Anthony Kronman have argued that previous generations of lawyers were focused upon the acquisition of understanding and insights into human nature.[11] Other authors, such as the UK legal academic Donald Nicolson, argue that a return is needed to an emphasis on a passion for justice and a desire to contribute to promoting the ideals which follow from this.[12]

The next sync gives you an opportunity to think about your perceptions of a lawyer and also to consider what the professional identity of a digital lawyer in particular might involve.

Sync 2: Who are "lawyers" and "digital lawyers"?

You should allow around 30 minutes for this activity

This activity is based on Sommerlad's experiment (described earlier). You need to draw two pictures:

- A traditional lawyer
- A digital lawyer

10 Charles Dickens, *Bleak House* (Bradbury and Evans 1853).

11 Anthony T. Kronman, *The Lost Lawyer: Failing Ideals of the Legal Profession* (Harvard UP 1993).

12 Donald Nicolson, 'Calling, Character and Clinical Legal Education: A Cradle-to-Grave Approach to Inculcating a Love for Justice' (2013) 16(1) *Legal Ethics* 36.

Next to both images, write five words or phrases to describe the person you have drawn.

When you have finished, spend some time thinking about the following questions:

- Are either or both of your images similar to the description of the images in the Sommerlad experiment?
- What factors influenced your images and choice of descriptions?
- Do your two images and descriptions differ? If so, in what ways and why?

You may have come up with a range of drawings and descriptions, based on your personal experiences (and perhaps even some of the content of this textbook!). You may have felt it was artificial to make a distinction between "lawyers" and "digital lawyers" because virtually all legal professionals today use digital technology in some form. Alternatively, you may have felt that a digital lawyer is likely to be quite different from a traditional lawyer. In the next section, we will consider the potential differences between a traditional lawyer and a digital lawyer, and what elements may form part of a digital lawyer's professional identity.

THE DIGITAL LAWYER AND PROFESSIONAL IDENTITY

In the previous section we considered a range of factors which could influence the professional identity of a traditional lawyer. Each of these is also likely to impact on the professional identity of a digital lawyer, but within these there may be significant differences.

- *Legal education.* A digital lawyer may have undertaken a traditional form of legal education, but they may also have taken other routes into the legal profession; for example, by starting out with a first degree in computer science or digital and technology solutions. In England and Wales, the introduction of the Solicitors Qualifying Examination means that individuals can take two examinations to become a solicitor regardless of what degree they have previously studied, potentially making alternative routes more likely. Even if a digital lawyer has studied a law degree, they may well have chosen options focused on digital technology. These could be specifically on digital lawyering; for example, Monash University in Australia has a suite of Legal Technology Clinics, where students work with industry experts to design solutions to real-life business and legal issues.[13] In the United States, the Legal Design Lab at Stanford Law School and d.school encourages law students to design and build a wide variety of legal services and products,[14] including a new online platform to provide help for individuals facing eviction or other landlord-tenant issues.[15] Alternatively, or in addition, digital lawyers may have focused on modules looking at the ways in which the law regulates different types of technology (e.g. the internet) or the implications for traditional areas of law (e.g. intellectual property). An increasing number of law schools also offer extracurricular activities involving technology for students to undertake; for example, the University of Sheffield (UK) runs the Sheffield Digital Justice pro bono project, allowing law, criminology, and computer science students to explore the intersections of law and technology. Sometimes this type of activity is linked to clinical legal education, such as The Open University's Open Justice project, in which students design and create chatbots capable of providing legal information on specific topics to the general public.[16]

- *Professional bodies.* Digital lawyers may be required to be members of particular legal bodies, depending upon which role they have within the legal profession. However, they may also be involved in a range of different bodies which give them different perspectives and networks. For example, the Society of Computers and Law[17] offers a range of events and special interest groups, and the UK

13 Monash University, 'Clinical Placement Offerings' <https://www.monash.edu/law/current-students/cle/clinical-legal-education/clinical-placement-offerings> accessed 20 August 2025.

14 Legal Design Lab, 'Stanford Legal Design Lab' <https://www.legaltechdesign.com/> accessed 20 August 2025.

15 Legal Design Lab, 'Legal FAQ' <https://legalfaq.org/> accessed 20 April 2025.

16 The Open University, 'Digital Justice' <https://university.open.ac.uk/open-justice/public-understanding-law/legal-technology> accessed 20 August 2025.

17 <https://www.scl.org/society>

organisation BIMA is open to anyone working within digital, tech and creative industries.[18]

- *The legal workplace.* Digital lawyers may work in more innovative and cutting-edge environments which have the resources and the dynamism to embrace new ways of working and practising law. Chapter 2 referred to the growth of alternative business structures and NewLaw, all of which are closely related to technological developments. These challenge many traditional elements of the legal workplace; for example, how often would such a law firm have a secretary? It is quite possible a form of virtual assistant will become more prevalent to reflect the norms of work in lawtech. It is also possible that more interdisciplinary, collaborative, and design-led approaches will be integrated into the work of digital lawyering and that this will be reflected in the professional identity of individuals. For example, a digital lawyer may not relate to the hierarchical structure of traditional law firms. Instead of measuring success in terms of promotion to partner or having a secretary working for them, they may use alternative measures such as the prestige of the organisations they have worked in partnership with and the ways in which they have innovated within a particular sector.
- *Popular culture.* Images of people working in digital technology are often different from the ways in which members of the legal profession are depicted. If a digital lawyer views themselves more as a technologist or an entrepreneur than a legal professional, they may identify more with these images and attempt to align themselves with them. This could be a deliberate attempt to remove themselves from images of lawyers as perhaps rather bland or boring and/or perhaps part of an attempt to market themselves to potential clients as someone who is at the cutting edge of digital lawyering.
- *Role models.* Following on from the ideas of digital technology in popular culture, rather than identifying with a partner in a law firm or a judge as a potential role model, a digital lawyer may have different role models. This could be figures such as Richard Susskind or Bill Gates (to take two quite different examples!), or other individuals working within the fields of technology and/or law. This may influence their behaviour and approach to their role and their career aspirations.

18 <https://bima.co.uk>

A recent set of interviews with 33 legal tech lawyers across six different countries illustrates a number of the factors highlighted here. It found that the interviewees viewed themselves as very different from traditional lawyers and were motivated by their interest in technology and entrepreneurship. They favoured flat organisational structures, casual dress codes, and working with a broad range of other professionals.[19] The authors note that there was a 'deliberate stepping away from traditional practice and identity' to demonstrate that law tech lawyers are different.[20]

Sync 3: Other influences on the digital lawyer

You should allow around 10 minutes for this activity.

What other influences do you think may influence the professional identity of the digital lawyer? You may draw on your own experiences, or those of others around you, as well as any reading and research you have previously conducted.

You may have thought of a range of influences. You may have also identified that these influences will probably vary significantly between individuals depending upon their role within the workplace, experience, interests, and background. One idea could include experience within non-legal workplaces; for example, an individual could have used their digital skills within a different profession or as an entrepreneur before moving into law. This could mean that they are used to different professional standards and norms around issues such as confidentiality and privacy. They may find it challenging or even frustrating to adapt to a legal environment, which has traditionally been viewed as highly regulated and potentially as stifling to creativity. They may see themselves as an entrepreneur or innovator rather than predominantly as a legal professional (although as discussed in previous chapters, the two are not mutually exclusive!). It is also interesting to consider what values these individuals may hold. Are they motivated by a passion for

19 Charlotta Kronblad and Søren Henning Jensen, 'Being a Professional Is Not the Same as Acting Professionally—How Digital Technologies Have Empowered the Creation and Enactment of a New Professional Identity in Law' (2023) 10(2) *Journal of Professions and Organization* 99.

20 Ibid., p. 116.

justice, a desire for profit or perhaps something else; for example, a love of technology and a belief in its transformative potential?

The client role in shaping identity

When thinking about the professional identity of both lawyers and digital lawyers, it is important to acknowledge the role that clients can play in shaping this. In fact, this could be existing clients or even potential clients which an individual or firm is seeking to attract. This can affect people's professional identity in a range of ways, from altering your dress (e.g. feeling obliged to wear a suit when meeting with a corporate client) to seeking to align yourself with a large client's values and motivation.

It is important for a legal professional to consider who they are working with and to what extent they are willing or able to adjust some of their professional attributes to work with those clients. Sometimes this may involve assessing whether you feel ethically and morally comfortable with what you are being asked to do. At other times, it may simply be a case of ensuring that you put strict lawyer–client boundaries in place from the start of your relationship. What is crucial is that you are aware of how such relationships can impact on your professional identity and professionalism.

LEGAL EDUCATION AND DIGITAL LAWYERING

THE ROLE OF LEGAL EDUCATION

A legal educator's duty goes beyond teaching the law and shaping analytical minds; one additional responsibility is to model behavior desired in the profession.[21]

The term "legal education" is in fact very broad. It encompasses topics such as citizenship in schools and colleges, as well as the more formal academic and vocational training that law schools commonly offer. To some extent, the purpose of legal education will vary depending on what type we are referring to. Within law schools there often exist tensions over whether the law degree should be viewed as purely intellectual or as vocational in nature (in other words, the start of preparing students for life as a lawyer). Different jurisdictions and law schools

21 Christine Cerniglia Brown, 'Professional Identity Formation: Working Backwards to Move the Profession Forward' (2015) 61 *Loyola Law Review* 313, 314.

take a variety of approaches to this; for example, in the United States the law degree is postgraduate and therefore more commonly associated with forms of vocational training. In jurisdictions where the law degree is undergraduate, such as the UK and Australia, there has traditionally been a tendency to focus more on purely intellectual development. However, many law schools aim for some combination of the two approaches. Given the growing recognition and emphasis on employability skills in higher education (as discussed in Chapter 11), there is also arguably increasing pressure on law schools to at least acknowledge the requirements of the legal workplace. Whether or not this is the right approach is heavily debated in law schools, particularly given that not all law students want (or are given the opportunity) to pursue a legal career. However, the reality is that most law schools and law degrees will try—at least to some extent—to prepare or shape students for legal practice.

This means that notions of professional identity and professionalism do form a part of legal education within law schools. Sometimes this may be through specific modules on topics to do with lawyering, digital lawyering, or legal practice. At other times, it may be through extracurricular activities to do with employability, such as talks from local law firms and help preparing for job interviews. Even if the law school is not actively trying to take such steps, it is arguable that students will absorb ideas about professional identity and professionalism in any event (as demonstrated by Sommerlad's experiment). This may be through their reading and research, participating in clinical legal education, interacting with fellow students who aspire to become lawyers, or by observing and absorbing ways of behaving from staff. Any staff who have themselves worked in the legal profession may well have become used to doing things or acting in certain ways which are the norm within the profession. They are therefore likely to demonstrate this in their teaching and interactions with students.

Sync 4: Your experience of law school

You should allow around 15 minutes for this activity.

Reflect on your own experience of law school and think about the following questions:

- What was your "professional identity" as a student?
- To what extent is your law degree preparing you to become a member of the legal profession?

- To what extent (if any) is your law degree preparing you to become a digital lawyer?

If you are not studying law, you can still think about these questions, as it might well be that your degree has given you valuable transferable skills and knowledge. Alternatively, you may want to compare your studies with what you have learnt about legal studies in this textbook: How similar do you think your study experience is to that of a law student?

Thinking about your professional identity as a law student can help you identify elements which you are likely to take forward into the legal profession. It can also help you understand what has influenced your perceptions of law, the legal profession, and digital lawyering to date. Although being a student is not commonly referred to as a "profession", when people begin law school they are likely to develop a new identity. This will partly be shaped by the fact that they are transitioning into higher education and a new phase of their life. However, it is also likely to be influenced by the fact they have specifically chosen to study law, and whether or not they aspire to enter the legal profession. When thinking about your professional identity as a law student, you may have felt that as a student you have more freedom than a legal professional with a greater focus on socialising and having fun. Alternatively, maybe your focus was on your intellectual development and ensuring you absorb as much knowledge and learning as possible. Another option is that you may have felt that you were using your studies to prepare you for the workplace and to develop the types of characteristics (e.g. being conscientious and reliable) that you are likely to need to display in a working environment. Perhaps you thought of some combination of the three, or something else entirely! Figure 13.3 identifies some of the potential influences that could shape the professional identity of a law student and their journey onwards into the legal profession.

Just as you probably had ideas about the legal profession before studying law, you are also likely to have had some ideas about what being a law student was likely to entail. This may have been from your family and friends, social media (e.g. following students or universities on Instagram or joining relevant WhatsApp groups), or from your initial contact with law schools on open days or through their prospectuses. It may also be that you had previously studied law at school or college as

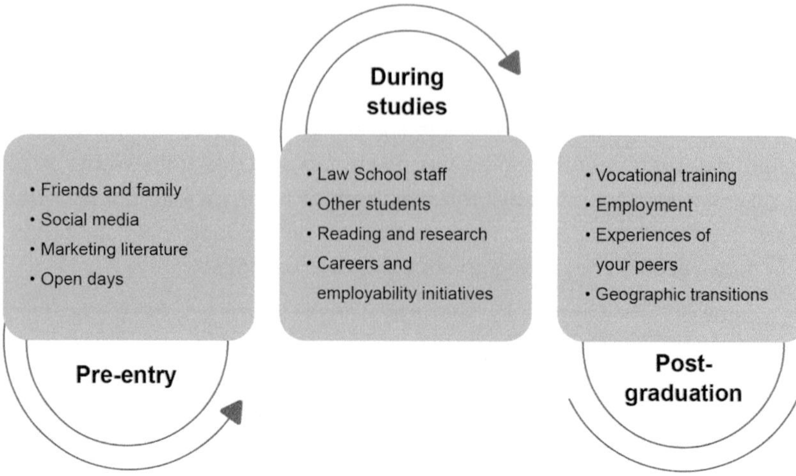

Figure 13.3 Factors influencing the identity of a law student

well. As discussed previously, once you begin law school, that is when it is likely that staff, students and your study experience will begin to impact your ideas. After graduation, it is likely that further training, the experience of your fellow graduates and your subsequent employment will change and develop your professional identity, so you move away from seeing yourself as a student and begin to see yourself as a professional. Often students have moved for university and end up moving again for work; this type of physical move can also have a psychological impact in distancing yourself from aspects of your previous identity.

When answering Sync 4, you may have found that your law degree focused more on preparing you for the legal profession generally, but not so much for digital lawyering in particular. This probably reflects the background and interests of the staff within your law school, which in turn shapes the curriculum that is offered. It may also be a result of the constraints on resources (both in terms of finance and time) that all universities have to face. However, it is likely that the current focus will change over the next few years as an acknowledgement of digital lawyering becomes increasingly common. It will be interesting to see whether this impacts upon the professional identity of law students and whether they begin to view themselves in new ways; for example, as digital citizens or innovators.

EMBEDDING DIGITAL LAWYERING WITHIN THE CURRICULUM

Preparing law students to participate and contribute to legal practice in the digital age will require an awareness of the application of law in a digitally networked society and digital living and practices. As such, it is likely that the study of how law interacts with technology, the breadth of technological influence on the law and gaps in the application of current laws on technology will increasingly become an important part of the curriculum. The ways in which this happens are likely to differ between law schools and jurisdictions. The following are some examples of how this could happen, drawing upon some commonly taught subjects from the law degree.

LEGAL SYSTEMS

A law degree will introduce you to the legal system of the jurisdiction in which you are studying and will often also encourage you to compare and contrast this with other legal systems. Some ways in which digital lawyering may be incorporated include:

- Questioning the current interpretations of various pieces of existing laws for application in a digital landscape; for example, the impact of social media on regulations around reporting upon court cases.
- Discussing the adequacy of public policy in regulating the digital world; for example, the application of the Universal Declaration of Human Rights and the European Convention on Human Rights.
- Identifying gaps where there is a need for the development of new legal doctrine as a result of developments in technology; for example, the increased collection by the state of biometric data (such as fingerprints and facial images).
- Developing a detailed understanding of the relationship between ethics, law, technology and public policy, and questioning the doctrine of justice when administered online.

CONTRACT LAW

A law degree will usually cover the law of obligations as a fundamental legal element required for the smooth running of society. Some ways in which digital lawyering may be incorporated include:

- Considering the functionality and impact of blockchain technology, its affordances across a wide variety of industries and its formation of smart contracts (as discussed in Chapter 10).
- Encouraging a deep understanding of smart contracts and how and when they operate, including the differences between traditional contracts and smart contracts.
- Raising awareness of the multi-jurisdictional locality of blockchains giving rise to complex jurisdictional issues.
- Determining the difference in contractual relationships, legal certainty, applicable laws, rights and obligations between smart contracts and traditional contracts.
- Understanding how blockchain commands operate and leave room for errors and omissions.

CRIMINAL LAW AND EVIDENCE

Criminal law is seen as essential for regulating the relationship between individuals and society and is therefore a key component of law degrees. The law of evidence is also critical in legal practice, although it is perhaps less frequently studied at the undergraduate level. Some ways in which digital lawyering may be incorporated include:

- Developing an appreciation for the multidisciplinary components which make up the subject area, such as components of law, criminology, ethics, and forensics.
- Discussing the ways in which the rapid advancement of technologies is changing the types of crimes to be investigated, the ways in which evidence is collected and disclosed and the ways of working in the law enforcement and criminal justice services.
- Exploring the challenges to the rule of law and the limitations on jurisdictional application of the law given that online crimes lack physical and geographical borders.
- Considering how law enforcers manage our obligations under the new data protection directives for the police, balancing the rights and freedoms of the public whilst protecting them, along with

issues such as the use of algorithms and artificial intelligence and its ethical impact on decision-making in law enforcement.

- Identifying that, because all activities online have a digital trail, digital evidence features prominently in many investigations.
- Encouraging a detailed understanding of how technologies have been used to determine evidence; for example, a case heard in the United States where the prosecution requested and obtained access to a conversation at home recorded by Alexa on Amazon Echo.[22]
- Understanding the role of digital evidence in court processes. Evaluating theoretical principles of admissibility of evidence and how these principles apply to digital evidence, how digital evidence is used in trial, methods of extracting and handling of evidence using admissible methods for use in court, the significance and use of the metadata contained in digital evidence and the methods of recovering deleted evidence via a digital trail.
- Considering broader issues also raise awareness of how evidence can be collected across jurisdictions and the transfer of evidence between different jurisdictions.

Sync 5: Design your own curriculum

You should allow around 60 minutes for this activity.

Imagine you are a member of staff at a law school who wants to design a curriculum which incorporates digital lawyering. Using the preceding examples for inspiration, pick three existing subjects commonly found within the law school curriculum; for each one, write down at least five ways in which you could integrate digital lawyering.

If you are struggling to think of a subject, you could choose from tort law, family law, public law, land law, and/or equity and trusts.

The ways that you choose could relate to the content of the module and identifying topics and issues that relate to digital technologies. They could also be related to the way in which the module is taught, using digital technologies to enhance its delivery.

You may have identified a wide range of ideas. If you are currently studying any of these modules, perhaps you could share your ideas with your tutor or the module convenor.

22 Anthony Cuthbertson, 'Amazon Ordered to Give Alexa Evidence in Double Murder Case' (*Independent*, 18 November 2018) <https://www.independent.co.uk/tech/amazon-echo-alexa-evidence-murder-case-a8633551.html> accessed 20 August 2025.

Other examples of aspects of legal education which can be used (and already are) to integrate digital technologies with the law degree include:

- *Skills and legal education.* Chapter 11 highlighted that law schools today do not just focus on legal knowledge; they also emphasise the importance of developing a range of skills, including employability skills. Throughout this textbook we have highlighted a range of skills which can be developed during your legal education and which are valuable to apply to legal practice and digital lawyering. These were drawn together into some key themes in Chapter 12.
- *Clinical legal education.* An important aspect of legal education which affords significant opportunities to encourage the incorporation and discussion of digital technologies is clinical legal education, whether this is through using online case management systems, communicating with clients remotely or using technology to organise documents and information and conduct research. Various examples have been given throughout this textbook, and these are likely to become more common in the next few years.

The COVID-19 pandemic also required law schools (and universities more widely) to think about the role of technology within their provision. Just as law firms shifted to remote working, legal studies were also moved online. This provided new challenges in terms of students and staff learning to use different forms of technology quickly, ensuring individuals had access to the equipment and Wi-Fi to participate, and thinking about the best ways to facilitate learning remotely. However, it has also brought new opportunities; for example, instead of sitting in a crowded lecture theatre, students were able to access pre-recorded lectures at a time of their choosing, listening, and taking notes at their own pace. The ways in which both students and staff have been forced to upskill and adapt have had some long-term consequences for legal education, accelerating shifts towards a focus on digital technologies.

THINKING LIKE A LAWYER

The term "thinking like a lawyer" is commonly used to describe the types of thinking that students are introduced to within law school. This is sometimes referred to as a process of socialisation—in other words, familiarising students with the culture and attitudes that commonly exist within law and the legal profession. It has often been associated with a very rigid form of legal analysis,[23] the type of analysis you often see applied in problem-style questions during assessments.

The discussion of skills which runs throughout this textbook has demonstrated that the lawyers of the future will need a broad range of skills to not only survive but also thrive in the digital world. Although thinking like a lawyer will always have a place, it is increasingly being recognised as just one element of the skill set needed to practise law successfully. The types of changes that are and will occur within the law school curriculum are likely to begin to challenge the concept of thinking like a lawyer so that it will widen (e.g. to include the forms of technical knowledge referred to in Chapter 3 and the types of soft skills referred to in Chapter 11). Alternatively, it may wither away to be replaced by a new notion of "thinking like a digital lawyer".

Sync 6: Thinking like a digital lawyer

You should allow around 20 minutes for this activity.

Drawing on your reading of this textbook and your wider reading and research, write a brief summary of:

- Your definition of digital lawyering.
- Your explanation of what "thinking like a digital lawyer" would entail.

Hopefully, Sync 6 will help you to draw together some of the ideas and themes you have identified as you have worked through this textbook. In the next chapter, as authors, we will explain our own understanding of these. Your answers can also form part of the reflection process, as you can continue to develop and enhance your understanding and insight as you continue to learn more about digital lawyering.

CONCLUSION: FUTURE IDENTITIES

Professional identity is important. It shapes how we behave, act, and even think within the workplace. It can also affect our personal lives, as

23 Colin James, 'Lawyers' Wellbeing and Professional Legal Education' (2008) 42(1) *The Law Teacher* 85–97.

few people can entirely compartmentalise their work and home personalities and attitudes. Professional identity is formed by a range of factors and shapes the notions of professionalism which become accepted (and largely complied with) throughout the profession.

Within law, professional identity begins to be shaped even before a student enters law school. Their legal studies are likely to have a significant influence upon this. Once they enter the legal workplace (assuming they choose to do so), their professional identity will also continue to develop and evolve, depending upon their roles, workplaces, and experiences.

The changes and shifts within the legal profession caused or influenced by the development of digital technologies will impact on the professional identity of both law students and lawyers. They will challenge some long-held assumptions and norms within the legal profession and require new skills and ways of thinking. The traditional notion of thinking like a lawyer will no longer be fit for purpose, and both legal education and the legal profession will need to adapt and evolve to exploit the new opportunities offered.

ADDITIONAL RESOURCES

- For a discussion of post-COVID changes in legal education, see <https://clp.law.harvard.edu/knowledge-hub/magazine/issues/transformation-in-the-latin-american-legal-market/reimagining-legal-education/>
- For an in-depth consideration of changes to the legal profession (from an Australian perspective), see Webb J and Paterson JM, 'The Evolution of Legal Knowledge Work in an Age of Brilliant(?) Technologies: From Robo-Lawyer to Digital Law Clerk' (2 April 2025) <https://ssrn.com/abstract=5371536> or <http://dx.doi.org/10.2139/ssrn.5371536> accessed 20 August 2025.
- For a discussion of the professional identity of lawyers providing both online and offline legal services, see Yao Y, 'One Foot in the Online Gig Economy: Coping with a Splitting Professional Identity' (2022) 9(3) *Journal of Professions and Organization* 273.
- For a discussion of the professional identity of lawtech start-up founders, see Goto M, Kotosaka M and Sako M, 'When Professionals Become Entrepreneurs: Identity Construction of Lawtech Startup Founders in Japan' (2025) 12(1) *Journal of Professions and Organization*.

14 CONCLUSION

SHAPING THE FUTURE OF DIGITAL LAWYERING

Emma Jones, Francine Ryan, Ann Thanaraj, and Terry Wong

INTRODUCTION

This chapter concludes our exploration of digital lawyering in the 21st century. It begins by drawing out key themes that have emerged through the previous chapters within this textbook. These include the concept of the digital lawyer; technology, innovation, and regulation; ethics and conduct; challenges and critiques; and skills and opportunities. Drawing upon these themes, it then considers what the future of digital lawyering might look like. To do so, each author takes one theme (digital lawyering and the legal profession, the effects of technology development and innovation, dispute resolution and ethics, and legal education and skills) and considers what the position may be 30 years into the future.

Based on your reading of this textbook, we hope that you will feel able to critique these visions of the future, and the themes they draw upon, by applying your own knowledge and understanding. Have we missed any key themes? Are the views of the future we present realistic, or overly optimistic or pessimistic? What challenges and opportunities do these ideas present? As you are a potential digital lawyer of the future, this is an opportunity for you to develop your skills of evaluation and critical thinking as you work through this chapter.

KEY THEMES IN DIGITAL LAWYERING

THE CONCEPT OF A DIGITAL LAWYER

The digital lawyer is a digitally fluent professional thriving in their legal practice. They flourish in a professional environment that is a hybrid

DOI: 10.4324/9781003602323-14

of face-to-face and online settings. They use various digital solutions to communicate in compelling ways and engage with clients seamlessly using tools that have the greatest impact. They will be working with a wide spectrum of individuals, drawing on interdisciplinary knowledge and methodologies. To do this will require a lifelong commitment to one's own professional and personal development and reflection, evolving their mindset, skills, and knowledge as digital solutions develop in fast-paced environments. Although other professions, industries, and sectors are also changing and adapting to the technological revolution, the ongoing transformation of the legal profession is arguably particularly radical, reshaping existing roles, careers, ways of working and even fundamental notions of professional identity and professionalism. This textbook has included considerations of how existing roles are changing due to the advancement of technologies in the profession and also the types of new roles being developed within it. At the heart of this change is the question of how the study of law and digital literacies and fluencies can be merged to create dynamic roles to serve clients.

A digital lawyer has a unique ability to thrive in the changing workplace, particularly in the legal profession, with agility, creativity, confidence, and adaptability. This enables them to learn and utilise new technologies and to work in ways which are augmented by technology and legal expertise. They need to be equipped with a foundational understanding of some of the complex and disruptive changes brought about by technologically mediated practices, and their impact in the current and fast-developing future of legal practice. To do this, they will need to use a blend of legal knowledge and interdisciplinary knowledge and methodologies beyond the components of subjects and modules that make up a traditional law degree The digital lawyer will need to be prepared with an understanding of the art and science of lawyering and the needs of legal practice but should also have a focus upon the digital transformation of practice, delivery, and user experience.

The fluency of the digital lawyer is captured through their deep understanding of core technologies, their features, and functionalities, how they are being utilised and the impact of these technologies on the role of legal professionals. Another dimension of digital lawyering lies in understanding the gaps in the profession and the opportunities to merge law with technology to create hybrid professions within the legal sector. A further dimension is in exploring the limitations and gaps in legislation and how these can be interpreted more broadly to capture the physical and digital worlds and the intersection between technology, law and society. With a need for horizon scanning, a digital lawyer will be expected to become aware of the current and emerging trends in the delivery of legal services. They will need to utilise the new technologies required to meet those demands through the use of appropriate, safe, and effective digital technological innovations and techniques for delivering legal services. This will also require being self-aware, collaborating with clients, peers, instructors, and other professionals, developing judgement skills and professional responsibility as well as evaluating professional identity and values.

Digital lawyers are also leaders, equipped with the leadership needed to shape the conversation around regulation in the digital age. They will use new and existing laws and the notion of the rule of law to shape the (digital) transformation of social, economic, democratic, political, and ethical structures which are being reimagined in the landscape of the Fourth Industrial Revolution. Drawing on solid legal knowledge, a digital lawyer frames the discussion of technologies, innovation and law around use and impact in legal services, grounded in one's values, ethics and professional responsibilities in a rapidly evolving legal profession and practice.

Success as a digital lawyer, or any digitally proficient professional, is less about the technology itself and more about understanding what technology works best in a given situation and how to optimise and use it within that situation. This means that the digitally proficient lawyer understands a legal or business problem, can appreciate the transcending boundaries of their client's problem across the physical and digital worlds, and has innovative ideas about how to solve it through the medium of technological tools and solutions where appropriate. This is where old legal problems can be approached in new ways by working out which tasks are repetitive or time-intensive, which require express legal knowledge, and which are most important to the client. A digital lawyer embraces lifelong and continual learning, which is absolutely necessary in today's fast-paced world to develop a new and improved understanding of the benefits and limitations of particular technologies and an appreciation for a digitally networked environment.

TECHNOLOGY, INNOVATION, AND REGULATION

In this book, we have offered an introduction to the foundations of modern computing technology in Chapter 3. In subsequent chapters we have illustrated the role of networks, Big Data, analytics, machine learning, and artificial intelligence (AI), as well as emerging distributed ledger applications on blockchain technology (Chapters 6, 7, 8 and 10). Each of these technologies presents significant, even transformative opportunities to clients and the lawyers who advise them.

The digital lawyer faces three challenges with respect to technology:

1 *Technology itself.* With many varied branches of practice, technology is complicated, jargon-filled, and apparently arcane and unusable for the average person. New technologies often require new ways of use, compel new ways to relate to technology and, in some cases, present challenges to safety and privacy. A lawyer, bearing an already great cognitive load in meeting the tasks of understanding rules and regulations, drafting documents and navigating the vagaries of human interaction, might find reason to question the utility or relevance of most technology and technology-related learning to the daily practice of law. We hope that we have demonstrated the connections to legal practice and the advantages that can be realised within this textbook.
2 *Rapid innovation.* The change and evolution of technology continue to accelerate, rendering many tools and ways of working increasingly dated, if not obsolete. Significant shocks such as the COVID-19 pandemic forced many to accept and apply many technologies long avoided by the legal profession, such as video conferencing and other remote working technologies, with astonishing rapidity. Before the pandemic, the attitude was one of "wait and see", if not of deep reservation or outright rejection. Continued acceleration of change is an inescapable reality against which we have offered the reader some techniques for understanding and formulating personal and professional strategies.
3 *Regulation.* New technologies and new applications bring new uses. As we have seen with distributed ledger applications using blockchain, such as cryptocurrencies, non-fungible tokens, and smart contracts, new applications raise many questions in real life. The legality of certain transactions, the concrete conception of smart contracts under the law, their enforceability, and the validity of exchange conducted with them are all questions we have examined. We have highlighted areas of development in the law as well as resources for understanding. We encourage a form of legal agility akin to agile technology practice, in which collaborating teams observe systems in

action and adjust their tactics in an iterative fashion, based on experimentation and interpretation of new information.

Staying abreast of technological developments need not mean abandoning the lawyer's calling for one of a technologist or data scientist, but rather following developments with healthy curiosity, basing one's views on emerging evidence as the technology is adopted and used in real-world applications. It means engaging and relying on the help of technology specialists to understand the opportunities and risks, all the while asking hard questions in the interest of the client or of one's own practice. As with all lawyerly pursuits, good relationships and open, mutually respectful dialogue in pursuit of facts and acceptable options will serve one well in learning and problem-solving.

While technologies can support trust, they cannot necessarily prevent breaches of privacy in highly complex modern systems, regardless of the care put into their engineering and implementation. This reality exists because such systems are built by humans with limitations, often labouring under conditions where scope, schedule, and budget are traded off in a sometimes ill-informed calculus of economic viability. Operating with technology will always involve three forces, each in a state of tension and yet complementary to the others: Innovation, risk management, and continuous improvement. It is said that lawyers are trained first and foremost in risk management, but that they do better when they also support innovators by questioning and examining shortcomings in improvement activities, even as they serve as a line of defence in risk management.

The legal profession has until recently been slow to adopt technologies, though it has at times appeared keen, rightly or wrongly, to call itself the "legal industry" despite (in a sweeping generalisation) casting itself in many settings as an individual craft, holding up the superiority and excellence of the individual legal mind over "mere machines" in sometimes self-limiting expressions of legal professional exceptionalism. While we do not debate the merits of this sentiment here, we can highlight the opportunity for lawyers to take advantage of emerging technologies that they learn about and trust to gain advantage in their daily practice: To use technology as a force multiplier for the excellence of the legal mind.

Technology can now reduce the time spent on background research and identify relevant material more accurately and more thoroughly than large teams of lawyers. This fact is cited in a negative, backward-looking manner when viewing technology as a threat to the profession, stoking fears that "AI will destroy the legal profession" and turn it into a dystopian manifestation of the "legal industry". We assert that both positive and negative aspects of emergent outcomes in the struggle for change are in the hands of energetic, informed members of the profession, theirs to shape with care, informed deliberation and a spirit of humility.

The empowered digital lawyer will see technology allowing all those lawyers previously fated to toiling on research free to spend more time thinking more deeply about the problems they are trying to solve on behalf of their clients. As clients look to manage their legal expenses more closely in the context of the hourly billing model, technology could be viewed to support more, not less, value delivered to the client per billable hour. Viewed as a tool, even a partner, technology and technologists working side by side with digital lawyers have many opportunities to remake the profession and professional practice into forms that better serve society, clients and lawyers.

ETHICS AND CONDUCT

Ethics goes to the very heart of what it means to be a lawyer. Legal ethics cover a range of matters such as confidentiality, upholding the rule of law, competence, acting with integrity, acting in the best interests of clients, and professional judgment. Lawyers are regulated by the relevant codes in their jurisdiction, and they must be committed to acting ethically based on those particular standards and requirements.

Lawyers will face difficult situations and dilemmas in their professional lives, and ethical principles help lawyers know how to respond when they have these challenges. Lawyers owe their clients ethical obligations and can be brought to account by their regulatory body if they do not meet those responsibilities.

Lawyers have a fundamental duty to deliver legal services competently and need to have the required legal knowledge and skills to discharge this duty. As discussed in Chapter 11, in 2012, the American Bar Association introduced the ethical duty of "technological competence" to Model Rule 1.1, which states that for lawyers to effectively represent their clients, they have a responsibility to be competent in technology.[1] Lawyers have a professional responsibility to be familiar with and understand the workings

1 ABA, 'Comment to the Model Rules of Professional Conduct' <https://www.americanbar.org/groups/professional_responsibility/publications/model_rules_of_professional_conduct/rule_1_1_competence/comment_on_rule_1_1.html.> accessed 20 August 2025.

of technology. Although there is no equivalent standard set out in the SRA Code of Conduct for Solicitors in England and Wales, you could argue that technological competence falls within Rule 3.3, which provides that lawyers must keep their knowledge and skills up to date.[2]

There is a difference between being confident using technology and understanding how technology is deployed within legal practice. It is not sufficient for lawyers to be comfortable using applications such as PowerPoint and Microsoft Teams. All lawyers, irrespective of their jurisdictions, need to ensure that as new technologies emerge, they have the knowledge and skills to understand the implications for their practice. Lawyers are not required to be technology experts, but they have a responsibility to ensure as part of their continuing professional development that they have the requisite knowledge to understand the impact technology is having on the practice of law.

In this textbook we have discussed the professional workings of lawyers and the ways that technological competence is required across all areas of practice. Chapter 7 identified myriad ethical issues that arise out of the use of AI, from data privacy and bias to automated decision-making. AI will continue to raise new and challenging legal and ethical questions, and lawyers will need to know how to navigate these as technology advances. It is not yet clear how the law will evolve and respond to these questions, and it is likely to be different across jurisdictions. Lawyers must be prepared to raise and discuss the ethical dimensions of technology innovation.

The consequences of the lack of physical and geographical borders were highlighted in Chapter 8 in the discussion on policing in a digital age. Lawyers are already involved in, and advising across, jurisdictional borders. With increasing connectivity, law firms will want to take further advantage of global developments and leverage the benefits from globalisation. Lawyers will be required to understand legal and ethical issues from a global perspective. Technology and globalisation will have a significant impact on the way in which law students of the future practise law.

In Chapter 9 we discussed how technology is changing the way in which courts resolve legal disputes. The increased adoption of online dispute resolution (ODR) systems means that we must consider the ethical principles that should underpin the design and implementation

2 Solicitors Regulation Authority, 'SRA Code of Conduct for Solicitors, RELs, RFLs and RSLs' <https://www.sra.org.uk/solicitors/standards-regulations/code-conduct-solicitors/> accessed 20 August 2025.

of ODR. The National Center for Technology and Dispute Resolution developed a framework that outlines the ethical principles that should be adopted for ODR.[3] As jurisdictions around the world explore the increased use of technology within different forms of dispute resolution, it is increasingly incumbent on lawyers and law students to be aware of the ethical challenges that arise within the field of ODR. Chapters 4, 9, and 11 highlighted the issue of digital exclusion and marginalisation of vulnerable parts of our society; we have to ensure that those with less access and power are still able to exercise their legal rights, and that requires paying particular attention to ethics in developing ODR systems.

In Chapter 5 we discussed ethics and social media. There are important ethical issues for lawyers in their personal and professional use of social media. Lawyers are required to understand social media and how social media platforms work so they can competently advise their clients. The content from social media sites is now a feature of legal proceedings, and lawyers need to be able to advise their clients on their social media presence. The rules on spoliation and preservation of evidence will be different across jurisdictions, but wherever you practise law, you need to understand how social media evidence can be used in legal proceedings. Beyond the ethical issues that are raised with social media in legal matters, there are also professional competence issues, such as how a lawyer maintains their own social media presence. Law students must also be aware of the risks and consider very carefully how they conduct themselves on social media. There are high standards of conduct that apply to lawyers, so it is essential that the duty to act professionally permeates all social media activity to ensure that professional conduct rules are not breached.

As technology further impacts on the practice of law, lawyers will need to leverage a new digital lawyering skill set which will include developing new ethical and professional competencies to respond to a disrupted legal environment.

CHALLENGES AND CRITIQUES

Each of the chapters within this textbook has highlighted the potential of existing and future technological developments, and the role of digital lawyering. However, we have also been careful to emphasise

3 National Center for Technology and Dispute Resolution, 'Ethical Principles for ODR Initiative' (2016) <https://odr.info/ethics-and-odr/> accessed 20 August 2025.

the challenges and critiques involved in such changes and shifts. It is important to take a balanced approach when assessing the benefits and challenges of digital technology within the legal profession and not seek to view it as a form of panacea or assume that its impact will be wholly positive.

At the most basic level, there is the impact of individual perceptions and preferences. As human beings, we have to learn to adapt to new digital technologies and the new ways of living, working and even being that they bring. We may feel unwilling, unable or reluctant to embrace such change. For example, a partner or principal in a law firm may be reluctant to invest in new technology because they feel "things are fine as they are". There are also some fears around the consequences of incorporating technology, which can lead to suspicion and resistance. These are understandable when it is acknowledged that, for some sectors of the legal profession, there may be negative consequences for individuals. For example, the adoption of AI is likely to bring a reduction in the need for paralegals for routine tasks which can be automated. This can lead to people feeling that their income and job security is under threat.

There is also a need for lawyers to understand clients' wants and expectations. For example, you may be used to communicating with people via emails and assume that clients are also happy with this means of communication. However, a client may prefer a telephone call or even a letter. There may be a sense of mistrust from some clients if processes they expect to be done "in person" are instead automated. Conversely, some clients may expect a high level of technological input and may struggle to see the value that can sometimes be added by a "human touch" in legal practice.

There is also the possibility of human error impacting on the adoption and use of digital technologies. This could involve practical issues around lack of digital literacy, digital poverty and digital exclusion. It can also be related to a plethora of ethical issues where inappropriate conduct and poor decision-making impact on clients and colleagues and have possible repercussions for the career and reputation of the individual involved. The examples given in Chapter 5 relating to social media demonstrate the challenges involved in applying professional codes of conduct and ethical standards to new issues raised by digital technologies. The blurring of lines between personal and professional lives is also highlighted by this.

The affordances of digital technology can also lead to challenges. The process of legal design should uncover these, and lead to potential solutions, at an early stage. However, this process itself can take considerable resources in terms of expertise, time, and finance. It often requires interdisciplinary work with expert input from a range of professionals and involves an iterative process of testing and refining. It may be that some emerging digital technologies are not yet well enough developed to meet the needs of the legal profession. The stringent regulatory requirements in most, if not all, jurisdictions may mean that lawyers may not always be able to act as early adopters of innovative new technologies. There is also the potential for errors and biases (e.g. an algorithm which is inaccurate in its predictions). This requires the individual(s) using the technology to have the knowledge and understanding to be able to assess the affordances of technology and adapt their working practices accordingly.

The use of information generated and processed via digital technologies also raises significant issues which need to be considered. In an era of Big Data, questions over how to securely and appropriately collect, store, and destroy data have become increasingly important. The need to comply with data protection regulations and be able to advise clients upon the implications of these are now important parts of legal practice. The balance that often needs to be struck with privacy issues also raises ethical issues and adds complexity to the way information is handled.

There are also broader challenges relating to the wider role of the legal profession in society. Questions such as how we can utilise digital technologies to promote access to justice are key. ODR and legal advice and assistance provided without the input of lawyers can all promote better access. However, this is not always the case. As previously discussed, issues such as digital poverty and a lack of digital literacy can exacerbate barriers to access, potentially for those groups who need it most. This raises vital questions about how we can best use technology to promote values which are crucial to the rule of law and the flourishing of society.

SKILLS AND OPPORTUNITIES

Although Chapter 11 focused specifically on digital skills, in fact the importance of understanding and developing the appropriate skills for digital lawyering have been emphasised in several chapters. We have highlighted some of these skills which digital lawyers will be expected to use within legal practice and which you can also begin to develop as a law student and whilst reading this textbook. Although these can involve technical know-how, many are much broader in scope, such as creativity and the ability to communicate clearly with clients via a range of mediums. As digital technology becomes more prevalent in legal practice, there has also been a move towards lawyers demonstrating increasing soft skills to ensure that the client care they provide is individualised and involves building rapport and empathy in ways which (as yet!) cannot be emulated by AI or other machine learning.

This textbook has noted the general issues around digital literacy within wider society. Although such literacy levels have been increasing, it has been emphasised that there are areas of digital poverty and problems with digital exclusion. It cannot be assumed that law students themselves have all the digital skills that may be required within legal practice (perhaps you noticed this in the skills audit within Chapter 4). There are a range of digital skills frameworks which can be used to identify and assess relevant skills, but these are not specific to law. Even within the legal profession, the type and extent of digital skills required have not always been fully acknowledged or understood. Different jurisdictions demonstrate different levels of engagement with digital lawyering skills. The extent to which such skills are embedded within skills and competency frameworks also varies.

It should also be acknowledged that different digital skills will be required within different legal roles. Although the contemporary lawyer, however "traditional", will require some level of digital literacy, this may be very different from those skills required by those who work within digital lawyering, or those who are involved in the types of new legal roles referred to in Chapter 12. As such skills become increasingly specialised, this raises interesting questions around whether and to what extent they can be fostered within legal education and training.

These changes in "legal skills" will also impact more widely upon notions of professional identity and professionalism within law. People's perception of themselves as digital lawyers may challenge existing notions of what makes a good or successful lawyer. This may alter or adapt the influences which currently shape ideas of lawyering both within the legal profession and more widely within society and popular culture. This may in turn impact on the aspirations and perceptions of law students and other aspiring entrants into the legal profession.

At the heart of these changes and developments around skills is an understanding that digital technology offers great opportunities and potential for the legal profession. Despite the challenges and critiques presented here, the transformative potential of digital lawyering should not be overlooked. In fact, aspects of the legal profession and lawyering have already been transformed. Examples within this textbook range from the use of smart contracts in conveyancing and other fields to the ways in which law firms have transformed in terms of communications, staff, strategy, and working methods. The COVID-19 pandemic has illustrated the capabilities of technology to transform many aspects of law and the workplace. Although for many this increased reliance on digital technology was from necessity rather than choice, it has demonstrated its potential in a way which is continuing to shape the legal profession's future.

OUR VISION FOR 30 YEARS IN THE FUTURE

In this section, each author sets out their vision of the future of digital lawyering, drawing on the themes previously discussed within this chapter and the content of their individual chapters.

DIGITAL LAWYERING AND THE LEGAL PROFESSION (ANN THANARAJ)

In 30 years, the profession will be unrecognisable. From the manner of operating to the roles and responsibilities of practising lawyers, I believe that everything we do as lawyers in the very near future will be creative, with a move away from a heavily laden knowledge sector with highly specialised skill sets to an industry that operates a service model based on creativity in problem-solving for clients. Much of the work paralegals and junior lawyers do will be automated. Hybrid careers in legaltech and in other professional business sectors will emerge. Creativity will be in the art and craft of the legal professional and digital lawyer.

More interdisciplinarily qualified lawyers will exist. The world faces a host of wicked and grand challenges that cannot be addressed by any one discipline in isolation. This is a powerful beginning in my reimagination of the future of the legal profession: To survive and thrive in a disruptive yet opportune world. This is also where creativity integrates with how the legal services industry will evolve and thrive.

There will be much more automation with technologies such as different aspects of AI (for example, natural language processing, chatbots, and sophisticated knowledge database search engines) tailored to niche areas of problems with legal and practical solutions. These will help clients find answers to their questions. The ability to research and understand one's route to a legal claim and compensation can be automated reasonably easily with high levels of accuracy as AI technology develops, which is trained with data sets to recognise patterns and draw from its machine learning and predictability functionalities about things such as family law, traffic tickets, and contracts. Outsourced companies are building affordable legal solutions using technology to do this at a fraction of the cost, including niche areas such as contracts drafting. Opinion writing (providing legal advice on an issue) can be made much easier through predictions technology and automatic research databases.

Litigation will continue, but it will be about handling certain large, high-stakes cases which will require interdisciplinary knowledge, legal knowledge, and skills of persuasion and asking different questions with alternative solutions to problem-solving across a variety of domains. Perhaps the role of a lawyer will change to one that has specialist and niche expertise to advise on unique and complex matters in creative ways requiring high-end specialisms that technology cannot automate. The ability to advise in this way may require experience and knowledge of working in other industries, acquiring grounding in understanding the practice of that discipline to bring expert knowledge which can be integrated with law. For example, advising on a criminal matter may require experience of previous work in digital forensics or IT security to demonstrate an understanding of new and emerging threats in the digital world and an appreciation of the application of law on people from other dimensions. Ethics and digital technologies will play a fundamental role in the work lawyers do. All areas of the law will be involved in dimensions of the digital world, and there will be a need to seamlessly transfer legal knowledge and acumen between problem-solving for the physical and digital worlds. As new technology is rolled out, litigation around those technologies and its impact on the digital and physical worlds will be on the rise.

Lawyers will also develop and improve the legal processes to regulate technologies and other innovations, to adapt to changes in technologies and interpretation of the law. They will also be fine-tuning the data sets that are used by algorithms in producing outcomes for and solutions to problems, so that AI can support the less complex work that can be easily automated and does not require human intervention or special consideration.

More hybrid careers will exist. Legal services will be delivered alongside other professional services that offer multidisciplinary business advice. They will be delivered by those qualified as lawyers and by those qualified in a variety of service industries, such as in banking and accountancy. Professional services, particularly those with a global footprint putting legaltech at the forefront of their offering, will be leading the way in how the delivery of legal services will operate. Agility and seamless and integrated automated services will be in high demand at low cost. Therefore, more packaged business services with streamlined processes that do not require a specialist skill set will be on the rise.

Creativity will be at the heart of a thriving legal profession. Creativity is occasionally misunderstood. It is the ability to demonstrate an approach or methodology in a unique and new way, thereby solving problems differently. The knowledge of law needs to be coupled with other disciplines such as science, ethics, humanities, and philosophy, applied in a new way within the context of solving legal problems, taking an exploratory approach that extends beyond devising clever legal arguments to think about what alternatives might exist for solving their problems, bringing changes to the way the law operates in contexts that require innovating and regulations. Creativity becomes an indispensable trait, and one that is not capable of automation.

THE EFFECTS OF TECHNOLOGY DEVELOPMENT AND INNOVATION (TERRY WONG)

In the coming decades, we can expect to see continued acceleration in the development of technology, with a greater focus on its application to augment human experience and performance. Increasingly, technology will be seen as a set of indispensable tools. In nearly all aspects of daily life, including legal practice, the condition in which digital technology is interwoven with everyday practice has already lost its novelty. Perhaps counterintuitively, improved technology will become less visible, as human–computer interfaces become more capable and more fluid, achieving a sought-after state in interface design parlance known as ambience.

Ambient interfaces are so functional and so fitted to their use that they cease to be novel and assertive in their presence, receding into the background and supporting their delivery of function in as fluid and intuitive a manner as possible. Put in other terms, “they get out of the way”. While we do not care to speculate as to the exact nature and manifestation of these developments, we can say that some continue to believe that natural language interactions with spoken word and text-chat interfaces will become more the primary mode of everyday interaction with computing technology.

Blockchain and cryptocurrencies around the world and in space

In the coming years, we will surely see case law, if not legislation, adjudicated or enacted to settle significant questions of law regarding the validity and execution of smart contracts, as well as clarifications of their role as the memorial of agreement or even active arbiter in resolving disputes. We can look for the clarification of the limits of recourse in case of dispute, or codification of the process of finding by the parties or a competent authority that they are in some way deficient or defective.

We will also see the consolidation of cryptocurrencies, with dominant solutions or emerging leaders and subsequent consolidation in the market. Governments will enact policy, clarify regulatory positions and set limits on the use of various cryptocurrencies and related technologies such as tokens. Some have banned mining, handling or using cryptocurrencies within their borders, creating significant challenges for compliance or enforcement in some cases. What effects these bans will have on the overall use of cryptocurrencies worldwide remains to be seen.

Legal clarification, mainstream adoption of technologies, and trust will also fuel another movement in technology. This will be a culmination of trends in trust, encryption technologies, and hardware evolution: the continued decentralisation—one may go as far as to say atomisation—of applications. This atomisation will be enabled by and rely upon the dispersal of computing power through the internet away from central servers to devices "at the edge"—in other words, to webs of devices that include not only mobile phones and personal computing devices, but also devices such as cameras and household smart devices (such as locks, alarms, and thermostats). Such applications will continue to build on the foundations of technology we have discussed in this textbook, enabling uses and opening opportunities yet unforeseen.

Quantum computing and huge data

Advances in quantum computing, a computing technology harnessing the properties of nature at the scale of atomic particles, may lead to a possible breaking of encryption algorithms which much of the current internet relies upon for security and authentication. This will represent a crisis moment not only for technology and technologists but for society as a whole, if a range of new algorithms and methods are not developed and proven successful ahead of such an event.

Data continues to grow at exponential rates. The emergence of Big Data sets enabled astonishing advances and the realisation of previously inaccessible predictive capabilities. Recent years have begun to show that the frontiers of technology problem-solving lie not where there is a dearth of data, but where there are poor methods. Indeed, if data sets and data generation trends continue, Big Data will certainly become Huge Data. The current crisis in methods and training in the disciplines of data management, data science, machine learning, and AI will likely continue, if not continue to compound. While the legal issues may remain the same, the focus on training and growing talent to serve the demand for data and data-dependent applications in industry will continue—if not greatly increase—the demand for lawyers able to navigate the issues for technology and technology management, with a savvy approach to creating options for their clients and their collaborators and service providers.

Laws in space

As we see the resurgence of space flight, its commercialisation and the establishment of a more permanent human presence in low Earth orbit and beyond, issues of jurisdiction and applicable law will be raised among the new pioneers in space. As settlements beyond the Earth's gravity eventually take root and develop, difficult questions of governance, independence and changes in legal tradition will likely arise. Enormous distances preventing real-time communications will require new protocols for the observance of proper legal forms, or perhaps they will require society to return to wisdom, courtesies and even protocols left behind with the inventions of the telegraph and telephone.

For now, even simple practical questions of law will arise, with the paths to resolution unclear. For instance, there has already been a report of a crime alleged to have been committed in space aboard the International Space Station. Science fiction literature has many rich speculations for the future of life in space, with varying suggestions with respect to the law. As always, in periods of great change, the genre provides ways to define, debate, and understand the issues that emerge. It is likely that some readers of this text, enjoying now the contemplation of that future, will in time become involved as leaders in the lawyering that will be critically needed.

DISPUTE RESOLUTION AND ETHICS (FRANCINE RYAN)

Dispute resolution

Over the next 30 years we are going to see exponential growth in ODR, but we are also going to see how technology can be used for conflict prevention. Court systems are expensive, slow and difficult for self-represented litigants to navigate. New technologies have the potential to help people resolve their problems before they escalate into a legal dispute. ODR is already firmly embedded within the private sector and resolves millions of disputes online with minimal human interaction. These platforms have demonstrated how technologies can be leveraged to provide quick and efficient resolution of disputes, and AI will accelerate these processes further. There are already examples of ODR being used in court services, but over the next decade ODR is going to become an integral part of the court system. The expansion of ODR will also include the expansion of online courts., The pandemic accelerated the use of online hearings: It allowed the courts to keep functioning when court buildings were closed. It also shifted attitudes towards technology and has provided opportunities for research into the strengths and weaknesses of technologically assisted justice. It will also afford opportunities to build that learning into the future direction of dispute resolution. If we envision the future, technology will have transformed the court system. Disputes will be categorised in relation to complexity and value and allocated accordingly to an online process. Some of those processes are likely to be fully automated where all the interaction with the court is digitalised. ODR is currently considered particularly suitable for low-value claims where automation can support users to navigate the process, including systems to draft court documents and where decisions can be made through a form of online judging. If the predictions about ODR are right, ODR will be expanded to resolve higher-value claims. With the development of AI, there is further scope for the expansion of ODR, and there is potential for a global platform that can be enabled for different jurisdictions.

Lawyers are already working online, but we need to ensure that we are equipping our future lawyers with the right skills and competencies to succeed in new forms of legal practice. By 2051 our court systems will be unrecognisable, and new technologies will displace current ways of working and replace them in ways we cannot yet imagine. At The Open University we are developing a virtual reality courtroom, and there are other similar projects around the world that are harnessing the benefits of virtual reality to train future lawyers, but there is potential for the use of virtual reality in court proceedings. The future of dispute resolution will be radically different to our current traditional court system, but there needs to be careful consideration of how we create a system that is fair, efficient and accessible to all. Technology innovation must ensure access to justice and strengthen the rule of law.

Ethics

Ethics is an integral part of being a lawyer, but as technology evolves, lawyers must have an ethical tech mindset. Lawyers need to have a robust understanding of the potential ethical issues that arise with the use of technology and will need to be able to design systems and policies to be able to respond. Over the next 30 years we will see a rapid rate of technology innovation, particularly with AI, which will give rise to greater ethical challenges, and lawyers and law firms will need to think carefully about the development and utilisation of technology. Technology has consequences, some of which have been explored in this textbook and some that are only starting to emerge. Lawyers have responsibilities around decisions that are made about the use of technology and will need to have the required skills and competencies to scrutinise and challenge decisions to ensure they are ethically grounded.

Technology is permeating all aspects of law and the practice of law. Lawyers are required to advise clients on the ethical challenges that arise from the development of machine learning and the algorithms that underpin these systems. There are significant issues in the development of AI in how to respond to the challenges of minimising bias. It is likely that those who design and develop new technologies are going to be responsible for the legal and ethical issues that might arise. There are myriad ethical issues that relate to emerging technologies such as privacy, trust, values, rights, and risk, all of which will underpin their future development and use. The regulatory and legal landscape is going to change, and lawyers are going to require a sufficient grounding in technology to effectively advise their clients.

In addition to advising clients, technology is having an impact on the future of employment. Automation is impacting on the delivery of legal services, and over the next 30 years the future work opportunities for lawyers will change. AI is already being used in legal practice, legal research, document management, predictive analytics, e-discovery, and contract and litigation management. The traditional work done by lawyers is changing; lawyers will still have important roles to play, but it will evolve. This will have an impact on the composition and economics of legal practice. Law firms are going to face ethical challenges about the meaning of legal work and around the place of work. Cybersecurity is a significant concern for law firms, requiring robust policies around data access and security. As more and more work is conducted online, new threats from attackers will emerge, and lawyers will face increasing obligations and responsibilities to ensure they protect the data of their clients.

Over the next 30 years we will see the emergence of new types of legal service delivery, increased use of technology and AI leading to ethical challenges. It is therefore essential that ethical obligations are not overlooked and that ethical integrity remains a core attribute of a lawyer and a digital lawyer.

LEGAL EDUCATION AND SKILLS (EMMA JONES)

Legal education

The law student of the future is likely to face changes in content and delivery, both significantly influenced by the continued development of digital technology. In terms of content, it is inevitable that digital lawyering and law and technology will increasingly become mainstream parts of the curriculum. They will move from being often regarded as "extras" into integrated parts of teaching and learning throughout a law degree. If such degrees remain largely broken down into courses or modules, the likelihood is digital technology will be acknowledged within each and every subject, from smart contracts in the law of obligations to data protection and privacy in human rights law.

However, it may well be that more law schools begin to move away from the current form of the modularised system. Instead, there is likely to be a shift towards approaches which avoid rigidly separating out different legal subjects and instead integrate them into an overall approach. For example, the University of York (UK) takes a problem-based learning approach, where students' study is based around a series of problem scenarios, each of which incorporates a range of different legal topics and areas.[4] The range of topics covered within digital law-

4 University of York, 'Problem Based Learning: York Law School' (2025) <https://www.york.ac.uk/teaching-innovation/case-studies/problem-based/> accessed 20 August 2025.

yering suggests endless possibilities for adopting this type of approach. This could involve not only combining a range of legal topics but also working with staff and students from other disciplines.

Digital lawyering is an interdisciplinary topic involving insights from technology, business, sociology, and other subjects. This could well involve students from, for example, computing, marketing and communications, sociology, and law all working together on long-term problems and projects. Such a process has already started within some law schools, particularly within law clinics (see Chapter 13). However, in 30 years it is likely to have become far more deeply embedded across law schools and jurisdictions as a central part of a law degree.

Of course, there will be barriers and challenges in adopting this type of approach. For example, staff may feel more comfortable and well-equipped to deliver "traditional" forms of law teaching. Law schools and universities more widely may find difficulties arise in finding the resources (including finance and time) to facilitate the transition to a different mode of delivery (not to mention the paperwork involved!). It may well be that law schools which adopt this approach decide to use these in their marketing strategies as a unique selling point to encourage students to join them. This in turn will promote the profile of digital lawyering even further.

In terms of delivery of teaching and learning, there likely will also be an increasing reliance on technology. Forms of blended learning, combining online and face-to-face learning, are already becoming more common. For example, traditional lectures are now often being converted into a series of shorter online videos which are easily accessible to students. This then frees up face-to-face teaching time to focus upon interactive activities and group work. Thinking ahead, it is possible that there will be classes run in virtual worlds, such as the Metaverse, which combine elements of in-person and online engagement.[5]

The advent of Generative AI has already seen debates around how law schools should assess students, with a particular emphasis on issues of academic misconduct and plagiarism. Some law schools may choose to significantly alter their assessment methods, for example, by reverting to in-person "closed-book" examinations, or instead conducting individual oral "vivas" on topics. Some courses may choose to incorporate AI into assessment formats, e.g. asking students to critique an AI output.

5 <https://www.meta.com/en-gb/metaverse/>

So far, this vision of legal education has focused upon law schools. However, legal education is far broader than just the law degree. It encompasses teaching and learning law in schools and colleges, vocational training for the legal profession, and continuing professional development for practitioners. Each of these is also likely to change to embrace digital technology. For example, schools and colleges may begin to teach students about the law and citizenship using examples drawn from digital technology (such as the use of social media, discussed in Chapter 5). Bespoke courses may be developed by vocational training providers for specific roles within the legal profession, such as legal engineers and legal project managers (see Chapter 12). It may also be that large tech companies begin to partner with education providers to create their own colleges and universities.

Skills

The importance of developing and adapting skills is likely to increase, rather than decrease, over the next 30 years. Competition for jobs and increases in precarious models of employment (such as fixed-term or zero-hour contracts) mean that individuals must focus on enhancing their employability skills as much as possible. Although there remains a digital divide and areas of digital poverty (see Chapter 4), there will increasingly be an expectation that individuals within any role (legal or non-legal) have at least a basic level of digital literacy. For example, a receptionist at a law firm is likely to use a computer system to organise room bookings and schedule meetings.

As new models of lawyering emerge, law firms and other employers will want to recruit people who can show they understand the importance of a broad skill set. Skills that are currently seen as "soft skills" or "non-legal skills" will increasingly become a part of accepted skills and competencies frameworks within legal roles; for example, being creative, innovative, and entrepreneurial in approaches to problem-solving. This will impact on the notion of professionalism and ideas of what being a legal professional involves. The cartoon stereotypes of lawyers in 30 years may well replace the individual in a suit at a desk surrounded by shelves of law books with someone who has digital devices stashed all over their person working at a "hot desk", with a technologist sitting next door.

TAKING DIGITAL LAWYERING INTO THE FUTURE

If you are reading this textbook, it is quite possible that you will be a part of the future of digital lawyering. In fact, as someone studying the topic, you are already contributing to the shaping of its future development. We hope that this textbook also empowers you to continue to do so in future. It is impossible to predict all the new developments that will arise, both in digital technology and in legal practice, or to say with 100% certainty where emerging fields of interest will lead. However, that is one of the appeals of digital lawyering: It is about engaging with and contributing to dynamic, innovative and creative solutions to key problems, and issues within society and the workplace. As authors, we sincerely hope that you continue your digital lawyering journey, whether as a practitioner, a researcher, or an interested observer. In doing so, you will be a part of a vibrant, exciting, and impactful community with a shared passion for digital lawyering. Whether considering your local town, your wider jurisdiction or even space, digital technology and law are intertwined and increasingly pervasive.

REFERENCES LIST

A&O Shearman, 'Fuse' (2020) <https://www.aoshearman.com/en/expertise/fuse> accessed 13 August 2025.

'ABA Comment to the Model Rules of Professional Conduct' <http://www.americanbar.org/groups/professional_responsibility/publications/model_rules_of_professional_conduct/rule_1_1_competence/comment_on_rule_1_1.html> accessed 20 August 2025.

ABA Commission on Ethics, '20/20 Introduction and Overview' <https://www.americanbar.org/content/dam/aba/administrative/ethics_2020/20120508_ethics_20_20_final_hod_introdution_and_overview_report.pdf> accessed 20 August 2025.

Abdeen M and others, 'Automatic Generation of Mind Maps from Text with M2Gen' (2009) *Science and Technology for Humanity* (TIC-STH) 95.

Acosta D, 'The Lawyer's Dilemma: Challenges for Law Firms Adopting Legal Tech' (*Legal Technologist*, September 2020) <https://www.legaltechnologist.co.uk/TheLegalTechnologistSept20.pdf> accessed 13 August 2025.

Addleshaw Goddard, 'Rev Up Your Legal Career with an Innovation and Legal Technology Seat: Accelerate Your Future' (22 June 2023) <https://www.addleshawgoddard.com/en/insights/insights-briefings/tech-talks/what-is-a-lawyer/> accessed 13 August 2023.

Allen LE, 'Symbolic Logic: A Razor-Edged Tool for Drafting and Interpreting Legal Documents' (1957) 66(6) *Yale Law Journal* <https://doi.org/10.2307/794073> accessed 1 January 2026.

'Alternative Legal Service Providers: Understanding the Growth and Benefits of These New Legal Providers' (2017) <https://static.legalsolutions.thomsonreuters.com/static/pdf/Alternative-Legal-Service-Providers_Long.pdf> accessed 13 October 2018.

American Bar Association, 'Comment to the Model Rules of Professional Conduct' <https://www.americanbar.org/groups/professional_responsibility/publications/model_rules_of_professional_conduct/rule_

1_1_competence/comment_on_rule_1_1.html> accessed 20 August 2025.

American Bar Association, 'Model Rules of Professional Conduct' <https://www.americanbar.org/groups/professional_responsibility/publications/model_rules_of_professional_conduct/rule_1_1_competence/comment_on_rule_1_1.html> accessed August 2025.

American Bar Association, 'Standing Committee on Ethics and Professional Responsibility' (Formal Opinion on Generative Artificial Intelligence Tools, 29 July 2024) <https://www.americanbar.org/content/dam/aba/administrative/professional_responsibility/ethics-opinions/aba-formal-opinion-512.pdf> assessed 30 September 2025.

American Bar Association, 'The Future Is Now: Artificial Intelligence and the Legal Profession' (2024) <https://www.ibanet.org/document?id=The-future-is%20now-AI-and-the-legal-profession-report> accessed 30 September 2025.

American Bar Association, '2025–2026 Standards and Rules of Procedure for Approval of Law Schools: Standard 301: Objectives of Program of Legal Education' <https://www.americanbar.org/content/dam/aba/administrative/legal_education_and_admissions_to_the_bar/standards/2025-2026/2025-2026-standards-chapter-3.pdf> accessed 19 August 2025.

Amghar L, 'How Generative AI Is Fueling Social Media Scams' (2023) <https://www.eydle.com/how-generative-ai-is-fueling-social-media-scams/?t>

Amnesty International, 'US: TikTok Ban Won't Solve Big Tech Harms' (17 January 2025) <https://www.amnesty.org/en/latest/news/2025/01/us-tiktok-ban-wont-solve-big-tech-harms/?t> accessed 2 January 2026.

Antwi-Boasiako A and Venter H, 'A Model for Digital Evidence Admissibility Assessment' in Peterson G and Shenoi S (eds) *Advances in Digital Forensics XIII, 511 Digital Forensics* (Springer and IFIP Advances in Information and Communication Technology 2017) <https://doi.org/10.1007/978-3-319-67208-3_2>

AUCyber, LexVeritas & Australasian Legal Practice Management Associations, '2024 State of Cyber Security in Law' (September 2024) <https://www.ft.com/content/4da1117e-756c-11e9-be7d-6d846537acab> accessed 18 October 2019; <https://aucyber.com.au/events/alpma-2024/report/> accessed 13 August 2025.

Australian Digital Inclusion Index, 'Key Findings and Next Steps' (2025) <https://www.digitalinclusionindex.org.au/key-findings-and-next-steps/> accessed 19 August 2025.

Aveni C, 'Alexa, How Private Is My Home?' (*Litigation News*, 2 December 2018) <https://www.cpmlaw.com/alexa-how-private-is-my-home> accessed 30 April 2021.

Backlinko, 'Social Media Usage & Growth Statistics' (19 November 2025) <https://backlinko.com/social-media-users?t> accessed 2 January 2026.

Bar Standards Board, 'Professional Statement for Barristers' <https://www.barstandardsboard.org.uk/uploads/assets/0279b209-dab6-40c9-a554af54994e2566/bsbprofessionalstatementandcompetences2016.pdf> accessed 20 August 2025.

BBC, 'Paris Brown: Kent Youth PCC Resigns after Twitter Row' (*BBC News*, 9 April 2013) <https://www.bbc.co.uk/news/uk-england-22083032> accessed 14 April 2021.

BBC News, 'Lawyer Gets Stuck with Cat Filter during Virtual Court Case' (*BBC News*, 9 February 2021) <https://www.bbc.co.uk/news/av/world-us-canada-56005428> accessed 19 August 2025.

BBC News, 'TikTok Sued for Billions over Use of Children's Data' (*BBC News*, 21 April 2021) <https://www.bbc.com/news/technology-56815480> accessed 29 April 2021

BBC Tech News Reports, 'Fitbit Data Used to Charge US Man with Murder' (*BBC News*, 4 October 2018) <https://www.bbc.co.uk/news/technology-45745366> accessed 3 January 2026.

Belshaw D, *The Essential Elements of Digital Literacies* [PDF] (Self-Published 2014), 11–12 <https://dougbelshaw.com/essential-elements-book.pdf> accessed 4 January 2026.

'Berne Convention Texts at the World Intellectual Property Organization' <https://www.wipo.int/treaties/en/ip/berne/>

Bindman D, 'The Danger of Instant E-mail Replies as SDT Reprimands Solicitor Who Called Opponent "a Plonker"' (20 July 2015) <https://www.legalfutures.co.uk/latest-news/the-danger-of-instant-email-replies-as-sdt-reprimands-solicitor-who-called-opponent-a-plonker> accessed 13 August 2025.

Blakeley V, Easteal P, Fitch E and Kennedy J, 'Social Media Evidence in Family Law: What Can Be Used and Its Probative Value' (2015) 5 *Family Law Review* 81–101.

Booth R, 'High Court Tells Lawyers to Stop Misuse of AI after Fake Case-Law Citations' (*The Guardian*, 6 June 2025) <https://www.theguardian.com/technology/2025/jun/06/high-court-tells-uk-lawyers-to-urgently-stop-misuse-of-ai-in-legal-work> accessed 30 September 2025.

Bowditch K and Williams A, *The Verdict: Social Media in the Legal Sector* (FTI Consulting 2016) <https://www.fticonsulting-emea.

com/~/media/Files/emea--files/insights/reports/legal-sector-social-media.pdf> accessed 14 April 2021.

Bradney A, *Conversations, Choices and Chances the Liberal Law School in the Twenty-First Century* (Hart Publishing 2003).

Brooks S, 'Fostering Wholehearted Lawyers: Practical Guidance for Supporting Law Students' Professional Identity Formation' (2018) 14 *University of St Thomas Law Journal* 412.

Brown CC, 'Professional Identity Formation: Working Backwards to Move the Profession Forward' (2015) 61 *Loyola Law Review* 313, 314.

Butler S and others, 'The Utah Online Dispute Resolution Platform: A Usability Evaluation, and Report' (September 2020) <https://law.arizona.edu/sites/default/files/i4J_Utah_ODR_Report.pdf> accessed 19 April 2021.

Byrom N and others, 'Rapid Review: The Impact of COVID-19 on the Civil Justice System' (2020) <https://www.judiciary.uk/wp-content/uploads/2020/06/FINAL-REPORT-CJC-4-June-2020.v2-accessible.pdf> accessed 4 January 2026.

Cambridge University, 'Helping Police Make Custody Decisions Using Artificial Intelligence' (Cambridge University Research, 26 February) <https://www.cam.ac.uk/research/features/helping-police-make-custody-decisions-using-artificial-intelligence>

Cappellino A, 'The Amazon Echo: Expert Witness in a Murder Trial?' (Expert Institute, 17 February 2021) <https://www.expertinstitute.com/resources/insights/amazon-echo-expert-witness-murder-trial/> accessed 3 January 2026.

'Card Spending Update' (*UK Finance*, June 2025) <https://www.ukfinance.org.uk/system/files/2025-09/Card%20Spending%20Update%20-%20June%202025.pdf> accessed 26 September 2025.

Carnegie Mellon University, 'Carnegie Mellon and Facebook AI Beats Professionals in Six-Player Poker' (Carnegie Mellon University, July 11) <https://www.cmu.edu/news/stories/archives/2019/july/cmu-facebook-ai-beatspoker-pros.html>

Charleton L, Kemp J and Bleasdale L, 'Interview with the 2024 ALT Best Paper in Legal Technology Prize Winners' (2024) 58(4) *The Law Teacher* 626–31.

Charlotin D, 'AI Hallucination Cases' <https://www.damiencharlotin.com/hallucinations/> accessed 30 September 2025.

Citizens Advice, 'Future of Advice: Our Strategic Framework 2019-22' <https://www.citizensadvice.org.uk/about-us/future-of-advice-our-strategic-framework-2019-22/> accessed 26 April 2021.

Civil Resolution Tribunal, 'Annual Report 2019/2020' <https://civilresolutionbc.ca/wp-content/uploads/2020/07/CRT-Annual-Report-2019-2020.pdf> accessed 25 April 2021.

Civin D, "Explainable AI Could Reduce the Impact of Biased Algorithms' (VentureBeat, May 2018) European Commission, White Paper on Artificial Intelligence – A European Approach to Excellence (COM 2020 65).

Clementi D, 'Review of the Regulatory Framework for Legal Services in England and Wales' (December 2004) <https://www.legal-services-review.org.uk/content/report/foreword> accessed 13 August 2025

Clifford A, 'Does the Online Safety Act Violate Privacy over Security Concerns Too Harshly' (2024) <https://www.lancaster.ac.uk/richardson-institute/blogs//does-the-online-safety-act-violate-privacy-too-harshly-over-security-concerns> accessed 6 August 2025.

Cohen MA, 'The Golden Age of The Legal Entrepreneur—Why Now and Why It Matters' (*Forbes*, 1 June 2018) <https://www.forbes.com/sites/markcohen1/2018/06/01/the-golden-age-of-the-legal-entrepreneur-why-now-and-why-it-matters/?sh=5a4496447803> accessed 19 August 2025.

Cohen MA, 'Why Is Law So Slow to Use Data?' (*Forbes*, 24 June 2019) <https://www.forbes.com/sites/markcohen1/2019/06/24/why-is-law-so-slow-to-use-data/> accessed 2 January 2026.

College of Policing, 'Authorised Professional Practice Extraction of Material from Digital Devices' (2021) <https://library.college.police.uk/docs/college-of-policing/APP-the-extraction-of-material-from-digital-devices-2021.pdf> accessed 13 January 2026.

Committee of Public Accounts, *Value for Money from Legal Aid* (NAO Findings on Legal Aid Deserts 2023) <https://publications.parliament.uk/pa/cm5804/cmselect/cmpubacc/481/report.html> accessed 30 September 2025.

Contend Legal <https://www.law.com/legaltechnews/2021/06/10/contend-legal-raises-new-questions-about-ai-and-legal-regulation/> accessed 30 September 2025.

Criddle C, 'Bitcoin Consumes "More Electricity than Argentina"' (*BBC News*, 10 February 2021) <https://www.bbc.com/news/technology-56012952> accessed 4 January 2026.

Crown Prosecution Service, 'Cybercrime—Prosecution Guidance' (2020) <https://www.cps.gov.uk/legal-guidance/cybercrime-prosecution-guidance> accessed 3 January 2026.

Crown Prosecution Service, 'How the CPS Will Use Artificial Intelligence' (*CPS.gov.uk*, 2023). <https://www.cps.gov.uk/how-cps-will-use-artificial-intelligence> accessed 30 September 2025.

Crown Prosecution Service, 'The Criminal Procedure Rules 2020, Part 19, Expert Evidence (updated 09/10/2019)' <https://www.cps.gov.uk/legal-guidance/expert-evidence#:~:text=The%20duty%20of%20an%20expert%20witness%20is%20to%20help%20the,to%20matters%20within%20their%20expertise> accessed 3 January 2026.

'Cryptocurrency Prices, Charts and Market Capitalizations' (*CoinMarketCap*) <https://coinmarketcap.com/> accessed 22 March 2021 and 4 August 2025.

Cueto E, 'Online Court Pilot Gets Low Marks Ahead of Wider Launch' (Law 360, 13 September 2020) <https://www.law360.com/access-to-justice/articles/1309437/online-court-pilot-gets-low-marks-ahead-of-wider-launch?nl_pk=77322a31-1bbc-4e35-8532-8a4ef2d22451&utm_source=newsletter&utm_medium=email&utm_campaign=access-to-justice&read_more=1> accessed 19 April 2021.

Cuckier K and Mayer-Schonberger V, 'The Dictatorship of Data' (*MIT Technology Review*, 31 May 2013) <https://www.technologyreview.com/2013/05/31/178263/the-dictatorship-of-data/> accessed 31 January 2021

Cunningham A and others, 'Disruptive Technologies & Legal Service Provision in the UK: A Preliminary Study' (7 December 2018) <https://ssrn.com/abstract=3297074 or http://dx.doi.org/10.2139/ssrn.3297074> accessed 20 August 2025.

Cuthbertson A, 'Amazon Ordered to Give Alexa Evidence in Double Murder Case' (*Independent*, 18 November 2018) <https://www.independent.co.uk/tech/amazon-echo-alexa-evidence-murder-case-a8633551.html> accessed 20 August 2025.

Data Reportal, 'Digital around the World' (July 2025) <https://datareportal.com/global-digital-overview> accessed 20 August 2025.

Davenport TH and Patil DJ, 'Data Scientist: The Sexiest Job of the 21st Century' (*Harvard Business Review*, 1 October 2012) <https://hbr.org/2012/10/data-scientist-the-sexiest-job-of-the-21st-century> accessed 2 January 2026.

Davis E, 'Mathematics, Word Problems, Common Sense, and Artificial Intelligence' (25 January 2023) <https://arxiv.org/abs/2301.09723> accessed 30 September 2025.

De La Garza E, 'Charges Dropped in Amazon Echo Murder Case' (Courthouse News Service, 29 November 2017) <https://www.courthousenews.com/charges-dropped-in-amazon-echo-murder-case/>

Deloitte, 'Developing Legal Talent: Stepping into the Future Law Firm' (February 2016) <https://www2.deloitte.com/content/dam/

Deloitte/uk/Documents/audit/deloitte-uk-developing-legal-talent-2016.pdf> accessed 12 October 2018.

Deloitte Legal, 'A Changing World Requires a New Approach to Law' (2017) <https://www2.deloitte.com/content/dam/Deloitte/global/Documents/Legal/dttl-legal-deloitte-approach-legal-management-consulting.pdf> accessed 12 October 2018.

Design Your Delta, 'Developing the Delta Model' <https://www.designyourdelta.com/about> accessed 19 August 2025.

Dickens C, *Bleak House* (Bradbury and Evans 1853).

Dickerson A and others, 'The Skills Imperative 2035: An Analysis of the Demand for Skills in the Labour Market in 2035' (National Foundation for Educational Research 2023) <https://www.nfer.ac.uk/media/utwf2grb/the_skills_imperative_2035_working_paper_3_an_analysis_of_the_demand_for_skills_in_the_labour_market_in_2035.pdf> accessed 2 January 2026.

Digital Government, 'Digital Inclusion and Wellbeing in New Zealand' (2025) <https://www.digital.govt.nz/dmsdocument/161~digital-inclusion-and-wellbeing-in-new-zealand/html#executive-summary> accessed 19 August 2025.

DoNotPay, 'The World's First Robot Lawyer' (2023) <https://donotpay.com> accessed 30 September 2025.

Duhigg C, 'How Companies Learn Your Secrets' (*The New York Times Magazine*, 16 February 2012) <https://www.nytimes.com/2012/02/19/magazine/shopping-habits.html> accessed 2 January 2026.

Embry S, 'Gen AI and Law: Perfection Is Not the Point' (*TechLaw Crossroads*, 20 July 2024) <https://www.techlawcrossroads.com/2024/07/gen-ai-and-law-perfection-is-not-the-point/> accessed 30 September 2025.

Enriquez J, 'Your Online Life, Permanent as a Tattoo' (*Ted2013*, February 2013) <https://www.ted.com/talks/juan_enriquez_how_to_think_about_digital_tattoos#t-338590> accessed 3 February 2021.

'European Network of Forensic Science Institute Best Practice Manual for the Forensic Examination of Digital Technology (ENFSI-BPM-FIT-01 2015)' <https://enfsi.eu/wp-content/uploads/2016/09/1._forensic_examination_of_digital_technology_0.pdf> accessed 3 January 2026.

'European Parliament Digital Agenda for Europe' (2008) <https://www.europarl.europa.eu/registre/docs_autres_institutions/commission_europeenne/sec/2008/2629/COM_SEC(2008)2629_EN.pdf; https://ec.europa.eu/digital-single-market/en/europe-2020-strategy>

Federation of Law Societies of Canada, 'Model Code of Professional Conduct as Amended April 2024' <https://flsc.ca/wp-content/uploads/2024/05/2024-Model-Code-of-Professional-Conduct-with-Changes-Marked.pdf?_rt=OHwxfGNvZGUgb2YgY29uZHVjdHwxNzU1Njk1MTA2&_rt_nonce=a6393033b0> accessed 20 August 2025.

Filing Fairness Project <https://filingfairnessproject.law.stanford.edu/#slsnav-history-and-theory-of-change> accessed 23 September 2025.

FisherBroyles, 'Law Firm 2.0®' (2025) <https://fisherbroyles.com/> accessed 13 August 2025.

Forensic Capability Network, 'Digital Forensic Science Strategy' (2020) <https://www.npcc.police.uk/SysSiteAssets/media/downloads/publications/publications-log/2020/national-digital-forensic-science-strategy.pdf>

Forensic Science Regulator, 'His Honour Judge Andrew Goymer, The Importance of Forensic Science to the Courts' (March 2014) <https://www.gov.uk/government/publications/his-honor-judge-andrew-goymer-oral-transcript> accessed 3 January 2026.

Forensic Science Regulator, 'Legal Obligations' (2020) <https://assets.publishing.service.gov.uk/government/uploads/system/uploads/attachment_data/file/882074/FSR_Legal_Obligations_-_Issue_8.pdf> accessed 3 January 2026.

Forensic Science Regulator, 'Newsletter' (2015), 3 <https://assets.publishing.service.gov.uk/government/uploads/system/uploads/attachment_data/file/470526/FSR_Newsletter_26__October_2015.pdf>, accessed 3 January 2026.

Franqueira VN and Horsman G, 'Towards Sound Forensic Arguments: Structured Argumentation Applied to Digital Forensics Practice' (2020) 32 *Forensic Science International Digital Investigation* 300923.

Furlong F, 'Why Law Firms Need R&D Investment' (*L21 Blog*, 2014) <https://www.law21.ca/2014/08/law-firms-need-rd-investment/> accessed 12 October 2018.

Garner v. Kandice, Court of Appeals of Utah <https://caselaw.findlaw.com/court/ut-court-of-appeals/117297291.html> accessed 30 September 2025.

Giancaspro M, 'The Consideration Myth about Smart Contracts' (2020) 1 *ANU Journal of Law and Technology* 11.

Gilster P, *Digital Literacy* (Wiley 1997) 2.

Goleman D, *Emotional Intelligence* (Bloomsbury 1996).

Goodison SE and others, *Digital Evidence, and the US Criminal Justice System. Identifying Technology and Other Needs to More Effectively Acquire and Utilize Digital Evidence. Priority Criminal Justice Needs Initiative* (Rand Corporation 2015).

Grother P, Ngan M and Hanaoka K, 'Face Recognition Vendor Test (FRVT) Part 3: Demographic Effects', *NISTIR 8280* (National Institute of Standards and Technology 2019) <https://doi.org/10.6028/NIST.IR.8280>

Gurin J, *Open Data Now* (McGraw-Hill Education 2014).

Hagan M, 'Design Thinking about Law: A Perfect Match' (Open Law Lab, January 2014) <www.openlawlab.com/2014/01/16/design-thinking-law-perfecr-match>

Hagan M, 'Law by Design' (2014) <http://www.lawbydesign.co/en/legal design/> accessed 5 January 2026.

Hagan M, 'The User Experience of the Internet as a Legal Help Service' (2016) 20 *Virginia Journal of Law & Technology* 394, 465.

Hall W and Pesenti J, *Growing the Artificial Intelligence Industry in the UK* (Department for Digital, Culture, Media and Sport' Department for Business, Energy 2017) <https://www.gov.uk/government/publications/growing-the-artificial-intelligence-industry-in-the-uk>

Her Majesty Courts and Tribunal Service and the Good Things Foundation, 'HMCTS Digital Support Service: Implementation Review' (2020) <https://www.goodthingsfoundation.org/sites/default/files/research-publications/digital_support_service_implementation_review_evaluation_report_-_september_2020.pdf> accessed 19 April 2021.

Her Majesty Government, 'Online Harms White Paper' (Gov.uk, April 2019) <https://assets.publishing.service.gov.uk/government/uploads/system/uploads/attachment_data/file/973939/Online_Harms_White_Paper_V2.pdf> accessed 14 April 2021.

HiiL, 'Understanding Justice Needs—The Elephant in the Courtroom, The Hague; Justice for All: The Report of the Task Force on Justice April 2019' (2018) <https://www.hiil.org/wp-content/uploads/2018/11/HiiL-Understanding-Justice-Needs-The-Elephant-in-the-Courtroom.pdf> accessed 30 September 2025.

Hill K, 'Wrongfully Accused by an Algorithm' (*New York Times*, 24 June 2020) <https://www.nytimes.com/2020/06/24/technology/facial-recognition-arrest.html> accessed 2 January 2026.

Hill K, 'How Target Figured Out a Teen Girl Was Pregnant before Her Father Did' (*Forbes*, 16 February 2012) <https://www.forbes.com/sites/kashmirhill/2012/02/16/how-target-figured-out-a-teen-girl-was-pregnant-before-her-father-did/> accessed 2 January 2026.

Home Office, 'Forensic Science Strategy' (2016) <https://assets.publishing.service.gov.uk/government/uploads/system/uploads/attachment_data/file/506683/54493_Cm_9217_Forensic_Science_Strategy_Print_ready.pdf> accessed 3 January 2026.

Horsman G, 'Can We Continue to Effectively Police Digital Crime?' (2017) 57(6) *Science & Justice* 448–54.

Horsman G, 'Raiders of the Lost Artefacts: Championing the Need for Digital Forensics Research' (2019) 1 *Forensic Science International: Reports* 100003.

Horsman G, 'Tool Testing and Reliability Issues in the Field of Digital Forensics' (2019) 28 *Digital Investigation* 163–75.

Horsman G, 'The COLLECTORS Ranking Scale for 'At-scene' Digital Device Triage' (2021) 66(1) *Journal of Forensic Sciences* 179–89.

Horsman G, 'When Is a Line of Inquiry "Reasonable"?—A Focus on Digital Devices' (2023) 55(4) *Australian Journal of Forensic Sciences* 560–71.

Horswill I, 'Polly: A Vision-based Artificial Agent' (1993) *Proceedings of the National Conference on Artificial Intelligence (AAAI)* 824–9.

House Committee on Oversight and Government Reform, 'Law Enforcement's Use of Facial Recognition Technology' (FBI.gov, 2017) <https://www.fbi.gov/news/testimony/law-enforcements-use-of-facial-recognition-technology> accessed 2 January 2026.

House of Commons, Science and Technology and House of Commons Science and Technology Committee, *Robotics and Artificial Intelligence Fifth Report of Session 2016–17* (House of Commons 2016) <https://publications.parliament.uk/pa/cm201617/cmselect/cmsctech/145/145.pdf>

House of Lords Select Committee on Digital Skills, 'Make or Break: The UK's Digital Future (February 2015) Chapter 3.

Huaixiu Z, 'COTA: Improving Uber Customer Care with NLP & Machine Learning' (Uber Engineering, 3 January 2018) <https://eng.uber.com/cota/>

Ibarra H, 'Provisional Selves: Experimenting with Image and Identity in Professional Adaptation' (1999) 44 *Administrative Science Quarterly* 764, 765.

IBM Cloud Education, 'What Is AI' (IBM, 3 June 2020) <https://www.ibm.com/cloud/learn/what-is-artificial-intelligence> accessed 25 April 2021

Information Commissioner's Office, 'Mobile Phone Data Extraction by Police Forces in England and Wales Investigation Report' (2020) <https://ico.org.uk/media2/migrated/2617838/ico-report-on-mpe-in-england-and-wales-v1_1.pdf>Institute for the Future (IFF), *Future Work Skills 2020* (University of Phoenix Research Institute 2011).

Institute for the Future for Dell Technologies, *The Next Era of Human Machine Partnerships* (2017) 14 <https://www.delltechnologies.com/content/dam/delltechnologies/assets/perspectives/2030/pdf/SR1940_IFTFforDellTechnologies_Human-Machine_070517_readerhigh-res.pdf> accessed 3 October 2018.

Institute of Student Employers, 'ISE's Student Development Survey Shows a Widening Gap between Student Education and Employer Skills Needs' (1 May 2024) <https://universitybusiness.co.uk/news/graduate-employability/> accessed 13 August 2025.

International Council for Online Dispute Regulation, 'ICODR Standards' <https://icodr.org/standards/> accessed 18 April 2021.

International Institute of Legal Project Management, '4-Phase LPM Framework' <https://www.iilpm.com/wp-content/uploads/2020/05/IILPM-LPM-Framework-English-Version_2020.png> accessed 19 August 2025.

Italian Institute for International Political Studies, 'The Digital Divide: A Barrier to Social, Economic and Political Equity' (4 April 2025) <https://www.ispionline.it/en/publication/the-digital-divide-a-barrier-to-social-economic-and-political-equity-204564> accessed 20 August 2025.

Ito J and others, 'The Blockchain Will Do to the Financial System What the Internet Did to Media' (*Harvard Business Review*, 2017) <https://hbr.org/2017/03/the-blockchain-will-do-to-banks-and-law-firms-what-the-internet-did-to-media> accessed 4 January 2026.

Jackson, G, Aitken, C and Roberts, P, 'Case Assessment and Interpretation of Expert Evidence: Guidance for Judges, Lawyers, Forensic Scientists and Expert Witnesses' (2015) <https://www.researchgate.net/publication/273698920_Case_Assessment_and_Interpretation_of_Expert_Evidence_Guidance_for_Judges_Lawyers_Forensic_Scientists_and_Expert_Witnesses>.

James C, 'Lawyers' Wellbeing and Professional Legal Education' (2008) 42(1) *The Law Teacher* 85–97.

Jisc, 'Building Digital Capabilities Framework: The Six Elements Defined' (January 2024) <https://repository.jisc.ac.uk/8846/1/2022_Jisc_BDC_Individual_Framework.pdf> accessed 19 August 2025.

Johnson CA and Donnelly B, 'If Only We Knew What We Know' (2013) 88 *Chicago-Kent Law Review* 729, 735.

Johnson T, 'Dish, NBCUniversal Settle AutoHop Ad-Skipping Lawsuit' (*Variety*, 17 June 2016): <https://variety.com/2016/biz/news/dish-nbc-autohop-lawsuit-settled-1201797895/> accessed 1 January 2026.

Jones E, 'Digital Lawyering and the Growing Importance of the Human Touch: Implications for Wellbeing' (October 2019) 7 *The Legal Technologist* 25 <https://www.legaltechnologist.co.uk/TheLegalTechnologistOct19.pdf> accessed 19 August 2025.

Jones E, 'Making Practice More Affective: Emotional Intelligence as a Legal Meta-Competency' (2018) 24(1) *European Journal of Current Legal Issues.*

Jones E and others, *Mental Health and Wellbeing in the Legal Profession* (Bristol UP 2020).

Justia, 'Bail Algorithms' (n.d.) <https://www.justia.com/criminal/bail-bonds/bail-algorithms/> accessed 2 January 2026.

Karol K and Zdonek D, 'Analytics Maturity Models: An Overview' (March 2020) 11 *Information* 142 <https://doi.org/10.3390/info11030142>.

Katsh E and Rabinovich-Einy O, *Digital Justice* (OUP 2017).

Katsch E and Rule C, 'What We Know and Need to Know about Online' Dispute Resolution' (2016) 67 *S.C.L. Rev.* 329, 343.

Kaye DH, 'R. v. Smith: Court of Appeal Rebukes Latent Fingerprint Identification in Britain for Being Out of Step with Modern Forensic Science' (June 2011) <https://for-sci-law.blogspot.com/2011/06/displaying-grave-dissatisfaction-with.html> accessed 3 January 2026

Kemp S, 'Digital 2021: "Global Overview Report"' (Datareportal, 27 January2021)<https://datareportal.com/reports/digital-2021-global-overview-report> accessed 14 April 2021.

Kolb D, *Experiential Learning: Experience as the Source of Learning and Development* (Vol. 1) (Prentice-Hall 1984).

Konle-Seidl R and Danes S, 'Digitalisation and Changes in the World of Work' (September 2022) <https://www.europarl.europa.eu/RegData/etudes/STUD/2022/733986/IPOL_STU(2022)733986_EN.pdf> accessed 20 August 2025.

Kronblad C and Henning Jensen S, 'Being a Professional Is Not the Same as Acting Professionally'—How Digital Technologies Have Empowered the Creation and Enactment of a New Professional Identity in Law' (2023) 10(2) *Journal of Professions and Organization* 99.

Kronman AT, *The Lost Lawyer: Failing Ideals of the Legal Profession* (Harvard UP 1993).

Lamport L and others, 'The Byzantine Generals Problem' (1982) 4 *ACM Trans. Program. Lang. Syst.* 382.

Law Commission, 'Evidence in Criminal Proceedings: Hearsay and Related Topics' (1997) *Law Commission Report* 245.

Law Council of Australia, 'Futures Committee' (19 August 2025) <https://lawcouncil.au/about-us/advisory-committees/futures-committee> accessed 20 August 2025.

Law for Life, 'LASPO Implementation Review Consultation Response' (September 2018) <https://www.lawforlife.org.uk/wp-content/uploads/LASPO-Implementation-Review-Consultation-Law-for-Life-Advicenow-response-Final-Sept-2018.pdf> accessed 30 April 2021.

Law Geex, 'Comparing the Performance of Artificial Intelligence to Human Lawyers in the Review of Standard Business Contracts' (LawGeex, 2018) <https://images.law.com/contrib/content/uploads/documents/397/5408/lawgeex.pdf>

Law Geex, 'How the Platform Works' <https://www.lawgeex.com/platform/>

Lawton D and others, 'eDiscovery in Digital Forensic Investigations' (UK Home Office 2014), CAST Publication Number 32/14 <https://assets.publishing.service.gov.uk/government/uploads/system/uploads/attachment_data/file/394779/ediscovery-digital-forensic-investigations-3214.pdf>

Lawyer Monthly, 'Robots and AI: Giving Robots "Personhood" Status' (*Lawyer Monthly*, 3 March 2017) <https://www.lawyer-monthly.com/2017/02/robots-and-ai-giving-robots-personhood-status/>

Leering MM, 'Conceptualizing Reflective Practice for Legal Professionals' (2014) 23 *Journal of Law and Social Policy* 83, 94.

Leering MM, 'Integrated Reflective Practice: A Critical Imperative for Enhancing Legal Education and Professionalism' (2017) 95 *The Canadian Bar Review* 47, 49.

Legal Design Lab, 'Legal FAQ' <https://legalfaq.org/> accessed 20 August 2025.

Legal Design Lab, 'Stamford Legal Design Lab' <https://www.legaltechdesign.com/> accessed 20 August 2025.

Legal Education and Training Review, 'Setting Standards. The Future of Legal Services Education and Training Regulation in England and Wales' (2013) <https://letr.org.uk/index.html> accessed 20 August 2025.

Legal Insights, 'When Big Data Meets Big Law' (Legal Insights Europe, 20 September 2019) <https://blogs.thomsonreuters.com/legal-uk/2019/09/20/when-big-data-meets-big-law/>

Legal Services Board, 'Technology and Innovation in Legal Services' (May 2023) <https://legalservicesboard.org.uk/wp-content/uploads/2023/06/20230425-Tech-and-Innov-survey-2022-Designed.pdf> accessed 13 August 2025.

Legal Services Consumer Panel, 'Tracker Survey 2019. Briefing Note: How Consumers Are Using Legal Services' <https://www.legalservicesconsumerpanel.org.uk/wp-content/uploads/2025/07/25.07.07-How-consumers-are-using-legal-services-report–2025.pdf> accessed 13 August 2025.

Lesk M, 'Automatic Sense Disambiguation Using Machine Readable Dictionaries: How to Tell a Pinecone from an Ice Cream Cone' (June 1986) *SIGDOC '86: Proceedings of the 5th Annual International Conference on Systems Documentation* 24–6 <https://doi.org/10.1145/318723.318728>

Li W and others, 'Law Is Code: A Software Engineering Approach to Analysing the United States Code' (2015) 10 *J. Bus. & Tech. L.* 297 <http://digitalcommons.law.umaryland.edu/jbtl/vol10/iss2/6> accessed 1 January 2026.

Linklaters, 'Scam and Fraudulent Communications' <https://www.linklaters.com/en/legal-notices/fraudulent-emails> accessed 13 August 2025.

Lloyds Bank, 'UK Customer Digital Index 2024' <https://www.lloydsbank.com/assets/media/pdfs/banking_with_us/whats-happening/lb-consumer-digital-index-2024-report.pdf> accessed 19 August 2025.

Lord Chancellor, 'The Lord Chief Justice and the Senior President of Tribunals, Transforming Our Justice System' (2016) <https://assets.publishing.service.gov.uk/government/uploads/system/uploads/attachment_data/file/553261/joint-vision-statement.pdf> accessed 19 April 2021.

Lord Chief Justice, 'Coronavirus (COVID-19): Message from the Lord Chief Justice to Judges in the Civil and Family Courts' (*Judiciary.Gov*, 19 March 2020) <https://www.judiciary.uk/announcements/coronavirus-covid-19-message-from-the-lord-chief-justice-to-judges-in-the-civil-and-family-courts/> accessed 19 April 2021.

Macdonald C and Liberatore S, 'The Robot That Could Get You Off a Parking Ticket: DoNotPay System Has Won 160,000 Disputes in London and New York' (*Daily Mail*, 28 June 2016) <https://www.dailymail.co.uk/sciencetech/article-3664413/The-

Robot-parking-ticket-DoNotPay-created-student-won-160-000-disputes-London-New-York.html> accessed 26 April 2021.

Magesh V and others, 'Hallucination-Free? Assessing the Reliability of Leading AI Legal Research Tools' (2025) *Journal of Empirical Legal Studies* 1–27 <https://dho.stanford.edu/wp-content/uploads/Legal_RAG_Hallucinations.pdf> assessed 30 September 2025.

'Man Jailed Over Suicide Bomb Book' (*BBC News*, 15 December 2009) <https://news.bbc.co.uk/2/hi/uk_news/england/derbyshire/8414527.stm> accessed 3 January 2026.

Mann WC and Thompson SA, 'Rhetorical Structure Theory: Toward a Functional Theory of Text Organization' (1981) 8(3) *Text & Talk.*

Manyika J and others, *Big Data: The Next Frontier for Innovation, Competition, and Productivity* (McKinsey Global Institute 2011).

Marr B, 'The Future of Lawyers: Legal Tech, AI, Big Data and Online Courts' (*Forbes*, 17 January 2020) <https://www.forbes.com/sites/bernardmarr/2020/01/17/the-future-of-lawyers-legal tech-ai-big-data-and-online-courts/> accessed 2 January 2026.

Marr B, 'Really Big Data at Walmart: Real-Time Insights From Their 40+ Petabyte Data Cloud' (*Forbes*, n.d.) <https://www.forbes.com/sites/bernardmarr/2017/01/23/really-big-data-at-walmart-real-time-insights-from-their-40-petabyte-data-cloud/> accessed 2 January 2021.

Maslen K, 'Teaching Law with Technology Prize 2020—Finalists Announced' (*Thomson Reuters*, 6 March 2020) <https://blogs.thomsonreuters.com/legal-uk/2020/03/06/teaching-law-with-technology-prize-2020-finalists-announced/> accessed 19 August 2025.

Matz A, 'In Pursuit of Proust' (*Slate*, 3 March 2005) <https://slate.com/culture/2005/03/the-new-proust-translation.html> accessed 1 January 2026.

McAffee A and Brynjolfsson E, 'Big Data: The Management Revolution' (*Harvard Business Review*, 2012) <https://hbr.org/2012/10/big-data-the-management-revolution> accessed 2 January 2026.

McFaul H and others, 'A Mobile App for Public Legal Education: A Case Study of Co-designing with Students' (2020) 28 Research in Learning Technology.

Mendez E, 'Dropping Dropbox in your Law Practice to Maintain Your Duty of Confidentiality' (2013) 36 *Campbell Law Review* 175, 190–2.

Michallon C, 'Johnny Depp and Amber Heard: A Timeline of Their Relationship, Allegations and Court Battles' (2023) <https://

www.independent.co.uk/news/world/americas/who-won-depp-v-heard-timeline-b2343074.html> accessed 6 August 2025.

Ministry of Justice, 'Open Justice the Way Forward' (2023) <https://assets.publishing.service.gov.uk/government/uploads/system/uploads/attachment_data/file/1155744/open-justice-cfe.pdf> accessed 23 September 2021.

Ministry of Justice, 'AI Action Plan for Justice' (2025) <https://www.gov.uk/government/publications/ai-action-plan-for-justice/ai-action-plan-for-justice> accessed 30 September 2025.

Ministry of Justice, 'Call for Evidence: Open Justice: The Way Forward' (2025) <https://assets.publishing.service.gov.uk/media/679a5a5161c295e9331f789a/open-justice-call-evidence-summary-responses.pdf> accessed 4 January 2026.

Ministry of Justice & The Alan Turing Institute, 'AI and Data Science Ethics Framework' (*GOV.UK.*, 2021) <https://www.gov.uk/government/publications/ministry-of-justice-ai-and-data-science-ethics-framework> accessed 30 September 2025.

Mohler GO and others, 'Randomized Controlled Field Trials of Predictive Policing' (2016) *Journal of the American Statistical Association* <https://amstat.tandfonline.com/doi/full/10.1080/01621459.2015.1077710>

Molag T, 'The Complete Guide to Social Media for Lawyers' (*Clio.com*, 23 February 2021) <https://www.clio.com/resources/digital-marketing-lawyers/social-media-lawyers/> accessed 12 April 2021.

Monash University, 'Clinical Placement Offerings' <https://www.monash.edu/law/current-students/cle/clinical-legal-education/clinical-placement-offerings> accessed 20 August 2025.

Moody R, 'Law Firms Hit with Average Ransom Demand of $2.5 Million' (1 August 2024) <https://www.comparitech.com/blog/information-security/ransomware-attacks-law-firms/> accessed 13 August 2025.

Moore GE, 'The Future of Integrated Electronics' (1965) 38 *Electronics* 4.

Morse J, 'Amazon Announces New Employee Tracking Tech, and Customers Are Lining Up' (Mashable UK, 2 December 2020) <https://mashable.com/article/amazon-aws-panorama-worker-customer-tracking-technology-smart-cameras/?europe=true> accessed 2 January 2026.

My Virtual Lawyer, 'About Our Team' (2021) <https://myvirtual.lawyer/our-team/> accessed 19 February 2021.

My Virtual Lawyer, 'You Should Become a Virtual Lawyer: Here's Why and How to Begin Your Law Firm' (2021) <https://myvirtual.

lawyer/why-and-how-to-become-a-virtual-lawyer/> accessed 19 February 2021.

Nakamoto S, 'Bitcoin: A Peer-to-Peer Electronic Cash System' (31 October 2008) <https://bitcoin.org/en/bitcoin-paper> accessed 4 January 2026.

National Center for Technology and Dispute Resolution, 'Ethical Principles for ODR Initiative' (2016) <https://odr.info/ethics-and-odr/> accessed 20 August 2025.

Naughton J, 'Is Blockchain the Most Important IT Invention of Our Age?' (*The Guardian*, 24 January 2016) <https://www.theguardian.com/commentisfree/2016/jan/24/blockchain-bitcoin-technology-most-important-tech-invention-of-our-age-sir-mark-walport> accessed 4 January 2026.

NBC News, 'Fitbit Murder Case: Richard Dabate Pleads Not Guilty in Wife's Death' (29 April 2017) <https://www.nbcnews.com/news/us-news/fitbit-murder-case-richard-dabate-pleads-not-guilty-wife-s-n752526> accessed 3 January 2026.

'Neural Nets Create Natural Speech Interaction' <https://www.eetimes.com/neural-nets-create-natural-speech-interaction/> accessed 30 September 2025.

Nicolson D, 'Calling, Character and Clinical Legal Education: A Cradle-to-grave Approach to Inculcating a Love for Justice' (2013) 16(1) *Legal Ethics* 36.

Nieto A and others, 'IoT-Forensics Meets Privacy: Towards Cooperative Digital Investigations' (2018) 18(2) *Sensors* 492.

Niven, K, 'DoNotPay Cases Underscores Hurdles for AI-Fueled Legal Help' (Technology Law, 2024) <https://technologylaw.fkks.com/post/102j901/donotpay-cases-underscore-hurdles-for-ai-fueled legal-help>

Ng A, 'Why Agentic AI Is the Smart Bet for Most Enterprises' <https://www.insightpartners.com/ideas/andrew-ng-why-agentic-ai-is-the-smart-bet-for-most-enterprises/> accessed 30 September 2025.

Norton Rose Fulbright, 'Business and Legal Operations Graduate Scheme' (2025) <https://www.nortonrosefulbright.com/en-gb/graduates/opportunities/business-and-legal-operations-graduate-scheme> accessed 13 August 2025.

OECD, 'OECD Principles on Artificial Intelligence' (2019) <https://www.oecd.org/going-digital/ai/principles/> accessed 30 September 2025.

OED, *Oxford Dictionary* (OUP 2021).

OFCOM, 'Ofcom's Approach to Implementing the Online Safety Act' (2023) <https://www.ofcom.org.uk/online-safety/illegal-and-harmful-content/roadmap-to-regulation> accessed 2 January 2026.

OFCOM, 'Online Nation 2024 Report' (2024) <https://www.ofcom.org.uk/siteassets/resources/documents/research-and-data/online-research/online-nation/2024/online-nation-2024-report.pdf?v=386238&t> accessed 23 September 2025.

Office of Lawyer Regulation Complainant v. Kristine A Peshek [2011] WI 47 <https://www.wicourts.gov/sc/opinion/DisplayDocument.pdf?content=pdf&seqNo=66464>

O'Kane S, 'A Second Apple Employee Was Charged with Stealing Self-Driving Car Project' (*The Verge*, 2019) <https://www.theverge.com/2019/1/30/18203718/apple-self-driving-trade-secrets-china-titan> accessed 3 January 2026.

O'Leary DL, '"Smart Lawyering": Integrating Technology Competence into the Legal Practice Curriculum' (2021) 19 *University of New Hampshire Law Review* 197–272, 199.

Online Rule Procedure Committee, 'About us—Online Procedure Rule Committee' <GOV.UK> accessed 23 September 2025.

Oswald M and others, 'Algorithmic Risk Assessment Policing Models: Lessons from the Durham HART Model and "Experimental" Proportionality' (2018) 27(2) *Information & Communications Technology Law* 223–50, 227–8.

Ozenc K and Hagan M, *Rituals for Work* (John Wiley & Sons 2019).

Pack L, 'Arson Suspect in Unique Case Featuring Pacemaker Data Is Back in Custody' (*Journal-News*, Hamilton, Ohio, 24 July 2018) <https://www.journal-news.com/news/arson-suspect-unique-case-featuring-pacemaker-data-back-custody/dn6JyzsOemZovpayJMZLNJ/> accessed 3 January 2026.

Page C, 'Legal Powerhouse Proskauer Exposed Clients' Confidential M&A Data' (TechCrunch, 6 April 2023) <https://techcrunch.com/2023/04/06/proskauer-confidential-client-data/> accessed 13 August 2025.

Palfrey J and Gasser U, *Born Digital, Understanding the First Generation of Digital Natives* (Basic Books 2008) ii.

Pleasance P, '"Legal Need" and Legal Needs Surveys: A Background Paper' (Open Society Foundations (online), 2016) <https://namati.org/wp-content/uploads/2016/11/OSJI-Legal-Needs-Surveys-Background-Materials-1-An-Introduction-to-Legal-Needs-Surveys-1-v3.6-2016-06-22-web_Pascoe.pdf> accessed 2 October 2019.

'PredPol Operational Review—Initial Findings' (Kent Police, 2013) <www.statewatch.org/docbin/uk-2013-11-kent-police-pp-report.pdf>

Preston CB, 'Lawyers' Abuse of Technology' (2018) 118 *Cornell Law Review* 881, 923.

Puiu T, 'Smartphone Is Millions of Times Faster than NASA's 1960s Computers' (*ZME Science*, 13 October 2015, updated 11 May 2023) <https://www.zmescience.com/science/news-science/smartphone-power-compared-to-apollo-432/> accessed 1 January 2026.

Purtill V, 'Lawtech: Standards for the Lawyers of the Future' <https://www.regulationmatters.uk/features/legal-tech-for-the-lawyers-of-the-future/> accessed 20 August 2025.

Quality Assurance Agency, 'Subject Benchmark Statement Law November' (March 2023) <https://www.qaa.ac.uk/docs/qaa/sbs/sbs-law–23.pdf?sfvrsn=c271a881_6https://www.qaa.ac.uk/docs/qaa/subject-benchmark-statements/subject-benchmark-statement-law.pdf?sfvrsn=b939c881_16> accessed 30 November 2025.

Queensland Association of Independent Legal Services Inc., 'Queensland Community Legal Centres Use of Technology Literature Review and Discussion Paper' (2014) 18 <https://law.uq.edu.au/files/1260/Qld-CLCs-and-technology-August-2014.pdf>.

'Redefining 21st Century Justice as a Vital Public Service' (The Law Society, 25 June 2025) <https://www.lawsociety.org.uk/contact-or-visit-us/press-office/press-releases/redefining-21st-century-justice-as-a-vital-public-service> accessed 3 January 2026.

Reith M and others, 'An Examination of Digital Forensic Models' (2002) 1(3) *International Journal of Digital Evidence* 1.

Reyburn S, 'The $69 Million Beeple NFT Was Bought With Cryptocurrency' (*The New York Times*, 12 March 2021) <https://www.nytimes.com/2021/03/12/arts/beeple-nft-buyer-ether.html> accessed 20 March 2021.

Reyes E, 'Who's Afraid of Computer Generation?' (*Law Society Gazette*, 28 October 2010) <https://www.lawgazette.co.uk/analysis/whos-afraid-of-computer-generation-/57836.article> accessed 12 November 2019.

Ritter C, 'Reach More Users: 4 Tips for Designing Accessible Apps and Websites' (2018), <https://www.thinkwithgoogle.com/marketing-strategies/app-and-mobile/website-app-accessibility-guidelines/> accessed 28 April 2021.

Rogers S, 'What Is a Data Scientist?' (*The Guardian*, 2012) <https://www.theguardian.com/news/datablog/2012/mar/02/data-scientist> accessed 12 October 2018.

Romm T and Lerman R, 'Amazon Suspends Parler, Taking Pro-Trump Site Offline Indefinitely' (*Washington Post*, 11 January 2021) <https://www.washingtonpost.com/technology/2021/01/09/amazon-parler-suspension/> accessed 2 January 2026.

Rose N, 'Lewis Case: "Wishing Death on Neo-Nazis" Went Too Far' (*Legal Futures*, 17 December 2018) <https://www.legalfutures.co.uk/latest-news/lewis-case-wishing-death-on-neo-nazis-went-too-far> accessed 29 April 2021.

Roux C and others, 'The End of the (Forensic Science) World as We Know It? The Example of Trace Evidence' (2015) 370(1674) *Philosophical Transactions of the Royal Society B: Biological Sciences* 20140260.

Rule C, 'Is ODR ADR?' (2016) 8 *Online Dispute Resolution* 8.

Ryan F and Hardie L, 'We Asked ChatGPT for Legal Advice—Here Are Five Reasons Why You Shouldn't' (*The Conversation*, 31 May 2024) <https://theconversation.com/we-asked-chatgpt-for-legal-advice-here-are-five-reasons-why-you-shouldnt-229147> accessed 5 January 2026.

S.1582—Genius Act (*Congress.gov*, 2025) <https://www.congress.gov/bill/119th-congress/senate-bill/1582> accessed 4 January 2026.

Salovey P and Mayer JD, 'Emotional Intelligence' (1990) 9(3) *Imagination, Cognition and Personality* 185.

Sandefur R, *Accessing Justice in the Contemporary USA: Findings from the Community Needs and Services Study* (American Bar Foundation 2014).

Sandefur R, 'Access to What?' (2019) 148(1) *Daedalus* 49–59. <https://direct.mit.edu/daed/article/148/1/49/27247/Access-to-What> accessed 30 September 2025.

Sandefur R, 'Legal Tech for Non-Lawyers: Report on the Survey of US Legal Technologies' (2019) <https://www.americanbarfoundation.org/wp-content/uploads/2023/04/report_us_digital_legal_tech_for_nonlawyers.pdf> accessed 12 January 2026

Sang-Hun C and Markoff J, 'Master of Go Board Game Is Walloped by Google Computer Program' (*New York Times*, 9 March 2016) <https://www.nytimes.com/2016/03/10/world/asia/google-alphago-lee-se-dol.html> accessed 30 September 2025.

Sarathy B and Ganesan R, 'Why AI Efficiency May Be Making Your Organization More Fragile' (*O'Reilly Radar*, 25 September 2025) <https://www.oreilly.com/radar/why-ai-efficiency-may-be-making-your-organization-more-fragile/> accessed 30 September 2025.

Scheiber N, 'Why Is This C.E.O. Bragging About Replacing Humans with A.I.?' (*New York Times*, 2 February 2025) <https://www.

nytimes.com/2025/02/02/business/klarna-ceo-ai.html> accessed 27 September 2025.

Schön DA, *Educating the Reflective Practitioner: Toward a New Design for Teaching and Learning in the Professions* (Jossey-Bass 1987).

Schwab K, 'The Fourth Industrial Revolution: What It Means, How to Respond' (World Economic Forum, 14 January 2016) <https://www.weforum.org/stories/2016/01/the-fourth-industrial-revolution-what-it-means-and-how-to-respond/> accessed 30 September 2025.

Scientific Working Group on Digital Evidence, 'SWGDE Multimedia and Digital Evidence Glossary, Ver 3.0' (June 2016) 6 <https://www.swgde.org/wp-content/uploads/2024/03/2016-06-23-SWGDE-Digital-and-Multimedia-Evidence-Glossary_v3-0.pdf>

Select Committee on Artificial Intelligence, 'AI in the UK: Ready, Willing, and Able?' (House of Lords, 2017–19) HL Paper 100, paras 10–19.

Select Committee on Artificial Intelligence, 'Report of Session 2017–19 AI in the UK: Ready, Willing and Able?' (*House of Lords*, 2018) HL Paper 100 <https://publications.parliament.uk/pa/ld201719/ldselect/ldai/100/100.pdf>

Sergot MJ and others, 'The British Nationality Act as a Logic Program' (1986) 29(5) *Communications of the ACM* <https://doi.org/10.1145/5689.5920>

Siegel DJ, 'Ethics Corner: 12 Rules for Ethically Dealing with Social Media' (*ABA*, 16 February 2017) <https://www.americanbar.org/groups/business_law/publications/blt/2017/02/ethics_corner/> accessed 11 April 2021.

Sky News, 'Mitesh Patel: Gay Pharmacist Jailed for Murdering Wife to Be with Boyfriend' (*Sky News*, 2018) <https://news.sky.com/story/mitesh-patel-pharmacist-who-murdered-wife-jailed-for-30-years-11572248> accessed 3 January 2026.

Smith A and Hutchinson T, 'Building Legal Project Management Skills and Organisational Capability' (2017) <https://gallery.mailchimp.com/ef0907072acfd9dfa8857ea40/files/d4eb13ae-8896-4b27-81ca-3ad6cf48e5ad/Building_LPM_Skills_Organisational_Capability.pdf> Sourced from: <https://legalprojectmanagement.co.uk> accessed 12 October 2018.

Society of Computers and Law, 'False Citations: AI and "Hallucination"' (26 February 2024) <https://www.scl.org/uk-litigant-found-to-have-cited-false-judgments-hallucinated-by-ai/> accessed 3 January 2006.

Solicitors Regulation Authority, 'Compliance Tips for Solicitors Regarding the Use of AI and Technology' <https://www.sra.org.

uk/solicitors/resources/innovate/compliance-tips-for-solicitors/> accessed 23 September 2025.

Solicitors Regulation Authority, 'Improving Access—Tackling Unmet Legal Needs' (2023) <https://www.sra.org.uk/sra/research-publications/improving-access---tackling-unmet-legal-needs/> accessed 2 January 2026.

Solicitors Regulation Authority, 'SRA Code of Conduct for Firms' <https://www.sra.org.uk/solicitors/standards-regulations/code-conduct-firms/> accessed 2 January 2026.

Solicitors Regulation Authority, 'SRA Code of Conduct for Solicitors, RELs, RFLs and RSLs' <https://www.sra.org.uk/solicitors/standards-regulations/code-conduct-solicitors/> accessed 2 January 2026.

Solicitors Regulation Authority, 'Statement of Solicitor Competence' <https://www.sra.org.uk/solicitors/resources/cpd/competence-statement/> accessed 20 August 2025.

Solicitors Regulation Authority, 'Technology and Legal Services' (Solicitors Regulatory Authority, 11 December 2018) <https://www.sra.org.uk/risk/risk-resources/technology-legal-services/> accessed 30 April 2021.

Solicitors Regulation Authority, 'Use of Social Media and Offensive Communications' (25 November 2019) <https://www.sra.org.uk/sra/corporate-strategy/sra-enforcement-strategy/enforcement-practice/social-media-offensive-communications/> accessed 29 April 2021.

Sommerlad H, 'Researching and Theorising the Process of Professional Identity Formation' (2007) 34(2) *Journal of Law and Society* 190.

South China Morning Post, 'Bitcoin Mining in Northern Chinese Province to Be Halted amid Energy-Saving Push' <https://www.scmp.com/economy/china-economy/article/3123633/bitcoin-mining-northern-chinese-province-be-halted-amid> accessed 22 March 2021.

'Speech by Lord Justice Colin Briggs: Online Dispute Resolution Forum' (7 June 2022) <https://www.judiciary.uk/speech-by-lord-justice-colin-birss-online-dispute-resolution-forum/> accessed 3 January 2026.

'Speech by the Master of the Rolls: AI—Transforming the Work of Lawyers and Judges' (11 March 2024) <https://www.judiciary.uk/speech-by-the-master-of-the-rolls-ai-transforming-the-work-of-lawyers-and-judges/> accessed 3 January 2026.

Staff C, 'Big Data' (2017) 60(6) *Communications of the ACM* 25 <https://doi.org/10.1145/3079064>

Statista, 'Internet usage in the United Kingdom' (13 June 2025) <https://www.statista.com/topics/3246/internet-usage-in-the-uk/#topicOverview>

Stubbings C, 'Foreword' in Price Waterhouse Cooper, 'The Workforce of the Future. The Competing Forces Shaping 2030' (2018) <https://www.pwc.com/gx/en/services/people-organisation/workforce-of-the-future/workforce-of-the-future-the-competing-forces-shaping-2030-pwc.pdf> accessed 17 October 2018.

'Suspected Undeclared Use of Artificial Intelligence in the Academic Literature: An Analysis of the Academ-AI Dataset' <https://arxiv.org/abs/2411.15218v1> accessed 30 September 2025.

Susskind R, *Online Courts and the Future of Justice* (OUP 2019).

Susskind R, *The End of Lawyers? Rethinking the Nature of Legal Services* (OUP 2010).

Susskind R, *Tomorrow's Lawyers: An Introduction to Your Future* (OUP 2013).

Sweeney M, 'Lord McAlpine Settles Libel Action with Alan Davies over Twitter Comment' (*The Guardian*, 24 October 2013) <https://www.theguardian.com/media/2013/oct/24/lord-mcalpine-libel-alan-davies> accessed 14 April 2021.

'System and Method of Handwritten Character Recognition' <https://patents.google.com/patent/US20030048948A1/en> accessed 30 September 2025.

Tang S, Holmes V and Foley T, 'Ethical Climate, Job Satisfaction and Wellbeing: Observations from an Empirical Study of New Australian Lawyers' (2020) 33 *Geo. J. Legal Ethics* 1035.

Tech Nation, 'The LawtechUK Panel' (*Tech Nation*, n.d.) <https://technation.io/lawtechukpanel/> accessed 21 March 2021.

TechTerms, 'Binary' (2020) <https://techterms.com/definition/binary> accessed 3 January 2026.

Thanaraj A, 'Making the Case for a Digital Lawyering Framework in Legal Education' (2017) (3) *International Review of Law* 17, 32.

The Association of Chief Police Officers, 'ACPO Good Practice Guide for Digital Evidence' (2012) <https://www.digital-detective.net/digital-forensics-documents/ACPO_Good_Practice_Guide_for_Digital_Evidence_v5.pdf> accessed 30 April 2021.

The Bar Standards Board Handbook, 'Social Media Guidance' (2023) <https://www.barstandardsboard.org.uk/static/61d13750-880c-4423-a4bf80cf96d3f06c/4590471b-3272-4f66-ad8684a76315cdd0/BSB-social-media-guidance-September-2023.pdf> accessed 23 September 2025.

The Economist, 'The World's Most Valuable Resource Is No Longer Oil, but Data' (*The Economist*, 2017) <https://www.economist.com/leaders/2017/05/06/the-worlds-most-valuable-resource-is-no-longer-oil-but-data> accessed 2 January 2026.

The House of Lords Library, 'The Criminal Procedure and Investigations Act 1996' (Code of Practice Order, 2020) <https://lordslibrary.parliament.uk/the-criminal-procedure-and-investigations-act-1996-code-of-practice-order-2020/> accessed 3 January 2026.

The House of Lords Library, 'AI Technology and the Justice System: Lords Committee Report' (2023) <https://lordslibrary.parliament.uk/ai-technology-and-the-justice-system-lords-committee-report/> accessed 30 September 2025.

'The Indiana Lawyer' <https://www.theindianalawyer.com/tags/mikayla-munn?__cf_chl_jschl_tk__=pmd_3a38ebf9bc89d30130627ffa18fc85682499f3ef-1627493748-0-gqNtZGzNAeKjcnBszQji> accessed 3 January 2026.

The Law Society of England and Wales, 'Access to Justice Crisis: Millions Left without Legal Aid' (21 February 2024) <https://www.solicitorsjournal.com/sjarticle/access-to-justice-crisis-millions-left-without-legal-aid> accessed 30 September 2025.

The Law Society of England and Wales, 'Civil Legal Aid: Millions Still without Access to Justice' (21 February 2024) <https://www.lawsociety.org.uk/contact-or-visit-us/press-office/press-releases/civil-legal-aid-millions-still-without-access-to-justice> assessed 30 September 2025.

The Law Society of England and Wales, 'Dispute Resolution Bridging the Gap: A Practical Guide to Generative AI in Legal Disclosure' (2 June 2025) <https://communities.lawsociety.org.uk/dispute-resolution/bridging-the-gap-a-practical-guide-to-generative-ai-in-legal-disclosure/6003339.article> accessed 30 September 2025.

The Law Society of England and Wales, 'Entry Trends' (28 January 2025) <https://www.lawsociety.org.uk/support-services/research-trends/annual-statistics-report-201 accessed 13 August 2025.

The Law Society of England and Wales, 'Ethics and Artificial Intelligence in the Justice System' (2020) <https://www.lawsociety.org.uk/topics/research/ethics-and-artificial-intelligence-in-the-justice-system> accessed 30 September 2025.

The Law Society of England and Wales, 'Generative AI: The Essentials' (20 May 2025) <https://www.lawsociety.org.uk/topics/ai-and-lawtech/generative-ai-the-essentials> accessed 30 September 2025.

The Law Society of England and Wales, 'How Can My Firm Use AI to Benefit Our Business? (27 January 2025) <https://www.lawsociety.org.uk/contact-or-visit-us/helplines/practice-advice-service/q-and-as/how-can-my-firm-use-ai-to-benefit-our-business> accessed 30 September 2025.

The Law Society of England and Wales, 'Introduction to LawTech 2019' (2019) <https://tlsprdsitecore.azureedge.net/-/media/files/campaigns/lawtech/introduction-to-lawtech-october-2019.pdf?rev=fc0013791e0c474198daaabd648a304d&hash=F030B90541BF66B22233A9702F4B22A5> accessed 30 April 2021.

The Law Society of England and Wales, 'Law Society Calls for "One-Stop Shop" AI Platform for Civil Justice' (24 June 2025) <https://www.legalfutures.co.uk/latest-news/law-society-calls-for-one-stop-shop-ai-platform-for-civil-justice> accessed 30 September 2025.

The Law Society of England and Wales, '21st Century Justice Report' (2021) <https://www.lawsociety.org.uk/topics/research/21st-century-justice-report> assessed 30 September 2025.

The Law Society of England and Wales, 'Unbundling Civil Legal Services' (12 April 2022) <https://www.lawsociety.org.uk/topics/civil-litigation/unbundling-civil-legal-services/> accessed 13 August 2025.

The Lawyer, 'The Watson Glaser and BCAT Critical Thinking Tests' (*The Lawyer*, 28 April 2015) <https://www.thelawyer.com/watson-glaser-test/> accessed 29 April 2021.

The Legal Technologist, 'Why Lawyers Should Learn to Code, but Not for the Reasons You Think' (*The Legal Technologist*, 25 November 2020) <https://www.legaltechnologist.co.uk/article/why-lawyers-should-learn-to-code-but-not-for-the-reasons-you-think/> accessed 19 August 2025.

The O Shaped Lawyer, 'Mindset & Attributes' <https://oshaped.com/the-o-shaped-mindset-and-attributes> accessed 19 August 2025.

The Open University, 'Digital Forensics' (2020) <https://www.open.edu/openlearn/science-maths-technology/digital-forensics/content-section–4.2#:~:text=Until%20the%20late%201990s%2C%20what,and%20Response%20Team%20(CART)>

The Open University, 'Digital Justice' <https://university.open.ac.uk/open-justice/public-understanding-law/legal-technology> accessed 20 August 2025.

The Pile <https://pile.eleuther.ai/> accessed 30 September 2025.

The Police Foundation, 'Digital Forensics: The Next Steps' (2020) <https://www.police-foundation.org.uk/project/the-next-steps-for-digital-forensics/> accessed 3 January 2026.

The Seattle Times, 'Soaring Bitcoin Prices Put Central Washington Electrical Utilities on Alert' (*The Seattle Times*, 9 January 2021) <https://www.seattletimes.com/business/technology/sunday-buzz-soaring-bitcoin-prices-put-central-washington-electrical-utilities-on-alert/> accessed 22 March 2021.

Thornton JI, 'The General Assumptions and Rationale of Forensic Identification' in Faigman DL and others (eds) *Modern Scientific Evidence: The Law and Science of Expert Testimony* (West Publishing Company 1997) 2.

Tiku N and others, 'Twitter Bans Trump's Account, Citing Risk of Further Violence' (*Washington Post*, 8 January 2021) <https://www.washingtonpost.com/technology/2021/01/08/twitter-trump-dorsey/> accessed 2 January 2026.

Tilstone WJ and others, *Forensic science: An Encyclopaedia of History, Methods, and Techniques* (ABC-CLIO 2006).

Thomson Reuters, 'Digital General Counsel are Transforming the Corporate Legal Department' (2020), 3 <https://legalsolutions.thomsonreuters.co.uk/content/dam/ewp-m/documents/legal-uk/en/pdf/reports/tr1135788-transforming-the-corporate.pdf> accessed 13 August 2025.

UK Government Press Release: New Cryptoasset Rules to Drive Growth and Protect Consumers <https://www.gov.uk/government/news/new-cryptoasset-rules-to-drive-growth-and-protect-consumers> accessed 13 August 2025.

UK International Development, 'Digital Development Strategy 2024–2030 Doing Development in a Digital World' (2024) <https://assets.publishing.service.gov.uk/media/6613e7f7c4c84d4b31346a68/FCDO-Digital-Development-Strategy-2024-2030.pdf> accessed 13 August 2023.

UN Trade & Development, '2025 Technology and Innovation Report' (7 April 2025) <https://unctad.org/publication/technology-and-innovation-report-2025> accessed 20 August 2025.

United Nations, 'The Impact of Digital Technologies6' (2025) <https://www.un.org/en/un75/impact-digital-technologies> accessed 20 August 2025.

Universities UK, 'New Analysis Shows That Graduates Will Be Key to Government's Industrial Strategy' (11 March 2025) <https://www.universitiesuk.ac.uk/latest/news/new-analysis-shows-graduates-will-be-key> accessed 19 August 2025.

University of York, 'Problem Based Learning: York Law School' (2025) <https://www.york.ac.uk/teaching-innovation/case-studies/problem-based//> accessed 20 August 2025.

US National Institute of Justice, 'Digital Evidence in the Courtroom: A Guide For Law Enforcement and Prosecutors' (2006) <https://www.ojp.gov/pdffiles1/nij/211314.pdf> accessed 30 April 2021.

Vijayanagar KR, 'EME, CDM, AES, CENC, and Keys—The Essential Building Blocks of DRM' (*OTTverse*, 28 August 2020) <https://ottverse.com/eme-cenc-cdm-aes-keys-drm-digital-rights-management/> accessed 1 January 2026.

Weizenbaum J, 'ELIZA—A Computer Program for the Study of Natural Language Communication between Man and Machine' (1966) 9 *Communications of the ACM* 36.

Wexler C, 'The Changing Nature of Crime And Criminal Investigations' (2018) <https://www.policeforum.org/assets/ChangingNatureofCrime.pdf> accessed 30 April 2021.

Wilkins J, 'Company Replaces Customer Support With AI, Then Panics and Forces Engineers to Work the Phones as the AI Fails' (*Futurism*, 4 September 2025) <https://futurism.com/klarna-ai-automation-engineers> accessed 27 September 2025.

WIRED, 'This Site Posted Every Face from Parler's Capitol Hill Insurrection Videos' (Ars Technica, 23 January 2021) <https://arstechnica.com/tech-policy/2021/01/this-site-posted-every-face-from-parlers-capitol-hill-insurrection-videos/> accessed 30 April 2021.

Woebbeking MK, 'The Impact of Smart Contracts on Traditional Concepts of Contract Law' (2019) 10 *JIPITEC* 8.

World Economic Forum, 'Putting Skills First: A Framework for Action' (May 2023) <https://www3.weforum.org/docs/WEF_CNES_Putting_Skills_First_2023.pdf> accessed 19 August 2025.

World Economic Forum, 'The Future of Jobs Report' (2023) <https://www.weforum.org/publications/the-future-of-jobs-report-2023/> accessed 19 August 2025.

World Economic Forum, 'The Future of Jobs Report 2025' (2025) <https://www.weforum.org/publications/the-future-of-jobs-report-2025/in-full/3-skills-outlook/#3-skills-outlook> accessed 19 August 2025.

World Justice Project, Global Insights on Access to Justice 2023' (2023) <https://worldjusticeproject.org> assessed 30 September 2025.

Wright A and De Filippi P, 'Decentralized Blockchain Technology and the Rise of Lex Cryptographia' (2015) *Social Science Research Network*, SSRN Scholarly Paper ID 2580664 <https://papers.ssrn.com/abstract=2580664> accessed 21 March 2021.

Yang KC, Singh D and Menczer F, 'Characteristics and Prevalence of Fake Social Media Profiles with AI-Generated Faces' (2024) *arXiv preprint* arXiv:2401.02627. 2024

Zhang L, 'Regulation of Cryptocurrency' (June 2018) <https://www.loc.gov/law/help/cryptocurrency/china.php> accessed 14 March 2021.

GLOSSARY

A number of key terms within this book are considered in detail within its chapters (e.g. digital lawyering). Others have short definitions next to them within the relevant sentences and paragraphs. This glossary contains a range of words used frequently within the legal profession and/or legal technology that may be less familiar to some readers than others.

Access to justice A basic principle, underpinning the rule of law, that everyone should have access to the courts and legal representation.

Adjudicator A person or body that makes a decision in a formal dispute.

Affordances Referring to user interfaces, the properties or features which give indications of a way to interact with the system or object, in order to achieve a specific outcome.

Algorithm A description of a computation or mathematical method, reduced to documentation or a software code executable by a computer.

Ambient A quality of computer interaction in which computer devices supporting a human–machine interaction are well-integrated into the experience, to the extent that the presence of the computing devices is not novel or noticed by the user and requires no additional cognitive load on the part of the user to accomplish the desired goal or task.

Analytics Systematic methods of processing and analysis for data or statistics.

App A vernacular shorthand for application, most often referring to those on mobile devices.

Application A computer program or programs packaged in such a way as to provide a ready-to-use object on a computer or mobile device.

Arbitration The settling of a dispute between parties by a mutually agreed other party outside a court of law.

Artificial intelligence (AI) The discipline concerned with the development of computer systems able to perform tasks normally performed by humans, requiring certain capabilities normally associated with humans such as decision-making, language translation and visual perception.

Attacker A malicious actor attempting to infiltrate a computer system or network to steal information, deny access to others, etc.

Attorney A term used in the United States to refer to a lawyer.

Audit trail A record of a step-by-step process where the data can be tracked to its source.

Automated The use of technology to replicate a process with limited human involvement.

(The) Bar The collective term for barristers.

Barrister A type of legal professional in common law jurisdictions whose work is often focused upon advocacy (representing clients in court).

Big Data A body of data that is too large to store and process using the capabilities of traditional single-computer systems.

Billable hours The amount of time billed to the client as a result of a legal professional's chargeable hours.

Bitcoin A market-leading cryptocurrency.

Block A unit of data on a blockchain that is introduced through a certain protocol and accepted using the blockchain's specified consensus mechanism.

Blockchain A distributed ledger technology duplicated and distributed to a network of participating computer systems, relying on a sequential series of data blocks created and managed according to a specific set of protocols for creating, validating and recording new blocks.

BYOD "Bring Your Own Device", a practice allowing business applications and communications to take place on employee-owned devices.

Chargeable hour Unit of time recorded by a legal professional when working on a particular issue.

Chartered legal executive A role in the legal profession within England and Wales, similar to that of a solicitor.

Classification Sorting a set of subjects into one or more categories.

Classifier A machine learning model that is trained to separate subjects into one or more categories based on specific characteristics measurable on each subject.

Client care The way in which a legal professional looks after and supports a client (similar to the more general term "customer service").

Client management system Software system that supports lawyers in tracking and managing the contact data of their clients, and in some cases including detailed collections of information, files and other supporting electronic documents related to specific matters for those clients.

Cloud A reference to the internet as a ubiquitous computing environment.

Cloud computing The provision and use of computing resources accessible via the internet in well-defined increments of resources for specified periods of time.

Coding See Programming.

Commodity computing Computers available at low unit cost, driving them to essentially interchangeable units, to be used and billed for use as utilities.

Common law jurisdiction A jurisdiction modelled on the English legal system which places a large reliance upon case law.

Communication The projecting of information to some destination or recipient over a distance.

Communications network A collection of two or more devices (computers, transmitters, receivers, radios, etc.) that can send and/or receive information, usually using electromagnetic signals carried by wire or wirelessly.

Computer vision A subdiscipline of AI concerned with the processing of image and video data.

Conditional fee agreement An agreement between the legal representative and their client in which legal fees are paid only in certain circumstances, normally if the client wins the case.

Consensus algorithm A mechanism by which new blocks are validated and accepted for incorporation into a blockchain.

Counterparties In a transaction, one or more other parties participating in that transaction.

Cryptocurrency A digital currency or means of facilitating exchange relying on cryptographic methods and often a blockchain for recording transactions and issuing units.

Cryptographic See Cryptography.

Cryptographic hash A large number of fixed size computed from a data input (e.g. a password or some other credential) used instead of storing the source value, as a means of authentication or validation in a secure computing system.

Cryptographic suites Collections of computer programs and reusable code containing implementations of cryptography that are used to secure communications and data storage from unauthorised access and use.

Cryptography The discipline of securing or protecting communications and data using certain mathematical methods and algorithms.

Curriculum Topics and subjects included in a programme, module or course.

Cyberattack A planned attempt by a hacker or an organisation to harm a computer system or network.

Dark web A collection of sites connected to the internet that require special software, configurations and techniques to access. Often referring to secret resources on the internet hosting or supporting illicit or controversial activity.

Data collection Accumulation and storage of data for specific (and sometimes non-specific) purposes.

Data custody The act of holding and maintaining bodies of data.

Data protection officer A person designated in an organisation who is responsible for advising and guiding that organisation's compliance to the General Data Protection Regulation (GDPR).

Data set A collection of discrete records collected for analysis and the support of some activity such as the delivery of a service or the delivery of information to support a decision.

Deep Learning The branch of AI focused on training neural networks with high numbers of layers, to handle highly complex problems

Deep Neural Network A neural network of three or more layers, though in modern practice over 1000 layers are possible.

Demographic shift A change in population that impacts society.

Desktop-as-a-service A form of virtual desktop interface allowing a user to see and use a desktop computer system in a physically separate, sometimes more secure location. Used to enhance security or to control costs in spending on desktop computing resources.

Digital presence How individuals or businesses appear online; what is found when people search on web pages, blogs and social media.

Digital rights management A body of tools and practices to restrict the distribution and access to digital media to paid or licensed users.

Distributed ledger A technology that supports the secure functioning of a decentralised database.

DRM See Digital Rights Management.

Due diligence The steps reasonable to take to ensure everything is as it appears.

Electronic signature A signature attached to a document which may involve either a graphical marking, a cryptographically supported annotation or both.

Encoding One of a range of methods for representing information in digital format.

Encrypted at rest The characteristic of data that is secured and stored in encrypted form, requiring decryption with an appropriate key or other secret before reading.

Encryption Security technology incorporating methods that scramble data into random, unreadable data using mathematical functions that can be reversed using other, complementary mathematical functions, requiring specific secret inputs that act as keys.

Ethereum A blockchain and smart contract platform supporting the creation of general-purpose applications.

Exculpatory evidence Evidence that establishes the innocence of a defendant.

Execution The running of a program on a computer (e.g. running a smart contract's code on a node on a blockchain distributed application network).

Expert system A computer system programmed with knowledge of a specific domain to emulate the decisions that would be made by a human in a well-defined set of conditions.

Fungible token A cryptocurrency unit that represents an asset or right which can be exchanged for a like asset or right.

Gas A unit of cryptocurrency for paying transaction fees related to applications built and run on the Ethereum blockchain.

GDPR The General Data Protection Regulation of the European Union. May also refer to the UK General Data Protection Regulation, depending on the context.

Generation Y Sometimes also known as Millennials, referring to people born from the late 1980s to the 1990s.

Generation Z People born between the mid-to-late 1990s and the early 2010s, often known as the tech-savvy generation because they were born into a time of fast digital growth.

Generative AI AI technology that creates content such as text, images and video, having been trained to do so on large bodies of representative content.

Globalisation The way in which the world has become increasingly more interconnected and interdependent.

Hallucination Incorrect but context-appropriate content generated by an AI model.

Hansard The records of a legislative body in jurisdictions following the British legal tradition.

Hardware technologies Physical components in computing systems including computers, storage, displays, networks and electrical power supplies.

HMCTS Her Majesty's Court and Tribunal Service.

HMCTS Reform Programme A reform of the court service to introduce new working practices and technology.

HTML Hyper Text Markup Language, a language used to create pages readable in a web browser, with rich formatting and multimedia, including graphics and video.

Human–computer interaction The ways in which humans effect, modify or receive the results of actions taken by a computer system.

ICO See Initial Coin Offering.

Immutability The property of data in certain systems that renders data unchangeable once accepted, whether for processing or storage.

Inculpatory evidence Evidence that shows a defendant's involvement in a crime.

Information retrieval The science of extracting information from bodies of data, including text and other forms of media.

Information theory A discipline focused on the encoding, transmission and retrieval of information.

Infrastructure Hardware and software that are assembled and managed together, to provide such services as processing, storage and communications for applications.

In-house Refers to an individual employed within a company or other organisation.

Initial coin offering An event where cryptocurrency units or tokens (coins) are purchased and issued to participants on a blockchain application network.

Input Data provided to a computer system by some means of interaction.

Instruct A client asking a legal professional to represent or advise them.

Interdisciplinary A combination of different disciplines (e.g. law and technology) within one activity.

Interfaces A hardware connection where two or more devices connect to each other.

Interlocutory hearing A hearing between the parties and the judge to decide procedural matters in a case.

Intermediary A party that acts as a carrier and conveyor of physical or virtual goods between two or more parties in a transaction.

Internet telephony Voice communications converted for transmission over the internet. Compare with traditional telephony, which uses analogue signals carried over wires.

Internetwork A network connecting smaller networks. The largest example of an internetwork is the internet itself.

Investigating authority An authority that is authorised to conduct investigations.

JSON JavaScript Object Notation, a standard text-based format for the encoding of data for reading by a machine.

Jurisdiction A defined set of boundaries, usually geographic, within which certain laws apply, or in which a court or other competent body may make a ruling.

K-means An unsupervised machine learning that divides a collection of subjects into K clusters based on a computation of similarity.

Known file matching This is the process of identifying known relevant files on a device using computational hashing and comparison methods. A digital forensics practitioner may maintain a "HashSet" containing the hashes of files known to be evidential (a common practice for IIoC cases). When a suspect device is scanned, any files which have the same hash value as those in the practitioner's HashSet must be the same (subject to collision caveats) and are therefore likely to be flagged for attention.

Large Language Model A machine learning model trained on a substantial body of text, used for natural language processing and text generation applications.

Law enforcement The term refers to the police as an authorised body empowered by the state to investigate and detect crime and prevent civil disorder.

Lawyer–client privilege A doctrine protecting the communications between a lawyer and a client from compelled disclosure.

Lawyers A collective term for legal professionals. Although commonly associated with the US legal profession, it is used in this book to refer to legal professionals generally.

Least squares A statistical method that determines the best fitted line to a set of sample points.

Legal aid If you cannot afford to pay for legal advice, you might be entitled to help to meet the costs of advice and representation through support provided by the government.

Legal brief A document that sets out the arguments in a legal case.

Legal executive A type of legal professional in England and Wales who performs similar work to a solicitor.

Legal practice The work undertaken by legal professionals.

Legal services The provision of legal advice and/or representation.

Legaltech A common vernacular term for legal technology, an emerging discipline at the intersection of legal practice and technology.

Litigation The legal process for resolving a dispute in a court of law.

Log parsing The systematic decomposition of events recorded in the log files of a software system for the purpose of extracting a usable data set describing the activity of that system or the users it serves for a specific period of time covered by those log files.

Machine learning A branch of AI that focuses on the development of computer systems that act without explicit programming, instead using data from previous experience to develop and improve models for action.

Machine learning tools Software and processes to support the training, evaluation and improvement of mathematical models incorporated in the construction and maintenance of machine learning systems.

Malware Malicious software designed to infiltrate and damage devices.

Marketing The promotion and selling of goods or services, often using advertising in various forms.

Mediation The act of resolving a dispute with the assistance of a neutral third party.

Metadata Data describing transactions or a larger body of data.

Microchip A small wafer of semiconductor material, usually silicon, containing extremely small electrical circuits.

Microcomputer A computer with power and capacity that fits on a desktop package.

Microgrid network A local electrical power generation and distribution system, usually associated with renewable energy initiatives, often supported by blockchain-powered applications for measurement and billing.

Millennial Sometimes also known as Generation Y, referring to people born from the late 1980s to the 1990s.

Mining The act of competitively verifying transactions to be incorporated into a blockchain, with a reward in cryptocurrency given to those who successfully complete validating a block, according to a certain selection protocol.

Mobile device A portable hand-sized device, usually (but not always) providing the capabilities of a mobile telephone and in many cases a general computing platform for running applications that use the communications capability of the device, such as voice, messaging and internet connectivity.

Moore's law An observation by the American engineer Gordon Moore that the number of transistors in a dense integrated circuit doubles every 18–24 months.

Natural language processing A discipline combining knowledge and methods from linguistics, computer science and artificial intelligence, concerned with developing computer systems to process and analyse data in the form of text or spoken word.

Neural Network A computational model simulating the activity of a network of neurons, which adjusts the connections among its layers in response to stimuli, having wide application in pattern recognition, classification and prediction.

Network A collection of computers connected and able to communicate with each other using wired or wireless links.

Networked A state of being connected over a communications network.

NFT See Non-Fungible Token.

NLP See Natural Language Processing.

Nodes Usually a single computer on a network, as in an application node for a network of computers servicing a blockchain application.

Non-fungible token A cryptocurrency unit that represents an asset or right which is in some way unique and cannot be exchanged for a like asset or right. Unique pieces of art or property are often exchanged using NFTs build with blockchain technology.

Non-repudiation The characteristic of certain systems where neither actions can be undone nor the records of such actions denied.

NoSQL database A database that supports the storage of data without requiring predefined definitions for the structure of that data. NoSQL databases are considered by technologists to provide more freedom for rapid development of solutions but can be more difficult to grow and maintain, given the lower requirements for structure.

Notarisation The act of certifying the authenticity of a legal instrument, often for the purpose of making that agreement legally binding according to the requirements of a jurisdiction governing the matter contained or described in that instrument.

Ontologies The practice of identifying, naming and categorising concepts, data and relationships as a means of facilitating of analysis, discourse and the creation of derivative works such as computer systems.

Open data Bodies of data available for public examination, copying, processing and redistribution, usually provided by a government or other large organisation as a means of providing transparency and accountability to citizens or other stakeholders.

Open source software Software provided with source code and licences that allow the viewing, modification and some permitted, possibly restricted forms of redistribution of the original and/or modified versions.

Optimisation In technological systems, the seeking of the shortest, most economical path for accomplishing a goal or delivering a service consuming the least amount of resources.

Output Data received from a computer system following some defined operation.

Paralegal A legal role often found in larger law firms. Sometimes viewed as a stepping stone to training as a lawyer.

Pattern recognition A branch of machine learning that exploits the mathematical characteristics of recurrent phenomena in data.

PBFT See Practical Byzantine Fault Tolerance.

PC A personal computer, referring to a desktop computer or laptop computing device, usually owned or provided for the use of a single individual.

Physical trace evidence Evidence that is found at the scene of a crime (e.g. fibres, hairs, gunshot residue) which is collected by the police for forensic examination.

PII Personally identifiable information.

PoS See Proof of Stake.

PoW See Proof of Work.

Place-shifting Use of a digital asset or capability held or provided in one place by a user physically located in another location, possibly in a different jurisdiction.

Practical Byzantine fault tolerance (PBFT) A characteristic of distributed computer systems that allows them to tolerate failure under conditions of imperfect information, such that they can continue to operate by reaching consensus. Blockchain consensus mechanisms incorporate PBFT.

Principal (of a law firm) A leader of a law firm, with strategic or fiduciary responsibility to the partners or shareholders.

Private practice Legal professionals who work for profit-making firms or other organisations rather than within the public sector.

Pro bono A lawyer who provides legal advice or representation free of charge.

Prompt A question or instruction used to effect an action from an AI model.

Prompt engineering The practice of developing instructions for an AI model, with a focus on best practices to achieve certain desired outcomes.

Prompting The act of writing an instruction or question for an AI model.

Processing The manipulation of data according to some specification.

Programming The creation of instructions for computer systems to execute and perform specific computations or tasks.

Proof of stake (PoS) A consensus mechanism for validating blocks on a blockchain that requires participants to show proof of investment or tenure on the network.

Proof of work (PoW) A consensus mechanism for validating blocks on a blockchain that requires the expenditure of a certain amount of computing resources in addition to a result shared by other participants in the network.

Pseudonymisation A personal data protection practice in which PII is obfuscated using masking or encryption when exposing data for allowed purposes in which the PII is present.

Quantum computing A branch of computing technology focused on building computing systems based on the characteristics of interactions between atomic and subatomic particles.

Queen's or King's Speech This speech, by the reigning monarch in the UK, sets out the government's agenda for the next session of Parliament and covers what legislation will be brought.

Regression A mathematical technique that determines the best-fitting mathematical function that describes a set of given data points.

Reinforcement Learning Training AI models with measurable outcomes, focusing on maximising or minimising a function computed from those outcomes, in order to obtain best performance from a given model.

Retainer A fee paid to a legal professional by a client in return for legal advice and/or representation.

Rhetorical structure theory A theory in linguistics that describes the relationships between parts of text.

Rule of law The principle that the law applies equally to everyone and we are all subject to the same laws.

SaaS Software as a service, a way of delivering computing services over the internet.

Scarcity of resources The demand for resources exceeds supply.

Search Retrieving specific data from a larger body of data based on certain characteristics, including keywords or metadata.

Self-represented litigants Sometimes also known as litigants in person, individuals who are representing themselves in legal proceedings.

Semantic analysis The practice of decomposing text into its underlying syntactic structures and determining their individual relationships to other structures and to the underlying text, allowing computers to interpret and act upon spoken or written text. A critical subdiscipline of natural language processing.

Server In hardware, usually a high-capacity computer providing the processing power, storage and network communications for a software program providing services for an application. In software, a program that contains the code implementation allowing a computer to provide services for an application communicating with remote devices over a network.

Smart contract A program that is part of a blockchain-based application that incorporates to a certain extent an agreement between two or more parties, and which may also take an active agency role in the execution and validation of the conditions specified in that agreement.

Smartphone A portable handheld device, providing mobile telephony capabilities (voice, short messaging and internet connectivity) and a general-purpose computing platform for running applications and internet browsing.

Social Credit System A system assigning a score to an individual based on observations of activity collected using mass surveillance and other methods of data collection mandated by the central government in the People's Republic of China.

Solicitor The most common type of legal professional in the UK who advises and represents clients on legal issues.

Solicitors Regulation Authority The independent regulatory body for solicitors in England and Wales.

Solidity A programming language for the authoring of smart contracts on the Ethereum blockchain.

Storage The reposing of data on an electronic medium for later retrieval and use.

Summarisation algorithms Certain classes of natural language processing techniques that extract a subset of data or text providing a capsule description of a body of underlying text.

Sync The act of connecting a device such as mobile phone to another device, such as a computer, to update and exchange data between the devices, such that the resulting copies are identical.

Telecommunications Communication over a distance, using electrical signals carried over a wire or electromagnetic waves such as radio.

Text mining The practice of using natural language processing methods and algorithms on large bodies of text to compute certain text characteristics such as word usage frequencies, relevant passages, etc.

Token A unit of cryptocurrency issued for the purpose of representing and facilitating the negotiation and exchange in assets or rights connected to the token.

Training A stage in setting up a machine learning or AI system whereby a set of example data, called training data, is used to compute parameters for a model addressing a given problem or problem domain.

Training Data Samples of data drawn from an AI model's intended problem domain, used to measure and tune the model's behaviour and performance prior to actual use.

Transformer An AI model that takes inputs and modifies (transforms) them into desired outputs.

Transistor component density A measure of the level of miniaturisation on a microchip, usually measured in transistor units per square millimetre. In general, the higher the density, the higher the capability and speed of the circuits on the microchip.

Transmission The projection of information to a destination or recipient at a distance, using an electronic means of communication.

Triage The sorting and allocation of legal cases.

Ubiquitous computing A state in which one's daily environment and lifestyle is supported by a range of computing devices.

Validation The act of verifying and certifying the data contained in a block to be incorporated into a blockchain.

Variables Data variables are things that can be changed and are used to store information on a computer program.

Virtual assistants A human person or digital assistant who provides support services to business from a remote location.

Virtual learning environment Online space designed for teaching and learning.

Virtual reality A computer-generated environment to create an authentic simulated experience.

Virus A unit of malicious code or a program which can infiltrate and harm devices.

Wallet A software application or hardware device built for the purpose of storing and managing units of cryptocurrency.

INDEX

For Product Safety Concerns and Information please contact our EU representative GPSR@taylorandfrancis.com Taylor & Francis Verlag GmbH, Kaufingerstraße 24, 80331 München, Germany